Foundation Marketing

Modular texts in business and economics

●●●●●●●●●●●●●●●●●

Series Editors
Geoff Black and Stuart Wall

Other titles in this series:

Business Information Technology: Systems, Theory and Practice
Geoffrey Elliott and Susan Starkings

The Macroeconomic Environment
Andrew Dunnett

Business Economics Second edition
Win Hornby, Bob Gammie and Stuart Wall

Management Accounting
David Wright

Financial Accounting Second edition
Christopher Waterson and Anne Britton

Introducing Human Resource Management Third edition
Margaret Foot and Caroline Hook

Quantitative Methods for Business and Economics
Glyn Burton, George Carrol and Stuart Wall

Introducing Organisational Behaviour
Jane Weightman

Introduction to International Business
Stuart Wall and Bronwen Rees

Introduction to Operations Management Second edition
John Naylor

Introduction to Accounting
Geoff Bank

Foundation Marketing

Third edition

Liz Hill **&** *Terry O'Sullivan*

Prentice Hall

FINANCIAL TIMES

An imprint of **Pearson Education**

Harlow, England • London • New York • Boston • San Francisco • Toronto • Sydney • Singapore • Hong Kong
Tokyo • Seoul • Taipei • New Delhi • Cape Town • Madrid • Mexico City • Amsterdam • Munich • Paris • Milan

Pearson Education Limited
Edinburgh Gate
Harlow
Essex CM20 2JE
England

and Associated Companies throughout the world

Visit us on the World Wide Web at:
www.pearsoneduc.com

First published 1996
Second edition published 1999
Third edition published 2004

ISBN 0 273 65532 9

British Library Cataloguing-in-Publication Data
A catalogue record for this book is
available from the British Library

Library of Congress Cataloging-in-Publication Data

Hill, Elizabeth, 1960–
    Foundation Marketing / Elizabeth Hill & Terry O'Sullivan. –– 3rd ed.
        p.   cm. –– (Modular texts in business and economics)
    Includes bibliographical references and index.
    ISBN 0–273–65532–9 (pbk.)
    1. Marketing.   I. O'Sullivan, Terry, 1957– .   II. Title.
III. Series.
    HF5415.H5166 1998
    658.8––DC21   98–42008
                                                                              CIP

Set in 9/12 Stone Serif
Typeset by 30

Printed and bound by Bell & Bain Limited, Glasgow

10 9 8 7 6 5 4 3 2
04 03 02 01 00

The publisher's policy is to use paper manufactured from sustainable forests.

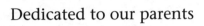

Dedicated to our parents

Contents

Preface

Marketing is one of the most popular topics on any college syllabus. Why? Because no matter what business you are in, or plan to be in, you will find a marketing perspective gives you the key to sustainable success in a competitive environment. Marketing involves all aspects of an organisation's activities, seen from a point of view with which we are all familiar – that of the customer. *Foundation Marketing*, as an introduction to this engrossing subject, takes that view very seriously – both in how it covers the subject, and with the support it offers both students and instructors looking for a straightforward and comprehensive treatment of the essentials.

Building on success

This book is the completely updated third edition of a widely adopted text originally published as *Marketing* in the popular Modular Texts in Business and Economics series. We have retitled it for this new edition to emphasise its coverage of the fundamentals of the subject. The new title underlines its suitability for use in courses which include marketing either at an introductory stage or as a component of a modular degree with other subjects. As well as being the recommended text for the Chartered Institute of Marketing's Introductory Certificate, this new edition of *Foundation Marketing* has been rewritten to suit the needs of the growing number of students taking Foundation degrees.

A foundation is something on which you build. It needs to be sturdy and sufficiently broad to support a variety of different structures. *Foundation Marketing* lives up to this image by being robust without being simplistic. It covers a broad swathe of marketing applications – including services and non-profit marketing – in order to equip its users with a sound basis for further study or the immediate practical application of its ideas. With a wealth of examples and case studies, memorable learning features, and an uncomplicated way of putting things, *Foundation Marketing* offers the learner a solid platform of knowledge, understanding and practical examples.

Market research has been an important part of the preparation for this new edition. As a result we have retained the following features which reviewers and users (including the authors' own students) enthused about in the second edition:

- ▶ 100% waffle-free.
- ▶ Practical know-how combined with academic rigour.
- ▶ Examples feature well-known organisations.

▶ Free-standing chapters in a logical order, so you can dip in and out as you need.

▶ Useful features designed to accelerate your learning: overviews, key words, arresting facts, self-test questions and in-chapter activities.

The book's coverage of topics by chapter, and its modular design, make it flexible enough to be customised to individual learning and teaching requirements. Most of the activities, and all of the self-test material, can be used by individual learners just as effectively as by groups, making the book highly suitable for distance learning courses.

What's new for the third edition?

▶ Completely revised selection of case studies with questions focused on chapter topics to help you grasp marketing ideas in practice.

▶ Enhanced focus on hot marketing applications such as communications, services and fashion.

▶ Totally new 'Foundation focus' feature at the start of each chapter, offering you a 20-second digest of what's to come.

▶ Updated references and refreshed links to further study.

▶ Key skill activities to link marketing knowledge with the essential areas of communication, application of number, information technology, working with others, improving own learning and performance, and problem solving.

▶ Revised selection of marketing facts to make you sit up and think in the popular 'Did you know?' feature dotted throughout the text.

▶ All-new coverage of emerging areas in marketing such as e-marketing, ethics and internal marketing.

▶ New key skill icons help reinforce important issues; the following six icons appear throughout the text:

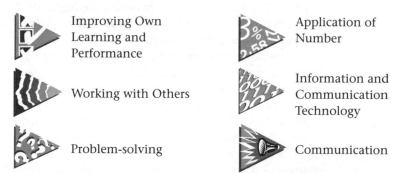

Improving Own Learning and Performance

Application of Number

Working with Others

Information and Communication Technology

Problem-solving

Communication

Other features of *Foundation Marketing* designed to help you get the most out of your study time include:

▶ Clutter-free visual design to provide clear signposts for the reader, and white space for your own notes.

▶ Enhanced use of icons.

▶ Revised index to get you to the information you need right when you need it.

There is also a dedicated website with clear learning/review objectives for each chapter. Visit **www.booksites.net/hill** to access additional learning resources, including:

▶ Up-to-the-minute links to Chartered Institute of Marketing Introductory Certificate syllabus.
▶ Overheads and lecture outlines.
▶ Tutorial plans.
▶ Supplementary case material.

Acknowledgements

We would like to take this opportunity to thank those individuals and organisations that have given us permission to use and adapt material for this book. Every effort has been made to trace the owners of copyright material, though in a few cases this has proved impossible and we apologise to any copyright holders whose rights may have been unwittingly infringed. We trust that in the event of any accidental infringement, the owners of the material will contact us directly.

Special thanks are due to Karen Beamish, Jackie Church, John Newsome, Catherine O'Sullivan, Brian Whitehead, Chris, Jo, Tom, Belle, Ollie, Ruari, Ned and Haydn Blackey, who have all, in their separate ways, been a lot of help.

The publishers would like to thank the following for permission to reproduce copyright material: Butterworth Heinemann Ltd for the figure 'Key stages in conducting a survey' in *Creative Arts Marketing*, Hill, L., O'Sullivan, C. and O'Sullivan, T. (2003).

Trademarks

CHAPTER 1

Introduction to marketing

Objectives

When you have read this chapter you will be able to:

➤ Define marketing.
➤ Identify the key characteristics of marketing-led organisations.
➤ Explain the difference between marketing, societal marketing and relationship marketing.
➤ Understand why marketing has grown in importance.
➤ Debate the advantages of marketing over other business approaches.
➤ List the tasks for which marketers are responsible.
➤ Illustrate the relevance of marketing to different types of organisation.

> ### *Foundation focus: the 20-second takeaway*
>
> The term 'marketing' is one that carries a number of connotations – some of them very negative. It is often wrongly used to describe high-pressure sales tactics, junk mail leaflets and street-corner research surveys, but in fact, while these are indeed forms of (sometimes inappropriate) marketing activity, they do not reflect what marketing really is. Marketing is potentially a very positive activity, which most people – if they knew what it really was – would probably approve of. It is an approach to doing business that recognises the utmost importance of meeting the customer's needs. Marketing activity seeks to understand those needs and to deliver products and services in such a way as to keep customers happy and coming back for more.

Introduction

This chapter introduces the topic of marketing. It discusses the fundamental characteristics of firms which can claim to be marketing-oriented, examining the reasons for the growth of marketing in recent years and the problems associated with alternative approaches to doing business. The primary activities for which the marketing function is responsible are explained, and the contexts in which they can be usefully applied are also discussed. This chapter also sets the framework for the rest of the book, indicating how the various elements which comprise the discipline of marketing fit together, and introduces concepts that are explored in more detail in later chapters.

What is marketing?
·······················

Most people think they know what marketing is and what marketers do. Marketing has become widely synonymous with the ways in which organisations attract their customers and persuade them to buy products and services. The marketing department is seen as being responsible for launching new products, for generating good press coverage, for placing advertisements, for conducting research and for supporting the salesforce. Marketing staff are expected to liaise with advertising agencies, to deal with customer complaints, to advise on product ranges and to arrange promotions. Such descriptions imply that the main function of marketing is to present an organisation and its products to its potential customers.

This, however, is by no means the whole story. Organisations who see their marketing activity as no more than a ploy to take them to their customers are missing the point altogether. The discipline of marketing is both broader and more meaningful than this. It is *a business philosophy that regards customer satisfaction as the key to successful trading and advocates the use of management practices that help identify and respond to customer needs*. An examination of some more definitions of marketing helps to clarify this. They tend to fall into two categories: those that emphasise a philosophical dimension and those that focus on the more concrete managerial processes of marketing.

Marketing as a business philosophy

An organisation that adopts the concept of marketing as a philosophy sees the customer as the central driving force behind its activities, recognising that businesses only survive if they meet customer needs. In a free-market economy, consumers have a choice of what to buy, when to buy, and where to buy, as well as whether to buy at all. Therefore, to be successful at attracting consumers, the most logical starting point for an organisation is to identify what customers want and then to attempt to supply it more effectively and efficiently than the competition. To thrive in the long term, an organisation must meet customer needs over a period of time and make money from its transactions. The closer the fit between the customer's needs and what the organisation supplies, the more the customer is willing to pay and the more profits the business will generate.

To summarise, marketing as a business philosophy is really all about creating and keeping profitable customers:

▶ *Creating* customers requires an organisation constantly to monitor its environment to ensure that it recognises and acts upon the opportunities presented by the changing needs of its potential customers, so that they become actual customers.

▶ *Keeping* customers means that organisations must minimise or avoid threats to an established customer base, either from changes in existing customer needs or from competitor activities.

▶ *Profitable* customers are those who have the potential to generate revenues that will more than exceed the costs of the business. Organisations must ensure that they focus their attentions on profitable business rather than pursue any customers at any price.

Efficiency versus effectiveness

A marketing-oriented organisation understands that in the long run, meeting the customer's needs is what leads to success. This exercise will help you to recognise the key things that create marketing orientation and understand the implications of taking a different approach.

Efficiency is a goal that is hotly pursued by most organisations. It is concerned with producing products at minimum cost, so as to maximise profitability, sometimes dubbed '*doing the right things*'. Consequently, hardly a day goes by without announcements being made in the press about job losses being incurred to improve productivity and make companies more efficient. But marketing-oriented firms place their emphasis primarily on being effective. *Effectiveness* is concerned with satisfying the needs of the market and '*doing things right*' in the eyes of the customers. Efficiency is seen as a means of enhancing profitability rather than the primary means of achieving it.

Of course, the ideal is for a business to be both effective and efficient, in which case it will thrive. But there are three other categories that firms can fall into:

	Effective	*Ineffective*
Efficient	1 Thrive	2 ?
Inefficient	3 ?	4 ?

What is the outlook for firms that are

▶ efficient but ineffective
▶ effective but inefficient
▶ neither effective nor efficient (4)?

Find examples of businesses that you believe fall into each of the four categories and suggest actions that they could take to improve their performance.

Marketing as a managerial function

Many definitions of marketing refer not specifically to the philosophy of marketing, but to the managerial processes that are inherent in 'creating and keeping profitable customers'.

Marketing is the management process responsible for identifying, anticipating and satisfying customer requirements profitably. (The Chartered Institute of Marketing, UK)

Marketing is the process of planning and executing the conception, pricing, promotion and distribution of ideas, goods and services to create exchanges that satisfy individual and organisational goals. (American Marketing Association)

Marketing is a social and managerial process by which individuals and groups obtain what they need and want through creating, offering and exchanging products of value with others. (Kotler, 2003)

These definitions help us to build up a picture of the role of marketing in an organisation. They portray marketers as facilitators, helping individuals to satisfy their needs and organisations to reach their goals. The task of the marketer is to arrange exchanges: usually customers' money in exchange for the organisation's products and services. A car manufacturer, for example, designs a range of models to meet the needs of its potential customers and requires them to pay a sum of money in exchange for the benefits that they will reap from ownership of their car. This is an example of a monetary transaction, but not all exchanges will be financial and the benefits sought by customers will not always be so tangible. A political party, for example, offers promises of prosperity and social harmony in exchange for the electorate's votes. A charity offers people clear consciences in exchange for their money or their time as volunteers.

These definitions of marketing also offer guidance as to how marketers should go about their task of facilitating exchange processes. Attention is drawn to the importance of researching customers' needs (identifying and anticipating needs). The creation of value is emphasised, indicating that marketers are responsible for developing products and services that offer sufficient benefits to induce customers to participate in the exchange process. Pricing is also mentioned, being an activity that assesses the value the customer places on the product and sets the terms under which exchange can take place. Promotion and distribution are both means by which the exchange process is made easier: promotion by raising awareness of products, services and the benefits they offer, and distribution by making them available in a convenient location for the potential customer.

The managerial function of marketing, therefore, goes way beyond the rather limited administrative activities suggested at the beginning of this chapter. It is an integrative function which helps match the needs of actual and potential customers with the goals of the organisation through desirable exchanges. Marketing management is:

. . . the process of planning and executing the conception, pricing, promotion and distribution of goods and services to create exchanges that satisfy individual and organisational goals. (Bennett, 1995)

CASE STUDY **1.1**   **Morgan moves ahead**

The Morgan Motor Company was founded by H.F.S Morgan in 1909. It is the world's oldest privately owned motor company, producing the last coach-built car. Still actively managed by members of the Morgan family, the company is very much a family business where the whole workforce is committed to the success of the product. The tradition of craftsmanship has been passed down the generations and the atmosphere at the factory is that of one family with a strong community spirit, and commitment to the development of the industry. In August 2000, the Motor and Allied Trades Benevolent Fund presented Morgan with a certificate in recognition of the excellent support given by the company and its staff to the Motor Industry.

The business is very much an international one, with 50 per cent of demand coming from the overseas markets. Morgan owners are regarded as part of the family, and visitors are welcome to come to see for themselves the loving care that is lavished on each new vehicle in production. A Morgan is generally bought as a second car by male drivers from all walks of life.

The car itself is unique in design, conveying the image of a vintage 1930s sports car while incorporating engineering features that offer high levels of reliability, performance and safety. It is quite literally a tailor-made vehicle, coming with a choice of body colours and optional features which include authentic walnut fascia panels, leather upholstery, coloured hoods and badge bars. The level of customisation is made possible by the existence of extensive waiting lists for the product, which have stretched as long as six years, with production volume as low as 500 vehicles a year. Despite this, the prices have always been considered extremely reasonable, starting at under £21,000 for the 2-seater model (2003).

In the 1990s The Morgan Motor Company was the subject of a BBC documentary presented by the former head of ICI, Sir John Harvey-Jones. He expressed some reservations about its highly labour-intensive production techniques, the desire to produce even small components in-house and the low price levels, given the high waiting lists. His intervention was a catalyst for several changes, including new investment in plant and production capacity to enable higher production volumes, cutting waiting lists for some models to around a year. Changing vehicle legislation has also led to new developments, and all models now come complete with airbags, low speed bumpers and meet emissions requirements. Positive decisions have been made over the years to keep the character of the car intact, but engineering developments have enabled the car to break new ground. 2000 saw the launch of Morgan's Aero 8 model at the Geneva Motor Show. The new all-aluminium Morgan, which benefited from the full and enthusiastic support of BMW in the development and testing process, has a distinctly twenty-first-century feel to it – and with prices starting at over £47,000 looks set to generate a valuable new income stream for the organisation.

Questions

1 List the characteristics that make Morgan cars desirable in the eyes of the customers.
2 Is The Morgan Motor Company product-oriented or customer-oriented? Or is it possible to be both?
3 Which companies do you think The Morgan Motor Company competes with?

Sources: Morgan literature; www.morgan-motor.co.uk; Ashton (1994); Economist (1994/95); Laban (2001); Rhys (1992).

Societal marketing

All of the discussion about the nature and role of marketing so far has assumed that the firm is responsible for satisfying the needs of individual consumers. What may be best for individuals, though, may not be best for society: individuals may like powerful cars with large engines, but the effects of the pollution they generate on air quality may be lethal to others; non-returnable bottles may be more convenient for consumers, but do not help to preserve natural resources and cause problems of waste management; more and cheaper beef-burger outlets may be demanded on the high street but if the grazing of the cattle to produce the beef requires the rainforests to be cut down, then the environmental impact may be detrimental to many more people than those who enjoy the product. This has led to the development of a business philosophy known as societal marketing, which advocates attempts to satisfy consumer needs in line with the objectives of the organisation as well as the needs of society. It has been adopted by a number of organisations, which see their role as balancing the interests of not just the firm and the individual, but also society as a whole. Resistance to this concept comes from those who argue that marketing executives are taking on the role of guardianship of public standards, which should be the role of democratically elected politicians. Nonetheless, organisations such as the Body Shop have proved that financial success and social responsibility are not necessarily mutually exclusive. Cause-related marketing schemes are also becoming more popular. These involve companies linking their promotional campaigns with charities for the mutual benefit of both parties.

CASE STUDY 1.2
....

Self-assembled success

The multinational furniture retailer Ikea has around 170 stores in 30 countries, has an annual sales value of over £5 billion, and employs workers in some of the world's most impoverished countries. Yet it does not generally suffer from the wrath of anti-globalisation protesters in the same way as other global firms such as McDonald's and Nike. To a large extent this can be put down to the philosophy of the store's founder, Ingvar Kamparad, who sees the business as having a cultural mission – to create a better life for people of limited means. The business's vision, ideas and values point towards taking social and environmental responsibility in various ways.

Since, in the early 1990s, a Swedish documentary showed children chained to weaving looms at a supplier in Pakistan, Ikea has taken its social responsibility very seriously. It has given money to Unicef to set up schools in India and to Greenpeace's campaign to save ancient forests. Its catalogue – the longest print run in the world – is printed on chlorine-free paper, and it sources its wood only from forests certified by the Forest Stewardship Council. To avoid accusations of exploitation, a single set of standards and a code of conduct are applied to all 1,400 of its suppliers across the world. The same rules apply in Sweden as in China.

The minimum service, flat-pack mentality at the stores themselves widens access by enabling costs and prices to be cut to the bone. Customers are encouraged to become highly involved in the shopping process and make a commitment to the products. The store is designed as a cross between a museum and a theme park, with 'visitors' being provided with a shopping experience which includes a full tour, following arrows on the floor, from the entrance right through to the cash desks by the exit. Whereas traditional stores appeal to individual consumers, Ikea is keen to create the chance for people to do something communal and aims to attract families and groups.

But ironically, the store's immense popularity has created its own environmental and service problems. Customer gridlock is a common feature at the stores, as people queue to get into the car park and out at the checkout. In the local neighbourhood, the traffic generated around its superstore warehouses is threatening the company's expansion ambitions as town planners turn down applications for new sites. With government policy firmly committed to promoting retail developments which do not rely on excessive car use, the company's stated aim of gearing its trade to car-borne shoppers is likely to continue to meet fierce resistance in many quarters.

Questions

1   To what extent is Ikea embracing societal marketing rather than simply implementing a good commercial marketing strategy?
2   Should Ikea bow to government pressure to downsize its new stores and locate them at sites where public transport is accessible?
3   Which has had more impact on Ikea's fortunes: fashion or vision?

Sources: Hetherington (2002); Moss (2000); Slavin (2001).

Relationship marketing

The discussion of marketing so far has concentrated on its role in developing mutually beneficial transactions between two parties (and in the case of societal marketing, transactions which are also of benefit – or at least harmless – to society as a whole). Marketing techniques are generally viewed as vehicles for attracting new customers and preventing existing ones from being lured away by the competition. The more recent theoretical concept of 'relationship marketing' looks at things in a slightly different way. Marketing activities are seen as a means for supporting long-term customer relationships through which transactions can take place (Berry, 1983); they are seen as much more than just a stimulus to encourage a purchase response. Whereas traditional marketing thinking focuses on a business's ability to make a series of single sales to a group of potential customers, relationship marketing focuses on building high levels of customer commitment by offering exceptional service levels over a long timescale, and generating customers' loyalty by treating them as individuals rather than small elements of large markets. Peppers and Rogers (1997) recommend that marketers move away from 'market-share thinking' to 'share-of-customer' thinking. If florists take a traditional marketing approach, then come Mother's Day and Valentine's Day when people buy a lot of flowers, they will all be competing to get as much business as possible from potential customers who are unknown to them, and will probably need to attract such customers with advertising or special price offers. On the other hand, if they concentrate instead on getting a larger share of each customer's patronage, perhaps by offering a superior service – more efficient deliveries, better gift-wrapping, or even a friendly welcome in the shop – then that customer is more likely to return, less likely to defect to the competition, and may even increase his or her overall expenditure on flowers in preference to other forms of gift.

Christopher and McDonald (1995) argue that relationships should be cultivated, not just with potential consumers of a company's products and services, but with a whole range of other parties who could influence that company's ability to reach and serve its customers effectively – including employees and suppliers, for example. Philip Kotler (1986) has coined the term 'megamarketing' to describe a strategic approach to relationships beyond those of the immediate parties to a transaction. In practice, such relationships require high levels of trust to be built up between all the parties concerned, and when that trust is in place, the potential for everyone to benefit from the resultant transactions is at its highest.

KEY SKILLS
ACTIVITY **1.2**
· · · · · · · · · · · · · ·
Communication

Dispelling the myths

A lot of people are very confused about what marketing is, and may mistake it for advertising, market research, direct mail and other activities which are simply some of the tools of marketing. This exercise will help you to clarify in your own mind exactly what marketing really is, and communicate it to others.

Prepare a PowerPoint presentation aimed at (a) a class of 7 year olds, (b) a meeting of your local Women's Institute, or (c) the Chamber of Commerce in your area, to explain to them what marketing is.

The growth of marketing
· ·

The number and range of organisations having adopted a marketing orientation in recent years can be attributed to changes in the social, business and economic environments and the growing complexities of doing business in modern industrial nations. Five factors have been instrumental in raising the importance of marketing orientation in today's world.

More sophisticated consumers

Maslow (1970) suggests that each individual is motivated by a series of needs, which range from those that are most fundamental to all human beings, to those that are highly specific to each individual. (See Figure 1.1.)

People are motivated to satisfy their needs sequentially, only attempting to satisfy social needs, for example, when their physiological and safety needs have been met. In subsistence economies, a high proportion of the population will be striving to meet the lower-level needs – for food, water, shelter and warmth – universal needs that are easy to identify and anticipate. In the Western world, though, consumers are increasingly in a position of having disposable income that is more than sufficient for supplying their basic needs. They are looking to satisfy higher-order needs, and the individuality of these needs makes it much more difficult for the producers of products and services to know exactly what to supply. Take motor cars as an example. A family looking to satisfy its social needs may be looking for a car that can carry two adults and two children in comfort, with room for the dog in the back and a roof-rack for luggage on holiday. On the other hand, the social needs of a teenager looking for a first car may be defined more by the need to build relationships with other young people and consequently the most 'sociable' vehicle may be a small sporty model with economic fuel consumption. Esteem needs may motivate some people to buy a vehicle offering them comfort and style on a grand scale, such as a Rolls Royce, while others may feel that their status is better reflected in the purchase of a vehicle with a reputation for speed, such as a Ferrari or a Porsche. Those who view cars as objects of intrinsic interest rather than means of transport may be seeking to satisfy self-development needs in their choice of car – they may choose a classic car, spend many a happy evening with their heads under the bonnet and only drive it to shows and owners' club rallies.

The key point here is that while it is easy to predict and supply lower-order needs, the task of anticipating, identifying and satisfying the more complex

figure 1.1
Maslow's hierarchy of needs

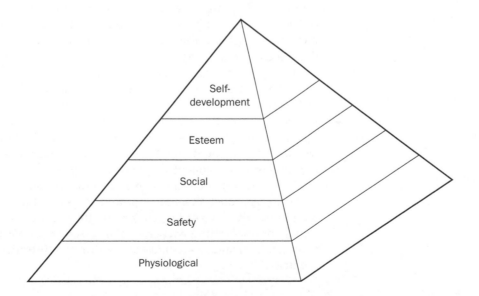

and individual human needs, and matching them with the capabilities and objectives of an organisation, is a complex and difficult one. A marketing orientation, putting customers at the centre of a business and making concerted efforts to find out just what they do want, is the approach most likely to encourage a successful match.

Greater competition

Firms are facing ever increasing competition from a number of sources:

▶ *International competition*: As global communication systems improve, the potential for organisations to supply customers from whom they are geographically remote increases dramatically. This poses both opportunities and threats for businesses: opportunities to search for customers abroad, but also threats from foreign competitors, eager to find markets where they can supply customers more effectively than the current domestic suppliers. Foreign firms may have certain competitive advantages, stemming from access to raw materials, from superior technologies, from lower costs (particularly those from low labour-cost countries) and even from a better understanding of customer needs, built up from experience in other parts of the world.

▶ *New technologies*: It is inevitable that from time to time new technologies will challenge and ultimately cannibalise existing industries. Described as a force for 'creative destruction' (Levitt, 1960), major innovation is increasingly likely to come from new classes of competitors emerging outside existing industries rather than from within them. History has proved this to be the case. For example, watchmakers were overtaken by electronics firms as customers are wooed by the benefits of accuracy and reliability over craftsmanship. These days, a range of diverse sectors are being threatened by the ever increasing penetration of Internet access. Bookshops are closing as online suppliers such as Amazon grow in strength; the printing industry is threatened as catalogues, books and directories are increasingly launched online; and the postal service is under threat as email becomes the preferred means of communication for many types of correspondence. As the speed of technological change gathers pace, organisations must adapt to survive, and recognise that the better they understand the needs of their customers, the better they can anticipate changes in demand and avoid extinction at the hands of these new competitors.

▶ *Imitators*: Although the law gives some protection to the originators of products through the granting of patents and copyright protection, whenever an organisation establishes a new product in a market and starts to gain business, competitors will be keen to attract a share of the new market. They will often launch 'me-too' products, adapted versions of the innovator's product, in an attempt to take a slice of the profitable new business for themselves. To gain ground they may use heavy promotional activity or price-cutting tactics, thereby posing a serious threat to both the potential sales and profitability of the firm that introduced the product in the first place.

A marketing orientation is one defence against such tactics. The better an innovating organisation understands the motivations and buying habits of its potential customers, the more prepared it can be to take pre-emptive action and the better will be its defences against this form of competition.

CASE STUDY **1.3**

Rewarding loyalty

So-called loyalty cards, offering discounts and benefits to regular shoppers, were once trumpeted as a nifty way of stopping promiscuous consumers buying from competitors; but they have failed to fulfil initial expectations. More than half of all consumers still report no particular commitment to any retailer, and the 35–55s are the most likely of all to eschew attempts to stop them straying to the competition. They are more likely to seek out the best deals and shop to fit in with their own lifestyle patterns, rather than stick with a single supermarket.

Often used by retailers as a simple promotional tool, many schemes have come and gone as their rivals jumped on the bandwagon and started to compete with each other to provide the best benefits. Supermarket group Asda scrapped its loyalty card scheme after a customer survey showed only a handful of shoppers wanted it, and introduced an across-the-board low price policy in its place. Investigations by research group Mintel and the University of Stirling have also found that loyalty schemes are expensive to maintain, estimated to cost around 1p per cardholder per week.

Despite this, points-mean-prizes schemes are still popular with many customers and if used as more than simply tactical means for boosting sales, can create tremendous relationship-building opportunities for retailers. The potential the cards create for building one-to-one relationships with customers is more highly valued by some than its impact on repeat purchase and loyalty. The Boots Advantage card, introduced in 1997, is held by half the UK's female population. It is judged to be the most technically advanced card available, allowing points to be held on the card and redeemed in store at any time. Described by Boots as a 'treat-based proposition', it encourages customers to save points by buying basic toiletries, then prompts increased sales by encouraging them to spend their points on extra treats such as fragrances or cosmetics. But more important than the uplift in sales is the card's role as a vehicle by which the store exchanges value for information. Transaction data is used to build a profile of customers at different stores, which feeds back into decisions about store layout, new product development and sales promotions. Accurately targeted special offers are mailed to appropriate people, and super-loyal customers are rewarded with extra elements, such as a customer magazine.

Questions

1 Cards are relatively ineffective at generating retailer loyalty. Suggest strategies which may be more effective.
2 In what ways can a database recording customer transactions be used for marketing purposes?
3 To what extent would the loyalty being generated by Boots through its scheme be sustainable if the scheme was terminated?

Sources: Finch (1999); Hiscock (2001); James (2003).

Separation of production and consumption

In days gone by, if a man needed a new suit, he would go to a tailor who would take his measurements, offer him a selection of cloths, discuss appropriate styles and invite him to return for fittings as the garment was being prepared. With the coming of mass production, such immediate contact between producer and consumer is lost. Cloth manufacturers will have to anticipate the fashion for forthcoming seasons, often years in advance of their sale on the high street. They will have to predict the popularity of raw materials, patterns and colours, and must understand the potential benefits of any new man-made fibres becoming available. Garment manufacturers are then responsible for choosing cloth, colour and styles on behalf of a large number of potential customers, who are unknown to them at the time the production decisions are made. They must decide how many of which sizes to produce, and in so doing will be making assumptions about the tolerance of their customers in buying garments that nearly fit but are not made-to-measure. Finally, retailers must assess which type, style and sizes of garment to stock to attract potential buyers into their stores. Chain stores may be making decisions for shops that are geographically very separate and whose average shoppers may be very different from each other.

In this process, unlike a visit to the tailor, the customer is not automatically consulted. Others are making decisions on his behalf. However, if he is unhappy with the decisions made by the cloth producer, the garment manufacturer or the retailer, he is in a position to take his business elsewhere, to others who can satisfy his particular requirements better.

The moral of this tale is that unless organisations make conscious, co-ordinated and consistent efforts to identify the changing needs of their potential customers, they are always in danger of missing vital signals from the market which would have been more evident had they had face-to-face contact with them during the buying process. A marketing orientation encourages contact with customers, in particular through market research.

> **DID YOU KNOW?**
>
> *'Mass customisation' is the twenty-first century's solution to achieving economies of scale while at the same time delivering a bespoke product to the customer. Nike iD is a web-based facility that enables people to create their own limited edition trainers, by customising some of its styles with different materials and logo colours. They can then add an eight letter personal ID that is stitched into the heel of the shoe. Each stage of the selection process updates the on-screen illustration, viewable from several angles. Nike has limited the options and hand-checks all IDs to ensure that the shoes don't look ugly, and to check that offensive names don't end up on their shoes. The shoes, which normally cost around £100, are sold at a premium of £8 for the custom design and are delivered within five weeks (www.nike.com).*

More complex organisations

As firms increase in size, their staff usually become more and more distant from the end-user of the organisation's product. Two significant problems emerge as a result of this:

► *Conflicting demands*: In all but the smallest organisations, employees are likely to be more responsible to 'internal' customers – normally their bosses, or other departments for whom they perform a service – than to those who buy the organisation's products and services. From time to time, the demands of these internal customers will conflict with the needs of the real customer. Suppose, for example, in an attempt to maintain high-quality standards, a fashion store's policy requires shop assistants to remove shop-soiled goods from display to be destroyed, and not to offer them at a discount. But then, after a long day's shopping, a customer finds the perfect dress in the store – the last one in her size. However, the previous person who had tried it on left a lipstick mark on it. The customer offers to purchase the dress, but asks for a 20 per cent discount. Organisations that have adopted a marketing orientation will put into practice the principles of 'customer focus' and 'goal orientation' and will empower the shop assistant to make a decision that will send the customer away happy, regardless of the rule book. Organisations whose own procedures are given precedence over responding to customer needs will gradually find themselves being labelled as bureaucrats and ultimately running out of customers!

▶ *Separation of ownership and control*: Employees tend to be less profit-oriented than owner-managers. If management fails to communicate effectively, the correlation in the minds of employees between serving customers, making profits and getting paid can be lost: in the short term, most employees will take home a wage packet or salary cheque whether or not the organisation's customers are satisfied. Compare this with the self-employed person who knows that failing to meet customer needs equates with a reduction in take-home pay.

To overcome the problems that emerge from this, marketing-oriented firms have started to design their organisational structures, their operating and communication systems, their remuneration packages, their staff appraisal and their training activity in such a way as to motivate employees to attend first to the needs of the customer.

Faster environmental change

There is more discussion of this in Chapter 3. However, it is worth noting here that the world is changing more rapidly and that if there ever was such a thing, a stable business environment is a thing of the past. New technology, as we have already seen, is making whole industries redundant. Social change is occurring as more of the world is educated at higher levels and is demanding more and better products. The environmental movement is gaining pace and influence over business practices. Economic influences are being felt globally rather than nationally, with events in Japan, the US and Europe affecting the world rather than just their own trading blocs. Firms that fail to integrate their own efforts in responding to changing customer needs in such a turbulent environment are in danger of being left behind in current markets and left out of new ones.

DID YOU KNOW?
The number of UK households with access to the Internet has risen from 18 per cent in 1999 to 46 per cent in 2002, a year in which 62 per cent of all adults in Britain accessed the Internet at some time. Computers continue to dominate as the preferred method for accessing the Internet in 2002, with 99 per cent using this method. But 11 per cent of adults have now done so using a mobile phone and around 7 per cent using Digital Television. Only 1 per cent had used each of these in July 2000 (www.statistics.gov.uk).

Alternative approaches to marketing

Looking at alternatives to marketing orientation, it is clear that they are becoming more and more difficult to justify.

Production orientation

Mass-production industries rely on economies of scale to reduce their unit costs and enable them to supply mass markets at prices that people can afford and that are simultaneously profitable to the organisation itself. The greater the number of units produced, the lower the cost per unit – known as productivity. If we assume that customers are primarily price-driven, then the reduction of price is an effective tool for generating new business and retaining existing customers. The temptation in industries characterised by economies of scale, therefore, is to become preoccupied with producing as much and as efficiently as possible without much thought as to whether customers want or need large supplies of uniform products. This is known as a production orientation.

As a rule of thumb, a production orientation can be considered as an appropriate short-term approach to business under two circumstances:

▶ *Shortage*: If customer demand exceeds what businesses can supply, prices in the market will be artificially high and competitors will be attracted by the high profit margins that can be generated. If a firm wishes to deter competitors, it may seek to raise its own production levels so that there are fewer customers left for potential new competitors. Any that do choose to enter the market will have to undercut existing firms and operate on reduced profit, just to get a foothold.

▶ *High unit costs*: If the unit cost of producing an item is high, then the prices that need to be charged to cover costs may deter customers and slow down or even prevent the growth of a potential market. Improved productivity and reduced unit costs may be brought about by concentration on increasing production, and this in turn may stimulate market growth.

CASE STUDY **1.4**

The magic of book marketing

Marketing in the book publishing industry is a sales-oriented process. Publishers acquire the rights to publish from their authors in the hope of persuading readers to go out and buy the books in the shops. Books by little-known authors pose a particular challenge, effectively having to be sold four times: the literary agent sells the manuscript to a publisher; the editor sells the concept of the book to the internal sales team; the sales team persuades the bookshop to stock the book; and the bookshop promotes it to the reader. In-store marketing is particularly crucial to success, as 70 per cent of people buy a book because they see it in a shop.

The market for children's books is a particularly tough one for new authors. 10,000 new titles are published every year, into a market worth £140 million a year – 24 per cent of the general retail market. J.K. Rowling's Harry Potter series was launched in 1997 by Bloomsbury Publishing (editors at Penguin, Transworld and HarperCollins had already rejected the manuscripts), with a print run of 500 for *Harry Potter and the Philosopher's Stone*. Three years and three books later, more than 35 million copies had been sold, and the fourth – *Harry Potter and the Goblet of Fire* – had an initial print run of 1.5 million copies, 30 per cent of which were sold on the day of publication. The series now accounts for over 19 per cent of children's book sales, compared to 3.9 per cent for the next best-selling series.

The first Harry Potter book had made its mark through word-of-mouth, helped considerably when it won the Smarties book prize in 1997. As the word spread, so distribution quickly developed, with supermarkets, service stations, and corner shops as well as book stores and online book sellers all clamouring for stock. And it wasn't only children who wanted to read Harry Potter. Discovering an adult market for the books, the publishers re-jacketed them and created cloth-bound editions for collectors, and boxed sets of both paperbacks and hardbacks.

Sales were helped by the very distinctive cover design, featuring the name Harry Potter in the largest type size as the main brand, with the title of the book in smaller type below. Press coverage of the books was exceptional, and helped by the additional angle about author J.K. Rowling herself, a single mother who wrote the stories in cafés because she was too poor to afford heating at home. Marketing campaigns for later books involved 'denial marketing' to create pent-up demand – the new books went on sale at precisely 3.45pm, timed at the end of the school day to prevent children playing truant to get hold of their copy. In another campaign, the title of the new book wasn't revealed until a week before publication. A Harry Potter Club and website are available for fans, and Warner Brothers now control digital rights to the title. Two movies have been produced by them, with Mattel having acquired the rights to toy licensing for the film.

Questions

1   What other sectors are likely to be at least to some extent sales-oriented? Why is this the case?
2   Can the Harry Potter phenomenon be attributed more to luck than judgement?
3   Is research of any value to the publishing industry?

Sources: Cassy and Moss (2000); Hattenstone (2000); Marketing Business (2001).

Product orientation

Organisations that are product-oriented define their businesses in terms of the products they sell, rather than the needs of their customers. As such, preoccupied with the addition of ever more intricate features, improving product quality or enhancing product performance or appearance, they often misunderstand the core benefits that their customers are seeking from their products. Manufacturers of video recorders were originally accused of having fallen into this trap. Keen to outdo their competitors in terms of the number of functions that their equipment would perform, they lost sight of the difficulties faced by their customers in operating the increasingly complex technology. Simpler operating procedures were a much sought-after benefit, and new, simpler control mechanisms were subsequently brought on to the market to help solve the problem. The same accusations could these days be levied at mobile phone manufacturers, who introduce models with features such as predictive texting, photography, Internet access and soon video conferencing, leaving less sophisticated users in confusion.

> **DID YOU KNOW?**
>
> *When Dyson launched the Contrarotator washing machine, the company claimed that its new product would give the 'cleanest wash results in the fastest time'. But when the Consumers' Association tested the new product against its closest rival, the Bosch Maxx WFL, it concluded, much to Dyson's dismay, that the Bosch model remained the best buy for all-round value as the Dyson was priced at £1,200 and the Bosch a mere £480 (Field, 2001).*

Another symptom of product orientation is the failure to recognise that a product is becoming obsolete. By defining their markets and customers in terms of their products, companies may fall into the trap of 'marketing myopia' (Levitt, 1960) and fail to see the threat posed by product developments in other industries. Marketing history is littered with casualties from product orientation – the growth of the 'dry-cleaning' industry was halted by developments in fabric technology as well as domestic laundry equipment. People wanted clean clothes, not dry-cleaners. Fax machines have limited appeal now that email permits the instant transfer of documents at virtually no cost across the world. People wanted fast, high-quality communication, not fax machines.

Sales orientation

This approach assumes that customers will not be willing to buy an organisation's products or services unless considerable effort is put into influencing them through persuasion and promotion. This is quite the contrary of a marketing orientation, which seeks such a close match between what the organisation is offering and what the customer wants that the product should virtually sell itself. A sales orientation considers the customer only after decisions have been made about what to produce, and this implies that the organisation is more interested in its own goals – converting products into sales revenues – than in satisfying customer needs and generating customer loyalty. (See Figure 1.2.)

As a result, a sales orientation can only prove effective in the short term, and then only if the organisation wishes to create customers but is not worried about keeping them. This may be the case in markets characterised by few repeat purchases – items such as fitted kitchens, sets of encyclopaedias and double glazing, where the customer is unlikely to want the item again for a long while. The organisation does not have to consider the possibility of a repeat purchase and may decide that 'getting the sale' is more important than post-purchase satisfaction. Election campaigns are characterised by similar approaches: promises may be made that prove impossible to fulfil, but once elected a candidate needn't worry about getting votes for another five years.

figure 1.2
**Marketing is NOT...
HARD SELLING!**

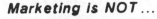

In the long term, even if individual customers are not in a position to repurchase, by undermining the company's reputation they can be a powerful force in damaging future sales. If they are dissatisfied with the products or services they were persuaded to buy, they are likely to spread the word and warn others not to make the same mistake. Research suggests that bad word-of-mouth travels far faster than good, with dissatisfied customers commenting on disappointments more than three times as often as satisfied customers comment on good experiences (Kotler and Armstrong, 2001).

The practice of marketing

As explained earlier, marketing is a philosophy that should underpin the business activities of an organisation, but it is also a managerial function that takes responsibility for the matching of customer needs with an organisation's products and services. The most fundamental tasks that fall to marketers are analysis, strategy, tactics and management. As Chapter 2 explains, the context in which these tasks take place is by no means limited to the familiar territory of the supermarket or high street. While consumer goods like baked beans or detergent provided the inspiration for what we have now come to call marketing theory, marketing now extends to services such as banking and insurance, industrial equipment and services, and even to non-commercial areas such as charities and the arts. The broad processes are similar in each case, even though organisational objectives may vary.

Analysis

This helps organisations to answer the question 'where are we now?' Effective marketing requires that firms understand their current position and anticipate any changes that may affect their abilities to serve customers. Therefore, marketing-oriented firms are committed to gathering and analysing information from their environment and their customers to build up a picture of the opportunities and threats facing them in their markets and enable them to respond to them in appropriate ways.

Environmental scanning is undertaken to identify the forces that surround the buyer and the firm and are beyond the control of the organisation itself. Changes in legislation, for example, may render an existing product obsolete or encourage demand from customers who had previously had no need for a particular product. The arrival of foreign competitors may start a price war which a domestic firm with high costs may find very difficult to win. An increase in disposable income brought about by falls in the mortgage rate may lead to increased demand for luxury goods and better quality products. (Further discussion of this appears in Chapter 3.)

Buyer behaviour needs to be assessed so that firms have a good understanding of what makes their customers buy. It is a critical role of marketing to identify the buyers of their products and services, the decision processes that they go through in making their purchase choices and the way in which their personal motivations and attitudes, educational levels, social class, age and many other factors influence their buying decisions. Individuals wanting to go on holiday, for example, may be motivated by a need for a rest, a desire to make new friends or a wish to explore new places. Their choices are likely to be influenced by their age, their family commitments, their budget and even their susceptibility to sunburn. (Chapter 4 explains the concept of buyer behaviour in more detail.)

Marketing research is the process by which much of the information about customers and the environment is collected. The marketing function is responsible for identifying information needs, gathering data and systematically feeding information into the organisation to help it make better marketing decisions. Without marketing research an organisation has to make guesses about its customers – a dangerous stance to take if you think about the sheer diversity of opinions, tastes and preferences that are evident when we look at buyer behaviour. (Chapter 5 looks at the applications and implementation of marketing research.)

Strategy

Designing a marketing strategy is about setting the direction for marketing activity. As a result of thorough analysis, appropriate decisions can be made about the types of customer that the organisation wants to reach and the ways in which it will attempt to satisfy their needs.

Market segmentation recognises that not all customers for a particular type of product or service are looking to satisfy exactly the same needs, though there are likely to be some similarities between them and a number of common needs. It is a process in which marketers examine all the potential customers for a particular product or service and divide them into groups with similar characteristics or buying habits, with members of each group having similar product requirements. Take the holiday example given earlier. Segments can be identified in terms of holidays for young people, holidays for families with children, activity holidays for active adults (or children), cultural holidays for those interested in history, walking holidays for those wanting to explore, country retreats for those in search of peace, and beach holidays for those in search of the sun, etc. The list is endless. The groups, or segments, with the closest match between their needs and what the organisation can potentially offer will form the basis for target marketing.

Target marketing decisions involve the organisation in deciding whether simply to address a single segment with their products, whether it is possible to offer the same products to a number of segments, or whether it needs a range of different products to meet the needs of different segments. Take holiday companies such as Saga or Club 18–30. Their products are carefully targeted at the needs of different age segments. Others, such as Thomson, offer a wider range of holidays of a more general nature with a view to attracting a range of different segments with overlapping needs. Such decisions on target markets have a major impact on both the organisation's resources and customer perceptions of it. (A full discussion of target marketing appears in Chapter 6.)

Product positioning takes place when decisions have been made about target markets. The needs and wants of the various market segments to be served have to be translated into a tangible set of features which an organisation will design to give its products a unique position in the minds of both actual and potential customers, so that members of its target segments see it as offering advantages over competitor products. This requires not only that the products themselves are tailored to the needs of the targeted segment or segments, but that their price levels are in line with customers' willingness to pay, that the promotional activity used to communicate with customers about the products puts across an image that appeals to them, and that the distribution of the products makes them fully accessible to their key potential customers. In other words, the organisation must develop a marketing mix strategy that supports its products' positions in the market.

The *marketing mix* consists of those features of the organisation's activities that have a primary influence on sales: namely the product itself, price levels, promotional activity and distribution (also known as 'place', hence the four elements are often referred to as the '4 Ps'). At the strategic level decisions are made on a variety of issues:

▶ Which products should be targeted at which market segments?
▶ Should any new products be introduced?
▶ How high should prices be set compared with the competition?
▶ What do we need to communicate to our target markets?
▶ Could distributors be used to reach the customer more effectively than selling direct?

These strategic decisions (in other words, decisions that affect the future direction of the business) then form the basis for the formulation of marketing tactics, which should be designed to fine-tune the match between customer needs and what the organisation supplies.

Tactics

Marketing tactics are the specific activities undertaken to implement the marketing strategy. These build on the broad outlines given in the strategy by providing more detailed descriptions of precisely how the elements of the marketing mix should be developed.

Products and services have to be carefully designed to provide the characteristics sought by the target market segments. In implementing a product strategy, marketers must recommend the most appropriate tangible features, such as colour, style, size and functionality, but they must also look at some of the less tangible elements that make up the 'total' product in the eyes of the customer. For example, a customer thinking of buying a carpet is certainly going to be interested in its colour, pattern and durability, but might also be concerned about it being a 'good make', whether it can be delivered and fitted and whether it is possible to pay in instalments. So responsibility for creating brand image, appropriate packaging, associated services and other intangible aspects of what the customer buys also falls to the marketing function. (This is discussed further in Chapters 7 and 8.)

Price levels have strategic and long-term implications for an organisation as they are related to the image of the product and will partly determine the nature and strength of competition that a firm faces in the market. Price levels should be set as a reflection of the value that customers place on the product – not always easy to determine, particularly as different market segments may be willing to pay different amounts. Tactical decisions have to be made if sales are not to be lost due to the inevitable mismatches that will occur between prices set and customers' perceptions of the value of the product. Price discrimination may be appropriate, whereby certain buyers are charged more than others – if so, under what circumstances? Discounts may be required to attract less enthusiastic potential buyers – to whom should they be given? how much of a reduction? (These and other pricing issues are dealt with in Chapter 9.)

Promotion is the means of communicating with potential customers about an organisation and its products and services. Promotional strategy will determine what needs to be communicated and to whom, but tactical decisions then have to be made as to how that is best achieved. Marketing communications can take a variety of forms, but they are usually described in terms of a promotional mix, namely advertising (promotion using mass media), sales promotion (incentives such as a holiday competition or cash-back vouchers), public relations (including the generation of editorial coverage, known as press relations) and personal selling (one-to-one communications, either face-to-face or over the phone). This list is not exhaustive though. Exhibitions, corporate hospitality and direct marketing, for example, are other forms of promotional activity which don't sit comfortably in any one of the above categories. Depending on the promotional strategy it may be necessary to use a range of methods. (Promotion is fully considered in Chapters 11 and 12.)

Place is the term used to represent the task of making products and services available to customers – it is also known as distribution. An important distribution decision is whether to use intermediaries to reach end-users (intermediaries being independent organisations whose primary function is distribution), or whether to attempt to reach customers directly. Take financial services, for example. Traditionally, most insurance companies sold their products through agents and brokers who were paid commission for arranging sales. In recent years, though, there has been a growth in direct distribution, particularly over the telephone, with customers arranging their policies with the insurance companies themselves and benefiting from the reduced prices offered as a consequence of avoiding payments to middle-men. Decisions relating to the use of intermediaries are known as marketing channel decisions. Organisations have to determine not only whether to use intermediaries, but if so, how many of what sort in which locations? Another set of distribution decisions relate to what is known as physical distribution, including order processing, transportation, warehousing and stock-holding. Marketers have to face an inevitable trade-off here. These are the activities that ensure widespread and consistent availability of products and services for customers, but they are expensive. Investment in improving service through better physical distribution may not always lead to proportionately greater levels of sales. (There is more discussion of this in Chapter 10.)

Management

The management of the marketing function involves the planning, control and organisation of marketing activity so that it can be effectively integrated across the whole organisation.

Planning is the process of assessing market opportunities and matching them with the resources and capabilities of the organisation in order to achieve the objectives of the firm. By encouraging a systematic approach to marketing decision-making, planning should lead to the more effective identification of customer needs and the more efficient use of resources in meeting those needs. It also ensures that organisations are constantly forced to address emerging issues in their uncertain environments, thereby improving the chances of success and reducing the risk of failure. The forecasts that are made during the planning process have a major influence on production, financial decisions, research and development and human resource planning. (The process of marketing planning is more fully explored in Chapter 14.)

Control of marketing activity is an important process for ensuring that things are going according to plan. It involves monitoring the progress of the marketing strategies being implemented and measuring their relative success or failure against the objectives they were designed to achieve. Control mechanisms enable corrective action to be taken where necessary before it is too late. If failure occurs, the cause can be investigated; it may be that the objectives set were too ambitious, or that the tactics chosen to implement the strategy were inappropriate or badly executed. Both can be changed if necessary, when it becomes clear that plans will not be fulfilled.

Organising the marketing function requires the allocation of responsibility for different tasks to different individuals. This is not always as straightforward as it may seem. Should managers be responsible for groups of products (and known as 'product' managers)? or should they be responsible for groups of customers (known as 'market' managers) to reflect the different segments in their markets? or should they be responsible for specific geographical regions, and be called 'territory' managers, particularly if their markets are international? Should a manager be responsible for all the market research, or all the advertising, or should these tasks reside with those who look after the product or customer groups? Such questions arise with regularity in many organisations, and the decisions made will affect levels of customer service – not just people's job descriptions. (There is more discussion of marketing organisation and control in Chapter 14.)

The scope of marketing

The origins of marketing lie in the post-war US consumer boom, when firms such as Proctor and Gamble, General Motors and Whirlpool pioneered attempts to introduce a consumer orientation to the supply of their manufactured goods. But the universal significance of a marketing approach has, in recent years, encouraged a wide range of very different types of organisation to adopt the marketing concept and introduce marketing techniques and practices in an attempt to 'create and keep profitable customers'.

Product suppliers and service deliverers

A product is normally seen as being tangible, while a service is more intangible, consisting of a process or activity aimed at satisfying customer needs. However, the distinction between the two is blurred. Most product suppliers add elements of service to their products to enhance the benefits they offer to potential customers. Few people buy carpets, for example, without the opportunity of having them fitted. 'White' goods such as washing machines are normally offered with service and repair contracts. Similarly, many services are accompanied by tangible features. Theatre audiences may experience the performance (a service) but may wish to consume drinks in the interval and purchase a programme to take home. Restaurants will be judged on the quality of their food (products) but their reputation is equally established on the basis of their speed of service and courtesy of waiting staff. Clearly, the concept of customer orientation is equally valid whether a business considers itself to be primarily a product supplier or service deliverer. In both situations, an understanding of customer needs should underpin decisions about what to supply and how to do it.

KEY SKILLS
ACTIVITY **1.3**
••••••••••••••
Working with others

University challenge!

To ensure that you meet the needs of your customers, it is always vital to find out what they want from your product and what influences their purchasing decisions. This is covered in more detail in Chapter 4. This exercise will help you to understand that people have a variety of different needs, and that successful marketers are the ones whose products and services best meet those needs, and who communicate the benefits of those products and services most effectively.

Traditionally, universities and colleges haven't had to take marketing very seriously. Demand for places from students outstripped the supply of places on university courses, so many institutions limited their efforts to the production of a prospectus and would fill any spare places through the clearing system. Times have changed. A large increase in the numbers of degree courses available has made it more difficult for universities to recruit students for some of their courses, and a more proactive approach is required if they are to attract good students to fill their places.

1   Make a list of all the sources of information you consulted in deciding which course to take. Do the same for four other members of your course.
2   Make a list of the key factors that determined your, and their, ultimate choice of institution and course.
3   Using this marketing research, recommend the most effective ways for your institution to attract future students to your course.

Consumer goods and industrial products

Some organisations sell to consumers, who purchase for their own use or that of their immediate household. Some supply other businesses with the goods and services they need, ranging from capital equipment to raw materials and business services such as accountancy. Organisational or industrial markets can be quite different from consumer markets: buyers are motivated by different factors, display different patterns of demand, tend to want long-term relationships with their suppliers and often involve a number of people in the buying decision. Nonetheless, the principles of marketing can be equally well applied, even if the marketing tactics used are slightly different. Customer needs must be identified (perhaps involving collaborative research) and efforts made to supply them with products and services that offer greater benefits than the competition. These benefits should then be communicated to target markets, often one-to-one, using selling rather than advertising as the main promotional tool. Distribution may have to be managed to accommodate a customer's just-in-time production plan (this is discussed in Chapter 10).

For profit and not for profit

The marketing concept emphasises that an organisation should only concentrate on performing 'exchanges' that will help it to achieve its own objectives. In the commercial world, the long-term objective for firms is likely to be profitability and marketing is well established as a doctrine that can help organisations improve their profitability. Not-for-profit organisations have non-financial goals, but marketing can be equally effective in helping them achieve these. Churches, political parties, universities, hospitals, museums and charities have all adopted marketing approaches in recent years, recognising that if they want to attract donations, votes, students, worshippers or visitors, they must first find out about their potential customers and set about matching what they offer with their customer needs. They too can benefit from studying 'buyer' behaviour, conducting marketing research and applying the tools of the marketing mix.

CASE STUDY **1.5**
....

Marketing charity to children

More and more charities are becoming sophisticated users of marketing techniques. The National Society for the Prevention of Cruelty to Children (NSPCC) is well known for its hard-hitting campaigns, which are based on a solid foundation of research findings. A two-year planning process led up to the launch of its FULL STOP campaign, which aimed to end cruelty to children through the education and support of families. Research revealed that, although the public cared passionately about cruelty to children, they often turned away from it because it was too difficult and painful to face up to. So a subsequent poster and TV advertising campaign showed a number of children's icons, including Rupert the Bear and Action Man, covering their eyes while a scene of abuse could be heard in the background. This left the viewer to infer cruelty, without it being made explicit. An estimated 85 per cent of the population saw the TV campaign, either on satellite or terrestrial channels, and over 8,000 poster sites also delivered the message, as well as a door drop of leaflets to every home in the UK. New supporters generated by the campaign were 70 per cent above target, and awareness of the work of the NSPCC rose by 42 per cent.

Calls to the NSPCC helpline also increased, by 280 per cent during the campaign's launch period, including many from children. Indeed, children themselves are an important target audience for the NSPCC. Research shows that even 7–10 year olds show a high degree of concern about many of the issues that trouble the adult population, with 'Cruelty to Children' at the top of the list. 73 per cent describe themselves as 'very worried' about this. So as part of the FULL STOP campaign, the NSPCC linked up with the Early Learning Centre (ELC) in a major cause-related marketing push at Christmas. The store felt that there was a strong fit between its own brand values and the principles and objectives of the NSPCC, as both aim to promote healthy, happy and safe child development. Fundraising initiatives involving the company's staff and customers were held over several months, including the sale of FULL STOP Campaign badges in stores, the donation of toys to NSPCC projects and an ELC employee ran the London Marathon for the charity, raising over £10,000.

Questions

1 Why do some charities such as the NSPCC feel that mass media promotional activity is an appropriate use for the funds they raise?

2 How important is it that companies such as the Early Learning Centre embrace the vision of the charities they support?

3 What factors should the NSPCC be considering when deciding (a) whether or not to become involved with a company and (b) how much money it should expect in return for its involvement?

Sources: Bedwell (2001); Early Learning Centre (1999); Wyatt (2000).

Domestic, international and global markets

As international transport and communications become ever more feasible, organisations frequently look beyond their domestic markets for business opportunities. The more involvement with foreign markets, the more important the marketing concept. Understanding the needs of customers who speak the same language and have similar cultural predispositions is difficult enough, but there are high risks involved in determining needs and the best ways of supplying them to markets that are culturally, economically and politically diverse and are thousands of miles away. Organisations have to determine whether foreign markets are similar enough to each other and to the domestic market to accept standardised products with minor adaptations to suit their local environment, or whether their needs are quite different from other countries, in which case products will have to be designed specifically to suit their needs, and promotion, distribution and pricing will have to be considered country by country. (These and other international marketing issues are considered in Chapter 13.)

Large businesses and small businesses

Small businesses often complain that they cannot afford to 'do marketing' properly, as if marketing is a set of activities with a price tag attached. It is not, of course, and there is no reason why a small business, any less than a multinational corporation, cannot attempt to identify the needs of its customers before deciding what to supply, and then to attract those customers with an appropriate marketing mix. The only real difference is likely to be the level of resources that can feasibly be committed to marketing strategies, and this is likely to mean that markets will have to be carefully targeted and that marketing tactics will have to be low-cost and innovative – this doesn't mean that they will be any less effective.

External markets and internal markets

Most people working in organisations are aware of marketing as a function that encourages mutually beneficial relationships with its external customers, those with whom the organisation trades its output. The term 'internal marketing' has arisen to describe the application of marketing *within* the firm, as opposed to *between* the firm and its external customers. As discussed in more detail in Chapter 2, internal marketing suggests that all employees should treat each other as if they are each other's customers, and are dependent on them to perform their own jobs. Thus a salesperson's external customer will be the buyer in another organisation, but his or her internal customers may include the order-processing team, which needs accurate information to ensure that the right goods are dispatched at the right time to the right destination, and the boss, who may need feedback on reactions to new products or details of competitive activity to be able to plan future sales strategies. At the same time the order-processing team and the boss may be the salesperson's suppliers, perhaps providing up-to-date information about orders placed or negotiating the purchase of appropriate technology to enable the salesperson to work as effectively and efficiently as possible. In practice, formalised internal marketing is seldom a recognised function in organisations, but its application is evident in businesses whose human resource management strategies place considerable emphasis on internal communications, responsiveness, personal responsibility and common purpose.

Key concepts
••••••••••••••••••

Cause-related marketing: linking marketing activities with good causes for the benefit of both parties.

Customer orientation: finding out what customers want before deciding what to produce and sell.

Economies of scale: when the cost of producing each product falls as the total volume of products being produced increases.

Effectiveness: producing products that satisfy customers (also known as 'doing things right').

Efficiency: producing output at the minimum cost (also known as 'doing the right things').

Goal focus: aiming to achieve an organisation's objectives.

Integrated effort: co-ordinating the efforts of different departments to satisfy the needs of customers.

Internal markets: customers within an organisation, such as colleagues in other departments.

Marketing mix: the marketing tools that an organisation can use to influence demand (product, price, promotion and place).

Marketing orientation: an approach to business that places customer needs at the heart of an organisation.

Maslow's hierarchy of needs: a framework that describes the different types of need that motivate people.

Product orientation: an overriding preoccupation with producing the products a firm would like to make rather than satisfying customer needs.

Production orientation: an overriding preoccupation with sustaining efficient production rather than satisfying customer needs.

Relationship marketing: a concept that emphasises long-term customer value rather than individual transactions.

Sales orientation: an overriding preoccupation with persuading people to buy rather than satisfying their needs.

Societal marketing: an approach to business that considers the interests of society as a whole as well as trying to satisfy individual customer's needs.

SELF-CHECK QUESTIONS

1 Marketing-led firms are driven by the needs of:
   a The product.
   b The organisation.
   c The employees.
   d The salesforce.
   e The customer.

2 Marketing is:
   (i) A business philosophy that emphasises the importance of meeting customer needs.
   (ii) A set of promotional activities designed to help a firm appeal to its potential customers.
   a Both (i) and (ii).
   b (i) but not (ii).
   c (ii) but not (i).
   d Neither (i) nor (ii).

3 What are the three elements of the marketing concept?
   a Customer orientation, product focus and employee motivation.
   b Product development, profitability and productivity.
   c Sales, advertising and market research.
   d Customer orientation, integrated effort and goal focus.
   e Analysis, strategy and tactics.

4 A sales orientation emphasises:
   a The need for economies of scale.
   b The importance of after-sales services.
   c Generating repeat business from satisfied customers.
   d Persuading customers to buy products or services.
   e Improving product quality and performance.

5 Environmental scanning is:
   a A process for identifying changes in markets.
   b A promotional technique.
   c An attempt to respond to the Green movement.
   d A system of reading bar-codes on packages.
   e A part of the marketing mix.

Which of the following are true and which are false?
   6 Income and age are likely to influence consumers' decisions when buying furniture.
   7 Grocery manufacturers usually distribute their products using intermediaries.
   8 You should never change a marketing plan once it is in place.
   9 The principles of marketing cannot be applied in public sector organisations.
   10 Many people have customers within their organisations as well as those outside.

Discuss the following

11 Under what circumstances might a firm adopt a sales rather than marketing orientation? Do you think such an approach is ever excusable, or even desirable?

12 Some authors suggest that the marketing mix has more than just the '4 Ps'. Suggest some other types of business activity that can affect demand for an organisation's products.

13 To what extent is the marketing concept relevant to the public utilities?

14 Do you think your university or college has adopted the marketing concept? If not, what alternative approach do you feel it is pursuing?

15 Explain the similarities and differences between the marketing of toothpaste and the marketing of a political party.

Further study
• • • • • • • • • • • • • • • •

Davidson, H. (1997) *Even More Offensive Marketing*, Penguin.
An enjoyable read about a whole range of marketing issues.

Kotler, P., Armstrong, G., Saunders, J. and Wong, V. (2001) *Principles of Marketing*, 3rd European edn, Prentice Hall.
A comprehensive coverage of the fundamental principles of marketing.

Payne, A., Christopher, M., Clark, M. and Peck, H. (1998) *Relationship Marketing for Competitive Advantage*, Butterworth Heinemann.
A closer look at the philosophy and implementation of relationship marketing.

Peppers, D. and Rogers, M. (1997) *The One to One Future: Building Relationships One Customer at a Time*, Bantam Doubleday Dell.
More about the personal relationships organisations can develop with their customers.

Several now classic articles give a good insight into the origins of marketing and the reasons for its growth and development:

Abell, Derek (1978) 'Strategic windows', *Journal of Marketing*, 42, July.
Borden, Neil H. (1964) 'The concept of the marketing mix', *Journal of Advertising Research*, June.
Bower, Marvin and Garda, Robert A. (1985) 'The role of marketing in management', *The McKinsey Quarterly*, Autumn.
Brown, Rick (1987) 'Marketing: a function and a philosophy', *The Quarterly Review of Marketing*, Spring/Summer.
Levitt, Theodore (1960) 'Marketing myopia', *Harvard Business Review*, July/August.

References
• • • • • • • • • • • • • •

Ashton, C. (1994) 'Morgan faces the future', *Organisational Excellence*, April.
Bedwell, R. (2001) 'The effectiveness of charity-promotion marketing', *Media Week*, 20 December, www.mediaweek.co.uk
Bennett, P. (1995) *Dictionary of Marketing Terms*, 2nd edn, American Marketing Association, Chicago.

Berry, L. (1983) 'Relationship marketing', in Leonard L. Berry, G. Lynn Shostack and Gregory D. Upah (eds), *Emerging Perspectives in Services Marketing*, Proceedings of the American Marketing Association, Chicago, pp.25–8.

Cassy, J. and Moss, S. (2000) 'The Boy Wonder', *The Guardian*, 28 June, www.guardian.co.uk

Christopher, M. and McDonald, M. (1995) *Marketing: An Introductory Text*, Macmillan.

Early Leaning Centre (1999) Press Release, 24 May.

Ely Ensign (2002) 'Church attack on commercial christmas', *Ely Ensign*, No. 157, December, p.9.

Economist (1994/95) 'Family values', *The Economist*, 25 December–7 January.

Field, M. (2001) 'How to put a spin on your new washing machine', *The Independent on Sunday*, 7 January, p. 17.

Finch, J. (1999) 'No cards for ASDA shoppers', *The Guardian*, 7 August, www.guardian.co.uk.

Hattenstone, S. (2000) 'Harry, Jessie and me', *The Guardian*, 8 July, www.guardian.co.uk

Hetherington, R. (2002) 'Prescott dashes Ikea hopes', *The Guardian*, 16 November, www.guardian.co.uk

Hiscock, J. (2001) 'Disloyal becomes the norm', *Marketing*, 21 June, pp.24–5.

James, M. (2003) 'The quest for fidelity', *Marketing Business*, January, pp.20–2.

Kotler, P. (1986) 'Megamarketing', *Harvard Business Review*, March/April, pp.117–24.

Kotler, P. (2003) *Marketing Management: Analysis, Planning and Control*, 11th edn, Prentice Hall.

Kotler, P. and Armstrong, G. (2001) *Principles of Marketing*, 9th edn, FT Prentice Hall.

Laban, B. (2001) *'Morgan: First and Last of Real Sports Cars'*, Virgin Books.

Levitt, T. (1960) 'Marketing myopia', *Harvard Business Review*, July–August. Reprinted in B. Enis and K. Cox (1980), *Marketing Classics*, Allyn and Bacon, pp.3–21.

Lewis, E. (2001) 'Combating the brand pirates and logo thieves', *The Guardian* (New Media), 3 September, pp.58–9.

Marketing Business (2001) 'Marketing Magic', *Marketing Business*, November, pp.10–13.

Maslow, A.H. (1970) *Motivation and Personality*, Harper and Row, pp.80–106.

McNeil, R. and Mirfin, V. (1998) 'Reaping benefits', *Marketing*, 26 March, p.33.

Moss, S. (2000) 'The gospel according to Ikea', *The Guardian*, 26 June, www.guardian.co.uk

Nayak, P.R. and Ketteringham, J.M. (1993) '3M's little yellow note pads: "never mind. I'll do it myself" ', in *Breakthroughs*, Prentice Hall and IBD, pp.53–69.

Peppers, D. and Rogers, M. (1997) *The One to One Future*, Doubleday, pp.20–1.

Rhys, G. (1992) 'Short-term, long-term', *Autocar and Motor*, 30 September.

Slavin, T. (2001) 'Trying to assemble a perfect reputation', *The Observer*, 25 November, www.observer.co.uk

Smith, A. (1776/1998) *Wealth of Nations*, ed. Katheryn Sunderland, Oxford Paperbacks.

Wyatt, J. (2000) 'Full marks for FULL STOP', *Marketing Business*, February, p.15.

CHAPTER **2**

Marketing in the real world

Objectives

When you have read this chapter you will be able to:

➤ Apply basic marketing principles to a wide range of situations.
➤ List the differences in emphasis between marketing a tangible good and a service.
➤ Tailor a marketing programme towards the needs of an organisational customer.
➤ Recognise the role of marketing in not-for-profit bodies, such as charities and cultural institutions.
➤ Describe the basic rationale and techniques of internal marketing.
➤ Understand some basic concepts relating to ethical decisions as they concern marketing.

Foundation focus: the 20-second takeaway

Marketing is not just for mega-corporations keen to make millions from packaged goods. Customers are equally important to organisations of all sizes, whether they manufacture physical products, provide intangible services, or sell things to other businesses rather than to ordinary shoppers. Even organisations for which profit is not an immediate objective (such as charities) can become more effective by applying marketing principles to their activities. So can organisations that treat their own staff as customers (internal marketing). In each of these contexts, the essential principles of marketing are the same. The variation occurs in how they are applied in each case. Marketing in any of these contexts raises important moral issues. Marketers can make better decisions and avoid costly long-term problems if they include ethical considerations in their thinking.

Introduction

This chapter looks at some of the ways the marketing concept has been extended to cover areas other than the profit-oriented, fast-moving consumer goods environment. We will examine marketing practice in services, non-consumer markets, and non-profit organisations (some of which can be openly hostile to the idea of commercial exchanges). We will also look at the growing area of internal marketing, whereby organisations are improving their ability to satisfy external customers by encouraging their own employees to see each other as customers. Finally, we will explore some of the ethical frameworks which are relevant to understanding marketing as an activity.

Extending the boundaries of marketing
···

Marketing, as we argued in Chapter 1, is a way of increasing an organisation's success by concentrating on customers as the justification for its existence. Instead of being inward-looking, a marketing-oriented organisation is recognisable by its external focus. Evidence for this comes from how it sees its mission, how information is gathered and shared, and whether decisions are made with the customer in mind. Experience suggests that organisations (of whatever size or purpose) which adopt this kind of approach enjoy long-term success. Organisations which neglect it tend to miss important opportunities and eventually go out of business.

Marketing as a named business discipline evolved in post-war America in fast-moving consumer goods industries – what the Americans call 'packaged goods' – such as soap powder and processed foods. At first, marketing experts tended to be housed in advertising agencies, acting as consultants to a number of clients. Then more and more manufacturing companies decided to create their own in-house departments. By the 1960s marketing was a recognised function on both sides of the Atlantic for manufacturers of consumer goods. Soon companies selling to buyers in other businesses rather than to ordinary consumers also started reaping the benefits of marketing.

The 1970s saw the spread of the marketing approach to the service sector, spurred by deregulation and increasing competition in areas such as banking and professional services. Such industries do not produce a tangible product for a customer to own and use, but an intangible service where the benefits are transferred directly at the time of purchase. For example, you don't 'own' a haircut (service) in the same way as you own a hat (product), but you can derive the benefit of looking smart from either. As we shall see, services create their own set of challenges for marketers but the basic principles of branding and customer focus remain the same as in product marketing.

To complicate matters further, some services have a cultural problem with marketing. At one stage in their history, institutions like banks and insurance companies would have rejected the idea of advertising and sales promotion as unprofessional. Having swallowed their misgivings, they are now among the most innovative practitioners of branding, customer care and direct marketing – although their adoption of marketing has not been without its problems.

DID YOU KNOW?

UK TV advertising legislation outlaws commercial spots for the following categories of services: betting tipsters, private detectives and escort agencies. So if you're after an accumulator, investigator or fornicator ... try the Yellow Pages!

In the late 1970s organisations in the non-profit sector began to explore the potential of marketing to increase their effectiveness. Charities, schools and colleges, health services, the arts and public sector organisations started to try out the vocabulary of customers, price and product. To some extent this has reflected a political environment that has seen market forces as the natural arbiter of what is possible (or even desirable) in society. But it also testifies to the versatility of customer focus as a successful operational principle. Non-profit marketing has become increasingly sophisticated and earned itself a new prominence on marketing's professional agenda. In its mission statement, the UK's Chartered Institute of Marketing extends the idea of 'business success' to the competitiveness, profitability and performance of industrial, commercial and not-for-profit organisations. On the other side of the Atlantic, Peter Drucker (1990) has written, 'non-profit institutions are central to American society, and are indeed its most distinguishing feature'. He sees non-profit organisations as being at the vanguard of marketing's future development.

The principle that unites organisational, service, non-profit and commercial marketing is that they all involve exchange relationships. In other words, they can be analysed in terms of customers and providers who exchange consideration (not necessarily just financial consideration, as will be seen in Chapter 9) for benefits. This kind of analysis opens the door to the application of marketing principles to facilitate all sorts of exchanges and to increase the value of the exchanges to the mutual benefit of those involved.

CASE STUDY **2.1**

Alpha's better . . .

Holy Trinity Brompton (or HTB as the church is known to its parishioners in London's ultra-fashionable Knightsbridge) is probably the richest parish church in the Church of England. Its annual income is over £2 million, and Sundays see a regular attendance by 2,500 enthusiastic worshippers. National statistics show that only 7.5 per cent of the UK population are churchgoers, but you'd be forgiven for some disbelief of the figures looking at HTB's miraculous success. And it is largely due to marketing – proving that the Devil does not have all the best tunes.

In 1993, the parish's dynamic curate, Nicky Gumbell, noticed that the introductory programme to the Christian religion he had been running in the parish was doing very well in attracting new parishioners. Called 'Alpha' (because of its position at the beginning of the Greek alphabet), the course provides a demystifying guide to the basic tenets of Christianity. Gumbell decided to offer the programme on a wider basis to other parishes and set up a number of conferences for other church leaders to show them how it worked. By the turn of the century, almost 8,000 courses were running in UK churches – not only Anglican churches but in other denominations as well. The international success of the scheme has been phenomenal, with three million graduates in over 130 different countries.

Marketing has been essential to Alpha's growth, particularly the poster advertising which has been a regular feature of its promotion. A typical annual campaign will feature 1,500 large billboards across the country, thousands of mobile sites on the back of buses, and coverage of London Underground stations to target the young professionals who have responded so positively to the scheme (accused by some of its critics as selling 'designer Christianity'). The real secret of the marketing is word-of-mouth, however. Hundreds and thousands of small posters and leaflets are used at grassroots level through homes and churches, and the most effective part of the process lies in people bringing their friends and family to see what's on offer. In this, Alpha's marketing has succeeded where many more expensive campaigns for commercial organisations have failed.

The attraction of Alpha seems to be the fact that it gives people a rare opportunity to talk about issues that concern them (such as life, death and eternity), which tend to receive short shrift in secular society. It is also good fun socially, revolving around shared meals and friendly conversation. Earnest bible-thumping is out; video-viewing and discussion are in. Questions and objections are welcome. Gumbel himself is well aware of the need to respect the position of those outside the conventional churches, having been a devout atheist until the age of 18. While studying law he decided to read the New Testament to prove it wasn't true. In fact, his reading had the opposite effect on him and, after a 10-year career as a barrister he was ordained priest in 1986.

Gumbel is still surprised by what he views as the 'accidental' success of the programme. He points to the Holy Spirit, the personification of divine inspiration, as the reason. On the other hand, Alpha has a staff of 64 (which is more people than work for the Archbishop of Canterbury) and has a vigorous publishing arm, producing videos, books and tapes, to generate a revenue of £400,000 per annum. Additional running costs are provided by donations from individuals and trusts of £1.7 million and from Holy Trinity Brompton's resources of £1 million. The course itself is offered free of charge to attenders, although there is an optional donation of £3 for the food each night, and a charge to cover costs for the weekend away which is part of the programme.

Much of the media interest in Alpha has focused on high-profile celebrities who have attended courses, prompting accusations of it being no more than a feel-good yuppie club. Popstars Gareth Gates and Geri Halliwell are among the Alpha set, as are disgraced UK politician Jonathan Aitken and ex-*Sun* page-three model Samantha Fox. It also runs in at least 60 UK universities. On the other hand, the scheme has enjoyed enormous success in 130 prisons in the UK. Some have waiting lists of six months. The prison ministry is changing the profile of the 'typical' Alpha graduate and providing a new opportunity for ordinary parishes to make themselves relevant to the challenges of contemporary society. On release, prison Alpha graduates are supported by parish groups in finding jobs, accommodation and a church at which to worship.

Questions
1 Make a list of how Alpha has used the 4 Ps of the marketing mix, and comment on the relationship between them.
2 How would you define customer needs in this case study, and how are they being met by Alpha?
3 Evaluate the role of 'word-of-mouth' marketing in Alpha's case and in two further markets of your choice – one a product, one a service. Are there lessons they could learn from the success of Alpha?

Sources: Bunting (1998); Combe (2001); Moore (2002).

Services versus physical products

The UK service economy is now outstripping the manufacturing economy in its value and the number of people employed in it. Service marketing has, therefore, assumed a new importance for marketing theorists. Of course, many predominantly physical products have an important 'service' element in them, such as ease of use, convenient packaging or clear instructions. At the same time, industries which we think as major players in the service field, such as fast food and entertainment, have a significant element of physical products involved in their consumption or delivery. For example, a visit to McDonalds (one of the biggest success stories of the service economy), will tend to involve the consumption of some kind of food. Similarly, the enjoyment of a television programme depends on access to a set. The 'continuum' between physical goods and services is explored in more detail at the beginning of Chapter 7. Suffice it to say here that customers are interested in benefits first and foremost, whether they are delivered via a physical good, a pure service, or something in between.

The basic principles of marketing a service are, therefore, the same as those involved in marketing a tangible product. However there are important differences in emphasis which are worth exploring further. Services have characteristics that separate them from physical products in a number of practical ways. Marketers need to understand what makes services different in order to present them to maximum advantage. Four widely-recognised differences between services and physical goods are as follows.

Intangibility

Unlike products, which can be handled and owned, services are intangible. They are experiences rather than objects. This means that potential customers cannot inspect or try out a service before purchase in the same way they might test-drive a car or sample some wine. The effect is to make promotion crucially important in service marketing. Communicating the benefits of what is on offer in a way that is accurate, attractive and credible is essential. Very often this means that techniques such as public relations (where a third party endorses the service) or word-of-mouth (where its reputation is spread by dedicated customers) have a more important role to play in promotional mixes for services than they do for products. We are likely to respond positively to a restaurant critic giving a good rating to the local Tandoori, even though we may take its advertising with a pinch of salt.

Another problem stemming from intangibility is that prices are difficult to set and justify in service industries. Customers cannot compare like with like in the same way they can compare physical products to assess their relative worth. So pricing needs to be carried out in a way that inspires customer confidence in the value of the offer. The perceived risk in buying a service is typically higher than in buying a product, so pricing needs to be explicitly linked to assurances of quality.

DID YOU KNOW?

Soaraway Service Sector ... About 80 per cent of the US's Gross Domestic Product (the value of what is produced by a country's economy each year) is in services rather than manufacturing. The UK is catching up with 74 per cent. Even in Germany, where manufacturing has long been the backbone of the economy, services now account for 68 per cent of economic output (CIA, 2002).

A further consequence of intangibility is the opportunity it creates for what are known as ancillary products. These are products that have a value from their association with the main offering. Tourism and the arts are essentially intangible services, but they are increasing their earnings through exploiting tangible merchandise such as apparel, books and recordings. These tangible products are reflections of the service experience which accompanies them.

Inseparability of production and consumption

Products are bought and used by consumers some time after manufacture. Services, on the other hand, are bought and consumed at one and the same time. This casts the customer in a more active role than is usually envisaged in marketing exchanges. The customer is more like a partner in the production process. As a result, the conditions under which the service is delivered need to be carefully considered. This is why banks and building societies pay so much attention to the design and layout of their branches. People need privacy and individual attention in transacting their personal financial affairs. They need to feel confident in the service provider, as well as comfortable in carrying out their side of the process. Easily-completed forms, queuing systems that minimise wasted time, even a relaxing colour scheme with appropriate fixtures and fittings can all provide sources of competitive advantage for financial institutions because of this human factor.

Another consequence of inseparability of production and consumption in services is the importance of the element of place, or distribution. Making services available to people when and where they need them has been the impetus behind the growth of direct insurance and telephone banking. Service industries such as theatre, opera and ballet companies often seek to extend their audiences by touring or playing in venues not normally associated with artistic performances.

Services are either administered directly by real people (such as physiotherapy), or mediated through technology of some sort (such as an internet-based information system). Whichever is the case, inseparability of production and consumption means that customers tend to associate the service with the person or machinery providing it. The result is that service providers need to pay special attention to the highest standards of customer care and convenience.

Heterogeneity

This is a long word for a simple concept – the impossibility of comparing like with like in services. Heterogeneity simply means 'differentness'. With products such as tins of baked beans, the manufacturing emphasis is on standardisation of production. One tin of Heinz Beans should be much the same as another tin of Heinz Beans to maintain consumer satisfaction with the brand. With services, on the other hand, the precise nature of what is being offered will depend on each transaction. No two visits to the doctor are ever quite the same, even though the benefit of improved health is the offer in each case. Sometimes the differentness of the service is key to the benefits involved. No two news broadcasts contain the same information, but every news broadcast offers the same benefit of keeping its audience up to date with events.

The consequence of heterogeneity for service marketers is to force them to be more active in explaining their advantages over competitive offerings. People in the market for life insurance or investments, for example, find it difficult to make sense of the choices available to them because there are so many imponderables. Different schemes offer different combinations of advantages and disadvantages. Sales advisors can play a crucial role in suiting the policy or scheme to the individual buyer.

Another consequence is the importance of umbrella branding. The power of a brandname like Rentokil, or a device like LloydsTSB's famous black horse, may well reassure an uncertain buyer in a confusing market. As a result, corporate advertising and public relations are particularly important in the service sector.

Perishability

Like the issue of intangibility, this is a fundamental source of difference between products and services. Many products are subject to perishability, as witnessed by 'best before' markings on grocery products, but even highly perishable products have got some kind of shelf life during which they can be stored, if not sold immediately. This is not the case with services. If an airliner departs with unsold seats, those seats will remain unsold forever. Synchronising supply and demand is a perennial dilemma for service marketers.

Pricing is an area where this is particularly apparent. Differential pricing, where different prices are charged for services at different times of the day, week or year, is a common response to the need to flatten out demand to meet availability (as we will see in Chapter 9). So theatregoers seeing a show early in the week will tend to pay less than those attending the more popular weekend performances. Similarly, the notorious complexities of fare structures on rail or air journeys reflect the need of those industries to recoup high fixed costs by maximising seat occupancy.

Here is a brief check-list of some of the main practical marketing consequences of service characteristics:

1 *Intangibility*:
   – An emphasis on promotion (especially public relations with third-party endorsement).
   – Higher perceived risk by consumers, so pricing needs to be linked with assurances of quality.
   – Opportunities for ancillary products.
2 *Inseparability of production and consumption*:
   – Customers participate in services, they need to feel confident and comfortable.
   – Distribution focuses on when and where the service is needed.
   – Customers identify service providers with the services themselves, so a high standard of customer care is essential.
3 *Heterogeneity*:
   – An emphasis on selling as a way of explaining comparative advantage in a confusing market-place.
   – Umbrella branding to reassure customers.
4 *Perishability*:
   – An emphasis on synchronising supply and demand.
   – Pricing techniques to maximise uptake across time.

Modelling service provision
• •

Chapter 7 will look at how we can analyse the nature of a company's product through looking at different levels: core, tangible, extended, and so on. Services can be usefully subjected to this kind of analysis, but marketers can also benefit from more specific attempts to model the way their services are produced. An influential approach, the Servuction model, has been proposed by Bateson and Hoffman (1999). It takes its name from the conflation of the two words 'service' and 'production'. (See Figure 2.1.)

The model emphasises the active role of the customer in producing the service with the service provider, rather than just passively accepting it. Services take place as a result of co-operation. The Servuction model explains the production of the service as the result of the customer's interaction with three other forces:

1   The invisible organisation (the service provider's internal systems and processes).
2   The visible organisation, consisting of the people (animate environment) and physical conditions (inanimate environment) which mediate the service.
3   Other customers.

The role of these three components may vary from one situation to another. Other customers, for example, may be very important if the service is a theatre performance or a football match where audience reaction is part of the atmosphere. However, in an individual medical consultation, other customers will not feature at all.

The Servuction model leads to a number of useful conclusions about service marketing, of which these are some of the most important:

▶   The active role of the customer means that if the way the service is provided changes, the customer needs to be educated into a different way of consuming. This can make it difficult for some service organisations to develop beyond a certain level of operations, as they risk confusing or disenchanting their existing customers.

figure 2.1
Servuction model

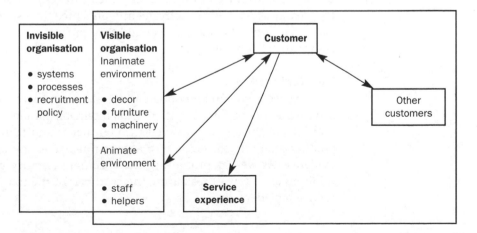

Adapted from: Bateson and Hoffman (1999).

▶ Mistakes made in services are much more difficult to conceal than problems on a production line for physical goods as they happen in the full gaze of the customer. Systems need to be in place to deal with customer feedback.

▶ Customers have a set of expectations when they approach a service encounter which some researchers have called a 'script'. For example, we all know (or dread) more or less what is going to happen when we visit the dentist. If the service provider departs from the kind of role the script expects, the customer becomes uncomfortable and dissatisfied. Staff training and internal communication thus assume a central role in service marketing.

Three more 'Ps'

These differences in emphasis between marketing services and marketing tangible goods mean that we can add three more 'Ps' to the four basic variables of product (what is on offer), price (how much it costs), place (how easy it is to get hold of) and promotion (how we hear about it). Service marketers can manipulate the elements of people, process and physical evidence.

People

Even though services can be administered mechanically (as in the case of an automated telling machine dispensing cash), people are involved in the vast majority of service situations. Profitable retailers, for example, concentrate on customer service in order to move the locus of competition away from price-cutting. Investing in training and delegating decision-making authority to customer-facing personnel are ways in which the quality of the personal aspect of service can be enhanced.

Process

Designing systems with customers in mind is essential to successful service delivery. A useful analogy with product marketing would be in the area of packaging. What might seem to a manufacturer to be a secure or economical form of packaging may strike a consumer as difficult to get into or tacky. Services need to be easily accessible and conveniently presented. In a service situation such as car rental or hotel booking, clear and easy procedures can provide a source of competitive advantage.

Physical evidence

The engineering of an appropriate physical environment for the delivery of the service is a way of compensating for its intangible nature. Assurances of quality and reliability can be conveyed through decor and furnishings. Uniform is another common expression of branding intangibles through tangible physical evidence. As well as promoting the corporate identity of the organisation, uniforms are a way of reassuring the customer of the roles and competence of service providers.

Non-consumer marketing

A significant proportion of marketing activity is directed not at consumers, but at organisations, industries or other businesses. As with services marketing, the fundamental principles do not differ from standard marketing. However, organisational needs are different from consumer needs. What organisations do with products (the mode of use) is different from what consumers do. Organisations tend to turn what they buy into goods and services for others, rather than using them directly. This affects the way in which products and services are marketed to them. We can use the structure of the traditional marketing mix to illuminate the main differences between organisational and consumer marketing.

> **DID YOU KNOW?**
> *Fear is the key, at least in organisational purchasing. Rarely invoked in consumer advertising, the fear appeal underlies one of the most famous advertising slogans in the history of industrial marketing: 'Nobody ever got fired for buying a Xerox'.*

Product in organisational marketing

Reliability is paramount in the minds of people carrying out purchasing for their organisations. Not only does the ability of their organisations to satisfy customer needs depend on the quality of the goods or services they buy, but their own professional success as buyers is tied to making the right decisions.

Organisations buy three kinds of goods and services: materials and parts that they process into their own products, capital items that are used to conduct the process, and supplies and services that maintain or facilitate the process.

Industrial marketers need to be aware of the different kinds of buying behaviour associated with these categories. For example, buying decisions about supplies and services such as those used for maintenance, repair and operating (MROs) will tend to be routine. At the other end of the scale are items of capital expenditure. These evoke protracted and difficult decisions on the part of their purchasers. Marketing capital goods such as installations (e.g. factory machinery) usually means a direct relationship between manufacturer and customer, with technically literate salespeople negotiating and advising on the right purchase.

Buying behaviour differs between consumer and organisational markets. Webster and Wind's (1972) classic study of the way people in organisations buy divides the roles involved into five main types (see Figure 2.2). Some of these roles may be shared by the same person, depending on the situation.

Users tend to start the ball rolling on a purchase by demonstrating or articulating a need. The opportunity exists, therefore, for industrial marketers to appeal directly to them in order to flag their brands as the obvious solution. Famous examples of this are Nutrasweet brand sweetner, Intel microchips and Lycra fabric component. None of these brands can be directly purchased by a consumer, but it is easier for their manufacturers to sell them to companies making beverages, computers and apparel because they make the finished product more appealing to the eventual user (whether in an organisation or on the high street).

Influencers act as reference points for others, while buyers are the professional purchasers, conducting negotiations with a number of suppliers in order

figure 2.2
**Organisational buying
behaviour**

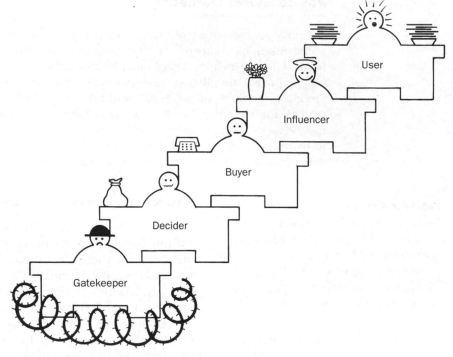

Adapted from: Webster and Wind (1972).

to get the best deal for the company. Their interests and priorities may be different from those of the users.

Deciders are those who can say yes or no to the purchase. As budget holders, they need to be confident in the decisions of their staff. This confidence can be enhanced by suppliers' branding activities. Finally, gatekeepers (such as determined secretaries) can make or break a supplier's marketing efforts by their capacity to allow or deny access to people within the organisation.

Industrial marketers spend time researching and envisaging the different motives and needs of each participant in the decision-making unit (DMU). The most important part of the process, however, is the organisation's own customer base. Canny industrial marketers sell 'through' the company in a way that guarantees that the benefits they are offering match the company's own customers' needs. In this way, successful industrial marketers are able to become more like business partners than suppliers to their customers.

Price

Price in organisational marketing is, generally, less important to customers than in consumer marketing. There are exceptions to this – such as the office stationery market, where competition between a number of very similar suppliers drives down prices. Also, negotiation on price (as one of a number of factors surrounding purchase) is far more common in industrial marketing than in consumer marketing. However, because of the need for industrial products to perform reliably and exactly, price is often a secondary issue in purchases of capital items. Their cost can be spread over a period of time (hence their capital status). Finally, the specialised nature of certain types of equipment market means that some manufacturers have very little competition on price, leaving purchasers little alternative.

Some pricing tactics are peculiar to organisational marketing. Contractors bidding for a new construction project, for example, will submit tenders for the work based not only on their own projected costs but also on what they expect their competitors will be bidding. Such 'sealed bid' pricing, where prices are submitted to buyers in confidence, relies on the bidders' ability to read the market.

KEY SKILLS
ACTIVITY **2.1**
• • • • • • • • • • • • •

Working with others

Organisational purchasing

This activity helps you to understand how your needs as a customer relate to the purchasing behaviour of an organisation of which you are a member.

Think of an organisational purchasing decision which affects you as a student or as an employee. It could be in an area like furniture, interior or exterior decoration, audio-visual equipment, stationery, catering – in fact anything which your organisation buys and which you use or experience. You may even have been involved in the purchasing process yourself. Like any purchase, it will have been made in order to satisfy a need or solve a problem (which is another way of putting the same thing).

1 Identify the people in your organisation or institution who fulfil the roles identified by Webster and Wind (1972) in the buying process for this service or product (illustrated in figure 2.2). You yourself will be the 'User'.
2 How could you as a user exert more influence on the buying process to make sure your needs were more fully met?
3 What advice would you give to a salesperson selling to your organisation or institution as a result of this exercise?

DID YOU KNOW?
When the UK government last auctioned independent television franchises in 1993 it did not expect there to be any shortage of applicants for the lucrative rights to sell TV advertising in the different regions of the UK. Cheeky Central Television (now part of Carlton) secured its broadcasting franchise for the Midlands with a sealed bid of only £6,000 – the minimum specified in the rules. In contrast Yorkshire Television (now part of Granada) misguidedly offered £43 million per year in its sealed bid – over £20 million more than its nearest rival – for its franchise.

Place

Distribution decisions in organisational marketing are subject to a wide variety of influences. Capital equipment and certain types of raw materials are frequently bulky and dangerous. This places pressure on the physical distribution operation, and explains why distribution channels connecting buyers to sellers in these markets are often very short.

Traditionally, industries have tended to concentrate in particular areas because of the proximity of energy supplies, raw materials or labour. In England the ceramic-producing potteries surround Stoke-on-Trent in Staffordshire, and the Black Country of the West Midlands is known for its sooty legacy of heavy industry. California boasts 'Silicon Valley', although information technology as an industry has the capacity to site itself more flexibly than manufacturing industries.

Time as a distribution variable is extremely important in industrial marketing. Manufacturers faced with the opportunity cost of lost output will pay a premium for prompt delivery. Industrial buyers try to insure themselves against discontinuity of supply by using a group of suppliers rather than just one. This is not so much to encourage competition on price as to make sure they are not left high and dry. With developments like just-in-time manufacturing (discussed in Chapter 10), the trend is for suppliers and buyers to become more closely involved in each other's planning.

Promotion

This is one of the major areas of difference between organisational and other forms of marketing. A typical consumer promotional mix will feature a large advertising spend, with extensive use of sales promotion, some public relations and personal selling limited to very expensive or complicated products or services such as cars, washing machines or life assurance. Industrial marketing tends to reverse the trend. Personal selling, because of the variety of members in the decision-making unit, is essential. And, because there are fewer buyers in the market than in consumer marketing, there is an even greater emphasis in industrial marketing on protecting and retaining existing business relationships.

Public relations, through the thousands of specialist magazines and journals that service UK trade and industry, is another key ingredient. Sales promotion of the consumer kind is relatively rare, but exhibitions are a key promotional resource (particularly for international business marketing). Printed material and publicity, carefully placed by direct marketing methods, are far more important than media advertising. In spite of this, business-to-business accounts are highly prized by advertising agencies, which find that the wide range of services their clients require (exhibitions, conferences, brochures, etc.) provides a continuous stream of profitable work.

CASE STUDY **2.2**

A licence to Rentokil

In 1982 the company that is now the UK businesses' services giant Rentokil Initial was a lowly pest control and wood preservation specialist. Then Clive (now Sir Clive) Thompson joined it from Cadbury Schweppes and determined to bring the rigours of FMCG (fast-moving consumer goods) marketing to bear on a company whose potential growth rate he promised as 20 per cent per annum. In fact for 17 years the average figure was nearer 22 per cent, a remarkable achievement. In 1999, however, growth dropped to 10 per cent. Other companies might have been pleased. For Rentokil, however, such a slowdown heralded disaster. Its shares fell to a quarter of their original value as the company's stocks were abandoned by fickle investors. Over the years of Thompson's stewardship the company had diversified into a portfolio of business-to-business services, including office cleaning, maintenance, delivery, and personnel services.

In fact, the problems of 1999 stemmed from an extremely ambitious attempt to expand by the £2 billion acquisition of a much larger company BET (British Electric Traction). At the time the move was likened to a horse trying to swallow an elephant. Because many of BET's businesses were very similar to Rentokil's, the move had the effect of reducing competition in a number of areas. However, alongside the highly successful Initial laundry and workwear company, BET owned several less impressive businesses which had an impact on the new group's overall profitability. The merger itself (which involved a leap in the number of worldwide employees from 36,000 to 130,000 overnight) created a temporary distraction from core business activities. Finally, Sir Clive's hands-on approach to managing the business immediately after the merger was diluted by a two-year stint heading the CBI (Confederation of British Industry) – a pressure group for industry leaders. While this may have been very good for raising the media profile of his company, it had a less healthy effect on the reality behind the image.

The recovery plan for the company has involved streamlining the business in order to focus on outperforming the business services sector in which it operates. As a result, one-third of the group has been sold off or closed, with the remainder targeting international growth markets, prioritising business that offers quick returns and customers who are likely to provide constant levels of high demand. The effect has been a share price recovery and renewed confidence in the prospects of the group.

Marketing at Rentokil Initial is not a functional specialism but a universally-held management responsibility. The traditional marketing mix is severely limited, with advertising and promotion a negligible expenditure compared to the focus on quality and customer satisfaction. The group has 110 branches operating in 40 countries, each one a profit centre. The majority of employees are blue-collar workers. They work largely unsupervised, conscious of their individual budget targets. Their individual salaries reflect whether they achieve their target. All training and motivation is in-house. The group's philosophy is simple – making profit by the most direct route possible. The overall strategy involves offering a high-quality service to customers who appreciate it and are prepared to pay a premium for it. The premium strategy means that Rentokil Initial is selective about its markets. Table 2.1 shows the turnover and profits achieved by the group in its international markets in 2001.

Table 2.1 Rentokil Initial turnover and profit by geographical market, 2001

Geographical Market	Turnover (£s million)	Profit (£s million)
United Kingdom	1,092.1	223.0
Continental Europe	660.5	140.6
North America	328.4	21.2
Asia Pacific and Africa	161.4	52.0
Total	2,242.4	436.8

Source: www.rentokil-initial.com (2002).

Almost half of turnover, and just over half of profits, come from the home market of the UK. Markets elsewhere are selected on the basis of their profit potential. Eastern Europe, China and most of Africa are avoided as not offering enough margin.

This geographical spread is unlikely to change in the foreseeable future, except that North America's importance in the portfolio is likely to increase.

The group's approach to segmenting its market also extends to customer size. While most business-to-business service companies aim at landing accounts within the Fortune 500 (America's biggest 500 companies), Rentokil Initial prefers to concentrate on middle-level businesses which are less capable of beating it down on price. The company is happy to leave the largest, and most powerful, customers to its competitors.

Simplicity is the key to the company's reporting structures. Management and financial systems are identical in each division in order to facilitate transparency. There are four major reviews of the business each year, each lasting 20 days. They are conducted by the board of a mere six directors, only two of whom are internal to the company. The common systems not only help senior management to control and guide the business, they mean that staff mobility is enhanced. Managers can move with ease between different parts of the group in different parts of the world because they already know the ropes. Just as marketing is everybody's job, so the personnel function, instead of being a separate department, is seen as the job of line management.

Questions

1 What evidence can you find in this case study for Rentokil being a marketing-oriented company?

2 Rentokil started off as a pest-control business. This is still an important part of its portfolio, but the business now extends to hygiene, security, conference services, tropical plant maintenance and parcels delivery. Comment on the advantages and disadvantages of a spread of business like this.

3 'Choosing the right customers is the secret of Rentokil's success, so far.' Discuss.

Sources: www.rentokil-initial.com; McClenahan and Bredin (1996); Shaw (1997); Simms (2001).

KEY SKILLS
ACTIVITY **2.2**
● ● ● ● ● ● ● ● ● ● ● ● ●

Application of number

Percentage perspective

This exercise gives you practice in using percentages to bring numerical data to life to back up arguments.

Look at the figures in Table 2.1 and fill in the following grid:

1 What percentage of total turnover does Continental Europe contribute?	
2 What percentage of total profit does Continental Europe contribute?	
3 What is the percentage profit on Continental Europe turnover?	
4 What percentage of total turnover does North America contribute?	
5 What is the percentage profit on North American turnover?	

Not-for-profit marketing

At first glance, marketing and profit seem to be interdependent as notions. However, marketing has proved an effective approach in the non-profit sector among organisations devoted to causes other than commercial gain (e.g. charities, health, social welfare, education and the arts). Marketing's association with big business means that some managers in non-profit organisations still treat it with suspicion. Common objections are as follows:

▶ Marketing is unnecessary: the advantages of good health or a sound education should be self-evident.

▶ Marketing is wasteful: it consumes scarce resources that would be better applied direct to the organisation's mission.

▶ Marketing is manipulative: its reduction of human behaviour to buying and selling is demeaning.

These misgivings are understandable, but they tend to stem from shoddy or misunderstood marketing rather than the effective application of genuine marketing principles. Marketing is a way of using scarce resources to maximum effect by agreeing on a focus for an organisation's activities: the customer. Rather than existing to serve their own ends, organisations need to find their justification outside themselves. In this sense, non-profit organisations need customers just as much as commercial organisations do. It is essential for them to articulate who their customers are, and to shape their efforts towards them.

Many non-profit organisations are therefore embracing marketing principles as a way of making themselves more effective in a competitive environment. However, just as organisational and services marketing display different emphases from FMCG marketing, so non-profit marketing has its own set of features. Again an analysis along the lines of the 4 Ps is a useful way of highlighting these.

Product

Most non-profit organisations are providing services, so what we have said about service marketing earlier will hold true for them. Their services link them to their users in a different way from commercial organisations, however. Instead of 'customers', organisations working in the social welfare sphere prefer the notion of 'clients'. This emphasises a more equal relationship between those who are helping and those being helped, as well as implying a professionalism on the part of the helpers which puts them on a par with firms like lawyers and accountants. In a classic article, Levitt (1986) described products as 'problem-solving tools'. Non-profits see themselves as empowering their clients to help themselves, rather than spoon-feeding them with pre-packaged benefits.

This means that sometimes the notion of what a customer wants is less relevant to effective non-profit marketing than what a customer needs (even though this sounds like marketing heresy!). A local authority housing unit, for example, may refuse requests for trivial repairs from its tenants (frustrating their short-term wants), but provide the facilities for them to carry out such repairs themselves. The money saved can be used to delay rent increases, satisfying the underlying long-term need for cheap accommodation (Harrow and Shaw, 1992).

Price

Although many charities make a charge of some sort for their services, pricing in the non-profit sector tends to be below cost. Prices to the target market are often subsidised by fundraising or government grants. This makes the management of non-financial price factors even more important in the non-profit sector than in the commercial sector. Someone going to the subsidised theatre in the UK, for example, will pay on average half of the true cost of a ticket. But there will be other elements of price – inconvenience, the conventions to be observed at the theatre, the need to concentrate, etc. Some of these aspects of price are integral to the experience. Others can be reduced by action on the part of the theatre. Clear signage, well-trained staff and a user-friendly atmosphere can reduce the non-financial price of a theatre visit by putting unfamiliar customers at their ease.

Voluntary organisations exact a price from their supporters in return for the benefits of involvement. This price can be financial, such as a donation, or expressed as a gift in kind such as unwanted computing equipment. By making it easier for their supporters to donate (by promoting payroll giving and other tax-efficient arrangements) charities can soften their financial prices in the same way that commercial organisations offer flexible payment schemes.

Time, given on an individual basis by many thousands of volunteers who participate in the work of the group, is perhaps the single most common form of price paid by a voluntary organisation's supporters. Again, the deterrent impact of such pricing can be reduced by action on the part of the organisation. Arranging for volunteers to staff a charity shop on rotas of short shifts rather than for full days is one way of doing this.

DID YOU KNOW?

Britain has got meaner – or bolder? – when it comes to door-to-door charity collections. A 1987 survey revealed that 57 per cent of respondents were too embarrassed to refuse doorstep appeals. By 2000 a similar survey put the figure at 25 per cent! In fact, only 30 per cent of UK households give to charity, with an accent on older donors. With income from individual donations declining, charities need to work hard to convince supporters of the worthiness of their cause (Walker and Pharaoh, 2002).

Place

Non-profits have the same need as commercial organisations to make themselves available to customers as and when required. Because so many of them are active in the service sector, the timing of their provision is very important (given the intangibility and perishability of services noted earlier in the chapter). Drop-in centres and telephone advice lines are two ways in which voluntary groups commonly administer their services in an attempt to strike the right balance between convenience to the customer and cost to the organisation.

CASE STUDY **2.3** **Final testament**

Smoking is the biggest cause of premature death and preventable illness in the UK: 98,000 people die per year as a result of smoking-related diseases. Unsurprisingly, smoking rates have declined since the 1960s when the link with cancer was established, but this decline has slowed in the 1990s. More alarmingly, smoking continues to be highly popular among teenagers. Government policy aims at reducing smoking by a combination of high taxation and public education.

But what is the best approach to take with such education campaigns? Do people pay any attention to messages in the mass media (such as press, TV and posters) about the dangers of smoking? And, given the difficulty of reaching the millions of men and women who smoke, what kind of priorities ought to govern targeting strategies? The UK's Health Education Authority (HEA) and its successor the Health Development Agency (HDA) has spent a lot of time and effort trying to answer these questions.

The good news is that evidence from research carried out in America, Australia and the UK shows that media campaigns are effective in prompting smokers to ditch the habit, with television emerging as the most powerful way of reaching them. As a result, television advertising forms a central plank of government smoking reduction campaigns. Such an expensive medium, however, needs to be carefully targeted in order to be effective. Campaigns run by the HEA since the early 1990s have therefore aimed at a range of target audiences within the smoking population, guided by age, family and class considerations. Another consideration has been how much the targeted groups want to quit. Parents who smoke were an early target audience (in order to prevent the habit from being picked up as normal by their children), then smokers who were close to giving up (given that a media campaign might just push them over the edge), and finally 16–24-year-old adults, especially women. This last group is currently seen as an urgent priority, as smoking shows least sign of diminishing in this section of the population. Table 2.2 provides details of how smoking in this segment was actually increasing in the mid-1990s.

Table 2.2 Percentages of men and women smoking by age, England 1994–96

	1994	*1995*	*1996*
Men			
16 – 24	32	32	34
25 – 34	33	31	31
35+	25	24	24
All Men	28	27	27
Women			
16 – 24	28	31	33
25 – 34	30	29	30
35+	22	21	21
All Women	24	24	25

Sources: www.hda-online.org.uk (2000); Grey et al. (2000).

Women are also seen as a key group because of the dangers of smoking during pregnancy. The proportion of pregnant mothers smoking rose from 27 per cent in 1992 to 32 per cent in 1996. Socio-economic groups C2DE (people in households with lower than average incomes) are also a high priority – 49 per cent of all women aged 16–24 in this group smoked in 1996.

Getting the anti-smoking message through to younger smokers is made more difficult by the fact that they are often less motivated to quit than older smokers. So the messages of encouragement and positive support which might be effective for older smokers fall on deaf ears for this group. Evidence from Australian research suggests, however, that younger smokers respond well to hard-hitting negative messages about smoking. On the other hand, it is clear that smokers of any age can seek escape routes of cynicism or disbelief about anti-smoking commercials. After all, television advertisements are scripted, and actors are paid to say lines. To block this avenue of escape, the 1997–99 Testimonials campaign featured real smokers who were as close as possible in age to the target audience talking about how the habit had ravaged their health. Television commercials containing their unscripted interviews were aired alongside other short interviews with health professionals talking about dealing with the consequences of smoking.

The personal testimonials to smoking's legacy of terminal illness, amputation and other serious disease made for disturbing, but riveting, commercials. Younger smokers found the campaign engaged their emotions and made them think seriously about giving up. The campaign succeeded in giving a powerful message without having to resort to the sometimes counter-productive shock tactics which had characterised some earlier approaches. Topline statistics for 2000 revealed that smoking among all women in the UK had declined to 25 per cent – although the percentage of younger women who smoke remained higher than average, and the proportion of all men who smoke remained more or less unchanged at 28 per cent.

Effectiveness apart, the campaign's use of real people raises some tough questions. The HDA's report on the campaign begins with an acknowledgement from Chris Neish, the advertising manager responsible, to the real people featured in the ads: 'Terminally ill with smoking-related diseases, the testimonees drew strength from "going public" and knowing that they could hopefully prevent others from suffering as a direct result of cigarette smoking. Without their help and the great support that we received from their partners and families, the advertisements could not have been made.'

Questions

1 The case study outlines an effective approach to educating younger smokers about the risks of smoking. Outline brief proposals for similar campaigns aimed at:
   ▶ men aged over 40 who would like to quit smoking;
   ▶ pregnant women smokers;
   ▶ smoking parents of children of primary school age.
2 The use of real cancer sufferers in the testimonials campaign was effective but controversial. There have also been recent examples of bereaved families allowing the use of images of dead family members in anti-drug publicity. What guidelines would you suggest for the use of 'real people' in campaigns to gather support for the following causes, and what alternatives would you propose if you felt such use was unacceptable?
   ▶ HIV/AIDS prevention;
   ▶ famine relief;
   ▶ a support centre for victims of domestic violence.

Sources: www.hda-online.org.uk (2000); Grey et al. (2000).

KEY SKILLS
ACTIVITY **2.3**
••••••••••••
Problem solving

Value exchange

Applying marketing principles to non-profit situations depends on recognising what is involved in the exchange between customer and supplier. This exercise helps you to identify the elements of an exchange from Case Study 2.3 by using a diagram – an important tool in diagnosing and solving problems.

1 Using the idea of marketing as an exchange, draw a diagram which shows what is being exchanged between a 16–24-year-old woman viewing the testimonials campaign and the Health Education Authority/Health Development Agency. For example, in Figure 2.3 the supplier is offering information, the customer is offering attention. What else might be involved?

figure 2.3
Exchange diagram

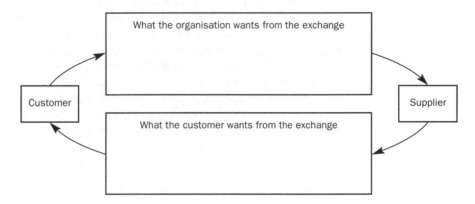

2 Use the diagram as a basis on which to suggest ways in which the exchange could be made more effective.

Promotion

Non-profits tend to have much smaller promotional budgets than their commercial counterparts, with an attendant reliance on public relations rather than paid-for advertising to get their message across. What advertising and printed publicity they do use, however, needs to be carefully conceived so as not to risk being counter-productive. Donors are unlikely to be impressed by publicity material that looks too expensive if it is pleading the case for urgent financial support.

A second consideration non-profits bear in mind with particular sensitivity is the moral dimension of imagery. Environmental pressure groups and charities will invariably use recycled materials for their literature. Charities working with the developing world or with disadvantaged people will studiously avoid stereotyped imagery portraying their clients as beggars. There is often a tension, especially in fundraising publicity material, between the emotional imagery which gets people to sit up and donate and the stereotypical imagery which voluntary groups are at pains to avoid.

CASE STUDY **2.4**

E is for Extracting donations...

e-Marketing is becoming big business for charities. It is particularly useful for targeting a group that has long posed a challenge to fundraisers – the young. Young people are vital to any marketer keen to recruit new customers, and charities are no different. So using a medium such as email or text messaging to contact them and arouse their interest is a natural choice.

World Vision, an overseas aid charity, has pioneered the use of e-marketing in its annual campaign directed at young people. Run each February, the 24 Hour Fast/Orangeapeel gives participants a chance to raise money for poverty relief and at the same time raise their own awareness of the issues being tackled by the charity. The event is targeted at 11–16 year olds, but feedback suggested that while girls were enthusiastic participants, boys were less responsive.

In order to attract more male participants, World Vision enlisted the football website Giveusthescore.com to include a message about Orangeapeel with the information and match updates it regularly sends to its subscribers. Many of them are teenage boys and the charity succeeded in reaching 3,000 new potential supporters as a result of the campaign.

Centrepoint, the homelessness charity, is using a similar tactic to try to rejuvenate its donor base. Like many charities, its typical donor is an older woman. In order to develop a greater proportion of younger supporters it has deliberately targeted recent marketing activity at the under-35s. An important part of the strategy is e-marketing, chosen by the charity not only for its popularity with younger people, but also because it is far cheaper than many traditional contact media, and thus makes Centrepoint's limited marketing funds go further.

Questions

1   List the strengths and weaknesses of SMS (short message service) and email as contact media aimed at 11–16 year olds.
2   What other incentives might World Vision use to interest 11–16-year-old males in its work?
3   How might an organisation like Centrepoint evaluate the success of its e-marketing activities?

Source: Ramrayka (2001).

Internal marketing

Non-profits such as the ones we have mentioned are often dedicated to selling an idea rather than a physical product. Many commercial companies have woken up to the need for selling ideas like their mission and objectives. Their target audience is not just external, however, but internal: their employees themselves. No matter how convincing a company's marketing mix, the deciding factor as to whether it can clinch regular repeat business is its people. Customer service, innovation and commitment to quality all stem from the workforce.

Internal marketing is an extension of the marketing concept that treats an organisation's employees as its internal customers, recognising their essential role in its external marketing success. It is still a relatively recent concept in marketing, but has been defined as 'attracting, developing, motivating qualified employees through job-products that satisfy their needs' (Berry and Parasuraman, 1991).

This idea of a job as itself a product is an intriguing one. Perhaps the best way to understand its relevance is to think back to our earlier discussion of business-to-business marketing. Companies buy products and services in order to enable them to serve their own customers better. If you are selling products or services to another business, an effective strategy is to emphasise how your product or service will help the business to serve its customers better than its competitors. For example, your oven equipment might not be the cheapest on the market but if it is the most reliable, then the bakery to which you are selling it will be able to produce high-quality bread on time and in the right quantities to its own customers. Similarly, if an organisation markets a 'job-product' successfully to an employee, that employee will be better equipped with motivation, knowledge and authority to keep his or her own customers coming back to the organisation as a preferred supplier. Furthermore, the employee will start to see his or her colleagues as internal customers and suppliers, linking each member of the organisation to the final customer.

Internal marketing has much in common with human resource management, but emphasises the priority of making sure that employees understand and can deliver the advantages of their company's product or service to their own customers. It impacts on organisations at three levels. First, at a basic policy level, internal marketing holds that it is no use having a mission and values unless they are communicated to staff. The development of a distinctive organisational culture, almost like an internal brand, is key to this process. Second, on the strategic level, internal marketing spreads ideas and techniques on how a company does business. Quality programmes, cost-saving exercises and team building are common strategic routes to success. Their establishment as strategic paths depends on a company's ability to enthuse its staff by satisfying their motivational needs like any other group of customers. Finally, on a tactical level, internal marketing can facilitate day-to-day operations like training (especially in customer service), recruitment and relocation.

The basic shift in perspective that internal marketing seeks to introduce is for employees to see themselves as linked to external customers by a series of marketing relationships inside the company. They are encouraged to see each other as suppliers and customers in this chain. This has the effect of allowing staff who are relatively remote from customer contact to realise that their contribution is vital to the whole company's ability to compete effectively. The concept of the internal customer can be embedded in a total quality scheme whereby people throughout the company are provided with the techniques to improve their service to each other and, by extension, to the final customer. Because the ideas come from themselves, the workers have ownership of them and their own customer needs (for job satisfaction and pride in their work) are satisfied.

The techniques of internal marketing revolve around effective communication. Information about the organisation is central to this – business gains, future developments, memorable details and news. Communicated via techniques such as internal briefings, newsletters and intranets, this kind of information can make each member of a company an invaluable ambassador to the external world. Second, the importance of marketing itself needs to be explained to workers throughout the organisation. Successful companies send staff from all functions on marketing courses in order to impress upon them the reasons behind decisions and working practices that may seem illogical from a non-marketing viewpoint. This has the result of gaining a company-wide acceptance of the rationale of marketing, with consequent gains in effectiveness.

Finally, internal marketing can be used to help allay the effects of crises – whether potential or actual. Well-briefed employees give credibility to the reactions of a company faced with serious adverse publicity. Observers will believe them. Indeed, a well-managed crisis can have a lasting beneficial effect on a company through uniting the workers in a kind of Dunkirk spirit that survives after the crisis has blown over.

CASE STUDY **2.5**

Dreaming of success

Lancashire-based Silentnight Beds is the UK's largest branded bed manufacturer, part of a furniture group which also includes Parker Knoll and Stag cabinets. Its Hippo and Duck characters, unlikely bedfellows as they are, have featured for years in the firm's advertising to demonstrate the advantages of its unique 'Miracoil' individual spring system. So popular have the characters proved that they are available in stuffed toy form from the company's website for mattress fanciers everywhere.

The company believes that a loyal, well-informed and highly motivated workforce is key to making the business more efficient and effective. It therefore places great store by internal marketing, which is co-ordinated by Silentnight's own marketing department.

The focus for a recent internal marketing campaign, which won *Marketing* magazine's coveted Internal Marketing award for 2002, came in the shape of the company's return (after a 15-year absence) to television advertising in 2001. The budget for the national advertising burst was £6.6 million, and the company felt that its workers needed to know the rationale for expenditure on this kind of scale. All staff were taken to head office for a 'Business Awareness Presentation', which set forth the business thinking behind the TV advertisement and the multi-million pound campaign. As well as receiving an exclusive preview of the advertisement itself, staff were regaled with a 'making of' documentary video explaining how and why it was put together.

To support its return to television advertising, Silentnight also embarked on a sponsorship deal with Anglia Television's popular drama series *Where the Heart Is*, set in a picturesque fictional village not far from the factory. Part of the package consisted of a staff competition with a walk-on part in the drama for the winner. The internal marketing strategy also featured a corporate citizenship campaign, linking with an appropriate charity and involving the efforts of 40 members of staff. The charity chosen was REACH – the national advice centre for children with reading difficulties. Silentnight launched the 'Biggest Bedtime Storytelling Event' where celebrities read their favourite stories to children.

Questions

1   List the ways in which Silentnight's customers are likely to be better served as a result of the internal marketing campaign described in this case study.

2   What challenges might a senior executive making a business awareness presentation to his or her staff face? How might marketing skills help overcome them?

3   The case study features a corporate citizenship campaign. What are the potential disadvantages of such a campaign in terms of staff morale, and how might an internal marketing plan seek to avoid them?

Sources: www.silentnight.co.uk/; Marketing (2002).

> ***DID YOU KNOW?***
>
> *Although it is illegal for companies to produce counterfeit goods which resemble leading brands, an estimated £2 billion of legitimate sales are lost to counterfeit traders in Britain each year. Far from boycotting such illegal practices, 40 per cent of consumers relish the prospect of buying fake brand names on the cheap. Of that 40 per cent, 76 per cent would buy clothing or footwear, 43 per cent would buy watches and 38 per cent would buy perfumes (Newland, 1998).*

Marketing ethics

Marketing involves moral choices. A retailer may, for example, be offered a very tempting incentive scheme by a supplier to sell off stocks of a product that will shortly become obsolete. Should that retailer tell the consumer that a brand new and better model is about to be launched? Alternatively, an advertising agency may come up with a highly effective campaign for a new kind of children's breakfast cereal, emphasising that it is full of vitamins but forgetting to mention its high levels of sugar and fat. The campaign will almost certainly boost sales, but should the client run it? The way in which a firm responds to questions such as these will reveal its marketing ethics – the values it holds and the principles that guide its conduct.

Normally, it is in an organisation's interest for its marketing ethics to match the norms and expectations of society. If they don't – if society judges a particular marketing activity to be unethical – then that business will lose sales, consumer protest may lead to legislation, and legislation will take away the organisation's choice. However, there are many grey areas where there are no clear-cut dividing lines between what is acceptable and what is not. Clothing retailer, Benetton, has provoked much controversy over the years for its press and poster advertising campaigns. The public generally accepted the picture of a baby having emerged from the womb covered in blood, but the scene of a grieving family around the bed-side of an AIDS victim was widely condemned and banned by various magazines. The issue is complicated further by the fact that public opinion is subject to change. The Advertising Standards Authority, for example, emphasises that its rulings on controversial advertising should not be taken as precedents. What it judges as acceptable one year might have become unacceptable two or three years on, and vice versa.

Companies could rely on the free market and legal systems to regulate their marketing activities. Under this principle, companies and their managers are not required to make any moral judgements, as they will simply behave within the formal rules of society. More commonly, however, a business will determine for itself what is acceptable behaviour in the market-place, and adopt a set of guidelines which may be more restrictive than the letter of the law. These moral philosophies are usually influenced by one of two principles.

▶ *Utilitarianism* is a philosophy which pursues the maximum good for the greatest number of people. Famous exponents of this view include John Stuart Mill (1806–73), Jeremy Bentham (1748–1832) and the contemporary Australian philosopher Peter Singer. From a utilitarian perspective, a cosmetics firm might argue that it is acceptable to test its products on animals as this may ensure that millions of women are protected from the risk of skin irritation. Utilitarians differ in their individual standpoints, however. Singer, for example, is a staunch defender of animal rights and so would abhor animal testing in general.

▶ *Ethical formalism*, on the other hand, is a philosophy which judges behaviour according to whether it infringes individual rights or universal rules. Probably the most famous philosopher to advocate this approach was the German, Emmanuel Kant (1724–1804), who argued that behaviour should be governed by duty rather than inclination. Such an approach might seem to be antagonistic to marketing, which works by responding to wants and needs, but Kant's 'universality test' of the morality of an action (by asking the question 'what would happen if everyone did this?') is actually quite a useful principle when weighing up marketing decisions. For example, if everyone delayed payment for as long as possible (in the hope that the companies to whom they owed money would go out of business before the debt was settled), the whole economy would grind to a halt.

Ethical dilemmas arise when a marketing activity, although it may benefit the organisation, the consumer, or both, may be considered unethical. Sometimes ethical dilemmas arise as a result of differences in cultural norms between countries. Bribery may be a perfectly acceptable means of securing a business contract in some parts of the world, but is illegal, or certainly unethical, in others. Firms wishing to trade in some countries may have to apply different standards in different regions if they are to stand any chance of gaining orders.

CASE STUDY **2.6**

Enough to make you spit?

Tobacco manufacturers defend the right of smokers to enjoy their products. At the same time, legislators (reflecting changing views of what is acceptable behaviour in society) have continued to restrict the places where smoking is permitted in public. Many businesses, spurred by fears of the effects of passive smoking on employees, have made their premises entirely non-smoking. As a result, smokers have fewer and fewer opportunities to light up outside their private spaces of home and car.

The answer (the industry hopes) seems to be smokeless tobacco products – ways in which smokers can indulge their craving for nicotine in a way which does not actually involve setting fire to anything. In one sense there is nothing new about alternatives to smoking. Chewing tobacco and taking snuff are both well-established ways of ingesting nicotine. Unfortunately, both have undesirable side-effects. Snuff tends to be accompanied by a certain amount of noseblowing, and chewing tobacco leaves the chewer with an irresistible urge to spit.

United States Smokeless Tobacco Co (USST) has come up with a solution – a product called Revel which it describes as premium tobacco flavoured with mint and packed in paper pouches. Packed in 'push and flip' plastic dispensers each containing 20 pouches, the product is inserted in the user's mouth, between gum and cheek. The nicotine is absorbed direct but, according to USST, the user feels no need to spit. Interestingly, USST is not the only company investigating a smoking alternative. Star Scientific, another American company, is introducing Ariva, a tobacco product it describes as a 'cigalett'. This is a lozenge of hard, compressed tobacco flavoured with mint and eucalyptus. Again, it is held in the mouth by the user, who will apparently feel no need to spit. Each lozenge will deliver about as much nicotine as a cigarette. A possible advantage being toted by Star is that the tobacco used contains low levels of nitrosamine (a particularly nasty chemical).

Lest Europe should be left behind in this race to join the smokeless zone, Swedish Match (now owned by Volvo) is also nursing a new product. Launched as Exalt in the US and Vazatek in the UK, this is described as a 'Tobacco Packet' providing 'a smokeless alternative for cigarette smokers when they cannot, or choose not, to smoke'. The launch press release draws attention to the manufacturing standard used, which 'works towards eliminating or reducing the elements in tobacco that have been identified by the scientific community as controversial'. What this means precisely is not clear, but the company (which may be familiar to students from its existing portfolio of Swan Vesta matches and rolling papers) is confident that Exalt will create a new smokers' alternative category within the OTP (other tobacco products) sector.

Questions

1 Swedish Match stopped selling cigarettes in 1999, concentrating instead on cigars, pipe tobacco, snuff and smoking paraphernalia. It aims 'to be a unique tobacco company, using its world leading brands and niche products to work in growing markets in harmony with current social and consumer trends'. How might the company be able to demonstrate that its activities are in line with current social and consumer trends, and how might this shape its marketing ethics?

2 Nicotine chewing gum and patches have tended to be marketed at smokers trying to give up the habit. In contrast, Revel, Ariva and Exalt could be seen as supporting smokers in their existing behaviour. List and discuss the ethical implications of marketing both sorts of product.

3 Compare and contrast what a utilitarian and an ethical formalist might have to say about marketing a smokeless tobacco product.

Sources: Bickers (2001); Swedish Match (2001).

Key concepts
....

Ancillary product: a product, such as a souvenir, sold alongside another product or service.

Animate and inanimate environment: the human (animate) and mechanical or physical (inanimate) environment in which a service is delivered.

Charity: an organisation (in UK law) that exists to do one of four things: the relief of poverty, the advancement of religion, the advancement of education, or any other purpose considered charitable. Eton school is a charity, but Greenpeace is not.

Customer script: the set of role expectations with which a customer approaches a service.

Ethical formalism: a philosophy which judges behaviour according to whether it infringes laws or universal prescriptions.

Exchange relationship: a basic unit of marketing, whereby something is given and received between parties to the relationship.

Internal marketing: marketing activity that treats the people inside an organisation as customers.

Marketing ethics: the values held by an organisation that guide its marketing activities.

Non-profit sector: organisations that exist for reasons other than commercial gain.

Pressure group: an organisation with a point to make in a democratic society.

Service characteristics: characteristics that distinguish services from tangible products such as intangibility, inseparability of production from consumption, heterogeneity and perishability.

Servuction: a model of service provision that emphasises the customer's role as partner in the process.

Stereotype: an unchanging (and therefore hackneyed) image. The origin of the expression is a printing term meaning an inflexible printing plate.

Utilitarianism: a philosophy which pursues the maximum good for the greatest number of people.

SELF-CHECK QUESTIONS

1 Marketing has been adopted by organisations such as schools, hospitals and charities to achieve which of the following objectives?
 a Increase profitability.
 b Reduce costs.
 c Widen earning potential.
 d Maximise efficiency.
 e Maximise effectiveness.

2 Services differ from products in a number of ways. Which two of the following are commonly acknowledged to be service characteristics?
 a Intangibility.
 b Imperishability.
 c Inscrutability.
 d Heterogeneity.
 e Homogeneity.

3 Industrial products fall into which of the following groups of three main categories?
 a Materials and parts; capital items; consultancy.
 b Mechanical material; investments; corporate resources.
 c Machine parts; installations; inventory.

d Material and parts; capital items; supplies and services.
e Material goods; invisibles; supernumerary supplies.

4 Common objections to marketing from managers in non-profit organisations include which of the following?
a Marketing is unnecessary.
b Marketing involves charging for things.
c Marketing is wasteful.
d Marketing is manipulative.
e Marketing involves stereotypes.

5 Which one of the following is the term used to describe the ethical approach which aims at the maximum good of the greatest number of people?
a Communism.
b Ethical Formalism.
c Taylorism.
d Utilitarianism.
e Uranianism.

Which of the following are true and which are false?
6 Customers are fussy about whether benefits are mediated by services or products.
7 Opportunities for ancillary products are created by the intangibility of services.
8 According to Webster and Wind (1972), deciders are the members of a DMU whose role is to negotiate with suppliers.
9 Geographical concentration is a feature of many industrial markets.
10 Relationship marketing concentrates on an organisation's efforts on finding customers.

Discuss the following
11 The reason for falling church attendance in the UK is poor marketing.
12 Industrial salespeople are a different breed from consumer salespeople.
13 The secret of successful service marketing lies not in a firm's marketing department but in its recruitment and training function.
14 Internal marketing is just another attempt at mind-control by management.
15 Relationship marketing is fine – unless your customers value privacy.

Further study

Bateson, J. and Hoffman, D. (1999) *Managing Services Marketing: Text and Readings*, 4th edn, Thomson Learning.

Bruce, I. W. (1994) *Meeting Need: Successful Charity Marketing*, ICSA Publishing.
A fascinating book by a leading commercial marketer who went to work for a major charity.

Ford, D. (1998) *Managing Business Relationships*, Wiley.
A collection of accessible and practical articles illuminating the world of industrial marketing from a perspective which emphasises the value of long-term customer relationships. Many of the book's ideas are very relevant to consumer marketing as well.

Hill, Elizabeth, O'Sullivan, Catherine and O'Sullivan, Terry (2003) *Creative Arts Marketing*, 2nd edn, Butterworth Heinemann.
Covers the fascinating world of arts marketing with a highly practical focus and lots of examples of cutting-edge practice in the UK and abroad.

Palmer, Adrian (1998) *Principles of Services Marketing*, 2nd edn, McGraw Hill.

Robinson, D. and Garratt, C. (1999) *Introducing Ethics*, Icon.
A highly accessible but intellectually respectable survey of the field of ethics.

References

Bateson, J. and Hoffman, D. (1999) *Managing Services Marketing: Text and Readings*, 4th edn, Thomson Learning.
Berry, L. L. and Parasuraman, A. (1991) *Marketing Services: Competing through Quality*, Free Press.
Bickers, C. (2001) 'Smokeless suppliers set sights on smokers', *World Tobacco*, 1 September, p.28.
Bunting, M. (1998) 'Happy, clappy . . . and zappy', *The Guardian*, G2, 4 March, pp.2–3.
Business Matters (1991) 'An audience with Tom Peters', BBC2 TV.
Central Intelligence Agency (2002) *The World Factbook 2001*, available at: http://www.odci.gov/cia/publications/factbook/, consulted 1 October 2002.
Combe, V. (2001) 'Curate's course feeds a spiritual hunger', *The Daily Telegraph*, 26 December, p.8.
Drucker, P. (1990) *Managing the Non-Profit Organisation*, Butterworth Heinemann.
Harrow, J. and Shaw, M. (1992) 'The manager faces the consumer', in L. Willcocks and J. Harrow (eds), *Rediscovering Public Services Marketing*, McGraw Hill.
Grey, A., Owen, L. and Bolling, K. (2000) *A Breath of Fresh Air: Tackling Smoking through the Media*, Health Development Agency.
Levitt, T. (1986) 'Differentiation – of anything', in T. levitt, *The Marketing Imagination*, 2nd edn, Free Press.
McClenahan, J. and Bredin, J. (1996) 'Simply model management', *Industry Week*, 18 March, p.13.
Marketing (2002) *Internal Marketing, Marketing Awards Supplement*, 6 June, p.223.
Moore, V. (2002) 'Beyond belief?', *Daily Mail*, 10 January, p.46.
Newland, F. (1998) 'Phoney wars', *Marketing Week*, 21 May, pp.43–6.
Ramrayka, L. (2001) 'Keep it personal', *The Guardian,* Media Section, 2 July, p.35.
Shaw, R. (1997) 'Does your marketing measure up?', *Marketing Business*, October, pp.26–9.
Simms, J. (2001) 'Target practice', *Director*, 54(12) July, pp. 70–5.
Swedish Match (2001) Press Release: Swedish Match announce test market of Exalt, 27 April, available at: http://www.swedishmatch.com/eng/media/pressreleaser/2001042700770.asp
Walker, C. and Pharaoh, C. (2002) *A Lot of Give: Trends in Charitable Giving for the 21st Century*, Hodder and Stoughton.
Webster, F. and Wind, Y. (1972) *Organisational Buying Behaviour*, Prentice Hall.

CHAPTER 3

The marketing environment

Objectives
··············

When you have read this chapter you will be able to:

➤ List the key forces in the marketing environment.

➤ Give examples to illustrate the potential impact of forces in the macro-environment.

➤ Discuss the means by which firms can exert control over different elements of their micro-environment.

➤ Suggest appropriate strategies and tactics for responding to changes in the marketing environment.

➤ Understand the key features of an environmental appraisal system.

Foundation focus: the 20-second takeaway
··

There is no doubt that the pace of change in society is such that the world today is a very different place from the one customers were experiencing just 10 years ago – let alone 20, or even 50 years ago. A combination of changes in social conventions, laws, technology, levels of wealth, transport infrastructures and many other factors means that marketers have to keep a close eye on the world around them and respond to the consequently changing needs of the people who live in that world. They must also be vigilant in their monitoring of specific factors that can potentially affect their own particular part of the market, which will be influenced by their competitors, their suppliers, their distributors and other stakeholders such as shareholders and the media. Monitoring and responding to the wide range of changes that take place in an organisation's immediate and broader environments is key to effective marketing practice.

Introduction
··················

An assessment of the environment should be the starting point for all marketing activity, because changes in the environment outside the firm will be continually affecting that firm's ability to 'create and keep profitable customers'. This chapter examines the nature of the marketing environment, distinguishing between those forces over which firms have very little control and those they can influence through their own marketing decisions. By using examples, it explains how changes in the environment can require marketers to adopt new strategies and tactics to assure continued relationships with their customers and the long-term survival and prosperity of their organisations.

Finally, this chapter provides a framework for organisations to use for the appraisal of their marketing environment, and suggests a process for prioritising action to meet the new demands and challenges posed by those factors beyond their immediate control.

What do we mean by 'the environment'?

The marketing environment consists of those factors outside the immediate control of the firm which influence its relationships with its target customers. Some environmental factors affect many firms and many industries, and cannot be pre-empted or forestalled by the activities of any one organisation: such factors comprise the *macro-environment*. There is little, if anything, that a firm can do to influence its macro-environment. It must simply monitor developments and prepare for the inevitability of changes. This involves forecasting the nature and extent of potential changes and putting plans in place for responding positively to them when the time comes. An interesting example of this relates to the structure of populations. It is possible to predict population trends many years ahead with reasonable certainty, based on birth rates and life expectancy. If there is a dip in the birth rate, manufacturers of children's toys, through no fault of their own, may soon be faced with a gradual decline in the size of their target markets. As this group grows up, there will be a corresponding decline in demand for products that appeal to teenagers (such as music systems and CDs), to young adults (household items for their first homes, for example), to families (food and transport, perhaps) and to retired groups (though this market may not contract as much as life expectancy continues to be extended). There is nothing that any one firm can do to change this pattern, but by recognising its inevitability, all firms can prepare to meet these changes by extending their target markets and reconsidering their marketing activities.

Other environmental factors are more specific to particular industries and individual firms, and will affect certain organisations more than others. Such factors comprise a firm's *micro-environment*. Competitors are a good example of this. Changes in the strategies or capabilities of one firm in an industry are likely to have fairly swift repercussions on their competitors as customers are persuaded to change their allegiances. But retaliatory strategies can then be implemented by the other firms in the industry to minimise the impact of competitive attack. In other words, firms can do more than simply anticipate and respond to changes in their micro-environment; they can influence the changes and control the extent to which they interfere with the relationship between themselves and their target markets.

The rest of this chapter examines the nature of the macro- and micro-environments in more detail, and looks at the marketing task of monitoring and evaluating environmental changes and their impact.

The macro-environment

This comprises a complex set of uncontrollable variables which collectively form a framework within which organisations conduct business. There are four categories of variable that will influence the way in which organisations approach their marketing activities. They are commonly known as the STEP factors:

▶ *Socio-cultural* factors are concerned with patterns of behaviour among populations.
▶ T*echnological* factors are concerned with the development of the physical potential of the world through its industries and its people.
▶ E*conomic* factors are concerned with the systems for allocating scarce resources in society.
▶ *Politico-legal* factors are concerned with the controls put in place to protect the interests of the society.

Socio-cultural factors

For those responsible for marketing, there are two important aspects of the socio-cultural environment. The first relates to the statistics of numbers and types of people in a society (known as demographics) and the second to the reasons for those patterns (known as culture).

Demographics

By looking at patterns and trends in population structure it is possible to pre-dict likely consumer behaviour and demand in different markets, as a large number of the needs and wants that people express are firmly related to demo-graphic features such as age, gender, marital status, race and occupation. Look at some of the changes in the UK's demographic profile over the past 20 years, such as

▶ *Population age distribution*: The UK has an ageing population. In 1961 around 12 per cent of the population were aged 65 or over and only 4 per cent were aged 75 or over. This compares with 16 per cent and 7 per cent respectively in 2000. Long-term projections indicate that the numbers aged 65 or over will peak at over 15 million during the 2030s.
▶ *Ethnic minority populations*: These have risen consistently since the early 1950s, and have more than trebled between 1971 and 2002, from 2.3 per cent to 7.6 per cent of the UK population. Targeting these sub-cultural segments has become increasingly viable where ethnic differences affect buyer needs. Producers of make-up and hair care, for example, have launched products specially tailored to meet the needs of this growing segment and have created well-established and profitable brands.
▶ *Average household size*: Higher divorce rates, later marriage and a lower birth rate have brought about a reduction in the average number of people living in each household (from 2.91 in 1971 to 2.33 in 2001) and an increase in the total number of households (from 18.6 million in 1971 to 24.1 million in 2001). Of particular interest to marketers are those households with high incomes and relatively low financial commitments, such as couples with no children, who are likely to spend disproportionate amounts on luxury durable goods and quality services, and are a good target for manufacturers of hi-fi systems, fashion retailers, holiday tour operators and restaurants.

Culture

By examining the cultural background of a society, it is possible to identify the prevailing beliefs, values, perceptions and behavioural norms that underpin that society, and this will give a strong indication of the likely preferences for products and services. Core beliefs are passed on from parents to children and will be reinforced by a society's educational, legal and social institutions. Some beliefs are enduring, and will not change much from generation to generation. Moral views, for example, on the importance of honesty and the value of human life have prevailed in most societies for centuries. But other cultural norms have changed quite dramatically. Marriage is no longer considered to be a prerequisite for family formation; divorce and remarriage are creating a new version of the extended family; religious observance has declined.

Some cultural changes have had a major impact on marketing activity. For example, the role of women in society has changed dramatically in most Western countries. Labour-saving products such as the deep-freeze and the washing machine released time from shopping, cooking and washing to enable women to work. Household income rose and more couples and families could afford cars and second cars. Limited opening hours and poor parking facilities made high street shopping a problem, so supermarkets moved out of town, built bigger car parks, stayed open after normal working hours and offered a wider range of products to enable a one-stop weekly shop. And for those too tired for this after a hard week at work, a booming take-away restaurant and fast-food sector has grown up to obviate the task of food preparation entirely! It is clear that cultural change and marketing opportunities have gone hand in hand. The businesses that have lost out are those that failed to respond to the changing social environment, such as the thousands of small retailers who went out of business when the supermarket chains started to dominate the grocery market.

KEY SKILLS
ACTIVITY **3.1**
· · · · · · · · · · · · · ·

Application of number

Population predictions

Some changes in the environment come with a fair amount of warning! Records of births and deaths allow statisticians to calculate how many people of what age are likely to make up the population at any given time. This exercise will help you to understand why these figures are so useful for marketers.

The Office for National Statistics has predicted the UK population to change as follows:

		Year		
		1991	*2001*	*2010 (prediction)*
Population size		*57.8m*	*58.8m*	*60.9m*
Age distribution	16	20%	20%	18%
	16–24	13%	11%	12%
	25–44	30%	29%	26%
	45–64	21%	23%	27%
	65+	16%	15%	17%

Source: www.statistics.gov.uk (2002).

1 How many more consumers will there be in the age group 45–64 in the year 2010 compared with 1991?

2 What will happen to the under 16 age group over the same period?

3 What should the following firms be doing now to prepare themselves for these changes?

a Gap.

b Nike.

c PC World.

d McDonalds.

DID YOU KNOW?

By stimulating genetic changes in crops, fruit and vegetables during their growth or production, scientists claim to have succeeded in finding a way of both extending the shelf-life of fresh foods and improving their flavour. These genetically-modified (GM) foods, dubbed 'Franken-foods' by their critics, are already finding their way on to supermarket shelves, but not without protest from some scientists who believe that GM food should be as rigorously tested as pharmaceutical products. Environmental pressure groups are also resisting them, and protest that inadequate labelling means consumers are often unaware of what they are eating.

Technological factors

Technology is a driving force for change in society and can be significant to the marketer for a number of reasons:

▶ It can create better ways of satisfying existing needs. Many products offer only partial solutions to customer needs: record players provided an opportunity to listen to music at home, but records were easily scratched and sound quality was poor; slide-rules enabled complex calculations to be performed, but their operation was difficult to master; soap powders removed everyday dirt from laundry, but couldn't shift marks or stains. It is hardly surprising that DVDs, CDs, calculators and biological washing powders have become so popular. Each of these has been developed from new technologies that have enabled customer needs to be met in more convenient and more effective ways.

▶ It can identify latent needs. Occasionally, new technologies even allow needs to be met that consumers have not recognised themselves. The concept of a non-stick saucepan was an off-shoot of the US space programme, the material Teflon having been developed for spacecraft, not kitchen pans. And before the days of bin-liners, who would have thought of using plastic film to reduce the number of times that kitchen bins needed washing out?

▶ It can enable new customers to be reached. Sometimes new technology makes it possible for firms to serve new groups of customers who previously offered insufficient potential for profitable transactions, or with whom it was physically impossible to trade. The multimillion-pound market for frozen confectionery, such as the Mars Bar ice-cream, has only been able to grow as a result of technological developments that have enabled chocolate (and not just 'chocolate-flavoured coating') to be successfully adhered to ice-cream.

▶ It can alter the patterns of demand. We have seen earlier how cultural trends such as the rising number of working women have created demand for new home technologies and retail formats. It is also possible that the reverse can occur, with changes in technologies affecting lifestyles and their associated patterns of demand. Much speculation goes on about the impact of information technology in the home. Toffler, as far back as 1980, predicted that new technologies would herald a return to a cottage-industry-style economy, with many more individuals working from home as freelance producers, not of manufactured goods, but of information. What then of the markets for transportation if commuting is replaced by home-working, and what will happen to the army of catering companies, cleaning companies and office furniture suppliers that rely on the existence of office buildings and groups of employees to create demand for their products and services?

▶ It can change the nature of competition in an industry. There was some discussion of this in Chapter 1. Consumers are not interested in the man-made boundaries between industries. They simply want better products and services to meet their needs, and it is quite possible that new technological developments will come from industries other than the ones whose products are being surpassed. The electronics industry, for example, is providing better solutions to a wide range of needs that were previously considered to be the domain of the service industries. Internet banking and cash-point machines are more convenient for customers than going to banks and building societies; email and the World Wide Web are reducing demand for postal delivery services; and online learning means that students are starting to learn from electronic sources instead of teachers!

▶ It can increase the efficiency of marketing activities. By using new technologies, businesses are able to improve the efficiency with which they serve their customers, not only saving themselves costs but also gaining customers by offering better service than competitors. Direct marketing (as explained in Chapter 11) uses digital technology to enable organisations to send their marketing communications direct to the homes and phones of those people most likely to respond to them. Electronic point of sale (EPOS) systems enable retailers to keep a close eye on stock levels without needing staff to audit the shelves.

KEY SKILLS
ACTIVITY **3.2**
....

**Information and
communication
technology**

Who's online?

New technologies have changed the face of marketing, and as more and more people gain domestic access to the Internet, opportunities for reaching the consumer through email and the Internet continue to expand. This exercise will help you find relevant information about key trends in consumer reactions to new technology.

Go to the website at www.statistics.gov.uk to find out about people's use of the Internet:

1   To what extent has the frequency of people's access to the Internet for personal use increased since 2000?
2   Has 'general browsing or surfing' become more or less popular since 2000?
3   Describe the growth in popularity of mobile phones and Digital TV as technologies for accessing the Internet?
4   Of those who do not access the Internet, what proportion say this is because they feel they have no need for it? How has this changed since 2000?

Explain the marketing implications of these figures for retailers.

DID YOU KNOW?

To mark the Queen's golden jubilee, Thinktank, Birmingham's museum of science and technology, ran an exhibition to celebrate the greatest scientific, medical and technical advances during her reign – one for every year she had been on the throne. The list, nominated by the public and filtered by a panel of scientists, included the pocket calculator (1972), IVF treatment (1978) and the DNA fingerprint (1984). However, a number of apparently trivial things have also changed the pattern of our lives in a remarkable way, such as the cassette tape (1962), the breathalyser (1967), bar-coding (1974), and Toy Story (1995), the first entirely computer-generated feature film (Branigan, 2002; Guardian, 2002b).

Economic factors

The economy influences the total amount of money available to consumers and businesses to make purchases. It affects the levels of income consumers retain to spend on themselves and has an impact on the amount of profit and cash that businesses generate, thereby influencing the ability and willingness of individuals and organisations to perform transactions to acquire the goods and services they want. There are a number of key economic variables that marketers should follow closely if they are to make relevant and timely decisions about their products and services and the markets that they should serve:

► *Income distribution* is important to marketers, as the rich tend to display quite different purchasing patterns from the poor. Perhaps unsurprisingly, as family income rises, the percentage spent on food declines and the proportion of expenditure on luxury goods increases. This becomes particularly significant in economies where income distribution is fairly uneven and there are sizeable groups of both 'haves' and 'have-nots' so that the economy is characterised by two quite separate groups of consumers. One (usually the larger of the two) is likely to be very price sensitive, looking for low prices to enable them to afford to make purchases at all, and the other is likely to be willing to pay much higher prices in return for superior quality and features.

▶ *Recession* reduces the total income and expenditure levels in an economy. Potential buyers tend to reduce their expenditure and focus on essential items only, either due to the fact or the fear of unemployment. Demand for consumer durables, such as cars, household goods, clothes and leisure products, usually suffers most. To overcome both the financial and psychological resistance that potential customers exhibit during a recession, marketers may need to emphasise the basic functionality and value for money of their products and services, rather than superior quality and performance.

▶ *Taxation* is a process by which governments divert money from the private sector of the economy to the public sector. Governments that impose high tax rates are effectively taking away purchasing power from individuals and spending money centrally on behalf of the whole community that they serve. High-tax economies tend to favour those businesses whose target markets consist of other organisations, rather than consumers. Educational suppliers, civil engineering contractors and manufacturers of defence equipment have traditionally thrived under centrally-driven economies, while a free-market philosophy is more conducive to profitable trading with individuals and households. Direct taxes, such as income tax, determine the amount of disposable income available to households to spend on goods and services of their own choosing, while indirect taxes, such as value added tax, increase the price of goods to the consumer. Products whose supply the government wishes to control for social reasons, such as tobacco, gambling and fuel, may be taxed more aggressively than others, and marketers are then left with relatively little influence over their own pricing strategies.

▶ *Interest rates* can have a major impact on consumer willingness to make non-essential purchases. There are two main reasons for this. First, credit of any kind gives people an ability to purchase now in anticipation of future income, and they tend to take advantage of this by using bank loans, mortgages and credit cards for major purchases such as cars, houses and holidays. But this facility has a price-tag attached in the form of interest payments and when interest rates rise, those with high levels of debt are faced with a rise in the cost of this borrowing. Consequently, they will have less money available to spend on other things, and discretionary expenditure on items such as entertainment, holidays, clothes and leisure may have to be curtailed to make ends meet. High interest rates do not only reduce current discretionary expenditure, though, they also deter people from taking out new loans for the purchase of major items, which means that total expenditure on luxury and non-essential purchases is curtailed even further. Consequently, for marketers in some industries, interest rate fluctuations can pose a serious problem. Demand for their goods may increase disproportionately under low interest rates, only to fall away rapidly when rates start to rise. When rates are high, attracting new customers becomes difficult and marketing emphasis may have to be refocused, concentrating predominantly on beating the competition to make sure of attracting a sufficient proportion of the lower level of demand that remains.

▶ *Inflation* can start if high levels of demand in the economy enable firms to start raising prices without losing sales. Expectations of further price rises fuel people's willingness to spend now in anticipation of price rises in the future. Businesses may do well in the short term and sell large quantities of their products at high prices, but in the long term this is likely to lead to higher wage claims as people see the value of their income being diminished. This in turn raises the costs of production, and businesses may try to raise prices again to prevent their profit declining as a result. The most immediate problem that inflation poses from a marketing perspective is that it may endanger international trade. If products become more expensive, sales are likely to fall in foreign countries which haven't experienced similar inflationary pressures as foreign buyers look for cheaper sources of supply. This is one of the reasons why governments are keen to keep inflation as low as possible and may raise interest rates in an attempt to dampen down demand that threatens to become inflationary.

▶ *Exchange rates* are another economic variable that affect international trade. If a country's currency increases in value against foreign currencies, products become more expensive in overseas markets, but if exchange rates fall, the prices paid by foreign buyers will also fall and demand is therefore likely to increase. One of the best defences a marketer can build against the fluctuations of the currency markets is to build market share in a number of countries, so that if the exchange rate becomes disadvantageous and undermines the marketing efforts in one, there are other markets that are not threatened and that may be sustained and grown.

CASE STUDY **3.1**   **New cars for new lifestyles**

Historically, the marketing of cars has revolved around brand choice, and the marketer's job has been to persuade car drivers to buy their brand of hatchback, saloon, estate or sports car rather than that of a competitor. But a number of social changes have had a major impact on the market for cars over the past 10 years. These have prompted new developments in the manufacturing and marketing of new cars, and have led to significant changes in the structure of the market:

▶ Increasing affluence coupled with a greater tolerance for debt has led to an expansion in second-car ownership.
▶ The growth in single person and affluent 'dual income no kids' households has been fuelled by the increasing number of women in the workforce and the postponement of childbirth.
▶ Separations, divorces and re-marriages increased, creating increasingly complex family units.

> ▶ Time poverty became a feature of life for the affluent middle classes, who spent money to save time and increased their expenditure on leisure.
>
> ▶ Parental choice over schooling was introduced, resulting in greater distances being travelled to school, and fears over road safety led to more children travelling to school by car.
>
> ▶ Total sales volume of cars rose from 2 million in 1990 to 2.2 million in 1999, and the breakdown of those sales changed radically.

Multi-purpose vehicles (MPVs), which did not exist 20 years ago, became the vehicles of choice for affluent extended families, taking 2 per cent of the market in 1999 compared with 0.4 per cent in 1990. Sports utility vehicles (SUVs), especially 4 × 4s, showed a similar increase, from 1.3 per cent to 4.5 per cent of the market; and sports coupés grew from 2.1 per cent to 3.2 per cent. Demand for small basic models also grew, but big volume losses arose in the traditional larger car market, especially the upper medium and executive models, whose share of the market declined from 36.3 per cent to 26.6 per cent during this period.

Questions

1   What benefits does the MPV offer to families? To what extent are they merely aesthetic? (For example, compare them with the benefits offered by a traditional estate car).

2   Account for the increase in demand for sport vehicles over the past 10 years.

3   List the socio-cultural trends that will have an impact on the market for cars over the next 10 years.

Sources: Living in Britain (2002); Simpson and Carpenter (2000).

Politico-legal factors

The economic factors discussed earlier often stem from political initiatives designed to improve the well-being of society, but the influence of governments is also felt through the legislation they introduce. Most legislation is created to protect people, though self-regulation by professional bodies with strict codes of practice is another means through which this protection is assured.

The laws affecting businesses tend to have one of three objectives: to protect consumers from businesses; to protect society from businesses; and to protect businesses from each other.

Protecting consumers

To prevent firms from taking advantage of consumers, laws have been introduced to ensure that products meet specific safety and quality standards, as well as controlling the way in which they are sold and the type and extent of information that must be given to the consumer in conducting a transaction (see Figure 3.1). Some of these laws relate specifically to marketing activities, for example, to prevent misleading pricing claims and stamp out dishonest selling practices. Others simply attempt to redress the balance between powerful organisations and relatively defenceless consumers, giving consumers the right to honest information about the goods and services they buy and an expectation that these will be fit for the purpose for which they were intended. Of

figure 3.1
**Legislation to
protect consumers**

> The following are just some of the Acts of Parliament designed to give consumers protection from undesirable business practices:
>
> Consumer Credit Act (1974)
> Consumer Protection Act (1987)
> Data Protection Act (1998)
> Fair Trading Act (1973)
> Financial Services Act (1986)
> Food Act (1984)
> Medicines Act (1968)
> Misrepresentations Act (1967)
> Prices Act (1974)
> Sale of Goods Act (1979)
> Sunday Trading Act (1994)
> Supply of Goods and Services Act (1982)
> Trade Descriptions Act (1968)
> Unfair Contract Terms Act (1977)
> Weights and Measures Act (1985)

course, a genuinely marketing-oriented business should have no need to fear such legislation as it will pre-empt the requirements of consumer legislation in trying to meet its customers' needs, recognising that dissatisfied customers who have to resort to the law because of deficiencies in the products they have bought or the way they have been treated are unlikely to remain customers for long!

DID YOU KNOW?
The Data Protection Act aims to give consumers more control over the ways that companies can use their personal details, and protect them from unwanted and intrusive communications. It is now illegal for a business to make unsolicited telephone calls to anyone who has registered with the Telephone Preference Service (TPS), so a firm undertaking any direct sales activity over the phone must first check their lists against the TPS list. Breaking the law can result in a fine of £5,000 (Dale, 2000).

Another type of legislation exists to encourage and protect competition. Competition between businesses is usually in the interest of consumers as it encourages businesses to focus on customers' needs. A monopoly is said to exist when a single organisation or related group of organisations supplies such a high proportion of the output of an industry that it is able to prevent, restrict or distort competition. When this occurs, the Competition Commission will review the situation and judge whether or not it is acting against the public interest and, if it is, recommend action that should be taken to restore competitive market activity. Similarly, the Restrictive Practices Court will review any trading agreement between two or more businesses that concerns issues such as setting price levels or terms and conditions of sale. Those agreements found to be acting against the public interest will be terminated by the court.

CASE STUDY **3.2**
....

Gambling hits the jackpot
In its heyday, the holiday destination of Blackpool attracted 17 million visitors a year, but the growth in international travel, changing lifestyles and unpredictable weather patterns have seen it lose its share of holiday-makers in recent years and visitor

numbers have dwindled to only 10 million. But the fortunes of Blackpool, and other coastal resorts such as Bournemouth, Southend and Margate, could change if UK gaming laws are liberalised, as planned in 2003.

The most radical shake-up of British gambling law since the 1960s will see an end to the restrictive rules imposed when casinos became the haunts of underworld gangsters. Gambling businesses will for the first time be permitted to bring together casinos, bingo and sport betting under one roof, and Las Vegas-style entertainment complexes offering a combination of gaming, restaurants and other leisure activities are being proposed to support the regeneration of fading seaside towns. Bournemouth, a traditional holiday haunt for the better-off middle classes, would like to develop as the British Monte Carlo, with a series of up-market casinos.

The changes in legislation will be music to the ears of bingo hall operators, who have been fighting to retain their markets since the launch of the National Lottery in 1994. Bingo is predominantly a working-class game, with more support in the north of England than the south and attracting many more women than men. Players currently have to be members. Traditionally, while men have gone to the pub, women have gone to bingo, and elderly women can still be found in the clubs chatting and knitting as they play. For younger women, the attraction is not so much the chance of winning as the entertainment, a sense of community and the opportunity for a girls' night out. The industry is keen to attract more high-spending groups, and the bigger prizes, including the £100,000 national games, are in the evenings when the over-60s give way to a younger, more mixed group. Under the new legislation, Gala, Britain's second biggest bingo operator, hopes to attract more well-off young adults by creating a series of gaming sheds on greenfield sites close to major cities, and will double their top prizes to £1 million.

But not everyone is delighted by the new rules. Gamblers Anonymous has expressed concern that more casinos and more relaxed rules on drinking and membership will lead to an increase in addiction, and pub owners fear that, because betting will still be forbidden on their premises, they will lose out.

Questions

1   What are the dangers for bingo hall operators in pursuing a wider market, and how might they minimise these?
2   How would you promote bingo to encourage people to go for the first time?
3   Who else might benefit from the proposed changes to legislation, and who else might face problems?

Sources: Ahmed and Mathiason (2002); Moss (2000).

Protecting society

As discussed in Chapter 1 (in relation to 'societal marketing'), the decisions that firms may make in the best interests of their own customers may not necessarily be in the best interests of society as a whole. As a result, legislation is created in an attempt to ensure that people and their environment are protected from the adverse consequences of their own buying decisions. Children are particularly shielded from products that may cause them harm, such as tobacco and alcohol, and they are prevented from driving cars until they are considered old enough to control them responsibly. Other legislation ensures that those who do drive cars are insured so that they can compensate others in the event of an accident. European law has been instrumental in the introduction of emissions control in cars and controlling the disposal of industrial pollutants, and in the US, plastic packaging has been banned in several cities. Such legislation creates both opportunities and threats in marketing. Although costs may be incurred in conforming to or pre-empting such legislation, those who respond soonest can potentially turn this to an advantage over their competitors.

Protecting businesses

Although competition is generally in the interest of consumers, there are certain circumstances under which businesses need protection from their competitors. In particular, if a new product or technology is to be brought to the market, its innovators need to be assured that competitors are not able to bypass what may be a lengthy and costly product development stage by simply copying the product when it is ultimately launched. Creativity and originality need to offer potential financial rewards if they are to flourish in profit-driven organisations. Legislation offers this protection in the form of patents, which are legal documents granting businesses that satisfy certain criteria the exclusive right to sell their own inventions. This type of exclusivity is very valuable in marketing terms. It enables firms to establish their products in their target markets without fear of competitive pressures, and usually this means that high price levels can be achieved and good profit margins sustained for the life of the patent.

The other form of protection offered against competitors is through the registration of trademarks. A trademark, which may include a logo, a word, a symbol, a design, or even distinctive colouring or lettering, cannot be copied within the geographical territory in which it is registered. Like a patent, it prevents imitators from bypassing a lengthy and costly process, but in this case the process is brand building rather than research and development.

DID YOU KNOW?
Complaints were made to the Advertising Standards Authority when a national press advertisement, appealing for donations to the charity Help the Aged, was published showing six pairs of feet all bearing death tags. The caption read: 'Thousands of elderly people will stop feeling the cold this winter'. Complaints objected that the references to death were offensive and frightening. But the complaints were overruled when the charity produced evidence to show a direct correlation between cold weather and a higher death rate, and that the risk of dying from a cold-related illness increased sharply with age. The Authority ruled that it was acceptable to shock to reflect this fact in a proportionately shocking way (www.asa.org.uk).

Self-regulation

Businesses are usually keen to keep the legislation of their industries to a minimum, as it can prove restrictive, costly to conform to, and even more costly if court actions have to be defended. Self-regulation through voluntary codes of conduct is one of the ways in which businesses can forestall the legislation of their industries. In the UK, broadcast and print advertising and market research are two areas where strict codes of conduct are policed almost exclusively by self-regulation. The Code of Advertising Practice (administered by the Advertising Standards Authority) governs non-broadcast advertising on a self-regulatory basis. Television and radio advertising are regulated separately, by a mixture of legislation and self-regulation.

On the other hand, market research, which has an equally responsible set of guidelines, is beset by problems arising from 'cowboy' outfits which refuse to conform to the rules and become involved in 'sugging' (selling under the guise of market research) and 'frugging' (fundraising under the guise of market research), both of which undermine the activities of organisations that are genuinely attempting to use market research to gauge consumer attitudes and behaviour.

The micro-environment

This comprises those factors external to a business that directly affect the running of that business and over which it can exert some control. Changes in this sector of the business environment are of major significance to the marketing department, and are likely to influence marketing decisions at both the strategic and tactical levels. Five key factors can be identified:

▶ *Customers*: Those whom an organisation wishes to engage in exchange processes (discussed in Chapter 1), usually by selling them something.
▶ *Competitors*: Other organisations attempting to sell similar products to meet similar customer needs.
▶ *Suppliers*: Those who provide the inputs to enable a business to produce its products and services.
▶ *Intermediaries*: Those who make an organisation's products available to their end-users.
▶ *Stakeholders*: Individuals or groups who have a vested interest in the activities of the business.

Customers

Those to whom an organisation supplies its products or services are described as *customers*. A *market* consists of all the customers of all the organisations supplying a particular product or service (groups of customers within a market who exhibit similar specific needs are called *market segments*, as discussed in Chapter 6). Markets express *demand* for products and services as customers acquire goods to satisfy their needs. The task of the marketing department in an organisation is to maximise demand for its own firm's products and services. To do this existing customers must be satisfied and not tempted to buy from another supplier, while competitors' customers must be persuaded to change their allegiances. Alternatively (or additionally), potential new customers can be attracted – those who have not previously been buyers of the product or service at all – and this will lead to an expansion of the market.

To enable them to perform any of these tasks, marketers need to understand as much as possible about the nature of their customers, their competitors' customers and their potential customers. They need to know:

▶ What are the characteristics of customers? Where do they live? How old are they? What lifestyles do they lead? What social class are they? How educated are they? What businesses are they in? etc. A profile of customers can be compared with a profile of the market to identify whether a particular organisation's products and services appeal more to some types of people than others. Such knowledge also enables organisations to decide whether new product features, price levels or different advertising messages are appropriate to their target markets.

► What needs are customers satisfying by using a particular product or service? In other words, what benefits are they seeking? People don't buy washing powders, they buy the promise of clean clothes. People don't buy theatre tickets, they buy an evening's entertainment. So if a better means of meeting their needs is made available, customers will switch to the product that offers them the most benefits.

► What criteria do customers use to choose between products? What makes one product or service better than another in the eyes of the customer? What features deliver most benefits to the customer? For example, when people decide which supermarket to shop in, some may choose on the basis of price levels, but others are more interested in the variety of goods available, the convenient location of the store, the perceived quality of the merchandise or the facilities they offer for parents with children.

► How valuable is the product or service to customers? If an organisation supplies an item that its customers find indispensable, those customers are likely to be relatively insensitive to price levels and the organisation has a good opportunity to trade very profitably. Undervaluing the benefits offered may mean that customers see themselves as getting a 'bargain' as opposed to good 'value for money'. While bargain offers have their role to play in promotional activity, consistently charging less than what the customer is willing to pay is a lost profit opportunity.

► Where do customers find information that influences their buying decisions? Some types of buying decision are made spontaneously, and the sight of a TV advertisement can trigger a consumer's intention to try a new food product or buy an unfamiliar brand. Other buying decisions are more carefully considered, particularly more expensive items such as cars, home furnishings and insurance policies. Buyers who purchase products for their organisations as opposed to their personal use are the most likely to make strenuous efforts to gather information which will help them make a rational choice.

These issues and others are raised again in Chapter 4, where the nature of consumer and organisational buyer behaviour is examined in more detail, and Chapter 5 looks at the role of marketing research in helping to answer some of these questions.

Competitors

Types of competitor
Competitors are organisations trying to satisfy similar customer needs and producing products that customers see as being alternatives for satisfying their needs. Having said this, it isn't always that easy for a business to identify its competitors, and it is probably best to consider them as being in one of four categories, as shown in Figure 3.2.

figure 3.2
Competitor typologies

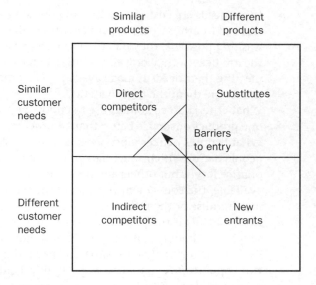

Direct competitors

These are usually the easiest to identify and comprise organisations offering similar types of product or service to satisfy similar types of customer needs. Normally these products are also sold at similar price levels and possibly through similar distribution outlets. Coca-Cola and Pepsi, Persil and Ariel, Sainsbury's and Tesco, and Ford and General Motors have all been direct competitors for many years. Because of the similarities of the physical characteristics of their products or product ranges, they have all made considerable efforts to differentiate themselves from their rivals in other ways. In particular, they spend large sums on advertising in an attempt to enhance the benefits that customers will gain from buying their product as opposed to their competitors' products. But from time to time they use price as a persuader and undercut their competitors in an aggressive bid to gain market share. Direct competition can therefore be very costly. The strongest and the most soundly financed are likely to be the only ones to survive in the long term. Those contemplating entering into battle with their direct competitors should first consider whether it is necessary, as there may be some customers in the market who can be profitably served without being drawn into expensive head-on competition. If there is no opportunity for this, the potential reaction of competitors will be critical in determining whether it is a fight worth taking on, or whether it is a market best left alone.

CASE STUDY **3.3**   **Cold wars**

Unbeknown to most ice-cream lovers, for whom the product represents sheer pleasure and self-indulgence, two of the world's largest FMCG manufacturers spent almost a decade fighting a bitter battle over the distribution of this frozen dairy treat. The two opponents in the cold war were Unilever, producers of the long-established brand, Walls, and Mars, a new entrant in 1989. Unilever is the world's biggest ice-cream producer with a market share of 40 per cent in Europe, including 50 per cent of the UK market. Mars is the US's largest privately-owned company. It found its market niche by modelling ice-cream brands on its chocolate countline bars such as Snickers, Bounty and the Mars Bar, particularly aiming to attract customers in the summer – a time when chocolate sales are traditionally low.

The cost of developing ice-cream products, marketing them and keeping them at the right temperature right through to the point of purchase is very high. The secret of profitable trading lies in being able to make the product available in perfect condition when the consumer's ice-cream-eating impulse strikes. To achieve this, the strategy adopted by Unilever and other ice-cream manufacturers had been to supply exclusive freezer cabinets to a large number of small local retailers, insisting that rival products may not be stocked in the same freezer. Small shops, short of space, could not then make room for new lines produced by other manufacturers as they didn't have enough room for another freezer cabinet. Hence new entrant, Mars, found it difficult to establish a strong foothold in the market.

In Ireland, where Mars was at first successful in persuading a number of retailers to stock its new range of ice-creams in its competitors' freezers, Unilever took it to court and won the case, but Mars appealed against the decision under EC law and the legal wrangling went on for years – Mars arguing that the consumer loses out from the exclusivity clause in Unilever's freezer provision, and asserting that more choice would be in consumers' best interests. It also pointed out that the distribution of other impulse products, such as sweets and cigarettes, often involves the supply of expensive display cabinets, but with no requirement on the retailer to exclude competitors' brands. Unilever responded that exclusive freezers enabled it to control the quality of its ice-creams very closely and to offer retailers a 24-hour service. It accused Mars of 'hitching a ride on the industry'.

The matter was considered in the UK by the Monopolies and Mergers Commission (MMC) in 1994, and freezer exclusivity was given a clean bill of health. But by the late 1990s it was clear that the market had not developed as anticipated. The MMC's successor, the Competition Commission, re-opened the case. In 2000, the whole practice of freezer exclusivity was condemned as anti-competitive. Unilever was barred from keeping other brands out of its freezers, and retailers with Walls cabinets were permitted to use 50 per cent of the space in those cabinets to stock other manufacturers' products. Mars and Nestlé were allowed to continue to operate exclusively in an effort to strengthen their competitive position.

The announcement was a particularly welcome one for Fredericks Dairies Ltd, which in 1998 had launched a range of Cadbury ice-creams and added to it in 1999 with Trebor Bassett brands, resulting in £10 million sales. However, even for such major brand names, growth has been hindered by limited access to freezers, and Peter Elvin, Marketing Director at Fredericks concluded 'without the changes in the market resulting from the Competition Commission Report, Cadbury's Impulse Ice Cream would probably never have been able to reach consumers in sufficient numbers to make a real impact on the market, but with the ending of exclusivity agreements, distributors and retailers will be able to offer consumers complete freedom of choice for the first time' (Willman, 1998).

Questions
1   How should Unilever react to the loss of its freezer exclusivity arrangements?
2   How should Fredericks Dairies react to the Competition Commission ruling?

3   What other marketing mix decisions does Mars have to consider now it is permitted to share other suppliers' freezer cabinets?

Sources: www.ice-cream.org; BBC News online (2000); Cowe (1999, 2000); Willman (1998).

DID YOU KNOW?

Competition from the National Lottery has been blamed for a significant downturn in business at bingo halls across the UK. Despite the fact that advertising restrictions preventing bingo hall operators from promoting themselves were lifted in April 1997, and that the industry has partially succeeded in shaking off its image as a game played by elderly women in dingy converted cinemas by opening new purpose-built clubs, most firms have experienced declining profits. Prize money, currently capped by law at £250,000, is thought to be too low to attract new players when lottery winners regularly pocket millions, a situation which is set to change when further liberalisation of the gaming laws in 2003 will permit top prize pay-outs of £1 million (Ahmed and Mathiason, 2002; Daneshkhu, 1997).

Indirect competitors

These are organisations producing similar products but serving customers with different characteristics, preferences or needs. For example, Aldi and Marks & Spencer both sell food, but are trying to attract customers in different socio-economic groups. Molnlyke and Andrex are both brands of toilet paper, but the former is sold predominantly into businesses while Andrex is a household brand. Halfords sells car spares and accessories to DIY mechanics, while automotive parts distributors such as Partco and Brown Brothers sell to the motor trade. Although indirect competitors are less threatening than direct competitors, they have the potential to encroach on an established customer base if they try. This has been particularly apparent with the growth of international marketing. Businesses that used to confine their activities to their domestic markets have sought to increase demand for their products and services by moving into foreign geographical territories that were previously the domain of domestic suppliers. Some domestic suppliers, failing to recognise the severity of the threat from the new arrivals, simply buried their heads in the sand and refused to defend themselves from rivals whom they had difficulty taking seriously.

It is worth noting here that competitors producing similar products, whether they are direct or indirect competitors, are described as being in the same *industry*. Marketers must be aware, however, that competitive threats can also come from outside their own industry, from firms producing substitutes, or from potential new entrants to the industry.

KEY SKILLS
ACTIVITY **3.3**
● ● ● ● ● ● ● ● ● ● ● ● ●

Improving own learning and performance

Webwise

A library of up-to-date information about market trends is always useful for marketers. Start your library now!

Compile a directory of useful websites to which a marketer may like to refer when considering the macro- or micro-environment of an organisation. Include the site mentioned In Activity 3.2, at www.statistics.gov.uk. You could also include some of the national newspapers, trade associations and the research agencies that conduct regular omnibus surveys.

Substitutes

Competitors offering substitute products may be selling very different product forms but are satisfying very similar customer needs. Hand-drills are mechanical tools and electric drills are power-driven, but they both enable a customer to make a hole in a wall. A paint manufacturer is in competition with a wall-paper manufacturer, even though the two products are produced by quite different industries, if the customer need is for home decoration. Substitutes often take organisations unawares. As discussed in Chapter 1 and earlier in this chapter, changing technology can create substitute products that improve the ways in which customer needs can be satisfied.

New entrants

There are two main types of potential new competitor in a market:

▶ Firms which already sell to a particular group of customers sometimes decide to extend the range of products that they offer them. The move of both Sainsbury's and Tesco into insurance and investments was an example of this. Their entry into the market for financial services took advantage of the confidence their customers have in the dependability and consistency of their retailing performance. Their good reputations acted to reassure potential customers that their investments would be in safe hands.

▶ The other type of new entrant into a market usually comes from within the industry, by firms in 'upstream' or 'downstream' businesses trying to secure themselves either a source of supply or a tied distribution route. Paper mills, for example, have acquired paper merchants to ensure that they can influence the end-user markets for their products.

The likelihood of new entrants emerging to compete in a market depends on the extent to which existing competitors are able to create 'barriers to entry' to keep them out. Some of the strategies for doing this are beyond the scope of this book, but are covered extensively by Michael Porter (1980) in his book *Competitive Strategy*, in which he gives a comprehensive explanation of the dynamics of competition. Marketers are in a good position to raise two barriers to entry to deter new entrants, namely those of product differentiation and customer loyalty. First, the more efforts they make to design products that meet the variety of different needs within the overall market, the less chance that a new entrant has of finding a foothold for itself, and second, the more satisfied their customers are with the products and services they buy, the less likely they are to change, even if a new supplier does enter the market.

Number of competitors

The number of competitors in an industry is of relevance to marketers, as it will partially determine the most appropriate type of competitive strategies.

A firm holds a *monopoly* when it faces no competitors in its markets. In this situation, any potential customers who need a firm's product have no option but to buy it from that company; they cannot shop around for lower prices, better product features or superior service levels as they do normally. This could enable organisations to exert a lot of power over their customers, and particularly to charge and maintain very high price levels. Clearly this is against the interest of the consumer, which is why the government goes to so much trouble to abolish monopoly power in markets. The few monopolies that still survive tend to be the public utilities, and these are heavily regulated to prevent them abusing their power.

> **DID YOU KNOW?**
>
> *In the past 40 years, the market share of large multiple stores has almost doubled to 65 per cent of retail turnover in the UK. The popularity of these – and in particular out-of-town superstores – has led to a decline in the number of small grocers, from 275,000 in 1950 to fewer than 80,000 today (Economist, 2000).*

An *oligopoly* exists when an industry comprises only a few competitors. This situation has often arisen because between them, the firms in the industry have successfully deterred new entrants. Industries characterised by high capital costs, such as petrochemical production, and those that are highly differentiated and spend a lot of money on promotional activity, such as cigarettes, confectionery and cars, are the most common oligopolies, as the costs of entering these markets are too high for most would-be competitors. Marketing in an oligopoly requires all firms to be sensitive to the activities of the others, particularly those of their direct competitors. Pricing is the most difficult issue. If one firm reduces its prices, the others are obliged to follow suit, or else they are likely to lose customers. On the other hand, if one firm in the industry raises its prices, its competitors may not follow as they may hope to take advantage of their position as a lower-priced supplier to gain market share. The firm that increases its prices may be forced to retract this or risk losing customers to its competitors. The net result of this situation is that oligopolies are often at risk of a downwards price spiral which will undermine the profitability of them all. The obvious solution would be for the few firms in the industry to agree not to engage in such pricing tactics and to compete instead using other weapons such as service levels or promotion. But as explained earlier, such agreements are forbidden by governments who wish to maintain the highest levels of competition in the interest of consumers.

Perfect competition occurs when there are many competitors in an industry offering very similar products to customers with very similar needs and preferences. This is a very difficult situation for marketers, as the only criterion on which their customers are likely to base their buying decisions is price. A firm that is not the cheapest supplier will theoretically attract no customers, as buyers will shop around until they find the cheapest prices. In practice, there are very few, if any, perfectly competitive markets, as most consumers are unaware of the full range of suppliers for any particular product or service, are unwilling to go to the trouble of seeking them all out and have some non-price-based criteria for their buying decisions.

To avoid perfect competition, sellers attempt to differentiate their products from the other suppliers in their markets by creating unique features for their own products to give them an element of monopoly power. This is known as *monopolistic competition*. Some firms might specialise in a particular type of distribution outlet while others might offer a unique product feature or perhaps a higher (or more basic) level of quality. Different price levels can then be set according to the value that the consumer places on the particular benefits offered. An excellent understanding of customers is important for survival under this type of competition, and market research is usually fundamental to identifying the product benefits that are of value to the consumer and for which they will be willing to pay.

Suppliers

An organisation's suppliers are those firms and individuals that provide it with the resources it needs to produce its own goods and services. They may supply capital equipment or machinery that enable it to produce its own products. They may be suppliers of raw materials or components that will ultimately form a part of its own products. They may supply packaging materials or labels that enable its products to be safely and efficiently delivered to their end-users. Or they may provide services, such as photocopier repair and bookkeeping, which help with the running of the business. Because their suppliers provide them with the items they need to conduct their own businesses, under certain circumstances firms can be vulnerable to the power of suppliers. For example:

▶ if a supplier holds a patent on a product essential to its own production. For many years, Appleton Paper held a patent on 'NCR' paper (meaning 'no carbon required') and any printer wanting to produce carbonless business forms for its clients had no option but to buy from Appleton. When the patent eventually expired, printers were free to buy from other suppliers, who quickly entered the market and produced lower-priced versions of the paper.

▶ if an essential product has no effective substitute. Manufacturers of leather shoes would be ill-advised to make shoes out of synthetic material just because their suppliers increase the price of leather. They have little option but to pay the suppliers' prices, and may have to try to pass this increase on to their own customers to retain their profit margins.

▶ if customers specify (or even just prefer) products from certain suppliers. Builders may be required to conform to the specification laid down by an architect, involving a particular construction material from a particular supplier. Supermarkets' customers may prefer to buy the manufacturer brands that they see advertised on TV and expect to find them at their local retailer. This gives the retailer little option but to buy from those preferred manufacturers, though it may try to copy their products with an own-brand product to minimise the potential threat of this power.

▶ if it is expensive to change to a new supplier. This can happen if long-term commitments have been made to certain suppliers. If a business takes out a bank loan which subsequently fails to offer interest rates as low as those of another finance house, it may face high penalty costs if it wishes to repay the loan and move to another provider.

▶ if suppliers are more powerful than buyers. A small company buying from a big supplier is at a disadvantage. If the supplier loses one of its customers, its business will hardly be affected, so a big company may offer disadvantageous prices and lower service levels to those who place relatively small orders, as the cost of supplying them is disproportionately high in comparison with the value of those orders.

Marketing managers must monitor supplier activities carefully. Supply shortages that interrupt production, or cost increases that have to be passed on to consumers can both damage customer goodwill irreparably. Shortages will force customers to look to a company's competitors, and cost increases may require price increases that will be unacceptable to consumers. The potential seriousness of these problems has led many organisations to work much harder at establishing better relationships with their suppliers, based on the recognition of their mutual interdependence.

CASE STUDY **3.4**

Jeans on trial

A four-year courtroom battle ensued when Levi Strauss sought to prevent Tesco from importing Levi's jeans from outside the European Union and selling them back into the UK – a practice known as parallel trading – discounted at up to 50 per cent of their normal retail prices. A previous judgment in the UK meant that trademark owners who had not placed express restrictions on the importation of their goods were assumed to have consented to them being imported. But Levi Strauss objected to the sale of its brand on the so-called 'grey market', and argued that its brand values would be undermined if sold in a mass market store as opposed to a boutique-style environment. It claimed that the staff selling its products needed special training.

The European Court of Justice ultimately ruled that Tesco was not allowed to sell Levi's jeans without the manufacturer's consent, which had not been given. This decision was subsequently supported in the UK High Court, despite objections from Tesco on the grounds of human rights. Critics of the decision, including the Consumers' Association and other parallel traders who will be affected in the same way as Tesco, have dismissed the ruling as a licence to fix prices. They point to research showing that in eight out of nine cases, European consumers paid more for branded goods, partly due to the ban on parallel trade. The British Brands Group, however, representing trademark owners, applauded the courts' decisions and reiterated their belief that manufacturers who have the skills to develop brands and invest heavily to support them should be allowed to sell their goods to whoever they want.

Tesco has vowed to continue selling cheap Levi's and although its US sources of supply have been cut off, European sources, which are not affected by the ruling, can continue to be sold. But the viability of its sales operation may yet be undermined. Just three months after the High Court judgment, Levi Strauss announced a deal with Wal-mart, owners of Tesco's arch rival Asda, to sell specially-made Levi jeans across the US, and a UK launch could be next.

Questions

1 Why was Levi Strauss so determined to prevent Tesco from selling cheap imported jeans when it subsequently agreed a deal with a US supermarket?
2 Which laws are designed to protect consumers from the power of manufacturers?
3 How might the forthcoming expansion of the European Community affect retail prices?

Sources: Cozens (2002); Day (2001); Finch (2002); Smith (2002).

Intermediaries

These are independent organisations involved in the promotion, selling and distribution of a firm's goods to the end-users of its products and services. There are three types of intermediary that can support an organisation's marketing efforts:

▶ *Resellers* are organisations whose role is to make products more easily available to their end-users. They include retailers, wholesalers, merchants, agents and any other form of business whose purpose is to make money by distributing the goods of other organisations. Marketers must attempt to engage the most appropriate resellers to help them maximise the availability of their products and services in their target markets. A danger is that, due to their close relationships with the end-users, resellers become more powerful than the manufacturers whose products they are distributing, and start to use this power to dictate terms of trade that are highly unfavourable to manufacturers, and in some cases can prevent them reaching their markets at all.

▶ *Physical distribution intermediaries*, usually warehouse operators and transport firms, are organisations involved in moving goods from manufacturers to their destinations. If goods are out of stock because a warehouse has failed to control stocks properly, customers may be lost to the competition, and if customers are disappointed and delayed because the goods they have ordered arrive damaged, they are unlikely to place more orders.

▶ *Marketing services agencies* include advertising agencies, marketing research firms, marketing consultants and any other businesses supplying the advice or facilities to help their clients target and communicate with their customers. Their strengths usually lie in their expertise in certain marketing functions and their objectivity when addressing the market, and their weaknesses are most likely to lie in the extent of their understanding of customers, markets and the competitive environment.

Stakeholders

This is a diverse group consisting of all those with an interest in or impact on the way in which an organisation goes about its business. Some of these people are of only indirect relevance to the marketing function. Shareholders and banks, for example, are financial stakeholders who are particularly interested in the profitability of a business, but will have only indirect influence over marketing decisions. Local authorities and pressure groups are community stakeholders who may attempt to influence the environmental or employment practices of an organisation, but not necessarily its commercial activities. Having said this, there are two important stakeholder groups that marketers should monitor closely as a part of their micro-environment:

▶ The *media*, including TV, radio, local and national newspapers and magazines, can have a major influence over large proportions of an organisation's target markets. Readers tend to have greater trust in the accuracy and reliability of editorial comment than in the messages they receive from advertising and promotional materials, so by publishing favourable or unfavourable comments on products and services, the media can influence the purchasing habits of consumers. This can be very useful for marketers who persuade the press to give them positive coverage, but devastating if reviews are poor and the press are highly critical. The impact of the press is always highly visible on Broadway, where theatre critics can effectively close a show if they publish a damning indictment of the quality of a performance. Marketers who continually maintain good relations with the media are in a position to maximise the opportunities of gaining useful coverage and minimise the possibility of damaging criticism.

▶ The *consumer movement* consists of groups whose objectives are to identify good and bad marketing practices and to draw them to the attention of consumers. Organisations such as the Consumers' Association test wide ranges of competing products and publish league tables of product quality and utility. They also put pressure on the government to legislate against unsafe products and misleading marketing practices.

CASE STUDY **3.5**

Nestlé infant formula

The sale of breast-milk substitutes to less developed countries has long been an issue that has concerned the consumer movement throughout the world. Attention has been particularly focused on the marketing activities of Nestlé, who by 1981 (the year in which the World Health Organisation (WHO) voted to establish a code of practice specifically on this issue) had around 25 per cent of the worldwide market for infant formula. Over half of this market was in developing countries, where sales were growing annually by as much as 20 per cent – at least twice the rate of advanced countries.

Consumer protests centred on a number of issues:

▶ The product itself was unsafe in some circumstances if a population had only limited access to clean water and sterilising equipment.

▶ The price of infant formula was so high it would make a severe dent in a family budget and may mean that other members of the family have to go hungry; it also meant that the product was commonly over-diluted which could lead to infant malnutrition.

▶ Unethical promotional practices were being used to persuade mothers that infant formula was the best way of feeding a baby, the most controversial of which was the use of 'mothercraft nurses' who were company representatives dressed in nurses' uniforms who visited mothers after they left hospital, demonstrated how to bottle feed and left samples of the product or vouchers to be redeemed at retailers.

▶ Packaging and instructions were only given in English, even in countries where English was not the national language.

▶ The medical profession was sponsored in various ways and provided with educational materials as well as free samples of infant formula for both professional and personal use.

Public opposition to Nestlé's activities first surfaced in 1973 with the publication of a series of critical articles suggesting that the aggressive promotional tactics being used were ultimately contributing to infant mortality in less developed countries.

Initially Nestlé ignored the problem, but subsequently started to engage in lawsuits against the activists, a move that only served to bring the issue to wider public attention. In a further effort to quell public criticism, Nestlé and other manufacturers established a voluntary code of practice with a view to improving their image, but the code was not enforced and the attempt to self-regulate had clearly failed when a pressure group called the Infant Formula Action Coalition (INFACT) announced a US boycott of all Nestlé products – a boycott that later spread to nine other countries and resulted in the largest non-industrial boycott in history. Attempts by Nestlé to discredit the activists only led to further public relations difficulties.

When the WHO announced its intention to institute a Code of Marketing of Breast Milk Substitutes in 1981, Nestlé joined others in the industry to resist the move, but subsequently agreed to comply at a cost estimated around $10–20 million. However, this has proved insufficient to see off a vocal minority committed to undermining the company's reputation. The UK pressure group Baby Milk Action draws attention to recent violations by Nestlé, such as adverts for infant formula on the vans of distributors in Armenia and in parenting magazines in Bulgaria. It questions the effectiveness of many of the measures introduced by the company to tighten up its act and stem the tide of criticism.

Questions

1 Why might organisations fail to adhere to their industry's code of practice?
2 What do you think was the true cost to Nestlé of the consumer backlash against its sale of infant formula in less developed countries?
3 How have other companies fared when defending themselves against allegations of improper marketing and business practices?

Sources: www.babymilkaction.org; Akhter (1987); Guardian (2002a).

Assessing the marketing environment
....

As we have seen, changes in both the micro- and macro-environments of firms can have both positive and negative effects. They can create opportunities for generating more business from existing customers or the possibility of doing business with new ones. On the other hand, they can seriously damage an organisation's capability of serving its customers and create a mismatch between its products and the needs of its customers. For this reason, it is important that marketers adopt a systematic process of identifying the significant changes in their environment, analysing the relevance of those changes and forecasting their potential impact for the firm.

▶ Stage 1: *Scanning*. This requires the marketing department to review continually all aspects of its environment, so that any change can be identified at an early stage. Appropriate action can then be taken before the change becomes a threat to the way in which the business is meeting the needs of its customers, or so that the initiative can be snatched from competitors.
▶ Stage 2: *Monitoring*. When environmental change has been detected evidence must be collected as to the nature of the emerging trends and patterns so that

figure 3.3
Categories of response to environmental change

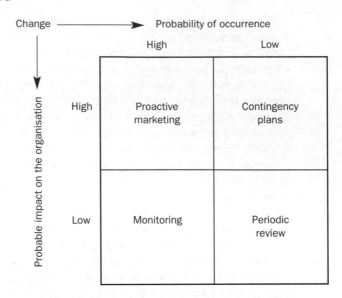

a more precise picture of current changes can be drawn. Some changes may prove to be temporary and insignificant, while others will start to grow and clear implications of potential opportunity or threat will start to emerge.

▶ Stage 3: *Forecasting*. When monitoring has identified issues of relevance, forecasting is used to project the likely scope, speed and intensity of the environmental change. Projective techniques may be used to draw up future scenarios that the business may have to face.

▶ Stage 4: *Assessment*. Finally, the potential effect of the change on the organisation's ability to serve its customers in the future has to be assessed. Four categories of impact can be identified, according to the probability of a particular change taking place and the likely impact of this change for the business (see Figure 3.3).

Pro-active marketers will start to prepare for new trading conditions when it becomes clear that a change in the environment is likely to have a significant impact on their future ability to meet the needs of their customers. Contingency planning should begin if the probability of change is less certain, but the impact of the change is equally serious. Monitoring should continue if change appears likely but the effects of the change appear to be less critical, and potential change that looks as if it will be slow to materialise and offer little in the way of opportunity or threat can be given the lowest priority.

Key concepts
··················

Competitors: organisations producing products and services that satisfy similar customer needs.
Culture: the set of beliefs, values and attitudes that underpin society.
Customers: individuals or organisations who buy a firm's products and services.
Demographics: the patterns and trends of population and social structures.

Industry: a group of organisations producing similar products or services.

Intermediaries: organisations which help products and services to be transferred from producer to consumer.

Macro-environment: events that influence more than one industry and over which firms have very little control.

Market: a group of people who wish to buy a certain type of product or service.

Market segment: a group of people with similar needs who wish to buy a certain type of product or service.

Micro-environment: forces that directly affect the running of a business and over which that business has some control.

New entrants: organisations that start to trade in a market after existing competitors have established their presence in it.

Stakeholders: organisations or individuals that have an interest in or influence over the fortunes of a business.

Substitutes: products or services that satisfy similar needs but have a different physical form.

Suppliers: organisations which provide the resources needed by other firms to produce their own goods and services.

SELF-CHECK QUESTIONS

1   A competitor selling a similar type of product to satisfy different customer needs is described as being:

   a A substitute.

   b A new entrant.

   c A direct competitor.

   d An intermediary.

   e An indirect competitor.

2   Suppliers can become more powerful than the firms that buy from them if:

   (i) They sell an essential product that has no effective substitute.

   (ii) They are large organisations supplying a wide range of businesses.

   a (i) only.

   b (ii) only.

   c (i) and (ii).

   d Neither (i) nor (ii).

3   What does patent legislation do?

   a Prevents firms from communicating false information about their goods and services.

   b Protects consumers from monopolists charging high prices.

   c Ensures that firms use environmentally-friendly business practices.

   d Prevents competitors from imitating a firm's corporate logo.

   e Enables a business to enjoy monopoly power for a period of time after it has invented a new product.

4   What action should an organisation take if it forecasts a likely change in its environment that will increase the market strength of its competitors?

   a Leave the market.

   b Launch a new product.

    c Prepare plans to minimise the competitive threat.
    d Run a promotional campaign.
    e Reduce its prices.

5 If the inflation rate increases in the UK, British firms:
    a will become more competitive in overseas markets.
    b are likely to suffer from weak domestic demand.
    c should reduce their prices.
    d should reduce their marketing budgets.
    e are likely to be subject to rising interest rates.

Which of the following are true and which are false?

6 Cars and holidays both represent major purchases for consumers, who will use the same criteria in making purchasing decisions for both types of product.

7 Marketers have no reason to be involved in decisions about the warehousing and transportation of their products.

8 The market for breakfast cereal is characterised by monopolistic competition.

9 Businesses can influence demographic trends in their macro-environment.

10 Cultural trends can create demand for new technologies and new technologies can influence cultural trends.

Discuss the following

11 To which industries does the development of the Internet offer marketing opportunities and to which does it pose threats?

12 What are the advantages and disadvantages of competing in an oligopoly?

13 What initiatives have tobacco companies taken to avoid the threat of further legislation to restrict the consumption of cigarettes?

14 How have the big supermarket retailers, such as Sainsbury's and Tesco, become so powerful over the manufacturers who supply them? To what extent has Marks & Spencer used a similar strategy?

15 Why are universities and colleges vulnerable to demographic changes? What actions could they take to minimise the threats posed by this?

Further study
· · · · · · · · · · · · · · · · ·

Various sources can provide useful information for the assessment of the marketing environment, including:

▶ Government publications such as *The General Household* survey, *Regional Trends, Social Trends,* and *Retail Sales,* all of which, and more, can be found at www.statistics.gov.uk

▶ Market reports by research agencies such as Mintel (www.mintel.com) and Euromonitor (www.euromonitor.com).

▶ Reports by professional associations, such as the Institute of Grocery Distribution and the Society of Motor Manufacturers and Traders; and government-linked organisations such as the British Tourist Authority (www.britishtouristauthority.org) and Arts Council England (www.artscouncil.org.uk).

► Reports and accounts of organisations with a legal obligation to publish their figures (www.companieshouse.gov.uk).

► Trade magazines and publications such as the *Monthly Review of Packaging Material Prices*, *Petroleum Review*, *Campaign*, *Off Licence News*, and literally hundreds of others.

► A summary of useful statistics relating to a wide range of markets is published each year in the form of a *Marketing Pocket Book* (www.adassoc.org.uk).

Books on the subject tend to be written from the perspective of corporate strategy rather than marketing, but the following is a relevant and comprehensive text:
Oldroyd, M. (2002) *CIM Coursebook 02/03: Marketing Environment*, Butterworth Heinemann.

For an interesting classic article relating to the marketing environment, read
Kotler, P. (1986) 'Megamarketing', *Harvard Business Review*, March/April.

References
Ahmed, K. and Mathiason, N. (2002) Britain goes for the jackpot, *The Observer*, 24 March.

Akhter, J. (1987) 'Nestlé's infant formula', in R.F. Lusch and V.N. Lusch, *Principles of Marketing*, Kent Publishing Co., pp.702–4.

BBC News Online (2000) Ice Cream Monopolies Banned, 28 January. Available at http://www.bbc.co.uk

Branigan, T. (2002) 'TV dinner served up as key invention', *The Guardian*, 17 July, www.guardian.co.uk

Cowe, R. (1999) 'Watchdog warns ice-cream makers on sales practices', *The Guardian*, 7 May, www.guardian.co.uk

Cowe, R. (2000) 'Court threat as competition ruling singles out market leader', *The Guardian*, 29 January, www.guardian.co.uk

Cozens, C. (2002) 'Levi performs U-turn over supermarket sales', *The Guardian*, 31 October, www.guardian.co.uk

Dale, K. (2000) 'Seeking permission', *Marketing Business*, February, pp.30–1.

Daneshkhu, S. (1997) 'Bingo operators try to weigh up the numbers game', *Financial Times*, 4 December, p.29.

Day, J. (2001) 'Tesco undaunted by Levi's ruling', *The Guardian*, 20 November, www.guardian.co.uk

Economist (2000) 'Market Forces', *The Economist*, 7 October, p.44.

Finch, J. (2002) 'Tesco loses fight to sell cheap Levi's', *The Guardian*, 1 August, www.guardian.co.uk

Guardian (2002a) 'Time to end boycott of food group', *The Guardian*, 29 March.

Guardian (2002b) 'Brainwaves that rocked the world', *The Guardian*, 17 July, p.22.

Living in Britain: Cars or Vans 1972–2000, 28 February 2002, www.statistics.gov.uk

MacErlean, N. (2002) 'Lighten up the shadow of debt', *The Observer*, 13 October, www.observer.co.uk

Moss, S. (2000) 'Step aside grandma', *The Guardian*, 13 November, www.guardian.co.uk

Porter, M. (1980) *Competitive Strategy*, Free Press.

Research (2001) 'Case Study: Kellogg's', *Research: Food & Drink*, November, p.18.

Simpson, T. and Carpenter, D. (2000) 'Car market in transit', *Research*, October, pp.44–5.

Smith, W. (2002) 'A question of choice', *Marketing Business*, March, pp.30–1.

Toffler, A. (1980) *The Third Wave*, Pan.

Willman, J. (1998) 'Cold cabinet warriors', *Financial Times*, 28 January, p.20.

CHAPTER **4**

Buyer behaviour

Objectives

When you have read this chapter you will be able to:

➤ Distinguish between consumers and organisational buyers.

➤ Identify the factors that influence buyer behaviour.

➤ Understand the stages people go through when making decisions about what to buy.

➤ Indicate how and why these stages may differ according to the nature of the product being sought.

➤ Explain the different roles that people take in buying decisions.

➤ Recognise the implications of buyer behaviour for the marketing of products and services to both consumers and organisational buyers.

Foundation focus: the 20-second takeaway

It is not always obvious why customers respond in the ways they do to the products that are available to them, or how they make the choices they are confronted with. For example, people buying a product for themselves, or for friends and family, tend to choose in quite a different way from someone making a purchase for the organisation they work for. In order to understand their different types of customer better, and ultimately to serve them better, marketers must identify the range of factors that will affect customers' preferences and unravel the thought processes they go through in making their decisions. As so many decisions are made in consultation with others, it is also important that marketers identify everyone who is likely to have a say, or at least an influence, on the decision being made.

Introduction

By studying buyer behaviour marketers aim to find out how people make their buying decisions and identify the factors that influence those decisions. This chapter looks at two types of buyer behaviour – that of consumers and that of organisational buyers – and considers the implications of both of these for the marketing of products and services.

Consumers are individuals who buy products and services for themselves or on behalf of their households. They are invariably either the users of these products or services, or responsible for the welfare and well-being of those who

89

are. They buy things that enable them to survive the physical demands of life, but they also use these purchases to indicate their roles in society, to express their personalities, to reveal their attitudes and opinions, to emphasise the values they hold and to demonstrate their wealth. In other words, the products and services they buy are selected not only to satisfy their physiological needs, but also their sociological and psychological needs.

Organisational buyers buy products and services on behalf of the organisations they work for. The needs they are trying to satisfy are the needs of the organisation. They buy components for the products that their organisations assemble; they buy accountancy services to enable their organisations to audit their finances; they buy capital equipment so that their organisations can produce goods and services for sale. As organisational buyers are human beings, unable to step out of their personal attitudes and preferences when they walk into their offices, their behaviour as buyers bears some fundamental similarities to consumers. However, their own personal needs are expected to be secondary to the objectives of their organisations and, consequently, the factors that influence their decisions and the way they go about making those decisions can be quite different from consumers.

This first part of the chapter will consider the nature of consumer buyer behaviour, which will then be compared with the behaviour of organisational buyers.

Consumer behaviour

Influences on decision-making

People are thought to develop their individuality through both nature and nurture. Consequently, their behaviour will partly reflect their intrinsic likes, dislikes, beliefs, attitudes and values, but their position in society and the influence of those with whom they live will also play a part. This is as true of buying behaviour as of any other type of behaviour. A consumer's social environment, individual circumstances and psychological characteristics combine to influence the decisions he or she makes about what to buy. (See Figure 4.1.)

figure 4.1
**Influences on
consumer behaviour**

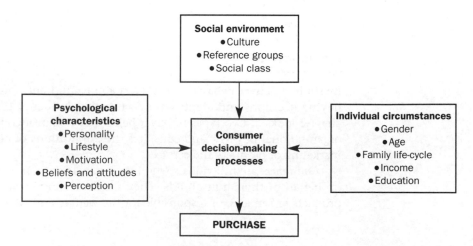

The practice of coffee drinking has deep cultural roots. While Parisians may associate it with smoky cafés, metallic espresso machines, miniature china cups, spoons and sugar cubes, Americans are more likely to envisage it as something to be consumed at the bookstore from a large cardboard cup. In Bangkok coffee is routinely sold by street vendors, poured into plastic bags of ice and mixed with evaporated milk (Sunderland, 2002).

Social environment

Culture

This refers to the prevailing beliefs, values, perceptions and behavioural norms that underpin a society. (Some explanation of these was given in Chapter 3.) They are usually reinforced by educational systems and legal and social institutions, and passed on from generation to generation, changing only slowly over time. Cultural differences may be apparent between nations or even groups of nations: the Western world strives to stay young and slim (hence the buoyant markets for hair colourants and low-calorie meals), while some Eastern cultures have more respect for age and associate slimness with poverty and starvation. Sub-cultural differences emerge between different religions, different regions and those of different social status. Food products are particularly sensitive to sub-cultural influences. The German bread market, for example, is characterised by hundreds of independent regional bakers producing local specialities for relatively small catchment areas. Mass production by national bakeries has failed to make any serious inroads into the market due to the strong and traditionally-held regional consumer preferences. As global communications have improved, so cultural divisions have been eroded and consumers have learned to tolerate a more diverse range of products (there is further discussion of this in Chapter 13), but nonetheless, cultural norms and practices remain a significant influence on consumer decision-making.

CASE STUDY **4.1**

An Asian experience

'We never get any Asian audiences coming to our theatre', is the woeful cry that often greets Asian theatre companies when they try to get bookings at theatre venues around the UK. Why not? Well, partly because those theatres have never programmed any productions aimed at Asian audiences; but even when they have, there are several more hurdles to jump. Research by Tamasha Theatre Company has shown that whenever it has performed in a new venue, over one-third of the audience, for the most part Asian, is also new to that venue. Perceptions are part of the problem. British arts institutions are seen as forbidding edifices and not at all user-friendly. In reality that may not be the case, but few will dare to walk through the portals of a large regional theatre unless they can identify with a face in the foyer. An average Gujarati family would find it difficult to cross the threshold into a traditional British theatre, but would happily go to the local town hall or cultural centre to see a Gujarati play.

Asian audiences also need to be targeted differently, and traditional marketing techniques using direct mail, posters and press advertising cut little ice with many potential Asian theatre-goers. The secret is word-of-mouth. Asian audiences like to have a direct relationship with the person or organisation selling the product, and this is a rule carved in stone. One promoter of Indian classical music concerts – not the easiest of things to sell – knows every core member of his audience, numbering about 500, by name. They spread the word.

Then, when Asian audiences get into a theatre, they discover British theatre conventions are alien to many of them. For instance, the concept of a performance starting at the time stated on the tickets is an unfamiliar one. They can cope with that idea when going to the cinema, but 'live' Asian events seldom start on time. Asian audiences are also noisy – as Indian and Pakistani cricket fans to the World Cup have demonstrated. They tend to come with the entire family – children to grandparents – and like to express themselves when they are enjoying something. If it is a music concert, people will go 'wah wah' or clap when a particularly good improvisation is in progress. Likewise, in the theatre auditorium, they will point to actors and say in a loud voice things like, 'That's Geeta from *Eastenders*', or, horror of horrors, start snapping pictures of the actors on stage.

The Royal Shakespeare Company's first-ever performance in China was an eye-opening experience for the actors. The volume of excited chatter in the theatre did not abate as the house lights went down – if anything, it intensified. Members of the audience strolled up and down the aisles. Mobile phones rang and flash photographs were taken, despite repeated instructions to the contrary. What nobody realised at first was that this was a great reaction. At the Chang'an Grand Theatre – Beijing's Covent Garden – the atmosphere is even less restrained. There, opera fans yell encouragement and abuse, as if attending a sports event. The audience sings along, and those in the premium seats in the front rows are served dinner.

Questions

1   How could British theatres make themselves more attractive to Asian audiences?

2   Should attempts be made to discourage white theatre-goers from attending performances primarily aimed at Asian audiences?

3   What measures could a marketer take to stimulate word-of-mouth communications among potential Asian audiences?

Sources: Bhuchar (1999); Hickling (2002).

Reference groups

These are the groups in society with which a person interacts. They are known as reference groups to indicate that they are a point of reference for consumers in making their decisions. Reference groups influence buying behaviour in several ways:

▶   *Informational influence* is exerted when a group is a credible source of knowledge, perhaps being expert or having experience in a particular field. This type of influence explains the power of word-of-mouth communications in some markets, particularly markets for services where it is not possible for consumers to try the product before actually committing themselves to a purchase (there was more about this in Chapter 2). People rely on the recommendations of friends and neighbours, regarding this as more reliable than the supplier's advertising claims.

▶   *Comparative influence* occurs when consumers attempt to make buying decisions that will associate them with groups they wish to be a part of, and dissociate themselves from others. Teenagers, for example, are keenly aware of the brands and labels that are acceptable to their peer groups, and the ones that would exclude them. Marketers have been quick to take advantage of this, charging high prices for strong brand images created for products, such as trainers, through powerful advertising campaigns directed at youth markets.

▶ *Normative influence* over consumer behaviour occurs when an individual experiences pressure to comply with the norms of a particular group. The reward for compliance is acceptance by the group, and sanctions may be taken against those who fail to conform. This type of influence is strongest with products that are highly visible, particularly clothing. In many organisations, executives will be under pressure to wear suits to work, regardless of the weather; members of a golf club may be forbidden from wearing denims; formal dress will often be expected of guests at a wedding. Different types of reference group exert different types of influence:

▶ *Primary groups* are those groups with whom a person has regular, but informal interaction. They include friends, neighbours, colleagues and the family. Their influence can be felt in all of the above ways, though in particular through informational and comparative influence.

▶ *The family* is one of the most important primary groups to influence buying behaviour, being the one with which most people will have maximum interaction over a lifetime.

▶ *The family of orientation* is the family a person is born into, consisting of parents, brothers and sisters, and in some countries more distant relatives too. This family grouping establishes purchasing patterns which a person learns during childhood. These can lead to entrenched attitudes towards favoured brands and suppliers. Selection of products and services as diverse as washing powders, instant coffee, banking services and holidays may all be influenced by family norms. To generate new customers, marketing activities may have to be designed to overcome the reluctance of consumers to break these norms.

▶ A *family of procreation* consists of a buyer's partner and children. This family has a more direct influence on everyday buying decisions. In particular, different members of the family tend to influence different buying decisions. Putnam and Davidson (1987) found that the male tends to dominate the purchase of sport equipment, lawnmowers and other domestic hardware, but kitchenware and food is mainly influenced by the female. Joint decisions are made on holidays, financial services and cars, but autonomous decisions may be made by either partner in the purchase of cameras, luggage and even the man's clothing! Where decisions may be made by either partner, marketers must recognise that they may have two distinct audiences, and two advertising campaigns may be needed to get messages across; using one campaign to appeal to both may be inadequate. Children's influence also varies by product category, predictably being strongest over toys and their own clothes, but also being significant in the purchase of breakfast cereals, fast foods and soft drinks.

▶ *Secondary groups* are those with whom people have more formal and less regular interaction. They may include religious groups, social or sports clubs and trade or professional bodies. Normative influence can be felt most strongly from these groups and the pressure to comply with their norms may even be enshrined in the constitution of the group – hence the threat of expulsion from some golf clubs for inappropriate dress.

Social class

Social classes (also known as socio-economic groupings) are groups consisting of individuals with similar social and economic circumstances who are considered to have similar status in society. The basis for defining this status will vary between societies, but is generally related to occupation, income, education and wealth. (See Figure 4.2.)

figure 4.2

Categories of social class

A	Higher managerial, administrative or professional
B	Intermediate managerial, administrative or professional
C1	Supervisory or clerical, and junior managerial, administrative or professional
C2	Skilled manual workers
D	Semi- and un-skilled manual workers
E	State pensioners or widows, casual or lowest grade workers, or long-term unemployed

Students living away from home are usually classified as C1.
Retired people with personal pensions retain their former social grade.

People tend to have far more interaction with their own social class than with others, and consequently, social classes usually display similar values and similar purchasing patterns. For example, some sections of society watch more TV than others; others have a greater likelihood of attending live arts performances; brand loyalty for grocery products is lower among the upper middle class than others. It is therefore very important for marketers to respond to different groups in different ways, however tempting it is to think of ourselves as being in a classless society.

KEY SKILLS
ACTIVITY **4.1**
· · · · · · · · · · · · · · ·
Communication

Categorising customers

Market research (covered in more detail in the next chapter) is often used to help marketers understand the factors that affect the attitudes and behaviour of their customers and potential customers. This exercise will give you some practice at phrasing the questions you would like to ask people in the most appropriate ways.

In conducting a survey it is normally important to ask people some personal questions about themselves – their age, gender, social class, ethnicity, etc. This enables their answers to be grouped and categorised so that their attitudes and buying behaviour can be compared and contrasted with other respondents. But writing questions that will be inoffensive, easy to answer and at the same time provide meaningful data for the researcher is a real art.

Assume that you are conducting a postal survey for the town or city council where you live, to investigate attitudes towards the council's transport policy. You would like to compare the responses of people in different

(a) age groups
(b) social classes
(c) geographical areas
(d) family sizes and
(e) ethnic groups

Write five questions that could be used on the questionnaire to enable you to categorise your findings in these ways.

Individual circumstances

Individual circumstances tend to stem from demographic characteristics. In Chapter 3, an explanation was given of the impact of changes in the demographic profile of a market, and the ways in which this can affect patterns of demand. At the individual level, a person's gender, age, family situation, income and education are likely to have a major influence on their buying decisions.

Gender

The influence of gender on consumer behaviour is highly visible. Mainly due to social norms, many of which can be traced back for centuries, men and women tend to buy different types of product and use different criteria when choosing what to buy. By identifying the behavioural differences between the sexes, marketers can reach huge untapped markets whose needs have never been fully satisfied. Car manufacturers, for example, responded to the increase in demand from female drivers by focusing their attention on safety features, which are frequently at the very top of the list of characteristics sought by women drivers. This was a radical departure from the emphasis on power and speed that had previously dominated car design, in response to the characteristics thought most desirable by male drivers.

Age

Age determines some of the buying decisions people make. The types of leisure activity they participate in, the likelihood of their being in education or at work, their need for health care and their preference for styles and fashions will all change through their lives and the products they purchase will change with them. Certain products and services emphasise these differences in their brand names and promotional campaigns. The tour operator Club 18–30 is quite evidently aiming at young people who see their holiday needs as being different from other age groups. Saga takes a similar view, but concentrates on a different age group, the over 50s.

Family life-cycle

This is another important marketing concept that influences behaviour, and is related to age. In 1966, Wells and Gubar described the stages of formation and progression of a typical family, and indicated the types of consumer expenditure most likely to be associated with those stages (see Figure 4.3). Much of this still applies even decades later. Young singles, for example, are likely to spend proportionately more on clothing, entertainment, fast food and leisure activities than other groups. They may have relatively low incomes, being at the start of their careers, but they have few financial responsibilities and are in a position to spend what they earn on their own pleasures. Compare this with the likely expenditure patterns of full-nest couples, who may have considerably higher income levels but will be spending much of this on maintaining their families, paying for food, education, insurance and household items. The stage a person is at in the family life-cycle is thus more significant in determining purchasing patterns than age alone.

figure 4.3
The family life-cycle

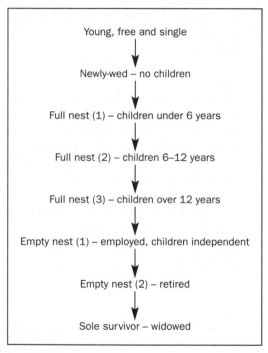

Adapted from: Wells and Gubar (1966).

Developments in society since the mid-1960s have led to the formation of new life-cycle categories which were relatively insignificant at that time. Childless couples have high levels of income and are willing to spend money to save time and to acquire quality and style. Single parents may be on severely restricted incomes as well as being under time pressure, trying to juggle the demands of work and children. Low-cost convenience is likely to be an important influence over purchasing decisions in this situation. This may also be the case in second families, when an estranged partner is financially responsible for children from a previous relationship, perhaps teenagers, as well as a new family of young children. Purchasing patterns in these situations are unlikely to conform to traditional norms either.

Income

Income is often linked to demographic characteristics, but not exclusively so. An individual's disposable income can vary for many reasons, in particular due to higher interest rates, unemployment or inflation (as discussed in Chapter 3). Certain products and services are more income sensitive than others. A person whose economic circumstances are suddenly reduced is likely to cut out discretionary expenditure, with consumer durables and leisure activities being hit the hardest. The criteria used in making buying decisions are likely to move away from style and, towards functionality and price.

Education

Levels of education are usually related to income and social class but have other interesting influences over consumer behaviour. People who left full-time education aged 16 display different purchasing behaviour from other groups. When choosing between products, they are less likely to evaluate unfamiliar brands or compare prices, but tend to make their decisions on the basis of tradition, brand image and personal experience. This has implications for the way marketers address this segment of their markets. Rather than providing detailed explanations and justifications of their products and services, they may be better off reinforcing reliability and corporate image.

Psychological characteristics

The decisions people make about the goods and services they buy are further influenced by a range of individual factors relating to their own psychology. It is quite normal for those of the same sex who are at similar stages in the family life-cycle and have the same levels of income to display quite different personalities and lifestyles, to be motivated by different goals, to hold different beliefs and attitudes and to see the same things in different ways.

Personality

Individuality is immediately obvious in a person's personality – character traits such as sociability, self-assuredness, shyness and aggression are what make individuals react in consistent and predictable ways to the situations they face. If marketers understand the reactions of different personalities to different types of product, they can design their brands to meet different needs. Painkillers are an interesting example. Sensitive, self-controlled and compliant types tend to buy brands that promise to gently soothe away pain, while more competitive, aggressive and dominant types want to actively fight the pain and look for brands that emphasise power, strength and speed.

Lifestyle
One of the ways in which consumers express their personalities is through the lifestyles they choose. Kotler and Armstrong (2001) describe lifestyle as 'a person's pattern of living as expressed in his or her activities, interests and opinions', activities such as work, entertainment, sports, hobbies, holidays and community involvement; interests such as family, food, recreation, media, fashion and music; opinions on education, politics, social welfare, personal relations and religion. The tangible evidence of lifestyle lies in the way people spend their time and money to interact with their environment. This can be measured (a technique known as psychographic profiling) to enable groupings with similar lifestyles to be identified. Different groups are likely to choose different products and respond positively to different images, giving marketers the opportunity to tailor their market offerings to meet these needs. (This is discussed further in Chapter 6.)

CASE STUDY 4.2

MOSAIC: patterns of lifestyle

MOSAIC is one of a number of commercially available databases that predict the 'lifestyle' of every household in the country. The system works on the assumption that people living in similar neighbourhoods are likely to have similar incomes, interests and purchasing habits.

By using information gathered from a diverse range of sources, including the Census, the Electoral Roll, County Court Judgments and the Postal Address File, its compilers have classified every group of households with the same postcode (usually around 10 addresses) into one of 12 'lifestyle' groups. Each group is then further divided into 52 types, each with its own highly descriptive title. For example, 'Clever Capitalists' and 'Ageing Professionals' are both types within group 1, the 'High Income Families', the 'Bohemian Melting Pot', 'Asian Heartlands' and 'Rootless Renters' are all types within group 6, 'Victorian Low Status' housing.

A description of each group and type is given, along with an indication of the likely demographic profile and financial status of residents. Those of the 'Clever Capitalist' type, for example, are described as 'wealthy people involved in business, particularly in the setting up and financial management of companies and in commercial trading, importing and exporting. The areas are characterised by company directors living in large detached houses though not necessarily with extensive grounds, in well-established residential areas within reasonable reach of city centres.' The demographic profiles indicate that people in these postcodes have a more than average likelihood of having children, though not very young children. They will probably be outright owners of their own homes and will be professionals or managers working in service industries.

For marketing purposes, this type of information can be invaluable. It can be used to investigate a customer database and identify the type of person currently buying a product or service; it can be used in direct marketing, for targeting specific types of household which are most likely to respond to a particular product offer. Retailers have used it to identify catchment areas with the best potential and to find the best sites for new stores, and theatres have used it to identify the best areas for leaflet drops.

Questions

1 How might the following use MOSAIC?

▶ A car manufacturer.

▶ A university.

▶ A charity.

2 Consider your own address. Do you think you are typical of the residents with your postcode?

3 What do you envisage as being the main disadvantages of using MOSAIC?

Source: www.micromarketing-online.com.

Motivation

Consumers are motivated to buy products when they believe that those products will satisfy their most immediate needs. In Chapter 1 there is a discussion of Maslow's hierarchy of needs. This explains that people are first motivated to meet their physiological needs, such as food, warmth, sex and safety, but when these needs have been met, they are motivated to satisfy their social and psychological needs. This creates important opportunities in marketing. Affluent consumers start to look for more than just the basic function from their products, which enables marketers to differentiate themselves from the competition by adding features to their products, both tangible and intangible, to meet the higher-level needs that motivate purchase.

CASE STUDY **4.3**
• • • • • • • • • • • • • • • •

From sex to sensuality

Maslow's hierarchy of needs (as described in Chapter 1) suggests that the human race is primarily motivated to satisfy its basic physiological needs, before attempting to satisfy higher-order needs for safety, friends, status and self-development. Sex is one of these fundamental physiological needs, so it is hardly surprising that marketers have long recognised its potential to sell products and services.

The approach used by advertisers to appeal to this basic level of motivation has changed with the times. In the early 1950s, the 'get-your-man' theme was a common one. Perfume promotions promised to lead their buyers to the men of their dreams, but the disappointment that followed when the bottles of scent failed to deliver such promises meant that brand loyalty was low. Research suggested that women's dressing tables were reminders of 'dead enthusiasm', which was hardly an incentive to make a repeat purchase. Perfume-makers responded to this by continually launching new brands, raising new hopes. But the effects of these were short-lived and served to confuse the customer – so much so that rumour persisted about the existence of a girl who, having looked at the mass of brands and promises for sale at the cosmetics counter, asked bashfully if there was a product suitable for beginners.

As time went on, permissiveness in society allowed more overt forms of sexual promise in daring advertisements. In one notable promotion for underwear, an attractive blonde woman was shown being dragged across the floor by a modern caveman, with the caption 'Come out of the bone age darling'. It is hardly surprising that more recent attempts at using sex to sell have required a more subtle approach, with sexism of this nature being firmly rejected. A 1980s poster campaign for the Fiat 127 Palio suggested that 'if this car was a lady she'd get her bottom pinched', but the graffiti that soon joined it said 'if this car was a lady, she'd run you over'. And in the 1990s men became the target of sexually suggestive advertising. A Body Shop poster showing a rear view of three naked men jumping for joy carried the caption 'new fragrances for every tom dick and harry'. In New York, a middle-aged woman lay down in the street outside a shopping mall and refused to move until the poster was taken down. She had to be forcibly removed by police. By 2000, the Advertising Standards Authority was reporting a dramatic increase in the number of men complaining about the sexual stereotyping used by advertisers, fed up with being depicted as sex objects with unfeasibly muscular bodies or as incompetent brow-beaten slobs, derided by women. With this in mind, Hägen-Dazs have abandoned their attempts to use sex to sell ice-cream in favour of a more spiritual approach featuring new-age hippies. A dedicated website welcomes visitors to a Californian-style new-age retreat called the Institute of Sensual Eating, which demonstrates how to tuck into ice-cream while adopting yoga positions, and features tongue-in-cheek video interviews with people who explain how ice-cream helps them find deep inner peace and happiness.

Questions

1   List some current advertising campaigns that use sex to sell. How successful do you think they are?
2   Do you think 'sex sells' better in some countries than others? If so, in which countries and why?
3   Identify advertisements that appeal to human motivation for:
    – safety
    – esteem
    – self-development
    to sell their products. Suggest why they have chosen these themes.

Sources: Arlidge (2001); Hunt (2001a); Packard (1957); Woolf (1996).

Consumers are seldom aware of their own motivations, which is why motivation research, using techniques such as role play, word association and psycho-drawing, is an important tool in helping marketers to understand the nature of these subconscious sociological and psychological needs.

Beliefs and attitudes

Each person holds views and opinions that stem from what they have learned in their lives, through personal experience or the experience of others. These views and opinions can lead to consistently held beliefs. Based on the account of a friend or an article in a newspaper, a consumer may believe that a certain brand is more reliable than others, or that another is more stylish, or more durable, or more expensive. Even if none of these beliefs are true, they will influence that person's buying behaviour as their expectations will cause them to reject the brands whose attributes are thought to be inferior to others. Beliefs can then lead to positive or negative attitudes which can be difficult to change. For example, beliefs about the negative environmental impact and health consequences of genetically modified foods has led many food producers to return to traditional ingredients and take advantage of the significant PR and sales benefits that can be gained from promoting their products as 'GM free'.

Perception

Perception refers to the way in which people make sense of the world. Consumers select, organise and interpret the marketing messages they are exposed to, protecting themselves from the barrage of information they are faced with every day by screening out those messages of no use to them (known as *selective perception*), and remembering only those deemed important (known as *selective retention*). These selections will depend on a wide range of factors, including their past experiences, their current needs, their beliefs and attitudes and the complexity of the messages they are faced with. This has a powerful impact on their buying behaviour. Marketers can only hope to persuade potential customers that a particular product will meet their needs if they can break through the perceptual barriers and reach them with a message that is understood, retained and acted upon.

The decision-making process

Consumers make buying decisions by responding to their own needs, taking a series of steps that enable them to select the right product from a series of alternatives (see Figure 4.4).

figure 4.4
The consumer decision-making process

Perception of need

Consumers may become aware of needs due to an internal imbalance, either physical or psychological, which can be met by the acquisition of products or services. Hunger may trigger a need for food and stress may trigger a need for a holiday. Only by purchasing those items can a person resolve the feelings of discomfort that arise from such needs. Alternatively, needs can arise as a result of exposure to some form of external stimulus. These are needs that would not have arisen spontaneously, but occur in response to changes in the external environment. A wedding invitation may trigger a need for a new suit, and a walk past an advertising hoarding may trigger a desire for a can of Coke or a bar of chocolate. Product sales can be increased if appropriate stimuli are used in promotional messages.

Information search

Having become aware of a need, a consumer starts to look for ways of meeting that need. This involves a search for information about potential products and services. Four sources may be used:

▶ *Internal sources:* Buyers search their own memories for previous experience of satisfying a particular need. This is probably the most convincing reason why firms must continually make every effort to satisfy the needs of their customers, rather than make one-off sales with no concern for customer satisfaction.

▶ *Word-of-mouth:* Trusted personal contacts are consulted as a source of unbiased advice. Their experience is used as a substitute for personal experience of the products or services in question.

▶ *Public information*: Independent reports of the comparative performance of similar products are published by consumer watchdogs, such as the Consumers' Association, newspapers and magazines. Consumers may consult these at the information search stage. Financial advice given in the broadsheet newspapers is widely read by those managing investments, for example, and book lovers examine critical reviews in the press before deciding what to read and buy.

▶ *Promotional messages*: These consist of information generated by the producers and sellers of products and services, including advertising messages, sales presentations, labels on packaging and sales literature. Although they are easily available, these information sources may be seen as the least credible in the eyes of consumers. This is particularly so in the case of services, such as hairdressing or insurance, when the consumer has no opportunity to sample the service before it is delivered. The high risk of such purchases encourages potential buyers to look for unbiased advice from those who have sampled the service before, rather than rely on company-sponsored information.

The information search enables consumers to narrow down the list of possible ways of satisfying their needs. Those that remain on a short-list at the end of the process are known as the evoked set. A consumer with a need for a long-term financial investment may start off considering possibilities such as property, shares, government bonds, endowment policies or building society accounts, but the information search may lead to the conclusion that the limited risk and ease of access to a building society account make this the best option. At this point, the different building societies and different types of account form the evoked set and the consumer is ready to evaluate these alternatives.

Evaluation of alternatives

This process involves the establishment of criteria that will be used to choose between options in the evoked set. One buyer may view proximity to a building society branch as a key criterion, while another may prefer an Internet account and place little value on a branch network. Others may feel secure only with a long-established society with a national reputation, or value high interest rates above all. Each buyer will have a hierarchy of criteria, ranging from the 'essential' to the 'would like' to the 'marginal benefit', and this hierarchy will enable the items in the evoked set to be ranked in order of preference, with the final purchase being made of the item that emerges at the top of the list.

DID YOU KNOW?

Dealer staff can exert a critical influence on the decision to buy a car. Research shows that about one-third of customers drop a model from their short-list because dealer staff show so little interest in them. Not having a car to test-drive is more likely to put them off than a pushy salesperson, and customers are likely to walk away if they sense anything is not quite as they would expect (O'Loughlin, 2002).

There are two important issues here for marketers. First, if the process of evaluation of alternatives is fully understood, there is less temptation to go in for price-cutting in response to what consumers often say is their key criterion for purchase. If consumer behaviour is carefully observed, factors such as quality, service and reliability often emerge as being the 'essential' attributes of a product, with low price simply being in the 'would like' category. Second, the selection criteria may include both tangible and intangible attributes of the product, as well as attributes of the seller of the product. Credit facilities, installation and after-sales service, brand image and the location and reputation of retailers may all be critical. In other words, the total product, and not just the core benefit offered, will be considered by the consumer at the evaluation stage in the decision-making process. (The total product concept is discussed further in Chapter 7.)

Purchase

This is the point at which a consumer makes a decision to buy and performs a transaction for the chosen product or service with the chosen seller, usually exchanging money for goods. Marketers must be aware that consumers can withdraw from the purchase process without completing the transaction. Suppose a chosen product is unavailable at a chosen retailer. Consumers may choose to buy an alternative product rather than switch retailers, particularly if brand loyalty is weak. Suppose they discover that the information they were given was inaccurate, and a product's price is higher than they were expecting. They may choose to delay or refrain from purchase altogether. Such issues reinforce the importance of consistency of service, product availability and truth in advertising.

Post-purchase evaluation

After they have purchased a product, consumers assess the extent to which it has satisfied their needs and met their expectations. As explained earlier, this assessment will then become part of their internal information search the next time they have a similar need. They will also share this evaluation with others who consult them for advice.

Cognitive dissonance can occur at this stage, particularly after the purchase of expensive or unfamiliar items. This refers to the doubts people feel after making such a purchase. It is common for consumers to continue 'shopping around' even after they have made a purchase, looking for information to reassure them that they have made a good choice. How often, having just bought a new pair of shoes or piece of kitchen equipment, have we then walked into the shop next door to see whether we could have found anything better or cheaper? How often have we glanced at the small ads in the newspaper just after we've bought a second-hand car? Supportive information at this stage can reduce this dissonance. If consumers are subsequently assured by their friends that they made a good choice, or are exposed to reassuring advertising messages, they are more likely to consolidate their satisfaction and are less likely to try to return the goods.

Purchase classes

The speed at which consumers pass through the various stages of the decision-making process varies widely according to the nature of the product and the perceived importance of the decision. Five distinct purchase classes can be observed, each of which is characterised by a different level of decision-making effort.

▶ *Impulse purchases* are made with no planning. The visual stimulus of seeing a product available on a shelf is what prompts a person to buy. The motivation is sudden and instant, and consequently such purchases can lead to feelings of guilt. After the purchase has been made, consumers may realise that they have little need for the product and may regret the failure to evaluate more carefully (though this may not deter them from making a similar purchase in the future). The powerful urge to buy seems to override conscious rationality. Marketers have long recognised the potential for the impulse purchase of non-essential items such as confectionery and magazines at supermarket check-outs. Faced with a short wait in a queue, shoppers are ideally placed to pick up the visual stimuli from such items, which are unlikely to have been on their shopping lists and would otherwise have been passed by in the aisles.

▶ *Routine purchases* are made of low-value items that are purchased on a regular basis. This normally includes grocery and household items that are consumed and replaced automatically, such as toothpaste, milk, detergent and pasta. Although these types of purchase are planned, consumers do not want to spend much time and effort on product choice. They will often have a preferred brand, but if that brand is unavailable when and where they wish to buy it, they will buy an alternative rather than wait or shop elsewhere. Manufacturers of these types of product become market leaders by establishing and sustaining these routine behaviour patterns. They ensure that their products are constantly available in as wide a network of retailers as possible, and advertise to reinforce the habit of buying their products. This makes it difficult for their competitors to threaten their position. Consumers will only change their behaviour if something new and different can encourage them to change their comfortable routines.

▶ *Familiar purchases* occur when a person is a frequent consumer of a product type, but is willing to put some effort into choosing a version or brand of that product. This is known as limited decision-making. It occurs when consumers are on the look-out for something new and different, but also when consumers are price conscious and looking for a better deal, or when they have become dissatisfied with their routine brand and are looking for a brand that meets their needs better. Product information is essential in this type of decision-making to enable people to make informed choices about the alternatives they are considering. Advertising can also be effective in encouraging consumers to shift away from routine purchasing and try something different.

▶ *Unfamiliar purchases* are subject to more extensive decision-making. These are products that consumers buy infrequently. They may be technologically complex and they are usually of higher value than impulse, routine or familiar purchases, though this is not always the case. A person who buys a dog for the first time may initially go to some lengths to choose an appropriate dog-food, even though the cost of dog-food is relatively low. More commonly, household appliances, sports equipment and holidays are all likely to be seen as unfamiliar purchases and be subject to extensive decision-making by most consumers. Buyers will use a wide range of criteria to evaluate them and will spend time weighing up the evidence and deciding what to buy.

▶ *Critical purchases* are usually high risk because the consequence of bad decisions can have serious implications. Where products such as houses, financial services and education are concerned, consumers often go to great lengths to ensure that they are well informed of all the relevant facts about their potential purchase before they decide to buy. They are likely to seek information from public as well as personal sources, and will be cynical of commercial messages unless they offer factual statements that can be substantiated.

Most products fall into different purchase classes under different circumstances. A tennis racquet may be an unfamiliar purchase for most of us, but for a tennis professional it is likely to be a familiar or even routine purchase. A shopper may buy crisps on impulse at the cinema, but see them as a routine purchase in the supermarket. By studying the decision processes that most commonly relate to their own products, marketers can identify any significant patterns and consequently provide the most appropriate messages to help consumers make informed decisions, and the best sales and service approaches to help draw them through those decision processes.

Consumer buying roles

Just as we have seen with organisational purchasing in Chapter 2, a lot of consumer buying decisions are not the sole responsibility of a single individual. Indeed, the whole decision-making process may be divided up between a group of people, collectively known as the decision-making unit (or DMU), which may be involved at different stages and play different roles in the final decision to purchase. There are five distinct consumer buying roles:

▶ *Initiator*: The one who first comes up with the idea to buy something and who may suggest it to others.
▶ *Influencer*: Someone whose advice carries weight in evaluating the alternatives. Sometimes this is a person whose opinions are respected by the other members in the DMU due to expertise or experience in buying the type of product in question.
▶ *Decider*: The person who makes the final decision as to whether to buy, what to buy, when to buy, how to buy, or any combination of these.
▶ *Buyer*: Someone who performs the transaction and exchanges money for products or services.

► *User*: The person who consumes, operates or experiences the product or service.

Sometimes a single buyer takes all of these roles him- or herself, particularly with products that are exclusively for personal use, such as shaving cream, make-up, hair-care products or hosiery. This is more likely to occur in single-person households than in families. As discussed earlier, family members are often jointly involved in purchasing decisions; even if a wife invariably does the household shopping, the influence of her husband and children may have been significant in shaping her behaviour as the buyer. Decisions may be made jointly between two partners for purchases such as holidays, with one deciding on the location and the other a particular hotel or apartment. Children are the users of many grocery products for which they are never the decider or buyer, and conversely parents are the buyers of many products for their children which they never use themselves. Marketers must identify the relevant buying roles for their products and services so that they can send appropriate messages to the different members of the DMU, according to their input into the purchasing decision.

KEY SKILLS
ACTIVITY **4.2**
• • • • • • • • • • • • • •

Problem solving

Making decisions

When you ask people whether they are influenced by advertising, they often say no – and if we take their word for it, we may conclude that advertising is a highly ineffective marketing technique. In fact, so long as it is a well thought-out campaign, advertising can be very effective at attracting customers. It is simply that people are often unaware of how they reach their decision. This exercise will help you to recognise the complexity of the decision-making process.

Think of the last time you bought the following products:

► A cinema ticket.
► Toothpaste.
► A pair of shoes.
► A music CD or tape.

For each of these products, draw up a 'mind map' that illustrates the links between the factors that influenced your decision to buy the item you finally chose. You will need to include all the sources of information you used to help you make your decision, and list all the people who were in the decision-making unit. How could maps such as these help the producers of these products improve their marketing?

Organisational buyer behaviour
• •

Influences on decision-making

Organisational buyers are subject to similar categories of influence over their buying decisions as consumers, but within these categories, different factors are significant (see Figure 4.5).

figure 4.5
**Influences on
organisational
buyer-behaviour**

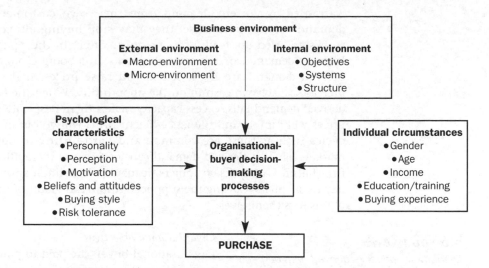

It is the business environment rather than the social environment that influences organisational buyer behaviour. The external business environment, namely the macro- and micro-environmental factors discussed in Chapter 3, will have an over-arching influence on the nature and quantity of products and services that an organisation buys, while the internal environment of the organisation itself will be important in the decision-making process.

The macro-environment
Factors such as the strength of the economy, the opportunities and threats posed by new legislation, interest rate changes, technological developments and environmental concerns may all affect the needs of a business. Organisational buyers will respond by increasing or decreasing their levels of purchase, looking for new suppliers as old ones become unable to supply new technologies and identifying new sources to meet new requirements. Even socio-cultural factors can have an influence. The unwritten rules of buying and selling in Japan, for example, are very different from those in Europe and the US, and the nature of the buying process may change accordingly.

The micro-environment
The most significant issue in the micro-environment which influences organisational buyers is the nature of demand from their own customers. Organisational buyers only buy goods and services if consumers or other businesses ultimately demand *their* products. This is known as *derived demand*. As a result of derived demand, they are less likely to stop buying a product or service altogether if the price goes up, as they need it to satisfy their own customers. Therefore, organisational buyers are also likely to exhibit *inelastic demand* (discussed in Chapter 9).

It is important to understand the significance of this from a marketer's point of view. First, demand from organisational buyers is likely to fluctuate more widely than from consumers. In anticipation of future increases in demand, buyers may increase the quantities they purchase by far more than is warranted by current demand from their own customers. If this forecast demand fails to materialise, they may stop buying altogether while excess stocks are used up, leading to a stop–go effect in their purchasing patterns. Inelastic demand can also cause problems. In a boom economy, when levels of derived demand are high, sellers will raise prices, make high profits and increase capacity to cash in on the opportunity. When the economy turns and derived demand falls, excess capacity makes them desperate to sell their goods, prices will tumble and the less efficient firms will go out of business. Business cycles such as these are common and hard-hitting in business-to-business markets. Finally, derived demand can lead to a vulnerability to bad debt. If a firm fails to satisfy its customers, it may go into liquidation and be unable to pay its suppliers, causing the suppliers, through no fault of their own, to go out of business themselves.

> **DID YOU KNOW?**
> Demand for paper is derived from demand for a wide range of consumer products. Although large quantities are used in publishing, stationery, packaging and domestic use, demand also derives from the automotive industry (filters for engines), the photographic industry (base paper) and even the furniture industry (the top surface of a laminated board is a sheet of printed paper).

Organisational objectives

Organisational buyers are paid to purchase the products and services their organisations need to conduct their business and achieve their objectives. Consequently, the business objectives and strategies of an organisation usually give direction to its buyers' decision-making processes. Suppose an organisation aims to be a cost-leader, undercutting other firms in its industry to become a market leader. The primary role of the buyer is to source products and services of an acceptable quality at the lowest possible price, so that costs can be kept low and profits can be made even at low prices. On the other hand, if an organisation wishes to be seen as the quality leader, the buyer may be willing to use higher-priced suppliers who offer a more reliable product and service, with a view to recouping these costs from higher prices to their own customers.

 KEY SKILLS
ACTIVITY **4.3**
. . . .
Application of number

Economic value to the customer

An element of both consumer and organisational buyer behaviour is usually related to very rational criteria, such as price. But the lowest price is not always the best value for money for customers. This exercise will help you to set a price for a product that takes into account what the product is really worth to the customer in tangible terms.

Although businesses are influenced by price-tags, they are often more interested in the 'economic value' of the purchase. The concept of 'economic value to the customer' is one that refers to the difference in *total* cost between an existing and a new product. This is a feature of some consumer markets too. Suppose a family needs replacement windows in their house. Although the *price* of single-glazed windows with wooden frames is likely to be lower than double glazing and UPVC frames, the cost over the lifetime of the window is likely to be higher if the cost of heat loss from the window and a regular need for repainting is taken into account.

Suppose a company is choosing between two suppliers to buy a new machine product (see Table 4.1).

Table 4.1

	Machine A	Machine B
Purchase price (£)	£20,000	?
Delivery (flat fee)	200	200
Installation and commissioning (flat fee)	600	1,000
Productivity (items per hour)	500	1,000
Annual maintenance (per annum)	1,000	2,000
Emergency call-out fee (per call)	200	200
Expected life (years)	10	8

Bearing this in mind, what would you charge for machine B?

Organisational systems

Organisations use a variety of formalised systems in an attempt to maximise their buying efficiency and effectiveness. As discussed in Chapter 10, the just-in-time production systems used by some manufacturers mean they carry very little stock and are dependent on their suppliers to deliver the right goods at the right time for their production lines. Under these circumstances, one of the essential evaluative criteria to be used in the buyer's decision-making process will be the reliability of the supplier.

Long-term supply contracts are a feature of the buying process in some organisations. Buyers can use them to exert buying power, requiring sealed bids from potential suppliers to ensure the lowest possible prices. More positively, though, long-term contracts can be used to develop better relationships between suppliers and buyers, recognising that the transactions between them must be in the interests of both parties. (Relationship marketing was discussed in Chapter 1.)

CASE STUDY 4.4

Stand and deliver

Online shopping is set to have a revolutionary impact on consumer buying habits, but its potential will be constrained, not so much by technological limitations as by the logistics industry responsible for delivering the desired objects to customers' doorsteps. The potential for dissatisfaction with this part of the transaction is legendary, and the subject of more complaints than many other aspects of online shopping which have much higher profile. Grievances about damaged goods, unfulfilled or incomplete orders, long lead times and badly timed deliveries are just some of the issues that have to be addressed by online suppliers who fail to get their logistics right. Poor service can kill off the relationship between an online supplier and its customers at a time when the 'doorstep experience' is fast becoming as important as it was in days gone by when the fishmonger arrived every Friday to sell a fresh catch off the back of his van. Yet many logistics and delivery companies, while well prepared to deliver goods in bulk to factories or shops, have little experience at picking and handling a high volume of individual stock items and delivering them to domestic addresses. Online book and clothing suppliers need watertight systems for effective returns handling; and technically complex products may need specialist handling and unpacking and even installation.

The Lane Group PLC is one of the UK's leading logistics companies with five years' experience of domestic deliveries. In 2002 it won over £1 million worth of new business, becoming the sole supplier for Parcelnet for the delivery of large-screen televisions, taking on the home delivery and installation of nursery products for Mamas and Papas, working for Tesco in a major product recall and re-delivery programme, and winning the Lilywhite's contract for the delivery of domestic gym equipment. But despite its success, profits were difficult to realise, as Sales Director Patrick Butler explained: 'We offer a professional two-man delivery and installation service, which many of our customers demand to complement their own quality products and brand image. However, there is still an unwillingness among retailers and manufacturers to pay for the added value elements of such a service … We have in the past come across customers who have expected a 48-hour service, installations, product testing and old product collection and removal – which is fine. What is unrealistic is that they often expect these services free of charge.'

Questions
1 What decision criteria should online retailers use in selecting a distribution service?
2 To what extent are the psychological characteristics of the buyer likely to have influenced the decision of companies such as Tesco, Parcelnet and Lilywhite to use the Lane Group?
3 Account for the reluctance of manufacturers and retailers to pay a premium for value-added distribution services.

Sources: www.lanegroup.co.uk; Reimen (2000).

Organisational structure

The way in which an organisation structures its buying function will influence the buying process itself. The roles, authority and domain of organisational buyers will vary between organisations, and identifying the decision-making unit is an important task for anyone trying to sell to organisations. For example, centralised buying is a feature of some large organisations. Its aim is usually to reduce costs by negotiating discounts for large quantities. This may mean that some organisational buyers do not have the authority to purchase certain products and services their organisations use. It may also mean that some organisations have the buying power to insist on buying direct from manufacturers instead of through distributors or agents.

Individual circumstances

Although organisational buyers are not buying for their own personal consumption, their age, gender, income (and therefore seniority) and education are still likely to affect their decision-making processes. In addition to these, training and experience in the role of buyer are other factors likely to affect buyers' behaviour. They may influence the rigour of their information search, their ability to evaluate, the value they place on personal contact with their suppliers and their willingness to try new sources of supply.

Psychological characteristics

Issues of personality, perception, motivation and beliefs apply just as firmly in organisational buying as in consumer buying but may exhibit themselves in different ways. Buyer motivation, for example, will stem primarily from the functional needs of the business, but the social and esteem needs of buyers may encourage them to prefer suppliers with whom they can enjoy social functions, or whose names are familiar and carry some prestige.

Personality characteristics can lead to different buying styles, with some buyers enjoying confrontation and the exercise of power over their suppliers, some being analytical and formally rational, and others encouraging open, honest discussion with suppliers, rather than win/lose negotiations. The extent to which risk will be tolerated is another psychological characteristic of buyers, with some willing to experiment with new technologies and new suppliers, while others wait for them to be tested with a proven track record before they are willing to consider them.

The organisational buyer decision-making process

Because of the complexity of some organisational buying decisions, more stages may be evident in the buyer decision-making process than in consumer markets (see Figure 4.6). There are six key stages:

▶ *Problem recognition*: Similar to the consumer's 'perception of need', someone in an organisation recognises that a problem may be solved by the acquisition of goods or services. Internally, this may occur due to a new product development, under-capacity or problems with quality control; externally this may occur when a buyer sees a product report in the trade press or is offered a promotional price by a potential new supplier.

▶ *Product specification*: Often in conjunction with other members of the decision-making unit who have expertise and can give technical advice, the buyer will draw up first a general description, and then a precise specification of the nature and quantity of the product required.

▶ *Supplier search*: The buyer will identify potential suppliers of the specified products and may ask them to submit proposals or give sales presentations to demonstrate their capabilities and indicate their prices. This will enable the organisation to draw up a short-list, similar to the consumer's 'evoked set'.

▶ *Supplier selection*: This is commonly done by ranking the desired attributes of potential suppliers in order of importance. The list is likely to include a number of purely functional attributes, such as price, delivery, quality and after-sales service, but may also include less tangible features, such as corporate ethics and communication skills. Suppliers will be chosen who most closely meet the key criteria. In many cases, organisations will choose more than one supplier for products they require on a regular basis, to ensure continuity of supply in case one supplier defaults and to allow the price and service comparison of different suppliers over a period of time.

▶ *Ordering*: The placing of an order with a supplier may be a one-off activity or may take the form of a contract to purchase under agreed terms over a period of time. Invariably these terms will include payment terms; while

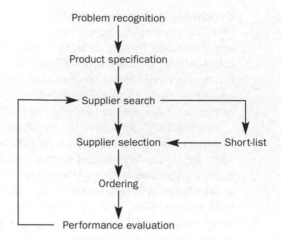

figure 4.6

The organisational buyer decision-making process

consumers usually pay cash up-front before they receive their products or services, organisations invariably set up accounts with their suppliers, receiving goods first and subsequently paying for them within a stipulated time period (though suppliers often insist on a credit reference with new customers).

► *Performance evaluation*: Buyers collect information about the performance of their suppliers and use this as an important source of information when a similar product is required again. Sometimes this information is used as part of a system for motivating suppliers to maintain excellent performance levels. Financial incentives may be offered for reaching delivery, service or quality targets.

This decision-making process has a number of implications for marketers. First, the earlier in the process they can make contact with the buyer, the more likely they are to be included in the supplier short-list. Many buyers appreciate the expertise of suppliers at the product specification stage and if a collaborative relationship can be formed, a phenomenon known as 'creeping commitment' may follow; the buyer will start to feel more comfortable with that supplier than others who are considered later on. Second, because the supplier search process is likely to be more disciplined and formal than in consumer markets, it is important that potential buyers can easily find information about sources of supply. Marketers must ensure that they are well represented in trade directories and the trade press, and that sales staff are as committed to building relationships with potential new customers as they are to 'closing a sale'. Finally, the monitoring of after-sales satisfaction is just as important for the seller as it is for the buyer. Particularly in the case of long-term contracts or repeat purchases, marketers should be fully aware of the levels of satisfaction of their customers so that they can use this in the negotiation of new business. The more satisfied the customers, the less likely they are to switch supplier on the grounds of price alone.

CASE STUDY **4.5**   **Driving a hard bargain**

So powerful are supermarkets as buyers of fruit and vegetables in the UK today that their desires have shaped the nature of an entire industry. Their product specifications are exacting. Fresh fruit and vegetables must be capable of being transported the length and breadth of the country without any signs of wear and tear; they must thrive in cold storage and have the longest possible shelf life; they must look immaculate and resemble customers' preconceptions of healthy produce, with no skin blemishes or unusual colours; and they have to fit nicely on the supermarket shelves. Mud and earth is a real problem, so wherever possible produce should be grown under cover to avoid rain, mess and cosmetic damage. Leeks must arrive in the stores without their green stalks; potato varieties must be round rather than oval, so that they don't get bruised in a mechanical harvester; carrots should all be identical to each other; and English varieties of strawberries, although winners in terms of taste, lose out to Dutch varieties which tend to survive transportation better.

Although growers and intermediate suppliers dislike the tight controls placed on them by supermarkets, they have little alternative but to try to meet them, as these clients now account for about 80 per cent of the UK's fruit and veg business. For the supermarkets, fresh produce can create an important competitive advantage, in that they can affect a consumer's choice of store. They also offer very high returns, with the standard mark-up being around 40 per cent. Some lines, such as fresh herbs, generate much more. Despite a wholesale price of £10.60 per kilo, herbs typically end up in small bags at 89p for 20g – equal to £44.50 per kilo.

One consequence of the supermarket dominance has been a decline in the proportion of fresh produce grown at home. Overseas varieties compete head on – and are often the ones preferred by consumers. The further internationalisation of buying by supermarkets seems set to continue as Internet auctions grow in popularity. Using an online exchange for retailers, supermarkets can now place their product specifications and supplier selection criteria on the Internet and invite bids from potential suppliers of the goods. The great advantages of the auction system are its speed and its potential for arriving at the lowest possible prices, as suppliers actively bid against each other to get the business. In one of the earliest transactions of this kind, Sainsbury's sourced its entire quarterly supply of economy mild cheddar using an Internet auction. A process that normally takes several weeks was reported to have been whittled down to just a few hours. Tesco, John Lewis, Safeway, Kingfisher and Marks & Spencer are all members of the Worldwide Retail Exchange (www.worldwideretailexchange.org), an organisation which facilitates transactions such as these.

Questions
1   What factors do you think influence the complex product specifications laid down by supermarkets for fruit and vegetables?
2   Who benefits from these tight controls?
3   In what ways do online business-to-business auctions alter the traditional patterns of the organisational buyer decision-making process?

Sources: Blythman (2002); Hunt (2001b); Islam (2000).

Organisational purchase classes

Just as consumers extend or curtail the efforts they put into the decision-making process according to the nature of the product they are buying, organisational buyers will approach the different stages in the decision-making process according to the nature of their buying task. There are three categories of buying situation:

▶ *Straight rebuy*: When the buying task is familiar and recurring, routine ordering procedures are used to place orders with acceptable suppliers. The supplier selection stage of the decision-making process is automatic, which makes it very difficult for new suppliers to break in. The buyer uses routine procedures to reduce the effort required for purchasing such products, and is likely to be reluctant to interrupt comfortable and established habits unless a problem occurs or a new supplier offers something with considerably more benefits. The buyer's selective perception may even mean that messages from alternative suppliers are screened out, including the avoidance of sales calls.

▶ *Modified rebuy*: If buyers become dissatisfied with their routine purchases for any reason, they may decide to consider new suppliers; their objectives may be to get better prices, to change the product specification, to improve the delivery times or simply to review the effectiveness of their routine purchases. This provides an opportunity for new firms to get on to the short-list and current suppliers must reassess what they offer and prepare for the likelihood of further negotiation.

▶ *New task*: Many buying decisions are likely to be new tasks that a buyer meets for the first time. In this situation, all the stages of the decision-making process are likely to be in evidence, though the amount of detail included in the product specification and the lengths to which buyers will go to find the best supplier are still likely to vary according to the value of the product and its importance in the operations of the organisation; capital equipment and component parts are more likely to be thoroughly scrutinised than office consumables or support services.

Organisational buying roles

Organisational buying roles are very similar to consumer buying roles and, as a result, the person entitled 'buyer' in an organisation is seldom the only important person in the decision-making process. One of the key tasks for marketers, therefore, is to identify the nature of organisations' decision-making units. These are likely to vary according to the nature of the products they are buying: the decision-making unit for computer systems is likely to be different from the one for office cleaning services, and those involved in deciding on company cars may have very little, if any, involvement in the purchase of raw materials or components. The buyer may be the person who arranges the transaction in all of these cases, but the users may be consulted in coming to a final decision and influence may be exerted by those with technical expertise or seniority. Even the final decision may not be the responsibility of the buyer, but perhaps a departmental manager whose budget may bear the cost.

The only members of organisational decision-making units who are seldom present in consumer buying are gatekeepers. These are people who control the flow of information in an organisation, normally with a view to preventing irrelevant information from reaching the decision-making unit. Secretaries often act as gate-keepers, turning away unwanted sales calls and diverting direct mail. If this is the case, the task of actually reaching relevant buyers becomes all the more difficult, and the role of marketing may need to encompass a strategy for breaking through this type of resistance.

Key concepts

Buying role: the nature of input a person has into the decision to buy a product or service.

Cognitive dissonance: doubts that arise after making a purchase and that lead to a feeling of discomfort.

Consumers: individuals who buy products and services for themselves or on behalf of their households.

Decision-making process: series of steps a buyer takes in selecting a product or service from a set of alternatives.

Decision-making unit: a group of people who exert an influence over a decision to buy a product or service.

Derived demand: demand for business products that originates from demand for consumer products.

Evoked set: a short-list of potential purchases that results from a search for information about products and services.

Family life-cycle: the stages of formation and progression of a typical family.

Gatekeepers: those who control the flow of information in the decision-making process.

Inelastic demand: when levels of demand for a product or service remain fairly stable, regardless of their prices.

Organisational buyers: those who buy products and services on behalf of the organisations they work for.

Primary group: groups of people with whom an individual has regular but informal interaction.

Purchase class: a product classification that indicates the level of effort a buyer will exert in deciding what to buy.

Reference group: any group that influences a person's buying behaviour.

Secondary groups: groups of people with whom an individual has formal and irregular interaction.

Social class: a group of people with similar levels of wealth and power who share similar values and attitudes.

1 Which of the following is the most commonly used indicator of social class?
   a Household size.
   b Car ownership.
   c Occupation.
   d Personality.
   e Life expectancy.

2 Derived demand is:
   a The motivation behind impulse purchases.
   b The motivation behind organisational purchases.
   c A feature of the family life-cycle.
   d A normative influence on consumer behaviour.
   e A stage in the organisational buyer decision-making process.

3 Which of the following is *not* a stage in the consumer decision-making process?
   a Post-purchase evaluation.
   b Straight rebuy.
   c Evaluation of alternatives.
   d Perception of need.
   e Purchase.

4 What role is a child likely to play in its parents' decision to buy a new car?
   a Influencer and decider.
   b Decider and buyer.
   c Initiator and decider.
   d Buyer and user.
   e None of these.

5 Which of the following elements of the business environment is most likely to influence the volume of raw materials and components an organisational buyer purchases?
   a Inflation.
   b Unemployment.
   c Recession.
   d Legislation.
   e Interest rates.

Which of the following are true and which are false?
   6 Internal sources of information are sufficient for making modified rebuy decisions.
   7 As organisational buyers are constrained by the systems of their firms, their personal characteristics do not affect their decision-making processes.
   8 Peer groups can exert comparative influence on consumer buying decisions.
   9 Marketers are unable to influence unfamiliar purchases with promotional messages.
   10 Consumers' lifestyles are reflected in the residential neighbourhoods they live in.

Discuss the following

11 To what extent can consumer perceptions of a product be influenced by advertising messages?

12 What criteria would you use to decide which products should be centrally purchased in an organisation and which should be purchased by individual departments?

13 Who are likely to be members of the decision-making unit for the purchase of a new house?

14 To what extent will the concept of social class be of use to marketers in the twenty-first century?

15 What information sources is an organisational buyer likely to consult in the search for a supplier of computers?

Further study
• • • • • • • • • • • • • • • •

The literature on the subject of consumer behaviour is extensive. Textbooks include:

Solomon, M., Bamossy, G. and Askegaard, S. (2001) *Consumer Behaviour*, 2nd edn, FT Prentice Hall.

Blythe, J. (1997) *The Essence of Consumer Behaviour*, FT Prentice Hall.

A fascinating reader on this subject is:

Packard, Vance (1957) *The Hidden Persuaders*, Pelican Books.
This is a seminal work on consumer motivation. Still in print more than 40 years after it was first published, it provides a fascinating perspective on a wide range of behavioural issues and also confronts the ethical dilemmas that they pose for marketers.

Organisational buyer behaviour is less well covered, but is included in most general texts on business-to-business marketing.

A useful book to help determine a person's social class based on their occupation is:

Market Research Society (2003) *Occupation Groupings: A Job Dictionary*, 5th edn, Market Research Society.

References
• • • • • • • • • • • • • •

Arlidge, J. (2001) 'Downtrodden, weak, outwitted and male', *The Observer*, 9 December, www.observer.co.uk

Bhuchar, S. (1999) 'What's different about Asian audiences?', *ArtsBusiness*, 32, 2, August, pp.5–6.

Blythman, J. (2002) 'Strange fruit', *The Guardian*, 7 September, www.guardian.co.uk

Hickling, A. (2002) 'Sit down and shut up', *The Guardian*, 12 June, www.guardian.co.uk

Hunt, J. (2001a) 'Cold sell', *The Guardian* (New Media), 20 August, pp.30–1.

Hunt, J. (2001b) 'Big names move in to e-markets', *The Guardian*, 25 January, www.guardian.co.uk

Islam, F. (2000) 'The whey ahead...', *The Observer*, 4 June, www.observer.co.uk

Kotler, P. and Armstrong, G. (2001) *Principles of Marketing*, Prentice Hall.

Museums Journal (2002) 'Free entry means traditional audiences keep coming back', *Museums Journal*, October, p.13.

O'Loughlin, J. (2002) 'Traffic report', *Research*, September, pp.32–4.

Packard, V. (1957) *The Hidden Persuaders*, Pelican Books.

Phillips, K. (2001) 'Marketing quality', *Research*, June, pp.30–1.

Putnam, M. and Davidson, W.R. (1987) *Family Purchasing Behaviour: Family Roles by Product Category*, Management Horizons Inc. (a division of Price Waterhouse).

Reiman, S. (2000) 'Coming up with the goods', *Research*, July, pp.38–9.

Sclater, I. (2002) 'Wish you were here', *Marketing Business*, July/August, pp.26–7.

Sunderland, P. (2002) 'Bean Counters', *Research*, November, pp.22–4.

Wells, W. and Gubar, G. (1966) 'Life cycle concept in marketing research', *Journal of Marketing Research*, 3, November, pp.355–63.

Woolf, M. (1996) 'Body Shop turns cheek to chic', *The Observer* (Business), 9 June, p.16.

CHAPTER 5

Marketing research

Objectives

When you have read this chapter you will be able to:

➤ Understand what marketing research can be used for.

➤ Recognise those situations in which marketing research is necessary.

➤ Set appropriate objectives for marketing research.

➤ Distinguish between primary and secondary data.

➤ Identify sources of secondary data.

➤ Explain the methods available for conducting qualitative and quantitative research.

➤ Describe the key stages of a marketing research survey.

Foundation focus: the 20-second takeaway

In marketing, the process of research helps generate a better understanding of customers (and potential customers) and provides clues as to how their needs can best be met. This process can take a number of forms. Sometimes, it is useful simply to browse through some websites or internal reports to find answers to key questions about products and markets. At other times, however, more specific information has to be gathered directly from customers themselves. Structured techniques involving questionnaires, discussion groups and interviews are often used for this. The most appropriate technique to use will depend on many factors, but especially the purpose of the research. The so-called 'quantitative' techniques are valuable for measuring the number of people who think or behave in a certain way, whereas 'qualitative' techniques are used to help understand the range of different attitudes, motivations and perceptions that people hold about something.

Introduction

The quality of marketing decisions is usually dependent on the quality of information that underpins those decisions. Questions such as 'who are my customers?' and 'what are their needs?' must be answered before decisions are made about what to produce, what to charge, how to promote and where to distribute. Marketing research is a process that organisations can use to generate the information they need to answer questions such as these. The term 'marketing research' is often shortened to 'market' research, though strictly speaking this is incorrect. *Market* research focuses simply on trends in the market related specifically to customer activity, whereas *marketing* research encompasses a much wider range of issues relating to an organisation and its environment.

This chapter looks at both the purpose and process of marketing research, examining a wide range of techniques and practices that can be used to gather data in the most effective and efficient ways.

What is marketing research?

Marketing research can be viewed in many ways. In essence, it is a systematic approach to gathering facts and figures related to the marketing of goods and services. Tull and Hawkins (1992) gave a very simple, but useful definition of marketing research, which emphasised the fundamental purpose of this activity. They described it as 'a formalised means of obtaining information to be used in making marketing decisions'. But the American Marketing Association (1995) puts more emphasis on marketing research as a function that creates an information channel between organisations and their customers:

> the function that links the consumer, customer, and public to the marketer through information – information used to identify and define marketing opportunities and problems; to generate, refine and evaluate marketing actions; to monitor marketing performance; and to improve understanding of the marketing process.

This definition recognises the wide range of decisions that marketing research can inform. Before, during and after the implementation of marketing activities, marketing research can be used to provide a basis for rational decision-making and help to avoid the problems that arise from acting on 'hunches'.

The scope of marketing research

Different types of research can be conducted according to the type of marketing information required:

> **DID YOU KNOW?**
> When a major office equipment manufacturer was investigating perceptions of its products, staff and customers were both asked 'If this company was an animal, which one would customers say it was?'
> On the staff picture-board were racehorses, jaguars, lions and antelopes; but the customer picture-board revealed donkeys, tortoises, monkeys and dinosaurs. The company was then able to take steps to correct both its image and its business practices (www.nop.co.uk).

▶ *Market research* is concerned with identifying the nature, composition and preferences of current and potential markets. This may be used to help organisations identify levels of potential sales in a particular market, or to identify regional differences (particularly important when considering exporting or overseas expansion, as discussed in Chapter 13). It can also be used to help firms identify differences between different sub-groups of their customers, known as market segments (further discussion of this in Chapter 6).

▶ *Behavioural research* attempts to establish the underlying factors that determine consumer behaviour in a market (as described in Chapter 4). It is used to develop an understanding of why people buy, and how they go about making their buying decisions.

► *Competitor research* is concerned with identifying the nature of current and potential competitors and their strengths and weaknesses. Changes in market share are of particular interest, as they indicate how well a business is performing relative to its competitors. Competitors' pricing and promotional policies may also need investigation, as may any new products that they launch.

► *Pricing research* can be undertaken to help understand the price sensitivity of customers: What proportion of sales will I lose if I put my prices up by 10 per cent? Are my prices too high relative to the competition? What price should I set for a new product? Experiments can be conducted to see just what sort of effect price changes might have on demand.

► *Promotional research* can be used to pre-test promotional campaigns before full-scale media costs are incurred, to see whether the chosen message, format and media will be effective. This is most easily done with direct mail letters, different versions of which can be sent to different addresses and the response rates compared. It can also be effective for TV advertising and sales promotion campaigns (discussed further in Chapters 11 and 12). Post-testing of promotions involves the evaluation of a campaign after it has run, to identify its impact and cost-effectiveness.

► *Distribution research* may be undertaken to identify the relative effectiveness of different retailers, distributors or agents. This can help businesses to identify any areas where their coverage is poor, and where they require a more significant presence. It can also help them use their own salesforce more effectively. Supermarkets use this type of research extensively to identify the best sites for the location of out-of-town superstores.

► *Product research* is particularly important when new products are developed (as discussed in Chapter 8), to ensure that their characteristics match those required by potential customers. It can also be used to help businesses improve existing products and to identify gaps in current provision.

► *Economic and social research* is concerned with identifying trends in the environment. As explained in Chapter 3, unemployment, interest rates, inflation and population trends can all affect the long-term well-being of an organisation, and such factors need to be monitored to enable firms to pre-empt any negative impacts of such changes.

DID YOU KNOW?

Research to develop the Ford Focus included the use of a Third Age Suit by the product's developers. The suit, which has 'stiff joints,' simulates the effects of ageing by restricting physical movement in such a way as to enable young designers and engineers to experience first hand how an older person might feel when moving around a vehicle (Hughes, 2002).

Is marketing research really necessary?

Needless to say, a lot of marketing decisions are taken every day without any marketing research being conducted. This begs questions as to whether marketing research is always appropriate. An organisation should ask itself a number of searching questions before embarking on a research programme:

► *Do I have enough information already?* It is always possible to generate more information to help make a decision, but at some point a manager will have to make a judgement that there is enough relevant information available to take a decision, and this may be before any research has been undertaken, especially if the problem is a straightforward one.

▶ *What difference will the findings make to my decision-making?* Some organisations commit themselves to certain courses of action and then conduct research to support their views, but there's no point conducting the research if the findings will have no influence on the decision. This also leads to the next question.

▶ *What if my research tells me something I don't want to hear?* The temptation is to dismiss the research as being wrong rather than to face up to the unpalatable implications of unwanted findings. Again, there is no point conducting the research if positive outcomes alone are to be heeded.

▶ *How quickly must I make a decision?* Some problems need to be resolved so urgently that there is no time for research. A good guess at the right time may be more advantageous than an informed decision that is made too late.

▶ *Can research give me accurate answers to my questions?* There are questions that research finds very difficult to answer. Consumer buying *intentions*, for example, may be measured but these intentions may never translate into purchasing. Conversely, consumers may reject new product ideas in research, but persuasive advertising campaigns may be very effective in breaking down negative attitudes if the product offers real benefits.

▶ *How much will research cost?* This is likely to determine the type of research to be undertaken, and may affect the process of research as well as the decision as to whether or not research should be conducted at all. An evaluation has to be made as to whether or not the research offers value for money.

▶ *What are the risks if I don't do any research?* Risk equals the potential cost of making the wrong decision. For example, suppose an organisation is considering adding a product to its line, but the cost of conducting appropriate research is high. If the costs of introducing the new line are low, it may be more cost-effective just to launch it and risk failure in the market than to incur the research costs. On the other hand, if a wrong decision could potentially undermine the reputation of the whole business, then the risks are too high to ignore research findings, whatever the cost.

CASE STUDY **5.1**
··················

Sinclair C5

Inventor Sir Clive Sinclair, who had achieved world firsts and technological breakthroughs with his executive pocket calculator and pocket TV, determined as far back as 1973 to produce an electric vehicle. When the UK government abolished tax on electric vehicles in 1980, and later passed legislation permitting anyone over 14 years of age to drive an electrically-assisted pedal cycle without a helmet or insurance, Sinclair took this as his cue to develop the one-seater, three-wheeler C5, which fell somewhere between the status of car and bicycle.

Sir Clive openly admitted that he did not believe in market research, claiming that it is impossible to assess demand for a new product accurately when there is nothing like it already on the market, but he confidently predicted sales of up to 100,000 vehicles per annum and reached an agreement with Hoover to start production in the autumn of 1984. The research he did undertake was mainly connected with product development and 63 families from urban and suburban areas were invited to try the prototype vehicle. They were also asked how much they thought such a vehicle might cost. The higher-income families thought about £1,000, while the lower-income families suggested around £2,500.

The product price was finally set at £399 and distribution was to be by mail order. Test-marketing was eschewed in favour of a single official launch which took place in January 1985 at Alexandra Palace, where journalists were invited to go for a test-drive through the hilly and snow-covered grounds. The few who did so expressed concerns about the road-worthiness of the vehicle under such conditions. Further complaints were soon forthcoming, and tests by the Consumers' Association produced a number of major criticisms:

▶ The height of the C5 on the road was at bumper-height of other cars, making it difficult to see and increasing the chance of injury in an accident.
▶ Spray, exhaust and the headlight beam from other vehicles affected visibility.
▶ The horn was ineffective, the headlight beam was insufficient and mirrors and indicators were optional extras.
▶ There was no reverse gear, so moving backwards usually meant getting out of the vehicle.
▶ The vehicle would travel no more than 15 miles on a fully-charged battery, as opposed to manufacturer claims of 20 miles.
▶ In hilly areas, drivers had to pedal a lot due to the motor cutting out.
▶ A maximum speed of 15 mph caused a hazard in urban areas with a traffic flow progressing at 30 mph.

It was subsequently revealed that, although safety consultations had taken place, the vehicle had been mainly tested on a test-track and in simulated accidents, not in heavy traffic.

Within three months of the launch of the C5 it was clear that sales would not meet targets. The root of Sinclair's problem seemed to be that it was being marketed as a serious means of transport – as a competitor to the moped and second car. Consumers, on the other hand, saw it as an upmarket plaything. Production was cut back by 90 per cent and within a further six months was halted altogether. The receivers were called in when only 14,000 had been produced. Businessman Maurice Levensohn, who bought nearly 7,000 of the trikes after the venture collapsed, eventually started marketing it as a collector's item and sold the whole lot at up to £700 each. They now fetch around £1,000 each at auctions.

Questions

1 Could market research have led to a happier ending for Sir Clive?
2 What else might you have wanted to know from the 63 families who tried the prototype?
3 What indicators might you look at to assess demand for a new product?

Sources: Griffiths (1985); Independent (1996); Marks (1990).

The marketing research process

The marketing research process should follow three key stages:

Planning

A clear purpose for marketing research needs to be identified before any action is taken. This purpose normally relates to a problem, issue or opportunity facing the organisation that is causing uncertainty as to which direction to take. When the purpose of the research is clear, it is possible to set specific objectives that will indicate what the research aims to find out and to identify the data (facts and figures) required to achieve those objectives.

Implementation

There is no single best way of collecting data. The way in which the research is implemented will depend on the research plan. Although a survey may be useful, it is by no means the only tool for implementing marketing research and may not be the most cost-effective way of achieving the objectives. Alternatives should always be considered.

Interpretation

'Information' is created when the data collected are interpreted in the context of the research objectives. The final stage of the process of marketing research is therefore to make sense of the findings and ensure that they are used to influence decision-making.

The rest of this chapter looks at these stages in more detail.

Planning marketing research

Identifying the problem

Organisations frequently meet business challenges that cause them uncertainty. They may be very positive challenges (sales are rising) or decidedly negative (market share is falling). There may be a hypothesis as to the reason the issue has arisen, and this hypothesis may need to be tested. Alternatively, there may be no apparent reason and the issue may need to be thoroughly explored. In both cases a manager may need information to help develop an appropriate response to the situation, and research will be required to provide some answers.

Setting objectives

Research objectives are statements that set out exactly what an organisation wants to know, explicitly establishing the information required to make a decision relating to the particular problem, issue or opportunity identified. They are important for three reasons:

▶ They are the starting point for the rest of the research process and are used as a guide to the type of data required and the best way of collecting them.
▶ They are used to help researchers highlight the most important findings when interpreting data and reporting results.
▶ They provide a benchmark for evaluating whether the research process was effective and cost-effective.

Objectives may be any one or a combination of three types: exploratory, descriptive or causal objectives.

Exploratory objectives

Exploratory research is conducted if the nature of a problem or issue is unclear, or if an organisation needs preliminary information to formulate a hypothesis that can subsequently be tested in further research. It is concerned with 'exploring' possibilities rather than finding specific answers. Exploratory objectives may be set if a firm has an idea that it wants to develop, but isn't sure which way to go next; or if it can find no apparent explanation for a fall (or increase) in sales and wants to identify possible reasons. Examples of exploratory objectives might be 'to identify areas of weakness in customer care' or 'to evaluate the impact of a new competitor'.

Descriptive objectives

When an organisation is seeking specific information to support specific decisions it will set descriptive objectives. In other words, it will use research to 'describe' the factors that will influence its decisions, such as the market potential for a product, customer attitudes, competitor strategies, price sensitivity or economic conditions. Descriptive objectives are very common, as the information obtained can be very cost-effective, helping to avoid the financial consequences of making bad decisions. Examples of descriptive objectives might be 'to determine the average frequency of purchase' of a product, or 'to identify the demographic profile of heavy users'.

Causal objectives

Causal objectives are set if an organisation wants to understand more about the relationship between two factors. For example, is TV advertising effective in generating charitable donations? To what extent are buying patterns influenced by store layout? By what percentage will sales volumes increase if prices are reduced by 10 per cent? Answers to cause-and-effect questions such as these can mean that firms are better placed to influence consumer behaviour, to eliminate inappropriate marketing tactics and to forecast demand.

Identifying data needs

When research objectives have been set, it is possible to identify data needs. *Data* are facts and figures used to generate *information*. The analysis of data (in the light of the objectives set) creates information that can be used in decision-making.

Conducting marketing research

When research objectives have been set and data requirements identified, it is possible to make decisions about the style and duration of research activities.

Quantitative research

If the research objectives require data to be collected about *how many* people hold similar views or display particular characteristics, the research is described as being quantitative. Conducting quantitative research usually requires data to be collected from only a small proportion (known as a sample) of the group of people of interest to the researcher. As long as the sample chosen is representative, statistical techniques can be used to make assumptions about the views of the whole group based on the responses from the sample.

Qualitative research

If the research objectives require information to be generated about *how* people think and feel about issues, or *why* they take certain decisions and behave as they do, then the research is described as being qualitative. Qualitative research is particularly useful for exploring the subtleties of consumer behaviour, when categorising and quantifying responses would be an inadequate means of drawing out individual characteristics. It tends to be conducted among very few individuals, and no attempts are made to draw conclusions as to the views of other people. Instead, the findings from qualitative research tend to be used either to set an agenda for further quantitative research (to see whether the views expressed are indeed representative of the views of others) or to add detail to some general findings that have emerged from quantitative research that has already been conducted.

Continuous research

Sometimes marketing research is needed to monitor changes that are occurring, for example in purchasing habits, in population trends, in customer satisfaction, or simply in sales figures. In this situation, the research has to be repeatedly conducted on an intermittent basis over a period of time, so that comparisons can be made and trends identified. This is known as continuous research.

CASE STUDY **5.2**

The TGI

The Target Group Index (TGI), published by BMRB International, is a continuous survey that has been running in Great Britain every year since 1969. Its primary objective is 'to describe, as accurately as possible, the characteristics of target groups of consumers'. It does this by asking questions about the buying habits of a sample of 25,000 consumers every year. The survey takes place on a weekly basis, with data being collected through detailed self-completion questionnaires. The questions themselves cover over 4,000 brands in more than 500 product areas, but also ask about other consumer behaviour such as newspaper readership and TV viewing. Lifestyle and attitude questions are also included and a full set of demographic data are gathered for each respondent.

By comparing the responses from one question with another (a technique known as cross-tabulation), profiles can be drawn up of different target groups. If the response to a question on mobile phones is compared with responses to questions on lifestyle and attitudes, the types of consumer who buy the different brands can be identified and compared. For example, heavy users of mobile phones are more likely than average to be cinema-goers and Internet users, but less likely to be TV viewers. And owners of Ericsson phones are more likely than other phone owners to work out regularly at a gym, to agree with the statement 'I like taking risks' and to have visited the Science Museum and the International Motor Show in the past 12 months.

One UK advertising agency used TGI data to create profiles of eight different types of housewives, for which it created names such as 'Take-away Tracey', 'Muesli Mum' and 'TV Dinah'. When one of its clients, Hellman's Mayonnaise, was concerned about the inroads being made into its market by supermarket own brands, it used TGI data about mayonnaise eaters to identify the types of housewife most likely to buy mayonnaise. It was found that 55 per cent of mayonnaise was bought by just 38 per cent of housewives, namely the 'Muesli Mums', 'Career and Connoisseurs' and 'Short-cut Gourmets'. Subsequent advertising campaigns then aimed at creating brand loyalty among these groups. Groups such as the 'Take-away Traceys' and 'Kids and Chips' were safely ignored, as they were much more likely to buy salad cream than mayonnaise.

Questions

1   What information can continuous surveys provide that *ad hoc* surveys cannot?
2   Given the evidence above, how would you promote Ericsson phones? What else would you like to know?
3   Would a continuous survey such as this be of any use in business-to-business markets? Discuss its limitations.

Sources: www.bmrb.co.uk; Tomlinson (1993).

Ad hoc *research*

This is a term given to describe one-off investigations of specific issues that will arise only once and for which more information is needed to make a particular marketing decision.

KEY SKILLS
ACTIVITY 5.1
·············
Improving own learning and performance

From theory to practice

The logistical issues that arise when you first undertake a research programme can be just as problematic as the methodological ones. Through this exercise you will consider the gaps that you will still have in your understanding – even having read this chapter!

Suppose you were appointed as a graduate trainee at a major international market research agency, and were given a budget of £10,000 to use for your training in your first year in the company. Plan a training programme for yourself, including courses you would like to attend and other learning approaches you would like to make use of, to prepare you for an account management role 12 months later.

Data collection
··················

Having identified the type of research to be undertaken, the researcher must decide upon the most appropriate method or methods for collecting the data.

First of all, sources of *secondary data* should be identified. Secondary data are facts and figures already available 'off the shelf', having been collected for another purpose or another organisation. The researcher is a secondary user of already existing data, so the research technique is known as *desk research*.

If, as is often the case, secondary data fail to provide sufficient evidence for a marketing decision to be made, then *primary data* will have to be collected. Primary data are facts and figures collected specifically to provide the information required to reach the research objectives. There are a wide variety of research techniques that can be used to collect primary data, and these are explored in the following sections.

Sources of secondary data

As explained above, secondary data already exist. If they exist within the organisation conducting the research, but were collected for a different purpose, they are described as *internal* sources of secondary data. On the other hand, if they were collected by another organisation, whether for the purpose of marketing research or any other purpose, they are known as *external* sources of primary data.

Both types have their advantages and disadvantages:

▶ They tend to be less expensive than primary data (available for free, internally, or at a relatively low cost from libraries and research publishers).

▶ They can provide data that would otherwise be impossible to collect (historical trends, for example).

▶ They can be used as a source of ideas and a starting point for further primary research.

But:

▶ The data required to reach the research objectives may not be available (either because no one has collected them or because the owner of the data refuses to release them).

▶ The data that *are* available may be irrelevant (perhaps being so general as to be of little use or only of use to other industries or markets).

▶ There may be doubts as to the accuracy of the data (such as errors in the original research design or an inappropriate sample).

▶ The data may be out of date (particularly in fast-moving markets driven by rapid technological change).

Internal data

A wide variety of potentially useful marketing data tends to be spread throughout the different departments of an organisation. Useful sources might include:

The customer database
This is likely to hold information about everyone that an organisation sells to. In some organisations this will include consumers or industrial buyers, but at a minimum the customer database will give details of retailers and other distributor customers. It is likely to give the name, address and sales history of anyone who has ever set up an account with the organisation and can be very useful for

investigations to identify groups of buyers with similar characteristics, known as market segments (as discussed in Chapter 6). It may also be useful for identifying trends in purchasing patterns and for forecasting future demand. More and more use is being made of customer databases as the growing capacity of computers makes possible the complex analysis of millions of records. This process is known as data mining.

Management accounts
These contain a lot of details about costs and revenues. They may be able to reveal the profitability of different product lines, and to provide direction for the allocation of marketing budgets.

Salesforce reports
As the salesforce usually comprise the members of an organisation who are closest to the customer, their observations of customer reactions can be very valuable. They may be able to spot needs for new products, to supply information about competitor activity, to pinpoint quality problems and to identify service deficiencies.

Website server logs
Server logs are generated for the activity at a website and provide a complete record of all the traffic to a site. An analysis of this data gives marketers information about the effectiveness of both the design and the content of a site.

Previous marketing research
Although probably out of date, the findings from previous market investigations may be used as a benchmark for comparison with new findings, and trends may be plotted if the research has been continuous.

External data
Other forms of useful marketing data may come from a range of sources, some of which are available for consultation free of charge through public libraries and others which are owned by private organisations who will charge for them.

Government statistics
In many countries throughout the world, governments publish statistics that have normally been collated to help them identify social and economic trends for the purpose of managing the economy and maintaining social welfare. UK statistics are considered to be some of the most accurate in the world and many of them are of direct relevance to businesses, the marketing function in particular. The *Business Monitor*, for example, includes sales figures for different industries, and may enable a firm selling business to business to identify growing and declining market sectors. *Social Trends* provides valuable information about consumer purchasing habits. These and all other UK government statistics are now available online at www.statistics.gov.uk.

Trade associations and professional bodies

These usually represent the interests of the members of a particular industry or profession and may produce their own research on matters of common interest to those members. They may also provide (or sell) lists of members which may be of use as a sample population for conducting primary research in a specific industry sector. Other representative agencies produce research across a range of industrial sectors, including the Chambers of Commerce, the Confederation of British Industries and the British Institute of Management.

Universities

Because they are primarily research institutions, universities are excellent sources of objective data. They tend to keep good stocks of useful publications in their libraries, and their staff and students are continually engaged in undertaking new research, some of which is published in the form of theses and dissertations and not available elsewhere. Different universities tend to specialise in different subjects, so it is wise to start a secondary data search at an institution with strong links with the industry sector under investigation.

The trade press

The UK is well served by trade, technical, business, professional and academic journals, and many foreign journals are also published in the English language. These can be invaluable sources of information about competitor activities, new product launches, technological developments and customer trends. To take advantage of these, organisations should consider setting up well-catalogued library systems to enable them to find the relevant material when it is needed.

> **DID YOU KNOW?**
> *Kids.net is a syndicated research study carried out every six months by research agency NOP (National Opinion Polls). Aimed at companies interested in education issues and the youth market, it combines quantitative interviewing and qualitative research, and monitors Internet usage among 7–16 year olds. Companies who join the syndicate can add their own confidential questions to both the questionnaire and focus groups (www.nop.co.uk).*

Syndicated research and omnibus surveys

Commercial market research organisations regularly publish reports of their own investigations into particular markets or industries, which they sell either to subscribers or on the open market. This type of syndicated research tends to be available when the cost to any one organisation of generating the data would outweigh its benefits. By sharing the findings, everyone can benefit from information that would otherwise be unavailable. Continuous research is often syndicated due to the cost of collecting data over a long period of time. Media viewing, listening and readership profiles, for example, are useful to all advertisers to help them decide on the most cost-effective way of reaching their target audiences. Some of this type of information is readily accessible on the World Wide Web. For example, NUA (www.nua.ie/surveys) and Cyberatlas (www.cyberatlas.com) both provide a searchable archive of research reports from different analysts, which summarise current and forecast future use of the Internet.

Another means of sharing costs is by using omnibus surveys, which are regular interviews with large samples of consumers conducted by market research firms, which sub-contract questions to anyone wishing to ask specific questions related to their own products.

Uses for secondary data

Internal and external data are commonly used for four purposes:

▶ To help clarify a problem, for example what exactly should we be investigating?
▶ To provide a background to a problem, for example a framework that puts the problem in context.
▶ To provide a benchmark for comparison with other research, for example to confirm or question the validity of new findings.
▶ To provide an answer to a problem, for example the problem has already been investigated by somebody else and the findings are available.

Whenever secondary data prove insufficient for reaching conclusions related to the research objectives, primary data must be generated.

Collecting primary data

Surveys are very useful and effective tools for collecting certain types of primary data and the final part of this chapter looks at the techniques associated specifically with this data collection method. However, a survey is but one of a range of methods available for generating primary data and is by no means the best in all circumstances. It is a very blunt instrument for conducting qualitative research, for example, where the nuances of behaviour patterns, attitudes and motivations may be lost in the attempts to make respondents conform to a predetermined mechanism for answering questions. It is also dependent upon respondents telling a researcher what they do, or think, or feel, though they may be unwilling or unable to give truthful answers. The research will be misleading unless their responses reflect their actions.

CASE STUDY **5.3**

Captured on film

The thought processes of today's shoppers are notoriously difficult to unravel using conventional research methods. Psychologists have identified that consumers have two buying modes: alpha and beta. In the alpha state, conscious decisions are made and the buyer is alert and attentive to the process. However, 80 per cent of shopping is carried out in beta mode, with decision-making taking place deep down in the unconscious. Consumers simply do not remember the individual elements of the experience that led to their purchase, and if they do, they find it difficult to describe that experience or express their feelings about it.

So to overcome the limitations of surveys, focus groups and other techniques which rely on a people's ability to recall and relate their experiences, film-based methodologies are growing in popularity. A typical approach uses in-store cameras, and individuals are filmed as they shop to record their reactions to the store environment or layout or any individual product category. Alternatively, eye-mark recorders, originally employed by NASA in the design of the space shuttle cockpit, are used to track volunteers' eye movement as they look at advertising materials, websites or point-of-sale offers. Subsequent analysis can reveal precisely what attracts and holds consumer attention.

But the use of film-based research is not limited to the retail environment. The new product development function is increasingly using it for 'Reality Research', to assess how people engage with new products in their domestic environments. In a study of how people use technology in their lives, 10 households, including a retired couple, six young professionals sharing a house, a single mother and a Bangladeshi family with five children, were all filmed over a four-day period by researchers who lived with them. A range of interesting findings emerged that would have undoubtedly been missed in focus groups. One family was using broadband to pipe sound from their local mosque; another had two Sony PlayStations – one exclusively for playing CDs and the other for games; and two families left their televisions on all day, regardless of whether they went out. Digital TV was found to be a refreshingly communal experience. As most households had only one digital TV, the families tended to gather together to watch programmes. Technical jargon relating to the Internet clearly baffled some. Internet service providers were confused with search engines, and while most participants knew what to do on the Internet, they couldn't accurately describe the process. One woman terminated an attempt to buy an airline ticket online as she did not understand the meaning of GBP when asked to enter a price.

Questions

1   What can focus groups reveal that film-based techniques cannot?
2   How else might new product ideas be effectively evaluated?
3   Should shoppers be told when they are being observed? Argue for and against covert in-store observation.

Sources: Cozens (2001); Scamell-Katz (2001).

DID YOU KNOW?

Interviewing techniques are of very little use with the under 5s, as their language is so unsophisticated. Observation is a far more important research technique with this group. The 'Teletubbies' TV series was researched at Ragdoll, a specially designed shop in Stratford-upon-Avon. Staff there keep a record of all adult and child comments that may be of interest to producers. They also regularly watch 'Teletubbies' with the children in the play centre and make notes about which elements of the programme appeal most to the young viewers (McKenzie, 1998).

In fact there are many ways to collect primary data, and it is important that the most appropriate method is used for the type of research being conducted. Four commonly used techniques include the following.

Observation

This technique involves watching people, their behaviour and their actions, or observing the results of those actions. It is a particularly useful technique in situations where people find it difficult to give accurate verbal accounts of their behaviour. Suppose, for example, the research objectives were to identify the most common route taken by shoppers through a supermarket. Few people would be able to report their movements accurately after their visit, but watching their progress through the store on closed-circuit TV provides all the data a researcher needs. This is an example of *covert* observation, with the shopper being unaware that the observation is taking place. Covert observation is also a feature of 'mystery shopping', a research method used by organisations to evaluate the quality of their own customer service. Researchers are sent to stores in the guise of ordinary shoppers and report back on their experiences.

Overt observation can also be useful. One way of measuring the impact of press or TV advertising is to monitor a viewer's pulse and eye movement when exposed to the advert, to assess levels of interest and see how much attention is given to the brand name (though, of course, this gives no indication as to whether the person liked or disliked the advert, or had favourable or unfavourable attitudes towards the brand). Another example is the observation of users that may take place before the launch of a new product, such as a computer program, to find out how easy it is to use and identify aspects of the software that need to be improved. TV viewing figures are calculated by attaching monitors to TV sets in a sample range of households. The monitor indicates whether a set is on or off, and which channels it is tuned to at every second of the day. (More on this in Chapter 11.) A new form of overt observation known as a Usability Lab is growing in popularity as a means for testing prototype websites, to see how easy they are to use and to navigate. These involve one-on-one accompanied web browsing, during which research participants 'think out loud' and the moderator asks questions and probes for subjective feedback on the site.

Indirect observation is concerned with observing the consequences of actions. Dustbin checks are an example of this. A selected sample of consumers (known as a panel) are paid to collect their domestic refuse in special sacks, which are taken away on a regular basis so that the consumption patterns of household products (as opposed to purchasing patterns) can be inferred from the discarded packaging.

Experimentation

This technique is concerned with measuring the relationship between two marketing variables that are thought to be related in some way. Using a technique borrowed from the sciences, the researcher will set up an experiment by initiating some sort of marketing activity on a small scale and monitoring the results. Attempts are made to keep all other factors constant, so as to be certain that any divergence from the norm stems from the marketing activity undertaken.

Suppose, for example, a food retail chain wanted to assess the price sensitivity of its own-brand products. The objective of an experiment would be to identify the relationship between sales of own-brand items and prices. The hypothesis might be that a 10 per cent increase in prices would lead only to a 5 per cent fall in sales volume (this information may encourage the retailer to increase prices, as it would lead to an increase in sales revenue). The experiment could be conducted by recording normal sales levels for a range of own-brand items over a period of a week in all stores and raising the prices of those items by 10 per cent in a sample of stores the following week. Electronic point-of-sale check-outs allow a rapid calculation of any differences in sales volume during the second week and statistical techniques can be used to decide whether there is sufficient evidence to accept the hypothesis. The extent to which 'extraneous' factors (perhaps the weather or school holidays) would have affected results can be assessed by comparing sales patterns for the second week in the non-experiment stores with the previous week. Provided there is no evidence to suggest that the sales trends observed have occurred everywhere, and not just in the stores with the higher prices, the retailer can be confident of the findings.

Unstructured interview

Qualitative data are often collected by means of unstructured interviews. Instead of using a formal response mechanism (such as a questionnaire) for recording respondents' views, the unstructured interview is used to probe beneath the surface of responses and encourages respondents to express their attitudes and motivations, rather than just their superficial views or observations. As a result, this technique is highly sensitive to the individual being questioned. The responses given cannot be quantified or assumed to be representative of others, but they are useful for giving the researcher deeper understanding of the issues under investigation. Two different approaches can be used to conduct unstructured interviews, namely the depth interview and the focus group.

Depth interviews

These are prolonged one-to-one interviews during which the interviewer asks questions on a series of topics, but is free to phrase the questions as seems most appropriate and to return to the most interesting points raised by respondents and probe them further. The interviewer has nothing more than a check-list of issues to explore and will use open-ended questions to encourage a full and explanatory response from the interviewee. Interviewers are a critical part of the research process in this type of investigation. The more skilled they are at leading respondents from topic to topic, and from the general to the specific, the more chance there is of getting to the bottom of hidden attitudes, motivations and opinions. Good interviewers are also aware of the non-verbal behaviour of their subjects, and will monitor and record the signals given out.

Focus groups

This type of research (also known as group discussion) involves an interviewer, known as a moderator, chairing a discussion among a group of six to eight respondents. The moderator has a minimal role in the discussion and simply intervenes to keep the conversation on the right lines, preventing it from wandering away from relevant topics and acting as a catalyst for new ideas when a subject is exhausted. The whole discussion is recorded on tape, preferably video so that the non-verbal behaviour accompanying the decision can be monitored. The sound track is normally transcribed word-for-word before interpretation to retain as much objectivity as possible, and quotations can be selectively used to support any observations.

The greatest advantage of focus groups comes from the effects of group dynamics, which stimulate members to reveal beliefs and views that may not have been so freely expressed in one-to-one interviews. The group situation also reflects the fact that many of the buying decisions people make are in reality influenced by the views of others. Conversely, though, if the ambience of the location is thought to be intimidating or the group comprises some dominant individuals, less assertive individuals may be unwilling to participate fully, and one of the most important tasks for the moderator will be to encourage everyone to give personal views, rather than simply conform to the norms of the group.

New forms of focus group are starting to find their feet as more and more people have access to the Internet. Chat-rooms and bulletin boards are a cheap and popular means of stimulating unstructured debate on single issues. Online real-time focus groups, though popular in the beginning, are generally thought these days to be of limited effectiveness, as moderators can exercise so little control over the 'conversation'. On the other hand, moderated email groups, comprising individuals who take part in a discussion via email over a 5–10-day period, are growing in popularity. The moderator emails discussion topics to participants, who are required to reply within a couple of days. The moderator then analyses the responses, including any minority views, and emails a summary along with the next set of topics for discussion. This approach is useful for reaching target groups which are geographically dispersed. It can involve more participants than a conventional focus group, and all participants will contribute, as there is no opportunity for a single group member to dominate. Participants can respond at a time and pace that suits them, allowing more considered answers to be put forward, and the marketer who has commissioned the research – as well as the moderator – has the opportunity to feed in questions and comments during the process.

Survey

If research requires quantitative data to be generated, it is likely that a survey will be required. This is a data collection method based on a questionnaire. Identical questions are asked of a large number of individuals and a systematic record is made of their responses. The following section examines the whole issue of conducting a survey, from design and implementation through to analysis and interpretation.

Conducting a survey
....

The survey is a tool for generating quantitative data and the findings tend to be used for generalising about the behaviour, attitudes and opinions of whole populations. It is therefore important that the way in which the survey is conducted does not bias the responses and that the data collected are indeed a reflection of the views of the whole population and not just a few individuals.

The most effective way of conducting a survey is to progress methodically through a series of key activities (see Figure 5.1).

1 Set survey objectives and identify data required

It is essential that a survey starts with a clear set of objectives that indicate precisely what information needs to be generated. This in turn enables the researcher to draw up a list of data requirements, which will form the basis for the questions to be asked. If it is difficult to state the objectives clearly at this stage, perhaps because the nature of the problem that prompted the survey in the first place is still unclear, it may be wise or even essential to conduct some exploratory research to refine the focus for the survey.

figure 5.1
**Key stages in
conducting a survey**

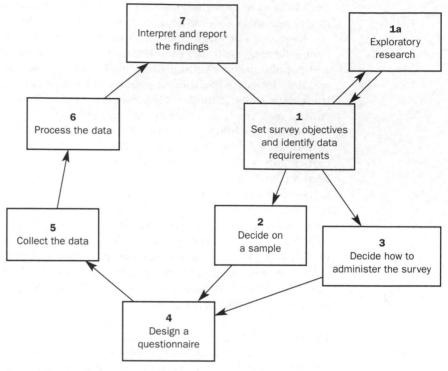

Source: Hill et al. (2003).

2 Decide on a sample

Surveys rely on the mathematical principle that the views expressed by a relatively small number of people (known as a *sample*) will be representative of a much wider group of people if the sample is of a certain size and composition. The researcher has to consider three parameters in deciding on the most appropriate sample for a particular survey.

The sampling frame

This is a term that describes the *type* of person to be questioned in the survey. The sex, age and other personal characteristics of potential respondents may be relevant, depending on the objectives of the survey. Should males, females or both be questioned? Should the sample contain all age groups or only certain age groups? Should the respondents have to fulfil certain criteria? The sampling frame for a survey of dog-food preferences, for example, is likely to consist solely of dog owners. All the people who are members of a sample frame for a particular survey are known as the 'population', or sometimes the 'population of interest'.

The sampling procedure

The next decision concerns who, from within the sample frame, should be selected to answer the survey questions. This can be done in one of two ways:

▶ *Random sampling* (also known as 'probability sampling') is a process that first of all identifies by name every single member of the population of interest and approaches a proportion of them completely at random. As each member of the population has an equal chance of being selected and there is no bias in the selection process, this sampling procedure enables researchers to gain a very accurate reflection of the views of the population. In reality, the practical difficulties and costs involved in identifying every member of a population and getting responses from all of those who are randomly identified normally outweigh the benefits of high accuracy. Take the dog-food example. Dog ownership is registered in the UK, so theoretically the population of interest should be easy to identify. But in reality, not all dog owners bother to buy a licence so the population of interest will be an incomplete list, and of those on the list, some may be unwilling to respond to the survey questions. Both of these factors will reduce the reliability and accuracy of the findings.

▶ Due to the high costs and logistical difficulties of finding a random sample, *non-probability sampling* is far more common. This is a term given to all sampling procedures that are not completely random. Normally they involve interviewers using their own judgement to select a sample, and this human intervention in the selection procedure introduces bias. With non-probability techniques, six times as many people need to be questioned to achieve the same levels of certainty given in a random sample. If large samples are not used, then sampling error creeps in, and the survey findings will be less trustworthy in terms of predicting the behaviour of the whole population and providing a firm basis for decision-making.

There are three popular non-probability sampling methods:

▶ *Convenience sampling* occurs when an interviewer selects the most available members of the population of interest. Bias creeps in here as certain members of the population are more likely to be available and willing to respond than others, so the responses may be disproportionately taken from people with similar characteristics, attitudes and motivations.

▶ *Quota sampling* aims to cut down bias by requiring that the interviewer find a prescribed number of respondents in each of several categories. For example, a survey into holiday preferences may require interviewers to find equal proportions of male and female respondents, a target number of respondents from different age groups and a specific proportion who have children.

▶ *Self-selection sampling* is the least reliable form of sampling. Respondents are not chosen by an interviewer, but decide themselves whether or not to complete a questionnaire and participate in the survey. Consequently, the sample tends to consist of those who have strong views about the subject being researched and the findings tend to polarise and reveal extreme attitudes and behaviour patterns only. Nonetheless, this type of sampling can enable large volumes of data to be collected very cheaply, so the benefits from the findings may outweigh the disadvantage of inaccuracy in some situations.

The sample size

There is no hard-and-fast rule as to the best size for a sample. It will depend on the size of the population, on the sampling procedure used, on the desired accuracy of results, and on cost, time and logistical limitations. As a rule-of-thumb, though, except in the case of very large populations of interest, figures of over 500 fully completed questionnaires usually give the researcher some confidence that the responses given reflect the views of more than just those who answered the questions. Certainly if the sample is any smaller than 500, it is difficult to make reliable comparisons between subsections of the populations, such as the difference between the views of men and women, or between different age groups.

CASE STUDY **5.4**

Unlucky seven?

1992 was the seventh time that opinion polls had been used to predict the outcome of a General Election in Britain, and the first to get the result quite dramatically wrong. On the day of the election, the pollsters were predicting a hung parliament or possibly a Labour victory. When the Conservatives swept home with a 21-seat majority, predictions were discovered to have been out by around 8.5 per cent. Similarly in 1997, although pollsters accurately predicted a Labour victory, it was not so much an improvement in predictive ability as the size of the Labour majority that led to their apparent success. In fact, the pollsters' error that year was the third worst result for the industry since 1945. With a sample of 1,500 people having been surveyed from a population of 40 million adult voters, statistical theory suggests that the responses of a representative sample should reflect the views of the whole population to within 2.5 per cent. So what went wrong?

The researchers were quick to point out that polls are not barometers of human behaviour, but simply measures of current opinions and views. Various hypotheses were put forward for the failure of this sample to represent the true intentions of the population. In 1992 it may have been that those who refused to co-operate with the survey were more likely to be Conservative voters, perhaps disaffected by issues such as the poll tax and unwilling to admit their intentions. Some blamed the inaccuracy of the predictions on floating voters who made a late switch to supporting the Tories. Others were willing to recognise that the system of quota sampling may be inadequate.

Samples for opinion polls are taken in 100 constituencies, selected at random. Interviewers are allocated to each area and required to ask questions of 15 people, who have to meet a number of criteria to ensure that the sample is as representative as possible of the constituency as a whole. The criteria relate to gender, age, social class and employment status. But age and sex are now thought to have little influence on voting behaviour. Social class is much more influential, but difficult to define, and many in the sample may be wrongly classified.

A better predictor of voting intentions is past voting behaviour, so in recent polls, adjustments have been made to ensure that the sample is not only representative of the nation demographically, but is also weighted according to how the nation actually voted at the last election. But even this creates problems for the pollsters. People forget who they voted for in previous elections and tend to think they voted for the winning party. Ask 1,000 voters how they voted in the last election, and you will find that Labour won by 25 points, not the 13-point lead Tony Blair actually secured.

Questions

1   Why might voters deliberately or inadvertently mislead researchers in opinion polls? Could this also happen in consumer surveys?
2   What other variables affect voting behaviour? To what extent can these be used to improve sampling techniques?
3   Does qualitative research have a role in predicting election results? Should it?

Sources: Sparrow (1999); Tomlinson (1993); Travis (2001).

KEY SKILLS
ACTIVITY **5.2**
. . . .

**Application of
number**

Slicing the cake!

Because surveys rely on the responses from samples to predict the behaviour of whole populations, it is important that researchers understand the extent to which predictive ability is limited by the size of the sample. This exercise will help you to do just that.

'You don't have to eat the whole cake to know what it tastes like!' Market researchers use this analogy to explain the use of samples to represent the views of a whole population. Statistical techniques enable us to predict just how similar to the population a sample will be. The size of the sample is critical to accuracy. An estimate of the population's response can be calculated from the sample's response by adding or subtracting the percentages given in the table below. So, from a random sample of 1,000, if the response rate from the sample is 30 per cent, the response for the whole population would fall somewhere between 27 per cent and 33 per cent.

	Response from sample				
Sample size	10%	20%	30%	40%	50%
100	6.0%	8.0%	9.0%	10.0%	10.0%
500	3.0%	4.0%	4.0%	4.0%	4.0%
1,000	2.0%	2.0%	3.0%	3.0%	3.0%
2,000	1.3%	1.8%	2.0%	2.1%	2.2%
4,000	0.9%	1.2%	1.4%	1.5%	1.5%

The table shows how the responses given by the sample more accurately reflect the views of the population as sample sizes increase. A sample of 500 can reflect the views of the whole population with at least twice the accuracy of a sample of 100.

Suppose an opinion poll is conducted among students to predict who is likely to be elected in the forthcoming Union elections. A random sample of 100 is taken from the enrolment list. When asked who they will vote for, the sample gives the following responses:

Frank Stein	31%
Jack Ripper	10%
Justin Time	36%
Daisy Roots	21%
No answer	2%

1 Do you think Justin Time will win the election?
2 Suppose 1,000 people had given these responses, not 100. How would this affect your prediction?
3 Suppose a quota sample of 1,000 were used instead of a random sample of the same size. How would this affect your prediction?
4 Suppose 20 per cent had refused to answer, rather than 2 per cent. How would this affect your prediction?

3 Decide how to administer the survey

There are four main types of survey, each with its own advantages and drawbacks.

Interview surveys

Face-to-face interviews, using the standardised framework of a questionnaire, are usually the most reliable way of obtaining accurate data from a large sample. The presence of an interviewer is shown to increase the likelihood of a respondent completing a questionnaire, and the response rate is found to be higher than for other data collection methods. This method also enables respondents to clarify any questions that are not understood and they can be shown visual aids such as advertising materials if required. However, as with depth interviews and focus groups, the skill of the interviewer will affect the quality of the results. 'The interviewer is, on the one hand, trying to be "standard" in all his or her approaches to respondents, but, on the other hand, may need to react to individual circumstances for the successful completion of the interview – in short, the interviewer needs to act like a robot but retain the appearance of a human being' (Kent, 1993). Bias may arise simply from the process of social interaction, with misunderstandings between interviewer and respondent arising from differences in age, sex, social class, dress, accent or personality.

Telephone surveys

Telephone interviews can be conducted fairly quickly, with interviewers under close supervision if required. If the questionnaire is fairly short, the telephone survey can be a relatively inexpensive way of collecting data; the cost of making the calls is likely to be lower than the expenses incurred by face-to-face interviewers. However, this technique quite obviously depends on respondents being on the phone and this fact alone may mean that a telephone survey is inappropriate in certain circumstances due to the bias it would introduce into the sample. It has other limitations too. The questions must be very simple to enable respondents to understand them quickly and without the use of visual aids. Interviewers need to be particularly skilled, as visual communication is excluded.

Mail surveys

Mail surveys are relatively inexpensive, incurring neither interviewer nor telephone costs. They can reach scattered populations easily and, if anonymous, respondents may give more honest answers to sensitive questions than they would face to face or over the phone. Interviewer bias is eliminated and because respondents can complete them at a time to suit themselves, they are usually willing to fill in longer questionnaires. There are, however, a number of serious disadvantages to this method of data collection, and whether or not this type of survey is cost-effective is less clear. Sampling is difficult to control, as response rates are likely to be low and the researcher has no control over who finally fills in the questionnaire. It may take a long time for responses to be received and some of these may be incomplete as there is no interviewer to clarify questions or encourage completion.

A lot of research has been undertaken to identify the factors that most encourage response to mail surveys. One of the most significant motivators is the inclusion of a covering letter that gives some background to the research, assures anonymity (or at least confidentiality) and gives clear instructions as to how to complete and return the questionnaire. A reply-paid envelope is essential in consumer surveys, and an incentive to respond, such as an entry in a prize draw or some discount vouchers, can also raise response rates. It can also help to send out reminders and a second copy of the questionnaire two or three weeks after the original one, making sure that accurate records are kept to enable those who have replied to be excluded from the follow-up mailing.

Email surveys

Email surveys are even cheaper than mail surveys, and generate responses almost as fast as the telephone. Very large samples can be approached, and international respondents are as cheap to reach as domestic ones. The data returned by respondents can be automatically dropped into appropriate software ready for analysis. But there are limitations to this approach. Email lists are difficult to compile and are often out of date; any unsolicited emails are often perceived to be junk mail, and are deleted before they are read; and penetration of email in the community, though growing, is not yet sufficient to provide a representative sample in many markets.

Self-completion surveys

Probably the least expensive method of all, the self-completion survey is a useful technique to use on a discrete and 'captive' population. It has traditionally been used to elicit views from those travelling on a train, boat or aeroplane, or sitting in a cinema or theatre seat. However, these days, even more common is its use on websites. Questionnaires are distributed to anyone who cares to fill one in and return it. It is also a method used by magazines and regional newspapers conducting simple polls on social or local issues. Readers are invited to complete a questionnaire included in the publication and return it by a certain date. As explained earlier, sampling error is very likely to creep in as those most likely to complete the questionnaires are those who hold the strongest views on the subject being investigated. Unless efforts are made by the researcher to encourage response from a representative sample, the findings may be worthless.

4 Design a questionnaire

Questionnaire design is critical to the findings of any survey. The style, length and layout of the questionnaire must be considered. Shorter questionnaires are generally better than longer ones, but there is no hard-and-fast rule as to how many questions should be asked. This will depend primarily on the objectives of the survey, but also on the data collection method. Layout is important too. Respondents must be given enough space so as not to be forced to shorten their responses.

The wording of individual questions is equally important. Each question should be evaluated against a series of criteria before its inclusion in the questionnaire. Questions should be:

▶ *Relevant* – so that the questionnaire length can be kept to a minimum, only those questions that will provide data to help reach the objectives of the survey should be included.

▶ *Clear* – technical jargon, complex terminology, long words and ambiguous statements must all be avoided. Respondents who do not understand a question will either miss it out altogether or, worse still, guess at its meaning and give a response to the question that they think is being asked, which may be quite different from what was intended.

▶ *Inoffensive* – questions relating to sensitive issues such as salary, age, social class and ethnicity may be thought offensive unless worded carefully. These types of question should be placed at the end of the questionnaire, to be answered after the respondent has built up a rapport with the interviewer (if any) and has already made a commitment to completing the questionnaire and is less likely to be put off.

▶ *Brief* – the meaning of questions of more than 20 words in length can be difficult for respondents to grasp quickly, particularly in an interview.

▶ *Precise* – each question should tackle only one issue at a time. If two issues are introduced, the respondent may have different views on the two issues but will be prevented from separating these if a single overall response is requested.

▶ *Impartial* – the wording or phrasing of questions can carry overtones that influence respondents to respond in a particular way. These are known as leading questions and should be avoided at all costs.

Before a questionnaire is administered, it should be tested on a very small number of people who are typical of the people to be included in the sample. This is know as the pilot stage, and is very important in ensuring that the questionnaire is adequate for collecting the data required. Questions that seem very straightforward to the researcher can be found confusing, incomprehensible or even offensive to the respondent!

KEY SKILLS
ACTIVITY **5.3**
• • • • • • • • • • • • • •

Communication

Asking the right questions

The quality of quantitative research data is only as good as the quality of the questions asked of respondents. The exercise will help you to understand the ways and extent to which ambiguities can creep into what may, at first, look like perfectly straightforward questions.

The manager of a small regional theatre is under pressure to generate more income from ticket sales. The problem is that people are not coming to see 'good' plays, but are only interested in pantomimes and well-known musicals. The trustees believe that to generate more money the theatre will have to put on a more popular programme. The manager has been resisting this idea and thinks that ticket prices should be raised instead, but he has agreed to conduct an audience survey to help him decide what to do next. This is the questionnaire he has designed.

1   Which age group are you in?
   1–16   ☐   40–50   ☐
   16–21 ☐   50–60   ☐
   21–30 ☐   60 +   ☐
   30–40 ☐

2   What is your occupation? ....

3   What is your income?
   Under £5,000   ☐   £25,000–£30,000   ☐
   £5,000–£10,000   ☐   £30,000–£35,000   ☐
   £10,000–£15,000   ☐   £35,000–£40,000   ☐
   £15,000–£20,000   ☐   over £40,000   ☐
   £20,000–£25,000   ☐

4   How often do you come to this theatre?
   Once a month   ☐
   Once every three months   ☐
   Once a year   ☐

5   What sort of theatrical performances have you been to in the past three years?
   a At this theatre

   ....
   ....

   b At other theatres

   ....
   ....

6   How much are you willing to pay for a theatre ticket?

Up to £3	☐	£10 to £15	☐
£3 to £5	☐	Over £15	☐
£5 to £10	☐		

7   'The role of this theatre is to provide the local community with theatrical performances that have artistic merit.'

> *Agree / Disagree*
> **1**   *What is wrong with each of these questions?*
> **2**   *What is wrong with the ordering of these questions?*
> **3**   *How would you select a sample for the survey?*
> **4**   *Design a questionnaire that would be more useful to the manager in deciding what to do next.*

Question techniques

There is a wide range of tried-and-tested styles for survey questions.

Open-ended questions

These allow respondents to provide answers using their own words, collecting data with the minimum of direction to respondents. This can be useful if the range of possible responses is very wide. Also, as people use their own words, they have the scope to articulate their true feelings more accurately than if they are constrained to a limited range of options. The main disadvantage of open-ended questions arises when they have to be interpreted. To enable them to be processed using computer software all the responses have to be read and categorised in a process known as *coding*. Inevitably, some responses will be ambiguous and difficult to code, introducing bias at this stage. Examples of open-ended questions are:

> How would you improve the service offered by your supermarket?
> What is your opinion of genetically modified foods?

Closed questions

Also known as 'closed-ended', 'forced-choice' or 'fixed-response' questions, these provide a limited number of possible responses that the respondent must choose between. Respondents tend to find these easier to complete than open questions and they are easier to code, so most surveys use predominantly this type of question to maintain high response rates.

Closed questions tend to be of one of three types:

▶   *Multiple response questions* offer a range of possible answers for respondents to choose between. Sometimes they are required to choose just one, and sometimes they can identify as many as are relevant, for example:

> What is your age? (tick one only)
> Under 18 ☐   18–64 ☐   65 or over ☐
> Have you ever been to the following countries? (tick as many as apply)
> France ☐   Germany ☐   Belgium ☐   The Netherlands ☐

Sometimes a category has to be included for those who are unable to respond (the 'don't know' box), and if there is some doubt as to whether all possible responses have been identified in advance, space should be provided for respondents to write in their own answers (the 'other' box), so that the answers can be coded when the results are analysed, for example:

Where did you last buy eggs?
Supermarket ☐   Butcher ☐   Greengrocer ☐   Farm ☐
Have never bought eggs ☐   Don't know ☐
Other (please specify)..

Closed questions offering only two options such as 'yes/no' or 'true/false' tend to be of limited use, as it is usually possible to find a different question style that elicits more information. The only important exception to this is when dealing with mutually exclusive categories such as gender.

▶ *Scaled questions* enable respondents to express the strength of their attitudes and opinions. Bipolar questions put forward widely differing opinions on a subject and invite respondents to place their own view somewhere between the two extremes offered, for example:

How do you rate the new flavour (of a food product)?
Much too sweet ☐
A little too sweet ☐
About the right sweetness ☐
Not quite sweet enough ☐
Not nearly sweet enough ☐

Another technique is to ask people to indicate the extent to which they agree or disagree with a particular statement. This is useful for measuring attitudes, for example:

To what extent do you agree or disagree with the following statement:
'It is impolite for women to drink pints of beer.'
Agree strongly ☐
Agree slightly ☐
Neither agree nor disagree ☐
Disagree slightly ☐
Disagree strongly ☐

A numbered scale can also be used to identify perceptions, using a question format known as Semantic Differential. Words of opposite meaning are placed at either end of the scale and respondents are asked to indicate their position between the two extremes, for example:

Compared with my own car, this car is:

Very quiet	1	2	3	4	5	6	7	Very noisy
Very attractive	1	2	3	4	5	6	7	Very ugly
Very cheap	1	2	3	4	5	6	7	Very expensive

The main problem with scaled questions is that respondents are reluctant to express very strong opinions and tend to avoid the first and last categories in any list. This reduces the ability of these types of question to capture true attitudes and opinions, which is why unstructured interviews are so useful for this task.

▶ *Ordering questions* enable respondents to express preferences and indicate priorities. Simple preference questions ask for one or more attributes or categories to be of more importance than others, but note that a box must be offered to accommodate those who are unwilling or unable to make a selection, for example:

DID YOU KNOW?

Research at Xerox in the early 1990s used a scale of 1 to 5 to measure customer satisfaction, with 1 as 'completely dissatisfied' and 5 as 'completely satisfied'. Customers who answered '5', indicating that they were 'completely satisfied', were found to be six times more likely to re-purchase Xerox products over the next 18 months than those who had answered '4' (Mazur, 1998).

Which three of the following reasons were most influential in your choice of university course?
Reputation of the institution ☐
Recommendation of friends/family ☐
Geographical location ☐
Nature of the course ☐
Accommodation provision ☐
Advice from careers officer ☐
Academic and social facilities ☐
Other (please specify)...................................
Can't say ☐

Ranking questions take respondents one step further by asking them to prioritise their preferences. In the example given above, respondents could have been asked to rank the influences in order, but this would have been a difficult task for such a long list. Ranking should be limited to short lists only, and even then it must be recognised that the intervals between ranked items may not be equal (the item ranked first may be seen as far more important than the rest of the list, with the others being seen as having almost equal importance).

5 Collect the data

The data collection method has already been identified by this stage (see stage 3) so the survey is ready to be administered. Interviewers must be briefed and trained for face-to-face and telephone data collection, and administrative systems must be set up for self-completion and mail surveys. If good preparation has been undertaken, this can be a very straightforward part of the research process.

6 Process the data

Data processing converts 'raw data' (i.e. the responses given on the question-naires) into a form that enables their underlying meaning to be identified. A range of computer software is available to make this task easier. A specialist data processing house may be required if sample sizes are large and the data are complex, but small businesses and those on low budgets can select from a number of relatively inexpensive packages to enable them to do the data processing themselves.

Data processing comprises three main stages:

▶ *Data input*: This involves the responses from each questionnaire being typed into the computer. It is a laborious process that requires no particular aptitude, though accurate keyboard skills are important for speeding up the process and avoiding the introduction of errors at this stage. Many interviewers now carry lap-top computers for instantaneous data entry, eliminating this time-consuming and expensive stage.

▶ *Data summary*: The computer will take the raw data and summarise how many people said what in response to each question. This is known as the *frequency* of the responses. As the sample has been designed to be representative of the whole population of interest, it can then be stated with some confidence that the frequency of response observed in the sample applies to the whole population. Visual displays of the data, in the form of pie-charts, histograms and tables, can then be produced to depict the frequencies more visually.

The computer is also able to calculate some summary statistics relating to the observed frequencies. The mean (arithmetic average), mode (most popular response) and median (mid-point of all the responses) can all help the researcher draw conclusions about the population. The dispersion (or standard deviation) of the findings is also important. The mean of a sample does not in itself imply that 'most people' hold a certain view. The dispersion of the views held must also be considered, as it indicates whether the mean was arrived at as a result of many people having similar views, or whether people have wide-ranging views on a subject so that the average is simply a half-way position on a very long scale. The larger the standard deviation, the wider the range of opinions on a subject.

▶ *Data analysis:* This involves the use of statistical techniques to identify interrelationships between the answers given, both within a single question and between different questions. Cross-tabulation, for example, is used to highlight any differences in the responses from different sectors of the sample. Do men and women hold similar views on a particular issue? Do young people have different attitudes from older people? These types of investigation can be undertaken with relative ease provided that the data have been input properly into appropriate computer software.

7 Interpreting and reporting findings

At this final stage, conclusions have to be drawn from the facts and figures to create information that relates to the objectives set, and this information has to be communicated to marketing decision-makers. This is usually done in the form of a written report which is presented orally and followed by a discussion.

The interpretation of data and the reporting of findings should be approached cautiously. Surveys produce a wide range of facts and figures, some of which are of little or no help in achieving the objectives set. These should be omitted from the report. Sufficient detail should be given to enable the decision-maker to act with confidence, but too much information is confusing and some responses may not need to be explored in detail. For example, there is no need to list all the responses to open questions, and if a large number of small frequency responses are given to a closed question, some of the categories may be collapsed into one and reported under the heading 'other responses'. Graphical illustrations can be useful for highlighting trends or relationships, but key issues should be discussed in accompanying text as well.

CASE STUDY **5.5**

Doom for the Dome

Britain's Millennium Dome got off to a disastrous start, and low attendance figures cast serious doubts on the integrity of the research that had led to estimates of visitor numbers.

Research had certainly informed the development of the Dome. Even before its concept was finalised, research had been done to help establish a suitable position for it in the context of the whole national Millennium programme. Subsequent qualitative research was used to establish a platform for the initial advertising, a full year before there was a product to show, in order to understand the significance that consumers felt the Millennium had, and how they would like to celebrate it. Rather than use traditional focus groups, 'cradles of opinion' were sought from groups of recruits, who included members of an amateur football team, workers in a Welsh crisp factory and a mother and toddler group. Further research took place among opinion leaders and trend-setters, including managers, academics and community leaders. The most significant finding was that many people had not picked up on the landmark nature of the Millennium, so the first wave of advertising attempted to raise the profile of the occasion. Subsequent campaigns were designed to build awareness of the content of the Dome, and that tickets had gone on sale.

But it was apparently an omnibus survey, used since mid-1997, that was used as a basis for visitor predictions of people who intended to go to the Dome. However, when chief executive Jennie Page was ousted just two months after it opened following revelations about the Dome's abysmal financial performance, the incoming chief executive P.Y. Gerbeau denounced the visitor forecasts around which the entire project had revolved as having been plucked from thin air. To his surprise, a thorough market survey, which he believes would have shown visitor figures of between 3 million and 6 million, had never been conducted. A subsequent government investigation was unable to pinpoint precisely how visitor projections had been arrived at, or why forecasts continually fluctuated from more than 15 million down to 10 million and finally to 6 million, without regard to the immense financial implications those changes entailed. The New Millennium Experience Company, which produced the initial business plan, and the Millennium Commission and the Department for Culture, Media and Sport which had agreed it, were all considered to have accepted the over-optimistic opinion polls without considering the underlying assumptions or exploring a new methodology on which to base the crucial figures.

Questions

1 Why are polls asking people whether they intend to do something notoriously unreliable?
2 To what extent could visitor forecasts have been improved with better research, and what methodology would have been most helpful?
3 When the research found that people had not picked up on the landmark nature of the Millennium, was it appropriate to advertise to change their perceptions?

Sources: Culture, Media and Sport Select Committee (2000); Mazur (2001).

Throughout the reporting of the findings, it should be made clear that it is impossible to make predictions with certainty based on a survey. No survey is absolutely definitive. Unless sample sizes are exceptionally large, sampling error alone makes it impossible to state categorically that the behaviour, attitudes and opinions of the sample are representative of the whole population of interest. To reflect this uncertainty, frequencies should usually be reported as integers rather than giving decimal places. The means, modes and medians observed in the data should be recognised as indicators of average views, and not as representing the opinions of Mr and Mrs Average.

Not every reader will want to look at the whole report, so it is advisable to write an Executive Summary which should appear at the front of the report. This is merely a brief summary of the findings, and main conclusions from the research, and recommendations if appropriate. More complex analysis, tables and graphical representations should be kept until later.

Marketing information systems

If marketing research is to play a useful part in a marketing strategy, it must be delivered to managers in a suitable form, as and when it is needed. Therefore, many firms take an integrated approach to the various types of information they generate and create what is known as a 'Marketing Information System'. Primary and secondary data sources are linked together to provide managers with a comprehensive package of marketing information which will be used to inform the planning, implementation and control of their marketing activity. Three key questions should be asked before a marketing information system is set up:

▶ *What information is necessary?* Information overload is as much of a problem as lack of information. If the system delivers too much information too quickly, managers will either ignore it or spend too much time on it, and may panic and over-react to minor temporary trends.

▶ *In what form should information be provided?* Raw data, such as customer sales records, completed questionnaires or transcripts of focus groups are of limited use for decision-making until they have been collated and analysed. A report of total monthly sales by product group can help managers identify trends, whereas copies of individual invoices are of little use.

▶ *To whom should information be made available?* Not all information is relevant to all managers. A good information system will only deliver information to the people who will find it helpful.

Key concepts

***Ad hoc* research**: an investigation to provide information about a specific issue.

Closed question: a question that provides a limited number of possible answers for the respondent to choose between.

Continuous research: an investigation that is repeated on an intermittent basis over a period of time.

Data mining: the analysis of transaction records held in customer databases.

Depth interview: a prolonged one-to-one interview in which the interviewer probes the answers given by respondents.

Desk research: the collection of secondary data.

Experimentation: an investigation that measures the relationship between two marketing variables.

Focus group: a group interview conducted by a moderator.

Frequency: a summary of the different responses to a question.

Marketing information system: a means of integrating all the different forms of data generated by an organisation.

Omnibus survey: a set of interviews with a large sample of consumers conducted by market research firms on a regular basis.

Open-ended question: a question that allows respondents to reply in their own words.

Population: the total group of people from whom information would be useful.

Primary data: facts and figures that are collected specifically to provide information that will help achieve the research objectives.

Qualitative research: an investigation to generate information about how people feel and why they behave as they do.

Quantitative research: an investigation to discover how many people hold similar views or display particular characteristics.

Questionnaire: a standardised set of questions designed to gather data that are relevant to the research objectives.

Sample: a small proportion of the population whose views are representative of the views of the whole population.

Secondary data: facts and figures that are already available, having been collected for another purpose or for/by another organisation.

Survey: a data collection method that makes a systematic record of the responses of a number of people to the same questions.

Syndicated research: market research data that is generated by a market research firm and sold to many organisations.

SELF-CHECK QUESTIONS

1 Which of the following may be an internal source of secondary data?
   a The Chambers of Commerce.
   b A customer database.
   c Government statistics.
   d The trade press.
   e Syndicated research.

2 Which of these descriptions fits the following question?
   a A multiple response question.
   b A semantic differential.
   c A scaled question.
   d An open question.
   e A coded question.

   To what extent do you agree or disagree with the following statement: 'Students should be required to complete their degrees in two years.'?
   Strongly agree ☐
   Agree slightly ☐

Neither agree nor disagree ☐
Disagree slightly ☐
Disagree strongly ☐

3 The frequency of responses to questions is a term referring to:
   a The number of respondents.
   b The profile of the whole sample's responses to each question.
   c The population of interest.
   d The central tendency of the sample.
   e The size of a sample quota.

4 Which of the following would be described as exploratory objectives?
   a To determine the relationship between price and sales volume.
   b To calculate the market potential for a new product.
   c To identify the relative spending power of different market segments.
   d To investigate the possible reasons for a decrease in sales.
   e To create a profile of competitors' customers.

5 Which of the following are *not* appropriate in a focus group?
   a Video recording of the discussion.
   b Audio tape recording of the discussion.
   c Transcription of the discussion after the discussion.
   d An interviewee leads the discussion.
   e Timid individuals are encouraged to speak.

Which of the following are true and which are false?
   6 Primary data should be collected before secondary data.
   7 More respondents are needed for statistical accuracy with a random sample than with a non-probability sample.
   8 Qualitative research requires a large sample if it is to be statistically reliable.
   9 Information can be generated from data.
   10 Direct observation is less reliable than indirect observation.

Discuss the following
   11 What are the main advantages and disadvantages of using syndicated research instead of collecting your own primary data?
   12 How would you sample students from your university, college or work place if you were conducting a survey to identify perceptions of catering provision?
   13 Under what circumstances might you choose to conduct a telephone survey rather than use face-to-face interviews?
   14 Why might it be useful to calculate the mean, the mode, the median and the standard deviation of responses in a survey to identify customer attitudes towards a new product?
   15 Is it possible to collect too much marketing information?

Further study
. . . .

There are many excellent textbooks available which look at marketing research in far more detail than this chapter, including:

Chisnall, Peter (2001) *Marketing Research*, 6th edn, McGraw Hill Education.

American texts on this subject tend to give more examples of marketing research in practice. Take a look at:

McDaniel, Carl and Gates, Roger (2001) *Contemporary Marketing Research*, 5th edn, South Western College Publishing.

To complete a study of marketing research, it is important to be aware that software is available for data processing and analysis. One of the more popular systems is SPSS for Windows, for which a guide is available:

Pallant, J. (2001) *SPSS Survival Manual: A Step-by-Step Guide to Data Analysis Using SPSS for Windows (version 10)*, Open University Press.

References

American Marketing Association (1995) Official definition of 'Marketing Research', cited at www.marketingteacher.com

Cozens, C. (2001) 'Sharpening the focus', *Media Guardian*, 21 May, www.guardian.co.uk

Culture, Media and Sport Select Comittee (2000) Marking the Millennium in the United Kingdom. Government Response to the Eighth Report from Session 1999–2000, October.

Gofton, K. (2000) 'Dome and gloom', *Research*, March, pp.28–30.

Griffiths, J. (1985) 'C5's road to the receiver', *The Financial Times*, 15 October.

Hill, E., O'Sullivan, C. and O'Sullivan, T. (2003) *Creative Arts Marketing*, 2nd edn, Butterworth Heinemann.

Hughes, M. (2002) 'Need for a new look at "old age" ', *The Guardian* (Money), 9 November, p.18.

Independent (1996) 'Whatever happened to the Sinclair C5?', *The Independent*, 2 November.

Kent, R. (1993) *Marketing Research in Action*, Routledge.

Marks, A.P. (1990) 'The Sinclair C5 – why did it fail?', *Management Decision* (UK), 28,4, pp.9–14.

Mazur, L. (1998) 'Copy cats', *Marketing Business*, February, p.16.

Mazur, L. (2001) 'What PY did next', *Marketing Business,* July/August, pp.16–19.

McKenzie, S. (1998) 'Early learners', *Marketing Week*, 30 April, pp.39–42.

Miller, J. (2000) 'Net v phone: the great debate', *Research*, August, pp.26–7.

Scamell-Katz, S. (2001) 'Brain sell', *Research, Food and Drink,* November, pp.26–7.

Sparrow, N. (1999) 'Labour's landslide saves pollsters', *The Guardian*, 27 October, www.guardian.co.uk

Stewart-Sandeman, P. (2001) 'The customer can have any colour he wants as long as it's black', *Research,* October, pp.38–9.

Tomlinson, M. (1993) 'Suggers, mugger and data fruggers', *Horizon*, Orlando TV Productions for BBC Television.

Travis, A. (2001) 'Embarrassing switch by pollsters', *The Guardian*, 1 June, www.guardian.co.uk

Tull, D.S. and Hawkins, D.I. (1992) *Industrial Marketing Research*, Kogan Page.

CHAPTER 6

Target marketing

Objectives

When you have read this chapter you will be able to:

➤ Distinguish between undifferentiated, product differentiated and target marketing.

➤ Identify ways in which a range of different markets could be segmented.

➤ Apply key assessment criteria to identify viable market segments.

➤ Discuss the relative advantages and disadvantages of concentration strategies and multi-segment marketing strategies.

➤ Explain the process of market positioning.

➤ Draw a perceptual map and evaluate the relative merits of different competitive strategies.

Foundation focus: the 20-second takeaway

Because people have such wide-ranging likes and dislikes, and needs and wants, it is rare that a single product or service will satisfy everyone. Consequently, it is often more effective for marketers to think about how to identify groups of people with similar needs, within the overall market, and to target them separately rather than trying to reach everyone with the same product offering. It may be best to aim for people who live in certain geographic locations, or who are at similar stages in their lives. But sometimes, it is more appropriate to target people who have similar outlook on life – regardless of where they come from or how old they are. Alternatively, it may be possible to group together people who want to use products in very similar ways, and attempt to meet their specific needs. Having identified appropriate groupings, it then remains for marketers to decide how many groups to target, and how to make their products and services as appealing as possible to members of those groups.

Introduction

As a result of studying consumer behaviour and conducting market research, organisations often come to the conclusion that it is not possible or desirable for them to attempt to sell their products and services to all the potential customers in their markets. This may be because the potential market is so large that the organisation has insufficient resources to supply it; it may be because customers are geographically very scattered; it may be because competitors have a strong foothold; or it may be because customer requirements from the product or service vary widely. Under these circumstances, firms have to decide which types of customer to aim for and then target their products and services only at selected parts of the market (known as segments). The process of identifying market

figure 6.1
**The process of target
marketing**

segments, selecting one or more of them and developing a marketing mix to meet their needs is known as target marketing and is the subject of this chapter. (See Figure 6.1.)

The development of target marketing

The concept of target marketing has grown in importance as markets have grown and become more complex. New markets often develop when a producer recognises common needs among potential customers and tries to meet those needs by producing products or services that satisfy as many people as possible. At this early stage in the development of the market it is usually possible to sustain an *undifferentiated* marketing strategy and produce a single product to satisfy the whole market. The example of the Model T Ford given in Chapter 1 illustrates this. This mass-market approach is seldom sustainable though. As a market grows, and in particular if competitors emerge with alternatives to the single product offered, it is usually found that some variations in the preferences of different customers emerge. In response to this, organisations sometimes adopt a *differentiated* strategy, producing different versions of the product, all still offering the core benefit but using a range of alternative features to give customers choice. The range of extensions that are often introduced to food products are an example of this, offering different flavours to cater for different tastes.

DID YOU KNOW?

Product variants are seldom more popular than their original version, but the exception to prove this rule is Nestlé's, peppermint Aero, which has consistently outsold the original chocolate bar.

The whole philosophy behind both undifferentiated and product differentiated marketing is to find sufficient similarities between customers to be able to sell products that will appeal widely across the whole market. (See Figure 6.2.)

A *target marketing* strategy takes a different approach. It starts off by recognising that different groups of customers often have different needs and may even want different core benefits from the same products. Rather than trying to satisfy these sub-groups with the same products, or different versions of the same products, complete marketing programmes are designed to meet the specific needs of the members of these sub-groups. Target marketing is an approach that concentrates on identifying similarities between customers but also *differences* between similar *groups* of customers. Again the motor car provides a good example here. Although most people thinking of buying a car are fundamentally looking for a means of transport of some sort, the key criteria they take into consideration when deciding which model to buy may vary tremendously.

figure 6.2
The development of target marketing

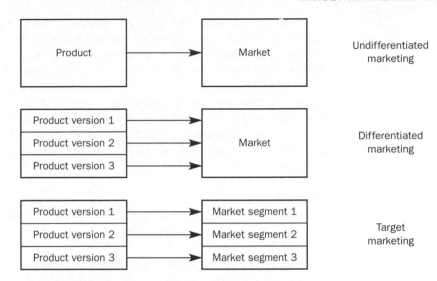

For some people, the car is a means for reflecting their status; for some it is a means of saving time; others want it to give them the thrill and excitement of travelling at speed; and some may see it as no more than a business asset, perhaps for making deliveries. Each of these groups of customers is looking for something quite different when they decide to make a purchase. This enables the manufacturers to design a range of models and back them up with promotional campaigns to reinforce the ways in which these different models can satisfy different needs.

CASE STUDY **6.1**

Harnessing the pink pound

Although the prospect of harnessing the spending power of the gay community is an attractive one for marketers in many sectors, the practicalities of targeting the so-called 'pink pound' are challenging ones. There is limited tangible data available that measures sexual orientation, and if there was, its reliability would be questionable. Instead, marketers attempting to target gay and lesbian communities have to rely on anecdotal claims and observations of the market. The casual observer will no doubt conclude that the majority of spending power in this market is focused on large urban areas such as London, Manchester, Brighton and Glasgow; but many marketers believe that there are more gay men and women living lives comparable with their heterosexual counterparts than frequenting known gay villages. And claims that 10 per cent of adults are gay, and that the number of ABC1 gay men is vastly higher than the UK average, can be little more than speculation; a *Gay Times* readership survey in 1998 revealed that the average reader earned only £14,969, compared with the then national average of £16,000.

   More to the point, perhaps, is the question as to whether gay men and women, even those who are quite open about their sexuality, want to be marketed to in a way that singles them out from the rest of society. Overt promotional campaigns targeting gay men and women can easily be seen as tokenistic and result in the alienation of the very group being targeted, as well as antagonising more mainstream audiences. More appropriate is the inclusion of gay characters and scenarios in mainstream marketing campaigns.

Products and services aimed at gay consumers can be equally badly received. G&L bank, the only Internet bank created specifically to serve gay and lesbian people, closed after just two years, with losses of £7 million. It welcomed users to its site with a rendering of 'We are family', a song by Sister Sledge, and offered a choice of 40 cheque designs, from rainbows to puppies. But the gay community was not so easily bought, and one former customer attributed its demise to the inadequacies of its service, saying 'why should I put up with crappy services simply because they're provided by my own community?' He cited a long list of problems, including botched balance transfers, interest rates not being honoured and repeated problems with web access.

Questions

1   Why is it difficult to estimate the size of the gay population?
2   For what, if any, products might the gay community be considered to be a viable market segment?
3   Would you describe market segmentation according to sexual orientation as a form of demographic segmentation, psychographic segmentation or behavioural segmentation?

Sources: Burrows (2000); Hill (2002); Jones (2001).

Market segmentation

This is the first stage in the process of target marketing, and is defined as 'dividing a market into distinct groups of buyers with different needs, characteristics, or behaviour who might require separate products or marketing mixes' (Kotler and Armstrong, 2001). It involves an analysis of the nature and composition of a market to identify groups of potential buyers who have similar needs or characteristics, or display similar behaviour. These groups are known as market segments. The differences between segments may mean that different groups of buyers need to be offered slightly different products, or should be communicated with in different ways. They may find different price levels acceptable, or look for different levels of service from their retailers or distributors. Look at the market for shampoo, for example. There are different products for people with different hair types, for babies and children, for women and men, for those who have permed or coloured hair, for people with dandruff and hair loss, for those who wash their hair frequently, for those who are in a hurry and want to condition at the same time as washing, and for those who simply want a basic product as cheaply as possible. Shampoo manufacturers have responded to the different needs and preferences of different groups of consumers and produced a wide variety of products to match the demands of the different segments they have identified.

Segmenting consumer markets

There are four possible starting points when considering how best to segment a consumer market. These should all be explored before making a decision as to the most appropriate ways of dividing up the market.

Geographic segmentation

In some markets there are identifiable differences in buyer needs according to where people live. Different geographical areas, whether they be towns and cities, regions, countries or even continents, may have different needs. In international marketing, for example, it is common to have to adapt a product or promotional campaign to suit local tastes and needs (see Chapter 13). This may be due to characteristics which are related to geography, such as climate, but may equally reflect cultural differences. In northern Europe, for example, dental health and oral hygiene are the main benefits sought from toothpaste, so brands tend to be promoted by emphasising features such as fluoride and other properties that prevent tooth decay and gum disease. In southern Europe, however, the cosmetic properties of the product are promoted more heavily, as these are of more interest to buyers.

Demographic segmentation

In other markets, geography is less relevant as a basis for segmentation but buyer behaviour is found to change according to the demographic characteristics of consumers. Depending on their age, their gender, the size of their families, their religion, their educational background, their income or their occupation, different people are found to want different features and benefits from the products and services they buy. They will choose different types of holiday at different ages, they may pursue different leisure activities according to their educational background and they will celebrate marriage in different ways according to their religion (some of these issues are discussed in Chapter 3). There are many interesting examples of demographic segmentation. Pharmaceutical manufacturers produce reduced-strength drugs for children; low-cost retail formats are designed for low income brackets; and car manufacturers have designed 'people carriers' for families.

Multi-variable segmentation is also quite common. Saga holidays are exclusively aimed at the over 50s, but are also tailored to meet the needs of single people, recognising that many people in this age bracket may have lost their partners. Single-room supplements which are commonly levied by other tour operators are waived on many of Saga's holidays.

Psychographic segmentation

As discussed in Chapter 4, the decisions people make about the goods and services they buy are influenced by a range of factors relating to their own personal characteristics: the things that motivate them, their personalities, lifestyles and attitudes, etc. This provides opportunities for psychographic segmentation – to divide up markets based on the ways people think.

In the US, socio-economic grouping is usually identified by classifying people according to their occupation, a demographic variable, but in the UK *social class* tends to reflect the ways people think and the beliefs they hold, and so is considered to be an important basis for psychographic segmentation. Social class affects the ways in which people spend money and the value they place on different types of product and service. Leisure activities tend to be related to social class, as do preferences for reading matter, home furnishings, clothing and even food.

Personality can be used as a basis for segmentation if product preference is shown to be influenced by individuals' personality traits. Brands can then be designed with characteristics that reflect the personalities of their target markets. Certain brands of household products, for example, are designed to appeal to anxious or obsessive personality types. White-coated scientists are used to promote toilet cleaning products, to demonstrate their germ-killing properties and to satisfy housewives as to their power. The effectiveness of washing powders is assured in testimonials from smiling customers, comparing the whiteness of their laundry with that of their neighbours.

CASE STUDY **6.2**

Who's online?

Understanding how to get the best out of a website is a difficult task, given that consumers display widely differing attitudes and behaviour towards the Internet. To help their clients make the most of the opportunities created by their websites, CACI, the company which originally created the ACORN system of classification (see below), has devised a profiling system known as 'e-types', which permits the behavioural segmentation of the population according to its relationship with the Internet. Seven types of behavioural groupings have been identified, and their predominance within the UK population aged 18 and over has been calculated:

Wired 4 Life (9.2 per cent of the UK population): The most extensive online purchasers, these people are interested in all forms of online shopping and use the Internet for all forms of activity, including finance and email. They are likely to have Internet access at work.

Surfing Suits (10.5 per cent): These people spend a more than average amount of time online. They look for information and enjoy news groups and current affairs, but are not keen on chatting or games. They purchase tickets, hotel rooms, travel, groceries and gifts.

Generation E (6.3 per cent): Mostly under the age of 25, these are avid users but only occasional buyers, and are likely to access the Internet at college or school. Their email usage is high, and they are interested in games and football scores as well as news and shopping.

Dot Com Dabblers (14.5 per cent): These people spend a shorter than average time online, though the value of their purchases are above average. Hotels, holidays and travel are all possible purchase categories.

Silver surfers (10.5 per cent): These are older people who are average users of the Internet but high users compared with many their own age. They prefer shorter online sessions and use travel, hotel, car rental and financial sites.

Virtual virgins (22.5 per cent): For these people online activities are limited to entertainment, such as games and football, though they may purchase toys and mobile phones online. The value of their online expenditure will be lower than average.

Wireless wonders (26.5 per cent): Overall, this group is not interested in the Internet. It shows the lowest level of usage by a considerable margin, and the few who are online don't tend to purchase.

Questions
1   How might an understanding of the e-type profile of its website users be useful to a holiday tour operator?
2   To what extent are the 'Wireless Wonders' of interest to marketers?
3   What type of functionality and design features are likely to appeal to Generation E? Compare these with the characteristics that would be favoured by Dot Com Dabblers.

Source: www.caci.co.uk

Lifestyle is another basis for psychographic segmentation, as discussed in Chapter 4. In recent years different lifestyles have been categorised by examining the geographic, demographic and other characteristics of the population, based on the premise that households with similar demographic characteristics tend to live in similar types of house and display similar lifestyles. These households tend to be grouped together in certain postcode areas, which can be identified from census data and other forms of market research. A number of firms have designed similar systems in which every residential postcode in the country has been classified according to the characteristics of people living at those addresses.

The first of these systems was ACORN, which stands for 'A Classification of Residential Neighbourhoods'. It is a system that uses information from the UK census on the characteristics of households, including age, family size, occupation and type and size of dwelling, to divide the UK population into primary categories, according to lifestyle. For example, category C consists of those described as 'rising', and comprises young professionals and executives in towns and cities who are either working or studying to make their way up in society. They tend to be relatively young, highly educated, live in high-status neighbourhoods, and the level of mobility of this group is high. Each category is then broken down into groups, with category C, for example, being subdivided into three groups, namely the 'affluent urbanites in town and city areas', 'better-off executives in inner-city areas' and 'prosperous professionals in metropolitan areas'. Finally, each of these groups is broken down further into types, according to any distinctive differences within the group. Within Group 6, for example, are the 'well-off town and city areas', 'flats and mortgages, singles and young working couples' and 'furnished flats and bed-sits, younger single people'. In total there are six primary categories, 17 groups and a total of 54 types, all of which can be identified by postcode. (See Figure 6.3.)

figure 6.3
ACORN categories and groups

Category A: 'Thriving'
▶ Group 1 Wealthy suburbs, large detached houses
▶ Group 2 Affluent greys, rural communities
▶ Group 3 Prosperous pensioners, retirement areas

Category B: 'Expanding'
▶ Group 4 Affluent executives, family areas
▶ Group 5 Well-off workers, family areas

Category C: 'Rising'
▶ Group 6 Affluent urbanites, town and city areas
▶ Group 7 Prosperous professionals, metropolitan areas
▶ Group 8 Better-off executives, inner city areas

Category D: 'Settling'
▶ Group 9 Comfortable middle-agers, mature home-owning areas
▶ Group 10 Skilled workers, home-owning areas

Category E: 'Aspiring'
▶ Group 11 New home-owners, mature communities
▶ Group 12 White-collar workers, better-off multi-ethnic areas

Category F: 'Striving'
▶ Group 13 Older people, less prosperous areas
▶ Group 14 Council estate residents, better-off homes
▶ Group 15 Council estate residents, high unemployment
▶ Group 16 Council estate residents, greatest hardship
▶ Group 17 People in multi-ethnic low-income areas

Source: www.caci.co.uk

Another system, MOSAIC, approaches things in a slightly different way. This classification system was compiled using data from a wider range of sources, which have resulted in the division of the population into 12 lifestyle groupings (see Figure 6.4) and 52 types. Case study 4.2 in Chapter 4 looks at the MOSAIC classification system in more detail.

figure 6.4
MOSAIC groupings

1 High-income families	7 Town houses and flats
2 Suburban semis	8 Stylish singles
3 Blue-collar owners	9 Independent elders
4 Low-rise council	10 Mortgaged families
5 Council flats	11 Country dwellers
6 Victorian low status	12 Institutional areas

Source: www.micromarketing-online.com

Systems such as ACORN and MOSAIC can be very useful when trying to identify discrete lifestyle groupings for target marketing. Retailers use them to estimate the potential for the catchment areas of proposed new stores; sales territory planning can be done more efficiently; appropriate areas can be identified for direct mail and door-to-door leaflet campaigns; and organisations' own databases can be analysed and categorised to enable them to profile their 'typical' customer and look for others like them.

CASE STUDY **6.3**
. . . .

Cash-rich, time-poor, information-starved

Research findings are starting to reveal a new basis on which lifestyle segmentation can be applied. Statistics show that 33 per cent of the hard-working British public now say that they would be willing to spend more money to save time. This is hardly surprising when you consider some figures relating to working patterns in the UK. The British working week is the longest in Europe at an average of 43 hours, compared with 40.3 for the rest of Europe; 33 per cent of full-time employed men do not take their full holiday entitlement; and the 1990s saw an increase of 30 per cent in the number of women in management and professional jobs. The working family is one of the most time-pressurised segments of all.

As a result of this, demand patterns are changing. 80 per cent of people say that companies should provide customer care over the telephone out-of-hours, and 35 per cent admit to wanting to shop-around-the-clock. Sunday shopping has continued to grow in popularity, and many retailers who initially refused to open their doors on the Sabbath have subsequently changed their policy. The domestic services sector is also growing all the time. In 1987, a total of £524 million was spent by UK households on cooks, cleaners, child-minders and gardeners, but by 1997 that figure had risen to £3 billion.

Time-poverty also means that consumers are harder to hit with advertising messages. Although people are being bombarded with more and more commercial information, they have less and less time in which to process it. Only those messages which reach their targets at those times in the day when busy consumers have enough time to absorb them will have an impact.

As a consequence of all this, suppliers of consumer goods and services are starting to direct their efforts at identifying and targeting the growing proportion of the population for whom parts of the day are so busy that their buying behaviour and limited exposure to media mean that traditional marketing tactics fail to make an impact. First Direct bank was one of the first companies to target the time-poor by offering telephone banking services out-of-hours, and has prospered ever since. It found that 66 per cent of its customers watch less than one hour of commercial TV per day, and consequently spread its choice of advertising media very widely.

Questions

1   Describe the demographic characteristics of the people most likely to fall into the 'time-poor' segment. Which media are likely to be most effective at reaching them?

2   What sort of people are most likely to be 'time-rich'? Why might these be a less attractive target market?

3   How well have high street travel agents responded to the needs of 24-hour society?

Sources: Cobb (1999); Curtis (1997).

Behavioural segmentation

Markets can be divided into discrete sub-groups according to the way people react to and interact with the product itself. Although a more difficult concept to grasp, in markets where other forms of segmentation are found to have little relevance, behavioural segmentation probably holds the key to effective and innovative marketing. Behavioural segmentation can be based on:

Time of use
Different people consume the same products at different times. Although the conventional image of Corn Flakes is as a breakfast cereal, Kellogg's identified that a significant proportion of its customers ate Corn Flakes as a snack food later in the day. To sustain sales in the face of fierce competition, it decided to promote Corn Flakes to evening snackers, and on the side of box it now runs self-advertising with a picture of a TV remote control and the slogan 'Prime Time? Fancy a Snack … Reach for the Kellogg's.'

KEY SKILLS
ACTIVITY **6.1**
••••••••••••••
Working with others

Timing it right
An understanding of the ways that people use products and services enables marketers to identify different ways to target new customers, and may suggest a route to finding a secure position in the market. This exercise will reveal how the time of the day, the month or the year can affect the way that people interact with the things they buy.

Interview five of your friends, colleagues, neighbours or family to find out more about the times at which they use or consume the following products or services, and indicate how this might affect the way you might promote and price them:

▶   Cereals.
▶   Coffee.
▶   Chocolate.
▶   Package holidays.
▶   Mobile phones.

Benefits sought
Different people want products to benefit them in different ways. Consider the yellow fats market: butter is an ideal product for those who are most interested in taste; low-calorie spread is aimed at those who want to lose weight; polyun-saturated margarine will appeal to those who are health conscious; block margarine is preferred by those who want to make good pastry; and basic own-label spreads will satisfy those for whom economy is paramount. Different brands have been created to provide the benefits sought by these and many other groups and combinations of groups in this heavily segmented market.

Applications

Different people want to use products for different purposes. Cotton wool, for example, has three primary applications: baby-care, child-care and cosmetic use. These three uses can then be subdivided into a number of further segments. In baby-care and cosmetic use, for example, cotton wool is used both to apply substances such as lotions and make-up, as well as for cleansing. Consequently, the market is characterised by product forms that are suited to these tasks. Flat cotton-wool pads are sold in polythene tubes for convenience for make-up removal, cotton-wool buds are an easy shape to use for make-up application, and cotton wool balls are ideal for general cleansing.

Related activities and products

Products are sometimes used because of, or in conjunction with, another product or activity. Car manufacturers, for example, have traditionally been very successful at selling spare parts to drivers of their cars. They assure their customers that only their own brands will give the quality and reliability they are looking for when their car is repaired, though generic alternatives are often much cheaper.

Expertise

Different people have different requirements from products because of their levels of expertise. The most obvious segmentation takes place between amateur and professional markets, with amateur musicians, for example, seldom demanding the same quality of instrument that professionals require for public performance. Differences in expertise also arise at the purely domestic level though. Enthusiasts of any description are likely to be more discerning in their purchasing habits. Keen gardeners, for example, are likely to be highly selective and discerning in their choice of stock from a specialist garden centre, while others are more likely to be looking for simple selections of hardy plants that offer them a reasonable certainty of successful blooms.

Purchase patterns

Different people buy products at different time intervals. Some people are regular buyers of certain brands while others only buy them on special occasions. Theatre audiences tend to be characterised by a core of regular attenders, a proportion of irregular attenders who come from time to time, and a large 'tail' of infrequent or one-off attenders who seldom or never return. These patterns can be scrutinised to ensure that appropriate promotional messages can be sent by direct mail to the right individuals – subscription offers for a series of performances, for example, are likely to be successful among the regular attenders but fall on deaf ears with the infrequent attenders.

Brand loyalty

Purchase patterns can also be examined in terms of brand loyalty. Some people, known as 'long loyals', always buy the same brand, regardless of price or competition, and are difficult to persuade otherwise. 'Rotators' stick to two or three brands, moving only between their favourites. The 'deal sensitives' shift between brands easily in response to price and promotions, while the 'price sensitives' will purchase whatever product is cheapest, regardless of brand. The proportion of shoppers in each of these segments varies widely from product to product. The key for marketers is to understand the composition of their markets so that the impact of pricing and promotional strategy can be maximised.

Segmenting industrial markets

Most of the bases for the segmentation of consumer markets are equally relevant in industrial or business-to-business markets. Organisational buyers can be divided up according to their geographical locations, their frequency of purchase, the benefits they are seeking from their products and the purposes for which they use them. There are, however, five other useful dimensions to consider:

▶ *Industry type*: Different industries may have different requirements for, say, quality or design features, depending on the nature of their own products and target markets.

▶ *Technology base:* Even within the same industry, different organisations using different technologies can be identified as being in separate market segments. Printing technology, for example, encompasses lithographic, flexographic, screen and digital printing processes, each of which may print on different types of material and is suitable for different types of print job. Even among litho-printers there are both sheet-fed and reel-fed (known as web) machines. Paper suppliers may need to recognise where their own strengths lie as they may not be in a good position to supply the whole industry.

▶ *Company size*: Large companies with factories, depots or warehouses in a wide range of locations are likely to have different requirements for service from small businesses. They may have specific delivery instructions; they may require different invoicing procedures due to a central buying function; or they may have less need for after-sales service due to in-house repair and installation facilities. They may also prefer to deal with other large businesses and perceive small businesses to be less reliable.

▶ *Urgency of demand*: Some organisations are willing to hold stocks of products in anticipation of their own future needs, yet others wish to rely upon the speedy and efficient delivery of components, raw materials or services by their suppliers on a regular basis so that they can save themselves the costs of stock-holding. Another category here is the organisation that only ever needs a particular product in an emergency. A company may need to segment its market according to the urgency of demand if it is unable to meet the delivery service levels demanded by some customers in its markets.

▶ *Size of order*: The so-called 'Pareto effect' suggests that in many businesses approximately 80 per cent of turnover will be generated by only 20 per cent of customers. If a segment of the market can be identified as comprising consistently heavy users of a product, an organisation may choose to focus on this group to achieve economies of scale in distribution; it may allow competitors to occupy the rest of the market unchallenged, leaving them the task of selling and distributing small quantities to a large number of dispersed buyers. This sounds a very profitable strategy, but it should be remembered that turnover doesn't always equate with profit, and that small but growing businesses may be allowed to develop a loyalty to competitors in their early years, which will not be forgotten when they develop far greater buying requirements.

Criteria for assessing viable market segments

Having identified possible segments to target, it is important to assess their viability. There are four key criteria to bear in mind when assessing whether a segment has the potential to be commercially exploited:

▶ *Size:* Is the segment a worthwhile target? A segment should not be so large as to be indistinct from the mass market, but it should be large enough for it to be worthwhile treating its members as being different from others. Car manufacturers, for example, are sometimes approached by very tall drivers for whom there is insufficient headroom in their cars, and very short drivers who find visibility difficult. While some vehicles attempt to meet their needs with adjustable seats, there is currently insufficient demand from these groups to make it worthwhile launching a new range of vehicles to meet their specific needs.

▶ *Relevance*: Do differences between groups of consumers affect their buying behaviour? It may be possible to identify groups of people with similar characteristics, but they should only be recognised as a market segment if the characteristics or needs relate to the product or service being supplied. For example, the market for toothpaste may be segmented to appeal to children and adults, those with different dental conditions, and smokers and non-smokers, as buyers' dental needs and taste preferences may be affected by these. It is probably not very relevant, however, to segment the market for toothpaste according to gender as there is no obvious connection between gender and dental needs.

▶ *Identity:* Does this group of buyers have significantly different needs? The most promising segments, and the easiest to target, are those that are distinctly different from other segments, where the identity of the group of buyers is quite different from other groups. Buyers of business stationery, for example, demand different sizes and styles of paper and envelopes from domestic users and there is relatively little overlap between the two segments. But in the

DID YOU KNOW?

Marketing to ethnic minorities in the UK is in its infancy in comparison with the US, where targeted marketing to the Hispanic, black and Asian communities is intrinsic to any major campaign. But reticence on the part of UK companies is more to do with numbers than attitudes. As the US population approaches a third of a billion, even the smallest ethnic group represents a significant audience, making it cost-effective to implement ethnic-based strategies. The black market alone comprises 30 million, whereas in the UK the entire ethnic population is around 3 million. So instead of using multi-segment marketing based on ethnicity, some brand leaders in the UK favour a more inclusive approach which uses other variables to segment the market (Sclater, 2002).

market for shampoo there is considerable overlap in what the different brands are offering to the market, and it is not so obvious why buyers should choose one brand over another. This makes it more difficult to attract buyers, who may be torn between two or more options.

▶ *Accessibility*: Is it possible to communicate with buyers in the segment? It must be possible for segments that are identified to be reached with marketing messages aimed specifically at them. This is not always easy. Young men have traditionally been quite difficult to reach, as they tend to read relatively few newspapers or magazines and watch less TV than other groups. The media costs of reaching them to tell them of a new product or service designed with their needs in mind can be prohibitive. However, given the relatively high Internet usage of this group, this segment has in recent years become far more accessible.

CASE STUDY **6.4**

Grey power

For many years, the over 50s were dismissed by marketers as offering little potential for profitable sales. Many consumers in this age bracket were on low incomes after retirement and conservative in outlook, so the booming youth markets were the segments that drew most of the attention.

But times are changing. Demographically, this group is becoming more attractive by the day. About 32 per cent of the UK population is currently aged over 50, and this proportion is projected to peak in the year 2021 when half of the adult population will be in this age group. Even by 2010 this segment will have more consumers than the 15–44 age group. They are also the wealthiest of age groups, owning about 80 per cent of the nation's private capital. Even though much of this is tied up in their houses, they tend to have low or negligible mortgages, which means that their disposable income is also relatively high compared with the cash-strapped youth of today. They out-spend younger consumers in many categories, including food, gardening and DIY products.

Psychographically, this group is also becoming more attractive to marketers. The over 50s are less convinced of the importance of saving than previous generations and are characterised by a mood of 'safe rebellion', and a belief that spending is justified as 'you can't take it with you'. Having sacrificed personal pleasure and time to provide for the family, the 'Greys' (as they are dubbed in the US) are wanting to break free from their roles as parents and home-makers and treat themselves to luxuries, including hi-tech gadgets such as video cameras and hi-fi systems, as well as holidays and cars.

Targeting this segment of the market must be undertaken with considerable sensitivity, as this is not a homogeneous group. The 60–70 year olds remember rationing, and have a cautious attitude to consumerism. They pay in cash and like saving. The over 70s are even more entrenched. Exhibiting Peter Pan-like tendencies, the last thing the over 50s see themselves as is old, and any direct reminders of ageing are likely to be rejected. Images of granddads and grandmas are scorned, and role models like Joanna Lumley are embraced. One of the key questions for marketers is whether to create specific products for this group or simply adapt the advertising for mainstream products. Seven Seas and Sanatogen have both created new health supplements aimed specifically at the over 50s, whereas Levi's simply chose older models for its press advertising to emphasise the heritage and longevity of the brand.

Questions

1   Suppose a car manufacturer wanted to increase its sales to the recently retired who have just given up their company cars. What imagery and media should it use?

2   To what extent are the 'over 50s' accessible to marketers? How might a financial services provider best reach this segment?

3   How should retailers respond to the growth of population in this age group?

Sources: Fry (1997); Hughes (2002); Pryke (1993).

KEY SKILLS
ACTIVITY **6.2**
● ● ● ● ● ● ● ● ● ● ● ● ●

Communication

Meet the Tweenager

Some market segments do not fit very well into the classic theoretical categories. Young people, for example, even though they share an 'age group', are certainly not a homogeneous bunch. This exercise will help you to understand the key characteristics of a sub-segment of this demographic segment.

Go to the website at www.guardian.co.uk and search the archive for the article entitled 'What are little girls made of?' by Maureen Rice, which was first published in *The Observer* on 3 December 2000. Write a 300-word summary of the main characteristics of the market segment described as 'Tweenagers' in this article.

Market targeting
● ●

Having identified relevant and viable segments in a market, an organisation is faced with the decision as to which segment or segments to serve. There are two possible strategies: concentration strategies, whereby an organisation focuses all its attention on a single segment in the market (known as a *niche*); and multi-segment strategies, where a series of separate marketing activities is designed for different market segments. (See Figure 6.5.)

figure 6.5
Market targeting strategies

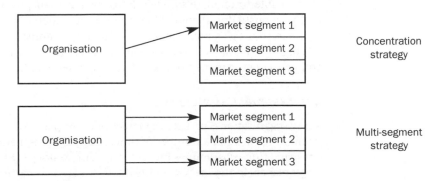

Concentration strategies

Directing all the marketing effort of an organisation towards a single market segment is known as niche marketing. It can be very advantageous in certain circumstances. When a concentration strategy is implemented, there is seldom any confusion in the eyes of potential customers as to whether or not that organisation is able to meet its needs, and the needs of the customers who are targeted are usually so closely scrutinised that even small organisations can realistically aim to be market leaders in their chosen market segment. The manufacturer of cereal-based health-foods, Jordans, clearly concentrates on health-conscious consumers and has succeeded in retaining a strong position in this segment even though other larger manufacturers dominate the market as a whole.

Aiming at a small niche in the market can enable firms with limited resources to compete with better financed organisations. The family-owned firm Start rite, for example, is well known for the production of high-quality, well-fitting children's shoes, yet is competing with much larger global manufacturers.

There are, however, two important disadvantages of niche marketing. First, an organisation can be vulnerable if powerful competitors turn their attention to that niche. Suppose, for example, a particular segment in a market starts to grow rapidly. The niche marketer will be faced by an increase in demand which may be difficult to satisfy in the short term, and it is very likely that competitors, who may previously have ignored that segment as it was considered too small to be of interest, will suddenly invest heavily to attract new business in this area, and severely undermine the efforts of the niche marketer to take advantage of the market growth. This occurred to some extent in the 'Green' revolution of the late 1980s. Niche marketers had previously sold environmentally-friendly products quite profitably through outlets such as health-food stores and specialist mail order. An upturn in demand for ecologically-sound products was recognised by large manufacturers who put tremendous efforts into promotional campaigns and achieving mainstream distribution through large retail chains. Much of the growth in the market benefited them, rather than the smaller niche players who were unable to retaliate sufficiently to sustain their positions in the niches they had previously dominated. What to do under such circumstances is the second problem that faces niche marketers. Having established a strong reputation in serving a particular market segment, it is relatively difficult to change direction and persuade the market that a different segment can be served equally well.

Multi-segment strategies

Many organisations, particularly larger ones, implement multi-segment strategies, attempting to reach a number of different market segments by developing different marketing programmes for each segment. Kellogg's, for example, is one of the larger players in the market for breakfast cereals. It is particularly successful at targeting children, but also has a strong presence in the health segments, among weight-watchers and in mainstream adult markets, which are sub-segmented in various ways. Recent advertising campaigns for Corn Flakes have addressed the 'lapsed user' segment using the slogan 'Have you forgotten how good they are?'

Multi-segment strategies tend to offer greater scope for expansion and growth than concentration strategies. The combined size of the different segments aimed at tends to increase sales revenue and this can also lead to economies of scale in production. The main disadvantage of this approach is that it requires a high level of marketing expertise and will incur higher marketing costs than concentration strategies. Resources are spread more widely and without sound financial backing it may be that they are also spread too thinly to be effective in establishing a presence in the chosen segments. This can lead to a further disadvantage of mixed messages being received by consumers, with no segment really understanding that the product or service is aimed at satisfying its particular needs.

Market positioning

This final stage of the process of target marketing involves designing product features and creating a distinct image that appeals specifically to the chosen

figure 6.6
The process of market positioning

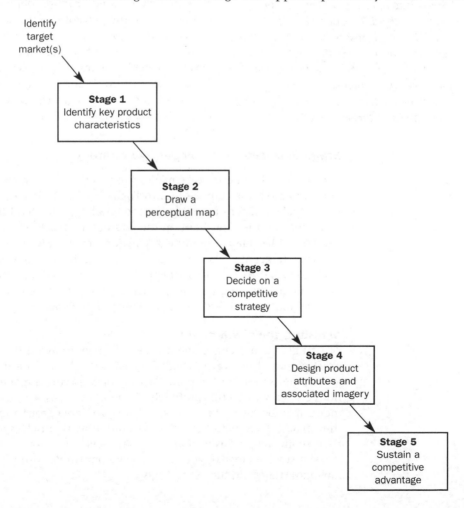

target market segment and sets the product apart from the competition. The term *positioning* refers to the way in which the product is positioned in the mind of the consumer – it is designed so that members of the target market segment will recognise that it is the best product for them. (See Figure 6.6.)

Product positioning involves a number of important stages.

Stage 1: Identify key product characteristics

The product features that members of the target market segment consider to be most important when considering which product to buy should be identified and given some sort of weighting. Note that these features may be tangible (such as colour, size, design), but also intangible (such as reputation or guarantees). This is discussed further in Chapter 7.

Stage 2: Draw up a perceptual map

This is a useful tool by which the current brands available to a market segment can be depicted visually. In its simplest form, the perceptual map consists of a grid that shows the two most important product attributes identified at Stage 1 placed on two axes of a grid (see Figure 6.7). Qualitative marketing research enables consumer perceptions about the current brands to be plotted, so that an organisation can see at a glance where competition is at its most intense and where there might be gaps in the market.

Stage 3: Decide on a competitive strategy

The decision then needs to be made as to whether to compete head-on or to position away from the competition. In Figure 6.7 it can be seen that different retail formats take different positions in food retailing. They tend to compete head-on with others in their quadrant on the grid but are less likely to see those in different areas of the map as holding any major attraction for consumers in their own particular target markets. A new organisation trying to enter this market will have to decide whether it should attempt to compete head-on with existing suppliers or to find a position on the map, such as the bottom right quadrant, where little competition exists. There are advantages and disadvantages to both strategies.

Avoiding the competition

At first glance it seems evident that a strategy to avoid the competition holds most potential. However, there is often a quadrant on a perceptual map that looks promising from the point of view of satisfying a market need, but it may not be so easy to do this profitably. Sometimes, firms who launch into such segments may be successful to a point, but profitable growth may be difficult and they may be faced with the task of repositioning themselves if they wish to build their profit margins as well as their sales revenues. Note that costs involved in stocking a wide range of goods may be incompatible with sustaining a profitable low-price strategy in the example given.

figure 6.7
**A perceptual map of
food retailing**

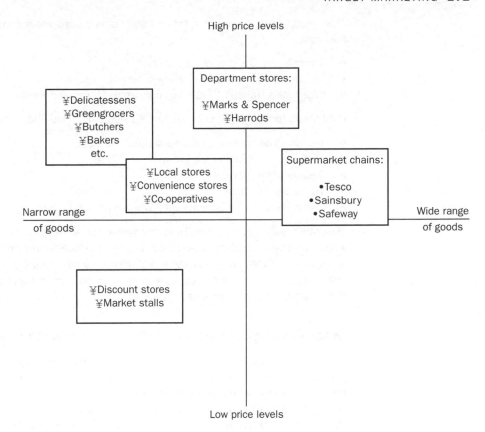

DID YOU KNOW?

*Growing competition in the canine treats
market led Friskies Petcare to re-launch
and reposition its 'Bonio' dog biscuit brand.
To differentiate the product from its rivals, a
new biscuit was developed to enhance the
oral hygiene properties of the brand, with a
formula that was proven to reduce the build-
up of doggie plaque by 20 per cent and
tartar by 25 per cent (Knott, 2002).*

Head-on competition

This may be equally, if not more, problematic. Unless the
market is growing significantly there may be no room for
extra supply without the profitability of all firms suffering
badly. Nonetheless, large and well-financed firms are often
reluctant to leave a segment unchallenged and are sometimes willing to challenge a leader head-on. Sales growth
in Cadbury's Caramel, for example, spawned 'me-too'
products in the form of Galaxy toffee bars and Rolo bars.
Smaller firms with less financial backing may be squeezed
out or will fail to find a foothold unless their product offering is demonstrably better than existing brands.

KEY SKILLS
ACTIVITY **6.3**
· · · · · · · · · · · · · ·

**Information and
communication
technology**

On target with air freight

*For many people, visualising a problem can make it easier to understand and
unravel. The perceptual map is one way of helping marketers to understand the
nature of the competition they face. This exercise will demonstrate this.*

The role of an air freight forwarder is to pick up freight from a client, place it with the
most suitable air carrier and collect it at the other end of the flight for delivery to its

final destination. Competition for air freight service operators comes from three sources:

▶ Other air freight service operators.
▶ Air freight divisions of the airlines themselves.
▶ Alternative transport systems, notably road, rail and sea.

Customers for air freight services are wide-ranging, including:

▶ General industrial and commercial enterprises.
▶ Producers of medical supplies.
▶ Sellers of cut flowers.
▶ Dealers in precious stones.
▶ International organisations with overseas sales depots.

Describe the different segments in the market for air freight. For each segment, which two characteristics do you think are most critical in influencing the decision to purchase? Create a spreadsheet and draw up a perceptual map with these characteristics on the two axes. Then complete the map indicating on the grid where the different freight options lie.

Stage 4: Design product attributes and associated imagery

At this stage the features of the product should be designed, along with the type of imagery that will be used to help the targeted customers identify the benefits being offered to them. Features such as brand name, packaging, advertising themes, price levels and distribution outlets are all important in creating this position in the mind of the customer – in other words, the marketing mix is the tool box that enables that position to be established. (This is the subject of the following chapters.)

CASE STUDY **6.5**

New look for Levi's

For many years, Levi's jeans were a potent symbol of Western youth culture. The young Berliner who, as the Berlin Wall came tumbling down, unfurled a banner proclaiming 'You can have Marx or you can have Levi's' summed up the brand's distinctive position in the young consumer mind. A disastrous 1970s foray for the brand into other areas, from baby clothing to polyester suits, focused the company's mind very clearly on the source of its success – it was its status as the original blue jeans maker that enabled it to charge premium prices. Consequently, for years afterwards the company firmly positioned itself as a manufacturer in the denim jeans market. A back-to-basics policy in the 1980s reinforced the fact that the flagship 501s were essentially the same as the jeans sold to miners and cowboys in the 1800s, and this, coupled with a now legendary advertising campaign in which Nick Kamen stripped off his 501s at the launderette, sealed a decade of unprecedented success for the company. This culminated with global sales of $7.1 billion in 1996.

But in 1997 the bottom finally dropped out of the jeans market. Young men in particular drifted off to new competitors such as Gap and Diesel, and were wearing other garments, such as combat pants and casual trousers. Over the next three years Levi Strauss lost over 50 per cent of its consumption among young people. Fashion marketing is always vulnerable to sudden changes in taste. Young consumers in particular are keen on trying new things, resisting the idea of brand loyalty. This was clearly a major problem for a brand that had nailed its colours so firmly to the youth market. The historical marketing strategy which nurtured 'cool' consumers and expected the mainstream market to follow was clearly no longer going to work. Different kinds of 'cool' kids, who behaved and influenced the market in different ways, were emerging. Furthermore, 'occasion' was found to be having an increasing role in the decision about what to wear, and among mainstream consumers there were different attitudes and needs relating to which product is right for which occasion. The brand's strong advertising emphasis on 'originality' had possibly become negatively associated with 'tradition' in the eyes of its core market.

Research was conducted to underpin a strategy for the brand's revival, using youth panels comprising both trend-setters and mainstream consumers to comment on the product. The most startling revelation was summed up by one participant: 'It's not that we're down on denim, it's just that no one has done anything interesting with denim for so long that we are bored – more bored than you can possibly imagine.' A series of design changes and new-style advertising campaigns were implemented as a result. Other findings led to retailing changes, including more displays which allowed people to touch and discover the product range. Training programmes were introduced for staff to help them recognise different shopping modes, so that a person wanting to 'replacement shop' can get a pair of jeans and leave the shop quickly, but someone wanting to take time to browse and explore is left alone.

Questions

1   Is the market for jeans a mass market or a niche market?
2   Is Levi Strauss right to continue positioning Levi's as a brand of denim jeans?
3   Levi Strauss has recently announced a deal to distribute jeans through the supermarket chain Wal-Mart (see Chapter 3, Case Study 3.4). What type of market segment(s) will this strategy attract?

Sources: Bannister (1999); Ellsworth (2000); McGowan and Thygesen (2002).

Stage 5: Sustain a competitive advantage

The establishing of a market position that sets a product apart from competitors' products in the eyes of its target market is known as creating a *competitive advantage*. For an organisation to be successful, it needs to sustain that competitive advantage over a period of time and fight off those who would like to have a share of any profitable business that is established. The fundamental principles of marketing apply here. To sustain a competitive advantage requires the continual collection and use of marketing information to ensure that the needs of target markets are being met more effectively and efficiently than by the competition and that adjustments to the marketing mix – or even to the positioning strategy – are made if changes in the environment threaten the business.

Key concepts

....

ACORN: a system that classifies residential neighbourhoods into groups of households which are likely to display similar lifestyles.

Behavioural segmentation: dividing markets into clusters of people who react to, and interact with, a product in similar ways.

Competitive advantage: the reason why a customer might choose a certain product rather than its competitors.

Concentration strategy: directing all the marketing efforts of an organisation towards a single market segment.

Demographic segmentation: dividing markets into clusters of people who share a demographic characteristic, such as age, gender, income bracket.

Geographic segmentation: dividing markets into clusters of people who live in the same area.

Market segmentation: dividing markets into clusters of people who are looking for similar benefits from the products and services they buy.

Market targeting: attempting to attract a specific market segment or segments.

MOSAIC: a system that classifies residential neighbourhoods into groups of households which are likely to display similar lifestyles.

Multi-segment marketing: attempting to attract a number of different market segments.

Niche marketing: attempting to attract a single market segment.

Perceptual map: a grid that depicts consumer perceptions of the attributes of competing products in a market.

Positioning: using the marketing mix to distinguish a product from its competitors and appeal to a target market.

Product differentiated marketing: supplying different versions of a product to give customers choice.

Psychographic segmentation: dividing markets into clusters of people who have a similar approach to life.

Target marketing: designing complete marketing programmes to meet the needs of different segments in a market.

Undifferentiated marketing: attempting to meet the needs of as many people as possible with a single marketing programme.

SELF-CHECK QUESTIONS

1 Which of the following are not bases on which to segment markets?
   a Climate and income.
   b Price and urgency of demand.
   c Time of use and application.
   d Company size and technology base.
   e Lifestyle and occupation.

2 ACORN and MOSAIC are most useful for segmenting markets on which of the following bases?
   a Geography.
   b Demographic features.
   c Lifestyle.
   d Purchase patterns.
   e Income.

3 Perceptual mapping is used to:
   a Enable different market segments to be visualised.
   b Indicate the relative market position of different competitors.
   c Determine the viability of different market segments.
   d Identify the psychographic segments of a market.
   e Distinguish between product differentiation and target marketing.

4 Which of the following is *not* particularly useful as a criterion for assessing the viability of targeting a new market segment?
   a The number of potential customers in the segment.
   b The number of competitors targeting other segments of the market.
   c The availability of media through which to communicate with the segment.
   d The extent to which the needs of a segment are significantly different from other segments.
   e The extent to which the proposed basis for segmentation is of relevance to potential customers.

5 Head-on competition may be the best positioning strategy for an organisation if:
   a Its competitors are strong and powerful.
   b Its competitors are concentrated in one quadrant of a perceptual map.
   c Customer needs in the market are highly differentiated.
   d Alternative positioning strategies hold insufficient volume potential to sustain the cost base of the organisation.
   e It does not currently hold a sustainable competitive advantage in any market position.

Which of the following are true and which are false?
6 Product differentiated marketing and multi-segment marketing strategies are both likely to involve creating a range of different products.
7 Behavioural segmentation is based on the way people interact with the product.
8 A concentration strategy is also known as a niche marketing strategy.
9 The marketing mix should be determined after the market has been segmented but before decisions have been made about market targets or positioning.
10 Customers who are consistently loyal to one brand may need to be treated as a separate segment from those who continually shop around to find the lowest prices.

Discuss the following
11 To what extent is demographic segmentation used by soap manufacturers to segment the UK market?
12 In what ways might pricing, promotion and distribution activity need to be changed if an organisation chooses to target 'deal sensitives' as opposed to 'rotators'?
13 How might store loyalty cards help make students a more desirable target market for supermarkets?
14 For what type of organisation might niche marketing be preferable to a multi-segment marketing strategy?
15 What do you think are the key product characteristics that suppliers of home computer software might place on the axes of a positioning map?

Further study
• • • • • • • • • • • • • • • •

Every textbook of marketing principles will contain some explanations of target marketing, but a more extensive discussion is given in:
McDonald, M. and Dunbar, I. (1998) *Market Segmentation*, Palgrave.

For an interesting reader on this topic:
Ries, Al and Trout, Jack (2001) Positioning: *The Battle for Your Mind: How To Be Seen and Heard in the Overcrowded Marketplace*, McGraw Hill Education.

Some of the early articles on the subject are still of interest today:

Haley, Russell (1968) 'Benefit segmentation: a decision-oriented research tool', *Journal of Marketing*, July.
This looks at aspects of behavioural segmentation and gives an interesting example of benefit segmentation in the market for toothpaste.

Johnson, Richard M. (1971) 'Market segmentation: a strategic management tool', *Journal of Marketing Research*, February.
A more difficult read but provides useful material linking marketing research to target marketing, and the ways in which positioning maps can be constructed.

Smith, Wendell R. (1956) 'Product differentiation and market segmentation as alternative marketing strategies', *Journal of Marketing*, July.
Compares and contrasts these two approaches.

References
• • • • • • • • • • • • • •

Bannister, N. (1999) 'Riveting the market', *The Guardian*, 3 July, www.guardian.co.uk
Burrows, S. (2000) 'Pink £', *Research*, February, pp.27–9.
Cobb, R. (1999) 'Open all hours', *Marketing Business*, November, pp.21–3.
Curtis, J. (1997) 'Out of time, out of mind', *Marketing*, 16 October, pp.22–3.
Day, J. (2002) 'Black Tower rebuilt for unsuspecting generation', *The Guardian*, 3 April, www.mediaguardian.co.uk
Ellsworth, J. (2000) 'Engineering a revival for Levi's', *Marketing*, 19 October, p.25.
Frost, B. (1995) 'Babycham's pioneer purveyor dies at 83', *The Times*, 7 September, p.2.
Fry, A. (1997) 'Shades of grey', *Marketing*, 24 April, p.23.
Hill, A. (2002) 'Pink bank slips into the red', *The Observer*, 17 February, www.observer.co.uk
Hughes, M. (2002) 'Need for a new look at "old age"', *The Guardian* (Money), 9 November, p.18.
Jones, L. (2002) 'School fate?', *Research*, *Special Report*, August, pp.26–7.
Jones, R. (2001) 'The Pulse: exploding the myth of the pink pound', *Media Guardian*, 5 June, www.guardian.co.uk

Knott, J. (2002) 'Canine treats', *Marketing Business*, February, p.14.

Kotler, P. and Armstrong, G. (2001) *Principles of Marketing*, 9th edn, Prentice Hall.

Marketing Business (2002) 'Top of the World', *Marketing Business*, July/August, p.10.

McGowan, P. and Thygesen, F. (2002) 'Defying labels', *Research*, July, pp.22–4.

Pryke, S. (1993) 'Generation gain', *Marketing Week*, 2 July, p.46.

Rankine, K. (2002) 'Tesco rises 13pc and claims more share', *The Telegraph*, 18 September, www.telegraph.co.uk

Sclater, I. (2002) 'Race relations', *Marketing Business*, September, pp.30–2.

CHAPTER 7

Product

Objectives
··············

When you have read this chapter you will be able to:

➤ Define the concept of a product.
➤ Distinguish between the core, actual and extended product.
➤ Classify a variety of consumer and organisational products.
➤ Evaluate the alternative ways of building a product range.
➤ Draw a diagram of the product life-cycle and discuss its key features.
➤ Recommend appropriate marketing activity at different stages of the product life-cycle.
➤ Use the Boston matrix to assess a portfolio of products.
➤ Explain the benefits of branding.

Foundation focus: the 20-second takeaway
··

Marketers are responsible for determining the types of product and service that will both generate satisfied customers and meet the organisation's financial or other objectives. There is a fine balance to be struck, particularly as competitors' offerings influence how customers perceive different products and services, and how likely they are to buy them. In order to protect themselves from the threat of competitors, most organisations try to develop a portfolio of products and services, some well-established and others new, so that the less successful ones can be financially supported until such time that they become successful or are ready to be discontinued. They also try to create unique personalities for their products and services, known as brands, which will establish them positively in the minds of customers and make it less likely that those customers will defect to the competition.

Introduction
··················

This chapter focuses on the nature of a product and its role as part of the marketing mix. The different ways of classifying products are examined, and as most products have a limited life before they are replaced by something new and better, the concept of the product life-cycle and its implications are also considered. The key factors that influence decisions as to which products to sell are discussed, and the importance of branding in helping an organisation to create a unique identity for its products is highlighted.

What is a product?
··························

Fundamentally, a product comprises the tangible and intangible attributes that a seller offers to a buyer in an exchange process. Consequently, a product may be a physical good, or a service, but more often is a blend of both. (See Figure 7.1.)

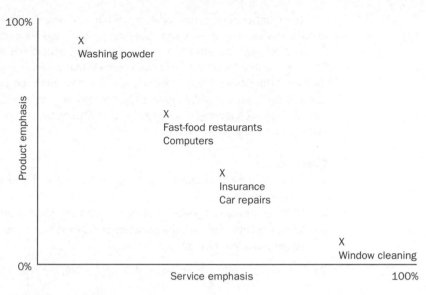

figure 7.1
Product and service components of domestic items

CASE STUDY **7.1**
....

A new start for art

Just a year after its opening in May 2000, Tate Modern emerged as the most popular museum in the world, with 5.25 million visitors – twice the projected number. It also became one of the ten most talked-about brands of the year.

While the quality of the art it displays is undoubtedly part of Tate Modern's attraction, this did not appear to be the primary reason for attending for many of its visitors in its early days. The experience of Tate Modern has been likened to a theme park, where the architecture, the restaurant with a bird's eye view overlooking the river Thames, and the trend-setting brand identity are as important as the exhibitions themselves. 21 per cent of early visitors cited the building as a major factor for visiting. Entry to the gallery's permanent collection is free, courtesy of a special grant from government, but only 100,000 of its visitors were sufficiently enthusiastic to pay to see the first major international charging exhibition, Century Cities.

Before its opening, Tate had taken care to establish its brand firmly in people's minds: one Tate, comprising four galleries – the new Tate Modern and its forerunner, now Tate Britain, in London, plus smaller galleries in St Ives and Liverpool. The aim of the associated marketing activity was to target the 'cuspers' – people who had the potential to attend a gallery, but needed enticing. Tate was careful to distance itself from the image of galleries as boring and fuddy-duddy, and sought a market position as a place which always had something new, different and challenging to offer. A new corporate identity was created to cover all four sites, including four versions of a new logo, new print and signage, front-of-house uniforms by designer Paul Smith and a branded range of shop merchandise. A range of non-commercial promotions trumpeted the coming of the new Tate, including 6 million Tate-branded coffee cups for Coffee Republic, Wagamana chopsticks promoting the Friends of Tate scheme, an in-store concession at the department store Selfridges, a special Tate Beer and a Royal Mail stamp. Merchandising and catering remain a key element of Tate's operations. During its first year visitors bought 1.5 million postcards and 850,000 teas and coffees were served. Ranges of merchandise are continually refreshed, and include items inspired by top designers and exhibitions, and special Christmas ranges.

The most popular exhibition ever held at Tate was the Matisse Picasso in 2002, in collaboration with the national galleries in Paris and New York. The UK exhibition ran for 100 days and attracted over half a million people between May and August. To accommodate the crowds, extended opening hours were a key feature. The exhibition ran until 10pm every Friday, Saturday and Sunday, and then every night in August, culminating in an all-night session to complete the run. Over 100,000 people attended during a late-night opening. 24,100 catalogues and 400,000 exhibition postcards were sold on site.

Questions

1 Describe the core product, the actual product and the extended product being offered by Tate.

2 What factors will influence whether Tate can sustain its current levels of success?

3 What implications does the success of Tate Modern have for the other galleries under the same brand?

Sources: www.tate.org.uk/home/news; Kellaway (2000); Kennedy (2001).

DID YOU KNOW?

Mobile phones provide functionality which goes way beyond simply making calls and sending text messages. The facility to change ring tones is used at least once a month by 3.4 million people in the UK and is particularly popular among 15–24 year olds. Of these, 4 per cent have changed to a tune they have composed themselves, and 8 per cent admit to changing their ring tone deliberately to annoy someone else (www.MORI.com).

'Goods' have physical form and can be seen and touched. They are tangible, and when purchased, the buyer becomes their owner. A service, on the other hand, is a deed performed for the buyer to experience rather than own (as discussed in Chapter 2). Thus a train ride is a service, as the customer can experience the journey but does not own the train. However, the quality of the journey will be partly determined by the tangible features of the carriage, so the tangible and intangible elements of the service are closely related and will both contribute to the buyer's satisfaction or otherwise with their journey. Similarly, when people buy food in supermarkets, although they are buying tangible goods they will own, store and ultimately consume, the quality of service provided by the supermarket will also affect their levels of satisfaction and influence their purchasing decisions. Thus the concept of a product encompasses all the physical, aesthetic, emotional and psychological elements that people buy when they engage in a transaction with a supplier.

KEY SKILLS
ACTIVITY **7.1**
• • • • • • • • • • • • • •

Information and communication technology

Who needs what?

Customers buy benefits, not features. But when marketing a product or service it is important to understand how features are responsible for delivering those benefits. This exercise illustrates how different features are capable of delivering exactly the same benefit.

Listed below are three very different customer needs.

▶ To travel from London to Aberdeen.

▶ To improve my game of tennis.

▶ To keep my dog healthy.

1　Surf around the Internet to identify all the products that could help satisfy these needs.

2　List the criteria that potential customers will use in deciding which of these products to choose.

3　How many of these criteria are tangible and how many are intangible?

4　How might this influence (a) the price you charge for these products and (b) the messages that you use to promote them?

The total product concept

Rather than try to distinguish between goods and services, it is perhaps easier to envisage all products as combining three distinct elements, as shown in Figure 7.2 and described below.

The core product

As the definition suggests, every product provides a basic function that solves a customer problem and satisfies a human need. This is the *core* product, without which the product would have no purpose. It is the core product that offers benefits to potential customers. Suppose, for example, a person is concerned about the increasing level of burglary in his or her neighbourhood. This problem could be resolved in a number of ways. A burglar alarm, a set of window locks and a large dog all offer the same core product, namely a feeling of security, and any of these could potentially supply the desired benefit of relieving the person's anxiety. The decision as to which of these items to buy will therefore depend upon more than just the core product.

figure 7.2
The total product concept

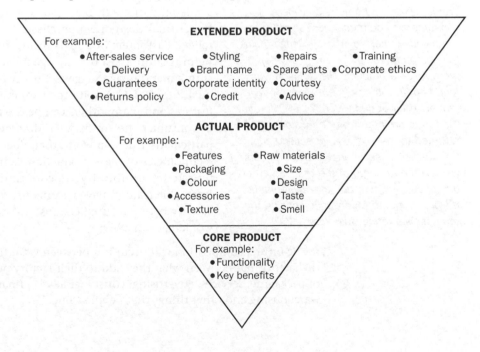

The actual product

This consists of the *tangible* features associated with the core product, which are designed to deliver the desired benefits as effectively as possible. These features are an important vehicle for differentiating a product from its competitors. In the case of the security product, the window locks may deter casual thieves and offer the advantage of minimum disruption and DIY installation; the alarm will be better for alerting neighbours in the event of a break-in; and the dog may be the best for deterring would-be burglars from even attempting to enter a property. Different solutions are likely to appeal to different segments of the market, according to their perceived needs.

Within each product form there is also potential for differentiating the tangible features so as to distinguish a product from competitors and more closely meet the needs of a target market segment. Window locks are produced of different materials to give greater or lesser strength; alarms may be activated by pressure pads under carpets or by infra-red movement detectors; dogs may be trained to attack or simply to bark! All of these features may influence the customer's final selection of a solution to the security problem.

DID YOU KNOW?

Research by Lyons Tetley discovered that the consumption of tea outside the home was much lower than in the home, yet the reduction in coffee consumption outside the home was far less significant. This was found to be because the quality of tea drunk away from home is considered by consumers to be much more variable than the quality of coffee. The challenge facing the company was therefore to develop a more reliable product. The solution was found not in a tea bag, but in a new-style teapot. The pot had a control lever to allow the tea to be lifted from the water and returned to make a perfect second cup, a transparent base to enable users to control visually the strength of the tea, and a non-drip spout. It was made of robust plastic, making it cool to touch while keeping the tea hot (Marketing Business, 2000).

The extended product

This consists of the intangible features of a product that influence buyer choice. These intangible features tend to offer psychological benefits that enhance the value of the core and actual product in the consumer's mind. For example, the existence of guarantees, exchange policies or free service agreements imply product reliability; the availability of credit may enable customers to buy now rather than postpone a purchase; a delivery service can relieve customers of a logistical difficulty; a polite and helpful shop assistant can create store loyalty; and a strong brand image suggests a trustworthy company and quality product. Despite their intangibility, all of these features and many others can be the key deciding factor in consumer choices between different suppliers. This is particularly true in a world that, due to the standardised technologies of mass production, is increasingly characterised by uniformity of core and actual products. Intangible features have become the focus of competitive activity between suppliers, just as Levitt suggested they would back in 1969:

> In the future, competition will occur not between what firms produce in the factory, but between what they add to their factory output in the form of packaging, services, advertising, consumer advice, financing, delivery, warehousing and other things that people value.

Product classifications

As we have defined a product as embracing everything that a seller offers to a buyer in an exchange process, we can include a very wide range of items when we start to classify different types of product. Product classifications are useful when planning marketing strategies as they focus on the similarities between groups of products, and similar products usually respond well to similar marketing activities.

The most important distinction to make is between consumer and business products.

Consumer products

These are products purchased by consumers for their own consumption or that of their households. They can be classified further according to the levels of the decision-making effort that consumers are willing to expend in making their product selections (this is also discussed in Chapter 4).

Convenience products

These are products purchased frequently and with minimum effort on the part of buyers. Also known as 'low-involvement' products, they include:

▶ *Staples* (also known as fast-moving consumer goods or FMCGs) such as bread, shampoo, coffee and all other food or household products bought on a regular basis, often by habit. With this type of product a well-established brand name gives consumers confidence to repeat their purchasing habits on a regular basis without reconsidering their choice, but maximum retail distribution is also important as consumers may not shop around if their preferred brand is unavailable in their normal store.

▶ *Impulse products* are unplanned purchases, usually triggered by some form of visual signal, particularly packaging. This category includes confectionery and magazines at the supermarket check-out, but also travel insurance at airports and ice-creams and popcorn at cinemas. Availability at the right time and in the right place is critical in the marketing of these types of product.

▶ *Emergency products* are purchased not because of sudden desire (as impulse purchases), but rather due to sudden need. This is an important distinction. The customer doesn't have time to shop around for bargains when a crisis occurs, so is unlikely to be very sensitive to high prices: the value of an umbrella to those faced with a long walk in the rain is far higher than to those who have no such immediate and pressing need.

Shopping products

These are products that the consumer feels are worth comparing with other products before making a final selection, the term being derived from the expression 'shopping around'.

▶ *Homogeneous products* are those seen as being basically the same as each other, so the consumer is willing to look around for the lowest prices. Car insurance has moved into this category in recent years. However much insurance companies try to emphasise the quality, reliability and other features of the services they offer, many consumers are willing to phone around for comparable quotations and will normally choose the lowest. This has created an opportunity for low-cost direct operators such as Direct Line to gain considerable business at the expense of large companies with high overheads, and in particular at the expense of insurance brokers.

▶ *Heterogeneous products* are compared on the basis of more than just price. Many consumer durables, which are products designed for use over a period of time, fall into this category. Clothing, 'white' goods (such as washing machines and fridges), 'brown' goods (such as TVs and hi-fi equipment), household linens, cars and sports goods are all examples of heterogeneous products. Consumers will consider the tangible features of these products and, if appropriate, the associated services on offer, before making their decisions to buy. Within limits, customers are not especially sensitive to prices provided that the product they are considering has some demonstrable advantage over its competitors, so promotional activity should focus on pointing out unique attributes rather than low prices.

Speciality products

These possess unique characteristics that consumers are willing to seek out and alternatives are not considered to be satisfactory. This uniqueness usually stems from undisputed quality superiority or design exclusivity. Steinway pianos are an example of the former; they are actively sought by professional musicians and concert venues for their quality and reliability of tone. Design exclusivity is a hallmark of Laura Ashley fabrics and Jaguar cars, both of which are considered to be quite different from other products with similar functions.

Speciality brands can be created even in the absence of unique functional or tangible attributes of a product. Nike trainers, Levi Strauss jeans and Rolex watches are always likely to be treated as speciality products by some segments of the population, even if their competitors produce items that are virtually indistinguishable in all but name. The status of these products is unparalleled, even if their physical uniqueness cannot be sustained.

Unsought products

These are products that consumers have no particular desire to buy, but can be persuaded to buy through active selling and promotion.

▶ *New products* fall into this category if they are introducing a completely new concept to the market. As we have seen, few consumers felt the need for bin-liners until the product was launched and people began to recognise the inconvenience of having to wash out their kitchen bins on a regular basis. The microwave oven was another example of a product for which consumers had to be persuaded of their need. Conventional cooking times had never been considered a particular problem until the benefits of quick defrosting and cooking were demonstrated.

▶ *Peripheral products* are unsought, not because they are new and untried, but because consumers' need for them is marginal. Prepaid funeral plans, timeshare apartments and double glazing are all products that many consumers feel they can live happily without, but can be persuaded of their importance by heavy promotional influence, particularly in the form of personal selling.

Business products

These include all products that enable a business to function; this in turn enables businesses to produce and supply products to consumers. As explained in Chapter 4, demand for business products is known as derived demand. If consumer demand for a company's products falls, whether this is due to seasonal factors, a down-turn in the economy or competitor activity, that firm will subsequently cut back on its own purchases of raw materials, components, operating supplies and even business services. Consequently, organisations that sell business products need to be aware not only of current trends among their own customers, but also of trends among end-user consumers so that they can anticipate any future changes in levels of demand. Business products fall into three main categories.

Process products

These ultimately become part of a producer's own product.

▶ *Raw materials* are unprocessed items that are converted into more useful forms during a further manufacturing process. They may take the form of *farm products*, which are commercially grown or reared with the express purpose of supplying other businesses. Wheat and hops are key supplies in the baking and brewing industries, cotton and flax are converted in textile manufacture, and farm animals are reared for use in the food processing industry. *Natural products*, on the other hand, are not produced but extracted. They exist naturally, and the task of the producer is to extract them from the environment, as in the case of oil, minerals, and even fish. The market for raw materials is often characterised by perfect competition (as explained in Chapter 3), as it is virtually impossible for producers to differentiate their products from those of other producers. Consequently, the key marketing tasks for these businesses are to ensure consistent quality, and if possible to get their customers to commit themselves to long-term contracts.

▶ *Components* are processed parts or materials that ultimately become part of a finished product. *Component materials* are raw materials that have been through the first stage of processing. Businesses convert iron ore into iron, wool into yarn and timber into wood pulp, and then sell these manufactured materials on to other manufacturers for further processing. *Component parts* are one step further down the conversion process, consisting of manufactured products, such as wire, motors, batteries and switches. Both component materials and parts may have two key markets through which sales can be made: OEMs (or *original equipment manufacturers*) and the *aftermarket*, where spares are sold for repairs to the original equipment. Motor vehicle parts, such as tyres and batteries, are extensively sold through both markets, but the more profitable of the two is the aftermarket. OEMs are generally large companies who buy such large quantities they are able to secure big discounts, whereas the aftermarket consists of a much greater number of smaller buyers, including many local garages and shops. They have far less, and in many cases no, bargaining power over their suppliers and consequently must pay higher prices.

CASE STUDY **7.2**
· · · · · · · · · · · · · · · · · ·

Beans means profits

Coffee beans are the second most traded commodity after oil, and given the explosion of coffee shops on to just about every high street in the UK – not to mention the rest of the world – one might suspect that coffee-growers in developing countries across the world are experiencing an unprecedented boom. But nothing could be further from the truth.

The apparent coffee boom is little more than a complex illusion. For example, while the UK has seen a 55 per cent increase in the size of the coffee shop market between 1997 and 2000, the drinks being sold by the high street chains contain more milk than coffee, and actual consumption of coffee has remained at roughly 2.4 kilos per head during this period.

At the same time, the world supply of coffee beans has increased dramatically. As new strains of coffee and intensive farming methods create bigger yields, the market has been flooded with beans, meaning only one thing for price levels. They fall.

Coffee prices have been volatile since an agreement guaranteeing a minimum price for coffee producers was scrapped in 1989, and more recently they have taken a nosedive. Since 1999 the commodity price of coffee has fallen from around $1.20 a pound to a low of 45c – even less for lower-quality beans. In 1997 consumers across the world spent $30 billion on coffee, and coffee-producing countries received $12 billion (40 per cent) of this for their beans. Five years later, consumers are spending $66 billion a year – more than twice the 1997 figure – but coffee producers' slice of the cake has fallen to just $5.5 billion (9 per cent). The problem is partly attributable to the complex supply chain for coffee. From tree to supermarket shelf or coffee bar, it is estimated that coffee beans can change hands as many as 150 times, each party wanting payment for their services. Producers sell to local traders, who sell on to international traders, who sell on to commodity traders. At the very end of the line are just four major companies, the largest of which is the Nestlé Corporation, makers of Nescafé, which supplies over half of the instant coffee that is drunk across the world. Nestlé admits that recent growth in profits, estimated at $1 billion from coffee alone, have been generated thanks to low commodity prices.

Meanwhile, coffee prices in the shops have stayed pretty constant. A jar of instant coffee has fallen just 4.9 per cent since 1997, according to the Office for National Statistics, and Starbucks still manage to sell plenty of their raspberry mocha chip cream frappucinos at £3.35 a go, and regular cappuccinos at £1.75. More worrying still, though, is the impact on the growers. Many are now laying off workers and leaving their crops to rot on the trees because they are no longer worth picking. According to the World Bank, around 500,000 jobs were lost in Central America and Mexico alone in 2000–01 as a direct result of the crisis.

Questions

1   Should the multinational companies involved in the coffee market act to protect the livelihoods of their suppliers? If so how?
2   If governments were to step in to regulate the commodity market for coffee, what impact would this have on consumers?
3   Could any other commodity growers face the same fate as the coffee growers? If so, what actions could they take to protect themselves?

Sources: Garratt (2002); Mathiason and Tooher (2001).

Plant and equipment

These are purchased by businesses to enable them to produce their finished products. They are generally long-lasting products, which are considered to be assets of the business and may be depreciated over many years.

▶ *Capital goods* are installations such as buildings and fixed equipment at which the production process is located. This includes paper machines in the paper industry, radar systems and aeroplanes in the aviation industry and even shops in the retailing industry. Businesses that supply such products are usually faced with the task of high-level negotiations with potential buyers over considerable periods of time. Their customers' decision-making processes and decision-making units are likely to be highly complex, and the product will often have to be specially designed or customised to meet their needs. This type of product is also vulnerable to a down-turn in the economy. Firms cut back or even cancel investments such as these during recession, and suppliers are forced to reduce their prices as a result of their industry's over-supply relative to demand.

▶ *Accessory equipment* consists of shorter-lived durable items used in production or office activities, such as fork-lift trucks, hand tools, filing cabinets and computer hardware. Standardised products are usually acceptable, and markets often span more than one industry. Fewer people tend to be involved in the buying process, and they are likely to be less senior in their organisations than the buyers for capital equipment. While price is important to customers for these products, it may be of less importance than the facility to rent or lease, which may help them to manage cash flow better.

Supplies and services

These are products consumed during the running of a business:

▶ *Maintenance, repair and operating supplies* (known as MROs) are items used in the running of a business or the production of a product but never become part of the product itself. These are the equivalent of consumer convenience products, ordered when required on a routine basis, and tend to be purchased across a range of industries. Maintenance items include paint, light bulbs and cleaning fluids; operating supplies include ink cartridges for computer printers, lubricating oil for machinery and paper for photocopiers; repair supplies are used to mend broken or damaged equipment, including adhesives, bearings and electrical fuses. Buyers are generally reluctant to spend much energy on product selection for any MROs, so contracts for supply over a period of time are often negotiated. Many suppliers of these products choose to distribute through industrial distributors (the equivalent of retailers for business products) rather than deal direct with the end-user business, as distributors can enhance the benefits to the buyer by offering an assortment of products, which can save time and effort in the purchasing process.

▶ *Business services* are purchased if a business needs to enhance its expertise in a particular area. Suppliers of skills to businesses include advertising agencies and accountants, but also data-processing houses, recruitment consultants, cleaning services and even landscape gardeners. Service supply is the fastest-growing sector in the UK economy, as many organisations have reduced their own employed staff to a bare minimum and contracted-out all the non-core services they require.

Creating a product range

It is very unusual for a firm to offer only a single product item. This may be the case for a new firm setting up in business for the first time, but in order to grow and protect themselves from competition businesses usually expand the range of products that they sell.

The *product mix* refers to the total set of all product items sold by an organisation. It can be expanded in three ways: by creating a product line, and then by increasing the number of product items within each product line, or by increasing the number of product lines in the mix.

The *product line* is a group of closely-related product items. The range of digital cameras produced by Kodak, for example, would be considered as a single product line as they are all intended for the same end-use. Other product lines are defined on the basis of being aimed at the same type of customer, such as a range of toiletries designed for baby-care, or low-calorie foods aimed at dieters. Even price levels can define a product range, such as the budget range of own-label groceries sold by some supermarkets under logos such as 'plain and simple' or 'back to basics'. Design is another factor that can distinguish a product line. Most car manufacturers have relatively few product lines, consisting of certain basic models, but they create a range of versions of each model and extend these from time to time by bringing out new editions that have the same basic design but include slightly different features and accessories.

The *depth of the product mix* refers to the number of items within each product line. For example, a sports apparel manufacturer whose product lines include sports shoes can demonstrate depth of product mix if the sports shoes line includes models for aerobics, basketball, cricket, dance etc., in a variety of colours, sizes and fittings, instead of just a limited choice of white trainers. If there are insufficient items in a product line to satisfy customer demands fully, a gap can be left open for a competitor to enter the market, so product lines tend to deepen over time as firms attempt to grow, to expand their market share and to deter competitors. However, careful consideration should always be given to the extra costs involved in extending a product line. New production capacity may be needed and additional promotional and distribution costs will almost always be incurred, so firms should plan the growth of their product lines with concern for marginal costs as well as potential future revenues.

The *breadth of the product mix* refers to the number of different product lines a firm sells. Some manufacturers specialise in one product line only, while others offer a range of product lines, sometimes aimed at completely different target markets. Large multinational companies such as ICI provide good examples of this. ICI supplies product lines that range from paints to synthetic fibres, chemicals and petrochemicals, with different product lines being aimed at consumer markets and industrial markets and different marketing activities and structures being used to support the different product lines. The breadth of the product mix is a key consideration in retailing too. Department stores usually carry a very wide product mix, but may stock only a limited number of items in each product line. Speciality stores, however, have the opposite policy. They may carry just one or only a few product lines, but attempt to carry a wide range of items within each product line. The Tie Rack is a good example of this, specialising in a comprehensive selection of ties and scarves but offering little else: lots of depth but little breadth.

Even if an organisation has a broad product mix, it may be involved in common marketing activities across the product lines, which can lead to economies of scale. Convenience products, for example, may all be sold through supermarkets, regardless of their product lines, and distribution costs may be reduced as a result. Any planned broadening of the product mix should take into account this type of consistency, which can improve the viability of a new product line.

The product life-cycle

After a product is launched there will be times when its sales levels will grow, times when they will be relatively static, and ultimately it is likely that its sales will start to fall, particularly if a new product comes along that satisfies consumer needs better (think, for example, of the gradual disappearance of vinyl records as consumers favour the superior quality and convenience of CD recordings, and how launderettes have become rare sightings in town centres, abandoned by most in favour of domestic washing machines). The concept of the product life-cycle is a useful model for describing these common patterns of sales growth and decline that can be observed over the lifetime of a product. Although not all products will follow this pattern precisely, and different products will move through their life-cycles at different speeds (some seeming to go on for ever and others disappearing after only a fleeting period of success), the concept is still very useful for helping marketers to identify likely sales trends and plan appropriate marketing activities. (See Figure 7.3.)

Characteristics of the product life-cycle

The product life-cycle depicts four key stages that a product is likely to pass through between its launch on to the market and its disappearance from it.

Introduction

The introduction stage is the period just after the launch of a product during which sales growth is likely to be slow. The product is new and untested, so potential customers are likely to be wary of it and resistant to buying something new. Only the most innovative buyers will experiment and try out the new product. (There is more discussion about the rate at which customers adopt new products in Chapter 8.) Consequently, sales revenue from the new product is likely to be low. However, product costs are likely to be high. Not only will the firm be incurring heavy expenses for promoting the new product, but in addition it is unlikely to be fully utilising its production capacity and there will be few economies of scale to be enjoyed with such a low level of output. As a result, many products make a loss at the introductory stage, and firms should identify in advance how they are going to find the cash to see them through this difficult period.

Many products make it no further than the introduction stage of the product life-cycle. If customers try the product but find that it doesn't satisfy their

figure 7.3
Characteristics of the product life-cycle

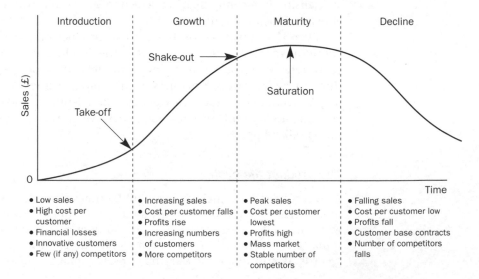

needs, then there will be no repeat purchases, no recommendations made to friends and colleagues, and sales will gradually fall away. The take-off point is the point at which the products offering customers genuine benefits will survive and move into much more rapid growth, while those tried and found to be unsatisfactory will start to move into decline.

Growth

Providing a new product satisfies customer needs, it will be fuelled by repeat purchases and word-of-mouth publicity, and sales will start to climb rapidly as a large number of new customers are attracted to the product for the first time. Profits start to be made as sales revenues increase faster than costs. Confident that the product is likely to be a success, competitors start to enter the market, copying much of the pioneer's basic idea but perhaps introducing new product features too. As the total size of the market is growing the new competitors can increase their sales by attracting new customers rather than undercutting each other on price, so they too are likely to be able to trade profitably. Only when the market starts to move towards maturity and fewer new customers are buying the product for the first time is price competition likely to increase, undermining levels of profitability.

Maturity

The stage at which a product's sales growth slows down is known as maturity. This slow-down is likely to lead to over-capacity in the industry as a whole, so at this stage there is a tendency for firms to start trying to attract customers away from their competitors by offering cheaper prices and increasing their promotional efforts. As this type of competitive activity intensifies, the least effective competitors are forced out of the market (known as the shake-out point), leaving just the strongest players to dominate a more stable market.

Saturation occurs during the maturity stage, at the point when sales growth slows down to zero. From this point on there will be no further net increase in the size of the market. Any new customers entering the market are simply replacing customers who have stopped buying the product, and all other sales are simply replacement sales or repeat purchases by the same customers.

High profits can be made at the maturity stage as sales revenues are high but costs can be kept quite low, with firms benefiting from economies of scale in both production and promotional activity.

Decline

The decline stage is the period when sales of a product start to fall. This usually occurs because a substitute product has been launched that offers the consumer superior benefits, so buyers are switching their allegiance to the new product. Competitive activity starts to intensify further at this stage, as the existing firms are chasing fewer customers to make their sales. Consequently, profitability is usually weakened and competitors have to consider whether it is worthwhile remaining in the market. Some choose to leave the market altogether, while others choose to curtail some of their promotional expenses, reduce their number of distribution outlets and focus solely on any remaining buoyant segments of the market.

Responses to the product life-cycle

Because the characteristics of the market change at the different stages of the product life-cycle, different marketing emphases are also appropriate. (See Figure 7.4.)

	Introduction	Growth	Maturity	Decline
Marketing emphasis	Create product awareness Encourage product trial	Establish high market share	Fight off competition Generate profits	Minimise marketing expenditure
Product strategy	Introduce basic products	Improve features of basic products	Design product versions for different segments	Rationalise the product range
Pricing strategy	Price skimming or price penetration	Reduce prices enough to expand the market and establish market share	Match or beat the competition	Reduce prices further
Promotional strategy	Advertising and sales promotion to end-users and dealers	Mass media advertising to establish brand image	Emphasise brand strengths to different segments	Minimal level to retain loyal customers
Distribution strategy	Build selective distribution outlets	Increase the number of outlets	Maintain intensive distribution	Rationalise outlets to minimise distribution costs

figure 7.4 **Marketing responses to the product life-cycle**

At the *introduction* stage, the firm that has pioneered the new product should be attempting to create wide product awareness and encourage product trial, so that the more profitable growth stage can be entered as soon as possible. The marketing mix should be managed to help achieve this objective. It is normally adequate to start off with a fairly basic product form, which satisfies a core customer need but offers a minimum of additional features. These can be added later as customer tastes and preferences start to develop and distinct market segments start to emerge. Prices charged are unlikely to cover costs, but one of two pricing strategies may be appropriate depending on the nature of the product and the likely competition: price skimming involves charging a high initial price, with a view to reducing it as the market grows, and price penetration involves setting a lower price than is likely to be maintained over the long term, so as to expand the market as quickly as possible. (Both of these strategies are discussed in some detail in Chapter 9.) It is sometimes difficult to encourage distributors to sell new products; they are concerned that the product will not reach the growth stage and that they will invest time and money in a product that will not bring them any long-term revenues. Therefore, concentrating on securing distribution through just a few key outlets is likely to be a more successful strategy than attempting to gain wide-scale distribution from the word go. Promotional activity also needs to be fairly selective, and may be aimed at both distributors (to encourage them to stock the product) and end-user markets. Some sales promotion techniques can be particularly effective at this stage, to give potential customers an incentive to try the product.

DID YOU KNOW?

No other media have ever grown as fast as the Internet, which by the end of 2005 is predicted to grow to 1 billion users across the world, from 445 million users at the end of 2001. But although consumption of other media has already reduced slightly, the Internet is likely to complement, rather than replace, other media – just as radio didn't replace print and TV didn't replace radio (Chaffey, 2002).

At the *growth stage* it is important for the pioneer to try to maximise its own market share in the face of new competitors now entering the growing market. This normally involves sacrificing some short-term profitability, as high costs are incurred in improving product features and distribution intensity, and in extending promotional activity to reach mass markets. Advertising often replaces sales promotion as the most important promotional technique as efforts are made to establish a strong brand image that will become a valuable asset during maturity. (The importance of the brand is discussed further at the end of this chapter.) Prices may have to be reduced slightly to reach the more price-sensitive potential customers, but only as the market moves towards maturity should it become necessary to use pricing strategies to fight off the competition.

At *maturity* there is sufficient opportunity for some competitors to operate profitably, though the brand leader can hope to be more profitable than the rest. It is important for firms to focus on maximising profits as there is little, if any, prospect of further growth. Product lines may be modified or extended to include versions that appeal to the specific needs of segments within the total market. Prices in general should match or beat the competition in an attempt to prevent customers switching their allegiance, but this should not be taken to such extremes as to damage profitability.

Promotion is an alternative technique that can achieve the same aim as price-cutting, but without undermining the generation of sales revenue. Advertising is effective for reinforcing brand benefits, while sales promotion can encourage buyers to switch across from competitors.

There is little long-term potential left for products at the *decline* stage so it is important for firms to minimise their marketing expenditure on these and instead use their resources, especially cash, to support new, cash-hungry products at the introduction or growth stages in their life-cycles. Competition intensifies at the decline stage so prices will normally have to be cut and it may be necessary to rationalise the product range and retain only those items that appeal to the larger and more profitable remaining segments in the market. Distribution can be phased out among the least effective distributors, as all but the most loyal customers will ultimately be abandoning the product in favour of something new and those who do remain are usually willing to make some efforts to track the product down. Promotional expenditure can be reduced to a minimal level, aiming specifically at the remaining segments, but towards the end may be withdrawn altogether. This type of activity at the decline stage is known as a harvest strategy. The speed at which such a strategy should be implemented will depend first on the speed at which product demand is declining, and second on the reactions of competitors. If competitors leave the market quickly there will be more scope for a firm to remain profitable in a declining market for a much longer period of time.

CASE STUDY **7.3**   **Skoda gets serious**

Reviving a brand which, to outside observers, seems to have come to the end of its useful life is a particularly tricky feat to achieve, yet there are some classic success stories. One such revival has taken place for Skoda, which in the 1980s was better known for unkind jokes about it than for its brand attributes. Competing on price rather than quality had damaged the brand's reputation. Western European consumers did not take the Czech cars seriously and were sceptical of Eastern European quality standards. But following the collapse of communism in 1990 the company started systematically rebuilding its manufacturing expertise, helped by a massive investment from VW which by 1995 owned a 70 per cent stake in the business. This, coupled with award-winning promotional campaigns, has led to a dramatic turnaround in the fortunes of the firm.

When the Skoda Felicia was launched in the UK in 1995, the emphasis of the associated promotional campaign was to demonstrate that people's perceptions of Skoda as unreliable and poor quality were misplaced. The stance used in the UK brand advertising was 'We've changed our cars: can you change your mind?' And because VW has strong associations with quality and reliability, Skoda emphasised the involvement of its parent company. This made an important impression and the new car received six consecutive 'Budget car of the year' awards from *Auto Express* magazine.

However, a more significant marketing impact was achieved in 1998, when a simple but bold advertising campaign focused on the benefits of a new model, the Skoda Octavia, thus distancing it from its square and functional predecessors. Style, comfort, reliability and safety were emphasised, as well as the staggering 10-year warranty; and its prices were competitive with models such as Proton and Hyundai, as well as significantly undercutting mainstream rivals such as Ford and Vauxhall. Press coverage of the Octavia was universally positive. *The Sun* named it as its car of the year, and *Autocar* magazine pronounced that there had never been a better quality budget hatchback on sale. Customer surveys, which in 1994 ranked it twenty-first in terms of total customers satisfaction, now showed Skoda in first place.

Despite widespread recognition that the brand had changed beyond all recognition, however, deep-rooted prejudice among consumers still remained and the subsequent launch of the Fabia was a major challenge. Unlike previous models the Fabia was not a budget car, and the starting price was on a par with mainstream competitors. The promotional campaign focused on the gap between people's expectations of Skoda and the reality. Using self-deprecating humour to encourage potential customers to re-evaluate the brand, the advertising carried the copyline 'It's a Skoda. Honest'. The results exceeded all expectation, and sales reached their full-year target in the first three months. Furthermore, the figure of 60 per cent of people who said they would not consider buying a Skoda fell to 42 per cent.

Three years later, with press interest in Skoda dwindling, the challenge was to keep up the momentum. The Octavia was re-launched to breathe new life into a tired sales curve, and achieved a dramatic upturn in sales, at a much faster rate and with a lower advertising spend than during the model's initial launch. Plans to launch an entirely new model into the 'Executive' sector are now on the books.

Questions

1 To what extent is Skoda's revival attributable to its product range, as opposed to its marketing communications?
2 How should Skoda build on its success and sustain its growth?
3 Why didn't VW abandon the brand and badge all Skodas as VWs instead?

Sources: Marketing Business (2002); Simms (1998); Thatcher (2002).

Variations of the product life-cycle

The product life-cycle is an important tool which gives guidance to managers as to the likely developments in its markets and the types of marketing activity that should be considered at each stage. It is not, however, a definitive description of the development of all products. Some products survive no longer than the introduction stage; some appear to have a never-ending maturity stage; some start to go into decline but are revitalised after a successful repositioning campaign.

Product classes are generic names for groups of products that satisfy similar customer needs, such as cars, soap or margarine. Product classes tend to have the longest life-cycles, characterised by maturity periods that seem to go on indefinitely. Sales of product classes tend only to go into decline if changes occur in the macro-environment. Cars, for example, offer such unique benefits to customers over other forms of transport that they may never go into decline unless there is a change in legislation, perhaps to control their use or make them more expensive to buy or run. (See Figure 7.5.)

figure 7.5

The product life-cycle for product classes

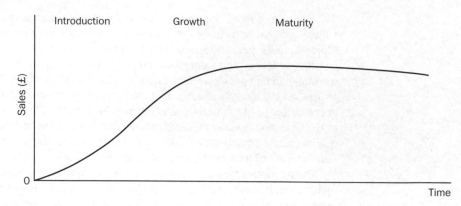

figure 7.5

The product life-cycle for product classes

Product forms are sub-sectors of product classes that deliver the benefits offered within a product class in different ways. Cars, for example, might be diesel- or petrol-driven; deodorants might be aerosols or roll-ons; computer printers might be laser or ink-jet. Even if a product class has an extended maturity period, the different product forms may not survive for that length of time, or may experience growth at different rates and at different times. Environmental concerns about the greenhouse gases emitted by petrol engines led to a resurgence in demand for diesel-powered cars in the 1980s, though this has since been reversed following concerns that diesel emissions are even more problematic. (See Figure 7.6.) When video cassettes were first launched, consumers were faced with two product forms – VHS and Betamax – though only the VHS product form survived into maturity. This is now itself moving into decline, as consumers are wooed by the superior facilities and quality offered by DVD.

Brands are products that belong uniquely to one producer. (There is more detail about the nature and purpose of brands at the end of this chapter.) The life-cycle of a brand is the most unpredictable of all, as firms attempt to create growth for their own brands by tempting customers away from competitors, thus causing their brands to move into decline. Successful brands may survive for many years if they can sustain some form of competitive advantage, but their life-cycles are often scalloped in appearance as firms start to lose market share in the face of competitive attack but then regain it when they retaliate with their own marketing campaigns. The big confectionery brands are typical examples of this. While new product launches can temporarily threaten the market leadership of the top brands, their success is seldom long lived. (See Figure 7.7.)

figure 7.6

The product life-cycle for product forms

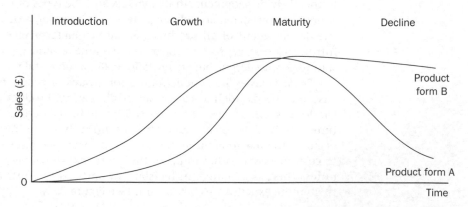

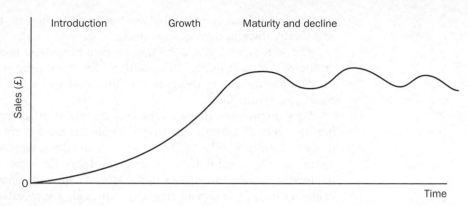

figure 7.7
The scalloped product life-cycle for brands

Fads may be product classes, forms or brands that are characterised by very short life-cycles. They are usually products that offer little in the way of benefits other than being unusual or exciting, and therefore lose popularity quickly when their novelty has worn off. Toys offered to children at Christmas often fall into this category; their producers need to be aware that, unless they have something new to offer the market, the following year they are unlikely to make any sales at all. (See Figure 7.8.)

The product portfolio

The product life-cycle has important implications for the overall portfolio of products that firms sell. If they have a lot of products moving towards the decline stage but few at the introduction or growth stages, they will have little opportunity for success in the future. On the other hand, if they have a lot of products at the introduction or growth stage, but very few generating profits at the maturity stage, they are likely to experience financial difficulties as they

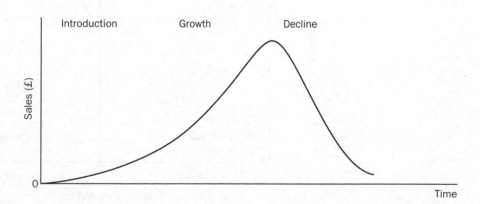

figure 7.8
The product life-cycle for fads

need to invest heavily in promotional activity to increase the brand awareness and loyalty towards their new products.

The Boston matrix is a useful tool for exploring these issues. It was developed by the Boston Consulting Group with a view to helping companies chart their product portfolios and recognise the financial and marketing implications of these. (See Figure 7.9.)

Stars are products that are achieving success at the growth stage of the product life-cycle. If a firm is gaining a dominant market share at this stage it is likely to continue to be successful at the maturity stage, so stars are important members of an organisation's product portfolio. However, heavy investment is required to sustain this success in the face of a growing competition (which is a characteristic of the growth stage), so although a star is likely to generate a lot of sales revenue, it will also incur heavy marketing costs. Hopefully the revenues will cover the costs, but if competition is particularly heavy they may not, and other sources of finance may be necessary.

Question marks are products that are failing to achieve success at the early stages of the product life-cycle. Competitors are dominating the market and, as a result, question marks incur high marketing costs in trying to get established but at the same time generate little revenue to sustain themselves. If question marks are thought to have long-term potential for success, it may be worthwhile supporting them through this difficult time with cash from other sources, but if the competition is thought to be too strong and aggressive for the situation to improve measurably, then they should be harvested even at this early stage before too many resources are wasted.

Cash cows may be one source of finance for supporting stars and question marks. These are products that are achieving success when the market is no

figure 7.9
The Boston matrix

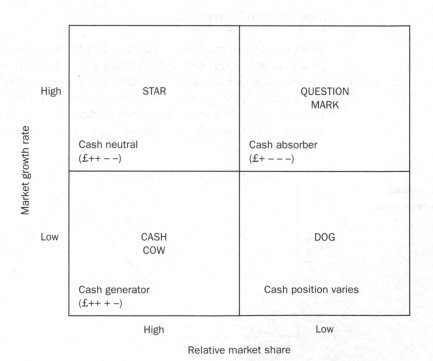

longer growing, usually at the maturity stage in the product life-cycle. Sales revenues are at their highest levels, but the marketing expenditure required to maintain a high market share is relatively low compared with the costs incurred when trying to build share in a growing market. Consequently, cash cows tend to generate more cash than they need to sustain themselves, thereby making funds available for use by other products in a portfolio.

Dogs are products that have failed to achieve the success being experienced by cash cows. In a market that is mature or in decline, these products have not succeeded in establishing a significant share of the market. At the decline stage competitors are likely to be aggressive, which may mean that a lot of money has to be spent merely in an attempt to survive in the market. However, if competitors are passive, it may be possible for a dog to thrive, particularly if the market is still at maturity, perhaps by concentrating on a single segment of the market of little interest to the market leaders. As a result, it is not always clear whether a dog is a net cash generator or a net cash drain. This needs to be monitored closely, and a harvest strategy implemented if it becomes apparent that the effort of supporting the product is not being repaid.

Branding

A brand is an element or combination of elements that uniquely identify a product as being produced by one particular supplier and thereby distinguish it from competitors' products. These elements usually include a particular name, logo, symbol and/or design that the customer then associates with a particular supplier and that the supplier, thanks to trademark law, has the exclusive rights to use for an unlimited period of time.

The importance of branding

Branding is an exceptionally important part of product strategy which offers important benefits to both customers and suppliers alike.

For customers, the brand:

- ▶ Saves time and effort, as customers know what to expect and do not have to go through an extended decision-making process every time they buy the product.
- ▶ Provides security and reduces the risk of purchase as the brand offers a consistency of quality. No one expects to fault Marks & Spencer on quality, whether it be in food, fashion or home furnishing products.
- ▶ Can offer psychological rewards by association with a sought-after image that can convey status on the buyer. The value of the perfume Chanel No. 5 was immediately enhanced by the announcement by Marilyn Monroe that it was all she wore in bed!

For suppliers, the brand:

- ▶ Can generate a loyal base of repeat customers who perceive it to be superior to competitor products in certain ways. This can then be used in promotional messages; for example, BMW emphasises good engineering; Volvo emphasises safety; Rolls Royce emphasises luxury.

▶ Can command higher prices because of the value placed by customers on the security offered by the brand, which is why well-known manufacturer brands of products are almost always more expensive than their supermarket own-label equivalents.

▶ Provides a platform from which to launch new products. Although a product may be new and uncertain, customers will be reassured if there are links with a well-established brand. Nokia has developed such a strong position in the mobile phone market that it has few problems persuading people to upgrade to more sophisticated handsets. The name carries with it connotations of style and quality.

▶ Can offer economies of scale in promotion if the brand is applied across a range of products. Whenever any Ford motor vehicle is advertised, the image of Ford is reinforced in the eyes of the customer. This is a benefit to Ford, but also to its dealerships, which rely on positive customer perceptions to attract their customers.

▶ Has value as an asset of the organisation. *Brand equity* can be valued, so a brand name can be sold if it is no longer required.

> **DID YOU KNOW?**
> *Using celebrity associations to develop brand personalities is a common but high-risk tactic. When Angus Deayton, presenter of the BBC's* Have I Got News for You, *was announced as the new face of Barclaycard advertising in April 2000, he was described by the marketing director as 'the perfect match for Barclaycard – intelligent, under-stated, yet always commanding respect'. But this respect proved to be short lived. In October 2002 he was finally sacked from the high-profile TV show following a series of Sunday newspaper accusations of drug-taking and involvement with a prostitute (http://news.bbc.co.uk; www.newsroombarclays.co.uk; Irwin, 2002).*

KEY SKILLS
ACTIVITY **7.2**
• • • • • • • • • • • • •

Working with others

Branding Britain

Communicating intangible brand attributes is a notoriously tricky activity. A brand such as 'Britain', can mean different things to different people. This exercise will help you to identify and communicate brand attributes more clearly, and by working in a group, you will see how one person's view may be quite different from another's.

The British Tourist Authority (www.britishtouristauthority.org) is charged with the task of attracting foreign tourists to England and encouraging English holiday-makers to stay at home.

1   In a group of four, discuss and list all the market segments you think are relevant for the UK tourist industry. What sort of product benefits would you emphasise to each of these segments to encourage them to take a holiday in the UK?

2   Each person in the group should then write a direct mail letter to one of these segments, encouraging them to phone the British Tourist Authority for more information about holidays in the UK. Take one of the following themes each as a basis for your letters:

▶   Historic buildings.
▶   Arts and entertainment.
▶   The royal family.
▶   Rural England.

3   Swap your letter with another person in the group, and ask them to edit your copy.

4   Give each other feedback as to the effectiveness of the letters.

Who creates brands?

Branding can be used by either manufacturers or resellers to establish their positions in the market. If they wish, they can then license others to use these brands for their products.

Manufacturer brands are the most common types of brand. These are created and owned by the producers of products, who are responsible for designing their marketing mix in a way that is consistent with the qualities of their brands. Product features such as quality, service levels and packaging must reflect the brand identity. Pricing must be at a level that reflects the value offered by the brand. Promotional activity must emphasise the key attributes of the brand and the personality and status associated with it. Distribution should be through channels that are attractive to the types of customer who will favour the brand, by reflecting its quality and image. Channel members should be able to provide an appropriate ambience and supply any services that form an integral part of the brand.

CASE STUDY **7.4**

Earth-moving brand extensions

Every year companies invest millions of pounds in new brands which ultimately fail – 19 out of 20 new brand launches are unsuccessful. Consequently, strategies for extending existing brands are very popular. Two out of every three new products are now brand extensions, and brand extension is seen by marketers as a lucrative way of maximising both customer loyalty and brand longevity.

Brand extensions often mean crossing product sectors and working with entirely new market sectors, and this has been successfully achieved in surprising areas. JCB was keen to capitalise on the high visibility and awareness of its brand in consumer markets. Despite such a high profile, the company was heavily reliant on sales in a relatively limited industrial sector, and perceived that its brand would have a value in consumer markets too. Fashion-conscious young people, children and DIY hobbyists were all thought to be relevant target markets.

An early step was to identify the core brand values. 'Yellow', 'diggers' and 'durable' were three themes common to all audiences; but while adults saw the brand as synonymous with quality and functionality, children saw is as big, muddy and therefore fun! Three areas of business were targeted with sub-brands – fashion, toys and hardware. JCB fashion is designed to be the epitome of urban credibility, with a range that includes outdoor and rugged clothing such as combat trousers, fleeces, footwear and sports equipment. The DIY series is marketed under the name JCB Sitemaster, the name of an actual JCB digger, and comprises quality power and hand tools. The toy range, JCB Junior, includes products which represent a return to traditional values. The theme underpinning the range is 'dads and lads', and is seen to be unpatronising and unlikely to undermine adult perceptions of the brand – especially important given that adults will be the actual purchasers of toys, as well as the fashion items and DIY equipment.

JCB is not short of rivals in any of these areas, and faces considerable competition, ironically from the same company it competes with for earth-moving contracts. Caterpillar has been a big name in merchandising for many years, and $1 billion of its $20 billion turnover comes from Cat-branded merchandising activity. The company sells machine products to more than 200 countries across the world, and so far has reached 132 by selling licences to market Cat-branded apparel and footwear. Core customers for merchandise are aged 18–26, but the product gains approval from a much wider age group, thanks to the established qualities of the brand. Recently, women have become a focus of marketing activity for boots, but the company is keen not to dilute what it considers to be its core brand values by feminising its products. Ladies lingerie would never be considered for a further brand extension, though men's underpants are a distinct possibility.

Questions

1   What characteristics of a brand make it suitable for brand extension into (a) related and (b) unrelated product categories?
2   What are the advantages and disadvantages of launching a completely new brand, compared with a brand extension.
3   What problems can arise when brands are licensed to third parties?

Sources: Irvin (2000); Law (2000).

Reseller brands are created and owned by retailers, wholesalers or distributors, who buy generic, unbranded products from manufacturers and take the responsibility for designing a marketing mix that will turn them into brands that are associated with themselves and not their manufacturers. Sometimes known as *own-label* products, these reseller brands have become more and more significant in recent years, particularly in the UK where the major supermarket chains, including Tesco and Sainsbury's, sell their own ranges very successfully in direct competition with the manufacturer brands on their shelves (own-label goods now account for more than 45 per cent of grocery expenditure in the UK, according to research analysts, Datamonitor). Other stores, including Marks & Spencer, have a policy of only selling own-labels.

Licensing brands are brands that manufacturers or resellers permit others to use under certain conditions and on payment of a fee. JCB, as we have seen, best known for its large-scale earth-moving machinery, has successfully licensed its brand for use in a wide range of consumer products, including men's, women's and children's clothing, toys, sports equipment and travel goods. Character licensing is very popular too, with film and TV companies offering the manufacturers of clothing, household products, stationery and even food the opportunity to associate its products with a popular media icon.

> **DID YOU KNOW?**
> Retailers have become adept at making their own brands look very similar to leading manufacturer brands, but usually manage to escape legal actions under the rather limited UK trademark laws. When McVities accused Asda's Puffin brand of copying their Penguin brand, the judge ruled that Puffin's packaging was deceptively similar to that of Penguin, and could lead to customer confusion. But he did not think there had been any trademark infringement, which meant that Asda could continue using the Puffin name and logo (Lomax and Todd, 1998).

What's in a name?

Firms have a number of options to choose between in deciding how to brand their products.

Individual branding occurs when a firm gives each product in its product mix a separate and distinct name. Nestlé, for example, sells a range of confectionery products under the names KitKat, Yorkie, After Eight, Polo and Quality Street, but other than the appearance of the manufacturer's name on the packet, there is little attempt made to associate each brand with its producer. This strategy is popular if firms wish to actively target different segments of the market which may be alienated if they are associated with other segments. Thus, although News International now owns both *The Times* and *The Sun*, it is unlikely that the company will ever make efforts to link the two as their readership profiles are almost mutually exclusive.

Family branding, on the other hand, is the practice of using a single brand name (often the name of the manufacturer) to link a range of products (and sometimes all products) in the product mix. Heinz uses its company name on its wide range of packaged foods, for example, to take advantage of its reputation as a quality supplier. Family branding can bring advantages by reducing the cost and risk of extending a product range, as customers will already be familiar with the organisation and are likely to be more prepared to experiment with something new. If, however, the new launch is unsuccessful, the negative impact can be very damaging to the core brand.

Other important decisions to make when selecting a brand name include the following:

▶ Might it be offensive or misunderstood (particularly in a foreign language)? Marketing textbooks are littered with examples of brands that would be very difficult to export, such as the French soft drink called Pschitt and the Chinese brand of men's underwear called Pansy.

▶ Should it be descriptive of the product? A brand such as 'I can't believe it's not butter' highlights the key benefit of the product, while others in the same market sector, such as Flora, Clover and Delight, offer few clues as to their superior features.

▶ Can it be remembered easily? Short, but meaningless words are easily remembered and quickly associated with a product – brands such as Cif and Kodak.

▶ Can it be registered? If a brand name has strong similarities with another in the market it may be refused registration on the grounds that consumers may inadvertently purchase a product by mistake.

KEY SKILLS
ACTIVITY **7.3**
••••••••••••
Problem solving

What's in a name?

A brand name will only be as successful as the product or service it is linked to – but an easily memorable and/or relevant name helps! This exercise will involve you in a process for generating a new brand name to arrive at the best option.

Famous examples of foreign product names that raise a smile in the UK include a washing powder called 'Colon', a toilet paper called 'Krapp', and a tin of tuna fish called 'grated Fanny'! But choosing a brand name that will work in international markets is more difficult than it sounds – Volkswagen launched the 'Sharan' in the knowledge that the name means 'Car of Kings', but in the UK it is associated more readily with 'Essex' girl. Mitsubishi's successor to the Colt was the Starion, a combination of 'Star' and 'Orion', but rumours soon started to circulate that it resulted from the Japanese mispronunciation of the word 'Stallion'.

Set up a brainstorming session with friends and colleagues to come up with ideas for new brand names for the following products.

- ▶ A tropical fruit juice.
- ▶ A roll-on deodorant.
- ▶ A domestic cleaning service.
- ▶ A low-calorie breakfast cereal.
- ▶ A satellite TV channel.

What criteria will you use to screen out those that may be worth pursuing from those that will not? Which is your preferred option, and why?

Source: Hewitt (1994).

CASE STUDY **7.5**

There's life in the Blue Nun yet

The concept of branded wines is one that is anathema to true wine connoisseurs, but given that they make up only a small proportion of the total wine-drinking public, the market for branded wines is a buoyant one. Branded wines in the UK have strong roots in the 1960s and 1970s, emerging just as the consumption of wine became a regular social phenomenon rather than the preserve of the upper classes, reserved for special occasions. Familiar brands were a welcome relief to consumers whose knowledge of and confidence with the new product was very limited. Le Piat D'Or, Black Tower, Mateus Rose and Blue Nun were the trendy labels that young people took to parties.

In some ways little has changed. In 2000, one in five of all bottles of wine purchased in the UK was branded, and some of the classics have hung on for a third or fourth decade. Le Piat D'Or and Stowells of Chelsea are still in the top 10 of the branded market, though the New World brands of Gallo, Jacob's Creek, Lindemans, Blossom Hill and Banrock Station have moved in to oust the likes of Veuve du Vernay.

Blue Nun, with its fashionably sweet taste, distinctive brown bottle and picturesque label, went into sharp decline in 1985, and in the UK acquired a somewhat mundane image. Its name was acquired 11 years later by Langguth Wine and Spirits who aimed to breathe life into the old brand. The first problem to resolve was that of its taste. The consumer market was demanding a drier, crisper wine, so out went the German Liebfraumilch and in came a whole range of new wines from various countries, including Merlot, Dry Reisling, Cabernet Sauvignon and even two sparkling wines. A narrower blue bottle with a simple label was designed to draw strongly on the Blue Nun name but take on a modern look. Market research led the company to find its new target market, and to define its core value – fun, easy and memories. It seemed that many people, now in their mid-30s, had positive memories of Blue Nun – not because of the drink *per se*, but because it reminded them of their youth. They have proved to be at the core of the new Blue Nun market in the UK, where sales tripled within five years. 500,000 bottles were sold in 2000, and in the run-up to Christmas 2000, it was the country's twelfth biggest selling wine.

Blue Nun is an international brand though, and is sold in over 80 countries, including most of Europe, the US, Australia, Japan, China, Taiwan and Singapore. In these markets the picture changes a little. In Asia, many consumers are drinking wine for the first time, similar to the UK in the 1960s, and a younger age group is attracted to the brand. China and Taiwan are experiencing the emergence of the middle classes, who also find Blue Nun attractive. To ensure that the core values are sustained across the world, a 'brand book', known as the Blue Nun bible, provides guidelines on the brand message, even detailing the use of fonts and colours to be used in advertising when local distributors market the wine themselves. A global press advertising campaign has focused on 'special moments' and how Blue Nun can enhance and intensify them. In the UK, US and Australian markets, a couple at a wedding are standing in sharp focus, looking at each other over a glass of wine, ignoring the out-of-focus bride and groom in the background. For the Asian markets, it is a group of friends who are in focus, laughing with their glasses of wine, because in Asian markets the more desirable norm is to socialise in groups, not just in couples.

Questions

1   What are the potential benefits and dangers for Blue Nun in creating a range of different wines under a single brand?
2   Why can global advertising be a problem when a product is at different stages in its life-cycle in different countries?
3   Are wine brands fashion products?

Sources: Armstrong (2001); Atkin (2000); Fellowes (2001).

Key concepts

Actual product: the tangible features of a product that deliver benefits to the customer.
Boston matrix: a portfolio planning chart used to classify products according to their market share and the growth rate of their markets.
Brand: a product that belongs uniquely to one producer.
Consumer durables: products designed for use over a period of time.
Core product: the basic function of a product that satisfies customer needs.
Extended product: intangible features of a product that provides additional psychological benefits to the customer.
Fast-moving consumer goods (FMCGs): household products that are bought on a regular basis.
Product life-cycle: a model for describing the common patterns of sales growth and decline that can be observed over the lifetime of a product.
Product line: a group of closely related products sold by an organisation.
Product mix: the total set of all product items sold by an organisation.
Total product concept: the combination of tangible and intangible attributes of a product that combine to offer benefits to the customer.

SELF-CHECK QUESTIONS

1 A guarantee is:
   a A tangible element of the core product.
   b A tangible element of the actual product.
   c An intangible element of the extended product.
   d An emergency product.
   e An unsought product.

2 Which of the following are not true about 'stars' in a product portfolio?
   a They are likely to be cash neutral.
   b They only exist in growing markets.
   c They have a high market share relative to their competitors.
   d They need no further investment.
   e They have the potential to become cash cows.

3 OEM stands for:
   a Original Equipment Manufacturer.
   b Operating Equipment Maintenance.
   c Operating Equipment Merchant.
   d Organisational End-User Market.
   e Operating Equipment and Materials.

4 Which of the following may also be convenience products?
   a Consumer durables.
   b Impulse products.
   c Speciality products.
   d Heterogeneous products.
   e Business services.

5 Which of the following products is not an example of a family brand?
   a Nissan Primera
   b Johnson's Baby Lotion
   c Campari
   d Body Shop
   e Slazenger

Which of the following are true and which are false?

6 Saturation occurs at the growth stage of the product life-cycle when competitors start to leave the market.
7 Component parts are only sold through the aftermarket.
8 A 'dog' in the product portfolio should be harvested if competitive activity in the market is aggressive.
9 The actual product comprises the tangible features that distinguish a firm's core product from those of its competitors.
10 A manufacturer brand may be sold by a retailer in competition with a reseller brand.

Discuss the following

11 Under what circumstances might household groceries be treated as shopping products or even speciality products?

12 What are the advantages and disadvantages of selling to the aftermarket as opposed to OEMs?

13 Describe the product life-cycle for recorded music. In what ways is this different from the life-cycle for tape cassettes?

14 Why might an organisation choose to invest further in its 'question marks'?

15 Family branding and product line extensions are becoming more and more popular. How do you account for this trend?

Further study
••••••••••••••••

Most of the introductory texts on marketing principles and marketing strategy also cover this area quite comprehensively. A particularly readable book on branding is:

Ries, A. and Ries, L. (2000) *The 22 Immutable laws of Branding*, HarperColllins.

A range of important articles develop some of the issues explored in this chapter, including classics such as:

Chematony, L. De (1993) 'Categorising brands', *Journal of Marketing Management*, April.

Day, George S. (1977) 'Diagnosing the product portfolio', *Journal of Marketing*, April.

Doyle, Peter (1976) 'The realities of the product life cycle', *Quarterly Review of Marketing*, Summer.

Levitt, Theodore (1965) 'Exploit the product life cycle', *Harvard Business Review*, 43, November/December.

References
••••••••••••••

Armstrong, S. (2001) 'Naff no more', *MediaGuardian*, 18 June, www.guardian.co.uk

Atkin, T. (2000) 'On the brand wagon', *The Observer*, 23 October, www.observer.co.uk

Buzzell, R.D.A. and Gale, B.T. (1987) *The PIMS Principles: Linking Strategy to Performance*, Free Press.

Chaffey, D. (2002) 'Is Internet marketing dead?', *Marketing Business,* May, pp.21–2.

Economist (1988) 'The year of the brand', *The Economist*, 24 December, p.93.

Fellowes, J. (2001) 'Message in a bottle', *Marketing Business,* May, pp.16–19.

Garratt, S. (2002) 'Wake up … and smell the money', *The Observer,* 8 September, www.observer.co.uk

Guardian (2002) 'Burberry set for London flotation', *The Guardian*, 29 May, www.guardian.co.uk

Hewitt, M. (1994) 'A car by any other name', *Marketing*, June, p.15.

Irvin, C. (2000) 'From crib to consumer', *Marketing Business*, March, pp.17–19.

Irvin, C. (2002) 'What's in a name?', *Marketing Business*, May, pp.33–5.

Kellaway, K. (2000) 'Get the T-shirt, read the book', *The Observer*, 14 May, www.observer.co.uk

Kennedy, M. (2001) 'The favourite exhibit in the world's favourite museum of modern art', *The Guardian*, 12 May, www.guardian.co.uk

Khan, Yasmeen (2001) 'Own labels go upmarket', *MediaGuardian*, 21 August, www.MediaGuardian.co.uk

Law, P. (2000) 'True grit', *Marketing Business*, June, pp.34–7.

Levitt, T. (1969) *The Marketing Mode*, McGraw Hill.

Lomax, W. and Todd, S. (1998) *Assessing the Risk of Consumer Confusion: Practical Test Results*, Kingston Business School Occasional Paper Series: No. 31, November.

Marketing Business (2000) 'A visible difference', *Marketing Business*, February, p.29.

Marketing Business (2002) 'Changing perceptions', *Marketing Business*, p.12.

Marsh, H. (1999) 'Making money from Monet', *Marketing*, 4 February , p.12.

Mathiason, N. and Tooher, P. (2001) 'World takes caffeine hit', *The Observer*, 12 August, www.observer.co.uk

Simms, J. (1998) 'Time to get serious', *Marketing Business*, November, pp.24–8.

Thatcher, M. (2002) 'Reviving brands', *Marketing Business*, February, pp.29–31.

CHAPTER 8

New product development

Objectives
. . . .

When you have read this chapter you will be able to:

➤ Distinguish between different types of new product.

➤ Understand why organisations choose to become innovators.

➤ Identify sources of new product ideas and use structured techniques for idea generation.

➤ Develop relevant criteria for the evaluation of new product ideas.

➤ Design appropriate market research programmes at different stages of the new product development process.

➤ Explain how buyer behaviour influences the rate at which markets adopt new products.

Foundation focus: the 20-second takeaway
. . . .

Marketing takes place in a fast-moving environment. Technology, legislation and social norms are all subject to rapid change. To keep their products and services relevant to the developing wants and needs of customers, marketers have to come up with a stream of new offerings. This process of innovation has been systematised into new product development (NPD). It is risky and expensive. Very few new product ideas make it into final production, and of those the majority fail for one reason or another. But in spite of the uncertain hit rate, companies invest vast amounts of time and money in NPD because they know that if they don't they will rapidly be left behind by more innovative competitors. By segmenting customers on the basis of their attitude to new ideas and products (from the innovation prone all the way through to the laggards, who avoid new things if possible), marketers can reduce some of the risks involved in new product launches.

Introduction
. . . .

This chapter defines new products and examines the reasons why firms introduce new products. It discusses the processes they go through in attempting to ensure that their new products will gain acceptance by customers and be successful at reaching their target markets. Techniques for identifying new product ideas are explored and explanations given of the different research techniques and types of analysis that should be undertaken before a decision is made to launch a new product. Influences on the speed and patterns of new product adoption by customers are identified to help explain the process by which innovations gradually penetrate markets.

What is a new product?
....

A new product is quite simply a product that is perceived as new by the customer. It may be a brand new technology for which its inventor won a Nobel prize, or simply a reworking of an age-old concept which, by virtue of its new design, offers new benefits to the customer. It may be tangible and have physical form, or intangible, such as a service or process. It may be unique and new-to-the-world, or simply a new brand that imitates a competitor's product or a new version of a product to extend a product line. The only important factor in defining a new product is that customers see it as being new and consequently change their normal buying behaviour patterns (more about this at the end of the chapter).

Having said this, it is possible to identify four broad categories of new product:

▶ *Major innovations* present radically new user benefits to customers, often through the development of new technologies. Compact discs, microwave ovens, the contraceptive pill and cellular telephones are all examples of new products that in their time have created new markets rather than entered old ones. These types of development are relatively rare as they usually require high levels of investment during the development process and run the ultimate risk of either technical or market failure. However, this type of new product also offers the potential for very high returns if it is successful.

▶ *Product improvements* are innovations within existing markets that have the potential mainly for taking market share from competitors rather than building extensive new primary demand. Windows 98, for example, offers little that is new to the computer software market but is presented in such a way as to improve the ease of use for customers.

▶ *Product additions* may offer new product features to a market, but offer limited new benefits to customers. This includes 'me-too' products, which are little more than copies of concepts that were developed by competitors. Alternatively, they may take the form of a product line extension, which perhaps offers a new flavour for a food product or a new colour and accessories for a car.

▶ *Repositioned products* can be considered as new products under the definition given above, but are normally thought of as product adaptations rather than new products. They tend to offer little, if anything, of a tangible nature that is new. Instead they create new intangible features through a change of promotional emphasis. (See Chapter 6 for a more detailed discussion of product positioning.)

> **DID YOU KNOW?**
>
> *Marketing's Hall of Blame is full of new products which failed to fizz. Take Crystal Pepsi which was launched to thirsty Americans in 1993. At first the prospects for the new product looked rosy. It had all the attributes of Pepsi Cola except the colour, and was to spearhead Pepsi's major offensive in the ongoing 'Cola Wars'. Crystal Pepsi sold well on launch, but nobody came back for more. The product simply did not offer a new benefit. It has achieved a lasting notoriety on the Internet, where unopened bottles and cans of the now defunct drink change hands for vastly inflated prices. Pepsicom's official website is strangely silent on this episode in the brand's history.*

Why launch a new product?

New product development is only one of four strategic options available to firms when planning their product/market development strategies (in Chapter 14 there is a full explanation of the four strategic options outlined by Ansoff's Matrix), but it can be very important under certain circumstances, for example:

▶ If consumer tastes are changing so that existing products no longer satisfy their needs, as is the case with any product that is susceptible to fashion or style preferences.
▶ If the environment has changed so as to create new needs in the market; out-of-town shopping malls, for example, have grown in popularity as more and more people become car owners and traffic restrictions make the high street an increasingly difficult and expensive place to park.
▶ If competitors are actively developing new products or technologies that will accelerate the decline of existing products (this is discussed in more detail in Chapter 3).
▶ If growth potential in a market is limited by the total size of the market or the intensity of the competition.
▶ If a firm has a portfolio of products that are generating a lot of cash at the maturity stage of their life-cycles (it needs to prepare to use its cash cows to support stars and question marks if it is to survive in the long term – see Chapter 7).
▶ If competition in a market is likely to intensify, for example if a patent is due to expire.
▶ If production capacity is under-utilised, perhaps due to seasonal variations in demand.
▶ If legislation threatens to curtail the marketing of existing products in the future, as is the case in the tobacco industry.

CASE STUDY **8.1**   **Guests for breakfast**

The first meal of the day has traditionally been a national institution in Britain. While the cholesterol-packed 'full English Breakfast' (which also crops up as Scottish, Welsh or Irish depending on where it is served) tends to be limited to weekends, a bowl of cereal is a staple of most people's morning ritual. 95 per cent of UK households have at least one packet in the cupboard, and 73 per cent of all consumers regularly eat cereal for breakfast. This means that the UK is the largest market for cereal manufacturers in Europe, and comes second only to the US globally. In terms of per capita consumption, we lead the world, munching our way through 7.7kg per person per year.

Cereal brands are classified either as 'staples' or as 'guests'. Staples, which include products such as Kellogg's Corn Flakes, Weetabix and Kellogg's Frosties, are the biggest sellers and are seen by consumers as the core choices for breakfast. Variety is important in food, however, especially for a family market, so there is also a large number of 'guest' brands bought intermittently. The market is divided into ready-to-eat cereals, which just require the addition of cold milk, and hot cereals, which require a little more preparation and have a distinctly seasonal pattern of consumption. Within the ready-to-eat sector (which accounts for about 96 per cent of sales) there are two distinct categories – family cereals (about 70 per cent of the total market) and children's cereals, where the emphasis is on fun. Because of their heavily-sweetened nature, however, parents tend to view them with caution. In fact much of the advertising in the market is driven by health claims, with 'organic' products showing strong growth.

Table 8.1 Breakfast cereals percentage value 2001

Kellogg's Company of Great Britain Ltd	42.0
Weetabix Ltd	19.0
Private label	17.6
Cereal Partners (UK) Ltd	12.2
Quaker Oats Ltd	4.0
W. Jordan Cereals Ltd	2.0

Source: Euromonitor.

But there are signs that the industry may be heading for the crunch. The continental breakfast, toast or a croissant with coffee, is making inroads, as is — more worryingly – the habit of skipping breakfast altogether. Concerned cereal giant Kellogg's has produced research which shows that 11 million Britons leave home without breakfast – most of them from households without children. On the other hand, many of those busy people do eat something before lunch, but they do so on the move or at work. If trends in the US are anything to go by, by the year 2020 we will consume half of all our food outside the home. So cereal manufacturers are faced with two kinds of new product challenge. How can they add interest to the British breakfast table to reinvigorate in-home consumption, and how can they create products which suit the needs of breakfasters on the go?

While product innovation is absolutely crucial to both of these challenges, the industry as a whole shows signs of maturity. Eight of today's top 10 brands would have been in the same list 20 years ago. The set of consumer needs which breakfast cereals satisfy appears to have been pretty well covered, leaving little opportunity for radical innovation. Having said that, the market-leading companies appear to be throwing a lot of resource and effort at developing new offerings.

Weetabix, the number two manufacturer in the UK, has added miniaturised versions of its famous breakfast biscuit to its porfolio of brands in order to widen choice for in-home consumers. Part of this effort has been to refocus recent new products in a way which will enhance the core Weetabix brand more single-mindedly. Originally launched as Crrrunch (a honey-crisped cereal designed to retain its crunch) and Minibix (a similar idea with a variety of ingredients), the miniatures range has been rationalised into four varieties of Weetabix Mini Crunch from 2002. At the same time, the company has also aimed for a more adult market with the development of its Alpen branding to cover a wider range of products. Launched in 1971, as the first TV-advertised muesli, Alpen is still a leader in its category. Weetabix has extended the Alpen brand to cover new cereal varieties and a family of cereal bars.

Cereal bars represent an attempt to cater for out-of-home breakfasters. Here, Kellogg's, the market leader in cereals, has scored a resounding success with its Nutri-Grain bar range. From its launch in 1997, the brand is now worth £37 million globally, and represents one-third of all cereal bar sales. The company has also tried to extend its existing successful cereal products into bar versions, launching a range of 'Cereal and Milk' bars and Rice Krispies Squares. Packaging innovations have led to a joint venture with a yoghurt manufacturer to offer split-pots of yoghurt and cereal, as well as complete servings of cereal, milk, sugar and (of course) a spoon, in Kellogg's To Go twinpots.

This kind of innovation is moving the company away from its core activities in cereal manufacturing towards a new positioning as a convenience food producer. A recent new venture has been Kellogg's Real Fruit Winders, fruit sweet strips sold as a coil which, for all the healthy associations of fruit, is really more like a confectionery item than something you would eat for breakfast.

Questions

1   List the factors which influence what consumers eat for breakfast. How does the case demonstrate cereal manufacturers developing new products in response to these factors?

2   Review the reasons why companies develop new products, presented at the start of this chapter. Which of them are relevant to Weetabix Mini Crunch, and why?

3   If, as is claimed in this case study, 50 per cent of food will be eaten outside the home by 2020, this will have consequences for other products and services. List three and briefly comment on what kinds of innovation are likely to occur in them.

Source: Euromonitor (2002); Marsh (2001).

Depending on their circumstances, firms will have a range of objectives for their new products. They may launch new products in an attempt to increase their market share or defend themselves from their competitors. Alternatively, they could be trying to improve their efficiency, exploit their strengths in areas such as research and development or distribution, or reduce their reliance on a single market.

Characteristics of successful new products

It is estimated that of the 90,000 new products launched in the UK each year, only 10 per cent manage to sustain success (A.C. Neilsen, 2000). The most successful new products are those that supply new and better benefits which provide improved solutions to customer problems. Doyle (2001) has identified four benefit criteria that new products should meet if they are to thrive in the market. They should be:

▶   *Important*: The customer must find the new benefit valuable. Many products fail to find a market because their inventors have overestimated the value placed on the new benefits by potential customers. Market research in this area is crucial.

▶   *Unique*: The customer must believe that the benefits offered cannot be obtained from existing products. Lack of differential advantage is one of the most significant reasons for product failure, and is responsible for the particularly high failure rate of me-too products and product line extensions.

▶ *Sustainable*: Competitors must find the new product difficult to copy. Patent protection can achieve this in industries such as pharmaceuticals, where the high costs of new product development can only be recouped if competitors are prevented from undercutting the innovating firm at the early stages of the product life-cycle.

▶ *Marketable*: The company must have the capability of producing, promoting and distributing the product at a price that is acceptable to customers.

What is innovation?

When a firm decides to launch a new product it has a number of strategic options:

▶ It can buy a branded product from another company and resell it as part of its own product mix.

▶ It can buy a generic product from another company, give it a brand name and resell as part of its own product line.

▶ It can negotiate a licence to produce and sell a product from the holder of a patent or trademark.

▶ It can acquire a company and produce and sell its product mix in addition to its own.

▶ It can develop a new product for the market using its own efforts and resources.

Only the last new product strategy on this list can be classed as *innovation*, defined as 'all the activities of bringing a new product or process to the market' (Clipson, 1991). Innovation, also known as New Product Development (or NPD), is a systematic process that begins with the identification and analysis of new product opportunities that fit within the mission of the organisation. The potential of these is then evaluated using financial, market and technological criteria, and finally the option or options that appear to offer the greatest benefits to the customer and the best opportunities for the company are selected and developed.

Why innovate?

Innovation can bring significant advantages compared with the other new product strategies if it enables the innovator to get to the market first with a new product that can satisfy previously unmet needs. Research carried out in the 1980s suggested that pioneers could earn an average return on investment 35 per cent higher than their followers, and that 70 per cent of market leaders described themselves as having been the pioneers of their products (Buzzell and Gale, 1987). Whether there is still such an advantage in being a first mover is debatable. In the twenty-first century ideas and products can be imitated rapidly (in spite of legal protections) and the rapid advance of technology in key product areas such as mobile telephones and computing, means that pioneers often lose their scalps!

Having said this, poor management of innovation can be responsible for the failure of new products which might otherwise have proved successful. Firms are sometimes too cautious, move too slowly and enable their competitors to launch first; they plan badly, resulting in ideas being poorly evaluated, markets being badly researched and insufficient budgets being allocated; and top managers may constrain their commitment to new products by refusing to sanction aggressive marketing activity if there are risks involved. Only when a new product that offers real benefits is coupled with an efficient process of innovation are the promised returns likely to be realised.

DID YOU KNOW?

A vibrant new product development programme has smoothed the path of 3M (originally Minnesota Mining and Manufacturing) from being a small business specialising in sandpaper to a multinational giant worth almost $16 billion, marketing more than 50,000 products across 200 countries. Innovation is key to the company's ethos. It aims to produce at least 30 per cent of annual sales from products less than four years old (Business Week Online, 2000).

Key stages in the process of innovation

'Innovation is work rather than genius' (Drucker, 2001). Most successful new products result from a conscious search for opportunities and a systematic attempt to remove the uncertainty surrounding them. This process needs to pass through seven key stages if mistakes are to be avoided and new product failures minimised. (See Figure 8.1.)

Stage 1: Idea generation

This is the starting point for new product development. For every new product that is finally launched on the market, a firm typically investigates seven other ideas

figure 8.1
The process of innovation

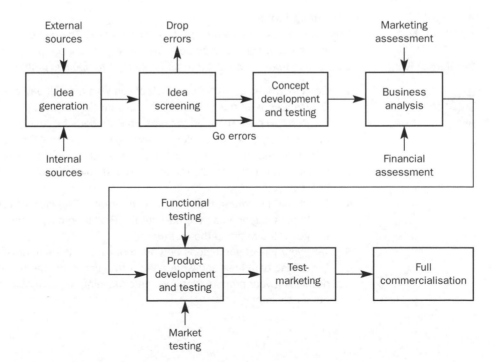

that don't make it as far as full commercialisation (Griffin, 1997). Consequently, it is important that organisations make continuous efforts to identify sources of potential new products and develop an organisational climate that is receptive to new ideas and will encourage them to emerge.

Internal sources of new product ideas are those generated within an organisation itself. They may emerge from:

▶ A research and development (R&D) department, motivated by technological possibilities.

▶ A production department, motivated by process possibilities, or attempts to fill capacity.

▶ A design department, motivated by aesthetic or ergonomic possibilities.

▶ A marketing department, motivated by a perception of customer needs.

▶ Senior management, motivated by strategic opportunity.

▶ Other employees, identifying opportunity in the course of their own work – perhaps as part of quality initiatives or through suggestion boxes.

Formal techniques to encourage idea generation can be used both within and across these functional areas. One such technique is *brainstorming*. This involves a group of individuals meeting together with a view to freely suggesting possible new product ideas, based on both their personal and work experience. The ideas are recorded, but there is no discussion or criticism of them, and their evaluation takes place at different times, often by different people. The great advantage of brainstorming is that it maximises the number of ideas generated, and allows even wild ideas, which are likely to be the most original, to be systematically assessed.

KEY SKILLS
ACTIVITY **8.1**
· · · · · · · · · · · · · ·

Problem solving

Spreading ideas

Brainstorming is an essential problem-solving skill. The purpose of brainstorming is to generate as many ideas as possible. By structuring a brainstorming session around a theme it is possible to find solutions to specific problems.

1 Get into groups of five or six, each of you with a small pad of Post-it notes. Designate one of the walls in the room your 'ideas' wall.

2 You are now each required to come up with ideas for 'things to spread on bread': every time you think of a new idea, write it on a Post-it note and go and stick it on the wall; take a look at the other ideas up there while you're there.

3 Continue doing this for 20 minutes – you should have at least 100 ideas between you.

4 Decide on the criteria that you will use for deciding which of your ideas may be worth pursuing and use them to put the Post-it notes into three piles of ideas: the good, the bad and the indifferent.

5 Take your pile of good ideas and attempt to rank them in order of merit.

6 Extract the best idea and write a letter to a company that might be interested in developing your product idea further, explaining why it should test the concept out on consumers.

Instead of things to spread on bread, you might like to work on the following:

- ► Alcoholic beverages.
- ► Hair care products.
- ► Kitchen appliances.
- ► Garden tools.

External sources of new product ideas are those that come from outside the organisation. They may emerge from:

- ► Customers, in particular end-users, who make suggestions and complain if their needs are not being fully satisfied.
- ► Distributors or retailers, who recognise the need for new products that their customers would like.
- ► Suppliers, who have identified ways in which their raw materials or components could be used to produce new consumer or industrial products.
- ► Competitors, who produce products that could be copied or improved.
- ► Universities, who identify potential new product applications as a result of scientific research.
- ► advertising and marketing agencies, who identify consumer or business needs in the process of researching markets.

DID YOU KNOW?

The inventor of the World Wide Web has not made any serious money from possibly the most important business idea of modern times. UK research scientist Tim Berners-Lee came up with the idea of the World Wide Web while working in a physics lab. As he modestly points out on his personal website, if he had tried to assert ownership of the idea it would have had little chance of catching on with other people. (http://www.w3.org/People /Berners-Lee/ShortHistory.html).

Stage 2: Idea screening

The purpose of this stage is to enable the organisation to eliminate any poor ideas before spending money on investigating and developing them further. Two errors are commonly made at this stage:

- ► *Drop-errors* are made when organisations fail to spot the potential of an idea, which subsequently proves to be successful in the market. Decca made a classic drop-error when it refused to give a recording contract to the Beatles! This type of error is relatively rare in comparison with the next type.
- ► *Go-errors* are decisions to continue with the development of a product idea that subsequently fails in the market. Different studies quote different figures, but up to 80 per cent of consumer products are thought to fail shortly after their launch. Famous go-errors include the Sinclair C5, which failed to meet the needs of its target market, and Concorde, which will never pay back its investment.

The process of idea screening usually has two levels. The first requires the new idea to be assessed in terms of its market potential and the organisation's capability of producing and selling it. The completion of a standard proforma is often required to ensure that the idea is evaluated against a comprehensive, objective and consistent set of criteria. Ideas that survive this stage can be further evaluated on a numerical basis, which is particularly useful if the relative merits of different ideas are to be systematically assessed. (See Figure 8.2.)

figure 8.2
Idea screening grid

Criteria for selection	Importance of criterion (1 = low, 10 = high) (X)	Rating of new product proposal (1 = poor, 10 = good) (Y)	Weighted score of new product proposal (X x Y)
Consistency with corporate mission			
Use of existing distribution channels			
Production economies of scale			
Technological capability			
Financial risk			
Market familiarity			

The importance of the different evaluative criteria are weighted, and the extent to which each new idea fulfils the criteria is assessed. The combination of these two numerical scores enables an overall score for each new product idea to be generated; only those with the highest scores should be permitted to proceed to the next stage.

Stage 3: Concept development and testing

Ideas that make it past the screening stage need to be tested out on their potential market. This can only be done if the *product idea* is at this stage converted into a *product concept*; in other words, the idea needs to be developed so that its features and benefits can be explained to potential customers, who will be able to envisage a product and indicate how they might use it, whether they might buy it, how much they might be willing to pay for it and express any concerns or reservations they may have about it. For example, a company might come up with the idea of producing a machine for peeling onions. A concept would have to be developed to describe the size of the machine, whether it would be manual or electric, how it would work and how it would be operated.

CASE STUDY **8.2**
· · · · · · · · · · · · · · · · · ·

Lukewarm reception for Hot When You Want It

Coffee giant Nescafé got financially scalded when it introduced a revolutionary new product in the UK. The company's launch plans included over £10 million in promotional support for what it claimed as the biggest single technological innovation since the development of instant coffee more than 60 years previously. Nestlé itself contributed £5 million to the development of the revolutionary self-heating can, in conjunction with packaging specialists Thermotic Developments.

The 210ml cans, which retailed at £1.19 contained an internal heat engine activated by pressing a button-like device on the base. Turning the can upside down and shaking it started a chemical reaction in the wall of the container. In three minutes' time the heat generated by the reaction was designed to provide a steaming cup of appetising coffee wherever and whenever the customer wanted it. The coffee was available with milk, with or without sugar.

Hot When You Want It was test-marketed through 5,000 outlets in the UK's Midlands region. Supermarkets and other retailers were extremely keen to stock it, spurred on by their faith that this was a genuinely innovative new product which would open up an entirely new category. The previous year, Nestlé had scored a success with a chilled product, Nescafé Ice, aimed at 16–24 year olds, and the wholesale and retail trade had even warmer expectations of the latest wonder-tin.

After five months of national availability, the brand reached a very satisfactory penetration of 15 per cent of the market. Problems became apparent, however, when customers failed to repurchase. The launch had hit two main snags. One was customers' disappointment that the standard 330ml size can only yielded 210ml of coffee. In spite of the fact that the quantity was marked clearly on the packaging, the overall size of the can (with its hollow wall containing the heat-producing reactive chemicals) had led to a psychological expectation of more. The second, perhaps more fundamental, problem was that the cans did not produce hot coffee in all circumstances. In colder weather, the coffee was still lukewarm after the three-minute heating period. The reaction was sufficient to raise the temperature of the beverage by 40 degrees centigrade. Fine in summer if the starting temperature was, say, 25 degrees. But on colder days, especially for a product designed to be consumed on the go, the boost was simply not enough to deliver the promise of heat. Company sources admitted that consumers were starting to call the drink 'Warm When You Want It'.

Nestlé withdrew the product from sale and handed the project of developing a more reliable offering in the 'hot drinks on the move' category to Beverage Partners Worldwide, its joint venture with Coca-Cola.

Questions

1   One of the reasons consumers failed to purchase Hot When You Want It was their disappointment at the serving size, in spite of the cans being clearly labelled as containing 210ml of product. What advice would you give Beverage Partners Worldwide as a result of this, and why?

2   What environmental factors might have contributed to Nestlé's decision to launch a product in the 'hot drinks on the move' category? Suggest at least one other new product idea for the company, justifying it from the same range of factors.

3   Hot When You Want It retailed at £1.19. Comment on the reasons for this pricing decision, and what alternatives Nestlé might have considered.

Sources: Kleinman (2001); Mason (2002).

It is common for more than one concept to be developed from each product idea, so that potential customers can be asked to react to a number of different styles or versions of a product and the company can decide which concept has the strongest appeal. (This has been made much easier and cheaper by the availability of computer-aided design systems, which make it relatively

> **DID YOU KNOW?**
> *The concept of the Sony Walkman failed in consumer tests? It was also resisted by marketers, engineers and accountants inside the company. It only survived due to the influence of Sony's founder, Akio Morita, who was determined to see the product on the market (du Gay et al., 1996).*

easy to generate drawings and models of different versions of proposed new products.) The onion peeler, for example, could be presented as a stand-alone mechanical device, a stand-alone electrical appliance or simply an attachment for a food processor, and potential customers would be asked which version they would prefer to use.

KEY SKILLS
ACTIVITY **8.2**
• • • • • • • • • • • • •

Communication

Apple appeal

Meetings are a great way to communicate ideas persuasively to others, share information, and work together on projects. More formal ones will involve the preparation of an agenda and noting down the decisions reached. This exercise gives you an opportunity to practise running and participating in a meeting about new product development in a hypothetical company.

Cider is as English as thatched cottages, cream teas and rain, but most of the cider sold and consumed in the UK is made by large companies from apple juice concentrate (often imported). Many of these products have a deliberately contemporary, urban image to escape what their makers see as old-fashioned and tired brand values. They are positioned to compete against products such as lager in what drinks marketers call the Long Alcoholic Drinks (LAD) sector.

There are, however, a number of successful niche marketers of more traditional varieties, based on authentic rustic recipes using native varieties of apple and organic ingredients. At the other end of the scale, some cider manufacturers have had considerable success with 'alcopops' – drinks which, while based on cider, have little or nothing to do with apples.

Your task in the Foundation Cider Company is to hold a new products meeting (of at least three people) in which you discuss which of the following new product ideas should progress to the next stage of development. You only have the resources to develop one of the products. Each should be championed by at least one person at the meeting, who will put forward arguments as to why it is more worthy of support than the other two. Come to a reasoned conclusion about which is the most likely prospect for further development.

1 Gala Light: A low-alcohol lager aimed at the health-conscious, younger drinker who enjoys other low-alcohol beverages but is looking for variety. Looking for distribution in wine bars, pubs and off licences. Available as draft, bottles or cans.
2 Chaucer Organic Reserve: Almost as strong as a white wine, and made from 100 per cent organic ingredients, this premium product competes head-to-head with wine as an upmarket aperitif or drink to accompany a meal. Its packaging, an earthernware 70cl flask, speaks exclusivity, tradition and quality – as does its price tag.
3 Newtonic: The cider that thinks it's a cocktail. Fizzy, fun and surprisingly potent, this sophisticated tipple is bound to be a hit with party people of all ages, but

particularly younger drinkers who are not too keen on the taste of alcohol. Named after the genius who discovered gravity when an apple hit him on the head.

Stage 4: Business analysis

As a result of concept testing, businesses gain a better understanding of the nature and specifications of the products that will be acceptable in the market. This enables them to undertake a much more comprehensive assessment of the commercial viability of the new product.

A *marketing assessment* will be the starting point. This will include:

▶ A description of target markets.
▶ A forecast of sales volume.
▶ An indication of product positioning.
▶ A judgement as to likely competitor reactions.
▶ A calculation of potential sales losses from existing products as customers switch to the new product (known as cannibalisation).
▶ A specification of the new product features, including quality levels.
▶ An assessment of achievable price levels.
▶ A strategy for distribution.
▶ A statement of promotional requirements.

A *financial assessment* will follow. Based on the marketing assessment, calculations can be made to project:

▶ Sales value.
▶ Variable costs of production.
▶ Incremental fixed costs.

These in turn will lead to an assessment of likely

▶ Contribution and profitability of the new product.

Products that appear to offer the opportunity for profitable trading can continue to the next stage of the innovation process.

Stage 5: Product development and testing

Up until this stage the new products do not physically exist, except perhaps in the form of models or drawings. It is only at this point that a company must confront the task of determining whether it is technically feasible to produce them and whether they can be produced at a sufficiently low cost to enable a realistic price to be set. This may take many years, particularly if a product is scientifically complex. Pharmaceutical products, for example, have to pass through a lengthy period of pure research to identify the relevant chemical and physiological reactions before they can develop a basic formulation for laboratory and clinical trials.

A prototype or working model of a new product must be produced at this stage to enable further testing to take place. The testing may take two forms:

▶ *Functional testing* should be conducted to identify the best materials and components, to make sure that the product works, to assess its reliability and to ensure that it works safely. Much of this testing will take place on the prototype itself, but it is also possible for some testing to be done using computer simulations which can reduce the time and costs involved in this process.

▶ *Market testing* often takes places in parallel to functional testing. This is a form of market research, usually qualitative research, which aims to check out the acceptability of the product in the market by testing out prototypes on potential customers. Whereas the concept test might only indicate possible product attributes, a market test enables potential customers to assess both the tangible and intangible attributes of a proposed product. The feedback provided at this stage can help to finalise decisions on minor styling and design features such as colour and user controls, as well as marketing decisions such as packaging and brand name. In other cases, the feedback may be so negative as to suggest that the product should be abandoned. At this late stage there is likely to be some resistance to such a move by the staff responsible for the new product development, who will have developed a psychological attachment to it. However, to ignore such signals from the market can have very costly implications as the final stages of the new product development process normally require a heavy commitment to investment in both production and marketing. It's better to acknowledge failure sooner than later.

CASE STUDY **8.3**
· · · · · · · · · · · · · · · · · · · ·

Happoshu Days

Malt is a key ingredient in beer. It is made by taking a grain such as barley, allowing it to germinate in water, and then drying the germinating grains in an air kiln. Boiling the result produces the 'wort' which eventually gets brewed into beer. The more malt there is, the stronger the resulting brew.

In Japan, the principle of beer taxation has traditionally been based on how much malt there is in the product – on the assumption that stronger beers should pay more tax. Not a bad idea, except that ingenious Japanese brewers have now discovered ways of making their tipples with less malt. Happoshu, the Japanese name for low-malt beer, looks and tastes (well almost) like real beer, has the same mellowing qualities, but costs two-thirds as much. The low-malt sector is therefore growing rapidly from a standing start in the late 1990s.

This has led to an intensification of competition between Kirin, the Japanese brewer which has dominated the beer market in Japan for years, and Asahi, whose Super Dry brand is the world's third best-selling beer. Asahi's recently-launched Honnama brand of Happoshu has been one of the great new-product success stories of Japanese brewing – with advance orders from distributors more than three times higher than normal for a new product. To a large extent this is because of Asahi's excellent marketing and branding skills, but Kirin is determined to fight back. Relaunching its own Happoshu offering, as well as changing the frequency with which it reports sales (to twice a year rather than once every month), are two of the ways in which it has tried to offset the effect of the rival launch on investor confidence.

Meanwhile, the Japanese government is thinking about changing its taxation laws again, in order to close the low-malt loophole. While the beermakers may protest, the change may not make that much difference to market shares. There is evidence to suggest that a growing number of customers are claiming to prefer the taste of low-malt beer to the 'real thing', and so may be prepared to pay more for it in the long run.

Questions

1   How might Asahi protect its Super Dry beer brand from losing sales to Honnama, its new brand of Happoshu?

2   What are the advantages and disadvantages of Kirin's decision to change the frequency with which it releases its sales figures from monthly to half-yearly?

3   Given that Happoshu is designed to be as similar to existing beer as possible, is it really a new product at all? Justify your answer.

Source: Economist (2001).

DID YOU KNOW?

Before launching the tortilla chip brand 'Doritos' in the UK, Walkers conducted 18 months of painstaking research. It found that British consumers like their tortilla chips to be four thousandths of an inch thinner than the American version (Mitchell, 1995).

Stage 6: Test-marketing

This is the stage at which a new product is first made available to potential customers under real market conditions, but on a smaller scale than for the full-scale launch that will follow.

The purpose of test-marketing is to enable a firm to find out about potential problems with its new product and associated marketing activity before going to the expense of a wider introduction. A lot of information can be gathered about customer and retailer or distributor reactions to the product: precisely who are the buyers, and how often do they make a repeat purchase? This, in turn, enables more accurate forecasts to be made of future sales and profitability, and appropriate corrective action to be instigated in the event of limited customer enthusiasm. (See Figure 8.3.)

figure 8.3
Implications of test market results

Standard test-markets

A standard test-market is commonly used for testing fast-moving consumer goods. It should, as far as possible, be a scaled-down version of an intended national market, involving:

▶ A geographical area that is representative of the future total market area.
▶ Similar advertising media.
▶ Equivalent distribution outlets and sales effort.
▶ Intended price levels.

Sometimes this is not easy, and compromises have to be made. Reaching a set of communities that will represent the tastes and preferences from across the wide range of regional sub-cultures in a country is either difficult and costly, or sometimes impossible. TV regions and provincial cities tend to be used for pragmatic reasons. Local media availability and newspaper readership patterns may be different from the national scene, which makes it difficult to translate national promotional campaigns into local equivalents. Dealers and retailers may have different concentrations in different parts of a country, so replicating distribution intensity can also be a problem.

Limited test-markets

If a firm cannot afford the time and expense of a standard test-market, or for some reason is keen to avoid alerting competitors to the potential of a new product, it may choose instead to conduct a mini test-market by making the product available through a selected store for a limited period of time only. Alternatively, it may create a *simulated test-market* by showing consumers advertisements for a number of different products, including the new product, and then giving them a sum of money to spend in a store or 'shopping laboratory' operated by a market research firm. Both of these methods have drawbacks because they do not recreate the true market conditions that will be experienced when the product is ultimately launched, but they can indicate if a new product is fatally flawed and draw attention to changes that are required in marketing activity.

In industrial markets, specialist trade shows and exhibitions are sometimes used as simulated test-markets. New products can be presented alongside all the other products on a firm's stand, and in the same arena as competitors' products. Visitors to the show are likely to be members of the target market, and their interest and reaction to the new product can be gauged. The main problems that can arise are when potential buyers want to place orders for products which are not yet in full-scale production. Unless the product is unique and technologically difficult to copy, this could provide an opening for competitors.

Product-use tests

Because of the difficulties of test-marketing industrial products, product-use tests are often conducted instead. A few potential customers are selected to borrow the product to use under normal conditions for a period of time. At the end of the trial they are allowed to keep the product in return for giving the company feedback on its performance.

Drawbacks of test-marketing

Although test-marketing can reduce the risks inherent in launching new products, it is not appropriate in all circumstances and can even encourage false perceptions of the strength of the new product. For example:

▶ If the new product does not represent a major commercial risk, the costs of staging a test-market may outweigh the potential benefits of risk-reduction it may bring.

▶ The economic environment may change between test-market and full commercialisation, changing customer willingness to pay for the product.

▶ Competitors may not retaliate at the test-market stage, but start gearing up for a me-too product if the new product seems to be damaging their market share in the test-market region.

▶ Innovative products may be brought by large numbers of consumers seeking to try them out once or twice, but prove to be fads with short product life-cycles.

▶ Competitors may attempt to undermine a test-market by price-cutting their own ranges for the duration of the test, so that the new product is less successful than it would otherwise have been.

CASE STUDY **8.4**

Boeing nowhere?

New product development can have a strategic value quite apart from creating new revenue flows for a company. Because of the news value of developments in big industries like aeronautics or cars, journalists flock to exhibitions and trade shows to hear manufacturers describe their dramatic plans for radical innovation.

March 2001 saw the announcement by Boeing that it was developing a revolutionary new passenger jet which would fly 20 per cent faster than conventional airliners. The 'sonic cruiser' would maintain a speed just below the speed of sound, and with its range of 8,600 miles (13,800 km) it would make it possible to knock three hours off a Pacific crossing. Not only would there be passengers willing to pay a premium for such speed, the company argued, but the immediate customers (the airline companies) would benefit from being able to squeeze more flights from each aircraft – a key variable in profitability calculations.

However, the industry's reaction was less enthusiastic than might have been expected. The sonic cruiser launch came soon after Boeing had unveiled rather less dramatic plans for an upgrade of its classic 747 – a range of aircraft that has been in service since the 1970s. (The product life-cycle of airlines is impressively long compared to some other high-tech industries.) Compared to its arch-rival Airbus's plans for a double-decker, 550-seat aircraft, the A380, the 747 revamp had fallen flat. Sceptics saw the speedy announcement of the sonic cruiser as an attempt to divert attention from the A380, and grab some headlines back.

However, 2001 was a bad year for order books for any kind of airliner. Not only was there a slow-down in business in the summer, but the tragic events of 11 September in the US gave the world's airline industry a traumatic shock. Prospects for any kind of new model suddenly looked grim as many companies faced possible bankruptcy because of passengers' reluctance to fly.

The name of the game for airlines now is to increase efficiencies and rebuild their finances after a difficult period. So the market for a superfast jet is less certain than it might have been. Boeing has responded flexibly. The computerised design process and application of new materials technology which yielded a 20 per cent speed increase has been drawn on to produce a more conventional plane which flies at the same speed as its competitors but is 20 per cent more fuel-efficient instead.

Questions

1   How might new product development differ between consumer and business-to-business markets?

2   Using the case study as an example, explain the importance of public relations in establishing confidence among investors and customers.

3   Discuss the view that innovation is less important in some industries than in others.

Source: Economist (2002).

Stage 7: Full commercialisation

The final stage of the innovation process is the launch and full-scale commercialisation of a new product. Production capacity is geared up to produce the quantities indicated in the sales forecast and the full marketing plan is activated.

Because of the enormity of this task, some organisations use a *roll-out* strategy to launch their new products. This involves sequentially targeting only selected geographical areas within the total target market over a period of time until all sectors have been covered. It is a particularly useful strategy for firms with limited resources, which can spread the costs of the launch over a longer period of time, during which they also hope to start generating sales revenues. Larger firms can afford to launch to much wider markets and progress more quickly into international markets; some even choose to launch globally and gain a rapid penetration of world markets.

CASE STUDY **8.5**

Critical success factors for new product development

Here are five new products which have enjoyed success since their launch at the beginning of the twenty-first century.

Brand	Manufacturer	Est. Annual Sales £	The story so far
Iams	Procter and Gamble	£16m	Already the second-largest pet-food brand in the US, Iams was tried by 2.5 million UK cats and dogs in its first year of launch there. The dry pet-food sector, where Iams is a leading player, is seen by owners as a healthier choice for their pets. The launch campaign, according to the company, achieved 70 per cent awareness within three weeks through intensive media coverage and widespead in-store presence.

Brand	Manufacturer	Est. Annual Sales £	The story so far
Fruit Shoot	Britvic	£21m	Aimed at sporty, active 5–11 year-olds, the brand's launch campaign involved extensive sampling, saturation TV advertising during school holidays, and a substantial sponsorship deal with Cartoon Network, a popular viewing choice for children. Its distinctive packaging (in bright colours and boasting a 'sports cap') reflects the vivid flavour variants of Orange & Peach and Apple & Blackcurrant.
Campino	Bendicks	£10m	A genuinely new addition to the £1bn (€1.6bn) sugar confectionery sector, Campino launched in two flavours – orange and strawberry – each combined with a distinctive 'cream' component. Heavyweight TV advertising, combined with impressive displays in outlets, fuelled significant growth in the dormant sugar confectionary market and prompted speedy entry with a 'me-too' offering from confectionery giant Nestlé.
Danone Activ	Danone Waters	£0.8m	A unique product proposition in the UK market on its launch, this 'functional' water offered consumers the opportunity to top up their calcium levels and thus, arguably, safeguard the health of their bones. The point was rammed home in a TV campaign which featured animated skeletons enjoying the drink. PR, sampling and education/health awareness work led to a phenomenal 90 per cent distribution in all major grocers in launch year.
Juice Up	Britvic	£0.7m	The phenonmenal success of Procter and Gamble's Sunny Delight opened up a 'fortified' fruit juice drink sector aimed at children. Britvic's challenger brand in the sector, appeals to parents because of its vitamins and added calcium and to children because of its flavours (Smooth Orange, Cool Berry and Sun-shine Tropical).

Experts maintain that successful new product launches are either the result of major promotional campaigns establishing awareness followed by trial and repurchase, or of smaller 'viral' marketing exercises where products are launched, perhaps just in test-markets at first, and then allowed to build through word-of-mouth. Sunny Delight is an example of the first kind of success, Red Bull is an example of the second.

What is clear is that successful new products offer something distinctive and new to consumers (even if this is just better value compared to what may seem very similar existing products).

Questions

1   From evidence in the case study and any further research you would like to undertake, list three characteristics that each of the new product launches dealt with here have in common.

2   Which of these five new products would you expect to sustain its success over the next decade, and why?

3   Is there any significance in the fact that at least two of these products are aimed at children? (That is, would you expect regular new product development activity to be more important than usual for this market?)

Source: Gray (2001).

Buyer behaviour and new products
••

The new product adoption process

Consumers and organisational buyers approach the decision to buy a new product using a process known as the *adoption process*. This is a sequential process consisting of five stages, each of which takes them closer to a decision to buy a new product and use it on a regular basis.

▶   *Awareness* is the first stage. The potential buyer knows of the existence of the new product but lacks information about it. Multimedia computers are currently at this stage in the adoption process for many households in the UK.

▶   *Knowledge* is the second stage. Potential buyers seek information about the product so that they have a basis on which to judge whether or not they have any need for it. Much knowledge about new products is acquired by word-of-mouth from those already using them, but informative advertising and PR activity are useful techniques for speeding up this stage. With regard to the multimedia computer, consumers will want to know what it can do, how easy it is to operate, and of course, how much it will cost.

▶   *Evaluation* is the third stage. The potential buyer weighs up the benefits and drawbacks of the new product and makes an assessment as to whether or not it could solve any problems.

▶   *Trial* is sometimes next. A trial is a process of acquiring or using a product on a limited basis before making a full (and usually financial) commitment to it. In the case of the multimedia computer, consumers may go along to their dealer showroom and ask to be allowed to use it in the shop. Fast-moving consumer goods are sometimes given away in sales promotions, either attached to the packets of existing products or pushed through consumers' letter-boxes, and food products can sometimes be sampled in in-store promotions. Car showrooms allow potential buyers to go for a drive in a demonstration vehicle. In resale markets, distributors may ask their suppliers to let them buy on a sale or return basis.

▶ *Adoption* finally occurs if the trial stage has proved satisfactory. The customer is willing to purchase it outright and uses it whenever the need for this type of product arises.

New product adoption rates

The speed at which different individuals pass through the adoption process affects the speed at which products penetrate their markets and move through growth towards maturity in their life-cycles. Two factors have a significant influence on the new product adoption rate: product characteristics and individual characteristics.

Product characteristics

These can affect the readiness of potential buyers to adopt a new product, and the following are particularly influential in speeding up, or slowing down, the adoption process:

▶ *Relative advantage* is a term that describes customers' perceptions of the benefits of a new product in comparison with existing alternatives. The greater the perceived relative advantage, the faster the rate of adoption. Mobile telephones have enjoyed what might seem surprising success in Central and Eastern Europe because of their greater reliability and availability than land lines in the same countries.

▶ *Compatibility* refers to the extent to which a product meets customer needs and reinforces existing attitudes and past experiences. The more closely a product meets a pressing customer need, the quicker it will be adopted. Perhaps this is why machines that stamp initials on golf-balls have never really taken off in a big way.

▶ *Observability* refers to the ease with which product benefits can be demonstrated and communicated to potential customers. The financial services industry experiences some problems persuading people to adopt products such as pension plans. The benefits of such policies are only realisable much later in life, and it is difficult to encourage people to plan so far ahead. By the time they do get around to thinking about them, their costs have risen substantially.

▶ *Simplicity* concerns the ease with which new products are understood. This is another problem facing the financial services industry. Frequent changes in taxation and social policy make it difficult for consumers to evaluate which is the best place to save and invest their money for the future, and the uncertainty of future returns deters many.

▶ *Trialability* refers to the extent to which a product can be sampled before it is adopted. Examples given in the previous section show how it is possible to offer tangible products to customers on a trial basis, but services are often more difficult as the customer and service provider are linked in the delivery of the service (discussed in Chapter 2). It would be too expensive for a package holiday company to allow its clients to sample a few days of a holiday before agreeing to stay the full fortnight, and a hairdresser is unable to offer just part of a new hair style.

Individual characteristics

These are also influential in the speed of adoption, though they are less easy to predict than product characteristics. Factors such as high educational levels, wealth and affiliation to both formal and informal groups tend to be characteristics shared by those who adopt new products first, but this will vary to some extent across product groups. Rogers (1995) identified five levels of innovativeness in individuals (Figure 8.4).

▶ *Innovators* comprise no more than 2.5 per cent of the population. These are people who are willing to try out new ideas and products first. Venturesome by nature, they are prepared to run the risk of buying a product that ultimately proves disappointing rather than miss out on the chance of being first to experience something new.

▶ *Early adopters* represent the next 13.5 per cent of the population to adopt a new product. This group is less willing to experiment and more conscious of social pressures to conform than innovators, so they adopt new ideas more carefully. They tend to be respected members of the community and therefore likely to be *opinion leaders* for others, who will only buy the new product when the early adopters have given their seal of approval.

▶ *The early majority* consists of those who are more cautious of new products than the early adopters, but if they are exposed to sufficient information to help them make their own evaluations, they will follow the example of the opinion leaders. Described as 'deliberate' in their actions, this group comprises a significant 34 per cent of the population, and is therefore an important target for firms looking to take their products from the introduction to the growth stage of their life-cycles.

▶ *The late majority* are followers, only tending to adopt new products when their friends have done so. Heavily influenced by pressures to conform to social norms, they are unlikely to buy anything that would make them stand out from the crowd. For this reason they tend to rely on word-of-mouth rather than media as their primary source of product information. Another 34 per cent of the population falls into this category.

▶ *Laggards* are described as being oriented to the past. They resist new products for as long as possible, preferring to stick to tried-and-trusted products. Sometimes they adopt new products only when they have been superseded by something else, and then may be forced into it by the discontinuation of the items they usually buy. 16 per cent of people fall into this category, usually older people and those in the lower socio-economic groups.

figure 8.4
The diffusion of innovation

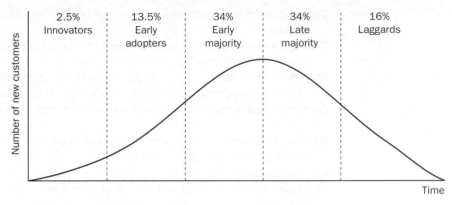

Source: Rogers (1995)

KEY SKILLS
ACTIVITY **8.3**
• • • • • • • • • • • • •

Working with others

Understanding the innovator

All marketing involves working with other people – colleagues inside an organisation, distributors outside and, ultimately, customers. Developing an understanding of your customer is a step towards empathy – a necessary quality for mutually-beneficial exchange activity. This exercise gives you the opportunity to develop an imaginative understanding of an important customer type. How might it help you work with others in a non-marketing context?

Innovators are those within the first 2.5 per cent of all people to adopt a product. For marketers they are an important group of consumers as they are willing to take the risk of buying new products before others have tried them and declared them satisfactory. Inside an organisation innovators are key colleagues in getting new ideas off the ground and driving change. But different people are likely to be innovators in different situations:

1   Create a pen-portrait of (and give a nick-name to) the sort of person that you think is likely to be an innovator in the markets for:
    – Computer software.
    – A new staff appraisal system.
    – Soft drinks.
    – A quality improvement initiative in your organisation.
    – Men's toiletries.
2   What product benefits are most likely to tempt these people to try something different?
3   What sort of promotional message and which media are most likely to attract them?

Key concepts
• • • • • • • • • • • • • • • • •

Adoption process: the stages an individual goes through on the way to accepting (or rejecting) a new product.
Brainstorming: a technique that uses free thinking to generate a wide range of new product ideas.

Business analysis: a systematic assessment of the commercial viability of a new product.

Concept test: research that aims to find out whether or not a new product idea meets customer needs.

Drop-error: the failure of a firm to recognise the potential of a new product idea, which subsequently proves to be successful for another firm.

Functional test: research that aims to assess how well a new product will perform.

Go-error: a decision to continue with the development of a product idea that subsequently fails in the market.

Idea generation: efforts to identify sources of potential new products.

Idea screening: identifying and dropping poor new product ideas before money is invested in their development.

Innovation: the activities involved in bringing a new product or process to the market.

Market test: research that aims to assess the reaction of potential customers to new products.

Me-too products: imitations of products originally developed by competitors.

Pioneer: the firm which gets to the market first with a new product which can satisfy previously unmet needs.

Roll-out strategy: launching a new product in different target markets at different times.

Test-market: introducing a product in a small sector of a target market to test its viability before incurring the expense of a full-scale launch.

SELF-CHECK
QUESTIONS

1 Which of the following is not an external source of new product ideas?
  a Distributors.
  b Employees.
  c Customers.
  d Universities.
  e Competitors.

2 Under which of the following circumstances would you say that a 'drop-error' has occurred?
  a When a consumer rejects a product at the trial stage.
  b When an idea is rejected during brainstorming.
  c When a product is developed but ultimately fails in the market.
  d When a simulated test-market is used instead of a standard test-market.
  e When an idea that could have been commercially successful is rejected during screening.

3 A financial assessment of a new product's viability is made at which of the following stages of the process of innovation?
  a Idea screening.
  b Concept development and testing.
  c Business analysis.
  d Product development and testing.
  e Test-marketing.

4 To which of the following categories of new product adopters are opinion leaders likely to belong?
   a Innovators.
   b Early adopters.
   c Early majority.
   d Late majority.
   e Laggards.

5 Which of the following sequences is the normal pattern for the adoption of new products?
   a Awareness, interest, desire, action.
   b Awareness, evaluation, desire, adoption.
   c Knowledge, evaluation, desire, adoption.
   d Awareness, interest, evaluation, desire, action.
   e Awareness, knowledge, evaluation, trial, adoption.

Which of the following are true and which are false?
   6 A new product that copies a concept that has already been developed and launched by a competitor is known as a 'mimic' product.
   7 The process of innovation always starts with a brainstorming session.
   8 Prototypes are made at the idea screening stage of the process of innovation.
   9 A product-use test is often used as an alternative to test-marketing in industrial markets.
   10 Laggards will never adopt a new product.

Discuss the following
   11 What are the advantages and disadvantages of launching a product line extension rather than a genuine innovation?
   12 Which are more acceptable – drop-errors or go-errors?
   13 What criteria would you use to decide whether to use a roll-out strategy or a global launch for a new product?
   14 Is there any point promoting to laggards?
   15 Is it necessary to pass through all seven stages of the process of innovation if you are thinking of launching a me-too product?

Further study
. . . .

A comprehensive core textbook on this subject is:

Trott, P. (1998) *Innovation Management and New Product Development*, Pitman.

But the subject of innovation is covered in a wide range of literature, beyond simply marketing texts. A good starting point for further reading is:

Gladwell, M. (2002) *The Tipping Point: How Little Things Can Make a Big Difference*, Back Bay Books.
A very readable book about how new ideas and social change comes about in contemporary society.

Henry, Jane and Walker, David (eds) (1991) *Managing Innovation*, Sage.
This looks at a wide range of issues related to new product development and provides a number of cases to illustrate the points made.

Rogers, E.M. (1995) *Diffusion of Innovations*, 4th edn, Free Press.
A seminal text in the literature of innovation.

There are also a number of key articles, some of which are now thought to be classics:

Alford, C.L. and Mason, J.B. (1975) 'Generating new product ideas', *Journal of Advertising Research*, December, pp.27–32.
Drucker, P. (1985) 'The discipline of innovation', *Harvard Business Review*, May–June, pp.67–72.
Moore, W.L. (1982) 'Concept testing', *Journal of Business Research*, 10, pp. 279–94.
Star, S.H. and Urban, G.L. (1988) 'The case of the test-market toss-up', *Harvard Business Review*, September–October, pp.10–27.

References

A.C. Neilsen (2000) 'New product launches: nine out of 10 set to fail', Press Release, 23 May, Oxford.
Business Week Online (2000) '3M glued to the Web', 20 November.
Buzzell, R.D. and Gale, B.T. (1987) *The PIMS Principles: Linking Strategy to Performance*, Free Press.
Clipson, C. (1991) 'Innovation by design', in J. Henry and D. Walker (eds), *Managing Innovation*, Sage, pp.96–105.
Doyle, P. (2001) *Marketing Management and Strategy*, 3rd edn, FT Prentice Hall.
Drucker, P. (2001) *The Essential Drucker*, HarperBusiness.
du Gay, P., Hall, S., Janes, L., Mackay, H. and Negus, K. (1996) *Doing Cultural Studies: The Story of the Sony Walkman*, Sage.
Economist (2001) 'A right old brewhaha in Japan', *The Economist*, 24 February, p.105.
Economist (2002) 'Sonic sinker', *The Economist*, 21 November, pp.72–3.
Euromonitor (2002) *Breakfast Cereals in the UK*, Report, July.
Gray, R. (2001) 'Taking the honours for 2001's launches', *Marketing*, 20 December, p.25.
Griffin, A. (1997) 'PDMA research on new product development practices: updating trends and benchmarking best practices', *Journal of Product Innovation Management*, 14, pp.429–58.
Kleinman, M. (2001) ' "Self-heating" Nescafé in £10m drive', *Marketing*, 5 October, p.5.
Marsh, H. (2001) 'Breakfast giants feed change', *Marketing*, 28 June, p.21.
Mason, T. (2002) 'Nescafe discards self-heating cans', *Marketing*, 15 August, p.1.
Mitchell, A. (1995) 'Fresh approach', *Marketing Business*, April, pp.6–8.
Pringle, H. (2002) 'The old ones are the best', *The Guardian*, 21 October, p.22.
Ray, A. (2001) 'What are you like? Early adopters', *Media Guardian*, 15 January.
Rogers, E.M. (1995) *Diffusion of Innovations*, 4th edn, Free Press.

CHAPTER **9**

Price

Objectives

When you have read this chapter you will be able to:

➤ Identify the four main types of objective that organisations address through pricing goods and services.

➤ Recommend an appropriate pricing strategy and tactics to maximise performance in a variety of situations.

➤ Justify pricing decisions on the basis of external and internal factors, including simple financial analysis covering cost-plus pricing, marginal-cost pricing and target return-on-investment pricing.

➤ Calculate the price elasticity of demand for a given product or service and understand how this knowledge is used in pricing decisions.

➤ Appreciate the organisational and ethical context surrounding price as part of the marketing mix.

Foundation focus: the 20-second takeaway

Price can make the difference between success and failure in marketing. Getting it right is the key to profitability. Getting it wrong can mean not making enough profit to survive, or being ignored by the market. Price tactics can affect how much money you make, or how many units you sell in the long term, how large a share of the available market you can take from competitors, and even your social mission as an organisation. Costs, competitors and corporate culture are important influences on the basic price-setting process. However, the relationship between price and cost is not a simple one. Knowing how price changes can affect the volume of your product or service's sales over time is extremely valuable in trying to anticipate the effects of pricing decisions, as is familiarity with the factors which sensitise customers to price in their purchasing behaviour.

Introduction

Price is one of the most important and far-reaching of the variables that marketing managers control. Pricing decisions affect profit, volume, share of market and social stance. In turn, pricing policy takes account of internal and external factors. Internal factors include costs and business objectives. However, the key to pricing success is the attractiveness of price to the consumer. External factors such as competition and customer expectation are paramount. Just as pricing carries image connotations for brands, so companies are increasingly being judged on the transparency and equity with which they treat price as a marketing variable.

Oscar Wilde wrote that a cynic is 'a man who knows the price of everything and the value of nothing'. But the concepts of price and value are hard to separate. As consumers, price is what we are prepared to pay in exchange for goods and

235

services. How much we are prepared to pay depends on how much we value what is on offer. At some times the purchase in question may be worth a great deal more than at others. A rose as a romantic gesture on Valentine's Day, strawberries on the lawn at Wimbledon, last-minute Christmas shopping – these are all things for which people are prepared to pay over the odds. Manufacturers propose prices to consumers, but at the end of the day what the consumer values is what counts. We can therefore define price as the expression, usually financial, of the value placed on a marketing exchange by the buyer. As well as money it can involve time, energy, attention, emotion and inconvenience.

Price in the marketing mix

Price is the only marketing mix element that generates income. The other variables – making the product, telling customers about it, and making it available to them – all generate costs. So getting the price right is a decision of fundamental importance. This is true even in markets such as luxury goods where, at first sight, price might not seem to be as important as outright quality. Boxed confectionery or scent, for example, are surprisingly sensitive to price. This is because of competition, often involving discount retailers operating in spite of manufacturers' concerns about the up-market image of their products. Luxury goods customers, usually buying the product as a gift, will insist on quality. But in choosing between alternative possibilities, even small variations in price can make a lot of difference.

In response to this, much recent marketing thought has emphasised the connection between price and quality in order to defend the idea of profitable business. 'Adding value' allows a manufacturer to widen the margin of available profit by offering the consumer more benefits. The justification for a higher price can come from any or all of the marketing mix variables:

▶ *Product* – offering extra features, individual specification or innovatory design.
▶ *Promotion* – increasing the prestige and reputation of the goods or services in question through regular advertising and promotion.
▶ *Price* – providing credit terms that spread payment but justify a higher eventual price.
▶ *Place* – guaranteeing a specific delivery date, or operating hours of business that allow the customer greater convenience.

CASE STUDY **9.1**

On a Roller

The super-luxury car category (i.e. hand-built and with a price tag of £150,000-plus) is showing a remarkable burst of entrepreneurial optimism. Not only has BMW launched its eagerly-awaited RR01, the first new model since its acquisition of Rolls Royce, but car makers around the world are unveiling plans for new and impressively expensive dream cars aimed at the more-than-comfortably off. The RR01 itself can be yours for £208,000 upwards – depending on what extras you regard as indispensable.

Standard on all models come refinements such as umbrella holders on the rear doors, heated side windows, and Rolls Royce logos on the hubcaps which rotate after the car has stopped to ensure that they finally come to rest upright. Ferrari's new model, the Enzo, sold out its initial production run (even though it was increased by 15 per cent) before its public launch. With a price tag of £434,000 and a top speed of 200 mph, the new Ferrari is named after the firm's founder. Bentley (now owned by Volkswagen), Daimler-Chrysler and Ford (through Aston Martin) are just three other major manufacturers currently lining up mouthwatering vehicles for the world's seriously rich drivers.

Super-luxury car sales averaged 7,000 a year in the late 1990s (that's barely one-hundredth of 1 per cent of total global car sales). The new wave of growth is targeting sales of nearer 17,000 per year towards the end of the first decade of the twenty-first century. Why are the car makers so optimistic? One reason is that they believe that sales in the past have been depressed through too little choice. Bernd Pischetsrieder, the new chairman of VW, feels that cars in this bracket are not about getting from A to B, but more akin to jewellery, powerboats or racehorses. He sees the recipe for success in sales is to tempt wealthy collectors with more and more sumptuous models.

The super-luxury car makers have in the past deliberately limited availability of their products in order to boost demand. Ferrari has traditionally aimed at sales of less than 4,000 models a year, in spite of waiting lists of customers in some countries of up to two years. In fact in some markets recent second-hand models have been changing hands at prices well above their official price tag – suggesting a good deal more unsatisfied demand than had previously been envisaged. With profit margins on super-luxury cars nearly ten times what they are on standard models, hard-pressed manufacturers may feel they can no longer afford to be coy with customers. But with sales of mansions, private jets and diamonds subdued by stockmarket uncertainties, might they be better off continuing to keep the brakes on?

Questions

1   What environmental factors might car manufacturers planning a super-luxury model take into account when deciding on timing?
2   Super-luxury cars have been the sole preserve of a small group of exclusive manufacturers. What advantages might entering this market offer more main-stream car makers?
3   The case study presents an example of manufacturers limiting supply in order to stimulate demand. (a) How viable is this in the long term? and (b) can you provide examples of it working in industries other than super-cars to support high prices?

Sources: Economist (2003); Griffiths (2003).

Just as each of the marketing mix variables can justify a higher price, so the price of a product will give the customer an impression of what to expect. In some markets, like champagne or theatre tickets, the lowest-priced choices are not always the fastest to sell because customers do not see them as having enough quality to make them good value. As we have seen, a sustained level of advertising may create a brand image that helps justify a higher price.

Conversely, charging a higher price can help fund this kind of regular promotional activity. On the distribution front, it may be that low prices can justify high levels of inconvenience – such as those endured by bargain-hunters in the traditional scrum of the January sales.

Price is the easiest marketing mix variable to change in the short term. But it should not be seen as a tactical variable which can be altered without affecting the strategic balance of the rest of the mix. It has its tactical uses, as we shall see. But its profound importance to the success of any marketing plan forces us to recognise price as a strategic issue rather than a tactical detail. There are a large number of factors to take into account in making and reviewing pricing decisions. Decisions on pricing should not be taken lightly or with an exclusively short-term focus. Pricing mistakes can lead to disaster in a spectacular way. Towards the end of this chapter we will look at some of the research and calculations that can help minimise the risk of taking bad pricing decisions.

Pricing objectives

There are four main types of objective that pricing decisions can help achieve. These are:

1   *Income related*: how much money can we make?
2   *Volume related*: how many units can we sell?
3   *Competition related*: what share of the available business do we want?
4   *Societal*: what are our responsibilities to our customers and society as a whole?

We will discuss these different kinds of objective and their accompanying strategies before moving on to illustrate relevant tactical support in each case. The techniques described are not necessarily exclusive to one objective. For example, selective discounting might be aimed at maximising income from a number of market segments, or at maximising volume through bringing in new business. Like any other aspect of marketing, pricing ought to combine creativity with flexibility.

Income-related objectives

Organisations need to make money to survive. Adjusting price is an obvious way of increasing the flow of money coming into an organisation.

The capacity to make more money in this way depends on the resilience of consumer demand to an increase in price. In other words, how many customers will go elsewhere or stop buying altogether if the price increases beyond a certain point? This question is what economists call price-elasticity of demand and later in the chapter we will be looking at how it is calculated.

It may be that an organisation can afford to lose some customers and still make more money so long as the remaining customers are paying enough. This process is often called moving 'up-market'. Decisions to move up-market to a more expensive positioning can mean fewer customers overall, but higher income. In other words, the company chooses to target market segments that are modest in size but have high spending power.

Another reason for focusing on income rather than volume is when a company is first into the market with an innovation and wants to recoup its research and development investment while it still has the field to itself. Here the decision to maximise income from price is the beginning of a race against time before competitors enter the market. We have seen this process at work in the product life-cycle, which is covered in Chapter 7.

A third reason to concentrate on the amount of money that can be made in the short term comes when a company is threatened by takeover. In order to convince shareholders of the financial health of the organisation, managers can take advantage of a number of measures to bolster profit figures. One of them is to impose price increases which may then be reconsidered once the shadow of takeover has receded.

DID YOU KNOW?

Marketers are pricing-shy. The late UK marketing guru Peter Doyle claimed that marketers are obsessed with advertising and promotion to the detriment of pricing. He pointed out that a 5 per cent improvement in price is worth more than a 5 per cent increase in market share (Doyle, 2002).

Volume-related objectives

Particularly in manufacturing industries, production capacity needs to be fully utilised or machines stand idle and employment opportunities decline. There is thus a good reason for seeing the overall health of an enterprise reflected first and foremost in the volume of sales it generates.

Price obviously has a role to play in determining the quantity of goods sold. The laws of supply and demand hold that the cheaper something is, the more of it will be bought. This holds true up to a point. There is, for example, a limit to the number of shoes even the most helpless fashion victim can find a use for. This is what the economists call 'utility'. But most things we buy, we would buy more of if the price came down.

CASE STUDY 9.2

Mobile groan

First-generation mobile phone networks provided simple analogue voice telephony. The second generation added some data services like fax and email, and more recent refinements have brought the capacity to send and receive larger files such as photographs via the mobile phone. The third generation (3G) of mobile telecommunications holds out the promise of data rates of up to 2 megabits per second, in addition to conventional voice, fax and data services. This should enable high-resolution video and multimedia services on the move, such as mobile office services, virtual banking and online billing, home shopping, video conferencing, online entertainment and Internet access.

Spurred by the prospect of such a potentially lucrative opportunity, mobile phone networks shelled out unprecedented amounts of money to national governments at the start of the twenty-first century for exclusive licences to allow them to operate 3G services. Meanwhile, hardware manufacturers bet their futures on developing handsets to cope with it. In all, something in the region of £71 billion was gambled on this new opportunity by 120 networks in 27 countries. Vodaphone spent £6 billion in the UK alone. But frustratingly, the technology has been slow developing. Third-generation mobile phones are struggling to deliver services that are as reliable or robust as their second-generation predecessors – so the revolution looks as if it is on hold for the moment.

In spite of this faltering start, Hutchinson, a relatively new entrant to the market, has faced up to the challenge of how to set prices for this remarkably expensive technology. It conducted extensive market research with over 150 focus groups over 18 months and found that by far the most popular option was an 'all you can eat' fixed monthly fee of between £59.99 to £99.99 for a 12-month contract. The packages are priced to reflect the different numbers of voice and video calls included in the deal. Each carries a bundle of voice call minutes, video call minutes, text, picture and video messages, email and multimedia content and services, but will exclude international calls, those made while abroad and premium rate calls. Services available include digital mapping and satellite location-based services and exclusive video clips of Premiership football highlights. Handsets cost between £400 and £600, with a fixed number of early purchasers being offered a discount.

Like most communication innovations, the phones are aimed at the business user, although the football clips suggest a degree of consumer appeal as well. However, considering that only 6 per cent of non-corporate mobile phone users in the UK spend over £50 per month on mobile calls, the all-important adoption of this product by consumers may be a long time coming.

Hutchinson's entry into the market comes against a background of allegations of over-pricing by the major mobile network operators for second-generation services. According to *Which?* magazine, published by the Consumers' Association, UK consumers are habitually paying more than £100 per year more than they have to because of the pricing policies of the big four networks: Vodaphone, O2 (previously BT CellNet), Orange and T-mobile. Cheaper entrants to the market, such as Virgin Mobile, are finding it hard to make an impact because of the entrenched position of the major operators, combined with the complexity of what is on offer to the UK's 43 million mobile phone users. There are currently over 250 different tariffs from which they can choose.

The problem is, of course, that there is no simple way of comparing like with like in this market as with many services. Pay-as-you-go phones offer the flexibility of not having a contract, but are expensive on a minute-by-minute basis. For example, Vodaphone peak pre-pay rates are 40p per minute, compared to their contract rates of nearer 10p per minute. On the other hand, sign a contract with a network and you find that you are locked in for 12 months, with swingeing charges for early cancellation.

Questions

1   Pricing a service (like equipment rental or call charges) is different from pricing a product. How do mobile phone tariffs demonstrate this? How might the large networks defend their pricing policies against *Which?* magazine's criticisms?

2   Hutchinson's 3G service is aimed at heavy business users. Give an example of two other markets that can be segmented usefully by people's willingness to

pay. What bases of segmentation would be relevant in such an exercise? (See Chapter 6 for a reminder about bases for segmentation.)

3 How useful is market research in helping to decide the appropriate level of tariffs for new mobile phone services?

Sources: Budden (2002); Harper (2002); Personal Computer World (2003).

Competition-based objectives

We have touched on the question of share of market when discussing the effect of price on volume. Obviously in a competitive market like confectionery that has been in existence for a long period of time (what is called a mature market) the overall growth in volume is likely to be slow. Organisations need either to create new customers or to steal customers from their competitors. Price can be a very useful tool in this war of attrition where success or failure is judged in terms of a few percentage points of market share, year on year.

Societal objectives

Competition between firms battling for market share has the effect of driving prices down. But in some markets competition is limited by the sheer size of the enterprises concerned. This can be seen to be against the public interest. Statutory controls are brought to bear to prevent such situations from developing, such as Anti-Trust Law in America or the activities of the Competition Commission in the UK. Certain industries, such as broadcasting, transport and public utilities, are subject to watchdog bodies with advisory or regulatory powers affecting pricing policies.

This kind of pricing control stems from the widely-held conviction that for certain essential services prices must be kept at a sufficiently low level to keep them within reach of all members of society. A similar kind of thinking applies to the pricing strategies of many non-profit organisations (particularly those in receipt of public funding). Such pricing decisions are a way of being seen to be accessible to a wide range of publics. But insofar as all organisations are subject to legislation, and particularly taxation, all organisations have an obligation to price in a way that is socially responsible. Potentially dangerous products, such as cigarettes and alcohol, attract high levels of duty which earn income for the public exchequer. This duty also helps to restrict their consumption to manageable levels by increasing their prices.

DID YOU KNOW?

Mobile phones are likely to be 'the next big thing' in paying for goods and services, especially on the Internet. They offer secure authorisation, everyone's got one and they are networked. It's like having a talking switch card. In a number of European Union countries 'Pay Box', part owned by Deutsche Bank, offers mobile users the facility to pay for things direct from their bank accounts using a pin number. At the same time, the telephone networks themselves are likely to start competing with credit card companies as customers get used to paying for items on their monthly telephone bill (Economist, 2002).

Putting pricing into practice
·······································

Tactics that focus on income

Skimming

Price skimming takes its name from the image of 'skimming the cream' from a market. In other words, it aims high, at a limited number of customers whose need for the product is great enough to justify a high price. It is a common approach on the part of high-tech and pharmaceutical companies which are keen to capitalise on an innovatory product which may have cost many millions of pounds to develop. By going for a small market segment which is willing to pay over the odds, the innovating company improves its chances of recouping its investment in research and development before competitors have an opportunity to enter the new market with their own offerings, or before patents expire. Mobile telephones, new drugs (such as Viagra) and digital pets are all examples of products whose early availability was characterised by skimming prices. The product life-cycle model explained in Chapter 7 is helpful in understanding this approach to pricing. It can only work for new products in their launch and early growth stages.

Differential pricing

Segmenting the market by ability (or willingness) to pay can maximise revenues by charging different groups different prices. A grocery manufacturer may segment its retailing customers by size and buying power and establish a pricing structure that offers the best terms to the largest customer. This can cause understandable aggravation for smaller retailers, but manufacturers defend the practice by arguing that the corner shop is competing on convenience rather than price.

Differential pricing is also common in service industries. Here the intangible nature of the offering means that income must be maximised at every opportunity (see Chapter 2 for more on service marketing). For example, airline seats cannot be stored – they are either occupied on a particular flight or they remain unsold for ever. As a result of this, travel operators aim pricing strategies at customer segments on the basis of when they are prepared to travel and when they are prepared to commit their money. Advance booking is encouraged by offering lower prices, as is travel at unpopular times. This policy can lead to disaffection among customers. It may be, for example, that two airline passengers in adjoining seats have paid radically different prices for no other reason than the times at which they made their bookings.

Bait pricing

This is a term given to a tactic that offers customers goods at a low price in order to attract them in the hope that they will buy other things. In the case of the supermarket loss leader, the low-priced goods may be offered at less than they cost the retailer. The loss is written off as a promotional expenditure. This can cause conflict between manufacturers and retailers (an example of vertical channel conflict is discussed in Chapter 10). Manufacturers oppose the practice on the grounds that such discounting devalues their brands. An additional reason for their opposition is their understandable reluctance to be pressured by other retailers into offering similar terms.

In some markets where personal selling is important (such as consumer durables like washing machines or cars) bait pricing can be used as a promotional device to lure customers into a showroom. This is often the case when an electrical retailer launches a new branch. Newspaper advertising announces that a product like a DVD player is available at a crazy discount to 'the first five customers'. Having attracted bargain-hunters inside the shop, the sales staff can offer alternatives at a higher price – a tactic sometimes known as 'bait and switch'. It is also possible to suggest complementary products and warranties in order to enhance the profitability of the basic offer.

Bait pricing raises a number of ethical questions. Used insensitively such tactics run the risk of becoming counter-productive, but the excitement and consumer interest special offers can create is considerable.

Auction

One of the oldest forms of pricing leaves it to customers, bidding against one another, to decide how much they will pay for something. This guarantees that the seller will achieve the maximum price available at a particular time in a particular market – making it a popular choice in markets, such as fine art, where price is a matter of fashion and opinion. The technique has always been popular in business-to-business marketing, where organisations tender for contracts by offering prices in competition with each other, either openly or by sealed bids (where nobody knows what anyone else is offering). Auction has received a new lease of life in consumer marketing largely due to Internet companies such as eBay.com.

Premium pricing

This aims at using price to maximise the image of quality in a product or service, often by positioning it at the top end of a range of goods or services at different price points. The relationship between price and quality can then be justified in the eyes of the customer by reference to the differences between each level when they can be displayed or demonstrated together.

This comparison can be used to legitimise a high price for the top range. But it can also make a middle-range offer look more attractive than it otherwise might by flattering it in comparison to a more expensive alternative. This kind of thinking affects how products are displayed in retail outlets or in catalogues. Here the relationship between items on offer is all important in guiding the consumer to make an appropriate purchase decision.

CASE STUDY **9.3**

What's it worth?

One of the marketing industry's favourite buzzwords is 'premium'. Premium products carry an exclusive image, accompanied by suitably elevated prices and attractive profit margins. But recent research casts doubt on consumers' continuing faith in the premium tag. 70 per cent of respondents agreed with the statement that the premium tag was 'an excuse to charge extra for products that don't always have extra benefits', and one in five dismissed it as a way of inflating prices.

Nevertheless, the research revealed what marketers have long suspected – that shoppers are keen on buying the best, although sceptical about paying over the odds for it. Moreover, premium positioning makes more sense in some types of market than others. Cars, alcoholic drink, clothes, grooming products are all examples of things for which customers will pay a higher price for a quality image. Premium price margins can range from as much as 300 per cent on grooming products to more than 500 per cent on consumer products such as hi-fis. On the other hand, image is less important in less visible purchases. As a result, marketers striving to create a premium image (and price) for services such as banking or insurance are probably wasting their time.

The research found that consumers pick up cues from packaging and product design when deciding on the quality of an item. This seems to be particularly the case for food, toiletries and electronics items. And the extra they are prepared to pay for a 'premium' experience is often out of proportion to the extra satisfaction they derive. This is good news for marketers keen to make profits. For example, wine buffs reported that they regularly paid 200 per cent more than the price of ordinary wine for drinks which they enjoyed only 20 per cent better. That 20 per cent extra satisfaction was still worth the extra money.

Another theme that emerged from the research was that customers value what they see as the genuine article. So, handmade or traditional products which have an 'authentic' image are seen to be worth paying more for, as are things used over a long period of time, such as a much-loved briefcase.

Questions

1 From your own experience as a consumer list at least one premium and one standard product in each of the following areas. How much more would you expect to have to pay for the premium offering in each case?

  ► Shoes.
  ► Ground coffee.
  ► Wrist watch.
  ► Hotel accommodation.
  ► Ready-made sandwich.

  Thinking in terms of the product life-cycle (PLC, described in Chapter 7), what parallels can you draw between what you expect to pay for any of these products or services and their position in the PLC?
2 What kinds of influence are active in pricing products which you can be seen consuming as opposed to less visible ones?
3 Are there any products or services (besides the financial services mentioned in the case study) where premium pricing would be completely inappropriate? Justify your answer.

Source: Matthews (2002).

Tactics that focus on volume

Penetration pricing

As its name implies, this pricing policy aims at penetrating the market as extensively as possible with the aim of recruiting the maximum number of customers. It is the opposite of skimming. Instead of going for a limited but highly profitable sector of the market, penetration pricing sacrifices immediate profit for the long-term security of buying a large market share.

It will be clear that penetration as an option is limited to those organisations that have the resources to make it work. Unless the company has a large enough production capacity to cope with the demand it expects to create, and can pass on the benefits of its economies of scale (i.e. its ability to use mass production to reduce its costs) in the form of low prices, penetration is unlikely to succeed. Furthermore, only companies that are large enough to be able to plan in the long term will be able to wait for the returns penetration brings.

The choice of this option also depends on market conditions. If a market is already mature – that is to say its expansion has slowed down – there may be little point in buying market share. So while a penetration policy might yield dividends in a market like health drinks (which is seen to be growing), it would be less successful for a new entrant in a market like desktop personal computers (where the market has reached saturation point). Davidson (1997) advises that the best thing to do in a market with falling prices is to get out quick.

Discounting

We have seen how differential pricing can maximise total income. Such a policy can work to protect and consolidate existing business. This is a very high priority in a competitive environment. But for firms wishing to recruit new customers and maximise volume, short-term discounts are a very important sales-generating tactic.

This is not only true of the kind of offer we might see on a supermarket shelf, tempting us to try a new product at a special price. It is also very popular in business-to-business marketing, for example in the field of television advertising sales. In order to attract new advertisers to the medium, television sales executives have an armoury of special rates. The effect of this kind of dealing, however, is often to alienate existing advertisers. They object that their television advertising expenditure, at full rates, ought not to be used to subsidise the activities of new users of the medium (some of whom may even be their direct competitors). As we have seen with other kinds of pricing strategy, discounting needs to be carefully weighed up for its potential ethical fall-out.

CASE STUDY **9.4** **Cruachan – the off-peak peak**

A power station inside a Scottish hill would not exist if it wasn't for off-peak discounts on electricity. Off-peak electricity is available at bargain rates during the night when demand for power is low. Cruachan (which means 'the hollow mountain') was opened in 1965 at a cost of £24 million specifically to take advantage of this.

At night, turbines powered by off-peak electricity pump water from Loch Awe at the base of the hill up tunnels hollowed out inside it to an artificial reservoir over 400 metres above. During the day, the turbines become generators driven by the water flowing back down through them to the Loch. In spite of an energy efficiency loss of between 10 and 15 per cent, this produces electricity that can be sold at peak rates, and is useful in meeting sudden surges of demand during the day.

Because of the way the respective prices of electricity and large-scale engineering projects have moved since the 1960s, building Cruachan would not be a viable proposition today. It remains, however, an ingenious feat of civil engineering that exploits a discount pricing opportunity. It also has a secondary function as a visitor attraction, complete with guided tours and an information centre visited by over 47,000 people in 2001.

Questions

1   To what extent can domestic consumers be encouraged to take advantage of off-peak electricity?
2   What alternatives are there to differential pricing (such as off-peak discounts) to spread demand for services such as electricity?
3   What changes in electricity pricing might threaten Cruachan's future viability?

Source: Company information.

Price bundling and multiple-unit pricing

As shoppers we are familiar with the idea of the multipack, whereby we buy items like confectionery, soft drinks, batteries or stationery in packets of more than one. Usually there is a bargain element in the pricing – bought separately the items would cost more. We are being offered a volume discount in miniature. For the manufacturer the advantage is in the increased volume sold. For the retailer the advantage is in increasing the value of individual transactions and simplifying merchandising and display procedures.

In a multipack each item is identical in value. But another form of multiple-unit pricing combines a number of different products or services into one offered at a particular price. This practice, which is very common in services marketing, is known as price bundling. Common examples include a package holiday, or a visit to the theatre which also includes a meal, interval drink and programme. Again the incentive for the customer is an overall bargain (as well as simplicity and convenience). The advantage for the service provider is the volume of business generated. Bought separately the various elements of a holiday or theatre visit would generate more revenue. But it is unlikely that the individual consumer could be relied upon to buy each one, so the overall effect is to increase volume.

The practice is also used in business-to-business marketing, where it can yield further benefits for the seller. In the international television programme market, for example, programming is sold by producers to broadcasters in negotiated packages. The price depends on stations being prepared to buy not only what they actively want, but to include in their purchases programmes which they might not otherwise have considered. Often this may be of questionable quality (as viewers of late night television can verify!).

DID YOU KNOW?

In spite of manufacturers' protests, retailers frequently split multipacks of crisps or soft drinks and offer the individual items at full price. As a response to this, individual multipack units usually carry a stern warning 'not to be sold separately' on their packaging to alert consumers. Furthermore, manufacturers weightmark the multipack wrapper rather than the individual units inside. This means that the retailer may be contravening labelling legislation by offering for sale products that should carry a weight statement at point of sale.

Clearance pricing

The ultimate gesture towards volume rather than profit is the clearance price. 'Everything must go' read the signs in the window of the shop about to close down. After all, it costs money to store goods – not only in overheads such as power and wages, but also in the cost of having their value tied up in stock rather than circulating in the organisation's cash flow. How much it costs to store goods depends on a number of factors (as discussed in Chapter 10 on physical distribution). Most estimates put the average cost of storage at about a quarter of the stock's sales value per year, which explains why businesses are keen on fast-selling lines. When stock becomes a liability, the idea of profit pales into insignificance beside the need to liquidate assets.

Clearance pricing is not just something that affects beleaguered chain stores in the high street. It also happens in international trade. Clearing stocks on an international level leads to the controversial practice of dumping. This involves selling goods at a price far below their normal domestic selling price in a foreign market. It has the advantage of getting rid of excess stock for the manufacturer with minimal impact on core business at home. Dumping is very unpopular with companies in the market where it takes place because of its destabilising effect. However, the practice of dumping can come home to roost when enterprising importers buy up large quantities of the dumped product in the export market and re-import them to sell in direct price competition with the domestic manufacturer.

Price promotion

Using price as the basis of promotional activity is a popular tactic within the overall strategy of going for volume. Certainly a reduced price offer (RPO) can bring business forward, even if its long-term effect is not to produce any net gains in volume. But RPOs do lead to the following identifiable advantages:

▶ They increase positive cash flow for the manufacturer.
▶ They create incentive for display by the retailer.
▶ They provide an opportunity to make the pack stand out: '5p OFF'.
▶ They flood distribution channels to crowd out rival products.
▶ They keep the brand fresh in the mind of fickle customers.
▶ They encourage new customers at least to sample the product, thus rendering it more likely that they will return in future as occasional, if not regular, users.

DID YOU KNOW?
Research conducted in 2001 by Professor Andrew Ehrenberg of South Bank University found that reduced-price offers on fast-moving consumer goods do not lead to increased sales once the incentive is withdrawn. His report, The Case Against Price-related Promotions, *also found that price promotions are mainly taken up by former customers of the brand. In spite of this, cut-price offers are one of the most popular marketing tactics used to drive sales (Gray, 2002).*

Tactics that focus on competition

Parity pricing

Parity pricing is the practice of setting prices which match what competitors are charging. The effect of this approach to pricing is to allow manufacturers to concentrate on non-price factors in their competitive activities. But it can quickly lead to collusion. In some markets, because of the limited range of alternatives available to consumers, a few manufacturers can get together and inflate prices to their mutual advantage. This does, however, present opportunities for innovative companies to make an impact by breaking ranks from the pack. A spectacular recent example has been the success of low-cost carriers, which have revolutionised the previously cosy and expensive air travel industry.

Undercutting

Porter (1980) sees 'cost leadership' as one of the prime strategic options open to successful companies. This involves reducing internal costs (often by massive investment in automation) in order to pass the savings on in the shape of permanently lower prices. An ability to undercut the opposition leads to a growth in market share for the cost leader. By the time the competition catches up (if it survives to do so) it may be too late. The wholesale rout of British motorcycle manufacturers by Japanese competition in the 1960s was an early example of how cheaper production practices leading to lower prices can successfully undercut an apparently impregnable industry.

Price leading

Prices in a number of markets are dominated by the decisions of a few well-established companies that have the weight and market share to set prices confident that their competitors will follow suit. Such confidence can come from the following sources of power:

- ▶ Control over distribution and availability (e.g. through owning their own network of outlets, as do many brewing companies).
- ▶ Dominant market share (often because of superior or improved quality, for which customers will pay).
- ▶ Strategic information systems (involving the collection and interpretation of sales/price/cost data which gives the organisation an advantage over its less well-informed rivals in forecasting and planning).
- ▶ A global perspective (taking the long view on how markets are developing, not only nationally but internationally, can lead to more accurate decisions).

Companies like this are known as price leaders. Smaller firms in the same market, or firms without the kinds of strategic advantage listed above, find themselves adjusting their prices in reaction to the leaders. They are known as price followers as a result.

Spoiling

Much competitive activity is aimed at frustrating, on a tactical basis, the plans of rival organisations. Pricing tactics are important here because of the speed with which they can be implemented, and their direct appeal to consumers. For example, if a competitor is conducting a test-market exercise with a new product in a particular area (as discussed in Chapter 8), the first a company may hear of it is from its salesforce. Or perhaps the news may come from the company's advertising agency, which has picked up increased media activity on the part of the rival as part of its media tracking. Speed of reaction is therefore essential. A surefire way to distort the results of such test-marketing is to lower prices –

perhaps by means of a special promotion limited to the area or to a specific group of retailers. The objective of such promotion would be to prevent the new product from gaining a foothold.

Survival pricing strategy

Because of the effects of competition, some organisations go to the wall, or face inevitable takeover. Pricing decisions can help them forestall closure for as long as possible, or survive as going concerns and offer a more attractive proposition to prospective purchasers. Pricing in these circumstances is aimed neither at income nor at volume so much as at mere organisational survival. It may be that a family firm, for example, is determined to see it out until the retirement of the owners. In this case, the long-term health of the company is irrelevant – what matters is the next three or four years. Alternatively, larger companies can afford to take losses in some markets just to retain a presence. Their more profitable activities elsewhere will help them over the lean times until market conditions are more favourable.

DID YOU KNOW?

People in Britain pay the highest prices in Europe for everyday goods. The Pricerunner survey compared a shopping basket of everyday products in 13 different countries. The basket included a Mars bar, Coca-Cola, potatoes, tomatoes, milk, a McChicken sandwich, and bus and cinema tickets. It revealed that the UK is at the top of the EU price league. At the other end of the scale is Portugal, where the same selection of goods cost less than half what Britons pay (Eurofood, 2002).

Tactics that focus on societal considerations

Differential discounts

As we have seen, differential pricing can be used to maximise income by charging a range of prices to match different segments of the market. Similarly, prices can be lowered on a long-term basis by differential discounts to encourage access to a product or service by certain target groups. Thus arts organisations or transport companies who are in receipt of public funding will often structure their prices to include discounts for retired people, students and children of school age. This is commonly known as 'concessionary' pricing (a rather grudging phrase).

Non-financial pricing

Pricing strategy is just as important to non-profit organisations as it is to commercial ones. Many non-profits charge for their services. For example, UK voluntary organisations are becoming increasingly involved in providing services like day-care for frail elderly people on a local basis on a contractual footing with local authorities. This involves the negotiation of a fee from the local authority as well as making a small charge to users for lunch and materials used.

We can also analyse their pricing activities on a non-financial basis. Volunteers, for example, will be involved in an exchange process with the organisation. In return for their time and commitment, the organisation will offer opportunities for involvement and achievement. Because of the limited pool of volunteer labour available, organisations depending on volunteers need to compete with each other to offer the best value for this non-financial commitment. Flexibility such as offering morning or afternoon sessions rather than expecting a whole day, or providing transport and training, can increase an organisation's competitive success in this respect by making the non-financial price more attractive to the volunteer.

Barter

A development of non-financial pricing, barter involves the exchange of goods or services without recourse to financial currency. A simple example of such a system would be a baby-sitting circle, whereby parents exchange the duty of looking after each other's children in order to free them for other activities. On a more sophisticated level, local and regional networks exist where skills can be traded – car maintenance in exchange for gardening, for example. But some kind of objective agreement on the respective value of the services involved is necessary. The system is attractive to many participants because of the community-based nature of the activities, a human alternative to the impersonal transactions of big business.

On the other hand, big business itself is no stranger to non-financial transactions. Counter-trade, whereby physical goods are exchanged without money changing hands, has shown itself to be a popular form of international trade. It not only takes care of currency difficulties, but it can be a way of avoiding tax.

> **DID YOU KNOW?**
>
> *ABBA, Sweden's record-breaking 1970s pop phenomenon, used to get paid in potatoes. The group had many fans in the former Eastern bloc countries. But because of hard currency shortages they were paid in kind for their performances, with goods ranging from heavy machinery and oil to potatoes. In order to convert these barter goods into cash they set up a subsidiary trading company.*

Public sector pricing

Although the major determinant of commercial price-setting is not so much what something costs to manufacture as what the market is prepared to pay for it, pricing in the public sector is a matter of public accountability. Taxation is a price we all have to pay, and its rationale needs to be clear. Government policy insists on transparency on costs in relation to prices from organisations like the police and health services. Value for money for the taxpayer seems a simple enough objective. But as with all pricing issues, this raises a number of ethical problems. For example, if value for money is to be stressed in the health service, hard decisions need to be taken in the face of conflicting priorities, as well as judgements about what measures are appropriate in assessing value.

How much is enough? Factors in setting prices

Our survey of pricing strategies, and the related tactics, has shown that price is a complex and flexible variable. But whether the objectives served by pricing strategy are predominantly related to income, volume, competition or social responsibility, the factors impacting on price-setting are the same. They come from three Cs: costs, competitive environment and corporate culture.

Costs

How costs are made up

Manufacturing a product or providing a service involves costs. These fall into two sorts:

► *Indirect costs* (often known as *fixed costs*): the overheads like lighting or heating which remain the same, whether you produce one thing or hundreds. Indirect costs are so called because they are not directly related to the amount made. But the organisation's accountants will establish a way to divide them up between the various product lines being made by a company so that each carries its share.

► *Direct costs* (often known as *variable costs*): costs such as ingredients which vary with the amount made. Thus the more loaves of bread a baker produces, the greater the variable costs represented by flour.

The distinction is a very simple one. Just remember that fixed costs don't change, but that variable costs vary with the amount produced. So, while permanent salaried employees will be a fixed cost, temporary labour bought in to cope with a large order will be a variable cost.

Added together the two sorts of cost become the total cost of production. It is easier to understand with a diagram (see Figure 9.1).

Let's stay with loaves of bread. As we would expect, the total variable cost goes up as each loaf is manufactured. But the fixed cost remains the same however many loaves are made. The average cost of each loaf, therefore, goes down as more are made – confirming our instinct as consumers that things ought to be cheaper by the dozen. In fact, as you can see towards the extreme right of the graph, the variable cost rises steeply after a certain point in this example. There might be a number of explanations for this. Perhaps the variable labour to achieve this level of output has involved expensive overtime working. Extra machines may have been hired to cope with the demand. Possibly ingredients have had to be bought short term. It is not always true to say that the more you make the cheaper each unit is.

Break-even analysis

In order to cover the costs, enough loaves need to be sold at a sufficient price. Calculating this requirement is known as a 'break-even analysis' and is a fundamental part of our understanding of the relationship between cost and

figure 9.1
Fixed and variable costs

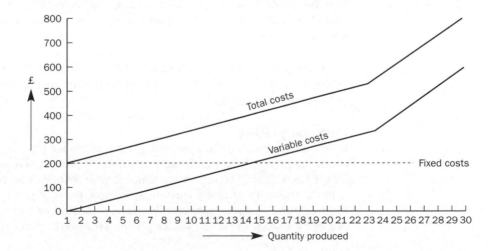

price. It is particularly useful when weighing up a business proposition. If we price our bread at 70p a loaf, how many do we need to sell to break even? If that price looks unrealistic, how many more units would we need to sell at 60p to make the same amount of money?

The answer can be expressed by an equation:

$$\text{Break-even point} = \frac{\text{Fixed costs}}{\text{Price per unit} - \text{Variable costs per unit}}$$

Returning to our graph of fixed, variable and total costs, we can draw another line (Figure 9.2). This represents the cumulative sales value of a quantity of loaves at a chosen price point. Where this line meets the total cost curve is called the break-even point. All income beyond this point is profit. The graph shows the revenue for a single price P1, but a number of alternative scenarios can be plotted to determine the optimum price.

KEY SKILLS
ACTIVITY **9.1**
· · · · · · · · · · · · · ·

Application of number

Break-even analysis

Break-even analysis is one of the most important techniques available to help with pricing decisions. The basic calculation is quite simple. The real complexity comes with trying to establish costs before production has happened. For this exercise, however, we have simplified this part of the process by giving you the fixed and variable costs in advance.

You run a small factory making and selling budget CDs (so you need not worry about margins to retailers in this example). Calculate the volumes necessary to break even at the following price points given the information in this example:

1   £4.50.
2   £5.50.
3   £6.95.

Your fixed costs (office overheads, recording and studio fees) are £28,000.
Your variable costs (manufacturing per CD, royalties and copyright) are £3.25 per CD.

It all seems so simple. It *is* simple. But this beautifully simple idea is not as useful as it might seem when it comes to pricing in the real world. Costs are only part of the picture.

Cost-plus pricing

If we know our costs, the argument goes, then all we have to do is to pass them on in the price, plus a percentage for profit. This is known as cost-plus pricing, and it has a kind of transparency about it which appeals to our common sense. It lies at the heart of many consumers' expectations of price, particularly in the kind of public sector examples we have discussed earlier. Certainly unless a company were using a loss-leader pricing strategy in order to generate volume

figure 9.2
Break-even analysis

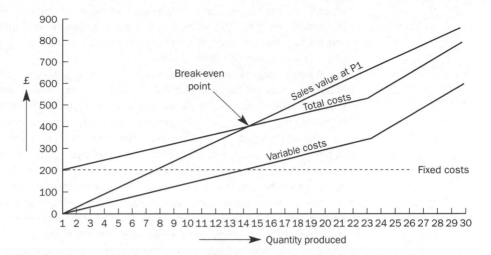

across a portfolio of products, or had reasons to liquidate stock in a hurry through clearance pricing, there would be little point in pricing at less than cost.

But the apparent simplicity of costs as the sole determinant of pricing is complicated by three considerations:

▶ It can be impossible to know your true costs until some time after you have manufactured your product, or provided your service. We have seen how the cost of individual units varies with the quantity produced. What happens if your estimated final costs are wrong in setting your price?

▶ A cost-plus price may be irrelevant to the market. It may either be more than the going rate (in which case you need to review your production procedures or find a different business to be in), or it may even be significantly less than you could get (in which case you are missing a valuable opportunity which is unlikely to last).

▶ It makes you a slave to your suppliers. Although price increases are invariably explained to consumers as the result of unavoidable fluctuations in the price of raw materials, successful organisations will have enough of a buffer in their pricing structures to be able to exercise some control over the timing of such increases with an eye to their possible effect on demand.

CASE STUDY **9.5**
· · · · · · · · · · · · · · · · ·

What price life?

Western pharmaceutical companies have been the subject of heated controversy for their apparent reluctance to make anti-AIDS drugs available in the developing world at a price which people who live in such economies can afford. Protestors have hit out at what they see as unscrupulous business practice, where the companies are putting profits ahead of the needs of desperately ill people whose poverty prevents them paying Western prices.

Against such criticism, several large companies have offered deeply-discounted supplies of HIV and AIDS drugs to a number of developing countries. The drugs are the same in every respect as the ones available in Europe and the US, even down to format and packaging. But the high prices available in the West for these identical drugs have led to a substantial problem in trafficking in grey-market imports. In fact, it is estimated that 20 per cent of Glaxo's marked-down AIDS drugs meant for impoverished

African patients have found their way back to the West, costing the British pharmaceutical giant £10 million. Police investigations have confirmed this figure. Arrests to date include a German businessman working from a garage near Bochum and a French pharmaceuticals trader.

A grey market is created as a result of manufacturers charging different prices in different national markets. Another name for this is 'parallel importing' as supplies of the goods to the market in question often take place 'in parallel' with legitimate distribution channels. Entrepreneurs buy up goods which are cheaper in one market than another and re-import them into the more expensive market to sell at a profit. Such flouting of official channels has been outlawed in the European Union following lengthy court battles between UK retailers and branded-goods companies (although the ban only applies to goods sourced outside the EU). Some see this as an affront to consumer choice. After all, if an organisation or individual is enterprising enough to take advantage of such pricing strategies, and the consumer is the beneficiary through lower prices, then what is the problem? Exclusive distribution activity by fashion or perfume companies is just another way to fix high prices according to this view.

The AIDS drugs case puts the practice in a much sterner light. The situation may be even more complicated than an unpleasant case of corrupt profiteering. One humanitarian organisation responsible for distributing the drugs in Africa appears to have been directly involved in the re-importation. Its chief executive was summarily dismissed by his national president when the scandal came to light. In his defence he stated that the drugs being sold were simply a surplus of Glaxo medication which he wanted to try to exchange for other desperately needed drugs and equipment. Indeed, even though the Glaxo drugs were being offered to African patients at a discount of 90 per cent, many activists claim that they are still far too expensive to achieve the necessary distribution.

Questions

1 Why do pharmaceutical firms charge such high prices for new drugs?
2 Parallel importing (at least in fashion and perfume markets) offers consumers a number of advantages. What disadvantages might it hold for them?
3 What advice can you offer Glaxo and its fellow pharmaceutical companies in order to protect themselves from parallel importing?

Source: Crouch (2002).

Target return-on-investment pricing

This has affinities with cost-plus pricing, insofar as it assumes that costs can be known (or estimated) with enough accuracy to feature in the calculation of price. But it represents a more pro-active stance on the part of the organisation to its objectives. It sees pricing as a means of obtaining a target level of financial return on the money invested in the business.

The calculation is as follows:

Price to achieve return on investment (ROI) =

$$\text{Unit cost} + \frac{\text{Target percentage return} \times \text{investment value}}{\text{Number of units sold}}$$

This approach to pricing is prone to the same difficulties as any cost-based approach, but it has the advantage of forcing the consideration of whether a proposed price is feasible from a purely commercial point of view.

Marginal-cost pricing

Like the previous two techniques this is cost-based, which rules it out as a stand-alone guide to the right price. But it helps to understand what is meant by marginal-cost pricing when weighing up certain kinds of marketing opportunity and examining the costs involved.

In a nutshell, the marginal cost of something is the cost of making one more unit. The related concept of marginal revenue is the income to the organisation of selling one more unit. As we have seen in our brief look at how costs behave as you produce more units (Figure 9.1), the marginal cost can start to accelerate after a while as the law of diminishing returns begins to set in. Marginal-cost pricing assumes we can draw a break-even analysis graph and put a marker on the spot where marginal cost equals marginal revenue, as shown in the graph in Figure 9.3.

Where the two lines intersect is the point of maximum profitability. Sell more than that quantity, and you begin to make less money – after a while you even begin to lose money. And having established the ideal quantity, all that remains is to establish the ideal price – a simple matter of checking up on the left-hand axis of the graph. But of course for the graph to work at all, you would have had to have made a pretty accurate stab at the right price in the first place.

Marginal-cost theory does provide a useful reminder, however, that organisations should consider profit as well as volume when assessing the terms on which they do business with large customers. Rentokil, one of the world's most consistently profitable companies in recent years, avoids very large customers because they do not offer sufficiently attractive profit margins, even though they guarantee high volume. Taking on more business is not enough to guarantee success – it needs to be business at the right price.

figure 9.3
Marginal cost and marginal revenue

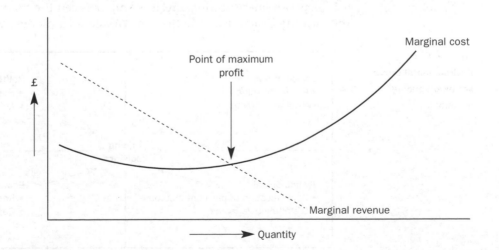

Competitive environment

As Figure 9.4 shows, all four of the environmental factors discussed in detail in Chapter 3 have a bearing on how pricing decisions are taken. Perhaps the most immediately important ones are economic and political. Changes in taxation, for example, can change the price of some goods and services overnight. Added to these general factors are industry-specific ones of competition (not only from existing rivals but from potential alternatives) and the ongoing struggle between suppliers and distributors. Monitoring and understanding the trends as they emerge can help organisations make better pricing decisions through planning.

Consumer expectations of what kind of price represents acceptable value will depend on two things – what they recognise as value themselves and what the competition is offering. This gives the marketing strategist the chance to sidestep the tyranny of cost as a factor in price-setting, and explore the opportunities afforded by perceived value.

DID YOU KNOW?

Toy giant Hasbro, maker of Action Man, Cluedo, Mr Potato Head and Monopoly, was fined almost £5 million for illegal price fixing. The company had been using its considerable muscle, according to the UK's Office of Fair Trading investigators, to force wholesalers not to discount the prices of Hasbro products. The fine would have been almost twice as much, but the OFT reduced it because of the co-operation shown by the company in the investigation (Bowers, 2002).

Elasticity of demand

The perceived value of a product varies from market to market and between brands in the same market. It is reflected in the propensity of customers to continue buying a product in the face of a price increase. One of the most important pieces of wisdom a brand manager can acquire is an understanding of the sensitivity of his or her brand to price increases. In the language of economics, this is known as its price elasticity of demand. It is difficult to generalise in any useful way about how brands respond to price increases, but on an individual level, especially looking at a number of years' back data, it can give an invaluable insight into the likely effect of future pricing decisions.

The concept of elasticity of demand is based on the idea that the cheaper a product is, the more of it will be sold – a principle acknowledged in our earlier discussion of volume-based pricing strategies. Another graph, shown in Figure 9.5, plots two lines showing a relationship between the price of a product and the quantity demanded. The first line (A) shows a product where, in spite of

figure 9.4
Environmental forces acting on pricing decisions

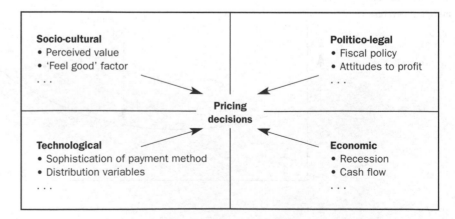

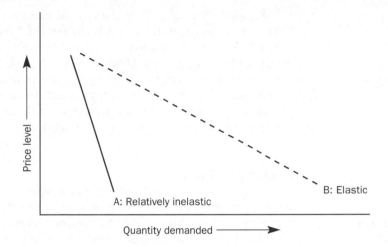

figure 9.5
Elasticity of demand

increases in price, demand remains at a relatively buoyant level. This is the pattern for products like cigarettes, or services like heating. Unless they become literally prohibitively expensive, our dependency on them means that we will continue buying them. They have what is known as inelastic demand.

The second line (B), however, shows a different story. Here, as the price goes up the quantity demanded falls steeply. In this kind of pattern we are looking at discretionary, non-essential purchases like foreign holidays or theatre tickets. Demand drops as soon as they become too expensive relative to the other purchases which consumers can use as substitutes (holidays at home or evenings in, respectively). This scenario is called elastic demand. It is as if the rising price is connected to the level of demand by an extremely stretchy piece of elastic which 'gives', rather than taking the quantity with it.

We can sharpen up this homely image of elasticity by putting some numbers on it. The formula is as follows:

$$\text{Price elasticity of demand} = \frac{\%\ \text{change in quantity demanded}}{\%\ \text{change in price}}$$

DID YOU KNOW?

In December 1966 the Catholic Church's 1,000-year ban on eating meat on Fridays was lifted. An American economist compared figures before and after 1966 in New England (which has a 45 per cent Catholic population). Having isolated other variables such as the price of competitive foods and trends in personal income, he concluded that, due to the reduced demand for fish, cod prices fell by 10 per cent and haddock by 20 per cent (Bell, 1968).

Where the answer to the formula is –1, the change in price is balanced out by the change in quantity demanded. In other words, the company sells fewer units but the extra money compensates for this exactly. A 2 per cent increase in price resulting in a 2 per cent decline in demand is a case in point.

When the formula yields less than –1, the demand is deemed elastic, that is the brand is sensitive to changes in price. An example would be a 5 per cent increase in price leading to a 10 per cent drop in quantity demanded. This would give an answer of –2. Unless an increase in sales could be expected for some other reason, like a price increase from competitors or an improvement in value, this would mean that total income would fall as a result of the increase.

Where the answer is more than –1, demand is inelastic, and price does not have such an effect on the quantity demanded. Thus a price increase of 10 per cent which yielded a sales decrease of 5 per cent would indicate a relatively inelastic elasticity of –0.5. This would suggest that the product actually sold better at the higher price – a marketer's vision of heaven.

Dreaming apart, the calculation based on historical information should yield a quantifiable insight into how much risk attaches to a price increase (or how much extra sales might result from a price cut).

KEY SKILLS
ACTIVITY **9.2**
• • • • • • • • • • • • • •

**Application of
number**

Elasticity of demand

According to Davidson (1997), assessing the elasticity of demand for your product in its particular market is one of the most useful calculations a marketer can perform. Yet, as this exercise shows, while the arithmetic is relatively simple, there are still important assumptions to be examined about environmental influences on demand other than price.

The most recent thriller by a best-selling author has been published in paperback at £8.99 in June. Its immediate predecessor in the same series (featuring the same detective) was published at £6.99 in paperback two months before Christmas. After three months, the new book has sold 10 per cent fewer copies than its predecessor had after the same length of time.

1 Calculate the price elasticity of demand for this author's books suggested by this evidence.
2 Comment on the accuracy and usefulness of elasticity of demand as a measure in these circumstances.

Price sensitivity

Gaining insight into the price elasticity of demand of a product or service can help marketers plan more effectively for price changes. But it also helps to have an idea of the factors which control the sensitivity of customers to price changes. These are not the same across all markets. Some of the most clearly identifiable ones are as follows:

▶ *Frequency of purchase*: How often does the customer buy the product or service? Price rises in frequently-purchased items like baby-food or petrol will have a more marked effect than in items like footwear or sporting goods, where purchases are more spread out over time.
▶ *Degree of need*: Inelasticity of demand is demonstrated more by necessities (such as food and fuel) than by discretionary purchases (such as holidays or new cars). However, necessities are culturally driven, so aspirational purchases such as alcohol and tobacco may have a higher priority than more 'necessary' goods in certain societies. Similarly, goods which are fashionable or which confer image benefits on their purchasers can often command much higher prices (at least in the short to medium term) than more immediately functional products and services.
▶ *Unit price*: High prices are often associated with high-involvement purchases such as consumer durables or holidays. Price changes here are influential because they are the subject of careful consideration and, frequently,

comparison. Here, as elsewhere, the greater the ease of comparison, the more sensitive customers are to price. With certain financial products, it is almost impossible to compare like with like, and so price sensitivity is not so pronounced as in other high-priced markets.

▶ *Price points*: Particular price points are important in markets like confectionery, cigarettes and newspapers. The price point may relate to the value of a certain coin, for example, or to assumptions about a consumer's concept of an appropriate limit (e.g. pub meals for 'under a fiver'). Sometimes, however, this issue appears more important to manufacturers than to customers.

Corporate culture

Who is involved in the pricing decision?

One of the problems of too rational an account of the factors affecting pricing decisions is that it runs the risk of ignoring the human side of the process in many organisations. Depending on the culture and structure of the organisation, a number of people's views may be involved in the decision. Typically the views of marketing, sales and finance will be represented.

Of these three, the finance department will see things in their most abstract terms. While marketing managers and accountants often view each other with mutual suspicion (as spendthrifts and bean-counters, respectively), they actually have a lot in common in terms of their interest in the long-term profitability of the brand.

The sales perspective, while having superficial similarities with the marketing position, will often be looking at a short-term orientation towards shifting volume rather than the long-term profitability of the brand. This can affect arguments about pricing for large customers, for example. The sales view will often argue that the volume to be gained is worth the sacrifice of some profit. The marketing view will counter that business on too generous terms with a large customer will destabilise the market in the short term and may even affect the brand's ability to sustain a higher price in the long term.

Successful organisations will seek to involve a range of inputs in determining their pricing strategy, but will have clear overall objectives and procedures to ensure that customer orientation is as important here as in any other marketing decisions.

Pricing and ethics

Since the abolition of Retail Price Maintenance in the 1960s, British retailers have been free to charge what they like for products and services. There is still the concept of the Recommended Retail Price (RRP) which is often featured on packaging showing details of Reduced Price Offers (RPOs) for purposes of comparison. Society relies on competition between sellers to keep prices at a reasonable level, with legal powers to enforce this. In the UK the Competition

Commission investigates any possible collusion between sellers to fix the price of goods or services to the disadvantage of the consumer. In the US the same process is fulfilled by Anti-Trust laws.

Legislation governing pricing can only hope to be effective within the bounds of national jurisdiction. The increase in international trade has opened up domestic industries to competition from economies with much lower labour costs. Textiles is one example of an industry where domestic producers have been unable to compete with cheap foreign imports. Protectionist legislation can help slow the collapse of such industries but their main hope lies in diversification or concentrating on market segments as yet uncatered for by their foreign rivals.

Such examples raise questions about the ultimate compatibility of corporate social responsibility with the profit motive. British consumers may regret the demise of their domestic coal industry, for example, but few are prepared to consider anything but the most economical option in terms of heating their own homes or businesses. There are, however, signs that in certain market sectors, segments are developing whose sensitivity to ethical issues makes them prepared to pay a premium. Recent marketing responses to this include Shared Interest, an investment company that offers modest returns on venture capital applied by individual investors to development projects: Clipper Tea and Cafédirect, which pay producers over the market rate for connoisseur teas and coffee; and a number of brands of detergent that guarantee a low environmental impact at a price. The green consumer, who became a force to be reckoned with as long ago as the 1980s, is maturing into a consumer who expects a great deal more, ethically, from suppliers than being environmentally friendly. Whether the majority of consumers will be prepared to pay the premium of more ethical pricing in the long term is another question.

KEY SKILLS
ACTIVITY **9.3**
. . . .

**Application of
number**

Business at any price?
Price changes affect profitability. Here is an example for you to explore.

Teriklene washing machines sell 500,000 units a year at £350 each. Their fixed costs associated with manufacturing and all other operations total £26 million. At unit sales of 500,000 a year, variable costs for manufacturing and all other operations total £64 million. Experience shows that raising the price of the machines by 10 per cent will lead to a sales decrease of 10 per cent. However, Teriklene's marketing department predicts that lowering the price by 10 per cent is likely to result in a sales increase of 20 per cent as the machines will then be the cheapest on the market in their class. The Teriklene production department is excited by the prospect of a 20 per cent surge in business.

Assuming that variable costs will increase by 10 per cent if unit sales go up by 10 per cent, or 20 per cent if sales go up by 20 per cent, calculate the effect on operating profits of increasing and reducing the price. Which is the better scenario, and why?

Key concepts
· · · · · · · · · · · · · · · · ·

Bait pricing: pricing a limited number of goods at rock-bottom levels to entice shoppers who may then pay full price on other purchases.

Barter: exchanging goods and services directly for other goods and services.

Break-even analysis: calculating the point at which goods sold at a certain price will equal in value the cost of their manufacture.

Captive pricing: pricing aimed at a committed market (e.g. for hardware-specific software).

Clearance pricing: low pricing aimed at clearing uneconomical stocks.

Cost-plus pricing: setting prices with reference to the cost of manufacture, adding a margin for profit.

Differential pricing: charging different prices for the same goods or services to different market segments.

Dumping: clearing stocks of goods in foreign markets at extremely low prices.

Elasticity of demand: a measure of how well demand for goods or services stands up in the face of price changes.

Fixed costs: overheads that do not change with the quantity of something produced (also known as indirect costs).

Marginal cost: where a quantity of a good is being manufactured, the cost of making one more unit. In combination with the idea of marginal revenue (the benefit of selling one more unit), it is used as a guide to optimising the relationship between price, profit and volume.

Parity pricing: pricing at the going rate for a particular industry.

Penetration: pricing at a level that maximises volume rather than profit.

Premium pricing: using price to enhance perceptions of quality or luxury.

Skimming: pricing at a level that maximises profit rather than volume.

Tariff: a structure of prices that often includes fixed charges and variable charges to the consumer.

Variable costs: costs that increase with the quantity of something produced (e.g. ingredients). Also known as direct costs.

SELF-CHECK QUESTIONS

1 Which of the following can be used as a reason to concentrate pricing strategy on income rather than volume?
   a Moving up-market.
   b Market penetration.
   c Recouping investment in an innovative product.
   d Cost leadership.
   e Countering the threat of takeover.

2 For which of the following might you expect penetration pricing to work best?
   a Organisations with substantial production capacity.
   b Small- to medium-sized enterprises.
   c Companies with strong financial reserves.
   d A competitor in a mature market.
   e A manufacturer in a growth market.

3 Demand is deemed relatively elastic when:
   a Any change in price is balanced by a change in quantity demanded with no overall effect on revenue.

    b Price changes have little effect on the overall demand for the good or service.
    c Putting the price up 10 per cent leads to a drop in volume of 2 per cent.
    d Putting the price up 10 per cent leads to a drop in volume of 15 per cent.
    e The answer to the price elasticity of demand formula is less than –1.

4 The break-even point is calculated by an equation involving which of the following groups of figures?
    a Elasticity of demand; fixed costs; marginal costs.
    b Selling price; fixed costs; variable costs.
    c Direct costs; overheads; indirect costs.
    d Variable costs; target return; marginal costs.
    e Selling price; variable costs; direct costs.

5 Variable costs are so called because:
    a They change with the time of year.
    b Exchange rates can send them up or down.
    c They change with the quantity of a product that is produced.
    d They cannot be added to fixed costs.
    e Services are variable in quality.

Which of the following are true and which are false?
  6 Price is an influence on consumer perceptions of quality.
  7 Societal pricing policies concentrate on satisfying the wants of the target market through low prices.
  8 Captive pricing is a technique that sometimes sacrifices profits on hardware to profits on supplies.
  9 RPOs rarely pay for themselves in generating net extra volume.
10 Costs are the most important influence on pricing decisions.

Discuss the following
11 How can companies assure their customers that their prices are fair and ethical?
12 Discuss the role of non-financial factors in pricing decisions.
13 Outline, with examples, the relationship of pricing decisions to the other parts of a marketing mix in the following areas: a consumer durable, a service and a fast-moving consumer good.
14 Reducing price as a promotional tactic is fraught with danger. Do you agree?
15 Why is it important for marketers to know the price elasticity of demand for their brands? What methods can they use to determine it?

Further study
••••••••••••••••

Ambler, T. (2003) *Marketing and the Bottom Line*, 2nd edn, FT Prentice Hall.
A new edition of a very practical guide to the financial implications of marketing decisions.

Dolan, R.J. and Simon, H. (1997) *Power Pricing: How Managing Price Transforms the Bottom Line*, Simon and Schuster.

Hirshleifer, Jack and Glazer, Amihai (1992) *Price Theory and Applications,*
    Prentice Hall.
Lots of detail, with some excellent examples.

Nagle, T. and Holder, R. (2001) *The Strategy and Tactics of Pricing*, 3rd edn,
    Prentice Hall.

Oxenfeldt, A. (1960) 'Multistage approach to pricing', *Harvard Business Review*,
    July–August.
*A classic paper proposing a six-step approach to setting prices which seeks to involve
every relevant aspect of a business's policy.*

The Economist and *Investors' Chronicle.*
*Both are useful, regular sources of information on the wider financial context in which
business pricing decisions are made.*
www.economist.com
www.investorschronicle.co.uk

Financial Times.
*Offers a daily perspective on the pricing environment, and is keen to target student
readers.*
www.ft.com

References
• • • • • • • • • • • • • •

Bell, F. (1968) 'The Pope and the price of fish', *American Economic Review*, 58,
    December, p.1348.
Bowers, S. (2002) 'OFT fines Hasbro £5 million for uncompetitive practices', 30
    November, p.27.
Budden, R. (2002) 'Hutchison 3G in tariff talks', *Financial Times*, 22 November,
    p.27.
Crouch, G. (2002) 'Europeans investigate resale of AIDS drugs', *The New York
    Times*, Section W, 29 October, p.1.
Davidson, H. (1997) *Even More Offensive Marketing*, Penguin.
Doyle, P. (2002) 'Why marketers must put price first', *Marketing*, 26 September,
    p.16.
Economist (2002) 'The telephone is the tool', *The Economist*, 27 April, p.75.
Economist (2003) 'Is one Rolls-Royce ever enough?', *The Economist*, 4 January,
    p.51.
Eurofood (2002) 'British pay more for everyday goods', *Eurofood,* 24 October.
Gray, R (2002) 'Driving sales at any price?', *Marketing*, 11 April, p.24.
Griffiths, J. (2003) 'Bavaria tries to make a British marque', *Financial Times*,
    4–5 January, p.9.
Harper, J. (2002) 'Ringing the changes', *Daily Mail*, 4 December, p.12.
Matthews, V. (2002) 'Shoppers wary of premium label', *Financial Times* (Inside
    Track), 29 July, p.12.

Personal Computer World (2003) 'Straight talking: what happened to 3G?', *Personal Computer World,* January, p.34.

Porter, M. (1980) *Competitive Strategy*, Free Press.

Ritson, M. (2002) 'Who needs marketers for price when vending machines will do?', *Marketing*, 27 June, p.16.

CHAPTER 10

Distribution

Objectives

When you have read this chapter you will be able to:

➤ Isolate the contribution that distribution makes to a successful marketing mix.

➤ Name the major channel intermediaries and describe their functions.

➤ Recommend appropriate distribution channels in a number of marketing situations.

➤ Appreciate the environmental forces operating on retailing in the UK and their relevance to goods and services marketing.

➤ Evaluate alternative strategies in physical distribution and logistics management.

Foundation focus: the 20-second takeaway

Distribution covers the activities of the many organisations and individuals that link suppliers to customers. They make life easier for suppliers by reducing the costs of doing business and facilitating exchanges. They increase convenience for customers by sorting products into categories, building up stocks and making appropriate quantities available. They also carry information and revenue between buyers and sellers. The Internet is changing the way goods and products are distributed, but has been slower to catch on with consumers than was at first predicted. By making a product or service available to the maximum number of relevant customers at the minimum cost, distribution makes a vital contribution to successful marketing. Furthermore, applying the same principles of efficient supply to all aspects of an organisation's processes can lead to significant improvements in costs and quality.

Introduction

This chapter introduces distribution, or place, the most mysterious of the four elements of the marketing mix. Traditional definitions tend to see it as moving goods or services from those who produce them to those who consume them, but all businesses are involved in purchasing as well as supply. Our examination of the topic will emphasise how businesses can sharpen their competitive edge by reviewing operations at both ends of the process, both as customers and suppliers.

Marketing involves a complex series of relationships between organisations. Distribution shows us how these relationships can be managed to increase the benefits available to the customer. An organisation's ability to satisfy consumer needs efficiently and effectively hangs on its relationships with its own suppliers.

Even something as apparently technical as the order in which goods are loaded on a lorry can give a business a competitive edge. The benefits can be passed on to the consumer as speed of availability, quality or price.

Distribution covers a range of operations and activities. We define it as the choice and management of ways to optimise the availability of a product or service to the maximum number of relevant customers at minimum cost. It not only involves the co-ordination of supply to the final customer, but also the movement of goods and services into the organisation.

In the past, some marketing writers have relegated distribution to the status of an 'order filling' activity in contrast to the 'order getting' function of advertising, selling, sales promotion and PR (Wilson et al., 1992). But it is a very powerful element of the marketing mix, capable of a much more active role than this classification suggests. The fact that it is less immediately obvious than the promotional side should not blind us to its power. Recent trends in telephone banking and Internet shopping show how whole new market sectors are created just by rethinking traditional forms of distribution.

KEY SKILLS
ACTIVITY **10.1**
••••••••••••••••

Communication

What is the point of distribution channels?

Being able to put your ideas across succinctly and clearly is a valuable skill. Sometimes it helps if you have an 'angle' around which to present your information. In this exercise you might expect your audience to be a little sceptical of the value that distribution intermediaries add to goods and services – they may start out by seeing them only as an extra source of cost to the shopper!

Write notes for a short presentation, explaining to a meeting of the local Women's Institute what a marketing channel is and what it does. Try to find examples of channels with four, three, two, one and no intermediaries to illustrate your explanation.

DID YOU KNOW?
Japan is truly a nation of shopkeepers. Products often travel through more than a dozen different intermediaries before reaching the final consumer. Frequent visits to the shop, buying goods in small quantities, and a taste for specialised products (especially in the area of food) have all led to the development of intricate distribution patterns. The mysteries of Japanese distribution are often cited as one of the main barriers to Western companies trying to crack the Japanese market.

Distribution channels
••••••••••••••••••••••••••

Distribution channels manage the series of exchanges that a product or service goes through as it is transferred from its producer to its final user. Channels can consist of a number of go-betweens or none at all, as in the case of direct marketing, which is discussed in Chapter 11. The intermediaries concerned can either be individuals or organisations, who may or may not take title to the product as it passes through their stage of the process. Taking title to something means owning it outright. This obviously involves more risk than merely acting on someone else's behalf, but it also gives the title-taker more control and a greater chance of profit. As is invariably the case in business, the greater the risk the greater the potential gain.

The idea of intermediaries is an uncomfortable one for many consumers. There is a distinct aroma of the 'gravy train' about the succession of different people waiting in line for their cut of the profit margin before a product reaches the final user. The consumer, after all, pays for all of this. But intermediaries justify their existence by providing useful services. There are four main reasons why businesses use them.

Specialisation

The mix of skills and experience that marks out successful manufacturers is not necessarily compatible with running a distribution operation. Using intermediaries leaves businesses free to focus more single-mindedly on their core functions. Distribution systems involve heavy investment and costs, so it usually makes better sense to contract this service out in whole or in part.

Customer utility

The consumer normally requires that a number of different products be available together at one place and time. This may be for the purposes of comparison or simply because of the limited time available for shopping. This kind of variety cannot be offered by a company dealing direct. The sharp end of customer contact is the job of the retailer.

Complexity

The growth in size and complexity of the manufacturing industry has required a similarly complex system for exchanging goods and services between companies, and getting them to the end-user. Think of all the various materials, ingredients and processes that go into something as commonplace as a jar of instant coffee. Bringing all these elements together into the finished product, and then getting that product into your home, requires an extensive network of distribution.

Distance

The increased geographical separation of the end-user from the producer of goods and services has ensured the growth of distribution systems. Traditionally, manufacturers have had strong markets in their immediate locality. We can still see concentrations of particular types of industry in specific areas, although this is becoming less and less the case as technology evolves. The greater geographical dispersion of customers means that distribution has become increasingly important as part of a successful marketing strategy.

KEY SKILLS
ACTIVITY **10.2**
· · · · · · · · · · · · · · · ·
Improving own learning and performance

Et in arcadia ego...

What kind of shopper are you? Retail groups such as the UK's Arcadia, whose portfolio of shop brands competes with such giants as Marks & Spencer and British Home Stores (BHS) for the lucrative 'mid-market' clothes buyer, are extremely interested to find out. Are you a careful consumer, guided by your head, or a hedonistic shopaholic, whose idea of fun involves giving your credit card a hammering every time you see something that takes your fancy? A more conscious awareness of the kind of shopper you are might improve your performance at maximising the benefits available to you. Are there other ways in which recognising your shopping personality might help you in your work or study?

Here is a list of Arcadia's shop brands, with a brief profile, including the kind of shopper at whom each is aimed. Check your understanding of yourself as a shopper against these categories.

Name	Profile
Burton	One-stop clothes shopping for men aged 24–49 looking for great value clothing with a fashionable edge. Versatile, affordable and practical clothes – both classic and contemporary. 380 shops in UK and Ireland and 100 years of tradition. Increasingly locating its stores alongside Dorothy Perkins, in order to attract women (who already influence 60 per cent of Burton purchases). Recent advertising campaigns have been fronted by UK style icons, including Martin Kemp and Ian Wright.
Dorothy Perkins	Strong regional presence outside London – 540 branches nationwide. A major force in high street fashion, aimed at women in their 20s and 30s who want wearable fashion without trend slavery. Appeals to the busy woman who can select a complete outfit confident that it will make her look and feel great without breaking the bank. Emphasis on practical, easy-care clothes (80 per cent of the range is machine washable) in a wide range of sizes (8–20). Range includes Dorothy Perkins Maternity, exquisite lingerie and exciting accessories.
Wallis	Distinctive, design-led range of clothes with a unique personality, like the women who wear them. The Wallis customer has high expectations of service, and knows what she likes. The range aims to interpret emerging trends, with an added extra in the way of colour, cut, style or detail. The 240 stores have a warm and feminine feel, with comfortable fitting rooms and lots of space and light.
Evans	Market leader for women size 16 plus. Appeals across the entire age spectrum with stylish and contemporary clothes for all occasions. Range includes casual to special occasion wear, swim and beach wear, lingerie, hosiery, accessories and sleepwear. Store staff throughout the 350 branches build relationships with customers and pride themselves in finding the right style to suit individual needs.
Top Shop/Top Man	Top Shop is a Mecca of affordable fashion for the style-conscious, independent-minded trend junkie. She will go shopping at least once a week for her regular fashion fix. Customers include models, stylists and musicians. The Talls range is a particular favourite with models, and the Petites range caters for the tinier figure. Top Shop offers a showcase for young designers through its TS Design label. 270 stores nationwide offer a lively and noisy ambience. International potential, with 49 stores abroad. Top Man is a 'safe haven' for the lad about town who loves clubs, pubs, sport and 'laydees'. He can manage to shop for clothes on his own, but also likes the chance to eye the girls in Top Shop with his mates on a Saturday.

Name	Profile
Miss Selfridge	Born in the swinging 60s, and still at the forefront of popular fashion trends. 120 high street outlets. The range evolves through the season, and aims to offer something special – whether it be fabric, trim or finish. The Miss Selfridge shopper is definitely 'up for it', with lots of attitude. She lives for the weekend, loves her friends, parties, gossip and fun.

Source: Marsh (2001); company information.

Having explained the growth of the distribution industry, let us now look at some typical distribution patterns, as shown in Figure 10.1.

There is no golden rule about what sort of pattern will suit what sort of business. The judgement needs to be taken on an individual basis. The more intermediaries there are, the longer the channel is deemed to be. For products like newspapers or perishable foodstuffs, this aspect of channel dimension is critical. Indeed, one of the historical reasons why England has a thriving national daily newspaper industry is that road and rail communications were good enough to allow wide distribution. Compare this situation with France where practically all the high-circulation dailies are regional.

Companies frequently use more than one distribution system at the same time. A major food manufacturer will tend to have its own salesforce directly servicing retail accounts above a particular size as well as a further tier of sales calls on wholesalers and cash and carries. Such companies are using at least two of the varieties of distribution channel shown in Figure 10.1 (manufacturer →

figure 10.1
Distribution channels of various lengths

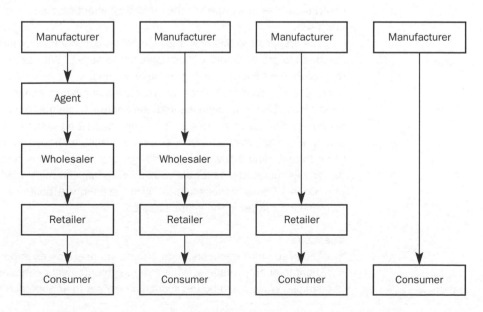

retailer → consumer, and manufacturer → wholesaler → retailer → consumer). In this way the varying service requirements of each size and type of customer can be met. Co-ordinating an exercise like this is a highly demanding management task.

All for Charidee...

Charity shops have been part of the retail landscape since the late nineteenth century, when the Salvation Army started selling cheap clothes and household goods to the urban poor. Yet it was only in 1947, when Oxfam opened its first shop, that the idea of fundraising through charity shops caught on. Oxfam now runs something like 850 shops throughout the UK, in an extremely sophisticated retail operation, and charity shops in general account for more than 7,000 outlets across Britain.

But an increasingly competitive environment has squeezed profits for many charities on the high street. The British Heart Foundation (BHF), for example, raised £9.5 million from sales of £34.4 million though 350 shops in 1997/98. The following year, in spite of having opened 33 new outlets, its profits had slumped to £7 million. The signs are that BHF is recovering, with a reported 7 per cent increase in profits in 2000, but charities everywhere are having to rethink their approach to trading in a tough environment.

Part of the problem is that they are facing new competitors in the market for cheap clothing. Charity shops used to be a popular choice for lower-income shoppers looking for cheap clothing for either themselves or their families. Now those core customers are being siphoned off by chains of fashion discount stores selling new clothes at cut prices. Another vital source of income has diminished with an overall fall in the price recycling companies are prepared to pay for 'rag' – the unsaleable clothes and textiles which still provide essential raw materials for many industries. Finally, charity shops face increasing competition from each other. With so many retailers deserting high street locations in favour of out-of-town developments, town centres have seen a growth in the number of charities occupying now difficult-to-rent premises.

The response to this new trading climate, particularly among the larger charities, has been to professionalise their approach to selling. With some notable exceptions (e.g. Save The Children Fund), the major charities have now replaced volunteer shop managers with paid employees. An increasing number of shops now take credit and debit cards. Scope, who pioneeered this approach, claims to have seen average spend per purchase rise from £3.50 to nearer £12 for credit card customers. Scope also uses sales promotion, from seasonal pushes on baby and maternity wear to a Chris Tarrant-fronted advertising campaign appealing for vinyl records. Cutting-edge design has replaced jumble-sale ambience. Oxfam commissioned a retail makeover from Conran Design Associates, to which the charity attributes a 20 per cent increase in turnover in the shops affected.

Questions
1 The case study mentions lower-income shoppers as an important market segment to charity retailers. What other segments might charities target for their shops? What would be the consequences for their approach to retailing?

2 Comment on the advantages and disadvantages to charities of having paid shop managers.

3 The case study mentions retail design, sales promotion and new payment methods as ways in which charities have modernised their retailing. Are there any other good ideas charities could borrow from what is happening in the commercial sector? Justify your answer.

Sources: Allsop (2001); Economist (2000).

What happens in distribution?

All channel members are involved in sorting activities: they sort out and keep stocks of various individual producers' or manufacturers' products. They also provide a means of breaking down bulk goods into appropriate quantities for the next channel stage, or for the consumer. They provide assortments of goods together in one location so that buyers are offered choice and convenience – the utilities of place and time. (See Figure 10.2).

Information flow

Channel members facilitate the flow of information between the market and the manufacturer. Regular contact with retailers and wholesalers is an important way for manufacturers to find out what is going on in the market. Often, the first a company will hear about the launch of a rival product is on the distribution grapevine.

Promotion

Distribution channels are also an essential link for information travelling from the manufacturer to the consumer. They participate in sales promotion, a subject we shall cover in greater depth in Chapter 12. Advertising aims direct at the consumer in order to create demand which will pull the product through the distribution channel. Concentrating on the channel itself, perhaps by offering intermediaries financial bonuses, free stock or other incentives, is known as a push strategy. Most manufacturers use a combination of both techniques.

Pre-sales services

Channel members reduce the number of contacts a manufacturer needs to make with customers. Depending on the type of intermediary, they can also get

figure 10.2
Distribution functions

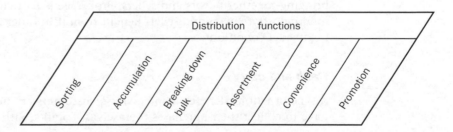

involved in pricing, packaging, grading or assembling products to suit the final customer's requirements.

Post-sales services

Channel members consolidate exchanges by transporting goods to their new owners, channelling money in the other direction. Wholesalers share the manufacturer's financial risk in tying up capital in stock, and take on the direct risk of financing the distribution process itself.

In spite of their profit margins, channel intermediaries can actually reduce the price consumers pay by offering manufacturers the benefit of their economies of scale.

Who does what in distribution?

Channel intermediaries fall into two main types: merchants and functional intermediaries. Merchants actually take title to (i.e. become the legal owners of) the goods they then resell. The risks are substantial in such a commitment. If the goods do not sell, it becomes the merchants' problem. But, at the same time, the potential profit to be made is correspondingly higher than in being an agent or functional intermediary.

Functional intermediaries never actually own the goods that pass through their hands. They earn a commission or fee for the services they provide. These can include transport, storage, finance or acting as the manufacturer's (or service provider's) agent in a particular market.

There follows an alphabetical guide to the main sorts of distribution intermediaries. It is not exhaustive (e.g. the various sorts of retailers are dealt with in greater detail in a later section), but it gives the essential information about the main players in the distribution process.

Agent

A functional intermediary with a contractual agreement to work on behalf of a particular buyer or seller. Agents find customers and negotiate, but never actually take title to the goods in question, receiving a fee or commission for their work.

Broker

Similar to an agent, but with fewer functions. These are mainly limited to bringing together buyers and sellers. Brokerage is particularly common in the food industry. Buyers and sellers benefit from it in order to cope with fluctuating market conditions.

Cash and carry

A type of wholesaler (see below) whose customers are not offered credit, and have to collect their purchases themselves. Popular with smaller independent retailers, who will often use the cash and carry in conjunction with traditional full-service wholesalers and company sales representatives in order to deal with their stock needs.

Direct marketer

Direct marketing is characterised by a direct relationship with the customer (including delivery of the goods) which circumvents all the traditional channel intermediaries. This kind of marketing approach is dealt with at greater length in Chapter 11.

Facilitator

Firms like hauliers, warehouses, banks and insurance companies help expedite exchanges without taking title to the goods concerned.

Franchisee

An individual or an organisation granted the exclusive right to exploit a successful business idea by its originator (franchisor) in return for a consideration. Examples include Tie Rack and Body Shop as well as services from fast food to rodent control.

Franchisor

The owner of a successful business idea who franchises it out to a number of franchisees (see above).

Industrial distributor

Similar to a wholesaler in consumer marketing terms, but offering industrial buyers the facility of inventory and location. Industrial distributors tend to specialise in particular product sectors.

In-home retailers

Companies, like Avon or Tupperware, who sell direct in people's homes rather than using traditional retail environments.

Licensee

Similar to franchisee (see above) but usually used in an international marketing context. The licensee (e.g. Coca-Cola Export Corporation in the UK) pays royalties on sales or supplies used in manufacturing the product to the licensor (in this case Coca-Cola in the US).

Merchandiser

A worker, sometimes freelance or part-time, who supervises displays and stocks for particular manufacturers in retail outlets. Merchandisers are often used tactically to supplement the efforts of a traditional permanent salesforce.

Retailer

The final link in the distribution channel with the consumer. Retailers frequently specialise in a certain product area (e.g. electrical equipment) and offer advice, credit and after-sales service to customers. A high level of service input is made at this stage, especially in product fields like food and fresh produce.

Wholesaler

An intermediary that buys stock from a manufacturer and sells to another reseller. Like retailers, wholesalers will sometimes specialise in a particular product area. They usually offer credit, delivery and frequently have their own sales representatives servicing retail accounts direct.

> **DID YOU KNOW?**
> *You spend about 135 hours a year waiting in queues: at check-outs, check-ins, or holding on the phone. Danish telephone company executive, Agner Kraup Erlang, published his first paper on queuing theory in 1909, paving the way for the modern call-centre (in fact, the standard unit of traffic in telecommunications is called the Erlang in his memory). His research claims that multiple queues are best for those who want to get ahead, as canny queuers can swap lines. The trouble with single queues (such as those found in most post offices) is that they are too fair, slowing down even the most strategic queuer (the business, 2001).*

Channel conflict

What is good for a manufacturer (outlets for all its brands) is not necessarily good for a retailer (who should only be interested in the fastest-selling products offered by each company). Even though both manufacturer and retailer are members of the same distribution channel, their priorities and interests are different. Distribution channels are made up of autonomous organisations with their own needs and agendas. This means that conflict can occur.

Let's look back at the diagram of typical distribution channels shown in Figure 10.1. Vertical conflict is the name given to conflict that travels 'down' the line of the distribution channel. It occurs between two or more members of the same channel, for example a wholesaler and a retailer having a spat about pricing policy.

Horizontal conflict is the name given to conflict that travels 'across' the line of the distribution channel. It occurs between two or more members of different channels who are at the same stage in each. Horizontal conflict might occur between two retailers, one of whom wanted to extend its opening hours in the face of opposition from the other.

CASE STUDY 10.2

Designer Olé-bel?

The international fashion retail industry is full of stylish success stories, such as Hennes and Mauritz (H&M), Gap and Benetton, but few can match the spectacular rise of Zara, the Spanish chain which started life in 1963 making ladies lingerie in the Galician town of La Coruña and now sells in 30 countries, through 500 outlets. Sales have increased by an average of 27 per cent each year since 1998, making Zara the world's fastest-growing retailer.

This success is largely due to the company's innovative approach to distribution. Because trends change so quickly in fashion, the key to success is lightning-fast reflexes. Zara manages to combine global reach to customers with a homespun approach to production. Unlike its rivals on the world's high streets, it manufactures more than half of its clothes in-house. H&M, on the other hand, uses a network of over 900 suppliers. An in-house operation means more control and fewer delays, from the basic fabric-dyeing to turning out the finished item in bulk. The company's design and manufacturing centre (still in La Coruña) is in daily contact with store managers to assess what is selling and what is being left on the shelves. As a result, production at the plant is planned in strict conformity with what is going on in the shops, giving it the opportunity to replace swift-selling lines immediately and allowing space in the schedule for new ideas from a team of in-house designers.

Here, too, the distribution systems used by Zara give it an edge. Being in touch with markets in 30 different countries is a fertile source of ideas. Zara's designers spend a lot of time travelling – scouring the world for 'cool' designs. By vertically integrating its manufacturing alongside its retailing, the company ensures that new product development can move rapidly. Zara claims to be able to produce an item from start to finish in three weeks, against an industry average of nine months.

The company runs very low stock levels, with deliveries to stores twice a week. This means that it never makes very much of any one particular line. Instead, it produces 10,000 new designs each year, which tend to be sold out within a month. Tellingly, José Maria Castellano Rios, Zara's chief executive, sees the shelf-life of a new garment much as that of a tub of yoghurt. The constant need to refresh what's on display before it goes 'out of code' creates an atmosphere of urgency and excitement in store. Zara does not claim to have a monopoly on fashion wisdom, but by avoiding building stocks it can minimise the effect of a bad decision. Most other retailers commit themselves to 60 per cent of their production at the start of a season. With Zara the figure is nearer 15 per cent – a much lower risk.

Questions

1 What are the disadvantages of vertical integration?
2 The case study suggests that speed of response is essential in fashion retailing. List three other 'essentials' related to distribution in this kind of business, and illustrate them – either from the case study or from your own experience as a consumer.
3 What is horizontal integration, and what would it look like in Zara's case?

Source: Economist (2001b).

Coping with channel conflict

Instead of having a collection of organisations working independently of each other in a distribution channel, there has been a growing trend towards integration by businesses keen to improve their profitability. The difference between autonomy (i.e. each channel member being independent) and integration is illustrated in Figure 10.3.

figure 10.3
**Conventional versus
vertical marketing
systems**

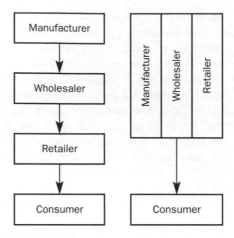

Integrated distribution channels are known as vertical marketing systems (VMS). Vertical conflict between members of a channel is prevented by an approach that treats the channel itself as a system. A system is a complex organisation that behaves as one unit. There are three main ways of establishing a vertical marketing system, and each method has been responsible for profit breakthroughs in companies enterprising enough to change their relationship with other channel members.

Corporate VMS

The first is the Corporate VMS, where two or more stages in the channel come under common ownership. Examples include off-licence chains and grocery retailers who service their outlets with stock from their own national network of depots. This is equivalent to owning the wholesaler stage of their distribution channel. The advantages in terms of payment systems, information flow and promotional co-operation are obvious.

Administered VMS

This form of integration sees one part of the chain assume control by co-ordinating the activities of other members (often its suppliers). Although there is no ownership involved, the bargaining power of the controlling organisation is sufficient to ensure co-operation from the other members. An example is the way major retailers specify clearly what is acceptable in terms of delivery and timing from suppliers. Such details can even include packaging specifications and label contents.

Contractual VMS

This controls channel conflict by establishing formal agreements between channel intermediaries. Examples include franchising and dealerships, where the exclusive rights to retail a product or service are granted to particular organisations or individuals. This ensures them a level of support (promotion, merchandising and a tried-and-tested business idea) as well as the absence of immediate competition. It also ensures the franchising organisation has a high degree of control. Contractual systems can also link organisations horizontally in distribution channels. For example, one way in which smaller independent retailers can challenge the buying might of their larger rivals is to form buying alliances themselves. This is the idea behind symbol grocers like SPAR, or chemists carrying the Numark brand.

Choosing the right channels

The factors that come into play in choosing the right distribution channels for a particular marketing purpose are illustrated in Figure 10.4. Some of these are internal considerations, others are external. Given that both types of circumstance change over time, it follows that successful companies keep their distribution arrangements under constant review. History is full of examples of companies which have come to grief by losing contact with their markets through inappropriate distribution channels. It makes sense to evaluate channel relevance every six months or so. It may be that a window of opportunity has opened through a change in only one of the six factors shown in Figure 10.4.

Consumers

Marketing organisations, by definition, put the consumer at the centre of every decision. This is nowhere more relevant than in decisions about distribution. Questions to be answered include the number of customers, their geographical distribution, how often they purchase, and where they expect to find the products or services in question.

Product or service characteristics

Mention has already been made of the particular needs of perishable goods like newspapers or fresh fruit and vegetables. Here time and channel length are crucial

figure 10.4
Factors in channel decisions

to getting the goods to the customer as quickly as possible. The features of many industrial products (e.g. size, heaviness, expense) will require a high level of involvement by the seller in the physical distribution process itself. Dangerous or very valuable substances will need systems that guarantee the maximum amount of security. This will cover aspects such as paperwork as well as the choice of warehousing and transport used. New technology offers considerable potential here, with the use of transponder devices attached to valuable parcels which can identify their precise location at any point throughout a distribution system.

Services need careful thought as to what distribution patterns fit their characteristics best. Where the service is an expert one, such as medicine or business consultancy, personal interaction is usually necessary. Choices here include where and when it should take place. On the other hand, there are certain sorts of service which can take place more efficiently without direct human intervention. To a large extent telephone banking and cash dispensers are the result of a drive to reduce fixed costs by financial institutions. But they also reflect modern patterns of consumer behaviour.

DID YOU KNOW?

On average, branches and their staff account for about half the costs of a typical retail bank. Banks hoped at one stage that they would be able to persuade their customers en masse *to do business over the Internet, slashing costs by closing branches. It now seems that customers want the convenience of the Internet as well as, not instead of, their high street branches (Economist, 2001a).*

Organisation

Organisational culture and characteristics influence distribution choice. Different businesses have different strengths and weaknesses which need to be borne in mind. Financial strength, market position, and quality of marketing information are all relevant factors in deciding what to delegate to intermediaries and what might be best done oneself.

Smaller organisations can find their size an advantage here. Their scale of operations allows them to experiment in a way that national concerns would find daunting and counter-productive. Distribution relationships are frequently long-term and difficult to change, especially for large and complex organisations.

Competition

It has already been stressed that channel intermediaries, unless they are part of a vertical marketing system, will each have their own business agenda. In spite of a perfectly good working relationship, there is no absolute claim on loyalty on either side. It is in the interests of channel intermediaries that competition for their services be maintained.

It is therefore prudent for firms to keep an eye on what the competition is doing. Channel intermediaries themselves may be a good source of information on this. Companies which have their own salesforces use them not only to sell their products, but also to gather information about what is going on in the market-place. Business contacts are an invaluable source of data.

Finally, under the heading of competition, it needs to be remembered that any channel choice has cost and revenue implications. Finding a cheaper way of getting the product to the consumer, or of ensuring early payment through systems management, can establish a long-term competitive advantage that it is difficult to undermine.

Environment

The external environment (political, economic, socio-cultural and technological) is constantly changing, and distribution patterns are changing alongside it.

Political change may make certain forms of channel irrelevant. The advent of the single European market, for example, has affected the way that new cars are sold in the UK. Traditionally in the UK, there had been a jealously guarded network of manufacturer-specific dealerships. But since the single market, dealers have been able to offer a much wider selection of manufacturers to their customers. Procedures for importing and exporting models have simplified.

Economic changes can also create new distribution opportunities. For example, the rise in 'hard discounters' such as Aldi or Netto has filled a gap in the UK retailing scene. This is because of their recognition of the value of a previously neglected class of shopper, the relatively economically disadvantaged. Food retailing always does better in recessions than non-food retailing, which means that large grocers need to review their mix of goods as the economic climate changes.

Socio-cultural changes, such as the growth in single-person households, have helped drive the development of direct marketing, and even basic distribution decisions by manufacturers, such as the most appropriate variety of pack sizes, will be affected by demographic changes.

Advances in communications technology have suggested new ways of making many goods and services available to users, with a particular focus since the 1990s on how marketers can harness the power of the Internet as a distribution tool.

Strategy

As an element of the marketing mix, distribution needs to work with the other elements in a strategic combination. The shorter the chain of distribution, the more control a manufacturer has over the presentation of the final product – a particularly important factor in the luxury goods market.

Price-setting also affects distribution. Merchant intermediaries fix their own resale prices. Agents, on the other hand, adhere to their clients' wishes in setting a price to the customer. The cost of the distribution channel needs to be included in pricing decisions. Especially for smaller businesses, this is a complex calculation where the actual cost of providing the goods or services to the consumer is frequently underestimated.

Another factor to bear in mind is that high-priced goods tend to be distributed differently from lower-priced goods. This reflects the different forms of buyer behaviour associated with different price levels. Higher-priced goods tend to be the object of extensive search behaviour, where consumers will take trouble to find out about alternatives and compare the value available in the market. This will involve visits to specialist retailers. Lower-priced, more frequently purchased goods, on the other hand, tend to be more widely available. They are bought more often, with less effort.

Finally, promotion is an important influence on distribution. We have mentioned the role that channel intermediaries can play in push and pull promotional strategies. For any promotional strategy to work, the distribution system has to be effective in getting the product to the consumer in the first place. It is no use advertising to empty shelves. It is nevertheless surprising how much more effective some manufacturers are at stimulating demand than they are at supplying it.

Consideration of these six factors ought to result in a distribution pattern that provides adequate outlets for a product or service in a way that maximises exposure to the target market at minimum cost.

The general pattern of distribution that emerges will be one of three main types.

Intensive distribution

This involves a presence in every conceivable outlet. It is ideal for frequently purchased, low-cost items that are easy to merchandise. Examples of products that follow this pattern include batteries, confectionery and soft drinks.

Selective distribution

Here the distribution pattern is less general, and customers will have a clear expectation of where to find what they are after. It is a typical pattern for what are known as shopping goods, where comparison on performance and price is common. Electrical equipment is a good example.

Exclusive distribution

In this pattern the goods or services are only available in contractually appointed outlets. Quality and service are reflected in premium prices. Luxury fashions and cars are typical of exclusive distribution, but so are other less expensive franchise operations such as fast-food chains and Body Shop.

E-commerce and distribution

Technological innovation has always been central to advances in distribution, from the invention of the wheel onwards. More recent developments in Information and Communication Technology (ICT) have included universal standards for bar-coding on packaging, which came in during the 1980s. Electronic Point of Sale (EPOS) scanning now allows speedier shopping for customers, and up-to-the-second stock control information for retailers and other distribution intermediaries. The combination of bar-code scanning with powerful database technology enables retailers to track the spending habits of loyalty card-holding customers to the point where they can predict individual tastes and match them with appropriate mail-order offers.

The technological innovation that is causing most excitement in marketing in general and distribution in particular is the Internet, which has created the concept of e-commerce. At its simplest, e-commerce is any trading activity that takes place on the Internet, usually through a purchaser visiting a seller's website and completing a transaction there. In spite of the enthusiastic predictions of e-commerce entrepreneurs in the late 1990s, whose dot.com start-ups lost investors significant amounts of money, consumers have been slow to take advantage of this new channel. To date, the real revolution has been in business-to-business (B2B) transactions, where electronic data interchange (EDI) has meant enormous cost-savings in the transactions between organisational customers and their suppliers.

There is evidence, however, with the wider penetration of Internet connections into people's homes, that e-commerce is catching on with consumers as well. Certainly the Internet plays an important role in the information-search stage of many consumer buying decisions (see Chapter 4), even if the actual transaction is then carried out in the real world. But companies such as Amazon.com, easyJet and TheTrainLine.com are warming buyers up to the advantages of purchasing certain sorts of product and service online. As with any form of innovation (see Chapter 8), it is only when a significant number of customers adopt a new form of behaviour that the mass market accepts it. This tipping point may not be far off for business-to-consumer (B2C) e-commerce.

As well as B2B and B2C, the Internet has provided a third form of distribution channel – C2C, or consumer-to-consumer. A good example is the American auction site, e-Bay, which acts like a vast electronic car boot sale as buyers and sellers are brought together by a website that takes on the role of broker.

Changes in distribution patterns threaten existing institutions, and the Internet is no exception. In fact some marketing writers have referred to 'disinter-mediation' to describe the way that the traditional functions of agents, wholesalers and retailers have been superseded by the direct link between buyer and seller created over the Internet. Functions such as breaking down bulk, assortment and convenience are all supplied by the seller on the website. On the other hand, companies that have tried to dispense with a physical retail presence completely have usually found that their customers resist the change. This is a particular problem with what are called 'legacy' retailers, that is retailers who are trying to develop an Internet presence even though they have an established real-world business and therefore have a 'legacy' of customer expectations of their availability on the high street. 'Pure' Internet retailers, who have never had a physical presence anywhere other than on a computer screen (like lastminute.com) have an easier time in convincing customers to adopt their systems.

In the early years of the twenty-first century it is likely that the predominant pattern of consumer distribution involving the Internet will be a combination of a virtual with a physical presence, as consumers seek to combine the convenience of ordering from a website with the reassurance of a real shop outlet which can be visited if necessary. 'Clicks'n'bricks' or 'clicks and mortar' has been a successful formula in the UK for a number of businesses, including Tesco, whose pioneering Internet shopping service, Tesco Direct, has inspired imitators in the US and beyond.

It may be that, rather than rendering traditional distribution intermediaries redundant, the effect of e-commerce in the longer term will be to give them a different role. It is already apparent that the growth of B2C transactions on the Internet has created the opportunity for new forms of intermediary, sometimes called 'infomediaries', to provide facilities such as credit card security and shopper privacy.

Retailing

Retailing has been the growth industry of the past 20 years in Britain. Much of this boom has been accounted for by the major multiple grocers like Tesco, ASDA and Sainsbury's. The food retailing sector is reckoned by many City analysts to be one of the most stable areas of the economy. On the other hand, the meteoric growth rate that many of these companies had become used to has slowed considerably, while specialist retailers such as Lush (whose no-holds-barred toiletries are merchandised to make a direct appeal to the senses) or Pret-à-Manger (which has revived the sandwich-shop formula) are turning in impressive performances.

CASE STUDY **10.3**

Putting the 'care' back in Mothercare

Table 10.1 Mothercare

	1998	1999	2000	2001	2002
Turnover (£m)	1335	1329	1266	509	427
Pre-tax profit (£m)	125	80.3	(389)	8.4	0.10
Earnings per share (p)	59.8	46.8	(0.65)	(3.73)	6.30

Figures in brackets represent losses

Source: Hemscott.com

Mothercare is still the only specialist UK retailer aimed at the expectant/recent mother and her young children, and is an established household name. Yet the chain has hit severe problems since it separated from British Home Stores in 2000, much of them caused by stock control.

Meanwhile, competition in the sector has been quietly growing. Adams, a chain specialising in childrens wear, has agreed a distribution deal with Sainsbury's, and Marks & Spencer has drafted in the assistance of style icon (and model parent) David Beckham in order to design and market a new range of apparel for the trendsetting toddler. Fashion retailer Next and grocery chain Tesco have also made credible entries into the field.

Mothercare has responded with a new impetus on marketing. A change of personnel at the top of the company has seen the appointment of senior marketers with a track record in other retail sectors. The chain's 245 shops are being repositioned as sources of advice for parents-to-be and new families, with clearly signposted ranges of products and equipment accompanied by well-trained personnel and information leaflets. The proposition is aimed at putting the 'care' back into Mothercare – taking into account the full range of needs presented by its customers and their children. The in-store makeover is being accompanied by redesigns of the company's other channels of distribution on the Internet and through catalogue sales. The overall effect, under the banner slogan 'Because little things matter', evokes a contemporary image, addressing customer perceptions about style and value for money where the chain is felt to have lost ground in recent years.

The image rethink has been accompanied by a fresh perspective on the range of outlets used by Mothercare to reach customers. An additional 35 out-of-town units are planned as part of the chain's longer-term expansion, as well as new retailing formats in city-centre and high street locations. Mothercare marketing director, Andy King, has very clear success criteria in mind for the repositioning. He wants to raise the absolute number of customer visits (from 1 million a week), increase the proportion of visitors who make a purchase (currently 56 per cent) and grow the average spend per purchase from its current level of £19.

Questions
1   What effect does poor stock control have on customer satisfaction?
2   What are the influences a retailer like Mothercare can bring to bear on its customers' perceptions of value for money?
3   The case mentions three success measures chosen by Mothercare's marketing director. What are the advantages and disadvantages of each? Can you suggest at least one other measure of success that Mothercare might find relevant?

Source: Kleinman (2002).

Place in retailing has a very literal meaning. The actual location of an outlet is of crucial importance. Pedestrian shopping malls in city centres are developed by property companies to exploit high foot traffic around business districts. There has been a parallel development of out-of-town shopping locations aimed at the car-bound shopper. Proximity to motorway junctions is a crucial priority for locations like Gateshead's Metro Centre and Sheffield's Meadowhall. They attempt to create a relaxed atmosphere that shoppers will find intriguing and enjoyable. Given the popularity of both destinations for coach-party excursions, it would seem that this has been achieved.

DID YOU KNOW?
Shopping-loving Britain now has more square metres of retail space per citizen than any other country in Europe.

Selling by design

Retail design aims at shepherding shoppers through the contents of a store in a way that helps them relate profitably to the merchandise available. The different assortments of goods on display as shoppers enter a shop are meant to draw them through into other areas. In a fashion shop, outer clothing gives place to informal clothing, then to night-attire, underwear and lingerie. Relationships between groups of merchandise are emphasised so that the shopper can contemplate a cluster of complementary purchases rather than isolated items. Even the carpet can come into operation to help guide the consumer. Darker colours indicate routes, lighter colours browsing areas.

Outside in the mall this theme of harmonious relationships continues. Competing businesses are not placed in juxtaposition. There is a natural pattern of different kinds of shops both in terms of their proximity to one another and the sort of location they favour on an individual basis. The maximum window space, but minimum floor space, of a corner position would, for example, be worth far more to a jeweller than to a clothing retailer.

Malls are a relatively recent import from North America. They represent a retail response to environmental and customer changes over the past two decades. Their basic technique of selling by association is one that can be profitably transferred to many other businesses.

CASE STUDY **10.4**

Net profits

The late 1990s and early years of the twenty-first century have seen a number of spectacular failures in online retailing as companies and investors, dazzled by the promise of Internet technology, have got their fingers badly burned. In spite of high hopes of the Internet as a consumer distribution channel offering global coverage, minimum cost and maximum convenience, prospects for it actually doing so in a sustainable and profitable way still look far from certain. In spite of the way in which the Internet has established itself as an essential part of how companies do business with each other (business-to-business, or B2B), its successful use as a way of reaching consumers (B2C) is still proving elusive.

Some organisations have, however, hit on a formula that works. Amazon.com, for example, leads the way in genuinely adding value to the experience of shopping online. Using powerful database technology, it 'remembers' the choices visitors make – not only things they bought but things they looked at. This means that the site can make recommendations about items individual shoppers may be interested in when they next log in. In certain areas of merchandise, such as books, this is a very useful feature, and one which few high street booksellers would be able to match. It is a good example of the 'mutual advantage' on which successful marketing is based – offering relevant choices to the customer and increased sales to the supplier.

Amazon has moved from specialising in books to offering a wide range of merchandise, having realised that what sets it apart from other retailers is not the mix of products or services on offer, but the way in which it establishes a relationship with customers. Other successful online companies, such as Expedia and Lastminute, are associated with a particular type of service (both are essentially travel agents) but are also capable of selling other goods and services to customers who are comfortable with this new way of shopping. Online retailing has focused marketers' attention anew on the importance of trust in marketing. Once this used to be seen in terms of brands and reputations. Now its meaning has extended to confidence in online security and delivering on promises – both key areas of concern for Internet shoppers.

The essential problem with e-tailing has been the cost. Promising start-ups, their business plans sustained by anticipated revenue from advertising, have bled cash to the despair of their backers as the advertising failed to materialise. Even giant players on the Internet, such as Yahoo! and AOL (America Online), have needed to search for non-advertising revenue. Yahoo! has led the way in encouraging its users to pay for services such as email with the promise of enhanced features. Again, in a classic illustration of traditional marketing wisdom, the company has found that consumers are willing to pay for quality, as services which used to be freely available on the Internet are becoming scarcer. Fee incomes increased 125 per cent in 2002, turning Yahoo! away from its unsatisfactory reliance on advertising to the more secure income base of subscription.

Information is a case in point. The Online Publishers Association (OPA), an American trade group, estimates that revenue from online content is doubling each year. In 2002, American consumers paid $1.2 billion to look at content (other than pornography and gambling) on the Web. Such content ranges from electronic greetings cards to dieting advice and to genealogy. Friendsreunited.co.uk will put you back in touch with old chums for an annual subscription of £5, and for rather more money (£115) Ancestry.com will put you back in touch with your forebears. By making useful information and services available to consumers who are prepared to pay for it, such organisations are unleashing the real potential of the Internet as a distribution channel.

Questions

1   List and justify three ways in which online retailers can add value to the experience of shopping.
2   What are the advantages and potential disadvantages of Amazon.com's ability to 'remember' customer choices between visits?
3   Online retailers such as Lastminute.com are moving away from specialising in a particular area of product or service to creating and exploiting information-based relationships with their customers. What lessons can a 'real' retailer learn from this, and is there evidence you can point to of this happening?

Source: Economist (2002b).

A–Z of retailing

The following is an alphabetical list of common sorts of retail outlets, each of which has a particular place in the market.

Category killers

This is a name given to any retailer who seeks to corner the market in a particular product category. Taking advantage of economies of scale, products are offered at substantial discounts to customers. Trading margins are slim, but the idea is to see off competition unable to match prices within the category in question (hence the rather melodramatic name). Examples of this sort of operation in the UK are the American import Toys 'R' Us, and the office stationery and equipment retailer Staples.

Convenience stores

These fill a gap left by the rise of the major multiples. They cater for shoppers who need the convenience of location and long opening hours that these general purpose grocers (frequently offering alcohol and video tape rental) offer. Located in residential areas, they are often operated as franchises (e.g. 7/Eleven) or symbol grocers. Petrol stations are finding the convenience store a useful profit enhancer in the face of slim margins on fuel.

CTNs

CTN stands for Confectioner, Tobacconist and Newsagent. This type of store is characterised by early opening, which leads to opportunities to augment sales of the basic product line with morning goods such as milk and bread, and close relationships with customers who are usually daily visitors.

DID YOU KNOW?

Distribution is good for your diet. 200 years ago most people in Britain lived through the winter almost exclusively on a diet of root vegetables and pickled meat, and had never tasted an orange or a banana in their lives. Now UK consumers have an unprecedented choice of out-of-season fruit and vegetables, many of which could not be grown in Britain's climate whatever the time of year (Jackson, 2001).

Department stores

Having been a dominant force in retailing in the 1950s, these have declined in importance. Their role in bringing together an assortment of different retailing concessions (like shops within shops) has largely been assumed by malls. On the other hand, there are still a number of very successful department stores which have bucked this trend. Their secret lies in targeting their customers carefully and supplying a high level of service (at a price) which differentiates them from the competition.

Hypermarkets

These are an even bigger version of superstores (see below). Precise definitions vary, but most analysts accord hypermarket status to stores with more than 100,000 square feet of selling space. They are more common in North America than in the UK, and their location makes them the exclusive domain of the motorised shopper.

Multiple grocers

The first supermarket chains began to develop multiple outlets in the 1960s. Succeeding decades have seen a concentration of more and more retail power in the hands of this sector. By the early 1980s, for example, two-thirds of all UK food purchases were made through multiple grocers. This is an alarming prospect for any manufacturer. Losing distribution through a major multiple can bring dire consequences for a brand's volume and market share, so the balance of power between manufacturers and retailers has shifted inexorably in the direction of the retailers.

The success of the multiples has stemmed largely from the following factors:

▶ Their realisation of their value as an intermediary to other parts of the chain.
▶ Investment in technology to improve their efficiency and information flow. Data collected from Electronic Point of Sale (EPOS) scanners enable large retailers to know exactly which lines are moving and which are staying on the shelf too long.
▶ Productivity. Concentrating on larger, more efficient, outlets, and cutting staff numbers, has yielded impressive productivity gains for many big retailers. They have also done deals with manufacturers to produce 'own label' versions of popular products which offer the retailer better margins than the branded alternative.

▶ Extended opening hours. Sunday trading is now an established part of shopping in the UK and the practice of 24-hour opening is spreading.

Speciality stores

These tend to be small, boutique-like enterprises dedicated to a single area of merchandise. They frequently offer subsets of a generic product (e.g. religious books, classical music, golf equipment, etc.) with well-informed personal service. Typically, they occupy city-centre locations, near established high street names, in order to benefit from the consumer traffic attracted by the bigger stores.

Supermarkets

See multiple grocers (above).

Superstores

These are similar to self-service supermarkets, but with a lot more space. Criteria vary, but most superstores have at least 60,000 square feet of selling space, and 15 check-outs. Out-of town locations are the norm, with adjacent parking and petrol availability. Analysts have varying views as to the number of large superstores a population can support, but the sector is a buoyant one in terms of new building projects. Grocery superstores have now been joined by others specialising in home improvement products and gardening.

Symbol grocer

This will form a network of independent grocers who share a common corporate identity, joint buying and promotion in order to muster more clout with manufacturers. A prime example of this is SPAR, whose accent on being local and convenient (with extended hours) brings together the two themes of the utility of time and place offered by the retailer.

Variety stores

These are similar to department stores (see above), but aim at the middle-market customer and will tend to specialise in a particular assortment of merchandise. This category of store includes the doyen of British retailing, Marks & Spencer, whose main strengths are in clothing and food. Other stores in this category include BHS (clothing and household goods) and Woolworths (houseware, children's clothing and home entertainment). Again, accurate positioning to appeal to distinct market segments has guaranteed these retailers their unique niche.

Voluntary groups

These are similar to symbol grocers (see above). This kind of shop includes outlets like Numark chemists, all of which are independent businesses but combine to increase their buying power.

Warehouse clubs

These outlets are an American idea whose time may not yet have come in the UK. The first in Britain was CostCo, which opened a branch in Essex in the early 1990s. Customers (members) pay a subscription for the privilege of shopping.

Their credit rating is scrupulously checked before admission to the select band of warehouse club shoppers. Once inside, shoppers have access to an amazing range of bargains – from power boats to toilet rolls. Discounts are very impressive. As a result, several manufacturers have refused to supply warehouse clubs for fear of appearing to cheapen their brands.

All of these retail businesses are catering for carefully-defined segments of the market. There is some overlap, admittedly, but even though the same consumers may use a convenience store and an out-of-town hypermarket, the occasions on which they do so will be different, as will their set of motivations when shopping. The retail trade is in a constant state of evolution to cope with this increasingly segmented market.

The wheel of retailing

An attractive theory that goes some of the way to describing this evolution is the wheel of retailing, popular with American academics in the 1960s. It suggests that retailing is a cyclical industry. Grocery outlets start out by trying to compete with their rivals on price. As they become established, the effect of this policy on their profit margins becomes a problem. They then try to move up-market to a better quality (and more highly priced) range of merchandise and selling style. This creates a gap at the lower end of the market for a new player to take the field with a low-price strategy.

This certainly fits the life-cycle of some famous retailers. Debenhams, now one of the most successful up-market department stores, began life in the 1920s as a cut-price retailer. Similarly, Tesco, which started in the 1960s as the original 'pile it high, sell it cheap' discount store, has moved up-market to a position not dissimilar from that of Marks & Spencer. This in turn has opened a gap in the market for the Scandinavian company, Netto, whose stores tend to be situated near less well-off council estates, and whose retailing atmosphere is very spartan. The choice available in Netto is limited, but all products are stocked on the basis of their cheapness.

Category management

As retailing has become more competitive, the pressure is on to squeeze as much profit as possible from each inch of shelf space. This has led to the development of a new marketing discipline – category management. Category management treats an entire product area as a strategic business unit (SBU) in order to maximise returns from it.

Pre-sweetened breakfast cereals form such a category. This product area features a number of well-known brands (Frosties, Sugar Puffs and Corn Pops to name but three), and has seen much new-product activity in recent years. Several own-label offerings have also made an impact on the market. Customers for the product category constitute a well-defined group – housewives with children. The variety such customers demand leads them to be purchasers of portfolios of brands rather than exclusively loyal to just one or two. Added to the variety of products on offer is a wide range of pack sizes and a high level of advertising and promotional activity. The in-pack free gift is a popular form of sales promotion in this category – and a frequent source of parental harassment by small children.

Such a product category presents the retailer with a series of choices. Quite apart from which product lines to stock, the optimum range of pack sizes needs to be determined. Furthermore, how should the products be displayed relative to one another on the shelf? And what should their merchandising relationship be with other 'morning goods', or with the entire range of other merchandise carried?

The temptation would be to class such decisions as an art rather than a science, but the advocates of category management argue that there are hard scientific principles waiting here to be uncovered and applied. Retailers now have an unprecedented wealth of information at their disposal. Electronic data capture at point of sale has meant that they know to the minute what is selling where.

The advent of smartcard customer loyalty schemes means that retailers can even track the buying behaviour of individual consumers. The accumulation and manipulation of such information using computers means that retailers can gauge very closely the effects of minute variations in pricing, display and stocking policies. A further stage of sophistication has been reached with the development of loyalty schemes between groups of non-competing retailers, which can now track purchasing behaviour within and between a complex range of categories.

DID YOU KNOW?

When Barclaycard, BP and Sainsbury's launched their joint loyalty card 'Nectar' in 2002, customers were so keen to register online that the scheme's website was unable to cope and promptly stopped working. The disaster ensured that the scheme received far more attention in TV, radio and newspaper reports than it would have done otherwise – one of the reasons for its eventual success.

Physical distribution and logistics

Physical distribution deals with the actual movement of products from suppliers to users. It concentrates on tangible products, but service providers can gain valuable insights from considering the strategic choices involved, and drawing parallels with their own operations. From a customer perspective, speed of delivery is often as important as price.

High-quality physical distribution can give a business an edge. The challenge is to balance the level of service with cost. It has been estimated that this part of the marketing mix accounts for something like one-third of all marketing expenditure, so it is an area offering rich rewards for companies which can successfully rationalise their operations.

The best way to examine the process of physical distribution is to look at it as a system. We have seen in our discussion of vertical marketing systems that this term implies a degree of control and interdependence. The relevance of the system concept here is that in order to improve the level of service offered in one aspect of the system, it may be necessary to compromise on another. The order of priorities each time will be dictated by considering the consumer's needs and attempting to satisfy them more accurately and profitably than the competition.

In fact this is the essential difference in meaning between the terms 'physical distribution' and 'logistics'. Logistics is the term favoured by marketing professionals. It starts with the consumer and works back through the entire system to ensure that each stage serves the needs and expectations of the end-user. Figure 10.5 illustrates the main functions carried out by a Physical Distribution/Logistics system. These are order processing, materials handling, warehousing, inventory management and transport. We will now examine each in turn.

Order processing

This first stage in a distribution system is a crucial one from the marketing point of view. It involves contact with the customer and offers an opportunity to introduce service advantages over the competition. The system design here should include speed, ease of use and efficiency.

Materials handling

Frequently, the physical attributes of the product (e.g. perishability, weight, bulk) will be the decisive influence in how it is stored and transported. Balancing service levels and cost here means working out the most efficient use of warehouse space, which will affect the shape, size and nature of the packaging used.

For services, which by their nature cannot be stored, this aspect of distribution is less relevant. However, there is a parallel with choices about whether the

figure 10.5
Physical distribution activities

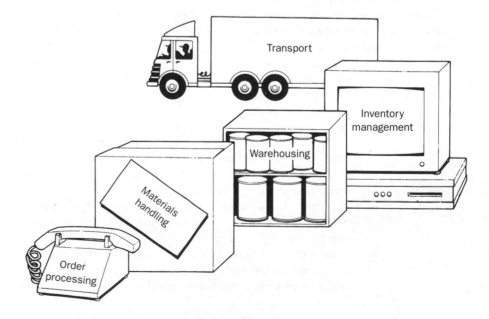

service is provided by its originator or is mediated through representatives or even reproduced through media of various sorts.

Warehousing

Again the focus here is on tangible products rather than services. The geographical location of warehouses relative to production and consumption locations is a key consideration for manufacturers. The functions that warehouses perform are several. They even out peaks and troughs in production by carrying a buffer of stock. Products are therefore immediately available to the next stage of the distributive process. A service analogy here can be drawn with information sources. Picture libraries, databases, information services and mailing list brokers are all service equivalents of warehousing.

Inventory management

Adequate stocks of working materials are vital. But too much money tied up in this way can spell cash-flow disaster. On average, stock will account for between one-third and a half of the assets of most businesses. Careful thought must be given to how much to reorder, and at what intervals. Typically the cost of storage averages out at about 25 per cent of the stock's value per year. This figure includes the opportunity cost of having money tied up in it (which could at least be earning interest) and the overheads (insurance, maintenance, security) involved in the process of storing itself.

There are two main lines of approach to solving the problem of having sufficient stock without tying up an excessive amount of capital. The first is to order the same amount of stock at each reorder but vary the intervals between each reorder according to your need. The second is to have regular intervals, but vary the quantity each time according to need. The first approach is called the 'fixed order approach', the second the 'fixed interval' approach. Over a wide range of stock the calculations involved in either approach are complex and cumbersome. As a result, this aspect of optimising distribution is usually handled by information technology, using computer models to gauge appropriate reorder quantities and intervals.

DID YOU KNOW?

Organising the supply of incoming parts and outgoing goods can acount for about 10 per cent of a company's total costs. According to TNT Logistics, the most expensive distribution mistake made by most companies is to hold too much stock, tying up money which could be better utilised elsewhere in the business (Economist, 2002b).

Just-in-time

What started as a stock control idea from Japan, has rapidly gained popularity with Western businesses. This technique, pioneered by car manufacturer Toyota in the 1980s, is called just-in-time manufacturing, or JIT for short. It aims at maximising the efficiency of the manufacturing process by carrying the minimum level of stock necessary. As a result there is increased attention to other aspects of manufacture (smaller manufacturing batches mean a greater emphasis on quality, more accountable use of time and resources, and finally a better product).

Advocates of just-in-time link its application to quality improvement. A favourite image is that of a flowing river. If you lower the amount of water that is in the river, hidden rocks and obstacles become apparent. By removing the rocks you can make the passage of a boat going down the river safer and more effective. Similarly, by lowering the level of stock flowing in a production system you can uncover snags and inefficiencies and eliminate them. This makes for a swifter and more effective production system, leading to fewer defects and an improvement in quality which the consumer will notice and appreciate.

CASE STUDY **10.5**

Exel excels

Exel is the world's biggest logistics company. Formed by a £2.75 billion merger between the UK-based National Freight Corporation (NFC) and Ocean Group, the company now solves distribution problems for a range of clients including some of the world's top names. Turnover in 2002 was £4.3 billion, with activities spanning 1,300 locations in 123 countries. A quarter of the group's business comes from the technology sector, with customers such as Nokia and Siemens struggling to get components and products to the right place at the right time in a fast-moving global market where even a week's delay can have disastrous consequences for profitability. Exel's other business is spread between consumer goods (22 per cent), retail (16 per cent), automotive (11 per cent), chemicals and industrial goods (14 per cent), miscellaneous goods (7 per cent) and health care (5 per cent).

Exel lead the field in 'third-party logistics' (3PL). This area, the outsourcing of supply and delivery across the whole of an organisation's activities, is a major focus of boardroom attention across the world. The kinds of just-in-time system which have revolutionised factory production methods since their inception in Japan in the 1980s are now taking effect outside the factory itself as companies struggle to streamline operations at the input and output stages of the process. A particular concern for automotive manufacturers, for example, is the sheer number of cars which build up in the system for up to 100 days between the factory and the showroom floor. The longer stock is held, the less it is worth (because of the costs of looking after it, and the opportunity cost of money tied up in it). By streamlining the flow of parts into and through the factory, inventory of finished goods can be slimmed down. The ideal for many companies is to copy Dell computers' principle of only manufacturing goods in response to firm orders. This philosophy of 'build to order' (BTO) means minimal resources being trapped in unsold goods, but requires extremely exacting systems to manage the availability of parts and components at the input stage. Companies such as Exel, often placing dedicated teams of logistics experts inside the organisations for which they work, can bring specialist knowledge and systems to bear on this problem.

Exel practises what it preaches. National Freight Corporation, one of its founding partners in 2000, was originally active in low-margin distribution and home-delivery services. It turned round its fortunes in the 1990s by concentrating on the much more profitable industrial sectors from which Exel now derives over two-thirds of its business. This trend towards non-consumer business was reinforced by the merger with Ocean Group, a shipping firm which traces its origins back to nineteenth-century Liverpool. As well as refocusing its targeting strategy, Exel also redefined what it offered to clients. It sold off its trucks and ships in order to release capital, repositioning itself as a co-ordinator of logistics strategy. Now it manages contracts rather than fleets of vehicles, and can concentrate on strategy rather than getting bogged down by fixed costs and maintenance worries.

The more that 3PL companies become involved in helping clients with input/output problems, the more likely it is that they will have to take on activities beyond what is normally seen as the remit of distribution. Exel re-packages and re-labels products for its pharmaceutical clients in purpose-built facilities. Such activities have traditionally fallen under the production function rather than distribution. One of Exel's competitors, TNT Logistics Corporation, carries out light assembly work for DaimerChrysler in America. Exel's intimate involvement with Ford means that such activities are likely to become part of its brief as well.

Questions

1   Just-in-time principles have influenced manufacturing and are now being applied directly to managing the flow of materials into the factory, and to what happens to finished goods after their manufacture. How might you apply just-in-time to a service industry such as a fast-food restaurant or a theatre?
2   What are the advantages and disadvantages of a company like Exel enhancing its logistics offering to its customers with services such as re-packaging or assembly?
3   How does successful logistics contribute to customer satisfaction? Illustrate your answer from your own experience if possible.

Sources: Chemist and Druggist (2002); Davey (2002); Economist (2002a).

Transport

This final aspect of physical distribution adds time and place utility to a product by moving it from where it is produced to where it is used. It is one of the most frequently contracted-out aspects of distribution, although many major manufacturers will maintain their own fleets of haulage vehicles. Typically, more than one form of transport will be used (e.g. road and rail, or canal and road) in the process of distributing any one produ.ct. As with other aspects of physical distribution, a balance needs to be struck between cost and service levels.

DID YOU KNOW?

A Carlisle-based haulier who specialises in the rapid despatch of fresh food around Europe has a fan club of 10,000 people. Eddie Stobart Jr runs a fleet of over 500 distinctively liveried trucks which top the lists of 'truck spotters' – bored motorway drivers and passengers who while away the time by looking out for the famous green, white and yellow Stobart vehicles. Stobart's nearest rival for spotularity is the exotically named Norbert Dentressangle, a French haulier (Wollaston, 2001).

Distributing a service
....

Services are distinguished from physical goods by their intangibility. You cannot store them or carry them, so many of the problems associated with physical distribution do not apply in the area of service marketing. However, some services rely on tangible products as part of their delivery (such as equipment or materials). Interpersonal contacts are usually essential to service delivery, a fact that influences their distribution patterns decisively.

Distributing a service through intermediaries has the advantage of encouraging clear thinking about the service itself. Just as agents and sales representatives need intimate knowledge of the product they are offering, so service agents and franchisees need to have an expert understanding of the service they are broking. Training, monitoring and systems aimed at consistency of presentation are essential prerequisites of reliable service delivery through intermediaries.

Location and time as elements in service distribution

A major distribution decision for any expert service (such as law or medicine) is quite literally to do with place. Where should the transaction happen? Either you visit your client, or your client comes to you. For many business services place decisions have a close bearing on the nature of what is being offered. It may be, for example, that a neutral location is the best choice: as in counselling and training.

Sometimes the service offered will depend very heavily on the personality and expertise of the individual at the centre of the company. This is frequently the case with design or PR consultancies, where the client is buying the insight or creativity of a particular director with whom they may have worked over a number of years. Using intermediaries such as other staff or agents in a situation like this needs to be done with care.

Time is as important as location in service delivery. By their very nature, emergency breakdown services have to be in distribution on a round-the-clock basis. Medical practitioners, on the other hand, have surgery hours for non-urgent cases which are handled on an appointment basis. These two examples illustrate how service distribution decisions are a matter of balancing cost (to the provider) and utility (to the consumer).

DID YOU KNOW?

Some Japanese companies have explored the use of aromatic effects to put their customers in a more relaxed and, possibly, free-spending mood. Smell is certainly an important element of some retailing operations in the UK such as Body Shop and the scented-candle specialist Wax Lyrical. More explicitly, experience museums, such as York's Jorvik Centre, use smells as an overt element in their created environments.

Physical environment in service distribution

Atmospherics is the name given to the distribution technique that seeks to create service delivery conditions that reinforce certain dispositions in customers (see Figure 10.6). The technique is particularly useful in a service environment such as health care (to reinforce feelings of safety or well-being) or financial services (reassurance and reliability). Major refits of banks and building societies in the UK have emphasised the importance of extending the corporate identity of the company concerned into the retail environment itself. Thus colours and textures that consumers have learned to associate with companies like LloydsTSB, HSBC or Barclays are now incorporated into the physical environment presented to their customers. The effect is not just a psychological one. Because of the intangible nature of services, it actually helps consumers to use them more easily if there is an element of consistency and familiarity in their presentation. So, a readily identifiable style of interior decor may be as important in financial services delivery as an easy-to-complete paying-in slip or a rational queuing arrangement.

figure 10.6
Atmospherics

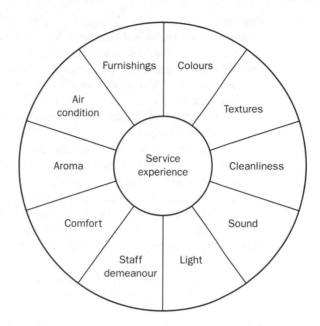

KEY SKILLS
ACTIVITY **10.3**
. . . .

Problem solving

Atmospherics audit
Gathering information is an essential step in the problem-solving process. This exercise gives you the chance to gather information in a structured way in order to diagnose potential problems and think about possible solutions.

Using the atmospherics diagram (Figure 10.6) as the basis, compile a check-list of atmospheric attributes. Use the check-list to conduct an audit of part of your college or organisation used for important service delivery (e.g. lecture theatre, common room, canteen, library). Rate each attribute on a scale of 1–6. It may be interesting to do this individually and then compare your ratings with those of other people to determine how subjective or objective atmospherics are. Having gathered this information in order to diagnose any potential problem with atmospherics, draw up a brief list of possible improvements that could be made.

Key concepts
. . . .

B2B, B2C: Business-to-business, business-to-consumer, respectively – terms used to describe e-commerce transactions.

C2C: e-commerce transactions carried out among consumers themselves (e.g. Internet auction sites).

Category management: a retailing philosophy that focuses on groups of products rather than individual brands.

Channel conflict: clashes of interest between distribution intermediaries. They can be horizontal (between intermediaries at the same stage in two separate channels) or vertical (between successive intermediaries in the same channel).

Channels: groupings of individuals or institutions linking buyers and sellers.

Clicks'n'bricks, clicks and mortar: a model of e-commerce which combines a presence on the Web with physical retail outlets.

Conventional distribution system: channel consisting of independent intermediaries (as opposed to a vertical marketing system where there is formal co-ordination).

Disintermediation: the replacement of traditional distribution channels with the use of the Internet.

e-commerce: trading activity that takes place on the Internet, usually through a buyer visiting a seller's website and completing a transaction there.

EPOS: Electronic Point of Sale information system involving laser technology to read bar-codes providing instant information on product movement.

Functional intermediaries: channel members whose activities do not involve ownership of the products with which they deal.

Infomediary: an organisation or individual providing services to facilitate e-commerce.

Inventory: the amount, and variety, of stock carried by a business.

Mall: architectural development combining an assortment of retail units in an indoor environment.

Merchandising: activity aimed at maximising the impact of display at point of sale.

Merchant intermediaries: channel members whose activities involve ownership of the products with which they deal.

Pull strategy: promotional activity that aims to stimulate demand in customers to 'pull' goods through the distribution system.

Push strategy: promotional activity that targets distribution intermediaries in order to 'push' goods through the system.

Vertical marketing system (VMS): a distribution system where two or more channel members are connected by ownership, administration or legal obligation.

SELF-CHECK QUESTIONS

1 Name six functions carried out by distribution intermediaries.

2 What is wrong with the following statements?
   a Distribution patterns are strictly industry specific.
   b Buyers and sellers only use one distribution pattern.
   c Push promotion aims to stimulate consumer demand.

3 Cash and carries are:
   a Discount retailers which do not accept credit cards.
   b Functional intermediaries which offer transport facilities to small- and medium-sized enterprises.
   c Wholesalers which offer credit facilities to club members.
   d Wholesalers which neither deliver nor offer credit facilities.
   e None of these.

4 Horizontal channel conflict occurs between:
   a Successive stages in a distribution chain.
   b Brokers in the UK and retailers in France.

  c Service providers and manufacturers.
  d Cable television operators and equipment manufacturers.
  e Two channel intermediaries at the same stage of parallel chains.

 5 VMS means:
    a Vertical management scenario.
    b Virtual management system.
    c Very major service.
    d Vertical marketing system.
    e Vertical matrix section.

Which of the following are true and which are false?

 6 Competition, environment and strategy are some of the influences on choosing
    the right distribution channels.
 7 Exclusive distribution is always connected with high-priced goods.
 8 Category management treats groups of products as SBUs.
 9 Hypermarkets have at least 60,000 square feet of selling space.
10 JIT leads to quality focus.

Discuss the following

11 Giving two examples of each, differentiate between merchant intermediaries and
    functional intermediaries.
12 What are the three main strategic options open to distribution patterns? Give
    examples of each type.
13 Explain the following terms:
    a Category killer.
    b CTN.
    c Symbol grocer.
    d Broker.
    e Inventory.
14 Outline the 'wheel of retailing' theory. What do you think are its limitations?
15 What are the five main functions fulfilled by a physical distribution system?

Further study
· · · · · · · · · · · · · · · · ·

*The following books offer a range of insights into the connections between distribution
and other areas of marketing and business:*

Baldwin, C.Y., Dyer, J.H., Fites, D.V. (2000) *Harvard Business Review on Managing
   the Supply Chain,* HBR Press.
Chopra, S. and Meindl, P. (2000) *Supply Chain Management: Strategy, Planning
   and Operations,* Prentice Hall.
Christopher, M. (1998) *Logistics and Supply Chain Management: Strategies for
   Reducing Cost and Improving Service,* 2nd edn, FT Prentice Hall.
Coughlan, A. (2001) *Marketing Channels,* Prentice Hall.

Retailing is a fascinating branch of marketing. Here are some useful books on the subject:

Seth, A. (2001) *The Grocers: The Rise and Rise of the Supermarket Chains,* Kogan Page.
Spector, R. (1999) *The Nordstrom Way: The Inside Story of America's Number 1 Customer Service Company*, John Wiley and Sons.

Sullivan, M. (2002) *Retail Marketing*, International Thomson Business Press.

E-commerce has been the subject of an avalanche of books recently. Here's a good place to start:

Chaffey, D. (2001) *E-business and E-commerce Management: Strategy, Management and Applications*, FT Prentice Hall.

References

Allsop, I. (2001) 'Charities attempt to arrest shop slide', *Charity Finance*, April, p.10.
the business (2001) 'Worth its wait in gold', *the business* (FT weekend magazine); 24 February, p.10.
Chemist and Druggist (2002) 'Logical route for logistics', *Chemist and Druggist*, 14 September, p.33.
Davey, J. (2002) 'Charting a profitable route across the globe', *The Times* (Business), 21 October, p.6.
Davis, J. (2001) 'The leisure principle', *Financial Times* (Creative Business), 20 February, pp.10–11.
Economist (2000) 'Chic-a-brac', *The Economist*, 20 May, p.41.
Economist (2001a) 'Beautifying branches', *The Economist*, 24 May, p.113.
Economist (2001b) 'Floating on air', *The Economist*, 19 May, pp.80–1.
Economist (2002a) 'A moving story',*The Economist*, 7 December, pp.93–4.
Economist (2002b) 'Profits at last', *The Economist*, 21 December, pp.95–6.
Jackson, T. (2001) 'The incompressible personal touch', *Financial Times,* 20 February, p.13.
Kleinman, M. (2002) 'Mothercare faces up to its failure', *Marketing*, 29 August, p.13.
Marsh, H. (2001) 'Arcadia focuses its interests', *Marketing*, 12 April, p.17.
Wilson, R., Gilligan, C. and Pearson, D. (1992) *Strategic Marketing Management: Planning, Implementation and Control*, Butterworth Heinemann.
Wollaston, S. (2001) 'King of the road', *The Guardian*, 17 October, p.15.

CHAPTER 11

Promotion – introduction, advertising and direct marketing

Objectives

When you have read this chapter you will be able to:

➤ Relate basic theories of communication to the practicalities of promotional management.

➤ Draw on the main practitioner theories of how advertising works.

➤ Explain the organisation of a typical advertising agency.

➤ Understand the client/agency relationship, especially in terms of selection, briefing, management and evaluation.

➤ Appreciate the contribution of media planning to successful campaigns.

➤ Explain the potential of new electronic media to revolutionise marketing communications.

➤ Recognise the relevance of direct marketing in a variety of marketing situations.

➤ Understand the self-regulatory framework of the UK advertising industry.

Foundation focus: the 20-second takeaway

Different organisations have different approaches to communication, but most subscribe to the idea that by attracting customers' attention, arousing their interest and stimulating their desire it is possible to encourage the action of purchase. Advertising is the most visible form of promotional activity for mass-market consumer goods and services. But encouraged by advances in technology and discouraged by the rising costs of traditional advertising, many organisations are experimenting with new routes to their customers. Direct marketing's emphasis on existing customers can be seen as a more efficient way of doing business. The prevailing economic climate is forcing a promotional rethink for many marketing organisations keen to integrate their promotional activities rather than keeping them in separate compartments. The opportunities offered by electronic media are making this approach, long an aspiration for marketers, into a practical reality.

Introduction

Promotion is the part of the marketing process that communicates the benefits of the product. In a competitive market-place, you cannot expect goods and services to sell themselves. No matter how high a product's quality, unless customers know about it you are unlikely to make a sale. Promotion has an essential role in winning new customers, and keeping existing ones.

The two promotional techniques we will focus on in this chapter, advertising and direct marketing, tend to be associated with new customers and existing customers respectively, although they are both highly flexible techniques. Other promotional methods such as sales promotion, public relations and direct selling are dealt with in Chapter 12. It is important, however, to see them all as aspects of the same process of informing and persuading customers of the advantages of your offer over the competition.

Integration – the way forward in promotion

In the past, promotional services have been offered by specialist agencies. Each discipline (such as advertising or sales promotion) argued its case to the client in competition with the alternatives. Very often this resulted in a tactical approach to promotion, with the various strands operating in separate compartments. Current thinking, however, advocates an approach called integrated marketing communications. This emphasises the use of appropriate promotional disciplines in combination with each other. Integrating its communications in this way recognises the fact that what an organisation is saying to its customers is more important than any single promotional technique. As a result, advertisers and agencies are becoming a great deal more flexible in how they contact their customers. 'Media-neutral planning', as this approach is often called, means that organisations try to avoid a bias towards particular ways of communication just because they are familiar with them (Ray, 2002). Instead, they start their planning with the customer and the message, taking advantage of the rich combination of different media and techniques available to the contemporary communicator.

The drive towards integrated marketing communications and media-neutral planning has resulted from the following factors:

▶ *Social* – increasingly sophisticated customers.
▶ *Technological* – computer databases, 'smartcard' electronics, new advertising media such as the Internet and digital TV.
▶ *Economic* – rising demands on marketing expenditure in a highly competitive environment.
▶ *Political* – deregulation of media, changing attitude to promotion.

CASE STUDY **11.1**

Oliver adds a billion-pound twist

Using the *Naked Chef* in its advertising campaigns has been a recipe for success, according to Sainsbury's, the leading UK grocery retailer. Cheeky Essex boy Jamie Oliver has been fronting its ads in 'slice of life' vignettes at a total cost of £41 million since the campaign started. The loveable mockney gets an estimated £1 million of this per year, but he is worth it according to the supermarket group whose internal research reveals his strong appeal to young mothers, a key food shopping demographic. The result, according to a case study presented at the Institute of Practitioners in Advertising (IPA) Effectiveness Awards, has been £5 extra profit for every £1 of advertising spend – a mouthwatering achievement. Sainsbury's has increased its turnover by £2 billion during the course of the campaign, and attributes half of this to the effects of the advertising.

Some business commentators have not been quite so sold on the influence of the popular TV chef. They argue that his tousled charm has been less of an influence on Sainsbury's fortunes than the fact that the group has been investing billions in upgrading its distribution and supply chain infrastructure, and on a programme of store refits and improvements. Furthermore, 4 per cent more selling space has been opened up over the relevant period.

Questions

1   Measuring advertising effects is always difficult. In what ways might Sainsbury's measure the effects of the Jamie Oliver campaign?
2   What are the potential dangers of using a celebrity to front an advertising campaign, and how might a company like Sainsbury's minimise them?
3   Along with other grocery retailers, Sainsbury's has been trying to widen its range of products into the non-food sector. What, if any, implications might this have for its advertising strategy?

Source: Blackstock (2002).

KEY SKILLS
ACTIVITY **11.1**
· · · · · · · · · · · · · · · ·

Problem solving

Technology and promotion

Creativity is at the heart of advertising and sales, just as it is at the heart of any kind of problem-solving. The challenge of inventing a value for a new advertising medium is a particularly interesting problem as success depends not only on assessing what advertisers are prepared to pay, but also on persuading them that the opportunity is worth their while.

New promotional media are continually becoming available as electronic and printing technology develops. Scratchcards, holographs, interactive video, the Internet, even something as relatively banal as advertising on supermarket trolleys ('the last advertisement the consumer sees before making a purchase') all took a leap of the imagination to conceive.

This exercise asks you to think of a new promotional medium aimed at one of the following groups:

1   Women aged 18–25.
2   People doing a weekly shop at an out-of-town supermarket (and therefore using a car).
3   AB men interested in sport.

For each group answer the following questions:

(a) What kind of companies would benefit from advertising on this new medium?
(b) How much could you charge them for doing so?

Understanding communication

The process at the heart of marketing communication can be seen as the journey of a message from its source to its target, to elicit a response. For example, a manufacturer sends a commercial message to a consumer who responds by purchase. This kind of 'process' model is certainly popular with marketing writers and features in many textbooks. It corresponds to most people's common-sense expectation of how promotion works: as a stimulus that can generate a predictable response in the market. (See Figure 11.1.)

The encoding and decoding involved in the model are similar to the way in which a marketing brief is turned into a commercial message from which the consumer is expected to take the intended meaning. The channel can stand for the medium used. Noise is anything that interferes with the successful transmission of the intended meaning (e.g. smudged printing, or even unclear language). While Figure 11.1 illustrates the stages in the process through events in an advertising campaign, it can just as easily be applied to public relations, direct marketing, sponsorship or any other promotional technique.

Hierarchy of effects models

While the academic field of communication studies has only really existed since the mid-twentieth century, advertising practitioners have been guided by common-sense models of communication for much longer. These are often called hierarchy of effects models because they suggest that customers have to pass through a number of stages to reach the desired response: a purchase. While each model has its own emphases, all of them move through three main stages: *cognitive* (making people aware of the product), *affective* (gaining approval of the product) and *behavioural* (prompting action about the product).

Hierarchy of effects models are open to criticism on two counts: they seem exclusively concerned with new business rather than regular purchases, and they imply that consumers are passive. But they help us think about planning and analysing marketing communications in a systematic way.

Three influential examples of such models are as follows.

Starch

Daniel Starch (1925): 'To be effective an advertisement must be seen, read, believed, remembered and acted upon.' An early, but still widely quoted, model emphasising the need to make advertising noticeable, easy to understand, credible, interesting and relevant to people's needs.

figure 11.1
Process model of communication adapted to advertising

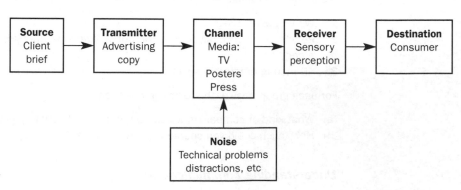

Adapted from: Shannon, C. and Weaver, W. (1949).

AIDA

E.K. Strong (1925): AIDA – Attention, Interest, Desire, Action. Another classic model. The idea of 'desire' is unique to AIDA. It means convincing the target group that this product is the one for them. Careful research into what they are looking for is therefore essential in order to stress the benefits that matter.

DAGMAR

Russell Colley (1961), in his book *Defining Advertising Goals for Measuring Advertising Results* (DAGMAR for short), claims that an advertisement must carry the customer along a continuum towards purchase. The four main stages are: awareness, comprehension, conviction, action. Colley's contribution was to focus attention on what exactly advertisers wished to achieve in particular campaigns in order to judge their success. So it might be that moving a target group from being aware of a complex new investment product to understanding it denoted a successful campaign, even if the act of purchase was still some way off.

In real life people are not as logical in their responses as sequential models assume, but this does not prevent the models from being useful. For example, AIDA can serve as a check-list for message structure, or as a guide to the layout and design of an advertisement or sales presentation. Practically any press advertisement will demonstrate the principle. A headline grabs the attention. The reader's interest is then captivated by an illustration or a photographic image. The words of the ad demonstrate how the product or service on offer will provide a sought-after benefit (thus stimulating desire). A coupon, or telephone number, or list of stockists, will complete the structure, allowing the reader to become a customer by converting interest and desire into the action of purchase.

An alternative view

In spite of appealing to our common sense, hierarchy of effects models often seem a million miles away from what is actually going on in the real world of customer communication. Far from being naive receivers for commercial messages, consumers are sophisticated and selective. They use advertising rather than being used by it. As we have seen, sequential models of communication have something to offer our understanding of what is going on in marketing communications, but they are by no means the end of the story. It is all too easy to end up talking at customers rather than seeking a dialogue with them. One-way communication can waste money and effort, at worst it can have a permanently alienating effect.

An alternative way of looking at communication is to start with the receiver and work back. Because any effective marketing starts with the customer, the relevance of such an approach to promotional communication ought to be clear. Instead of putting the onus on the effective transmission of intended meanings, this approach recognises that receivers create meanings themselves. As a result, the way in which the building blocks of meaning relate to each other becomes of crucial importance. These building blocks are called signs, the systems in which they operate are called codes, and their wider environment is called culture. The study of signs and their relationships is called semiology (or semiotics).

At its most basic level it is both a simple and a useful idea. It boils down to talking the right language to the customer. What this means in practice for communications management is an increased provision for qualitative research before campaigns are devised, and a willingness for clients to trust the more outlandish ideas of their promotional agencies (provided, of course, that they are backed by reasoned argument and evidence).

CASE STUDY **11.2**

Slice of life

Since its creation in 1890, Hovis has cultivated an image of natural, wholesomeness, building on the revolutionary idea of its inventor, Richard Smith, to retain the wheatgerm in the flour. This is one of the most valuable parts of the grain from a dietary point of view, yet it is removed from ordinary flour. One might expect Hovis advertising to concentrate on rational health claims as a result, but it has always been a classic example of the soft sell, using powerful images rather than rational arguments in its campaigns. The very name Hovis is rich in semiotic significance. It is derived from the two Latin words 'hominis vis' (meaning 'the strength of man') and replaced the less successful, and far more literal, original brand name 'Smith's Patent Germ Flour'.

Creative advertising methods have been a mainstay of the brand throughout its history. In 1898, for example, Hovis ran a magazine advertisement titled 'A list of principal bakers who do not sell Hovis bread'. Below the headline was a blank space. Later, in the early twentieth century, the firm tried to cash in on the cycling craze by issuing Hovis cycle maps and route guides, indicating the best places to stock up on the product. In the 1920s prominent artists and illustrators such as Heath Robinson and Mabel Lucy Atwell were behind the brand's posters and advertisements. 'Don't say brown, say Hovis', a line penned at about this time, continued in use until the 1950s when Hovis became one of the first food brands to take advantage of television as an advertising medium.

Hovis's 1974 TV ad featuring a young lad pushing his bike up a hill is possibly the most famous advertisement in the history of UK television. Directed by Ridley Scott, who graduated to feature films such as *Alien* and *Blade Runner*, the Hovis ad introduced the slow movement of Dvorak's New World symphony to a generation of viewers, and spawned countless parodies and imitations. It also created an image of nostalgia about the brand which served it well for a number of years, but was becoming somewhat tired by the mid-1990s, by which time the bread market had changed out of all recognition.

UK consumers spend something like £3 billion per year on bread, with the average family munching its way through eight loaves a week. British Bakeries, the group behind Hovis and Mothers Pride, slug it out with Allied Bakeries, who own the Kingsmill brand. Together with own-label sliced bread, at various price points including 'value brands', and unsliced product from in-store bakeries, the bread market is furiously competitive.

Research by Hovis suggested that while the brand had strong associations of warmth, natural goodness and family values, it was beginning to look outdated against the competition. In an attempt to make Hovis more relevant to contemporary needs, the brand went through a radical re-launch in 2001, involving new packaging, new advertising, and a new proposition aimed at families: 'something good inside'. Out went nostalgia, and in came a *Simpsons*-style cartoon family, Hugh and Hilary Hovis, and their squabble-prone children Harry and Hannah. The animated cartoons were aimed directly at families – the heartland of the brand's traditional success.

Packaging also got a revamp. It was updated to include photographs of traditional, wholesome British food connected with bread, such as cucumber slices on one style of loaf, and baked beans on another. In an innovative move (which did not prove very popular with some retailers) a new 'Best of Both' loaf was introduced which allowed mums to get the goodness of brown bread in a white loaf. Sales volumes went up by 20 per cent as a result of the £7 million re-launch, suggesting that there is plenty of life still remaining in the brand, in spite of the fact that it has been around for more than a century.

Questions

1   Why might imagery rather than rational argument be effective for a food product?
2   What are the advantages and disadvantages of using cartoon characters in advertising?
3   In the light of the case study, critically discuss the idea that while products have a limited life-cycle, a brand can go on forever.

Sources: Guardian (2002); Smith (2002); Taylor (2002).

Theories of advertising
....

Advertising is any form of paid-for media communication designed to inform and influence existing or potential customers. It is a major marketing expense, but in spite of the amount of money that is invested in it, there is relatively little scientific consensus about how advertising works. Clients and agencies invest plenty of time and money in trying to understand how their own advertising works, but this information is precious and confidential – and is likely to be specific to their own markets and brands. Advertising awards and case studies allow some insight into the process, but may not give the full picture.

DID YOU KNOW?

According to the Advertising Standards Authority, whose job it is to police them, there are approximately 30 million press advertisements each year in the UK (www.asa.org.uk).

It is almost impossible to generalise from advertising research. Experiments and surveys can only be carried out with specific examples of advertising. So a company might learn more about how its own press advertising works from research, but whether this would hold true for anyone else's advertising, or for advertising in a different medium, is another question entirely.

In spite of this, there is no shortage of advertising practitioners who are willing to share their philosophy of what constitutes effective advertising with prospective clients. The principles to which they subscribe are based not so much on scientific experimentation, as on common sense and experience. Each agency's distinctive approach to advertising will aim at differentiating it from its rivals in a highly competitive market-place. Yet there have always been two main schools of thought – those who believe in the hard sell, and those who favour gentler tactics.

Hard sell versus soft sell

Advocates of 'hard sell' believe an advertisement should have a simple and direct message, hammered home in an unforgettable way. This approach draws on a well-established practitioner theory of advertising – the Unique Selling Proposition, which was made famous in the early 1960s by Rosser Reeves, who worked for the American agency, Ted Bates. Reeves argued that advertising operated on a platform that was basically rational, and that to increase its memorability an advertisement should concentrate on just one powerful message. To pull users across to your product you needed to argue a case for it. Your advertising needed to stress your product's unique features, driving home its advantages over the competition with a compelling sales pitch.

An alternative approach to how advertising works avoids the question of rational arguments altogether. Instead of trying to prove a product's superiority over the competition by enumerating its features, it aims at endowing the product with an attractive personality with which its users can identify. This is true of a number of long-running campaigns where a brand is demonstrated in a family context (products like Oxo, Andrex and Persil have provided good examples in the past). This approach is in the tradition of brand image advertising, often identified with the name of David Ogilvy, who made it a hallmark of the famous agency he founded in the 1950s.

Brand image advertising takes the benefits of the product for granted, and focuses instead on creating positive emotional and psychological associations with the product. It is a gentle but confident approach, soft sell as opposed to hard sell. Its advocates maintain that it works best with expensive, highly visible purchases which are themselves connected with status (such as luxury goods), but experience suggests that even frequently-purchased items like clothes washing detergent and lavatory paper can be given an aura that reflects their performance and quality.

Of course many successful advertising campaigns contain elements of both approaches, varying the mixture according to the product and the market. Advertising for Fairy Liquid, for example, hammers home the benefits of effectiveness, kindness to hands and value for money, but also surrounds the product with warm associations. After all, as consumers we are driven by a combination of the rational and the emotional. We are therefore more comfortable with advertising that reflects this.

KEY SKILLS
ACTIVITY **11.2**
....

**Improving own
learning and
performance**

Hard sell and soft sell

Developing a variety of approaches to persuading a customer of the benefits of your product or service is a useful skill. This exercise gives you an opportunity to experiment with different styles.

Find one hard sell and one soft sell advertisement in a newspaper or magazine. Come up with a list of changes that would make the hard sell softer and the soft sell harder, and rewrite the ads accordingly. How appropriate are the revised approaches? Might they appeal to a different market segment from the current one?

Advertising and sales

Not all advertising activity is meant to have a direct effect on sales. For example, oil companies often run general advertising campaigns in order to improve their image with investors and environmentalists. This kind of advertising, known as corporate advertising, is not tied to any particular product, so its effects would be impossible to gauge from measuring increased sales. Research into attitudes or stock market prices would be a better method of seeing if it was working.

Some advertising activity is actually meant to deter sales. For example, the horrific drink-driving campaigns that are unveiled each year before the Christmas season aim to prevent the inappropriate purchase and use of alcoholic drinks by their target group.

All advertising has one thing in common, however. It aims at affecting behaviour (and we can include what people think as well as what people do in this category). The behaviour with which most advertising is associated is purchase behaviour – either to induce it in the first place, or (more commonly) to maintain it in the face of intense competition. The widely accepted model of how this works is that advertising supports sales with a short-term impetus whose effect survives after the advertising activity has finished. After a while, if no further advertising takes place, the effect decays. This may also be due to the activities of rival firms, whose advertising is now supplanting your own in the minds of the consumers to whose needs it is relevant.

Most advertising researchers agree that advertising cannot make you buy something you are not already in the market for, but that it can have an effect on the actual choice you make between the alternatives. Another way of putting this is that advertising cannot itself expand a market, but can affect brandshare within a market. So car advertising is unlikely to make the UK car market bigger (that will happen for other reasons, connected with lifestyles, income and technological infrastructure), but it might make the difference between whether you buy a Volvo or a Volkswagen, if you are looking for a family car of a certain size.

DID YOU KNOW?

The world's most expensive TV advertising campaign (so far!) was carried out by Pepsi Cola in the US. Fronted by pop idol Britney Spears, the ads cost £5.7 million and were first broadcast during the American Superbowl on 3 February 2002. The ads work out at £63,000 per second (Folkard, 2003).

Share of voice and share of market

Share of voice is the name advertising agencies give to this idea of how much advertising activity one company is conducting compared to its competition. There is an observable relationship between share of voice and share of market. So, for example, Ford's share of advertising in the UK car industry will have a relationship with its share of the number of cars sold in any year.

A long-standing American research project called PIMS (Profit Impact of Marketing Strategy) has collected information over the years about advertising and marketing activity from a large number of major companies (Buzzell and Gale, 1987). Participants are guaranteed anonymity in return for being able to share the results of the research. The findings suggest that in advertising, as in life, success breeds success. Increasing share of voice is most effective for brands that already have a very large share of the market. Similarly, a pound spent on advertising an already successful product in a growing market can be expected to yield more in benefit than a pound spent trying to resurrect the fortunes of an ailing brand.

How much is enough?

Given the high cost of advertising, and the uncertainty surrounding its precise effects, the question of how much to spend is a vexed one for many businesses. Yet precisely because of the vulnerability of advertising budgets, marketing managers need to be able to defend them on rational grounds. The following factors are commonly applied in decisions about how much to spend on advertising.

Competitive activity

Measuring the amount of advertising broadcast or published by competitors can lead to a pretty accurate estimate of the levels of their expenditure, and specialist monitoring companies exist to provide such a service. Armed with this knowledge, a company can then attempt to match the 'industry average' in its own efforts to advertise. Critics of competitive activity as a guide to advertising expenditure point out that setting budgets by this method alone is merely a recipe for maintaining the status quo.

History

Looking at what was spent last year and adding an element for inflation often features in budget preparation. Unfortunately the market may have changed, or the last few years may have represented an under-investment which, if continued, will only make matters worse.

DID YOU KNOW?

Sexist advertising is bad for your brain. In an experiment at Canada's University of Waterloo, groups of students were shown different selections of TV ads, some of which portrayed stereotypical women obsessed with cake mix and skincare products. In maths tests administered after the ads had been shown, women who had seen the sexist ads performed considerably worse than other respondents (Motluk, 1999).

Percentage of sales

Advertising Association figures reveal different going rates for what is known as the 'advertising to sales' ratio in different industries. A recent survey in Ireland revealed, unsurprisingly, that soap powder manufacturers spend most, with Persil committing 5 per cent of its total sales to advertising. At the other end of the scale were dairy products (where, no doubt, availability and price are more important than promotion). Avonmore Milk, Ireland's biggest selling grocery product according to industry figures, spent only 0.14 per cent of sales on advertising (O'Kane, 2001). The more important image is to the product, the higher the ratio is likely to be. However, if sales of a particular brand are going down due to too little advertising, this yardstick is not much help.

Objective and task

This is the most rational method of budget setting, and the most popular with marketing theorists. It operates on the principle that you should first decide what you want to do (objective) and then cost the necessary action (task). The problem is that the ideal programme of activity may well become so extensive as to exceed the availability of funds. But as an exercise in prioritisation, this approach has much to recommend it. It forces planners not to take anything for granted.

For example, the actual number of times an advertisement needs to be seen before it registers with its audience is likely to vary with the nature of the product and the nature of the advertisement itself. A reminder-type advertisement for a familiar product might only need to be seen once or twice, but a ground-breaking new advertisement for an unfamiliar product might need three or four exposures before it sinks in. Effective frequency, as this ideal number is called, is a key factor in trying to extract the maximum value from the advertising budget. Too few exposures and money will have been wasted in an ineffectual campaign, but too many exposures are just as wasteful – perhaps with the additional effect of irritating consumers into the bargain. Jones (1995) goes so far as to claim that in many cases only one exposure may be enough to trigger sales.

None of these factors in isolation offers a watertight solution to the problem of establishing an infallible figure. However, applied together, they can provide marketing managers with a degree of confidence about the size of their budget.

KEY SKILLS
ACTIVITY **11.3**
· · · · · · · · · · · · · · · ·
Information and communication technology

Irritating advertisements

The best place to get a feel for Internet advertising is probably on the Internet itself, and who better to tell you about it than Microsoft? In fact, any of the major portals such as Yahoo! or Lycos will have a section which informs advertisers of the benefits, technical details and cost of various advertising opportunities. Browse their sites to see what is available.

Pop-up ads on the Internet are a source of irritation to many surfers. They appear on your computer screen unbidden and need to be actively closed by a mouse click. This slows things down and is frustrating if you are in a hurry to find information on another page. Advertisers claim that because such ads are harder to ignore than the banner ads which simply wait to be noticed (and, ideally, clicked) they are more effective at raising the profile of goods and services.

Visit the Microsoft Network Advantage Marketing network Website (www.advantage.msn.co.uk) and browse the resources there on 'Next Generation Ad Products', which include pop-up ads.

Agencies and clients
· ·

Advertising, like many other marketing services, is usually entrusted to a specialist company called an agency. Agents act on behalf of others – so the relationship with the client, the person who is actually footing the bill for the advertising at the end of the day, is crucial.

How agencies make money

In the beginning advertising agencies used to work for media owners rather than advertisers. In nineteenth-century America they acted as sales representatives for media owners, selling space to advertisers and taking a commission from the media owner for doing so. As time went on they also began writing ads to fill the space for their customers, and then added on more services until they emerged as fully-fledged agencies. From these roots the traditional 'commission' system of agency remuneration developed.

Media owners pay recognised advertising agencies a standard commission of 15 per cent on the time or space bought. So, if the price of a TV spot is £1,000, the agency only pays £850 to the station (i.e. 85 per cent – the full price, minus the agency's 15 per cent commission). When the agency bills the client it adds 17.65 per cent to the figure to make it back up to £1,000. On activity that is non-commissionable, such as buying artwork or research, the agency bases the price to the client on the same kind of principle, grossing up the cost price of the purchase by 17.65 per cent. In all these transactions the agency is acting as the principal. In other words, if the client goes bust, the agency is still responsible for paying the media owner – a further justification of its right to commission. If an agency goes bust, which sometimes happens, the media owner cannot get redress from the client for any outstanding debts. So media owners will only offer commission to recognised advertising agencies whose management and finances are regularly reviewed by a number of trade bodies.

There is, however, an increasing move towards charging for work on a fee basis. This makes sense for smaller clients and for special projects, like new product development, where advertising expenditure may be out of the question for several years until the new product finally makes it to the launch stage. In the era of media-neutral planning, where agencies no longer take it for granted that media advertising is the best or only option, the idea of remuneration by commission is looking increasingly outmoded.

Why use an agency at all?

There are a number of reasons why clients prefer to use agencies, as follows.

Reduced contact costs

Like the distribution intermediaries discussed in Chapter 10, they reduce costs and inconvenience. The countless transactions involved in creating, producing and placing advertising are consolidated into one relationship for the client.

Advertising expertise

Agencies are full of specialists who, between them, can offer many lifetimes' worth of experience in areas such as media research, campaign planning, buying advertising space and time. An agency can offer a client a fresh perspective, but needs to work hard to understand the whole of the business – not just the communications end.

Economy

Because of their buying power agencies can achieve prices for services like market research or printing which their clients would have difficulty matching.

Creativity

This is probably the single most important reason for using an agency. It's the one thing that clients cannot do for themselves. Agencies can view their clients' business dispassionately, providing insight and objectivity. But most of all they can come up with the Big Idea and have the skills to make it work.

Who's who?

The way that advertising agencies are structured reflects the kind of work they do. Some are very specialised, such as media buying shops. Others, known as full-service agencies, will be of a size that reflects their capacity to offer clients the full gamut of advertising services – from planning and devising advertising strategies to realising and carrying them out. Figure 11.2 shows the structure of a typical agency of this sort, offering account handling and planning, creative and production, and media planning and buying.

The main point of contact with the client will be the account director. It is a common joke about advertising agencies that everyone is a director (as it impresses clients to have senior-sounding personnel on their business). But the job title implies a real degree of autonomy and responsibility. In a fast-moving service environment, account directors organise the agency's top players to achieve the client's goals.

Although the precise job titles may differ from agency to agency, Figure 11.2 is a guide to the main roles in any advertising agency structure.

Senior account director

The team captain – maximising the service to the client, while watching profitability. Will have a number of account groups, not unlike the way a senior marketing manager is responsible for several groups of products.

Account director

Dubbed 'the Suit' by the rest of the team. Needs a strategic and diplomatic approach in order to be able to deliver the (near) impossible to impatient clients.

figure 11.2
Agency structure

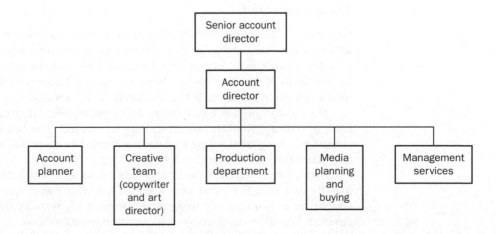

Account planner

The brains of the team – thinking long-term, representing the customer, updating the creative brief, researching and evaluating. Wins arguments without shouting.

Creative team: copywriter and art director

Usually hired as a team of two – one for words the other for pictures. Sensitive, observant, insecure. Under enormous pressure, which is why they need to be managed carefully and well.

Production department

Some agencies have in-house artwork studios, but much print production (and all radio or TV) will be placed externally. The production department co-ordinates, spots talent and negotiates to get the best deal.

Media planners and buyers

Often a dual role (particularly for press planning/buying). Plan where to spend the media money to best effect, and negotiate for the lowest price as they spend it.

General management services

A good financial controller (backed by reliable systems) is essential to a successful agency because of the need to maintain positive cash flow. Only the largest agencies will have a personnel function – usually recruitment and training is handled by staff active in other areas.

Account management requires a clear head and a tough skin. Acting as the point of contact with the client means that sales skills and diplomacy are at a premium. But business insight and strategic skills are just as necessary. The account director will work closely with the client in order to understand the problem that the advertising will aim at solving to their mutual benefit. In most agencies the account planner will make a significant input at this stage, to create something called the creative brief. This is the first step in the process of managing the advertising process.

The creative brief

Creativity is the most important aspect of what clients demand from their agencies. But it is a very difficult commodity to manage. Ingenious advertising may win awards, but truly creative advertising needs to be relevant and effective. In the words of Bill Bernbach, whose ads for Volkswagen in the 1960s made it into a cult car in America: 'If it doesn't sell, it isn't creative.'

The creative brief is a systematic technique to help clients clarify their problems so that appropriate solutions may be offered. The full brief will usually consist of a lengthy document, detailing market background and outlining the characteristics of the target audience.

It will be crystallised on to one side of A4 as a summary creative brief – usually cast into the form of a series of questions and answers. The precise format varies from agency to agency, but most are broadly similar in the areas covered. The three most important questions are as follows.

What is the problem/opportunity?

As we have observed, no one spends advertising money lightly. There has to be a problem to solve, and the more tightly defined the problem the more capable it will be of solution. In this sense a problem (like a declining brand) is an opportunity (to revitalise it). Skoda's renaissance as a credible car maker in the wake of its takeover by Volkswagen in the early 1990s was in large part due to advertising which humorously, but effectively, addressed the issue of the brand's perceived quality.

Whose behaviour are we trying to affect?

Advertising aims at changing behaviour, even if that behaviour is the way we think about something. Trying to define the audience for the campaign is crucial in order to set realistic objectives in this respect. Are we talking about encouraging existing users to consume more, or reminding lapsed users of the virtue of our brand, for example? And what kind of people are they? Talking your audience's language is the first step to getting through to them. The careful segmentation that is an aspect of all successful media campaigns will be evident here in a precise definition of the target market, often using demographic terms.

What is the single most important message we want them to take from the advertising?

Thinking back to the section on communication theory at the beginning of this chapter, this is where common-sense semiotics comes in. The question as posed here recognises that the audience are active interpreters of the advertising rather than passive recipients of its message on the advertiser's terms. It is vital to envisage the advertising from their viewpoint in order to articulate the desired effect. So, to pick a famous example of advertising, Nestlé urges us not to have a delicious chocolate biscuit snack (which might be how a less canny advertiser would see the proposition) but to 'Have a Break – have a KitKat'. The core benefit of a KitKat is the excuse it gives us to relax, and that is what we recognise in the advertising.

The brief will also include any other information that can be pressed into creating the right kind of advertising results. This can include details of recent market research surveys, articles from magazines or journals, guidelines on media preferences expressed by the client, seasonal trends, news of competitive activity and so on. The essence of the brief, though, will be contained in the answers to the three main questions we have looked at – defining the problem, focusing on the market and articulating the benefit.

The creative brief is thrashed out and agreed by the client working in close co-operation with the account director and the account planner. The problem is now presented to the creative team. They need to respond with a compelling interpretation in words and images. Creative teams comprise an art director, providing pictures and visuals, and a copywriter responsible for the verbal side. Even in an apparently non-visual medium like radio, an art director can help a copywriter by visualising the pictures being evoked. And in a poster or press ad that consists entirely of words, the art director can advise on the style of typography used.

Managing the relationship

The creative brief is just one technique for managing the relationship between client and agency. As in any partnership involving a service, at all times it must be clear what action is approved. There is plenty of room for confusion. Many students who do placements in advertising agencies are amazed by the complexity of the processes involved in getting something as apparently simple as a press ad into the paper. Another common observation is how last-minute everything seems to be – due to the time pressures involved in servicing a number of demanding clients. These conditions require robust systems to make them work without getting wires crossed. Some of the most useful ones in an A–Z of popular advertising jargon are as follows.

Brand reviews

A periodic, usually annual, assessment of the standing of each brand in the agency's care. The review involves substantial input from the client's marketing team as well as reports from the account planner and media personnel. This is an opportunity to stand back and take a strategic perspective, which will then feed in to a medium- and short-term action plan.

Call reports

Decisions taken in meetings or telephone calls, with action responsibilities, will be recorded in what is known as a Call Report (a business call rather than a social call). This is circulated immediately after the meeting.

Client meetings

Reviewing progress, approving creative work, sharing information, effective meetings are a cornerstone of successful client/agency relations. They are expensive because of the amount of time they tie up, so need clear objectives and outcomes.

DID YOU KNOW?
How much does a televison 30-second ad cost to broadcast? It depends where and when. A mid-evening weekday slot on Grampian (with 2 million homes viewing) costs approximately £870. The same spot on Carlton (with 5.6 million homes viewing) costs over 35 times as much (Advertising Association, 2001).

Media schedules

These are the written plans outlining advertising activity involving media expenditure. They need to be approved by the client before any money is committed. Usually advertising will take place in a series of bursts through the year – and frequently clients will insist on approving each burst of advertising separately. Alternatively, advertising that goes on continuously but at a lower level (called 'drip' advertising) may be approved by calendar period. Media owners are as anxious as anyone else to ensure that their services are sold, and will offer discounts to encourage early commitment of funds. So client approvals need to be clear and well-timed.

Production estimates

Advertising involves the production as well as the creation and placing of advertisements. Production budgets can vary enormously, from a few hundred pounds for a basic radio advertisement to half a million for a TV extravaganza. The production estimate is a way for agencies and clients to keep tabs on exactly what is being spent through a detailed breakdown of costs. The precise list will vary with the kind of medium being used, but is likely to include photography, actors and models, materials, sets and locations, typography, setting and reproduction. The more money that can be saved here, the more the advertiser can afford to spend on the media campaign itself.

Evaluating advertising

Having made the right selection of advertising agency, and managed the relationship carefully, how does a client evaluate the results? Like any marketing activity, advertising needs clear objectives. Measuring success against precisely defined objectives means that valuable experience can be built up.

As we have seen, the sales effects that advertising should help produce are hard to trace immediately or exclusively to advertising activity. It is easier, and more useful, to trace the effects of advertising through the following shorter-term measures:

► *Recall*: asking people what they can remember seeing advertised in a particular period.
► *Attitude*: measuring consumer attitudes to a product or idea before and after a campaign.
► *Exposure*: calculating, from regularly published viewing, listening and readership figures, how many people in your target group will have had a chance to be exposed to your advertisement and how often.

Recall and attitude surveys can be conducted on an occasional or a regular basis. Spontaneous recall is when respondents can remember an advertisement off the top of their head. Prompted recall is when respondents are given examples of products or advertisements, and agree that they have seen them recently. Such research provides many advertisers with a dispiriting reminder of how much work they still have to do to make any headway into people's attention or memory.

Media research

Measuring exposure keeps an entire industry busy. UK media research is a remarkably intricate network of regular surveys funded by media owners, advertisers and agencies, dedicated to establishing precisely what any kind of media exposure is worth. With billions of pounds being spent on advertising each year in the UK, this is far from an academic exercise.

Television advertising is measured by an organisation called BARB (Broadcasters' Audience Research Board). This reveals what the UK television audience are watching at any particular time, and is of keen interest not only to advertisers, but to programme makers from both commercial and public sector TV. It collates data from a sample of over 5,000 homes spread across all the TV regions, carefully selected for being representative of the population. It reveals that on average we watch three-and-a-half hours of television a day – less in summer and more in winter. The data is provided on a minute-by-minute basis, allowing advertisers to track precise performances of commercials in particular programme breaks.

The nation's reading habits are reported at six-monthly intervals through the National Readership Survey (NRS). This takes data from 35,000 interviews a year to assess what respondents have 'seen or looked at in the last 12 months' – a pretty rough measure of readership which nevertheless serves as the basis for audience calculations. Readership is always higher than circulation, of course, because a copy of a newspaper or magazine will tend to be read by more people than actually buy it. Readership varies from publication to publication – for a newspaper it can be as little as two or three readers per issue, for a trade magazine circulating in a company it could be six or seven. The number of times a publication is referred to (and thus offers a chance for an advertisement to be seen) also varies from title to title, with programme listings magazines like the *Radio Times* heading the ranks.

> **DID YOU KNOW?**
>
> *According to the chairman of Granada TV, television advertising produces an average 4.8 per cent uplift in sales for fast-moving consumer goods in the first month after advertising is seen by a consumer, and a significant number of incremental purchases for some time after (Allen, 2002).*

Other media have their respective research sources, each with its distinctive acronym. RAJAR (Radio Joint Audience Research) gives quarterly figures for radio listenership. Posters have been notoriously under-researched in the past, but since the 1990s POSTAR (Poster Audience Research) has provided credible statistics on audiences for UK poster sites.

Media research terminology

All of these media research sources have a common terminology to describe what is being bought and at what price. Crude as comparisons between media inevitably are, these terms nevertheless give us a framework for evaluating the effect of advertising in any medium:

▶ *Cost per thousand (CPT)*: The cost of reaching 1,000 members of your target audience in a particular medium.

Although it is a useful statistic when comparing like with like (e.g. two free newspapers in a specific circulation area), it is not very helpful in making comparisons between media. For example the cost per thousand for a poster is many times less than for a television spot, but the two forms of communication are very different.

▶ *Coverage*: The number of people reached at least once by an advertisement, or series of advertisements.

Within this number (usually expressed as a percentage of the target audience) many will have seen the ad more than once in the course of the campaign. A television campaign would have to run for a very long time in order to get 100 per cent coverage of the entire audience because of the recalcitrant 'light viewer', but coverage levels of 75 per cent to 80 per cent are common for most campaigns.

Television advertising has spawned its own terminology for coverage – the Television Rating Point (TVR) or 'ratings'. A TVR is equivalent to

1 per cent of your target audience viewing a particular spot. So if 30 per cent of London men are glued to the Bond movie on ITV, that means you have bought 30 London men TVRs. The problem is that this measurement does not take into account repetition of the same audience. The next spot you buy might score 20 TVRs, making a total of 50 TVRs in all. But the unit makes no distinction between those who have already seen your ad and those seeing it for the first time. So rather than having reached a total of 50 per cent of the target audience, your ad may still have reached only 30 per cent, but two-thirds of them will now have seen it twice. Only careful scheduling to include different sorts of programming will maximise the number of people who see your ad at least once.

▶ *Frequency*: The number of times an advertisement is seen.

Received advertising wisdom is that most ads need to be seen more than once in order to communicate effectively, although recent research has suggested that an interested buyer does not need much prompting. Effective frequency will differ from case to case, but exceeding it can be wasteful. The trick with clever media scheduling is to maximise the number of readers, listeners or viewers exposed to the advertisement the targeted number of times.

Which medium to use?

With nearly 600 paid-for newspapers, 3,300 consumer magazines and almost twice that number of business publications from which to choose, the inexperienced advertiser faces a bewildering variety of media. Which of them is best suited to advertise a particular service or product? The best kind of media planning starts out from the idea that what you are buying is not so many inches in a newspaper or seconds on a television screen, but people. What kind of people are your customers? What sort of media do they pay attention to? Where do you need to reach them in the best frame of mind?

As we have seen, the kind of media research carried out through large surveys like the NRS can link age and social characteristics to media usage. And media owners themselves can be a useful source of information on what kind of audience they can deliver. They have a vested interest (as agencies do) in a client's advertising being successful, so they can be listened to with confidence (although they are always selling in competition with other media).

An important source of information in this decision is a large-scale regular survey called the Target Group Index (TGI). This looks at the consumption patterns of a representative sample of consumers. It asks questions about the products they buy and use, but it also covers what they watch, read and listen to. Subscribing to this survey (an example of the omnibus type of survey mentioned in Chapter 5) allows a marketing organisation to draw direct correlations between its customers and the audience of certain media.

Media characteristics

Thinking in more general terms about choosing the right place for a promotional message, it is clear that different media have different strengths and weaknesses. Their characteristics can be borne in mind not only when planning an advertising campaign, but also for making sure a public relations programme is being accurately targeted.

A short guide to the strengths and weaknesses of the major UK media is as follows (with statistics from the Advertising Association (www.adassoc.org.uk, 2002).

Television (roughly a quarter of UK advertising expenditure)
On the positive side:

► High audiences, as many as 15 million people watch big films on ITV. But they are becoming increasingly spread over the viewing opportunities available from multi-channel television.
► TV is excellent for demonstrating product usage.
► Advent of digital TV offers marketers the potential for tighter targeting and powerful interactivity with customers.

On the minus side:

► The short time span of most commercials (30 seconds) is a limiting factor.
► High wastage (i.e. viewers not in your target market).
► There are a number of restrictions on what can be shown on television.

Press (roughly half of UK advertising expenditure)
On the positive side:

► Highly targetable.
► Can provide a very good environment for advertising matter.
► Handles detail well.
► Can be used to get direct response (e.g. from reply coupons).

On the minus side:

► There is a confusing profusion of titles available to the media buyer.
► Can be low-impact.
► Can present the advertiser with timing difficulties in co-ordinating the appearance of a campaign.

Radio (over 3 per cent of UK advertising expenditure)
On the positive side:

► Radio is a growing medium allowing accurate geographical targeting.
► Relatively low cost compared to other broadcast media, although digital services will increase the potential sophistication of activity.
► Speedy access to audiences.
► Stations such as Classic FM provide a national advertising presence, complemented by strong regional and local stations.

On the minus side:

► It is seen as a background medium – something you listen to when you are driving or doing housework.
► It cannot handle complex messages.

► In spite of its progress as a national advertising medium, it is still relatively fragmented.
► The absolute numbers of people it reaches can be low compared to other media.

Posters (5 per cent of UK advertising expenditure)

On the positive side:

► Possibly the oldest advertising medium.
► Impressive size and ubiquity. There are in excess of 100,000 panels in the UK.
► Like radio, posters are relatively cheap.

On the minus side:

► Tend to be seen as low-impact and are complicated to buy.
► They have to compete with a lot of visual clutter and are subject to damage and defacement.

CASE STUDY **11.3**

Leave them kids alone?

Sweden only started allowing advertising on television in 1990. It does not permit any advertising on television aimed at children under 12. Greece has a ban preventing toys being advertised on television, and Belgium does not allow advertising to children on TV in the Flemish part of the country. Denmark has a ban on advertising for five minutes before and after children's programming, and Ireland's broadcaster, RTE, does not carry advertising on children's television. Italy does not allow advertising in cartoons, and Poland has banned TV and radio marketing aimed at children.

The UK's regime looks pretty liberal compared to this, but there are very clear guidelines on what is and is not allowed on television and other media as far as advertising to children is concerned. The UK advertising industry argues that it is only by exposing children to advertising in a responsible and sensible way that they can learn how to make judgements in a commercial world, and that to prevent children from seeing advertising is to deprive them of information to which they have a legitimate right. Critics maintain that children are a soft touch for advertisers, and that advertising support for processed foods, expensive gadgets and designer labels leads to unhealthy diets and harassed parents. In a National Opinion Poll survey conducted in 2000, 54 per cent of respondents supported a ban on advertising to children in the UK, and in 2002 over 100 MPs put their names to an Early Day Motion in the House of Commons which proposed outlawing any TV advertising aimed at the under-fives.

Questions

1 If the issue at stake is the morality of advertising to children, why do the bans mentioned in this case study focus exclusively on television advertising?
2 Assess the argument that children need to be exposed to advertising in order to be able to make judgements in a commercial world.
3 The Greek advertising ban means that customers pay more for toys in Greece than they would pay for comparable purchases in other European countries. Comment on the reasons for this, and on the view that the Greek ban is just a form of protectionism.

Source: Incorporated Society of British Advertisers (2002).

New media

One of the driving forces behind media-neutral planning is the enormous potential offered by new electronic media, particularly the Internet, to extend relationships with customers. By using digital computer technology to integrate data, text, sound and all kinds of image within a single environment, 'multimedia' marketing widens the boundaries of traditional marketing in a way which threatens established business models. Technological developments happen fast in this area, but the available opportunities fall into four main categories:

▶ *The Internet* – mostly conveyed through computers, but increasingly featuring content available on portable devices such as mobile phones and personal digital assistants (PDAs).
▶ *Digital television* – offering advertisers and broadcasters unprecedented potential in the richness and interactivity of what can be broadcast. Effectively, digital broadcasting harnesses many of the creative and marketing capabilities of the Internet in the familiar shape of the television set.
▶ *Interactive kiosks* – devices with touch-screen technology which can be installed in venues such as tourist information centres, pubs and nightclubs.
▶ *Packaged media such as CD ROMs or Digital Video (Versatile) Discs (DVDs)* – these can either be used on their own, as multimedia catalogues, or in conjunction with online Internet resources to update their content. For example, a music CD might connect the playing device to an Internet website with details of forthcoming live performances by the artistes concerned.

Using the Internet

The common element in these applications is the Internet. Because of its rapid growth the Internet is still something of an unknown quantity, although it promises to be among the most accurately-trackable marketing technologies ever implemented. The one thing that all pundits agree upon is that the Internet is on an irresistible growth trend. Commentators are fond of pointing out that, while television took 15 years to establish 50 million viewers in the US, the Web will have reached that target in less than a third of the time (Mazur, 1998).

DID YOU KNOW?
While UK advertising spend on the Internet increased from £8 million in 1997 to £142 million in 2001, this still represents something less than 1 per cent of all advertising expenditure (Advertising Association, www.adassoc.org.uk, 2002).

The demographics of Internet users are highly attractive to advertisers. Innovation-prone by nature, they reveal many of the attributes associated with early adopters (see Chapter 9). Generally youthful, university-educated, male, with above-average earnings, the nature of the online population still reflects the predominant use of the Internet as a business or academic research tool – true to its origins in the 1960s as a network of information exchange between military and scientific research communities. However, the sharp growth in domestic connections through Internet Service Providers (ISPs), and the rapid adoption of broadband and 'always on' connectivity to homes as well as businesses, suggests that the

Internet has now turned the corner as a consumer medium rather than a professional one. In much the same way, mobile phones have migrated from being exclusively business tools to becoming consumer accessories.

The sheer amount of information on the Internet is overwhelming. There is also enormous variability in its usefulness and accuracy, given the absence of the quality control mechanisms associated with traditional publishing. This has led to the growth of what are known as portals – literally gateways into the Internet which offer users a reliable guide to what is on offer and act as a jumping-off point. Because portals tend to be built around a particular interest (such as an area of work or leisure), or around a search engine like Yahoo! or Lycos, they offer marketers a ready-built community of potential customers who might have needs and wants in common. Portals therefore use their position as gatekeepers to take advantage of the high traffic through their home pages and search pages, and sell advertising and sponsorship in much the same way as magazines or newspapers do.

> **DID YOU KNOW?**
> The average Internet user tends to concentrate his or her attention on no more than about a dozen frequently-visited sites. In spite (or perhaps because) of the millions of web pages out there, the Internet is a highly customised information resource.

Yahoo! is one of the most visited sites in the UK and is essentially a starting point for searching the Net. By offering space to advertisers that is visible alongside the search results, the company has been one of the first Internet businesses to show a healthy profit. The advertising that appears depends on the keywords used by the searcher. This 'self-selection' by potentially large audiences voluntarily forming themselves into smaller segments may have a profound effect on traditional marketing attitudes to segmentation and positioning.

> **DID YOU KNOW?**
> Yahoo! site visitors earn more than twice the national average, are ten times more likely to eat in restaurants, and eight times more likely to visit cinemas on a weekly basis than the rest of the UK population (Rosen, 1998).

Advertisers can buy space juxtaposed with the content (most often as 'banner' advertising, which takes the form of a clickable graphic link to the advertiser's own website), or they can opt to sponsor other people's websites. Research suggests that the most effective banner campaigns get click-through rates of 10 per cent and more (Hayter, 1998). Click-through is the proportion of people who see the ad and then use it as a link to the website of the advertiser for further information or to place an order.

The kind of advertising opportunities available on the Internet are in a state of constant development. For example, most banner ads now feature animation and sound in an attempt to engage the user's attention. Media-rich banners, as they are called, can be appreciated without having to leave the original site. A more obtrusive, and annoying, form of advertising on the Web is the interstitial ad – literally a web page that 'stands between' the user and the next page. There are also smaller ads known as 'pop-ups' which appear unbidden, and even 'pop-unders' which load behind the page being currently viewed and are not visible until that page is closed. Because these advertisements appear without being requested, and need to be closed by the viewer before moving on, they are noticeable, but can alienate the user very easily.

As a new medium, it is important to recognise that the Internet has distinctive capabilities and needs to be approached in a way that takes full advantage of them. The following criteria are worth bearing in mind when briefing or evaluating proposals for any online campaign (Owen, 1998):

▶ It should provide synergies with existing promotion in other media, contributing to the overall integration of a campaign message.

▶ It should be concise and snappy: time is a scarce resource on the Internet, as attention spans are short and pages can be frustratingly slow to load if they are too sophisticated.

▶ It should be visually arresting – the visual impact of the medium is judged by increasingly sophisticated standards.

▶ It should be tailored to its environment – even more than most advertising, because of the self-selecting nature of its audience, online work needs to be context-sensitive.

▶ It should offer some kind of interactive opportunity – one of the great strengths of Internet advertising is that it allows the consumer to do something (like a competition, game or in feedback form).

▶ Where purchasing is involved, delivery systems and pricing should be geared up to customers' expectations. Customers are likely to see the Internet as an alternative to established forms of ordering goods or services (phone or written media), rather than as a replacement. The success of BMW's Internet strategy has been largely due to its integration into the firm's existing ordering and distribution systems (Clarke, 1998).

The internet allows companies to capture data on customers automatically (e.g. tracking which pages they look at when visiting a website). This raises issues of privacy and consent with which not all customers are happy, although companies argue that such information helps them to develop offers tailored to a customer's individual needs. Research on consumers from a number of different EU countries suggests that younger consumers are less bothered about privacy, but that all Internet shoppers worry about security (Brand Strategy, 2002). The top four criteria revealed by the research for successful online shopping were security (71 per cent), competitive pricing (57 per cent), redress if there was a problem with the purchase (55 per cent) and delivery (50 per cent). Having said that, only 27 per cent of the sample were happy to shop online with a credit card, and then only if the website contained an explicit security statement.

Direct marketing
••••••••••••••••••••••

Internet marketing can be seen as an evolution of direct marketing, and both are growing for much the same reasons: pressure on marketing budgets, the growth of information technology, and increased competition in all markets.

Direct marketing is any form of marketing communication that adds value by establishing a direct relationship with the customer. It covers a wide range of activity. Sophisticated mailshots to known customers, mass leaflet drops in the hope of establishing a list of customers who may respond to future offers, magazine advertisements with a reply coupon, even customer care telephone numbers on low-fat spread or soft-drinks cans: all are forms of direct marketing. They are all aiming to forge an direct relationship between buyer and seller which will lead to long-term mutual benefit.

The mail is a particularly important medium for direct marketing, but it is by no means the only one. In fact any advertising medium can be used to foster a direct relationship with the customer – even a fleeting television or radio commercial can contain a telephone number, as pioneering insurance company Direct Line has proved. As well as promotion, direct marketing involves distribution – the actual delivery of the order is an essential part of the process. It can be seen as a whole philosophy of marketing – a way of doing business that creates and keeps a customer in a demonstrable relationship built on mutual advantage.

> **DID YOU KNOW?**
> The UK telemarketing business can be a pretty tough place to work. Bullying and humiliation by managers is not unknown, and staff turnover can be as high as 60 per cent per year. In one notorious case (a true story) a supervisor offered his staff nappies so that they could spend less time away from the phone on loo breaks! (Economist, 2001).

Database marketing

Direct marketing is often referred to as database marketing because of the way it stores and uses customer information. Knowledge is power, and in database marketing knowledge about customers empowers an organisation to satisfy customer needs more effectively than its competitors. A database is simply a list. But the enormous advantage of maintaining and manipulating databases on computers is that information on purchasing behaviour can be cross-referenced with other data. The result is that it becomes much easier to tailor marketing activity relevantly. This ability to customise marketing activity offers a dual benefit. The customer is only targeted with goods that are appropriate (and thus begins to see such promotion as helpful rather than intrusive). The organisation cuts down on inefficiencies in the marketing budget.

> **DID YOU KNOW?**
> Direct marketers tend to have more success during times of national crisis than national rejoicing. Industry pundits suggest that it may have something to do with consumers, depressed at the uncontrollable escalation of external events, trying to exercise some kind of control over their personal environment by buying things. On the other hand, the slow-down in direct marketing observed during, for example, royal weddings, may have something to do with customers' reluctance to cut out offers from magazines or newspapers with 'historic' celebratory value.

Customer acquisition

This is the most expensive part of the process. The phrase reflects the way in which direct marketing regards the customer as an appreciating asset. Another way of putting it would be to see customers as a portfolio of investments. They involve a substantial outlay and not all of them will perform as well as hoped. But by careful review and maintenance they can yield substantial dividends.

Customers are acquired in the following ways.

Collecting information from existing customers
Theatres can convert single-ticket buyers to subscribers, and mail-order companies can convert chance shoppers to regular purchasers, by data capture at point of sale.

Fishing for prospective customers
Trade exhibition stands offering the prize of a bottle of champagne for the first business card drawn out of the hat, advertisements inviting further enquiries, even leaflet drops to particular areas targeted through geodemographics are all ways of trawling the market-place in search of a group of people who are sufficiently interested to respond with their personal details.

Renting other people's customers

There is a burgeoning industry of list brokers fuelling direct marketing. List brokers can provide direct marketers with selections of potential customers to fit specific briefs. Lists can be sourced direct from their owners (e.g. specialist magazine publishers) or compiled fresh from existing sources. Because of the high cost, list renters or list purchasers often insist on testing a sample of the list first with a trial offer. In spite of the frequently high cost per thousand rentals and comparatively low response rates, commercially available lists can be a useful short-cut to establishing the best kind of list of all – a list of people who actually have bought from you.

Existing customers

Sociologists demonstrate that people tend to behave in similar ways within peer groups. As a result MGM (Member Get Member) or FGAF (Friend Get A Friend) are frequently-used tactics for customer acquisition. If they are sufficiently pleased with the service they receive, existing customers can even act as advocates (see Chapter 4 on buyer behaviour).

The test mentality

In spite of the popular image of junk mail, direct marketing in all its forms is one of the most rationally-driven of all marketing communication techniques. Every aspect of a direct marketing package is capable of being tested. For mailings the colour and shape of the envelope, for press ads the size of the illustration or the arrangement of copy, for charity requests the size and order of the suggested donations . . . the permutations are endless. The next time you receive a piece of direct mail, examine each element carefully. Each part will be identifiable by a small code – a guarantee that its effectiveness in generating response is being measured. It may be that half the mailing has gone out in one kind of envelope, the other half in another. Similarly with press ads that seek a direct response, a publication may be printed so that half of its edition carries one version of an advertisement and the other half an alternative version. All else being equal it should be possible to measure their relative effectiveness at pulling response.

One thing that this kind of test approach seems to confirm is that gimmicks work well, even in direct marketing aimed at what one might expect to be rational customers. *Which?* magazine, for example, avoids the newsagents stall and is distributed entirely by subscription. Its stern pages cut through marketing hype to test the true performance of products from family cars to blue jeans. Yet the Consumers' Association has no qualms about using blatant promises of inclusion in free draws and the lure of mystery free gifts to entice likely subscribers to its magazine. As it explains in one of the many inserts in its mailings, such techniques have been proved by research to work.

Five secrets of direct mail success

1   Start selling before they open the envelope. Thinking back to AIDA, this is the opportunity to grab the prospect's Attention. So a message on the envelope itself (perhaps a teaser to arouse curiosity), or an intriguing device seen through a window in the envelope, can save your mailing from the wastepaper basket.

2   Being interesting is more important than being brief. Research shows that people are willing to read four-page letters quite happily, so long as they are interesting. The following layout devices can help:

   ▶ try to end a page with a sentence that runs into the next page
   ▶ indent paragraphs to keep the eye moving down
   ▶ keep paragraphs short
   ▶ keep it personal.

3   Include a response device. If this has the name and address of the respondent pre-printed this makes life easier for them, and good marketing is all about making your customer's life as easy as possible.

4   The more items you put in a direct mail package, the more often the potential customer has to say no. Stickers, scratch cards, certificates, envelopes within envelopes, all promote involvement. The important rule is to be consistent – everything should have a common theme.

5   The most brilliant ideas are frequently the most simple. Charities are particularly good at this, faced as they frequently are with making minimal budgets stretch as creatively as possible. The asthma charity, which included a narrow drinking straw through which prospects were invited to breathe as they read the mailing (to simulate what an asthmatic attack felt like), provides a particularly impressive example of this.

CASE STUDY **11.4**

SMS mess?

Short Message Service (SMS) is marketing-speak for text messaging – a sure-fire way to establish a direct marketing relationship with young consumers. McDonalds, an expert at marketing to pre-teens, have been in the vanguard of this trend with its SMS-based McDs TXT Club aimed at young people of 12 and above. Part of its sponsorship of the ITV series *Popstars – The Rivals* included a Pop & Txt campaign which offered participants text vouchers, added-value content and games. With intensive advertising, blanket media coverage of the television series, and a Christmas Number One guaranteed, the burger chain certainly got value for money.

Marketing to young people is a legal and ethical minefield, however, particularly when data gathering is involved. The Direct Marketing Association recommends, for example, that information on anyone aged under 14 should not be included on any marketing database. While schemes such as McDonalds' can claim to have checked out the appropriate guidelines and to abide by them, there is still considerable misgiving among some parents about this kind of promotional technology. Icstis, the watch dog organisation covering the operators of premium-rate phone lines, is concerned about the number of unsolicited SMS messages being sent to youngsters. Many offer the receiver the chance to win a prize, but only if they phone a premium-rate number which can cost up to £1.50 a minute. While Icstis takes action to punish offenders (fining or barring about 30 services in 2002), there are still a number of unscrupulous companies willing to bend the rules.

Such dubious schemes are just the tip of the iceberg, if the experience of US direct marketers is anything to go by. E-scamming (the use of electronic media such as SMS and email to try to con unwary users out of money) is a significant problem there and threatens the credibility of the direct marketing industry as it tries to use such media for legitimate purposes. The UK government takes the view that self-regulation by the industry itself is likely to be a more effective safeguard for consumers than creating new laws, because of the speed with which the technology moves. There is also the problem that the majority of such scams originate outside the UK, from countries such as Canada and Malaysia. This means that the only effective course of action is to educate consumers to beware of the e-con artists, although the industry is reluctant to create a climate of suspicion around direct marketing through new media.

Questions

1 Assess the argument in the case study that government regulation is less effective than industry self-regulation in establishing appropriate guidelines for using SMS in marketing communications activity.

2 The DMA recommends that marketing data should not be stored on young people under the age of 14. Discuss (a) the ethics and (b) the usefulness of storing data on consumers this young.

3 What advice could you offer the direct marketing industry on how to preserve its credibility in the face of e-scamming?

Sources: Precision Marketing (2002a, 2002b).

DID YOU KNOW?

What's the definition of 'unsolicited'? Recent EU legislation forbids unsolicited direct marketing calling, by telephone, email or fax. But the legislation stops short of defining 'unsolicited'. The meaning accepted by the UK direct marketing industry is any call to a consumer with whom the caller does not have an ongoing relationship. So your bank getting you out of the shower with details of a new financial service will still be OK, even if you haven't asked them to!

Legal, decent, honest and truthful?

The British system of control of advertising and promotion (as with many other professions) works by self-regulation. The Advertising Standards Authority (ASA), set up in 1962, is the body that polices all British advertising in non-broadcast media. Television and radio advertising are policed by the Independent Television Commission (ITC) and the Radio Authority. The ASA re-routes many complaints addressed to it in the first instance to the appropriate body.

The ASA protects not only the interests of the consumer by ensuring fair dealing, but also the credibility of advertisers themselves. Although funded by a levy on all advertising expenditure, it is entirely independent both of the industry and of the government. It states as its primary objective: 'The promotion and enforcement throughout the UK of the highest standards of advertising in all media so as to ensure co-operation with all concerned that no advertising contravenes or offends against these standards, having regard *inter alia* to the

British Code of Advertising Practice.' Prospective advertisers therefore need to take account of the standards the ASA sets for advertising and sales promotion.

These are set out in a combined document available from the ASA website (www.asa.org.uk/). The codes specify that advertising and sales promotion be legal, decent, honest and truthful. Furthermore, they should be undertaken with a sense of responsibility to the consumer and society, and adhere to principles of fair competition in business.

The ASA has no powers of legislative enforcement itself. Instead it will refer complaints about breaches of the law to the appropriate body, for example the Trading Standards Department.

The ASA has got teeth, however, in the shape of the support that advertisers, agencies and media owners have pledged to it. A publisher can be warned not to accept advertisements that have not satisfied its requirements. In the vast majority of cases breaches of the code are accidental. Most advertisers and agencies value the free and confidential advice which the ASA gives, and demonstrate this by checking their creative material with the ASA before publication.

As well as responding to complaints from the public and requests from the industry, the ASA carries out about 150,000 spot checks itself each year. It keeps a special watching brief on certain areas, including alcohol, health-related products and environmental claims.

In 2001, a typical year, the ASA received over 12,000 complaints, of which 651 were upheld. Others were either outside the remit of the ASA (which is only responsible for non-broadcast advertising), not upheld, or resolved informally. Nine per cent of all complaints were actually not from members of the public at all, but from companies complaining about other companies' advertising! Decisions are published in the ASA's *Monthly Report*, which is circulated to the media industry and is universally available on the ASA website. If a complaint is upheld, the advertiser is asked to withdraw or amend the advertisement. If the advertiser's response is unsatisfactory, sanctions are applied.

Broadcast advertising is dealt with by the ITC for television and the Radio Authority for radio. Advertisement scripts need to be cleared before production with each body, and then the finished commercial needs to be seen and approved before it goes on air. This is usually a highly effective screening process, although there is always an element of subjective judgement about the decision. Famous advertisers whose work has been rejected as unsuitable for television include the ice-cream manufacturer Haagen-Dazs (some of whose very adult ice-cream work was deemed too steamy for the screen) and Unilever, whose original campaign for the UK launch of the brand 'I Can't Believe It's Not Butter' was thrown out because of its possibly confusing effects. Each of these companies happily used the rejection of their work as a public relations theme, suggesting that there is no such thing as bad publicity.

CASE STUDY **11.5**   ### Controversial advertising gets talked about

Since Benetton's much talked-about posters of the early 1990s, which avoided fashion to focus on controversial social issues instead, advertisers have been trying to stretch their budgets by generating word-of-mouth through controversy. A survey by

Propeller Marketing Communications in 2000 placed another clothing retailer, Marks & Spencer, at the top of its 'talked-about' advertising list for its infamous poster of an exultantly naked size 16 woman, with the slogan 'If you're not average, you're normal'. Part of the shock of the Marks & Spencer poster was its departure from the store's traditionally respectable image. While existing customers were not keen on the new look, the posters certainly made others reconsider the brand, and may have contributed to the revival of the troubled retailer's fortunes in the early years of the twenty-first century. Incidentally, Benetton was still in the thick of controversy that year with its death row poster campaign making fourth place in the Propeller list.

The ultimate accolade is, of course, to get a controversial poster 'banned' (or at least have the ASA ask you to withdraw it). Such was the fate of the Christmas 2000/01 Yves Saint Laurent poster for the popular scent Opium, featuring a starkly naked Sophie Dahl in an extremely provocative posture of what appeared to be sexual abandonment. The picture had passed without comment as a magazine advertisement, but aroused very strong reactions when it was plastered over enormous poster sites in time for the Christmas rush (chalking up 960 complaints, a new record for the ASA). Yves Saint Laurent must have been pleased with the controversy created, but were unamused when the brewers Scottish Courage ran a spoof of the ad, featuring a comatose Geordie in an identical (but, thankfully, clad in overalls) posture, clutching a bottle of Newcastle Brown and bearing the slogan 'Brown is the new brown'. Yves Saint Laurent lodged a formal complaint and threatened legal action if the posters were not withdrawn.

Sometimes the controversy is almost too carefully staged. *Viz*, the notorious 'adult' comic, carried advertisements deriding Skegness as filthy and boring. The publisher approached Skegness Town Council for a comment, and the resulting controversy raged in the pages of the *Daily Star* and on Channel 4's *Big Breakfast*. *Viz* then pulled a similar stunt by liverying several London cabs as 'Cockney Wan-Cabs' in commemoration of one of its more celebrated characters, himself a cabbie. The Licensed Taxi Drivers' Association were only too pleased to respond with official outrage, and again made it into the national media at a fraction of the cost of such coverage through legitimate means.

Questions

1 Are there any advertising campaigns (e.g. those with hard-hitting social messages) which are controversial by their nature? Does such an approach always risk being counter-productive?
2 Advertising does not take place in a vacuum. Discuss this idea with reference to the case study examples.
3 The ASA will act on relatively few complaints (e.g. the Opium poster was withdrawn after a record 960 letters had been received – a tiny fraction of the millions of people who saw it). How does this affect its ability to act authoritatively?

Source: Cowlett (2001).

Key concepts
....

Advertising: any form of paid-for media communication designed to inform and influence existing or potential customers.

Advertising to Sales (A/S) ratio: the ratio between the sales value of a product or service and the amount of its advertising budget. It is frequently used as a guide to how much to spend on advertising.

Banner ad: a rectangular advertisement which appears as part of a web page and acts as an active link to an advertiser's website.

Body copy: the words, other than headlines, of a press advertisement.

Broadcasters' Audience Research Board (BARB): the UK research body that commissions and publishes regular television viewing information for advertisers and programme makers.

Commission: traditionally the basis of advertising agency remuneration, a percentage of the purchase price of media (usually 15 per cent) which is returned to them by the media owner.

Copy: the words of an advertisement, or (more generally) advertising material of any sort.

Corporate advertising: advertising that promotes a company rather than an indivudual product brand.

Cost per thousand (CPT): the cost of reaching 1,000 of your target audience. Used as a yardstick to compare value for money in media.

Coverage: how many people in your target audience have been reached by your advertisement at least once.

Database: at its simplest, a list. Usually used to mean lists stored on computers.

Direct marketing: activity that develops and exploits a direct link between an organisation and its customers.

Frequency: the number of times your advertisement reaches your target audience.

Integration: the drive to co-ordinate promotional activity instead of regarding each element of the promotional mix as a separate tactic.

Interstitial: a web page which carries advertising and appears unbidden between other pages.

Media: literally meaning 'ways' – the vehicles such as press, television or posters that carry advertising.

Pop-up: an advertisement on the web which appears unasked-for on top of the page being currently viewed.

Semiotics: a theory of communication that stresses the creation of meaning in messages by their recipients.

Share of voice: the proportion of advertising accounted for by your advertising in its product category in a specified period.

Television Rating Point (TVR): a measure of advertising achievement, a rating point is 1 per cent of your target market seeing your advertisement.

Unique Selling Proposition (USP): the feature, unique to any successful long-term product, that differentiates it from any of its competitors.

SELF-CHECK QUESTIONS

1 Integrated marketing is:
   a An approach to marketing communications that values customer acquisition above customer retention.
   b Using communication to affect opinion rather than behaviour.
   c Marketing to organisations rather than individual consumers.
   d An approach to marketing communications that seeks to get the various communication disciplines working in harmony.
   e An approach to marketing that is led by technology.

2 Hierarchy of effects models:
  a Are an accurate description of what goes on in the communication process.
  b Are particularly useful when dealing with organisational hierarchy.
  c Suggest that consumers are taken through distinct stages from behavioural to cognitive to affective effects by communications.
  d Suggest that consumers create their own meanings for communications.
  e Suggest that consumers are taken through distinct stages from cognitive to affective to behavioural effects by communications.

3 Brand image advertising:
  a Sells the functional benefits of the product or service.
  b Surrounds the product with an aura of associations.
  c Was invented by Rosser Reeves.
  d Is not good for frequently-purchased items but fine for luxuries.
  e Is not as effective as more rational advertising methods.

4 BARB stands for:
  a British Audience Research Board.
  b Broadcast Advertising Research Body.
  c Broadcasters' Audience Research Board.
  d Broadcast Advertising Report Bulletin.
  e British American Research Body.

5 The Advertising Standards Authority:
  a Deals with complaints for all British advertising media.
  b Can only act in response to a complaint from a member of the public.
  c Charges for its services.
  d Has no powers of legislative enforcement.
  e Is a government-funded agency.

Which of the following are true and which are false?
6 All advertising activity is meant to have a direct effect on sales.
7 Advertising agencies are responsible for paying bills to media owners, even if their clients default.
8 Account planners in advertising agencies prepare estimates for how much the advertisements will cost to produce.
9 Drip advertising goes on continuously but at a low level.
10 Circulation is always higher than readership.

Discuss the following
11 If consumers are selective in their attention to advertising, what is the point of using mass media?
12 Creativity in advertising is all about selling things. Discuss.
13 Argue a case for a large advertiser to make more use of direct marketing to consumers.
14 Compare and contrast the strengths and weaknesses of any two of the following media (using examples as appropriate):

    a Radio.
    b Posters.
    c Press.

15 In an increasingly fragmented media environment, has self-regulation for advertisers got a future?

Further study
••••••••••••••••

On advertising:

Brierley, S. (2001) *The Advertising Handbook*, Routledge.
An interesting perspective on the advertising world by an ex-journalist.

Broadbent, Simon (1997) *Accountable Advertising: A Handbook for Managers and Analysts*, Admap/ISIA/IPA.
Articulate and challenging, it is well worth a read.

Butterfield, Leslie (ed.) (1997) *Excellence in Advertising: The IPA Guide to Good Practice*, IPA/Butterworth Heinemann.
A lively collection of essays and articles with a strong practical focus, written by the pick of UK advertising agency talent.

Ogilvy, David (1995) *Ogilvy on Advertising*, Prion Books.
Anything by David Ogilvy is worth a look, and this title has the advantage of being lavishly illustrated.

White, R. (1993) *Advertising: What It Is and How To Do It*, McGraw-Hill.
Still a very valuable book by a leading figure in the UK industry.

On direct marketing:

Bird, Drayton (2001) *Commonsense Direct Marketing*, 4th edn, Kogan Page.
On direct marketing, this book is hard to beat as a single recommendation, although some readers may find it too 'hands on'.

Godin, S. (1999) *Permission Marketing*, Simon and Schuster.
An insightful and challenging book with a particular emphasis on new media.

Peppers, D. and Rogers, M. (1996) *The One to One Future*, Piatkus.
A stimulating read, positing that the way forward in marketing is about quality rather than quantity of customers.

The following journals are invaluable:

Admap
Published monthly, it offers an excellent selection of informed articles about advertising practice.

Campaign
The UK advertising industry's 'house magazine' is a weekly dose of gossip interspersed with thoughtful articles and features.

Marketing Direct
Interesting and engaged accounts of developments in a wide spectrum of direct marketing activities.

Media Week
A very useful weekly for keeping up to date with developments in the world of advertising media.

Revolution
A lively, authoritative and highly practical magazine. Lots of useful insights into the fast-developing world of digital marketing.

Internet links

The Internet is a particularly good source of information about advertising, and most advertising agencies maintain extremely impressive websites as showcases for their work. We will not attempt anything like an exhaustive listing of sites here. Instead, here is a very small selection of valuable sites. Of course web addresses may change at short notice, but these organisations are sufficiently well-established for us to believe their addresses will be stable. You will find, too, that many of the sites contain large numbers of links to other useful resources.

www.asa.org.uk/
The Advertising Standards Authority website is a really terrific jumping off place for other links (e.g. the Advertising Association, which contains a number of invaluable student briefing pages on advertising). The website also contains the full text of the Codes of Advertising and Sales Promotion Practice, *as well as the monthly ASA reports on recent adjudications. It's searchable – an excellent resource for all marketing and advertising students, as well as practitioners. See Advertising Standers Authority (2003)* 11th British Codes of Advertising and Sales Promotional Practice, *available free from Brook House, 2–16 Torrington Place, London WC1E 7HN (Tel: 0207 580 5555) or website (see above).*

agb.mediatel.co.uk/tvtrack/glossary.cfm
A very useful glossary of terms to do with television advertising research from the company that runs the Broadcasters Audience Research Board.

www.mediauk.com/directory/
This is a classic website for anyone seeking information about television, radio or newspaper media. Its coverage is compendious and its organisation and navigability are exemplary.

www.nrs.co.uk/intro.htm
An extremely user friendly and genuinely informative website about the National Readership Survey. It covers history, funding and methodology (among other issues) and provides top-line results. Definitely worth a browse.

www.rab.co.uk/
The Radio Advertising Bureau's website is full of excellent information about all aspects of radio advertising. It is rather elegantly produced, although you may need a pretty recent computer to get the most out of it.

www.dma.org.uk/
The Direct Marketing Association website is geared towards its members, but has useful information and case studies.

References

Advertising Association (2001) 'Student Briefing No. 6: Facts and Figures on Advertising Expenditure', available at http://www.adassoc.org.uk/inform/in6.html.

Allen, C. (2002) 'Presentation to Lehman Brothers Media Conference', London, 17 September.

Blackstock, C. (2002) 'Pukka! TV chef serves tasty profit', *The Guardian*, 4 December, p.11.

Brand Strategy (2002) 'Research: building customer value through the Internet', *Brand Strategy*, April. p.37.

Buzzell, R.D. and Gale, B.T. (1987) *The PIMS Principles: Linking Strategy to Performance,* Free Press.

Cowlett, M. (2001) 'Taking control of the news agenda', *Marketing,* 15 March, pp.29–30.

Clarke, D. (1998) 'Taking business on-line', *Marketing Direct*, July/August, pp.45–6.

Colley, R. (1961) *Defining Advertising Goals for Measured Advertising Results*, Association of National Advertisers.

DMA (2001) *Direct Marketing Association Best Practice Guidelines: For Use of Data in Direct Marketing*, Direct Marketing Association. Available at: http://www.dma.org.uk.

Economist (2001) 'The Asians are coming, again', *The Economist*, 28 April, p.32.

Folkard, C. (eds) (2003) *Guinness World Records,* Gullane Entertainment.

Guardian (2002) 'Pass Notes No. 1,894 Hovis', *The Guardian*, 11 June, p.10.

Hayter, N. (1998) 'Stop the old-media comparisons', *Revolution*, May, p.23.

Incorporated Society of British Advertisers (2002) 'ISBA Briefing Paper: Advertising and Children', May. Available at: http://www.isba.co.uk.

Jones, J.P. (1995) *When Ads Work: New Proof that Advertising Triggers Sales,* Simon and Schuster.

Mazur, L. (1998) 'Marketers should sit back . . .', *Marketing Business*, December/January, p.28.

Motluk, A. (1999) 'Sexism takes its toll', *New Scientist,* 4 September, p.6.

Owen, J. (1998) 'So what is the secret of a good online campaign?', *Revolution*, May, p.7.

O'Kane, P. (2001) 'Ad Lib: media and marketing', *Sunday Tribune*, 26 August, p.5.

Precision Marketing (2002a) 'Can industry stem the new wave of conmen?', *Precision Marketing*, 22 November, p.11.

Precision Marketing (2002b) 'Preying on the young', *Precision Marketing*, 6 December, p.27.

Ray, A. (2002) 'Media neutrality – brand evolution', *MediaWeek*, 28 February, p.10.

Rosen, N. (1998) 'The end of the beginning', *Revolution*, May, pp.6–7.

Shannon, C. and Weaver, W. (1949) *The Mathematical Theory of Communication*, University of Illinois Press.

Smith, C. (ed.) (2002) *Marketing: Great British Brands*, 1 August, p.23.

Starch, D. (1925) *Principles of Advertising*, Shaw.

Taylor, D. (2002) 'Brands in training', *Brand Strategy*, 4 November, pp.20–1.

CHAPTER 12

Promotion – selling, sales promotion and public relations

Objectives
••••••••••••

When you have read this chapter you will be able to:

➤ Identify the contribution made by direct selling, sales promotion and public relations to the strategic marketing communications effort.

➤ Plan a sales call.

➤ Appreciate the human resource elements of the sales process.

➤ Recommend sales promotion responses to a variety of marketing situations.

➤ Differentiate between public relations and other forms of marketing communications.

➤ Apply the main public relations techniques to a selection of marketing problems and understand the basis for their evaluation.

Foundation focus – the 20-second takeaway
••

Personal selling is at the sharp end of marketing, when a customer transaction is finalised in a mutually satisfactory way. It's a vital part of the marketing process, although some marketing writers tend to relegate it to a less worthy position. As Robert Louis Stevenson once wrote, 'everyone lives by selling something' – so it's a skill well worth developing. Sales promotion is a support activity designed to make selling more effective by speeding up or intensifying buying response through temporary added value. Public relations aims at creating the right kind of environment (both inside and outside a company) for sustainable success. It actively manages the messages sent out by a company, usually with the assistance of third parties such as journalists.

Introduction
••••••••••••••••

In the previous chapter we looked at marketing communications, particularly at advertising and direct marketing, with their respective emphasis on creating and keeping customers. Three further techniques which play a vital role in successful communications are personal selling, sales promotion and public relations.

We might picture these activities layered in a kind of pyramid, with public relations at the base and selling at the apex, literally the sharp end (see Figure 12.1). But they interact in an effective promotional mix to the point where it is difficult to say which layer takes precedence, and the likely mix will vary from organisation to organisation. As with the techniques in Chapter 11, successful marketing communications involves the integration of these various disciplines into a seamless process involving an organisation and its customers or partners.

figure 12.1
**A promotional
pyramid?**

Selling
· · · · · · · · ·

Selling is interpersonal activity that completes a marketing exchange in terms of the transfer of ownership of a good or service. It can take place between any combination of groups and individuals. Selling is an essential part of the marketing mix. In a sense, selling is what everything else leads up to. Without a customer there is no business, and without selling there are no customers. Even in situations like self-service retailing, selling is going on. Instead of people doing the selling, interior design is taking on the job. Whether it is the bright airy ambience of Sainsbury's, or the discreet wooden panelling of a gentlemen's outfitter, retail appearance is capturing the attention of a prospective customer and convincing him or her that these particular products offer benefits more effectively and efficiently than the competition. Furthermore, the products would not be there at all were it not for the fact that a salesperson had sold them to a wholesaler or a retailer in the first place.

The importance of selling

Selling has long been seen as the poor relation of marketing. Definitions of marketing as a business philosophy often contrast the advantages of the marketing concept against sales-led thinking and production-led thinking (see Chapter 1). The selling concept is seen by Kotler et al. (2001) as a management orientation that fears the customer will not buy enough of the organisation's output unless a concerted promotional effort is made. As we have argued in Chapter 11, it is highly unlikely that people can be persuaded to buy what they do not want. Customer-led approaches work much better.

Companies that boast marketing excellence, such as Marks & Spencer or IBM, recognise the central importance of selling. Indeed, their selling operation is like a microcosm of marketing itself. Far from trying to load unwanted goods on to unsuspecting customers, these companies start by interpreting the needs of their customers and end by fulfilling them through personal service.

Much of the literature on selling dwells on closing individual sales. It is as if the writers or sales trainers expect the relationship with the customer to end with the sale, casting customers as only so many stepping stones on the way to organisational success. On the contrary, Levitt (1986) points out that even if companies see their part of the bargain ending in the sale, for their customers it is the beginning of the relationship. They have become customers by acquiring the product or service. Even the language of selling, which talks about closing the sale, has an air of finality about it that belies the reality of successful selling.

Companies like IBM see their sales relationships as ongoing. In a high-tech product field like information technology or office automation the relevance of after-sales service should be clear as advances in software lead to continuous improvement. But the way successful companies approach selling is based not so much on their product field as on the conviction that looking after existing customers is as important, if not more important, than winning new ones.

So, far from the stereotypical foot-in-the-door merchant immortalised in cartoons and situation comedy, the successful salesperson is likely to be some-one who works hard to understand customer needs, fulfils those needs appropriately, and takes the long view. At the same time, customer empathy has to be combined with commercial vision. The sales representative has to be pre-cisely that – a representative of the company's interests in the mutual relationship. So development of skills such as time management and presenta-tion technique are essential to maximise the effectiveness of the scarce resource represented by time available for selling.

Planning a sales call

Personal selling is the most expensive form of promotion, as well as being the most powerful. No other technique accommodates the range of feedback the customer can give a salesperson, allowing direct negotiation and customisation of the offer. But because of the power of the technique, its use needs to be care-fully planned. The kind of wastage that is taken for granted in impersonal forms of promotion such as advertising cannot be tolerated in selling. It is only to be expected that a large percentage of the audience seeing a television com-mercial will not be in the market for that particular product or service. But selling cannot afford to be anything less than 100 per cent relevant to its audi-ence all of the time.

We will address the issue of salesforce management a little later in this section. First let us follow the stages a salesperson will go through in planning and carrying out a sales visit. This encounter with the customer need not be face to face. The same broad considerations apply to selling over the telephone (although of course the opportunities for visual communication are limited to verbal pictures in such situations). What matters is the personal nature of the encounter – facilitated by comprehensive research and preparation before the event, convincing presentation during the sales call, and assiduous follow-up.

There are six main stages involved in planning and carrying out the personal selling process, as follows.

Stage 1 Prospecting

This is in many ways the most important part of the entire process. By identify-ing people who are likely to be interested in what you have to offer, selling becomes more efficient and successful. Screening out inappropriate customers at this stage will save much wasted effort and time later on.

As in direct marketing, it is often the case that existing customers will be the source of additional leads. Other useful sources include:

▶ Competitors.
▶ Exhibitions.

> ► Government information.
> ► Mailshots.
> ► Newspapers and journals.
> ► Professional and trade associations.
> ► Suppliers.
> ► Trade directories.

The importance of each type of source of leads will vary from industry to industry, but once possible customers have been identified, they have to be scrutinised to ascertain their suitability. This process, known as lead qualification, can involve gathering information about their size, creditworthiness and potential. Information here will tend to be qualitative, but a certain amount of quantitative data may be available in the shape of annual reports, company literature and the financial press. For business-to-business salespeople, just finding out who is the best person to approach in the organisation is often one of the most confusing and frustrating parts of the operation. The same job title often covers widely differing functions in different companies. To confuse matters further, in most organisational buying situations responsibility for the purchase will be spread among several people (as discussed in Chapter 4).

KEY SKILLS
ACTIVITY **12.1**
• • • • • • • • • • • • • • • • •

Improving own learning and performance

Information sources

Knowing where to look for the right kind of information is a vital skill for both learning and marketing activity. Research and preparation help ensure that a salesperson's (or a student's) valuable time is properly directed and their performance improved.

List the key information sources to which you would refer if you were prospecting for the following sorts of customers (please be as specific as possible):

1 Prospective students for a college of higher education.
2 Donors for a charity dedicated to funding bone cancer research.
3 Season ticket buyers for your local football team.
4 Potential sponsors for the Royal Opera House, Covent Garden.
5 Subscribers to a new magazine devoted to archery.

Stage 2 Approach

Just as the immediate objective of a job application is to secure an interview, so this stage of the sales planning process focuses single-mindedly on gaining personal access to the decision-maker. Research is very important here. The kinds of information sought falls into two types. There are objective facts about the company, its recent performance, its own customer base. But there is also what might be known as subjective information to do with company style, the way decisions are made, even the personal interests and characteristics of the people with whom you will be dealing. The unique strength of selling is, after all, its personal quality. Attention must therefore be paid both to the strictly functional and the more human aspects of the encounter.

Gaining the opportunity to get through to the targeted individual can be a challenge. Some secretaries are like brick walls and will fend off approaches with ruthless efficiency. With the growth in person-to-person media (email and the increased number of direct telephone lines are two recent developments) this is becoming less of a problem, but there is still no substitute for tact and determination. Lead qualification should have eliminated all those apparent prospects who are not in a position to take advantage of what you have to offer. So painstaking explanation of the relevance of your product or service to the targeted organisation should eventually pay dividends.

Stage 3 Presentation

This is the hoped-for culmination of the hard work and research that have gone into the first two stages. The sales presentation provides the chance to enjoy the undivided attention of the prospect while you put your case. Visual impressions are extremely important, so appropriate dress code and grooming must be observed. In international business transactions there is the added complication of different styles of business etiquette. This varies from the formal quasi-rituals that accompany business in Japan, to the casual back-slapping approach of some American companies. These cultural norms can be learned and adopted without too much trouble, but there are other aspects of business etiquette that constitute more of a problem. The expectation in some countries of business gifts that amount to little short of bribery can cause severe ethical difficulties for companies used to plain dealing.

DID YOU KNOW?

First impressions last. At least 70 per cent of what comes across during interpersonal communication is due to body language rather than words. This is even true on the telephone, where tone of voice is more important than the words being used (Wolfgang, 1984).

For all its weaknesses as a detailed account of what happens in advertising, the AIDA model discussed in Chapter 11 provides an excellent template for a sales call. Having a model in mind helps the salesperson to keep control of the encounter in a way that makes the best use of the time available. Here is how the AIDA model can be applied to the structure of a sales call, either in person, on the telephone or via video-conferencing:

► *Attention*: This can be gained by as simple a device as a friendly greeting. Often an attention-getting device can be used, such as a visual aid or a model or sample. Giving your counterpart in the negotiation something to hold and/or look at can focus both your minds on the matter in hand.

► *Interest*: Here we come to a fundamental principle in selling. Focus on the benefits. This entails engaging the customer's interest in what you are selling by allowing him or her to appreciate its relevance to their needs. Questions to diagnose the customer's sphere of interest are vital here. The temptation is always to dwell on product features (company perspective) rather than the benefits (customer perspective). An inexperienced computer salesperson might be carried away with the amount of memory that a new machine has as a feature. The customer is only likely to be interested in the fact that it will be able to store more information. Engaging the customer's interest will require careful judgement as to what the appropriate benefits are in each case. This question should be easy to answer because of the research involved in preparing for the sales call.

▶ *Desire*: This is when interest is personalised directly to the prospect. Dramatising the benefits to the customer involves seeking their co-operation in the process through questions. Open questions are particularly important in sales presentations at this point. They allow you to empathise with the customer and to produce genuine responses to the needs articulated. Another way of promoting interest to desire is to give the customer the opportunity to convince themselves of the desirability of the product. Test driving a car, using a software package for a limited trial period or taking an introductory flying lesson are all ways in which desire can be confirmed.

▶ *Action*: The outcome of the encounter needs to be clear. It may not always be an immediate purchase. At the very least the salesperson should aim to come away with valuable information from this kind of engagement with a customer. It may mean an order next time. But the prime objective of a sales call is a sale. In a real sense this is part of the service. The customer can actually be helped to resolve the purchase by a tactful and supportive approach.

Although an overall structure is always necessary, different situations call for different approaches to presentation format. Working in a mechanised and repetitive environment, telephone selling requires more formal discipline than working person-to-person over a longer period of time. Thus the use of a script for telephone selling can help maximise the effectiveness of the time spent on each call, and ensure that nothing is left out.

At the other end of the scale is the diagnostic, consultative selling process, where the encounter follows its own route. The skills required from the salesperson here consist of careful listening and conscious analysis of the customer's needs. Empathy, imagination and extensive product knowledge are essential for success here. The technique is best suited to markets where the sales function is combined with a high level of technical expertise such as industrial chemicals or telecommunications.

Stage 4 Handling objections

Using the terminology 'handling objections' is misleading insofar as it puts the salesperson and the customer in an adversarial role. Negotiation is a more helpful expression here. It recognises that there are two sets of interests which the sales process must reconcile into one outcome. The negotiation is a two-way process in which there will be give and take. Having said that, there are aspects of the relationship between buyer and seller that resemble a kind of game. It is therefore best to be aware of them and have a sense of how to cope with this side of the process.

What are often called psychological objections are various internal sorts of resistance to being sold something. It may simply be that the timing of the call is inappropriate. The customer may have had a bad day. There may be a feeling of antipathy with the salesperson, or it may just be that the customer is phased by having to commit themselves. Listening skills are important here, especially the ability to probe behind the external objection. If, for example, it turns out that you are dealing with the wrong person after all, it may be in your interest to curtail the sales call and wait for an opportunity to make the right contact later.

Logical objections are easier to deal with insofar as they are objective. The price may be too high, or some technical aspect of the product may be less than clearly understood. The way to deal with this aspect of negotiation is to ask questions. By questioning, it may even be possible to take the customer through his or her objection to an answer of their own devising. Objections to price can be resolved by concentrating on value, or misunderstandings as to function can be resolved by further demonstration. It is important to take objections of whatever sort seriously and respectfully. The last thing you want to do is to argue with the customer. Arguments create winners and losers, and put distance between buyer and seller. Working towards mutual understanding, on the other hand, creates a win/win scenario.

> **DID YOU KNOW?**
>
> *Silence is a powerful tool in sales presentations. Knowing when to shut up can help active listening, and encourage the customer to fill the gaps in the conversation. On the other hand, the salesperson's worst nightmare is silence from the customer. The lack of feedback, even negative feedback, can severely disorientate even the most experienced and well-informed product advocate (Argyle, 1990).*

Stage 5 Closing

Again, the term 'closing' sits uncomfortably with a view of selling as a strategic function. It sounds too final, as if the process is complete and the door can be shut on the relationship. In fact, good closing skills can be seen as part of the professionalism that salespeople offer as a service to their customers. Making the sale means that the customer's immediate problem has been solved. They are in the market for something, be it advertising, a new car, an order for a new product. Facilitating a purchase frees them of that immediate need and takes that particular job off their list of things to do.

Nevertheless it can be difficult to get to the point where the salesperson asks for the order. This may be due to a number of reasons, not the least of which is the anxiety a salesperson inevitably suffers about failure and rejection. Quite apart from the personal disappointment this causes, there is also the sense of needing to show a return for the enormous investment in time and preparation involved in a sales call. While things are still in the process of negotiation, there is still hope. The fear is that moving to a conclusion may decide events adversely.

Developing a conscious technique to cope with this delicate stage of the negotiations is therefore desirable. Sales training manuals offer many solutions. One piece of oft-repeated advice is to watch for buying signals. It may be that the kinds of question the customer asks lead naturally to the order. Spontaneous positive comment on the product or service can signal readiness to purchase. Body language becomes more relaxed, and often the customer will literally move closer to the salesperson. A number of popular closing techniques can be brought into play at this point to tie up the deal, as follows:

1 *Ask for the order*: Simple and straightforward, this consists of requesting the order directly. Pen and order form can be useful props here: 'Why don't you fill this form out right now and it can be yours today?'
2 *Trial close:* A number of techniques share the function of establishing how near the customer is to the point of purchase. For example, the 'alternative close' consists of asking a purchase-related question (e.g. whether the customer wants delivery now or next week). This flushes out the decision without a direct approach, and can therefore be used to keep the negotiation in play: 'Will you be paying by cheque or credit card?'

3 *Assumptive close*: Here the salesperson makes the positive assumption that the customer has said yes, and concentrates the negotiation on some less central aspect of the deal. As with the straightforward request, the appearance of pen and order form can be used to confirm this assumption in due course: 'So we're really only talking about whether you want electric or manual windows on the car.'

4 *Allocative close*: Allocation, or the sharing of an over-demanded product between keen customers, is one of the functions of a salesperson in an expanding market. The allocative close puts it to the customer that there is a shortage of the product or service, and that therefore speed of purchase is of the essence to avoid disappointment: 'I'll phone the warehouse to check, but we should still have just enough in stock for you to get delivery next week if you order now.'

5 *Summary close:* Another straightforward device, this simply consists of the salesperson summing up all the points made about the product, all the answered objections and all the benefits (often with the use of visual aids or graphics) and asking for the order. The momentum of such a close can be irresistible: 'It's got all the things you need, it's on special offer this week, we stock it in purple, we can have it to you by Friday. Now if you can just sign this, we can go to lunch!'

Stage 6 Follow-up

Estimates vary, but even the most conservative suggest that it is five times cheaper to do business with existing customers than it is with new ones (Gordon, 1998). It therefore makes a lot of sense to nurture relationships, and salespeople are in an excellent position to do this. Checking on delivery dates, keeping the customer informed if there are any changes to plan, contacting the customer after delivery in order to establish if everything is satisfactory are all ways in which the salesperson can use his or her front-line position to consolidate a relationship and win future business. Personal management software is making it easier to keep regular contact with a customer database by the power it offers to flag up appointments that need to be made or phone calls that need to be placed to keep in touch.

Sometimes follow-up is part of the product or service being sold. For example, computer equipment sales will tend to include training and consultancy as part of the package. But even if there is little or no service content in the offer itself, as in the case of office consumables such as stationery, good salespeople will concentrate on keeping customers as much as on creating them. A good personal relationship with a customer can give a salesperson an unshakeable competitive advantage over other companies, and make business more of a pleasure.

Motivating and managing the personal selling process
....

An organisation's salesforce is usually its largest single marketing communications expense. As such it needs careful management. Unlike impersonal promotional tools like advertising or sales promotion which operate through the media, direct selling involves people. The salesforce therefore needs a different kind of management from other areas of promotion, drawing heavily on human resource management ideas.

We can divide the salesforce management process into three main tasks: the three Ss of Strategy, Structure and Support.

Salesforce strategy

The organisation's marketing plan will break down into a number of complementary strategies to be implemented by its various divisions (see Chapter 14). Salesforce strategy will support clear objectives governing volume sales, revenue targets and market-share targets. For individual salespeople these objectives mean the setting of specific goals. These goals may cover any or all of the following:

▶ *Call frequency*: The number of times sales visits are made.
▶ *Growth*: The amount of development expected from existing customers.
▶ *New business*: The year-on-year increase in worthwhile new accounts.
▶ *Profitability*: The target for allowable discount.
▶ *Quota*: The volume of sales of each product carried.

The immediate targets for individuals in the front-line salesforce need to be realistic. There is the additional human resource consideration here that because of the motivational power of objectives, some sophistication may be called for in their setting. For example, volume targets might be set at three thresholds: minimum, probable and possible. This is especially important when performance is linked to remuneration, as we shall discuss later.

Salesforce structure

The second major area for salesforce management decisions is how the complex resource of the salesforce is best organised. There are three main approaches here, which are often reflected through into the organisation of the marketing department as a whole (see Chapter 13).

DID YOU KNOW?

If workers at the free ads paper LOOT *are among the most flexible and relaxed in advertising sales, it is because they benefit from the attention of two in-house, full-time masseurs. In addition, the paper's stressed-out telesales execs are encouraged to participate in exercise classes which are run on site three times a day (Management Today, 1999).*

Geographical structure

The basic idea of the salesforce territory is a logical response to the needs of companies whose products are in wide distribution, as in the case of a nationally-available grocery line. One salesperson is responsible for each territory. This means that there are no clashes between rival salespeople from the same company and that the customer has one simple point of contact with the organisation. The difficulty with this approach, however, is that a variety of different account sizes and types within the same area may reduce the efficiency of the individual salesperson's efforts. There is also the need for constant review of territory size as the business environment is a dynamic one.

Customer-type structure

This would appear to offer the most marketing-oriented solution to structuring the salesforce. After all, we are used to the idea in marketing that the customer should be at the centre of our thinking. Wrapping the salesforce round different customer types is therefore an attractive idea. It puts segmentation into practice. In certain markets it makes sense because of the concentration of certain types of customer in particular areas. But more usually this approach has the disadvantage that customers of the same salesperson can be widely dispersed, making it hard to provide a high level of personal service at an economic cost to the company. About half of the typical salesperson's time is spent travelling, so the disadvantage of increasing this inefficiency becomes apparent.

Product-line structure

At first sight this approach seems to contradict many of the ideas on which marketing is founded. Marketing adopts the customer's perspective rather than the organisation's. In other words, we should stress benefits not features. Customer needs rather than the available products ought to be the starting point in marketing decisions. But in spite of this, a product-based structure for a salesforce may offer the right solution in certain markets. Where a high level of technical expertise is demanded of the salesforce it may be the only way to provide the specialisation the customer will demand.

In fact most salesforce structures will have elements of each of these three approaches. A large, fast-moving consumer goods salesforce structure is illustrated in Figure 12.2. The pyramid starts at the level of the individual sales rep working his or her territory. Their work will involve managing accounts of a minimum size, and devoting time and attention to growing the most promising ones. Although they are each highly autonomous, they will report to sales managers, and take part in team meetings on an area-by-area basis.

figure 12.2
Salesforce structure for a national fast-moving consumer goods company

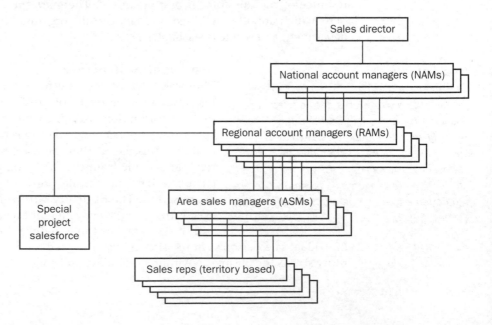

The next level up, the area sales managers, will motivate and direct the territorial sales staff, convening regular meetings and acting as a channel of information to and from the higher echelons of management. They will have direct sales responsibilities themselves for larger accounts.

The next line of management begins to blur the distinction between geographical and customer-type organisation. These regional account managers (RAMs) have line management responsibility for area sales managers (ASMs), but also deal with significant accounts that need constant personal attention. Retail groups often have a regional bias, and this kind of customer offers a great deal of potential for personalised promotions whereby significant volumes of stock can be moved in the context of a special offer. RAMs will be based in regional offices with administrative support.

National account managers (NAMs) are the aristocrats of the salesforce. Not only do they drive the best cars but they control the company's business from head office with the largest customers in the country. As well as being prestigious, these customers are very hard to deal with because of the level of power they command. As we have seen in Chapter 10, being delisted from a retail giant like ASDA or Sainsbury's can mean losing access to a very large slice of your customer base overnight. NAMs are under intense pressure to do business with the retail barons on terms advantageous to their company. They have strategic input to sales and marketing plans and communicate directly to the board via the sales director.

Bestriding this pyramid like a mighty colossus, a charismatic sales director is a considerable advantage to an organisation. His or her visibility and dynamism set the tone for the rest of the operation in what can be a very gruelling and competitive field. Credibility and leadership are at a premium here. Not only will the director motivate and inspire from the top down, but he or she will also fight for resources for the salesforce at board level – often in competition with colleagues arguing the merits of other forms of promotional expenditure.

Floating apart from this structure in Figure 12.2 is an example of a product-specific salesforce being used in tandem with the other two approaches. In this case it is a specially bought-in temporary salesforce from a broking company whose services have been engaged to launch a new product. The decision to hive off this activity from the main salesforce might be taken for a number of reasons. The product might, for example, be the result of a recent merger or acquisition and so not fit into the portfolio of products they are already selling. It might not be clear how the time and resource costs of carrying the new product might impact on the support the salesforce can give to its existing ranges. Or it might just be that, for political reasons, it is considered best to give the launch an independent chance of success.

Salesforce structure is the result both of planning and evolution. As will be clear from our discussion, there is no universally-applicable model. Instead, a flexible and responsive approach that takes into account the need to adapt to changing market conditions is most likely to offer success.

Salesforce support

Of the three Ss this is the one that raises most operational issues. There are five interlocked areas to cover:

► Recruitment.
► Training.
► Remuneration.
► Motivation.
► Evaluation.

This is the area where sales management draws most upon human resource management. As we shall see, however, the peculiar nature of the selling function throws up certain emphases unique to this area of management.

Recruitment

In any service environment the quality of the people involved is paramount. Sales is no exception, even though it is often perceived as a junior role. Some organisations, accepting this, resign themselves to a very high turnover of sales recruits, many of whom will have been far from suited to the real task of selling.

In contrast, companies with a real commitment to their customers are identifiable by their commitment to attracting the right kind of sales staff. Big money promises are less important than the training and development they can offer in a structured career. Instead of wanting to attract a continuous stream of sales-fodder, they are interested in selecting only those candidates who are likely to succeed in the long term.

Training

As we have seen in our review of how to plan and carry out a sales call, natural abilities can usefully be enhanced in order to maximise personal effectiveness. The number of different tasks involved in a selling role offer plenty of scope for training input:

► Time management is essential in order to maximise the effectiveness of the limited number of selling hours available in any day.
► Product knowledge needs to be constantly updated to keep pace with technical developments and customer expectations.
► Presentation and negotiation skills also need to be honed to perfection.

Because of the amount of reporting back and administration involved in controlling business with multiple clients, salespeople need to be very well versed in order processing and distribution systems. The amount of training investment necessary to an effective salesforce is one of the reasons why selling is such an expensive promotional tool.

Remuneration

Staff costs are the main item of expenditure in any salesforce management set-up. The way that salespeople are rewarded reflects the individual nature of their jobs. Performance-related pay tends to be a feature of salesforce remuneration.

Systems vary from company to company. One extreme is the commission-only sales job, where, apart from an initial investment in product and sales training, the recruit is left unsupported. Income depends entirely on performance. At the other end of the scale is the salary-only salesperson. Typically an employee like this will have a job description that includes responsibilities other than selling. Indeed, selling may not even be the most important part of what they do.

The majority of cases, however, feature a mixture of commission and salary. The trick is to get the balance right. Too heavy a dependence on commission, and variations in the salesperson's monthly amount may lead to instabilities elsewhere in his or her life. Instead of being performance enhancing, such uncertainty can have negative consequences. But balanced against this is the feeling that different levels of achievements among the salesforce ought to be recognised by different levels of reward. Remuneration arrangements need to be informed by the kind of realism that we have noted as an aspect of objective-setting in the strategic input necessary to salesforce management.

Motivation

Part of the problem with too heavy a reliance on commission is that it fails to take into account the classic work of Herzberg (1966) into motivation. Herzberg's research found that money was what he called a hygiene factor. Such factors need to be present in sufficient quantities to make a job tolerable – like office environment, proper lighting, ease of access, etc. But in themselves he found they were less powerful in enhancing performance than the factors he called motivators. These are things like status, interesting work, praise and peer esteem.

Most successful salespeople are self-motivated high achievers who thrive on stress. Their job means a high level of autonomy as they spend a great deal of time working on their own. Thus their need for motivation is different from the kind of motivation traditionally expected from managers. Sales managers can help their staff best by providing clear objectives and structuring what can appear to be dauntingly complex requirements. This kind of leadership is best given by example. Again we are reminded of the essentially personal nature of the selling process.

As an alternative to direct financial inducements, yet providing the simplicity of a common currency of reward across the salesforce, a number of major companies use an annual competition as an incentive for their salesforce. Performance is judged against agreed criteria and the winners are fêted with appropriate recognition at the annual sales conference. As a form of sales promotion this can motivate the salesforce to get behind a particular brand and boost its volume or distribution in a particular year.

CASE STUDY **12.1**
· · · · · · · · · · · · · · · · ·

E-salesmanship

Research into the effectiveness of personal selling to medical practitioners in the US reveals that, while pharmaceutical companies spend something like $8 billion a year on an army of 63,000 sales reps, only 60 per cent of their visits to medical practices result in meetings with the actual doctor. Even these meetings will necessarily be short – 90 per cent are over in two minutes or less. The problem is that, like their colleagues elsewhere in the world, American doctors are chronically short of time. While they are genuinely interested in what sales reps can tell them about new prescription drugs which might offer benefits to their patients, there are so many other calls on their attention during a busy day that visiting salespeople tend to get sidelined. This is frustrating for pharmaceutical companies anxious to get new products established ahead of rivals, and is less than ideal for patients (who may not get the opportunity to benefit from new drug therapies if doctors do not get to hear about them).

The solution to the problem may lie in electronic marketing. The American term for contacting doctors about new drugs is 'detailing' – so the use of new technology for this purpose has swiftly been dubbed 'e-detailing'. It has attracted a number of specialist companies already, keen to offer their expertise to pharmaceutical companies which need to get their message across.

One such firm, ePocrates, sends brief details of new products to doctors via their PDAs (personal digital assistants) – a popular productivity tool among American professionals. Like many forms of electronic marketing communication, the system requires an active response from the recipient. If the doctor is interested in the product, he or she sends a message to the manufacturer requesting a fuller brief. Thus a mutually beneficial relationship is built up.

A second firm, RxCentric.com, based in New York, has positioned itself as an exclusive Internet service provider (ISP) for the medical community. Drugs companies in the past have sponsored medical conferences, or kept doctors supplied with pens and notepads. Providing Internet connectivity is, perhaps, a development in this kind of tradition – with the added benefit that it facilitates keeping in contact with ISP members by email. As with ePocrates, RxCentric provides brief 'taster' information, and it is left up to the individual doctor to contact the manufacturer for more details.

A third variety of e-detailing is provided by iPhysician.net, based in Arizona. Going a step further than ISP services, this organisation has actually installed high-speed connections and video-conferencing-enabled terminals in the offices of almost 7,000 of America's heaviest-prescribing doctors. In exchange for the kit and services, the doctors agree to monthly video briefings from nine big drug makers, allowing sales personnel much more flexibility to suit their attentions to the availability of the doctors themselves. The video medium means that the salesperson can incorporate more sophisticated and complete visual information than would be possible in a fleeting personal encounter, so iPhysician.net claims that the system is not just a substitute for, but an improvement on, more traditional methods. There is a cost advantage, with each video-session costed at $110 compared with $200 for a face-to-face visit. Early figures attest to its effectiveness too, with a 14 per cent increase on new prescriptions compared with the result of the traditional sales call.

Questions

1   The case presents three methods of contacting doctors using electronic marketing – PDA messages, email and video-conferencing. From your knowledge of Information and Communication Technology, suggest and justify at least one further method.

2   Compare and contrast face-to-face selling with selling via a video-conferencing link. What adjustments might you have to make to your face-to-face sales presentation via video-conferencing?

3 Use the AIDA model to describe the approach undertaken by the three companies in this case study. What insights might they gain from your analysis?

Source: Economist (2001a).

Evaluation

Selling is one of the most accountable jobs in the marketing repertoire. As will be clear from the list of objective areas in the section on salesforce strategy, there is no shortage of performance indicators by which to judge the achievements of individual salespeople. The merciless measure of statistics can be applied to call frequency, sales against targets, sales against previous periods or in comparison with colleagues' performances. The profitability of sales efforts can be calculated in terms of return per call, and how accounts have grown or shrunk during the year.

This is a hard standard to be judged by, and can lead to insecurity and the temptation to massage figures. On the other hand, it provides an objective source of feedback which can be used by the sales manager and the salesperson to improve performance.

DID YOU KNOW?

'Spot the ball'-type competitions are taken very seriously indeed by the judges. Winners are selected with the aid of extremely powerful optical magnification, to determine the precise centre of the smudged biro crosses on entry forms – and eliminate the possibility of any disputes. In practice the chances of winning are as virtually remote as a game of chance, but the 'skill and judgement' aspect of the competition prevents it from falling under the remit of lottery laws – even though a purchase is necessary.

Sales promotion

Sales promotion is promotional activity designed to enhance the speed or volume of purchasing response. It operates through adding value on a temporary basis to a product or service in order to provide an extra incentive to purchase. It can be directed at consumers, distribution intermediaries, salespeople, or any combination of the three.

In the trade press sales promotion is often referred to as below-the-line expenditure. This is to differentiate it from media advertising expenditure, on which commission is payable (see Chapter 11 for a fuller explanation of this). The imaginary line of the expression is drawn to separate expenditure that is commissionable from that which is not.

Sales promotion often works better when combined with advertising. Indeed, in certain markets (such as petrol) the sales promotion can provide the central platform for advertising messages, because there is little else to say about the product to differentiate it from the competition. Advertising agencies sometimes refer to specific advertising in support of a sales promotion as 'scheme advertising', reserving the term 'theme advertising' for the mainstream, long-term brand-building campaign.

Sales promotion comes of age

Sales promotion, rather like sales itself, has tended to suffer from an image problem. Yet, as the idea of integrated marketing communications has gathered pace, the traditional antipathy of advertising agencies (with their long-term emphasis on building brands) to sales promotion agencies (with their more immediate concern to stimulate sales) has diminished. In fact, more and more advertising agencies have positioned themselves as one-stop shops for clients keen to buy a range of marketing communications services, and have set up or absorbed sales promotion businesses.

The main reason for sales promotion's image problem stems from the necessarily short-term nature of the kind of activity involved. Because the added value (of whatever sort) needs to be clearly seen as something above and beyond what is normally available, the life of any effective promotion rarely exceeds three months. As a result there has been a temptation to see promotional activity of this sort as tactical rather than strategic.

Sometimes the result has been activity that has no relevance to the core brand proposition, or whose timing has been less than optimum in relation to advertising. There has even been the fear, particularly with respect to price-based promotion, that the activity can undermine long-term marketing effort for the sake of a short-term jump in sales.

Yet sales promotion is booming for a number of reasons:

▶ Crowded markets offer shoppers an unprecedented number of products. Sales promotion can endow them with a temporary sparkle.
▶ Powerful retailers have put pressure on manufacturers to work harder. More promotional activity is one response to this.
▶ Advertisers frustrated by rising costs, media clutter and patchy coverage of their target audiences are moving more money from above-the-line media advertising to below-the-line sales promotion.
▶ Senior marketing decision-makers have grown up with sales promotion as a technique. It now has board level credibility.
▶ The quality of the people working in the industry itself has improved and there has been a move towards greater professionalism.
▶ Technology (scratch cards, printing processes, packaging and point-of-sale display) has favoured the growth of creativity.
▶ The legal climate governing games of chance is becoming relaxed, leading to a boom in instant-win promotions.

For all these steps forward, however, sales promotion has suffered some notable reverses in the public mind. Any industry that depends so much on novelty will inevitably suffer the difficulties associated with doing things for the first time. Pioneers, as they say, get scalped. Sales promotion history is littered with some spectacular wrecks, all the more embarrassing for being so deliberately visible.

CASE STUDY **12.2**
• • • • • • • • • • • • • • • • • • •

Great sales promotion disasters of our time

It's not often we get a chance to pity the poor marketing whizz kid, but here are a few of the most legendary sales promotions from hell.

Hoover free flights

Customers spending £100 or more on Hoover products qualified for two free flights to Europe or the US. Sounds like a good deal? A lot more people than Hoover expected thought so. As well as flooding the market with second-hand vacuum cleaners for the foreseeable future, the promotion resulted in law suits, media vilification, the departure of three senior managers and a £19 million provision to cover costs. American parent company Maytag ended by selling the European Hoover operation to Candy in 1994 at an £80 million loss.

Cadbury's Creme Eggs

A classic from 1984. Inspired by the success of puzzle-picture books like Kit Williams's *Masquerade* (containing clues to the location of a buried golden hare), Cadbury's buried 12 £10,000 golden eggs at secret locations around Britain. About 100,000 enthusiastic treasure-hunters dug large holes in the English countryside, many blithely ignoring the competition rules which stated that none were buried on private land, National Trust property or at ancient monuments. Some venerable sites still bear the scars. After intervention from the Environment Secretary, Cadbury's blew the whistle on the promotion with six eggs to go. Apart from the embarrassment, however, the £750,000 promotion led to record egg sales.

On the house

Oxfordshire brewery Brakspear ran a promotion in 1995 which offered an incentive of a free bottle of beer a day for a year to anyone who could visit all its 75 pubs in a specified time period. It under-estimated the determination of its drinkers, however, dozens of whom had qualified before the embarrassed brewers called time on what was becoming an impossibly expensive promotion. A few years earlier, the Mansfield brewery had run a similar promotion, with even more disastrous results. In a bizarre precursor of the Hoover fiasco, it offered a £500 holiday to anyone who could visit all of its 196 pubs. Five hundred holidays were claimed before it called a halt.

Pepsi in the Philippines

One to rival Hoover – but on the other side of the world. Pepsi offered a million pesos (a modest £26,000) to anyone finding a bottle top printed with the magic number 349. Due to a computer error, however, no fewer than 800,000 such bottle tops were in circulation. The potential payout was £19 billion. After a 3am crisis meeting, Pepsi management agreed to pay £13 to each winner – but withdrew the offer £8 million later. Factories and lorries were attacked, there were two fatalities, thousands of law suits and a reputation from which the fizz has vanished.

One in a million

The chickens flew home to roost for Michael O'Leary, the chief executive of low-cost airline Ryanair, in June 2002 when a judge ordered the company to pay £43,000 in damages to Jane O'Keefe, a Dublin mother of two. Mrs O'Keefe had been awarded free travel for life in 1988 by Mr O'Leary (then the airline's marketing manager) by virtue of being the company's millionth traveller. At the time, the award was announced amidst lashings of champagne and publicity, but when Mrs O'Keefe tried to book a flight to Scotland in 1997 she found her privileges had been cut off. She rang Mr O'Leary to query this, to be asked (in words quoted embarrassingly back at him in court) 'Who do you think you are, ringing up demanding flights?'

Understandably miffed, Mrs O'Keefe took the matter to court and found a judge who agreed with her that Ryanair's chief executive had been 'hostile, bullying and aggressive'.

Questions

1   The Hoover free flights disaster has been blamed on 'groupthink' – the tendency of people in organisations not to question decisions. Suggest ways in which this tendency might be reduced.

2   Is it possible to predict consumer uptake of sales promotions with any accuracy?

3   If you were a Pepsi manager in the Philippines, how might you have tried to deal with the lottery run?

Sources: Brown (2002); Colbey (1995); Denny (1994).

The role of sales promotion

Within its general remit of increasing the speed or intensity of purchasing response, sales promotion can help solve a number of specific marketing problems.

Prompting trial

For new products or reformulated existing products, sales promotion can tempt new or lapsed consumers to give a product a chance.

Increasing loyalty

To confirm consumers in their purchasing habits by encouraging multiple purchase.

Widening distribution

Prompting more retailers and wholesalers to stock a product either by offering them a direct incentive or through making the product demonstrably more attractive to the consumer through the promotion.

Increasing display opportunities

Rather than looking for extra volume as a direct result of the promotion, the marketing department may use it as a platform to refresh salesforce, trade and consumer interest in the product. Particularly in markets like confectionery which are largely driven by impulse purchase, display is an essential factor.

In order to work most effectively, sales promotion needs to enhance existing brand values as it solves these tactical problems. An inappropriately-conceived piece of activity can waste management time and resources, and confuse the customer into the bargain.

Sales promotion techniques

From the variety of sales promotional tools available, many can serve a number of different marketing ends. This allows established brands to offer their customers variety in the format and style of promotional activity – a considerable bonus given that an important part of the rationale for sales promotion is to provide a new perspective on the product.

Some of the most popular techniques, with some notes on their use, are as follows.

Advertising allowance

This is a sum of money paid by a manufacturer to a retailer or wholesaler on the understanding that it will contribute to joint advertising activity. This kind of approach is noticeable at Christmas, for example, when some major retailers publish catalogues or run substantial television advertisements detailing special offers. Manufacturers will usually have co-funded this activity. The definition of what constitutes advertising activity, however, can be rather loose. Often the allowance is merely a device for transferring extra margin to a powerful retailer.

Competitions

These can be used to generate salesforce, trade and consumer interest. The best response levels are achieved by the simplest ideas. Competitions like 'spot the ball', usually featuring the words 'Using your skill and judgement', are very popular because entrants recognise that very little skill and judgement are in fact needed. They are very nearly lotteries and, as such, find little favour with the small but vocal group of people whose main hobby is doing competitions. 'Compers', as they style themselves, have their own magazines and jargon. Avid for EFs (entry forms) and POPs (Proofs of Purchase), they despise what they see as skill-free contests. They are, however, a very small minority of anyone's market.

Coupons

Enormously flexible, these offer savings to consumers when redeemed against the purchase price of a particular product. Consumer-choice coupons allow the consumer to decide which pack size to use the coupon against – the largest savings being attached to the largest sizes. Friction can occur between manufacturers and retailers over the problem of malredemption whereby some stores allow coupons to be used against purchases that do not include the product in question. Technology is providing the answer to this in the shape of machine-readable coupons which will only work in combination with specific bar-codes when scanned at point of sale. A further recent development is the retailer-specific coupon issued to storecard customers. These not only guarantee secure redemption, but their use can be tracked to individual customers.

Dealer loaders

These are promotional gifts to wholesalers and retailers to encourage them to take on more than their usual stock levels of a promoted line. The old sales adage 'stock pressure sells' relies on the fact that if a wholesaler or retailer has a lot of stock, there is the immediate incentive for them to sell it more quickly.

Display allowance

This is a sum of money or free stock given to a distribution intermediary in order to guarantee a special display. This amounts to buying shelf space in prime locations, such as at gondola ends (the end of a fixture where shoppers will notice a featured product as they turn their trolleys).

Free gifts/trial

As the name implies, this involves giving something away with a purchase. In the 1960s plastic daffodils were all the rage with soap powder. These days the gift is more likely to be connected with the product (e.g. special glasses with whisky) and used as a branding device. Free trial can involve attaching sample packs to a purchased product, dropping free samples through selected letter-boxes, or using coupons.

Free draws/free mail-in

These are basically a free raffle. The magic words 'no purchase necessary' absolve them from the legal restrictions attached to lotteries (a form of regulated gambling) where no skill or judgement comes into participants' chances of winning. Conversely, as we have seen, virtual lotteries such as 'spot the ball'-type competitions are absolved from these same legal restrictions by insisting that skill and judgement are part of the competition. They are practically the same as free mail-ins, but tied to a purchase.

Instant-win promotions

Packaging which contains prizes or messages when opened are a very popular promotional gambit. As with other games of chance, the chance to enter without purchasing the product must be available (although the conditions in the small print usually specify that free entry will be limited to one per envelope sent to the competition address). This seems to be obeying the gambling regulations in the letter rather than in the spirit, but many in the marketing industry would argue that such legislation is now outmoded due to changing social mores concerning gambling. The advantage of such promotions is their simplicity. The disadvantage is that there are a great deal more instant losers than there are instant winners, so careful thought needs to be given to the creative side of the promotion and the number of prizes involved.

In-store promotions

These are any promotional activity that takes place in, and is exclusive to, a retailer. Merchandising, competitions, sampling and free draws are popular examples. To be successful, such activity needs the active support of the retailer.

On-pack promotions

These are any promotion whose details are communicated entirely on the packaging of the product. Because of the pressure on space in retail outlets it is virtually impossible to place manufacturers' promotional leaflets. Packaging and printing technology have facilitated the move to on-pack communication. In spite of the complications this presents in terms of stock control and materials purchasing, the special packaging often gives the manufacturer the chance to jazz up familiar packaging with attention-grabbing flashes.

Personality promotions

This technique uses real people, frequently models in fancy dress, mounting a particular drive – it is popular with newspapers and specialist foods. It is often used in conjunction with sampling and can create considerable goodwill. A number of brands including Lilt and Chicken Tonight have established advertising campaigns around the idea, using consumers as the personalities rather than paid models.

Reduced price offers (RPOs)

These have the advantage of being simple and effective. They can be used to gain extra display impact if the offer is communicated on-pack by a colourful flash. Used too often they soften prices and put margins at risk in the entire sector. In spite of this they are popular with frequently-purchased, low-priced goods.

Re-usable container premiums

These are good for products packaged in glass or metal. The customer can be persuaded to trade up to a larger size than normal by limiting the storage jar or tea caddy to a larger pack. A further advantage is that the branded item will remain in the kitchen for some time after the promotion, perhaps encouraging product loyalty.

DID YOU KNOW?

In 1995 a TV-supported Tango sales promotion offered Gotan, a little orange doll, to callers on a premium telephone line. In the event, 300,000 of the fruity plastic figurines were bought by besotted customers, increasing sales of the soft drink by 34 per cent year on year.

Sampling

This involves giving away small amounts of product. It is very powerful – the product sells itself to the consumer – but it is extremely expensive. Coupons that may be redeemed against a new product are less expensive because they will not be subject to 100 per cent use. They are less effective as a result, however.

Self-liquidating premiums (SLPs)

Here an exclusive item of branded merchandise is offered to consumers at little more than cost price. The benefit for the manufacturer is that the promotion should cover its costs. There are significant financial risks involved in the set-up costs, however. An economic quantity of the goods needs to be available from the chosen supplier, and sensible reorder quantities need to be on call at short notice. This can be difficult to get right. Quality problems or delays will impact directly on the reputation of the brand rather than the supplier. However, if things go well, the benefit for the consumer is an unusual item offering good value and positive brand associations. Such promotions inevitably require the use of intermediaries such as handling houses to deal with response and process applications.

CASE STUDY 12.3

Giving promotion the push?

Sales promotions such as multi-buys (e.g. buy three for the price of two) are beginning to attract criticism from some large companies for being counter-productive. Procter and Gamble's UK managing director, Paul Poltman, went on record in 1997 as saying that such marketing activity invests vast amounts of money in a way which neither enlarges market share nor value. It appeals to a minority of customers and encourages brand disloyalty. Instead of buying the product, consumers are encouraged to buy the 'deal'.

Why do companies still persist with this kind of 'push' strategy, which is aimed at forcing stock through distribution channels, rather than 'pull' strategy, where consumers themselves are targeted (usually through the media) with offers which make the brands more attractive? Is it pressure from excess stocks, perhaps generated by over-ambitious production targets, themselves based on unrealistic sales objectives? Faced with warehouses full of ageing inventory, marketers panic and try to speed up the rate of sale, sacrificing short-term profit and long-term brand values.

Promotions based on extra volume carry the added problem of clogging up distribution channels and creating post-promotional dips in demand. This could be because deal-happy consumers are trying to work their way through cupboards full of extra product bought as a result of the promotion. On the other hand, industry research suggests that it is also due to retailers buying extra promotional stock at discounted rate, and then selling it later at full price. At least this means that the promotion prevents a competitor from gaining distribution. But it is a very expensive way of doing so, and it may be that short-term benefits are outweighed by the overall cost to the company.

Defenders of 'push' promotions argue that many product categories (particularly impulse buys) respond well to this kind of treatment. And there are psychological advantages in focusing the attention of distribution intermediaries on your brand. It renews interest and commitment, gaining display opportunities which may make the final consumer reassess the brand in a positive light.

The main problem with many 'push' promotions, however, is a lack of shared objectives. Such objectives (for a retailer) might include building customer traffic through an outlet in the hope of growing volume and sales in non-promoted goods. A manufacturer, on the other hand, is more likely to want customers to switch brands. For a retailer this might mean no real increase in overall sales of coffee, just a temporary variation in where sales are coming from.

As a result, 'push' promotions are becoming an increasing source of irritation between manufacturers and retailers. This kind of irritation, known technically as vertical channel conflict (see Chapter 10) can be resolved by closer planning links between manufacturers and channel intermediaries. At the same time, many manufacturers are beginning to reconsider the balance between push and pull promotional strategies in their marketing operations, and are placing more emphasis on making a direct appeal to customers over the heads of wholesalers and retailers.

Questions
1 Give three examples of products which, in your opinion, might do well in push promotion.
2 Promotions can cause tensions between retailers and manufacturers. Suggest the kinds of negative tension they might create between the following members of the marketing chain:
   ▶ Manufacturers and consumers.
   ▶ Retailers and consumers.
3 What are the advantages and disadvantages of flooding a distribution channel with promotional stock?

Source: Mitchell (1997).

Strengths and weaknesses of sales promotion

The main advantages of sales promotion as a technique are as follows.

Something for nothing
The great strength of sales promotion is that it offers something for nothing. This stimulates a positive attitude to the product among consumers and intermediaries.

Short-term effectiveness
This tips customers over the edge of the decision to buy, thus leading to immediate sales increases.

Flexibility
Sales promotion can address a number of different marketing problems. The absolute costs and lead-times involved are frequently less daunting than for other kinds of marketing communication.

Sales promotion is most effective in certain situations. For example, when launching a new product, it can prompt early trial. It can be used to communicate a major product improvement, a new pack size or variant. Used in the trade it is excellent for increasing distribution (via incentives to middlemen). Dealer loaders, such as free gifts, can persuade channel intermediaries to accept much higher levels of stock than they might otherwise, thus bringing forward business. This increases cash flow and, by flooding the distribution channel, effectively crowds out the competition. Used in tandem with advertising, sales promotion can be very effective at increasing the impact of commercial messages.

The drawbacks of sales promotion are as follows:

Temporary effects
By their very nature these are short lived (usually less than 90 days). It is therefore very difficult to get strategic messages about your brand across by sales promotion alone.

Cost-effectiveness
At first sight this looks like one of the attractions of the technique. However, the need to support sales promotion with other techniques (scheme advertising, salesforce support, public relations activity) means that the real cost of a promotion can exceed its apparent budget by some way.

Lack of continuity
The 'one-off' dominates sales promotion as a technique. Only a few are recurring. The pressure to be original negates the economies of scale that might be possible from a long-running advertising campaign.

Too much activity can make a product look busy, although this depends on the size and traditions of the product and consumers' expectations. There is some evidence to suggest that continual cut-price promotion devalues the brand in the eyes of consumers. There is certainly a growth in the number of deal-prone customers who switch brands promiscuously in search of the cheapest alternative (see Chapter 9).

So sales promotion is best avoided as a technique on established brands with no improvements to tout. It cannot, on its own, restore the fortunes of brands in the decline stage of the product life-cycle. There may be more effective ways of supporting brands in markets where sales promotion is the norm (such as pre-sweetened breakfast cereals), but being first in with a new sales promotion idea may give you an edge, however temporary. Heavy price promotion offers short-term benefits to the consumer, but falling margins may deter participating companies from making the kind of investment in quality necessary to long-term consumer satisfaction.

In spite of its apparently tactical nature, it is essential to integrate the planning and timing of sales promotion activity across the range of a company's products or services to maximise its support for the sales effort. This involves looking at least a year ahead at timing, techniques, geographical areas, brand co-ordination, synergy with planned advertising and the need to create selling support material.

KEY SKILLS
ACTIVITY **12.2**
....

Working with others

Selling sales promotion

Part of the challenge of working with others lies in the need to divide up tasks and allocate responsibilities. This exercise gives you a clearly structured task, but you still need to decide who does what, and think about what each of you need to find out as you prepare your 'sales pitch' and responding role.

Working in pairs (if possible) take the roles of a new business executive in an established sales promotion agency and a new client who has not used the medium before. The client is one of the following (please choose whichever one you prefer):

1 Your college or business.
2 Your local crime prevention officer.
3 A new sports centre.

Prepare a five-minute presentation to the prospective new client, who must then give you constructive feedback on your performance and whether or not he or she is convinced of the relevance of sales promotion to his or her needs,

Public relations
....

A cynical view of public relations might describe it as applied conviviality to keep bad news out of the press and free advertising in. It is yet another marketing communications technique with an image problem in some quarters. But for a more comprehensive, and more useful, definition we can turn to the words of the Institute of Public Relations (IPR) definition. This bills it as 'the deliberate, planned and sustained effort to establish and maintain mutual understanding between an organisation and its publics'.

In fact you could extend the definition of public relations to cover every aspect of an organisation's interaction with its customers, external and internal. Corporate image, employee relations, investor relations, sponsorship, event management and hospitality – these are just some of the ways in which public relations operates.

We shall concentrate on how companies can manage public relations within their promotional mix to help achieve specific marketing communications tasks, with particular emphasis on editorial public relations, which uses third-party media to convey marketing messages to target publics.

Public relations in the strategic mix

Companies are free to choose whether or not to advertise, do direct marketing, run a salesforce or use sales promotion. But they have no choice about public relations. Public relations happens whether you like it or not. The only choice is whether to manage the process or let things drift along by themselves.

Companies that let things drift along are nevertheless still sending out messages. Product performance, packaging, what the reception area looks like, even the way the telephones are answered are beaming images to customers, employees, stakeholders, competitors and suppliers.

It makes sense to make a conscious effort to manage public relations, but it is a historical fact that practically all in-house PR departments have arisen from a crisis, rather than from planning. A company faced by a takeover threat, for example, suddenly realises that it matters very much indeed what people think about it. The confidence of City institutions can save its independence. The sudden threat posed by a contamination scare, an industrial disaster or a management gaffe can precipitate a programme of damage limitation. The best-prepared organisations are the best at weathering such storms. Companies have learned, if not from their own experience then from that of others, the value of a programme of pro-active public relations.

A further factor in the increased use of public relations as a marketing tool is its perceived cost-effectiveness. Advertising growth has slowed down as public relations expenditure has increased. Perhaps less enlightened companies expect PR to do their advertising on the cheap, and have therefore switched money from one budget into another. They are, however, two very different techniques, as Figure 12.3 shows. But there is evidence that public relations budgets are more likely to withstand the pressure of a recession.

Unlike advertising, which tends to flourish only in positive economic conditions, public relations is a wise investment in good and bad times. In adition, the absolute costs of public relations are l ess than those of advertising. Cost-cutting managers feel there is more fat to trim off their relatively substantial advertising appropriations. If a reduction of £50,000 means cancelling 5 per cent of the planned advertising or 80 per cent of the planned PR programme, there are persuasive grounds for retaining the latter unscathed.

figure 12.3
**Public relations
versus advertising**

Public relations	Advertising
● Informative	● Persuasive
● Background	● Foreground
● Editorial	● Identified sponsor
● Gratis	● Guaranteed
● Credible	● Biased
● Once only	● Repeatable

Public relations techniques usually involve a third party standing between the organisation and its audience. Often this is a journalist, whose work is facilitated by a PR professional with information and material. In the case of a PR technique like sponsorship, the third party will be the event, institution or individual whose reputation is being used as a way of getting a brand's message across. Techniques such as advertising and sales promotion offer organisations precise control of the content and presentation of their messages. They reach the public direct through paid-for media exposure. With public relations the messages are dependent on third parties.

This can give public relations greater credibility than advertising. Particularly for a service whose benefits are more difficult to convey than those of a tangible product, an expert's endorsement can work better than direct communication. We are more likely to trust a travel writer on the subject of an untried holiday destination, for example, than an adverisement.

This leads us to another difference between public relations and the other marketing communications disciplines. No other technique places the same emphasis on dialogue. In spite of the amount of research that goes into its creative development or campaign analysis, advertising tends to be a one-way process. Public relations, on the other hand, implies dialogue. Any worthwhile programme begins in research to find out what an organisation's publics are thinking and saying. This is why the IPR definition stresses 'mutual understanding'. Good public relations involves a lot of listening.

CASE STUDY **12.4**

On the ball . . .

Football's World Cup competition finals come once every four years. This is more than enough for some people, but it means that Adidas, the sporting goods and apparel supplier, needs to slot its new product development schedule carefully into a four-year cycle. This is because it makes a point of unveiling a new, 'state-of-the-art' football to be used for each set of finals. The influence this exerts on what the rest of the world then use to play the beautiful game should not be underestimated. For example, how many people know that the Adidas Telstar, official match ball of the 1970 Mexico finals, was the world's first combination white hexagon/black pentagon ball (now the most common design in use)? And how many footballing pundits realise that the first synthetic ball used in the World Cup finals was the Adidas Azteca, introduced in 1984 – again in Mexico?

The 2002 finals were no exception to the onward evolution of the football. For this tournament Adidas unveiled what the company described as its 'most accurate ball yet'. Using the 'syntactic foam layering system' (a mass of tiny bubbles aimed at distributing energy equally around the ball when kicked), the Adidas Fevernova set new standards in allowing footballers to get the ball to respond to their intentions. Another important feature of the Fevernova was its distinctive champagne colour with red and gold graphics reflecting the official World Cup logos.

The UK launch of this superball was entrusted to PR company Hill and Knowlton (most famous, perhaps, for their work on winning American hearts and minds in support of the Gulf War). Their campaign, which picked up the Institute of Public Relations' Excellence award for 2002 in the consumer category, aimed at stressing the ball's advanced technology as well as the strong link between Adidas and England through its sponsorship of David Beckham. There was also a strong imperative to boost sales of the ball to sports fans in the run up to Christmas 2001, preceding the World Cup finals themselves.

One of the challenges facing a PR company handling sports clients is time. Not only are celebrities such as international footballers available for very short periods, but the actual timing of news stories and press releases needs to be extremely carefully co-ordinated around the actual news stories that sporting events themselves. Beckham's very limited availability meant that rather than spending lots of time organising photo-shoots with the ball, Hill and Knowlton used digital manipulation to retouch existing photographs of the footballing idol, to include enhanced images of the Fevernova itself.

Another issue concerned the detailed timing of the launch. The PR agency knew that the draw for the finals was to be made on 1 December 2001, a Saturday, so it would dominate Sunday's sports reporting. By the following day, journalists would be casting round for fresh angles on the story, so it was decided to aim for coverage of Beckham and the Fevernova in Monday's papers. 45 personalised media packs were distributed to key sporting journalists. They included a metal mesh box (with astro turf base) containing the ball, wrapped in a red ribbon with a St George's cross motif to stress the England connection. Each package also contained media information prepared with the specific recipient in mind, drawing on Hill and Knowlton's detailed knowledge of, and relationship with, these specialised journalists.

The best-selling tabloid, *The Sun*, was given particular attention because of the demographics of its readers – avid football fans. By explaining exactly what they were sending other journalists, and promising an exclusive digital image of Beckham with three balls depicting the flags of the three countries facing England, Hill and Knowlton secured front-page coverage for their story on the nation's favourite tabloid.

The campaign worked for Adidas. Even though the Fevernova's unprecedented accuracy did not help England to get very far in the competition, the ball had sold out in sports shops across the UK by Christmas 2001, a rate of sale in its first month of availability more than ten times greater than any previous ball launch.

Questions

1 Adidas's launch of the Fevernova has been held up as a textbook example of how to handle a consumer product launch. How might other companies learn from its experience?
2 What are the advantages and disadvantages of using a sporting celebrity in a PR campaign?
3 Digital manipulation of photographic images has become a common technique in PR and popular journalism. What, if any, ethical issues does it raise?

Sources: Institute of Public Relations (2002); Weinberg (2002).

Strengths and weaknesses of public relations

The advantages of public relations as a promotional technique are as follows.

Coverage
It reaches people who are difficult to reach through advertising, either because they consciously avoid it or because they simply don't see much of it (like AB men or young people, both of which groups are notoriously difficult to reach through traditional advertising media).

Economy
The visible costs are considerably less than those of advertising. While the two techniques can hardly be compared on a like-with-like basis, this nevertheless looms large in what clients say about it. Administrative costs and time overheads can be heavy, though.

New products
Editorial public relations is particularly effective in support of new products, especially in the business-to-business sector where trade press can generate extensive coverage of the market.

Services
Third-party endorsement means that unfamiliar products or intangible services can be described more extensively and credibly than if they were merely being advertised.

The disadvantages of public relations are as follows.

Difficulty of control
Because of PR's reliance on third parties, exact details of message content, presentation or even appearance cannot be guaranteed.

Reliance on news values
The kind of repetition used in other forms of promotion is difficult. Sustaining a theme requires particularly careful planning and management.

Evaluation
Effectiveness is difficult to gauge in any promotional technique. But public relations campaigns offer a particular challenge. Pre-and post-campaign qualitative research is expensive, and relying on measures like editorial column inches is crude and subjective. The issue of evaluation is dealt with at greater length towards the end of the chapter.

Editorial PR techniques

The concept of 'publics' implies that different audiences will have particular preferences when it comes to how messages are mediated. In some cases the best way may be through a direct approach. Receptions, conferences, exhibitions are all tools that come under the heading of public relations. More often, however, because of the size of the publics you need to reach, the media will come into the equation. Knowing how to deal with the media and, in particular, how to write effective press releases, is a core skill in PR.

Journalists are busy people. Effective editorial PR aims to make their lives as easy as possible. One way of doing this is to be able to spot an angle to a story that is likely to interest readers, listeners or viewers. A second necessary skill is the ability to communicate the idea briefly and coherently in a press release. The most important knack to acquire, though, is an appreciation of what makes news.

What makes a story?

DID YOU KNOW?

News values haven't changed much over 100 years? 'When a dog bites a man that is not news, but when a man bites a dog that is news' (Charles Anderson Dana, 1882).

The simple answer is anything. But a brief glance through a local or national newspaper reveals that the stories they contain hang on some particular hook. Journalists are trained to look for what is newsworthy in a story. It needs to contain at least one of the following elements:

- ► Action.
- ► Conflict and debate.
- ► Unusualness.
- ► Local interest (for local media).
- ► Human interest.
- ► Topicality.
- ► Relevance to a national issue (e.g. a soap opera, politics, scandal, the Lottery, Christmas, etc.).

Different papers have different approaches to news. Some are very serious, others mix heavyweight stories with quirkier tittle-tattle. The same is true for radio programmes and television. The skill lies in matching a story or an angle with an appropriate outlet. After all, the media need an endless supply of material to fill their column inches or broadcast minutes, so there is no shortage of opportunity; but it needs to be the right kind of material.

Although this chapter uses the terminology 'press release', what is said about printed media does not always hold true for broadcast. Action is very important to television. Sound is important to radio. As with creative choices in advertising, a sensitivity to the strengths and potential of media is important in PR – and can enhance coverage of the target publics by maximising exposure across a number of media.

Another thing to bear in mind about the media is the deadline. As new technology tightens its grip on the traditional world of the newspaper, the time between receiving a news item and its publication is shortening. But the best story in the world is still no good to a journalist if it arrives too late to be used. Having clear policies can help a company minimise the delay in releasing news – especially in the case of a crisis where speed of reaction is essential.

Writing a press release

I keep six honest serving-men
(They taught me all I knew);
Their names are What and Why and When

And How and Where and Who.
Rudyard Kipling, *The Elephant's Child*

Good press releases bristle with facts, preferably in the first one or two sentences (the lead as journalists call it). What is happening? Who is involved? Where is it taking place? When is it happening? Why is it happening? These questions are as important for the launch of a new product as they are for a summit conference of world leaders or a major sporting event. The first couple of sentences of your release are crucial to the success or failure of what follows. They will be scanned by an extremely busy journalist. On them depends whether the press release ends up on the desk for further investigation, or in the bin.

Another good reason for starting with the essential facts is that sometimes editors print press releases without changing them, except for cutting them. Traditionally editors cut from the bottom. So the less important details should go into later paragraphs. This tradition has affected the way newspaper stories are written. Almost invariably, the reader can pick up the main point of the story (with the essential information) from the first paragraph of each news item.

The rest of the release should include supporting facts and details. If there is a personality involved in the story, it is a good idea to include a substantial quote. This means the journalist can select a few words to give his or her story a personal stamp. It is essential to provide a number for further information at the end of the release.

As in any other sort of marketing relationship, customer care is important when dealing with journalists and editors. Press releases can demonstrate this by catering for the needs of the journalist's own customers (by having news value). The more immediate needs of the journalist or editor can be catered for by following their professional conventions:

▶ Dates and other factual details should be exact and full to avoid misunderstandings. The release needs to be double-checked for accuracy. Getting things wrong makes both the issuer and the journalist look inept.

▶ Production details are important. Wide margins, double spacing, one side of the paper only. All these apparently aesthetic features actually affect how easily a press release can be used by a journalist.

▶ Brevity is the soul of wit, especially in a press release. It's useful to remember that one side of double-spaced A4 fills about six column inches in most newspapers (that's only about 150 words).

▶ Facts, not opinions, count. Opinions are for the journalist to form. Press releases that go over the top about the qualities of a product will be dismissed as an attempt to get free advertising.

▶ Simplicity pays dividends. The average reading age of the Great British public is lower than you think!

▶ Making your press releases (and other media resources such as speeches, fact files, images and graphics) available electronically on the Internet is another way of helping journalists get your story straight.

Impressing the press?

The knack of writing for different audiences is an essential skill for any public relations executive. Sometimes inexperience leads to a press release being written more like a piece of advertising copy than a stimulus for a reporter. This exercise gives you the opportunity to critique a press release, and to rewrite it for a different audience.

Here are two press releases for the same piece of news. Spot the differences and discuss why the second press release is better than the first. Are there any other improvements you can suggest? How would you rewrite the press release for use with a local radio station, Frutiton FM?

EMBARGO: 20th July, 9.30am
Do not use beforehand.

For the attention of the Editor, *Frutiton Gazette*

TFP are launching a great new product, the delicious and nutritious Rasp-o-foam. In two great value-for-money sizes, small and large, this fantastic new technological breakthrough offers housewives the highly convenient instant dessert of raspberry mousse dispensed from an aerosol can at the touch of a button. Tasty on its own, or teamed with TFP soya custard or TFP tinned wild rice pudding, this is another groundbreaking innovation from your local specialist in fruit (and fruit-flavoured) puddings. Rasp-o-foam, the delicious new fruit dessert in an aerosol can, is manufactured using double-helix polymer fused process bessamer twin cylinder technology, only the third new product in the north of England to do so. So point, shoot, and taste that fruit!

TFP is pleased to announce that their production line needs to be expanded in order to cope with the expected demand flooding in from all over the country for this extremely unique product. This increase in capacity is not likely to effect its reputation for quality and value. It's still absolutely fruitful!

We hope you will support this exciting new venture in your paper, especially as we have placed recruitment advertising regularly with your company now for nearly three years.

With best wishes,

Des Parette

Terrikin Fruit Puddings
Pudding House
Orchard Lane
Fruititon LS18 5HD
Tel: 0123 456789

T*F*P

Success in a Squirt for YOU

PRESS RELEASE: 20th July for immediate use

New jobs at local company on back of product launch

Terrikin Fruit Puddings, Frutiton's second-largest employer, yesterday announced plans to create ten new jobs on its production line. The jobs are a result of the launch of the company's third new product in five years, Rasp-o-foam.

Rasp-o-foam is a new concept in fruit puddings: raspberry mousse in an aerosol can. The company is launching it in two sizes: the 150 ml one-shot size aimed at the snack market, and the 550 ml aimed at the family shopper. 28 year-old engineering manager Dr Perry Terrikin, son of the managing director, said yesterday: 'This new fruit pudding is the result of two years' research and development into packaging fruit puree under pressure – and we have now patented it as a British invention. Although it's a very sophisticated process, I got the initial idea from watching my mother making jam.'

Journalists and photographers are invited to join the directors of TFP at the launch of Rasp-o-Foam on Tuesday 20th July at the Board Room, Pudding House, Frutiton at 2pm.

Samples and recipe leaflets will be available.

For further information
contact TFP press officer Des Parette

01234 56789 (8.30am – 6pm, Mondays to Fridays)

The feature article

This is when a PR practitioner offers an editor a complete article on a particular subject. It can be reprinted as it stands or rewritten by another journalist. The advantage is that it allows an issue to be treated in depth. The disadvantage is that such articles need to stand on their own two feet as editorial matter. They will tend to be useful as background material, but less so in support of specific products or services.

Visuals

The problem with press releases is that journalists can make of them what they like. This may not always accord with the issuer's interests, although it makes a good story. The beauty of pictures is that they are easier to control (in general) and have much more immediate impact than the written word. As with feature articles, publications frequently accept an organisation's own pictures. And, again, customer care is important here. Because of the format of newspapers and magazines, certain types of picture work better than others. Close-ups, upright images rather than sideways ones (i.e. portrait not landscape), people close together, people doing something that is easily understood. These are all characteristics of typical press photographs.

We live in an increasingly visual culture, dominated by television and video. So photographs are a very natural way of communicating. The main problem is keeping a supply of fresh ideas coming. At one stage, for example, no share flotation was complete without a photocall of abseilers descending the company HQ wall. This was, at least for a while, a good way of making a pretty dull event visually exciting. Banal as it may seem, pictures involving hats, children and animals (sometimes all three) are enduringly popular. And, despite changing attitudes, young women with 'nice smiles' tend to be seen as a safe bet as well.

> **DID YOU KNOW?**
> Public relations for celebrities is big business (largely because of the rapid rise in the number of new publications looking for stories). Hello! magazine pays up to £500,000 to big stars to show readers their 'beautiful homes' in lavish photo features. At the other end of the scale, an interview with an evicted housemate from Big Brother can be had for upwards of £10,000, depending on who their PR rep is (Economist, 2001b).

The video news release (VNR)

The ability to think in pictures is essential to securing time on television news programmes. This has been extended in recent years by organisations who supply video material to news programmes, thus saving the considerable cost of originating images to put over the words. Amnesty International is one of the most successful non-profit organisations to employ this technique. Its promotional campaigns highlight the plight of people whose stories would not normally make the news agenda, but by supplying video material it can often gain priority with television editors desperate for visuals.

The broadcast interview

Journalists, especially in the broadcast media, are keen to combine topicality and human interest via the technique of interviews. There is a burgeoning industry in media training for senior personnel from organisations like major companies and the police in order to optimise their performance in what can sometimes seem like a gladiatorial struggle.

Radio and television interviews can be very intimidating for the inexperienced. As with all media, it is essential to consider the special opportunities they present. For example, radio news bulletins tend to be very short, so simplified messages work best. Complex arguments should give way to one main point. The growth in popularity of the soundbite, a conveniently sized quote that can be worked into a news report, is a symptom of this.

For longer interviews, the object of the presenter will be to make entertaining programming. He or she will want to sound confident and in control. A positive manner on the part of the interviewee is therefore a real help. Whether the interview is to be recorded or is going out live on air or over the Internet may affect the best kind of answers to the questions posed, especially if the information might go out of date quickly. Life can be made easier for the interviewer by being briefed in advance with some written material about the product or organisation in question. To ensure their programme goes smoothly, most presenters will brief their subjects in advance on the shape the interview is to take.

Managing and evaluating public relations

Public relations can be carried out by an internal department, an external agency, or a mixture of both (the most common arrangement). When dealing with an external agency, the management of the relationship is an important element to get right for both parties. As with advertising agencies (see Chapter 11) the relationship will be the result of a period of courtship, cemented in agreed terms of business covering the following areas:

▶ Exclusivity (so the agency does not face competition in its territory or to its business, and the client does not have to share its services with a competitor).
▶ Scope of the services offered.
▶ Systems for approving and authorising work undertaken.
▶ Copyright and property responsibilities.
▶ Confidentiality.
▶ Fees and terms of payment. These are usually in the form of an agreed monthly fee called a retainer, supplemented by charges for expenses and services bought on the client's behalf, such as printing or copyright fees. Such expenditure will usually be marked up to offer the agency an agreed profit margin.
▶ Legal liability.

The areas covered are very similar to those governing relationships between advertising agencies and their clients. The payment method is different, however, in that public relations is a below-the-line expense. The media commission on which many advertising agencies still base their income does not form part of the picture.

The outline programme for the services to be offered to the client will also be agreed and updated at regular intervals. Such programmes will cover the background and objectives of the activity, and delineate the key messages that the programme will seek to communicate. Precise target audiences, the PR techniques to be used and budgets for the projected activity are also established and agreed as a result of this process.

As with advertising, client/agency meetings are a central technique in managing the PR process. The cycle of activity requires regular update meetings to report back on achievements and monitor media and other activity. Usually on a monthly basis, these are supplemented with quarterly or six-monthly planning meetings which respond to changing external conditions and trends. They are also an opportunity to evaluate the success of the activity carried out in the longer term.

Commonly-used measures of success include the following.

Cuttings book

A subjective measure, perhaps, the client needs to be satisfied with the amount of press coverage that can be demonstrated from a period of activity. While many PR practitioners condemn the comparison of their art to advertising, they often refer to how much their column inches or broadcast minutes would have cost to buy. Certainly a fat cuttings book can enhance a client's 'feel good' factor about PR.

Strategic messages

Key words and phrases are agreed and the success of the campaign is gauged by their appearance in editorial matter. This technique has the advantage of linking targeted media coverage closely to strategy, but it also means that the messages themselves have to be realistic. Also, the key words themselves must be well conceived. John Major's ill-fated 1994 'Back to Basics' campaign became a public relations disaster at the time, as rival politicians used the phrase to taunt his unsuccessful policies.

Market research

In an ideal world this would be the best way of evaluating PR effectiveness. The relevant key audiences would be sampled and polled before, during and after the activity. The major weakness with such an approach is its cost, which limits its use to the largest organisations.

Numerical targets

Influenced perhaps by the quantified media research that advertising agencies can invoke, this attempts to introduce a similar kind of rigour to PR. The requirement to register an agreed number of 'hits' certainly provides a measurable objective. But the problem is that numbers may not be the right currency in which to measure the quality of the activity.

Whatever the methods of evaluation used, the setting of realistic and clear objectives is the cornerstone of this kind of promotional activity.

Key concepts
··················

Below-the-line: promotional expenditure that is not commissionable (see Chapter 11). Commonly used to differentiate sales promotion expenditure from media advertising.

Closing: bringing a sales interview to the point of purchase.

Commission: a remuneration scheme whereby a salesperson is rewarded with a percentage of the value of achieved sales.

Feature article: a non-news story in a paper or magazine.

Hygiene factor: according to Herzberg (1966), a condition necessary to satisfaction in the workplace, but not necessary to increased performance.

Lead: the first couple of sentences of a press release or article.

On target earnings (OTE): expected, rather than guaranteed, earnings of a salesperson, taking into account commission and bonuses.

Prospects: potential customers. They need to be qualified by careful research.

Public relations: the management of mutual understanding by an organisation with its publics.

Sales promotion: promotional activity designed to increase the speed or volume of transactions.

Scheme and theme: two types of advertising – scheme is in support of a particular promotion, theme is general brand advertising activity.

Stakeholder: an individual or group with an interest in an organisation.

VNR: Video news release.

SELF-CHECK QUESTIONS

1 The six stages of the personal selling process consist of:
   a Prospecting, listening, arguing, handling objections, negotiation and closing.
   b Prospecting, approach, presentation, handling objections, closing and follow-up.
   c Approach, attention, interest, desire, action and follow-up.
   d Prospecting, presentation, punctuality, process, physical evidence and people.
   e Prospecting, approach, problem-solving, handling objections, probing and promising.

2 The allocative close:
   a Assumes that the customer has said yes.
   b Is a straightforward request for the order.
   c Puts it to the customer that there is a shortage of the product.
   d Sums up each point agreed in the presentation and ends with a request for the order.
   e Offers the customer a discount if he or she will agree the sale.

3 The salesforce management process can be divided into the three Ss of:
   a Subterfuge, structure and suspicion.
   b Strategy, structure and support.
   c Stratification, structure and stasis.
   d Situation, selling and sustenance.
   e Structure, stability and strategy.

4 Personality promotions:
   a Exploit psychological weaknesses in consumers' personalities.
   b Use models, often in fancy dress.
   c Are never used in conjunction with sampling.

   d Are an example of above-the-line expenditure.
   e Are a recent addition to the sales promotion repertoire.

5 Public relations can have greater credibility than advertising because:
   a It is planned and sustained.
   b It is more cost-effective.
   c It uses third-party endorsement.
   d It is for products not services.
   e It uses video news releases.

Which of the following are true and which are false?

6 Successful selling aims to look after existing customers as much if not more than winning new business.
7 Questions can be a useful way of diagnosing a customer's real needs.
8 Good salespeople always talk a lot.
9 Most successful sales promotions last for a maximum of three months.
10 Good press releases are full of honest opinions.

Discuss the following

11 Salespeople are born not made.
12 'Everyone lives by selling something' (Robert Louis Stevenson, 1850–94).
13 Sales promotion has no future as a form of strategic communication.
14 Public relations is an unethical imposition on journalists trying to present an objective view of the world to their audiences and readers.
15 The future of editorial public relations lies with the video news release.

Further study
....

Bernstein, David (1988) *Corporate Image and Reality*, Continuum International Publishing.
A classic account of public relations on a corporate level.

Carnegie, Dale (1992) *How to Win Friends and Influence People*, Cedar Books.
Offers a lot of farsighted wisdom and is extremely readable.

Cummins, J. and Mullin, R.(2002) *Sales Promotion: How to Create, Implement and Integrate Campaigns that Really Work*, Kogan Page.
A lively treatment of sales promotions from a practitioner perspective.

Hobday, P. (2001) *Managing the Message*, London House.
Plenty of relevant examples and some very thoughtful commentary from a broadcaster whose career has spanned advertising, PR and business journalism.

Theaker, A. (2001) *Public Relations Handbook,* Routledge.
Insightful and intelligent treatment of PR.

PR Week
The UK industry's chronicle of public relations news. A source of good ideas and stimulating case studies.

Internet links

Public relations, like advertising, is well served on the Internet. Here are three websites that are worth looking at:

www.martrex.co.uk/prca/index.htm
The Public Relations Consultants' Association (PRCA) website has codes of practice and information, and is geared primarily towards the 160 or so members of the Association. This gives it an authentic, practical feel.

www.ipr.org.uk/
The Institute of Public Relations site has lots of information, is well constructed and offers some extremely useful links to other sites, whether you are trying to research public relations as a subject, or doing some background research for some public relations of your own.

www.instituteforpr.com/
An American training and awards body – worth a browse.

Sales promotion is rather less well covered, but a good starting point is the Institute of Sales Promotion at www.isp.org.uk.

References
••••••••••••••

Argyle, M. (1990) *The Psychology of Interpersonal Behaviour,* Penguin.

Borkowski PR (2002) Improperganda press release, available at:
http://www.borkowski.co.ok/press/improperganda250400.html

Brown, J.M. (2002) 'Prize passenger beats Ryanair in court', *Financial Times,*
20 June, p.1.

Colbey, R. (1995) 'Brewer prevents customers from organising free party', *The Guardian*, 23 December.

Denny, N. (1994) 'Law of the bungle', *Promotions and Incentives*, October, pp.26–30.

Economist (2001a) 'Rebirth of a salesman', *The Economist*, 14 April, p.82.

Economist (2001b) 'PR man in father-in-law slur shock', *The Economist*, 7 July, p.35.

Gordon, I. (1998) *Relationship Marketing*, John Wiley.

Herzberg, F. (1966) *Work and the Nature of Man*, World Publishing Co.

Institute of Public Relations (2002). Award winners case study, available at:
http://www.ipr.org.uk/excellence/winners.htm

Killgren, L. and Edwards, P. (1999) 'Making a trauma out of a crisis', *Marketing Week,* 1 July, pp.26–9.

Kotler, P., Armstrong, G., Saunders, J., Wong, V. (2001) *Principles of Marketing,* 3rd European edn, FT Prentice Hall.

Levitt, T. (1986) *The Marketing Imagination*, Collier Macmillan.

Management Today (1999) 'Perk life: hands-on relaxation', *Management Today,* August, p.25.

Mitchell, A. (1997) 'Promotion fails to pull its weight', *Marketing Week*, 28 February, p.32.

Rigby, R. (1997) 'Cut out the middleman', *Management Today*, October, p.98.

Weinberg, A. (2002) Adidas Fevernova shines, Forbes.Com, 31 May, available at:
http://www.forbes.com/home/2002/05/31/0531tentech.html

Wolfgang, A. (1984) *Nonverbal Behaviour: Perspectives, Applications and Intercultural Insights*, Hogrete International.

CHAPTER 13

International marketing

Objectives
··············

When you have read this chapter you will be able to:

➤ Explain the major operational and theoretical differences between domestic marketing and international marketing.

➤ Assess the opportunities offered by the international marketing environment.

➤ Justify the selection of international markets and recommend appropriate entry decisions.

➤ Analyse product, price, promotion and distribution strategies in an international context.

➤ Apply basic marketing planning techniques to international business.

Foundation focus: the 20-second takeaway
···

In their search for new customers, or even as a result of new customers searching them out, most organisations get involved in marketing across borders sooner or later. Some industries, like information technology and computer games, are international by their very nature. International marketing offers the marketer considerable challenges in planning and operations. It presents increased levels of risk and uncertainty, requiring an organisation to widen its repertoire of skills and resources. The big decisions facing international marketers are which markets to choose, how to address them, and to what extent they can sell the same product the same way the world over (standardisation) or do they need to change methods to suit local markets (adaptation). This decision has important consequences for structure and strategy throughout an organisation's marketing activities.

Introduction
·················

Some businesses, such as electronics and cars, are international by nature. The high stakes involved in their research and development programmes necessitate international markets. There simply are not enough domestic consumers in any one country to make the game worthwhile. Other industries, which have started off on a purely domestic footing, have had to seek customers elsewhere in the world for a variety of reasons. Certainly the trend is towards more and more marketing taking place on an international footing, which has led to a growing interest in the whole area of international marketing theory and practice.

International marketing takes place across national boundaries. It embraces the activities of a range of companies from exporters (who remain based in one country) to transnationals or multinational companies (MNCs) whose operations and management span the world. A truly international company will display the following characteristics:

▶ Product planning, manufacturing and research and development in several countries.
▶ A wide distribution of sales volume throughout a number of markets.
▶ A mix of nationalities at senior management level.

International marketing involves risks and uncertainties that are many times greater than those facing a company operating in only one national market. There are a number of reasons why companies are prepared to overcome these difficulties and extend their marketing activities. Among the most common are the following:

▶ A limited market at home prompts the search for new markets overseas. The fine-arts sector in Eire targets Europe and North America rather than the tiny domestic art market, encouraged by marketing schemes sponsored by the An Chomhairle Ealaion (Arts Council of Ireland).
▶ A product's life-cycle needs extension (see Chapter 7). The original Volkswagen Beetle ceased production in Germany in 1978, but then started production, and sales, in South America as the 'Fusca'.
▶ The avoidance of domestic competition. UK confectionery giant Cadbury's operates in a highly competitive but stagnant domestic market. Its $4.2 billion purchase of Adams, a chewing gum business, from Pfizer in 2002 has opened up new distribution opportunities in America.
▶ The search for economies of scale. To reap the full benefits of investment in manufacturing plant, companies may be spurred to expand into markets that might otherwise have gone unconsidered.
▶ The need to get rid of excess stocks. International marketing's equivalent of clearance pricing (see Chapter 9) is an activity called dumping. Excess stock of a particular product is cleared on to another country's market at very low prices in order to liquidate capital. There is no long-term ambition to enter the market – it is just a hit-and-run exercise. Countries try to protect their domestic marketers from this destabilising phenomenon with legislation.
▶ Historical accident. Being in the right place at the right time is often cited as the reason behind one of the most successful international brands of all time – Coca-Cola. US forces took the drink with them wherever they went in the Second World War. An aggressive distribution policy on the part of the brand itself guaranteed that the footholds thus created would be exploited. As a result, Coca-Cola's red and white livery is one of the most immediately recognisable marketing devices anywhere in the world.

Whatever motivates a company to market its goods internationally, the differences between such marketing and domestic activity need to be understood and planned for. Figure 13.1 summarises some of the main points of divergence between international and domestic marketing.

figure 13.1
Domestic versus international marketing

Domestic marketing	International marketing
• Main language	• Many languages
• Dominant culture	• Multi-culture
• Research relatively straightforward	• Research complex
• Relatively stable environment	• Frequently unstable environment
• Single currency	• Exchange rate problems
• Business conventions understood	• Conventions diverse and unclear

As we shall see in the material that follows, international marketing is even more difficult to get right than domestic marketing for the following reasons:

▶ It places greater stress on environmental analysis.

▶ It makes more searching demands on a company's planning and control systems.

▶ It requires a more extensive repertoire of marketing and business skills (languages, treasury, law, etc.).

▶ It presents a greater diversity of manufacturing decisions (e.g. location of factories).

▶ It demands higher risks in terms of investment and market entry.

▶ It creates particular problems for debt-collection and payment methods.

▶ It offers less accumulated marketing experience and wisdom on which to draw.

DID YOU KNOW?

The Russian space station MIR might not have been the last word in technological breakthroughs (with a record of malfunctions and at least one near-disastrous collision with a cargo vessel) but it did notch up a notable international marketing first: the first television commercial from space. The brand was Tnuva – a kind of ultra-pasteurised milk from Israel which needs no refrigeration. Flight commander Vasily Tsibliyev was filmed swallowing a floating blob of the white stuff while his comrades quipped 'One small drop of milk, one giant leap for commercialisation' (Uhlig, 1997).

The international environment

As we have seen in Chapter 3, marketing responds to a number of variables in the external environment: socio-cultural, technological, economic and political. These variables present threats and opportunities to the firm, which need to be recognised and assessed. Because of the complexity and unfamiliarity of the international environment, successful international marketing requires vigilant attention to environmental factors. The process of scrutinising the business environment on a systematic basis is known as environmental scanning. Some of the most important issues for international marketers to consider are as follows.

Socio-cultural factors

Culture is a set of learned behaviours that unite a group of people, often along national lines. Language, education, religion, lifestyle, taboos, norms and values are some of the areas that culture embraces. Culture affects not only the way people define their wants and needs through consumption, it also influences the way they work and do business together. Clearly, for firms which are serious about international marketing, cultural sensitivity is paramount.

Coming to terms with it involves change. Dietary norms in certain countries mean that food products often have to be reformulated for export markets to avoid forbidden ingredients such as pork derivatives. Such adaptation is relatively straightforward compared to the kind of difficulty people from different cultures can find in working together. English managers tend to be pragmatic and informal. French managers, on the other hand, are trained to be far more analytical in the way they approach problems, and are expected to justify their solutions with argument and evidence. While both approaches work well in isolation, they can lead to misunderstanding and antagonism when combined. Mughan (1993) suggests that companies adapt best to cultural difference by:

- ▶ *Self-analysis* – recognising the situation from the customer's point of view and adapting behaviour accordingly.
- ▶ *Cultural training* – particularly for personnel working with counterparts from other countries or dealing direct with distributors or customers.
- ▶ *Recruitment* – the shortest route to widening the culture of an organisation is through direct recruitment in the international labour market. As we have noted, one of the characteristics of most international companies is the presence of a range of nationalities in its senior management.

> **DID YOU KNOW?**
>
> *Pepsi Cola was taken aback by the reaction when it extended its 1960s 'Come Alive With Pepsi' campaign to Taiwan. The literal interpretation of the slogan as used there was 'Pepsi brings your ancestors back from the grave'.*

Technological factors

Consumer needs and wants are bound up with technological infrastructure. The kind of fuel used for cooking, for example, will affect the type of oven, the choice of pan and utensil, even the sort of food cooked and the frequency of meals. The kind of transport used for getting to work will affect choice of garments and accessories. Instead of being the isolated events on which individual companies concentrate their marketing, consumers' choices are part of a whole pattern of consumption.

So the level of technology in a country will dictate appropriate product and service responses to consumer needs. Other aspects of marketing activity will also need to reflect this. Telephone-based market research, for example, is not much use in countries where levels of telephone ownership are low. The availability and scope of advertising media will affect the planning and execution of promotional strategies. Distribution channels are extremely sensitive to technology. It may well be that a company has to rethink its entire approach to distribution in a new geographic market because the systems on which it relies in its original market are not available.

Technology is a central factor in business-to-business marketing as well as consumer marketing. Different telecommunications standards have presented substantial difficulties to marketers even within the same continent. There has been a move to harmonise this and other aspects of business technology, but progress in such attempts is only as fast as the slowest member of the group. Initiatives from the European Union have helped speed up and co-ordinate technological harmonisation, which is a potential source of significant competitive advantage for European companies trading elsewhere in the world.

Economic factors

The potential of a market is governed by the number of likely customers it contains, and their ability (and willingness) to spend. Measures such as per capita income are often available, but can conceal enormous disparities between rich and poor in some countries. Evenly distributed income makes for better marketing prospects in a number of middle-income purchases such as consumer durables. Other yardsticks for purchasing power across the population include ownership rates of durables such as motor cars, the balance between urban and rural population, and the prevailing rate of inflation. It can be useful to look at Gross National Product (GNP). This figure is particularly relevant to the potential for industrial marketing. As ever with statistics from a number of sources, there can be problems with continuity of information and difficulties in comparing like with like.

Market size can also be assessed from the existing levels of activity in the sector in question. Are there domestic producers to provide competition, and how many other firms are already exporting? A very low level of activity might suggest that the opportunity is not yet ripe. Local firms may provide competition disproportionate to the quality of their offerings because of their control of existing distribution channels.

Fluctuations in currency exchange rates can wreck the soundest international marketing strategies, but they also provide attractive short-term opportunities in markets such as tourism. Visitor traffic to Europe from North America depends not only on the cultural and recreational delights awaiting tourists, but crucially on the standing of the dollar among international currencies. In 1985 a dollar bought ten French francs, making Paris a very attractive destination. Three years later American tourists were a much rarer sight on the Champs Elysees, as their currency now bought only five francs.

On a corporate level such fluctuations can mean the difference between profit and loss. Deciding when to buy and sell in the various markets in which a multinational company is involved is a high-risk, 24-hour responsibility. The international financial environment, accelerated by the spread of near-instantaneous computer-based information systems, has never been more volatile. This is one of the key differences between international marketing and domestic activity, but as well as increasing the risks involved it can offer significant windfall profit opportunities.

Politico-legal factors

Success in international marketing contributes to the balance of trade in the domestic economy by helping a country to sell abroad more than it buys in from other countries. When this balance is positive the domestic environment for business growth is much enhanced. As a result, governments tend to intervene in international marketing by assisting their countries' industries to make sales abroad, and by placing obstacles of various kinds in the way of prospective importers.

Governments are also under pressure to assist in alleviating unemployment and stimulating economic activity. Many countries actively court foreign investment, providing tax concessions and support of various kinds to persuade international companies to site their manufacturing units in depressed areas. This is true not only for production industries but also for service economies. Eire has had considerable success in establishing itself as a location for making films, aided in no small measure by favourable exchange rates between the dollar and the euro. Nevertheless, an enlightened policy offering generous tax incentives as well as a pro-active attitude to attracting film-makers, has helped Eire make the best of its largely non-industrial economic heritage.

On the other hand, political conditions can cause severe difficulties for international marketers, even to the point of having to withdraw completely from a market (as did Coca-Cola from India) or write off an entire operation (as did Chrysler in post-revolutionary Iran). The reaction to potential instability is to reduce the commitment of the company's relationship to the country. It may mean, for example, withdrawing direct manufacturing facilities in favour of a safer, but less profitable, exporting strategy. Some industries, such as mineral exploitation, do not have this option by their very nature. The host government's ultimate sanction here is expropriation – the confiscation of the assets of the industry involved (with or without compensation).

Less severe measures invoked by governments in order to protect their domestic industries include the following:

▶ Quotas to limit the numbers of goods allowed in.
▶ Duties, like a special tax on imports (which then makes them non-competitive on price).
▶ Non-tariff barriers such as product legislation which means that expensive adaptations need to be made before the item is legally saleable in the host country.

CASE STUDY **13.1**
....

Cuban crisis?

Fidel Castro led a rebel army to victory in Cuba in 1959, and during the subsequent decades it exported communist revolution, with Soviet Russian support, to nearby countries in Latin America and Africa. In 1990 the island was plunged into a severe economic recession, with the withdrawal of Soviet subsidies worth between $4 billion and $6 billion a year. The situation has not been helped by the fact that, since 1961, the US has operated a trade embargo against its nearest communist neighbour – only 150 km off Florida's Key West. But there are signs that the relationship is losing its frostiness. Since 2000, American companies have been allowed to sell food to Cuba – but only for cash. In 2002 they shipped food worth approximately $165 million, promoting the US to Cuba's tenth-biggest trading partner if unofficial estimates are to be believed. The need to import food is symptomatic of Cuba's peculiar economy, which is characterised by relatively efficient exporting industries (such as its famous cigars) and disastrously inefficient domestic sectors. The island's population is an estimated 11.2 million, with a labour force of 4.3 million. They are employed as follows: agriculture 24 per cent, industry 25 per cent and services 51 per cent. The respective contributions of these three sectors to Gross Domestic Product (the value of goods and services produced by a national economy) is 7.6 per cent, 34.5 per cent and 57.9 per cent respectively, illustrating the relative inefficiency of Cuban agriculture.

Tourism has also been an important source of trade from America. The Clinton administration eased the ban on travel to Cuba, allowing visits by professionals and Cuban-Americans. There are now 26 flights per week between the US and Cuba, and in 2001 there were 200,000 American visitors. The majority were officially sanctioned Cuban-Americans, but there were at least 50,000 Americans who arrived unofficially, travelling via a third country to escape red tape.

As well as income from American visitors, and the money that Cuban-Americans send home to their families, there is a growing tide of American investment in Cuba. This is indirect, insofar as it is from multinationals from Europe or Canada who are setting up operations in Cuba, but American institutions are prominent among the shareholders of such organisations.

America's ambivalent attitude to Cuba is causing some resentment among its more traditional trading partners. For example, it is still true that any foreign ship which docks at a Cuban port is banned from entering an American port for six months, even though American ships sail to Cuba at least once a week.

Questions

1 The case study illustrates an extreme version of the influence of the political environment on international marketing. What links can you suggest between the political situation in Cuba and socio-cultural, technological and economic factors influencing conditions for marketing there?

2 How sustainable is the idea of a trade embargo in the world of international business?

3 What are the advantages and disadvantages of international tourism as an industry for a relatively less developed country like Cuba?

Sources: CIA (2002); Economist (2003).

International marketing research

As we have seen in Chapter 5, marketing research reduces risk and aids effective decisions. For the international marketer, the research task of listening to the customer in a planned and systematic way is made more difficult by the unfamiliarity of the environment in which the research is conducted.

Secondary, or desk research, uses published sources of information such as censuses, directories or reports. International organisations such as the Organisation for Economic Co-operation and Development (OECD), International Monetary Fund (IMF) or European Union (EU) can provide useful statistics at a general level. However, in individual markets systematic research towards this kind of material may be in its infancy, preventing the detection of meaningful trends. In countries with a history of political instability, there may be large gaps of information. Problems of comparability of data between countries also dog the secondary research effort. How to define a particular sector and what to recognise as significant information are decisions that need to be taken carefully and applied consistently.

Primary research, where a company unearths information for the first time, is also vulnerable to special difficulties in the international context. Research methods that might be taken for granted in Western countries may prove culturally inappropriate in others. Survey methods that assume literacy and education levels, access to telephones, or even willingness to respond to questions, frequently need to be reassessed in the light of international conditions. Like advertising agencies, who are realigning themselves as transnational groupings in order to parallel their clients' promotional needs, market research agencies are facing the challenge of international market research by establishing international networks. Such research agencies can offer their clients local knowledge without losing a global perspective.

Other sources of market intelligence include national trade associations and chambers of commerce (or their equivalents). However unscientific it might appear, there is no substitute for personal visits to the targeted country to get a feeling for the customer and competitor environment. International trade shows and exhibitions are particularly useful in this respect, and are one of the most widely used techniques of information gathering for international marketing. One of the key characteristics of marketing across national boundaries is the length of distribution channels. Intermediaries such as agents and foreign distributors can provide very valuable information. While what they offer in the way of research is anecdotal, their appreciation through experience of what is important and relevant should never be underestimated.

KEY SKILLS
ACTIVITY **13.1**
. . . .

**Improving own
learning and
performance**

EU information

Information retrieval and handling is a vital skill for both study and professional life. Different sources require different approaches to get the best from them. Libraries and specialist collections in libraries are particularly useful to the researcher who knows his or her way round. This exercise invites you to visit and get acquainted with an information resource essential to anyone trying to explore international marketing in Europe.

The European Union has established over 300 European Documentation Centres (EDCs) around the UK. These centres are regularly updated with documents originating from the European Commission and European Parliament. Most of them have a direct bearing on conditions for international marketers in the single market. Find out the location of your nearest EDC (it may even be in your university library) and visit it to familiarise yourself with its resources.

Market selection
· ·

The process of selecting and targeting markets in international business is broadly the same as that described in Chapter 6. The criteria that govern what is a viable market segment discussed there are common to international market segments, but are particularly important when it comes to the areas of accessibility and size.

Accessibility means that customers can be reached with promotion and distribution. Market segmentation frequently identifies consumers with similar needs and aspirations across a number of national boundaries. A woman business executive living in Paris will have more in common with a working woman living in Turin than with a housewife in rural France. But reaching urban women with a promotional campaign that runs in precisely the same kind of media throughout Europe may be impossible because of differences in coverage between countries. Either the campaign execution or the limits of the segment will have to be adjusted in order to make the segment as a whole accessible.

Size means that the number of customers is of an order that can be dealt with by the organisation. International market segments are often attractive to firms because of the sheer number of consumers involved. This can tempt firms to enter markets on which they have no hope of making an impact, leading to their subsequent withdrawal. A common reaction to this problem for firms anxious to expand into new markets is to form alliances, either with other firms in the domestic market or with similar enterprises abroad. While seeming to turn the idea of competition on its head, this form of co-operation means that new market segments become feasible without affecting existing relationships.

Segmentation, and the targeting that follows, take place against a constantly shifting background of market dynamics. Certain areas in the world grow in attractiveness to certain marketers while others decline. Kenichi Ohmae (1985, 1992) was one of the first marketing writers to point to the domination of world markets by what he called the Triad – the three major world players of Europe, America and Japan. But the situation is capable of turbulent change. The rapidly-developing countries of the Pacific Rim (in particular Singapore, South Korea, Hong Kong and Taiwan) are going through a period of unparalleled economic growth. While income is still unevenly distributed throughout their populations, their increasing prosperity has created a market of consumers hungry for Western luxury brands to reflect their rising status.

> **DID YOU KNOW?**
>
> *DeBeers, which controls 80 per cent of the £32.5 billion world market in gem diamonds, markets them in different countries according to different cultural norms. In the UK a diamond ring is synonymous with getting engaged, in Spain it is bought after the birth of a child, and in Saudi Arabia diamonds are an important wedding gift – almost like a bridal nest-egg. Moreover, Saudi brides not only receive rings – necklaces, earrings and tiaras are usually included in the set (IPA, 1997).*

As a result, names like Burberrys and Ralph Lauren feature prominently in Singapore shopping arcades, and jobs in the aerospace industry are being lost by America to Taiwan. As industrial sectors have grown in these countries, agriculture has decreased in importance. This alters the mix of goods and services required in the business market, creating opportunities in information technology and construction among other areas. Finally, the governments enriched by their nations' developing prosperity are providing

Western armaments suppliers (many of them from the former Soviet Union) with rich pickings from swelling defence budgets.

As well as spotting the areas of growing demand for a particular product or service, the process of market selection needs to take into account the kind of trading environment that prevails in the segment under consideration. While liberalisation of trade, deregulation and privatisation have been worldwide trends since the 1980s, there has been a compensating response from regional trading blocks organising themselves against the depredations of economic invasion. Much of the impetus behind the establishment of the European Union, for example, has been from fear that otherwise the member countries will see their domestic industries shrivel as American or Japanese multinationals run riot. A frequent response to the establishment and growth of trading blocs is the phenomenon of insiderisation (Preston, 1993). This is when companies seeking a presence in a protected market will aim at a co-operative strategy involving joint ventures with domestic firms, or the foundation of a subsidiary company providing jobs and tax revenues within the host economy. The UK car industry provides several examples of this pattern.

Finally, competition is an important consideration when deciding on which segments to target. Growing sectors attract entrants which can quickly crowd out competitors who have insufficiently well-defined offerings. Market selection therefore requires careful consideration of the unique advantages of the company's offering to its prospective customers.

KEY SKILLS
ACTIVITY **13.2**
. . . .

**Application of
number**

Assessing markets

Statistics in international marketing need careful handling. As well as increasing your confidence about using numbers to back up an argument about how attractive a particular market is, this exercise suggests that numbers need to be set in context before they become meaningful.

Here are some statistics on four South American countries. Consider them carefully, and choose which one of the four would be the best market into which to launch a consumer durable product (such as a washing machine).

	Brazil	Colombia	Mexico	Peru
Population (millions) 2002	176	41	103	28
GDP (US $ billions) 2001 est.	1340	255	920	132
GDP per capita (US $) 2000 est.	7400	6300	9000	4800
Unemployment % in 2001 est.	6.4	17	3	9

Source: CIA (2002).

Gross Domestic Product (GDP) is the value of goods and services produced by a country's economy. It gives some indication of the level of prosperity of a country, but GDP per capita is a useful way of putting it into perspective. Remember, too, that the political situations in some of these countries can be volatile, so it is worth tempering your calculations with recent information about political developments.

Market entry decisions
••••••••••••••••••••••••••••••

Market entry is perhaps a misleading term for the way in which firms interface with their international customers. It gives the impression that such decisions are taken deliberately by companies free to choose between a number of alternatives. In fact, many companies fall into international marketing almost by accident. They find they have already made their entry into a market by the time they come to consider the best way of relating to it. Usually the nature of their relationship with their international customers will evolve with their business. It may be that, as with distribution patterns (see Chapter 10), a firm will use more than one method of accessing international business.

The various ways we shall review here range from low-risk, low-commitment indirect entry methods to high-risk, high-commitment direct entry methods, as illustrated in Figure 13.2. While some firms may move from one end of the spectrum to another as the importance of their international business develops, this is not always the case. Jumps can be made from exporting to direct manufacturing for political reasons before they make sense commercially. Nissan's establishment of a UK manufacturing base in the 1980s came at a time when the company's share of the British car market was still relatively weak. The long-term justification for the move was the advent of import restrictions connected with the coming European single market. Conversely, companies can move back along the spectrum from high commitment to low commitment for pragmatic reasons – such as a reaction to changing political circumstances which might increase the risk of their foreign investment. Finally, some of the most successful international marketing operations are franchise-based. In other words, the level of commitment of the parent firm is focused exclusively on a low-risk strategy as part of the business system it runs at home and abroad. There is thus no room for evolution to a more committed posture.

As with all strategic choices, the higher the risk the higher the likely rate of return. The option chosen depends on the firm's willingness and ability to commit its resources, managerial, financial and operational. Naturally the firm's

figure 13.2
Market entry methods

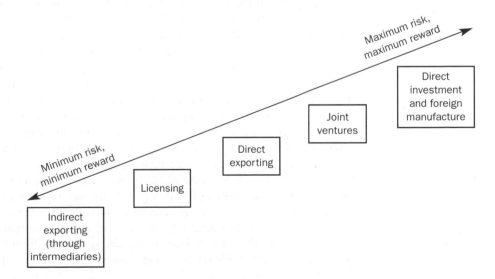

ambitions and size will influence how it orients itself to its target markets. Many of the kind of disciplines on distribution strategy we have observed in Chapter 10 also come into play for international market entry decisions. The kind of product or service involved, whether the firm is operating in the consumer or industrial sector, and the level and nature of competition, will all be contributory factors in choosing the best method of market entry. In most cases the most lucrative but economically binding method is to manufacture the product direct in the market concerned. This operational decision is one of the hallmarks of the truly international firm, carrying with it the advantages of proximity to customers and a range of stakeholders which includes host-country employees. Most companies' experience of international marketing, however, starts with indirect exporting.

DID YOU KNOW?

Mineral exploration needs to take place in some pretty dangerous places. In Algeria, where terrorists trade atrocities with pro-government militias, oil firms typically spend 8–9 per cent of their budgets on security. In Colombia, another international hot-spot for trouble, the average is between 4 and 6 per cent (Economist, 2000b).

Indirect exporting

Exporting, whether indirectly (involving the services of other companies to sell the product in the foreign market) or directly (where the firm deals direct with its overseas customers), assumes that production takes place in the home market. Products end up in export markets through a number of routes.

The least active, on the part of the manufacturing firm, is when a buying organisation from another country sources its product for sale in the foreign market. Domestic purchasing of this sort is becoming increasingly frequent as companies try to benefit from the price differences present in various markets. Import record shops are a good example of this kind of activity happening on a small scale. The dedicated fan is prepared to pay a premium for a recording available in the US which the record label has decided not to release in Europe.

A more active posture towards the issue of exporting is to use the services of an export management company. Sometimes this is an independent organisation which will handle export arrangements for a number of clients, like a functional distribution intermediary. Like advertising agencies, the management company will have several accounts competing for its attention, and the range of services and expertise offered will vary from one company to another. The kind of things likely to be offered will be purchasing, shipping, financing and negotiation of foreign orders. The establishment of the single European market has led to a rise in the number of small- to medium-sized enterprises (SMEs) from Britain seeking access to mainland Europe. For them, export management companies can act as fixers, setting up contacts and accelerating their acquisition of foreign market knowledge. Alternatively, a company can set up its own subsidiary export management company, as in the case of Unilever Bestfoods UK which has a division called Unilever Bestfoods UK Export. This enables a diverse range of the company's brands to access the expertise of a central export service, creating economies of scale similar to the ones provided to their clients by independent export management companies. The division manages a portfolio of well-known brands such as Hellmann's, Flora, PG Tips and Pot Noodle, by building up strong relationships with third-party distributors.

As we have seen, international marketing sometimes involves unexpected alliances rather than competition between firms. Piggybacking is an example of how different companies can share resources in order to access foreign markets more effectively. What happens is that a firm with a compatible product (known as the rider) pays to get on board the distribution system already operated by a firm active in the foreign market (known as the carrier). As a result, the rider gets access to an instant network of outlets, and the carrier can add more value to its activities by offering its intermediaries a greater product range.

DID YOU KNOW?

Two-thirds of Britons speak no foreign language at all compared to the EU average of 47 per cent. Luxembourgers are the best linguists of all, with nearly 98 per cent of the population confidently multilingual (Economist, 2001a).

Licensing

Licensing is the offer of a brand name, process or trade secret in return for a royalty or fee. It is a frequent method of entry in the drinks market. Budweiser, for example, is made in the UK under licence from the US brewing giant Anheuser-Busch. Interestingly, the beer has a premium positioning in the UK as a lager for trend-conscious yuppies. In America, on the other hand, it is very much a working man's beverage. While licensing offers many advantages as a low-risk and cheap method of accessing income from foreign markets, it offers little control and can create problems in the longer term. The licensee, having developed expertise with the product, can sometimes start manufacturing an alternative, offering dangerous competition. Licensors (the granters of licences) therefore have to keep devising innovations that increase their licensees' dependence on them in the relationship.

DID YOU KNOW?

Vending machines, a mainstay of Coca-Cola's distribution elsewhere in the world, are practically impossible to place legally in Russia. A mass of bylaws covering standards for food and drink retailing, real estate and taxation (which require all sales to be conducted with a cash register) means that vending machines only appear with the assistance of 'security firms'. Incidentally, Coca-Cola, which has sunk tens of millions of dollars into Russia since the collapse of communism, has yet to show a significant profit there (Economist, 2000c).

Direct exporting

Direct exporting involves the manufacturing firm itself in the task of distributing its products in the foreign market. In this respect it is treating its foreign customers as it would its domestic ones: choosing agents and distributors, and directly supporting their efforts. Expensive and time-consuming as this is, it offers greater control and profits than relying on intermediaries. There are the additional advantages of more immediate market intelligence and an enhanced experience curve. As a strategy it suits business-to-business marketing very well in the area of capital equipment such as printing presses or packaging machinery where there is a high degree of specialisation and a limited number of customers and suppliers.

Joint venturing

Joint ventures offer another example of co-operative rather than competitive operations in international marketing. A foreign company and a domestic company join forces, either by buying into each other or establishing a third jointly-owned enterprise. Complementary strengths facilitate success together which would elude each company on its own. Sometimes a joint venture is the only way a foreign firm can gain a toehold in the market. The number of joint ventures in the automotive sector has increased with liberalisation of trade in the former Eastern bloc, as European and US car manufacturers struggle to decrease costs and grow market share at the expense of their Japanese competitors. But even these voluntary arrangements are subject to difficulties that reveal themselves in the longer term. If the foreign partner wants to standardise aspects of its offering in line with global policy, the domestic partner may object. As a result, joint ventures tend to have limited lifespans. They work best in sectors where there is a high degree of local adaptation rather than in industries with a monolithic approach to their markets.

Foreign manufacture

In many situations some form of manufacturing in the host country may be the only way of accessing a new market. Although many companies may therefore be forced into this posture, it has many advantages over the alternatives. There is a clear sense of commitment to the local market, and the speedy availability of parts and spares provides a crucial source of competitive advantage against other suppliers. Finally, being on the scene directly allows a company to detect changes and developments in the external environment quickly enough to be able to plan round them effectively.

The extent of the host country's participation in the process of foreign manufacture can vary from superficial assembly to research and development-led innovation. At the superficial end, products can arrive in bits (completely knocked down, or CKD) and be reassembled in what are known as screwdriver plants, a name that denotes the level of manufacturing skills required. The idea here is to avoid import controls aimed at finished products. As a manufacturing policy, foreign assembly is usually merely a tactical response to protectionist measures.

At the other end of the scale is the kind of direct manufacturing investment that distinguishes the truly committed transnational company. While this kind of strategy is very popular with host country governments keen to grow their economic manufacturing base, it can also be perceived as economic colonialism. Care needs to be taken that the firm is contributing to its host economy as well as benefiting from the relationship.

CASE STUDY **13.2**

The World Wide Web?

Enthusiasts for the Internet as a marketing tool emphasise its international potential to put businesses in touch with customers the world over. But as far as language is concerned, the message seems to be that you can access websites in any language, so long as it's English. Although 85 per cent of all web pages are in English, only 45 per cent of users are native speakers of the language, and the proportion is dropping as Internet usership continues to internationalise beyond its home ground of North America.

As marketing on the Internet becomes more competitive, the imperative to address potential and actual customers in their own language becomes more pressing.

The results of launching local-language websites can be dramatic. Otis Elevator, the US-based lift company, saw sales shoot up 130 per cent after it introduced multilingual websites. But, of course, such flexibility comes at a cost. First of all there is the cost of translation itself, followed by the administrative nightmare of updating multiple versions of a website (co-ordinating content and branding accurately between them), together with the challenge of developing and running systems sufficiently robust to withstand international e-commerce.

However, the difficulties of building and maintaining multilingual websites are alleviated to some extent by the use of content management software. Essentially this gives site designers at company headquarters a series of templates which can be used to control the overall appearance of sites in several different languages. With the templates in place, web designers can publish information using simple web page forms. Transmission of new content to translators can be automated as part of the system, which speeds up the process of updating once local managers have approved the new translations.

Nintendo's promotional sites for the Gameboy Advance's launch in America were prepared by Blast Radius, a web design agency based in Vancouver, British Colombia. Using a content management system on the original development added an estimated 10 per cent to the initial design costs. This investment paid off, however, when Nintendo came to launch the Gameboy Advance in Europe since it was able to roll out translated versions of the existing site. This saved weeks of development time in a market where speed is of the essence.

Questions

1   Apart from translation, what other aspects of a website might need tailoring to specific local needs?
2   The case study provides a good example of the advantages and disadvantages of adaptation. What effects would you expect adaptation to have on the structure of an organisation?
3   The proportion of Internet users for whom English is a native language is predicted to decline to less than 30 per cent in the next few years. What are the consequences for international marketing on the Web?

Source: Tweney (2001).

The international marketing mix
·····································

Marketing, as we have seen in Chapter 1, is a business philosophy that puts customers at the centre of an organisation's thinking. This philosophy does not change, whether the marketing is carried out in one country or several. However, the task aspects of marketing – the management functions involved – do need to be tailored to the international environment. Reviewing the four elements of the marketing mix from an international standpoint highlights the major differences involved.

Product

Product is the fundamental component of any marketing mix. Promotion, price and distribution all take their cue from the basic offering to the consumer.

There are good business reasons for trying to make a standard product acceptable to as large a number of customers as possible. Thinking back to the material on market segmentation in Chapter 6, we can reflect that a segment's size is one of the key criteria in deciding its attractiveness. International segments are certainly sizeable, but are rarely as homogeneous as marketers might wish. There has to be a trade-off between the ideal economies of the one-product-suits-all approach of the truly global marketer, and the adaptation to individual tastes that complicates the production operations of most international suppliers.

DID YOU KNOW?
Although UK Smarties eaters will only find eight standard colours in their tubes, the sweets are produced in a total of 15 colours because of the complex product standards and dietary laws in the various markets in which they are sold throughout the world.

Standard or differentiated?

Some products are more amenable to a standardised global approach than others. Typically, areas like sporting goods, office and industrial equipment, toys and computer games are standardised. Food, on the other hand, is highly culturally conditioned. There are exceptions to this general principle, however. Chewing gum and soft drinks seem to have little trouble crossing borders, but office equipment manufacturer Xerox encountered early resistance to its copiers in the UK when it was found that the machines were too large to get through British office doorways (narrower by several inches than their American counterparts). Even companies like McDonald's, which are famous for their global marketing, make considerable adjustments to reflect tastes in local markets (although the basic format remains unchanged). The truly global brand may be condemned to be an eternal gleam in a marketing manager's eye rather than a reality on the supermarket shelf. Consumers are, after all, a highly unpredictable bunch. Their needs are in a state of continuous evolution – a fact that drives the product life-cycle (see Chapter 7). It could be argued that by the time a company has standardised its products to a global level, its consumers will have moved on.

DID YOU KNOW?
Attitudes to toilet paper set UK consumers apart from their continental neighbours, and make the UK one of the most lucrative markets for the product anywhere in the world, with a choice of over 50 pack sizes, colours and brands from which to choose. The secret is that Britons insist that their loo rolls match their bathroom decor, whereas the continentals are content to put up with white or, at a pinch, pink. One of the satisfying results for the paper industries is that the British pay twice as much as the French and Germans, and two-and-a-half times as much as the Americans, for one of life's little luxuries (Economist, 2000a).

Product life-cycle and new product development

Products and services, like their users, have life-cycles. As we have seen, profit levels vary at each stage of the cycle. Keeping a positive cash flow in the long term requires a company to make sure that its portfolio of products is in the right combination.

Moving into a new market with an established product can give it a new lease of life, but in the competitive international environment, companies need to extend their products swiftly if they are not to be forestalled in foreign markets by competitors.

CASE STUDY **13.3**   **Long distance**
India has a number of spectacular qualities as a country – art, architecture and landscape to name but three. But what really excites the telemarketing industry is

that it boasts world-class information technology, a highly-educated workforce who speak English, and wages that are 80 per cent lower than Europe's. As a result, it is gathering momentum as a world force in 'remote customer support' – the industry term for the fact that when you call a customer helpline, you are as likely to speak to an operator thousands of miles away as you are to one in your own country. UK calls can be routed direct to the subcontinent at no extra charge to the caller and with no discernible loss in sound quality thanks to advanced telecommunications technology.

In the UK personnel costs account for between 60 per cent and 65 per cent of a call centre's budget, with staff earning an average of £13,000 a year. In India, by contrast, labour accounts for between 20 per cent and 25 per cent of overheads, with starting salaries of as little as £1,300. While this might sound outrageously exploitative, it compares extremely well with Indian earnings in general, where the average annual per capita income is £316. Only 3.5 per cent of the population earn more than £1,600 per year. Furthermore, working in a call centre in India, while no less pressured than the equivalent job in Europe, is not seen as such a dead end. UK call centres turnover something like 60 per cent of their staff each year, many of whom are deliberately temporary workers such as students earning money to see themselves through college. In India the workers are likely to be graduates, keen to get a start in the booming telecommunications and customer service industry.

Their training involves not only how to deal with customers, but also an intensive course in Britishness. Most will never have visited the UK, so it is important to get them familiar with the environment from which their customers will be calling – from what's on television to what the weather is like. Their grasp of vernacular English is tested by the simple expedient of having them ring Bed and Breakfasts in Wales, Northumberland, Yorkshire and Scotland, asking for directions. They are also exposed to videos of *Rab C. Nesbitt, EastEnders* and *Brookside* to give them a grasp of regional dialects, and some call centres even have tabloids flown in so that the workers can keep up with the latest gossip on UK news and celebrities. Sometimes the operators themselves are encouraged to abandon their Indian names in favour of English versions to make it easier for them to identify themselves to their customers, and one call centre in Delhi supplies staff with name plates for their desks, in case they have difficulty remembering their aliases under pressure.

India's burgeoning IT and software industries mean that the newly-equipped centres have impressive reserves of expertise on which to draw, and practically all of the services offered are web-enabled. India's electricity industry is not renowned for its reliability, so disaster-recovery systems also come as standard, and several of the new centres have developed their own power-generation facilities.

Two early examples of Western companies which have outsourced to India are British Airways and GE Capital (which run store cards for UK retailers such as Top Shop and Debenhams). British Airways has had an office in Mumbai (Bombay) since the early 1990s, but now uses its Indian operation to handle key aspects of the airline's customer support, including services to its Asian Executive Club members. GE Capital now directs something like 2.5 million calls from the UK to its Delhi centre each year, and claims to have saved £108 million in its first three years of operations as a result.

Questions
1   What steps might you take, as a UK call centre operation, to safeguard your future against Indian competition?

2 Apart from 'managed customer contact' (telemarketing jargon for call centre business) what other services could be outsourced like this? What might the consequences be?

3 Discuss the ethics of training Indian call centre workers to appear more 'British'.

Sources: Curtis (2001); Economist (2001b).

New product development keeps a company in touch with the evolving needs of its customers. Certain international markets, known as lead markets, contain a higher than average number of consumers who respond well to innovation (see Chapter 4 on buyer behaviour). A presence in these markets is essential for the producer who wants to keep abreast of ideas and emerging technology in its product field. If you are a consumer electronics company, for example, you have to be active in the chaotically innovative Japanese market in order to be able to plan effectively for the slower markets of the West.

CASE STUDY **13.4**

Bottoms up from down under

The French are extremely good at making wine. The Australians are also extremely good at making wine (although they haven't been doing it for as long), but they have the additional virtue of being good at marketing. As a result, the Australian wine industry is posing a serious challenge to France for domination of the UK wine market. Given the centuries of tradition which have linked British drinkers to French vineyards, this might once have seemed unthinkable, but UK consumption of Australian wines gurgled up from 85,000 litres in 1990 to a millennium torrent of over 1.2 million litres. The trick which the Australians have managed to pull out of the bottle, so to speak, is the simple art of branding. The French, with their fastidious allegiance to unique vineyards and growths, have never descended to such a vulgar expedient. For them, each wine is essentially different from the next. The Australians, on the other hand, realise that if you are buying wine in a supermarket or an off licence, you can do without all the confusion and uncertainty of loads of different names and regions. So for some time they have been pushing brands like Jacob's Creek, Pinfold's, Rosemount or Hardy's. Each stands for a range of varieties from a particular region, but buyers immediately recognise what they are getting at the £5 or £10 price mark, and are confident of the quality and taste they can look forward to. In fact, it is an excellent example of why branding is a good idea for both customers and suppliers. The customer has a guarantee of performance, and the supplier has something to develop and promote in the customer's mind. French wines still dominate the eating-out market – a lucrative and prestigious niche from which it will be hard to unseat them. But Australian wines are romping to victory in the supermarket. That's probably the better place to be in the long run, as 84 per cent of all wine bought in the UK is consumed at home.

The other advantage being pressed home by the Australians is pronounceability. One of the problems with French wine for the less confident buff is the danger of getting the name wrong in front of a sniffy wine merchant or waiter. Furthermore, French wine labels are indecipherable to the average Briton. The Australians obligingly provide labels with helpful and interesting information in English.

The lessons have not been lost on the French, however. Traditionally they have concentrated on near and domestic markets, but have woken up to the fact that, in spite of concerns about whether wine 'travels' or not, the twenty-first-century wine trade is an international affair. So French makers are putting more emphasis on exporting, as well as using segmentation to target the luxury end of niche markets. They are even recruiting some of the more adventurous 'New World' wine makers to help them do it.

Questions

1 Wine consumption is increasing in the UK. What factors are responsible for this trend?

2 Branding seems to be working for Australian wines. What are the disadvantages (if any) of this approach in a market like wine?

3 Briefly comment on how wine growers can use market segmentation to boost sales and profits.

Source: Blackwell and Marsh (2001).

Branding

An important contribution in adding value to a product is made by branding. As discussed in Chapter 7, a brand is the identity of the product – its distinctive personality. While the basis for the brand identity must lie in the product's quality and performance, it can be extended into a communication separate from the product itself. Kotler and Armstrong (1994) make a useful distinction between the utterable brand (a name like Persil or Guinness) and the unutterable brand (a symbol, logo, colour scheme, or even the typeface in which a brand name usually appears). International branding works best on the unutterable level – although even here elements like colour can have an unexpected cultural significance. White, for example, denotes mourning in some Eastern societies; green is popular in Muslim countries, although its use for packaging materials is considered bad form in Egypt where it is the national colour; red and black are avoided in some other African countries. A number of popular international logos use a combination of yellow and red, including McDonald's and Shell. In fact, Shell revamped its logo in the late 1980s in order to eliminate the word 'shell', and now relies exclusively on the stylised shell symbol in its distinctive colours. This avoids the problems of pronunciation and translation that accompany international attempts at utterable branding.

The attraction of reputable brands to international consumers is such that a thriving trade in counterfeit goods has developed, and continues to develop, especially in product fields like fashion goods, publishing, computer software and cosmetics. It could be argued that the very existence of pirated goods indicates a

DID YOU KNOW?

What's in a name? The annals of international marketing are full of unfortunate examples of brand names that don't travel. Here are a few classics:

➤ *Vauxhall's Nova didn't go down too well in Spain, where the name literally means 'doesn't go'.*

➤ *Amorous types asking for Durex in Australia might find themselves in a sticky situation, as there it is a brand name for a kind of adhesive tape.*

➤ *Thirsty Japanese consumers can refresh themselves with a soft drink called 'Pocari Sweat', while their neighbours in Germany can purchase toilet paper called 'Bum'. Neither brand seems set for success in the UK.*

marketing failure on the part of the genuine manufacturers. After all, if their own marketing mix is on target there should be no room for imitations.

Country as brand

Country of Origin (COO) influences the perceived quality of a product. But such perceptions are often subjective. One of the difficulties of working with other people is the assumptions we make about how they see the world. This exercise explores country of origin perceptions as well as offering potential insights into why other people see things as they do.

First, choose a product type (such as cars, consumer electronics or sporting apparel). Working in pairs, write down your product type/quality expectations (three adjectives at most) with the following countries of origin. Do this exercise individually at first and then compare your list with that of your partner. What, if any, differences are there, and what does this reveal? Do your expectations change, for example, with product type? Are any of them based on actual experience as a customer?

▶ Ireland.
▶ New Zealand.
▶ Japan.
▶ Germany.
▶ UK.
▶ Korea.
▶ China.
▶ Finland.
▶ Italy.
▶ America.

Pricing

As we have seen in Chapter 9, pricing decisions are governed by competition, production costs and company objectives. International pricing decisions need also to take into account exchange rates, the difficulties of invoicing and collecting payment across borders, and company policy towards its activities in each market. Designing methods of invoicing and payment that are proof against all the vagaries of international trade has proved impossible, in spite of progress towards the standardisation of documentation. It is prudent to allow for a level of unrecoverable debt when setting price levels.

Tariffs and purchase taxes may have the effect of making imported goods expensive compared with host-country alternatives. The international marketer either absorbs the difference (sacrificing profit to remain competitive), or sacrifices volume in the hope of obtaining a premium positioning. In the long term the only way to get round the problem, however, is to lobby the host-country government and perhaps move to a different form of relationship with the market. Some multinational companies which have subsidiaries in other countries use a technique known as transfer pricing to minimise the effect of tariff barriers when possible. Tariffs are usually levied at a percentage of the price of a product. Transfer pricing involves selling-on goods to subsidiaries within another country at a price deliberately set as low as possible to attract the minimum taxation. The resale price to the end-user can then be set at a more realistic level.

Another way of avoiding taxation, and hedging against the deleterious effects of currency fluctuations, is to abandon money altogether and trade direct in goods and services. This form of international barter is known as counter-trade. According to the OECD, this form of trade accounts for 5 per cent of world trade as a whole, and up to 35 per cent of trade involving lesser developed countries and Eastern Europe where hard currency is in short supply (Bennett, 1995).

Companies active in a number of markets are at liberty to charge different prices for the same product in different markets (perhaps subsidising one with profits from another). The most extreme example of this practice is called dumping – when goods are off-loaded at uncommercial rates just to get rid of them. Charging a substantially lower price in a nearby country can cause the embarrassing phenomenon known as parallel importing. This is when an entrepreneur from the higher-price market imports large quantities of the goods from the low-price country and sells them cheaper than the official import. In the UK this has happened in markets as diverse as pharmaceuticals and soft drinks.

A final aspect of pricing in international marketing is the question of exactly what is included in the price paid by a distribution intermediary taking title to goods. Freight and insurance costs need to be paid, and all parties to the agreement need to be clear on whose responsibility this is. This need has spawned a technical vocabulary of pricing terminology known as incoterms (defined and updated by the International Chamber of Commerce). Here are some of the most common incoterms explained:

▶ *FOB (Free On Board)*: The price includes loading on to a ship at a specified port in the exporter's country, but after that the cost of freight is the buyer's responsibility.
▶ *CIF (Cost, Insurance and Freight)*: The exporter is responsible for the cost of freight and insurance for the goods to a named destination in the importing country.
▶ *CPT (Carriage Paid Too)*: This is similar to CIF above, but the buyer has responsibility for insuring against loss or damage to goods.

DID YOU KNOW?

Britons go on an estimated 3 million 'booze cruises' a year to nearby Calais to avoid UK prices for alcohol, tobacco and cigarettes. EU regulations allow them to bring back substantial quantities for personal use only. However, organised smuggling of booze and tobacco is also big business for criminal gangs. The result is that, of every five packets of cigarettes smoked in the UK each day, one is estimated to be illegal (Morris, 2002).

Promotion

This is one of the most interesting and challenging areas of international marketing, and is particularly sensitive to socio-cultural, technological and political factors. The international marketer's 'Holy Grail' of a global approach to the brand is nowhere more visibly evident than in international advertising. Unfortunately great advertising ideas do not always cross national boundaries.

The international Bond market

The James Bond film franchise, which celebrated its fortieth birthday with the launch of *Die Another Day* (officially the twentieth cinematic outing for 007), has grossed more than $3 billion worldwide since *Dr No* hit the screens in 1962. This makes it the most successful series of films ever made, reaching millions of people worldwide through cinema release and in-home media. It is not only an amazing international marketing success story in its own right, but has been latched onto by a horde of companies keen to share the glamour of the world's favourite secret agent by making sure their products and services are featured prominently in the films.

Die Another Day's Los Angeles and London premières followed years of hard-nosed negotiations between the film's producers and scores of international brands desperate to carve out their piece of the action. While figures on how much money actually changed hands are not available, the strategic placement of products in the film, as well as subsequent promotional spin-offs, is rumoured to have gone a long way towards subsidising its $100 million production budget.

Of course, many of the deals will not have involved the exchange of money at all – a good example of the tax-efficient practice of 'counter-trade'. For example, British Airways made one of their Boeing 747s available for filming on the understanding that in the film's final version, their luxurious first-class cabin accommodation would feature prominently. BA won the privilege to offer early screenings of the film as an in-flight movie, as well as to run a rather unlikely-sounding promotion urging prospective passengers to 'Save your Moneypennys, fly like Bond'.

A range of other brands litter the film – Kodak, Omega watches, Samsonite luggage are all visible. There is also some evidence that Bond's tastes in vodka and motor cars are changing. Out goes Smirnoff, to be replaced by Finlandia Vodka. And, after a brief flirtation with BMW in his last few films, Bond is now back at the wheels of an authentic Aston Martin sports car (following intensive negotiations with Ford, new owners of the luxury car brand). In fact Ford also threw in a selection of Jaguars and Ford Thunderbirds to make sure their products were sufficiently represented in the movie.

Sony scooped exclusive rights to all the audio-visual equipment which appears in the film. In exchange for supplying the goods on a barter basis, they secured valuable licensing rights to using James Bond branding in retail promotions. And, as far as personal care is concerned, super smoothie Bond is pictured grooming himself exclusively with Philips shavers. The relevant scenes had to be shot twice for different versions of the film on release, as the shaver in question is branded as a Norelco rather than a Philips in America.

Questions

1   Compare and contrast international sporting events and blockbuster films as promotional opportunities for international marketers.

2   What are the advantages, and disadvantages, of using product placement as an international promotional tool? Some of these are illustrated in the case study, but you may be able to come up with more from your own analysis.

3   The list of names associated with *Die Another Day* suggests that luxury brands are a key sector for international marketers. Explain why this might be the case.

Source: Burt (2002).

Technological factors affect the choice of promotional media in foreign markets. Many domestic brand managers anticipate that replicating their domestic promotional plans in foreign markets will be sufficient. However, there is little point in extending a successful print campaign to a country where print technology or magazine coverage is not competent to carry it off. As media empires grow through diversification and vertical integration this is becoming less of a problem, but it still presents difficulties to advertisers wanting to stage something as simple as a poster campaign using the same copy in a number of European countries. Panel sizes in the UK (where posters account for about 5 per cent of media expenditure) and France (where they account for 12 per cent) are different.

Exhibitions are a very important promotional medium for the international marketer, especially in the business-to-business field. It may be that a firm makes no use of this medium at all in its domestic business, so getting expert advice on the choice and use of trade shows is important. Such gatherings provide very useful first-hand contact with potential customers, and competitors, even if orders do not emerge immediately.

Regulation on what is and is not permissible in advertising varies greatly from country to country, although harmonisation in this field is another aspiration of the European Union. It is hard enough to find a formula that is culturally acceptable across national boundaries. Legal restrictions on direct marketing (involving as it does the computer storage of personal information) and sales promotion (free offers are banned in certain countries) make truly standardised promotional approaches very difficult across an international campaign. While the economic advantages of size and synergy are highly desirable, even global advertisers such as Benetton and Marlboro need to balance homogeneity of strategy and flexibility of execution in local markets.

DID YOU KNOW?

In spite of the rise of home cinema and the proliferation of television channels, worldwide cinema attendance is increasing. There are, however, important cultural differences in how we go to the movies. The French eat hardly any popcorn compared to the British, and Mexicans prefer it sprinkled with lime juice. Swedes don't go to the cinema much, preferring outdoor and sporting activities. In Spain, where lots of young people live at home with their parents, the cinema is a top spot for dating. Great fun, but does anyone remember the film? (Wright, 2002, personal communication).

Distribution

Making a product or service accessible to the maximum number of customers at the minimum cost is a challenge to the international marketer. The temptation is to concentrate on those aspects of the chain nearest to the manufacturer, rather than see the process from the customer's point of view. This is neglecting to give logistics (working back from the customer) as much importance as physical distribution (working from the manufacturer to the customer).

Distribution channels between nations are chosen with a number of considerations in mind: the value and type of product, the cost and speed of alternative methods of transport, the ease with which a channel can be managed. Once inside the country itself, however, the channel is more difficult to influence. The company needs to adapt its practices to local opportunities. In the West retailing patterns have emerged that assume that shoppers have access to cars and do their main shopping at intervals of a week or so. Elsewhere in the world shopping is a more frequent activity, and the amounts bought are smaller. These differences work their way back through the entire system. Countries like India have elaborate distribution systems, with goods passing through a lengthy chain of wholesalers before reaching the final customer. The distribution systems of Japan are so complex as to represent a challenge to foreign goods marketers every bit as difficult as an import tariff.

Using local agents and brokers who are familiar with the opportunities offered by such complex systems is the key to managing this difficult area. A large part of export management time is taken up by their careful recruitment, support and review.

International marketing planning

International marketing planning is the systematic and continuous attempt to match a company's capabilities to the opportunities presented by its international environment. It involves establishing the aims of the organisation, the analysis of its present position and the establishment of a programme of action to carry out the aims. Companies active in the international sphere need to be clear on what they are doing and why, so planning is particularly important for them. Their planning procedures will follow the basic template outlined in Chapter 14. However, the extended nature of their organisations makes the implementation of agreed plans difficult. Head office can have a very different perspective on the direction of the business from a local company, for example.

Many successful multinationals have developed a planning culture that allows strategy to be developed centrally, but implementation through short- and medium-term plans to be taken care of locally and regionally. Even with this kind of approach, however, international marketing planning is still rife with difficulties. Here are some of the main problems:

▶ Sketchy market intelligence limits the quality of the information on which planning is based.
▶ There is a scarcity of experience and theory available to international marketers.
▶ Many of the models available to planners have been developed from experience with FMCG markets in a domestic, usually North American, context. Too literal an application of them may have a distorting effect.

International business theory

International business has attracted some influential thinkers. One of the most far-reaching theorists has been Michael Porter of the Harvard Business School, whose work on international competition has helped set the planning agenda for contemporary marketing. He argues that companies operating in the international environment can gain competitive advantage from concentrating on what he calls the value chain (Porter, 1990). This is the sequence of operations in production and marketing through which products and services pass. Performing these stages better than competitors can give a company the edge.

A key factor here is the geographical location of each stage of the chain – playing to a country's particular strengths.

David Ricardo

Porter's thinking is reminiscent of the ideas of the very first theorist of international trade, the classical Scots economist David Ricardo (1772–1825). Ricardo developed a theory of what he called comparative advantage in which he argued the benefits of trade between nations on the grounds of efficiency. It is easy, he argued, to make good wine in Portugal because of the natural resources of that country. So rather than struggling to make indifferent wine in England, it makes better sense to import. In return, the importing country can offer what it has comparative advantage in – eliminating inefficiency and making greater wealth available to all.

Attractive though Ricardo's ideas are, they do not take into account the conditions of market turbulence in which international companies operate. As we have seen, rapid change is a characteristic of many international economies. This means that sources of comparative advantage may change. Taiwan was a low-wage economy making cheap shoes in the 1980s. It is now established as a world player in aerospace and technology, threatening jobs in traditionally high-skilled economies elsewhere in the world.

Life-cycle

Another influential theory of international trade that acknowledges the idea of change is the idea of the trade life-cycle. First advanced in the 1960s by the American theorists Vernon and Wells (1986), this traces a process that starts when a country targets a foreign market for its exports. The establishment of a new market for the product spurs production by native producers. The final stage is when the original exporters face competition themselves from imports. The Japanese car industry is often pointed to as a prime example of this. Japan, originally a market for American cars, is now a major player in the American car market itself. In broad terms the theory is a credible one. But as life-cycles of products become ever shorter, its reliability as an aid to planning is questionable.

Business gurus like Eisenhardt and Brown (1998) maintain that the only response to the chaotic international environment is to abandon strict planning in favour of a flexible approach. But even such a pragmatic prescription acknowledges that some kinds of objective are necessary. Planning pays, even if plans have to be changed. The process itself keeps the organisation focused on its purpose. This is no mean feat in the shifting international environment as business attitudes move from the ethnocentric (seeing a firm's operations as extended from its domestic base) to the geocentric (accepting the world itself as the primary market).

Key concepts
••••••••••••••••••

Comparative advantage: theory propounded by David Ricardo (1772–1825) maintaining the utilitarian benefits of international trade.
Culture: learned behaviour specific to a group of people.

Exporting: manufacturing goods in one country, but selling them to customers overseas.

Expropriation: confiscation of a firm's assets by a host government.

Gross National Product (GNP): the total domestic and foreign added value claimed by residents.

Host country: a country where international marketing operations take place.

Incoterms: standard terminology for international marketing agreed by the International Chamber of Commerce.

International marketing: marketing activity that crosses national borders.

Licensing: a low-risk form of market entry whereby the owner of a product or idea allows another company to use it in a foreign market in exchange for a royalty.

Non-tariff barrier: obstacle to international marketers from a non-fiscal source (e.g. product safety legislation).

Pacific Rim: the collection of newly-industrialised countries around the Pacific.

Quota: a non-tariff barrier that limits imports to an agreed percentage of the market.

Tariff barrier: a financial tax on imported goods.

Value chain: the processes whereby raw materials are converted into a finished product offering to the consumer. Its effectiveness can be enhanced by an international context.

SELF-CHECK QUESTIONS

1 Which of the following features of a company does not constitute proof of its involvement in international marketing?
   a Using foreign components in manufacturing.
   b A wide distribution of sales volume throughout several different countries.
   c Product planning, research and manufacturing in a number of countries.
   d Exporting activity on a small scale.
   e Foreign distribution intermediaries.

2 Which one of the following aspects of marketing management presents international and domestic marketer with the same level of complexity?
   a Environmental analysis.
   b Planning and control.
   c Product quality.
   d Manufacturing decisions.
   e Invoicing and payment.

3 Which of the following consumer characteristics is least affected by cultural factors?
   a Language.
   b Education.
   c Values.
   d Spending power.
   e Hair type.

4 Rank the following market entry methods in order of their potential risk:
   a Direct exporting.
   b Foreign manufacturing.

c Licensing.
d Joint venturing.
e Foreign assembly.

5 OECD stands for:
a Organisation of Economic Co-ordination and Development.
b Overseas Export Coalition Directorate.
c Open Export Channels Directive.
d Organisation for Economic Co-operation and Development.
e Overseas Economic Criteria Development.

Which of the following are true and which are false?

6 Joint ventures are an effective form of long-term market presence.
7 Sporting goods, office equipment and computer games offer manufacturers opportunities to standardise their products.
8 Lead markets contain a higher than normal number of innovation-prone customers.
9 Unutterable branding is preferred by global marketers.
10 The theory of international trade life-cycle holds that the final stage of the cycle comes when exporters are faced with competition in the host country from domestic manufacturers.

Discuss the following

11 What advice would you offer a small- to medium-sized business aiming to enter a new international market?
12 Promotional management is one of the most difficult areas of international marketing. Why is this, and what precautions can companies take to avoid pitfalls in this area?
13 Discuss the problems presented by international market research. Are they different in kind from those presented by domestic research?
14 With international marketing assuming an ever greater importance, what qualities will marketing managers require in the twenty-first century that their predecessors lacked?
15 What ethical problems are raised by companies from the developed world expanding into developing markets?

Further study

Albaum, G., Strandskov, J. and Duerr, E. (1998) *International Marketing and Export Management*, 3rd edn, Addison Wesley.
Extremely clear and well-planned study. Concentrates on export which is a highly relevant area for most firms involved in international marketing.

Doole, I. and Lowe, R. (2001) *International Marketing Strategy*, 3rd edn, International Thomson Business Press.
Straightforward and well written.

Terpstra, V. and Sarathy, R. (2000) *International Marketing*, 8th edn, Dryden Press.
A popular textbook which handles the subject in a well-structured format with interesting examples. In spite of the fact that this is a 'European edition' it is still predominantly American in tone.

Usenier, J.C. (2000) *Marketing Across Cultures*, 3rd edn, FT Prentice-Hall.

Levitt, T. (1960) 'Marketing myopia', *Harvard Business Review*, 38, 4, July/August, pp.45–56.
Much reprinted and referred to, this article got the ball rolling on 'global marketing' but is valuable for its visionary insights into marketing on a more general level as well.

International Journal of Advertising and *European Journal of Marketing*.
These are UK-based and carry accessible research and articles in their respective areas.

References

Bennett, R. (1995) *International Marketing: Strategy, Planning, Market Entry and Implementation*, Kogan Page.

Blackwell, D. and Marsh, V. (2001) 'Australian wines set to leapfrog the French', *Financial Times* (Weekend), 3–4 March, p.16.

Burt, T. (2002) 'He's Bond, James Bond, the man who's licensed to sell', *Financial Times*, 5 October, p.22.

CIA (2002) *The World Factbook 2002* available at http://www.cia.gov/cia/publications/factbook/

Curtis, J. (2001) 'The UK cashes in on Indian support', *Marketing*, 28 June, pp.39–40.

Economist (2000a) 'Going soft?', *The Economist*, 3 April, p.59.

Economist (2000b) 'Risky returns', *The Economist*, 20 May, pp.127–30.

Economist (2000c) 'A coke and a frown', *The Economist*, 7 October, p.115.

Economist (2001a) 'English is still on the march', *The Economist*, 24 February, p.50.

Economist (2001b) 'The Asians are coming, again', *The Economist*, 28 April, p.32.

Economist (2003) 'The Americans have come', *The Economist*, 3 January, p.45.

Eisenhardt, K.M. and Brown, S.L. (1998) *Competing on the Edge: Strategy as Structured Chaos*, Harvard Business School Press.

IPA (1997) 'International', *It Pays To Advertise* (video), Institute of Practitioners in Advertising.

Kotler, P. and Armstrong, G. (1994) *Principles of Marketing*, 6th edn, Prentice Hall.

Morris, S. (2002) 'Customs lose battle over booze cruisers', *The Guardian*, 1 August, p.10.

Mughan, T. (1993) 'Culture as an asset in international business', in J. Preston (ed.), *International Business: Text and Cases*, Pitman, pp.78–86.

Ohmae, K. (1985) *Triad Power*, Macmillan.

Ohmae, K. (1992) *The Borderless World: Power and Strategy in the Interlinked Economy*, Fontana.

Porter, M.E. (1990) *The Competitive Advantage of Nations*, Free Press.

Preston, J. (ed.) (1993) *International Business: Text and Cases*, Pitman.

Smith, D. (1998) 'European youth', *Marketing*, 22 January, pp.29–33.

Tweney, D. (2001) 'Think globally, act locally', *Asiaweek*, 16 November, p.10.

Uhlig, R. (1997) 'Russian agency's giant leap for the hard sell', *The Daily Telegraph*, 26th August, p.3, Connected@telegraph.co.uk.

Vernon, R. and Wells, L.T. (1986) *Manager in the International Economy*, 5th edn, Prentice-Hall.

CHAPTER 14

Strategic marketing management – planning, organisation and control

Objectives

When you have read this chapter you will be able to:

➤ List the major generic strategies available to marketers in a range of competitive situations.

➤ Justify marketing planning as a business discipline and use a selection of analytical frameworks.

➤ Prepare and present an outline marketing plan, with provision for evaluation and control.

➤ Identify a range of common marketing organisational structures.

➤ Determine and apply measures of marketing effectiveness.

Foundation focus: the 20-second takeaway

In spite of its 'back room' image of graphs and number-crunching, planning has a lot in common with marketing. They are both ways in which organisations try to match what they are good at with what customers want. Giving customers a reason to choose you rather than your competition is known as differential advantage. Planning your marketing thoroughly, and revising your plans in the light of what you learn from them, guarantees that you will keep pace with customers as their needs and wants change and develop. Marketers use frameworks to analyse opportunities and help them establish achievable objectives. They can call on a number of forecasting techniques (both quantitative, based on numbers, and qualitative, based on ideas) to assess future customer needs. They can choose from a range of classic marketing strategies based on market share, product/market relationships and competitive positioning. Checking progress and making adjustments are essential to implementing plans successfully. Planning helps marketers shape their organisations in ways which allow them to implement strategy more effectively. Planning and marketing go together because they both keep an organisation focused on its customers.

Introduction

Strategy is the overall vision of how an organisation's purposes are to be fulfilled. The term has its roots in a Greek word meaning the activity of generals. The traditional outcome of such activity was stratagems – ploys and ruses to win a battle, and eventually the war. Marketing strategy sounds a more civilised process, but the outcome is the same. In the commercial battlefield you may be fighting competitors, indifference or inertia, but a sound strategy is the key to long-term victory.

It is important to be clear about the distinction between strategy and tactics. The original meaning of tactics (another Greek word) was the arrangements made for individual battle. In marketing this means the day-to-day implementation of plans to achieve long-term aims. It's helpful to think of strategy as being a principle (the way we do things) and tactics being the practices based on that principle (what we do).

In the real world of business we can talk about two ways in which strategy comes about. The first is called deliberate strategy, the conscious pursuit of objectives through deliberate plans and their execution. The second is called emergent strategy, when a company falls less consciously into a way of doing things. Emergent strategy can, of course, be recognised and consolidated into deliberate strategy by evaluation and control. (See Figure 14.1.)

Furthermore, there are levels of strategy at work in an organisation. The governing principle of operation is the corporate strategy. It is long-term, and is concerned with the overall direction of the organisation. Corporate strategy is expressed in terms of the organisation's mission (we will look at the subject of the mission statement later in this chapter). In an organisation that places the customer at its centre, the corporate strategy will be imbued with the marketing philosophy. Within this overall framework, and supporting it, is the functional marketing strategy (along with the other sets of functional strategies, financial, production and human resources). Marketing strategy will be more specific and practical than corporate strategy, although customer orientation will link them.

Later in this section we will review a number of common strategies that can be identified in the way companies achieve their aims. Formulating strategy requires the kind of helicopter vision that is one of the characteristics of good marketing. Rather than seeing the organisation from the internal perspective of day-to-day operations, the strategist steps back and tries to see things from outside, just as the marketer tries to see things from the customer's point of view.

Searching for differential advantage

The key to success in a competitive environment is to maintain an advantage over rival firms that gives customers a reason to choose you. There are as many

figure 14.1
Levels of strategy

possible sources of this kind of advantage as there are dimensions of a business that are relevant to the customer. This creates considerable scope for discovering and developing them. The advantage may be lodged in the organisation's own capabilities, in the product or service, or in the nature of the relationship with the customer. Here are some examples of differential advantage in each of these three categories, which have already been mentioned in this book:

▶ *Organisational capacity*: Spanish clothing retailer Zara's in-house production capacity gives it an edge in restocking swift-selling lines, so that customers can get the clothes they want, when they want them.
▶ *Product or service:* First Direct's telephone banking lines are staffed by human beings rather than machines 24-hours a day, so account holders receive personal service whenever they call.
▶ *Nature of the relationship with the customer:* Amazon.com can target existing customers with offers it knows will be of interest because of purchase behaviour already logged.

The concept of differential advantage is similar to the classic idea of the Unique Selling Proposition described in Chapter 11 as the basis of effective promotional communication. Marketing strategy aims to uncover and enhance differential advantage to the long-term benefit of the organisation.

Strategic options

The search to establish differential advantage can take a number of directions. Businesses can take some guidance in this area from the findings of the long-standing American project known as PIMS (Profit Impact of Marketing Strategy). Originated in the 1960s by the American company General Electric, the project was brought under the wing of the Harvard Business School in the 1970s. Participating firms submit regular confidential information on the market conditions under which they have been operating, together with their performance in competitive and absolute terms. Most of the firms involved are large manufacturers (services are under-represented in the sample) but a significant proportion are active internationally. The project aims to discover which strategies are most profitable in which situations. Although its findings are not above reproach because of the causal links they assume, the following broad patterns have emerged (Buzzell and Gale, 1987):

▶ The single most important contribution to long-term competitive success comes from the quality of the product or service on offer.
▶ High market share means high profitability. Economies of scale, return on investment and the efficiency of marketing expenditure all increase with the size of market share.

These findings confirm the received wisdom of marketing that success breeds success. Traditional marketing strategy has always put a great deal of emphasis on building market share, in the belief that establishing a brand's position in the purchasing habits of a large volume of consumers must be good for its long-term profitability. The pricing strategy of penetration pricing discussed in Chapter 9 values market share above immediate revenue in support of this principle.

Market share-related strategy

Kotler and Armstrong (1998) sum up the kinds of strategy available to a firm as a function of its share of the market. They split the options four ways to suit the four kinds of competitive position that a firm can occupy: market leader, market challenger, market follower and niche player.

DID YOU KNOW?

Avis has made a virtue out of a necessity with its challenger strategy in the car hire business. It's 'We Try Harder' slogan, introduced as early as 1962, summed up the company's espoused philosophy of taking nothing for granted because it was not the market leader.

Market leaders

Market leaders are, as we have seen, likely to be the most profitable and therefore most powerful competitors. But they also have the most to lose. Their available strategies either defend what share they already have – this is made easier by the economies of scale that they enjoy – or they aim to expand their business, either by increasing share or by increasing the overall size of the market itself.

CASE STUDY **14.1**
··················

Reinventing the pub

Founded in 1979, the JD Wetherspoons pub chain is now one of the UK's fastest-growing businesses. The secret of its success lies in a very clear strategy of differentiation – using service and the marketing mix to set it apart from its competition. Like many good business ideas, it is not devastatingly complicated – just a case of serving good beer and good food at reasonable prices, served by friendly and well-trained staff who feel they have a stake in the success of the company.

Wetherspoons often opens outlets in renovated premises (one even used to be a funeral parlour!), so it has a positive effect on its local streetscape. The company claims that this encourages other businesses to smarten up, and also attracts new people into an area with positive economic results.

An important feature of its pubs is that they are music-free, catering for the art of conversation. Food is an important part of the offering, and is available up to an hour before closing time, in marked contrast to the limited availability of food in most other pubs. The success of this part of the business is reflected in the fact that food accounts for a quarter of all sales – even breakfast (up to midday) is available in most pubs. A relatively recent innovation is an initiative to welcome families with children as diners between 10am and 6pm in some outlets, although the bar areas themselves remain child-free zones.

At least one-quarter of each pub is designated non-smoking, with state-of-the-art ventilation systems meaning that nobody leaves the premises smelling like a kipper. Another point of pride with the chain is the design and upkeep of the toilets in its pubs, which have won several awards.

Any service marketer knows that people are an essential part of the offering. Wetherspoons' marketing approach recognises this, placing considerable emphasis on staff motivation. Unlike many pub operations, its working conditions stress work/life balance, with employees having two days off in seven to spend with family and friends. Pay is higher than the industry average, there are pub-by-pub incentive schemes, training linked to national vocational qualifications, and a share option scheme whereby staff can buy shares at a fixed price and participate directly in the success of the company as shareholders. All the chain's workers are encouraged to be innovative and responsible, and their ideas on how to improve the business are actively sought. As well as full-time employees, Wetherspoons have an army of 'associates', hourly-paid workers. They, too, are canvassed for ideas, as they are often much closer to the action than their managers can ever hope to be. The company reports that over half of its current management were formerly associates.

Questions

1 How does JD Wetherspoons' marketing mix create differential advantage?
2 Explain how JD Wetherspoons' human resource strategy supports its marketing strategy.
3 Name at least three examples of market segmentation in this case and explain how the company manages to keep each segment satisfied in spite of conflicting needs.

Source: JD Wetherspoons Company Information (2003).

Market challengers

Market challengers are the number two brands in each market. Often they will direct their competitive activity at smaller companies rather than at the dominant player, quietly growing share as a result. Confronting the market leader is unlikely to be successful. A flanking strategy often has better results. This borrows military terminology to describe an attack on the side of the army rather than head-on. It assumes that the market leader will be so preoccupied with its main business that it may leave parts of the market undefended. Australian wines are overtaking French wines in UK supermarkets because of the lack of attention given to this form of distribution by the less marketing-savvy French growers. On the other hand, French wines still outsell Australian ones in restaurants – a more traditional channel where retail marketing skills are less important.

> **DID YOU KNOW?**
> *Boston Consulting Group research suggests that competitor brand shares show a remarkable similarity in markets dominated by a few brands. Where three brands occupy 70 per cent of a market (often the case in a mature industry) the top brand usually has twice the share of the next largest, and four times the share of the third largest.*

Market followers

This group of companies are nowhere near the market leaders, but have found themselves a comfortable position and are therefore not keen to rock the boat. By careful market segmentation and an intelligent use of distinctive competences, such companies can maintain impressive profits. In spite of the price wars raging among their national counterparts, local newspapers in the UK provide an example of a market that is controlled by no more than half a dozen major companies. Instead of fighting each other, they actively manage their business so that the existing shares of the market are maintained whenever publications change hands.

Niche players

By selecting a precisely defined market segment that is too small to be of interest to a major competitor such companies can establish very lucrative businesses if they are content with low volume. Their success suggests that the correlation between size of market share and profitability works best at either end of the scale, leaving the middle ground to less profitable businesses. However, niche marketing, like market following, may not be a sustainable option. As soon as the major players notice the profits to be made there is a strong possibility that they will move in with their superior fire power. The growth of boutique biotechnology companies, developing innovative processes and products in the late 1990s, established a niche in the technology industry that led the major pharmaceuticals to either buy up the independents or launch their own.

Product/market strategies

Another way of looking at strategic options is to move away from market share and look at how an organisation relates to its customers and its offerings. Igor Ansoff (1987), who pioneered the treatment of strategic management as an academic discipline in the 1950s, identified four strategic options based on the firm's orientation to its markets and its offerings. (See Figure 14.2).

The first strategy, increasing sales of an existing product in an existing market, is known as penetration. As we have seen earlier, this can be a credible choice for market leaders keen to expand their business without excessive risk to existing share. Market penetration, as it is known, can be illustrated by brand leader Kellogg's Corn Flakes. Its promotional campaigns to persuade lapsed users to come back into the fold, 'Have you forgotten how good they taste?', represent an attempt to increase usage by the existing market.

The next strategy is more risky, taking an existing product and putting it into a new market. Mars pioneered the fun-size sector in the grocery trade by repackaging its existing product in a new format that would appeal to the family shopper. The needs of such a shopper differed markedly from those of the core Mars buyer, purchasing confectionery for themselves. Fun-size appealed to those buying for others, perhaps as a children's treat or something to put into lunch boxes. The market sector expanded rapidly to the point where practically all of the major confectionery brands have a fun-size incarnation available in supermarkets. This strategy is known as market development, and carries a medium level of risk.

figure 14.2
Ansoff's growth vector matrix

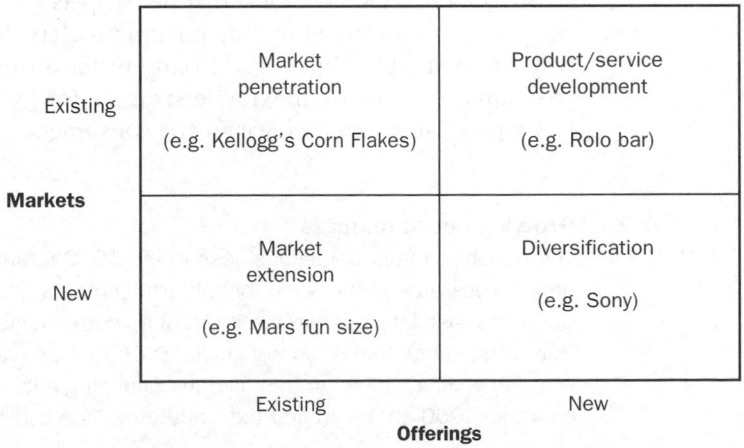

	Existing	New
Existing (Markets)	Market penetration (e.g. Kellogg's Corn Flakes)	Product/service development (e.g. Rolo bar)
New	Market extension (e.g. Mars fun size)	Diversification (e.g. Sony)

Offerings

The third option is product development. This is more risky than market development because the absolute costs of entry are usually higher. A product or service new to the organisation is offered to an existing market. Bic, which sells disposable pens, lighters and razors with great success, tried to introduce a line of disposable perfumes in the late 1980s. The introduction was a marketing disaster. The kind of exclusivity and personal imagery that people associate with perfume was missing from this kind of presentation. Customers who were happy with disposables in their other purchases could not accept the format for perfume.

Ansoff's final option is the most risky of all, although it offers compensatingly high rewards for those prepared to wager the high stakes involved. This is when an organisation diversifies, bringing new products and services to new markets. The double unfamiliarity here can provide the recipe for expensive failure. But an organisation with a sufficiently clear strategy can make a success of the process. The UK retailing industry provides some good examples of diversification. Sainsbury's and Tesco have both made successful entries into the financial services industry, using their power as brands and their pervasive distribution to challenge traditional providers. In one sense this development has taken them a considerable distance from their core business of grocery retailing, but it can also be seen as a natural development of their customer franchise.

In Chapter 10 we looked at the patterns of potential conflict in distribution channels, identifying their directions as horizontal (between parallel channels) and vertical (along the same channel). We can use the same terminology to describe the direction of diversification in related industries (or integration as it is known). Vertical integration is when an organisation like a publishing company buys into the industry that feeds it (e.g. a paper mill) or into the industry it feeds (e.g. a bookselling chain). In the example here, the purchase of the paper mill would be called backward integration (moving back up the supply chain) and the purchase of the bookseller would be forward integration (moving down the chain, closer to the final customer).

Horizontal integration is when companies buy into organisations that parallel their own. Rupert Murdoch's acquisition of both *The Sun* and *The Times* as part of his News International group clearly brought him two very different products addressing different markets, but they are both at the same stage of the newspaper business horizontally. The media industry arouses political sensitivities because of the role that newspapers and broadcasting have in keeping the electorate informed in a democratic society. 'Cross-media' ownership has thus aroused wide objections. In any other industry such integration might pass unnoticed as the inevitable struggle for greater efficiencies, leading to lower prices and better service for the consumer.

CASE STUDY **14.2**

Growing out of jumpers

The Benetton family began business in the 1960s, founding the clothing company now famous around the world for colourful jumpers and controversial advertising. But in the last 10 years the profits from its core business have come under pressure from competition in the form of chains such as Gap and Zara, and from customers who are getting cannier in their clothes shopping habits. The chain, which once boasted 7,000 shops around the world, now lists 5,000 outlets. This is still a very substantial business, but the family's strategic direction has now turned towards diversification, building a portfolio of profitable interests outside the clothing trade.

To date these include highway services, telecoms, property and agriculture. Benetton part-owns Olivetti, which has a controlling stake in the Italian telephone company Telecom Italia. Its hotels include prestigious sites in Venice, and the exclusive Asolo Golf Club. The family also have large investments in Autogrill, a catering firm which runs self-service restaurants, Sagat, which manages Turin airport, and Grandi Stazioni, which runs services on railway concourses. While this might seem a pretty random assortment of businesses, the Group's directors claim that transport and service-related businesses offer unlimited potential for expansion.

Its most recent diversification is into highway operation with a £5 billion bid for Autostrade, an Italian company which is Europe's largest toll-road manager. It operates a network of more than 3,100 km (1,900 miles) of roads, generating tolls of over €2 billion per year. The business has plenty of growth potential, as Italy not only has relatively free-flowing motorways, but it also boasts the lowest toll charges in Europe. So far the family's investments in the business have proved twice as profitable as their clothing operation, so they are keen to consolidate through a controlling stake.

Questions

1   What are the dangers of diversification away from clothing retailing for Benetton and how might the company safeguard against them?
2   What retailing skills do you consider important to successful road-toll operation?
3   Benetton's investments outside its original business are all concentrated in Italy. What are the marketing advantages and disadvantages of this for the group?

Source: Davey (2003).

Competition-based marketing strategies

The dominant voice in strategic thinking for much recent marketing has been that of Michael Porter, a Harvard professor whose diagnosis of strategic options focuses on the idea of competition between firms in mature markets (the situation in which most marketing strategy now takes place). Rather than wavering indecisively in the market-place, Porter (1980) recommends that a firm deliberately takes up its stand on one of three strategic platforms:

▶   *Cost leadership*, where it concentrates on its ability to exercise economies of scale in a number of different market sectors by investing heavily in technology to enable it to beat its rivals on price.
▶   *Differentiation*, where it concentrates on product quality to justify a premium price (thus generating more profit).
▶   *Focus*, where it devotes its efforts to servicing a narrow range of customers or segments rather like a niche marketer (with the same risk that too much success in growing the market will inevitably attract larger competitors).

Any of these three generic strategies should create the kind of differential advantage that will give a customer a reason to go to that particular supplier rather than a rival. We can illustrate cost leadership as a strategy from the intensely competitive market of short-haul air travel.

CASE STUDY **14.3**

Low cost airlines soar away

Budget airlines are the success story of the early twenty-first-century travel market. All of them unashamedly base their business model on the success of South West Airlines, the 1971 brainchild of Herb Kelleher, a hard-drinking, chain-smoking lawyer. Kelleher famously appeared in a TV commercial for his airline wearing a paper bag on his head, in order to reassure passengers who might be embarrassed to be seen using a no-frills carrier. The ad promised that passengers would be issued the bag free by the airline. Whether they wanted to use it to preserve their anonymity was up to them, but Kelleher insisted it would still be handy for keeping all the money they would save by travelling with his company.

South West Airlines flies only one kind of aeroplane and won't use airports whose slots it considers too expensive, or who spend too long turning aircraft around between journeys. Unlike other major airlines, which use a hub-and-spoke system that forces passengers to make lengthy journeys in and out of a central point in order to get from one location to another, its routes connect a number of popular destinations in sequence 'point to point' (rather like a train). Hub-and-spoke systems are high-cost but can generate a lot of revenue because of the vast number of destinations that can be offered. South West is happy to concentrate on a limited range of destinations at a much lower cost.

Productivity is key to airline profitability, in order to make as much return from the high capital investment as possible. Swift turnaround of aircraft is essential. South West averages between 20 and 25 minutes for each 'turn time', which helps generate as many passengers as possible. On the other hand, it does make check-in a very inflexible process for the budget traveller, and limits the possibility of holding a flight should there be a delayed connection. This can be extremely frustrating.

The company's informal style and sense of humour is a hall mark of its approach. Passengers are often greeted by singing staff, pilots pitching in to help with suitcases and the occasional flight attendant emerging from the overhead luggage compartment. The company's HQ in Dallas Texas is itself a popular destination for management students keen to find out how the company culture works to create such a positive buzz. The airline has a proud record on employment, never having made a single redundancy in its history – no mean feat after the downturn in aviation after the tragic events of 11 September 2001.

While subsequent low-cost operators have not been able to emulate all of the aspects of the original, some common features have emerged. Limited destinations, an optimum size, simplicity of operations and an emphasis on short-haul business are all features of low-cost carrier strategy. Indeed, no one has yet found a way to crack the lucrative long-haul market with a low-cost operation. It may well be that the standard of service, entertainment and comfort necessary on long-haul flights would put low-cost airlines out of the running.

As well as this possible limit to the expansion of the business, a low-cost model is no guarantee of success. There have been plenty of failures from start-up low-cost challengers, whereas the inefficient big carriers remain in business. Such failures may be explained by a poor business model, which was initially lucky, or by poor management. There is something romantic about airlines, and as a result many entrepreneurs get involved in them for the wrong reasons and with limited success. Finally, while low-cost airlines face direct competition on many routes from trains and ferries, there is no serious alternative for the long-haul traveller, so companies operating in this area benefit from something of a monopoly.

Pricing strategy is essential to the success of the no-frills operator. It actually costs EasyJet something like £45 to fly a passenger, so the amazing discounts on offer must be funded by other passengers paying a range of higher prices. Ticket yield – the amount of money made by charging different prices through the plane – is the crucial calculation here. Operators use computers to help them maximise revenue per flight. Filling the cabin is not the issue – it's how to make the flights pay that is the real challenge.

Some passengers are extraordinarily price sensitive. For example, one low-cost carrier put up its base price from £29 to £39 from Birmingham to Malaga and saw demand drop by one-third the following day. Equally there are some passengers who are relatively price inelastic, for example needing to travel at short notice whatever the cost because an urgent family issue has cropped up.

Questions

1 Illustrate the concept of a cost-leadership strategy from evidence in the case study.
2 What might be the disadvantages of a low-cost strategy in airline marketing?
3 What evidence is there in the case study that the long-haul sector is safe from low-cost challengers? How sustainable do you consider this position to be? (You may find it helpful to use analogies from other industries here).

Source: Day (2002).

Marketing planning

Why plan?

For something that appeals to common sense, planning meets with more than its fair share of resistance. When confronted by the need to plan, people in organisations often claim to be too busy, or too cynical, or think it's not their job, or protest they don't have enough information. These are all understandable objections, but they do not absolve anyone of the responsibility of planning. As somebody once said, 'To fail to plan is to plan to fail.'

Put simply, planning is the process of trying to match an organisation's capabilities to the opportunities around it. Looked at in those terms, planning and marketing are very similar. Marketing attempts to satisfy external demand by understanding it, and making it the justification for an organisation's activity. This requires answers to a number of key questions.

What business are we in?

This is the basis of an organisation's mission statement, the cornerstone of corporate strategy (and therefore a key determinant of marketing strategy). It is a question that needs to be asked on a regular basis. Otherwise the organisation will sink naturally into a state of self-maintenance, oblivious of the changing external environment. The answer to the question defines the organisation's customer(s) and the nature of the relationship sought.

Multinational food company, Nestlé, defines its mission as follows: 'Nestlé is dedicated to providing the best foods to people throughout their day, throughout their lives, throughout the world. With our unique experience of anticipating consumers' needs and creating solutions, Nestlé contributes to your well-being and enhances your quality of life' (www.nestle.com 2003). This statement reflects several decisions about what business Nestlé is in. Its desire to position itself internationally as a part of people's daily nutritional routine at different stages in their lives reflects its extremely broad product portfolio – from infant formula to convalescent food for the elderly, taking in convenience foods, breakfast cereals, pasta, ice-cream and confectionery on the way. Also implicit in the mission statement is the wide geographical spread of the company's operations, adapting its brands to each market in which it operates. Nestlé's emphasis on customer-led research and development is clear from the second part of the mission statement. Having made decisions about what is important, and enshrined them in its mission statement, the organisation can then go about implementing them and communicating them without fear of confusion or contradiction. A mission statement gives everyone confidence that they are going in the right direction to fulfil the purpose of the organisation.

This is not to say that organisations may not change their purpose. In the 1980s Dr Barnardo's (as it was then known) had to face up to the fact that its traditional role of looking after parentless children was becoming outmoded. Its Victorian heritage of institutional care was no longer relevant. But another need had taken its place – helping disadvantaged young people through training and family support. Recognising the new need, it changed its name in 1988 to Barnardos, dropping the 'Dr' to distance itself from the image of Victorian institutions, and finally closed its last orphanage a year later. More recently still, Barnardos has taken up a much more energetic advocacy and campaigning role, winning the 2002 Institute of Practitioners in Advertising's Advertising Effectiveness Awards for its hard-hitting campaign against child prostitution and adopting the strap line 'Giving Children Back Their Futures' in its corporate identity.

So the first step in marketing planning must be to identify and articulate the mission of an organisation. Is it appropriate and realistic? Does everyone in the organisation subscribe to it (what is known as goal congruency), or are there differences that need to be resolved?

Where are we now?

Having decided on the mission, the next question determines what stage the organisation has reached. The answer to this question requires research and analysis. Where information is not available, informed estimates must be made.

One of the advantages of planning is that it forces us to make our assumptions explicit. There are four areas to look at: internal capabilities and external opportunities, competition and business analysis (taking a strategic view of customers and markets).

Internal capabilities and external opportunities

Planners have evolved structured ways of looking at the current situation of an organisation. One of the simplest and most effective of these is called SWOT (strengths, weaknesses, opportunities and threats) analysis. We looked at this form of analysis in Chapter 3 in connection with the marketing environment. Revisiting the concept allows us to hone its use in a way that maximises its relevance to planning.

Strengths and weaknesses tend to be internal, and to do with the past or the present. Opportunities and threats tend to be outside the organisation, and to do with the future. When naming strengths and weaknesses it is essential to assume the perspective of the customer. It may be that the organisation sees efficiency of manufacturing process as one of its strengths. Unless this efficiency is passed on to consumers as superior product quality or lower prices it is unlikely to be of any relevance. Researching customer needs is dealt with at length in Chapter 5 on marketing research. It is important to check the relevance of the organisation's offerings to its customers on a regular basis. Usage and attitude surveys, or brand standing research, can help elucidate the true strengths and weaknesses of an organisation.

Often it appears that the same aspect of an organisation may be both a strength and a weakness, depending on how you look at it. This is not a very helpful finding in practical planning and signals the need for further analysis. Breaking down the aspect into its component parts will usually reveal a more useful pattern in this case. It helps to be as specific as possible. Another aspect of effective SWOT analysis is to prioritise. Ranking entries under each heading into an order of importance throws up the key issues facing an organisation. This can then feed into the formation of appropriate objectives.

KEY SKILLS
ACTIVITY **14.1**
· · · · · · · · · · · · · · · ·

Working with others

SWOT team

Working with others, and particularly with customers, requires empathy. This exercise asks you to put yourself and your colleagues deliberately in the role of customers. Working in a small group helps you to do this, as it gives you experience of other people's perspectives. On the other hand, you need to beware of group think (especially if you are all members of the same organisation or learners in the same class). 'Group think' means that the group do not question their own judgements sufficiently. It leads to bad decisions as it puts distance between organisations and their customers.

The SWOT analysis is a useful and simple tool which can be used by individuals or groups to solve problems. One of the drawbacks of the technique, however, is the difficulty of assuming the perspective of a customer. Strengths and weaknesses are only relevant to marketing success if they are important to customers. So, for example, a university might see one of its strengths as an excellent research rating, but if this translates into students never being able to find members of staff (because they are always off somewhere doing research) it can come across as a fatal weakness to a key customer group.

Working with at least one other person, conduct an audit of one aspect of your organisation from the customer's point of view. It might be how the telephones are answered, what the catering is like, the IT facilities — any aspect will do. In order to do this, you need to compile a customer check-list on which you chart your impressions as you work through each stage of the experience. Part of the groupwork is to negotiate an agreed list of what you see as important dimensions of the experience involved.

From your results construct a list of strengths, weaknesses, opportunities and threats which might be useful in developing marketing objectives. Here is a suggested check-list for a visit to a staff restaurant:

	Poor			Excellent	
	1	2	3	4	5
Walk to restaurant					
Initial impression of décor and ambience					
Noise level					
Queuing system					
Length of time in queue					
Staff friendliness					
Staff knowledge and helpfulness					
Staff appearance					
etc...					

Opportunities and threats: STEP factor analysis

Looking at opportunities and threats brings us to another useful check-list for analysis of the environment outside the organisation. This is called STEP factor analysis. It is discussed at length in Chapter 3 describing the socio-cultural, technological, economic and political environments in which an organisation's activities take place. As with SWOT analysis, the framework has to be used intelligently to avoid confusion about what is relevant. Prioritising aspects of the external environment helps reveal the main opportunities and threats facing the organisation.

Competitive analysis

A more customised vision of an organisation's external environment can be gleaned from scrutinising the competition it faces. Here we are still looking outside the organisation, but at the more immediate environment in which it operates. Michael Porter, whose ideas on generic strategy we have briefly reviewed earlier in this chapter, has contributed a useful model for this purpose, known as the 5-forces model. (See Figure 14.3.)

Porter's approach concentrates not only on the immediate rivalry among existing firms in the market-place, but recognises four further competitive pressures. These are:

▶ The threat of new entrants to the market who may change the rules of competition.
▶ The power of suppliers.
▶ The power of buyers.
▶ The threat of substitutes.

figure 14.3
Porter's '5-forces' model

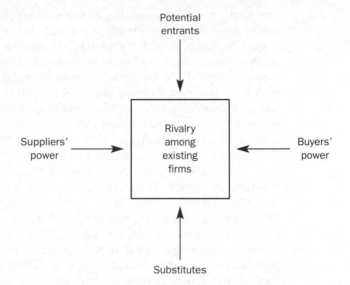

The model can be illustrated by looking at the UK retailing environment. Chapter 10 introduced the concept of multiple grocers – chains like Tesco and Sainsbury's which are locked in a fierce battle for share of the grocery market. This is the industry rivalry part of the model. The power of suppliers, the manufacturers of branded goods, appears to be on the wane. The power of buyers, consumers like ourselves, is also limited due to our lack of organisation (although groups of consumers can unite on issues such as boycotts). The threat of substitutes (other types of grocery shopping or even growing or hunting one's own food) has been minimised by the major multiples' careful market segmentation and positioning. They are aiming at the car-using customer, to whom time and convenience is as important as value for money.

There is, however, the threat of new entrants who may change the rules of engagement by introducing new formats for shopping. Warehouse clubs, such as the American chain CostCo, hard discounters from the continent such as Aldi and Netto, and even some of the existing grocers' Internet operations have all made successful entries to the retailing scene in the last decade and this has altered the balance of power.

Competitive analysis helps firms understand their position relative to customers and suppliers, encouraging them to apply the full range of marketing tools to develop sustainable advantage. Distribution, for example, becomes as important as promotion in this kind of competitive framework, even though traditional marketing thinking has tended to underrate its importance.

> **DID YOU KNOW?**
> *No matter how sophisticated your strategy, saying thank you helps. Australian marketing agency Proximity ran a 12-month test in the UK for a major credit card company. A pool of customers was split into two groups. One group received a thank you message from the firm for their custom, the other just got standard communications. At the end of the test period the thanked customers had spent between 10 per cent and 20 per cent more than the other group (McIntyre, 2002).*

Business analysis

As well as scrutinising its internal characteristics, and external settings (both wide-angle through STEP and narrow focus through competitive analysis), an organisation needs to examine its business activities itself. Portfolio models are useful here. We have already discussed the role of the Boston Consulting Group's portfolio model in Chapter 7, in relation to a firm's management of its product range. The model can also be applied to other aspects of its operations – groups of products, factories, divisions, international markets. All of these can be termed strategic business units (SBUs) and be subjected to classification as stars, cash cows, problem children and dogs. Recognising their position relative to one another in terms of their contribution to cash flow (or its equivalent in a non-profit organisation) can help decide appropriate strategies to maximise their value to the organisation as a whole.

Another useful matrix is the General Electric Business Planning Grid, from the same remarkable company that brought us management by objectives and the PIMS database. (See Figure 14.4.) This aims to refine the rather crude information inputs of the Boston Consulting Group (the brute measures of rate of market growth and relative market share). In their place it puts composite measures requiring a degree of judgement on the part of the planner. One axis plots market attractiveness and the other plots competitive business strength. Part of the challenge of using this matrix sensibly is to identify what, in a firm's sphere of operations, constitutes market attractiveness. Common features are size, rate of growth, number of competitors, susceptibility to change or regulation, and so on. Some of these will be more important than others, depending on the markets concerned. Similarly, the attributes required for competitive business strength will vary from industry to industry. What the model lacks in simplicity is made up for in the way it forces planners to quantify and test their assumptions.

figure 14.4
GE Business Planning Grid

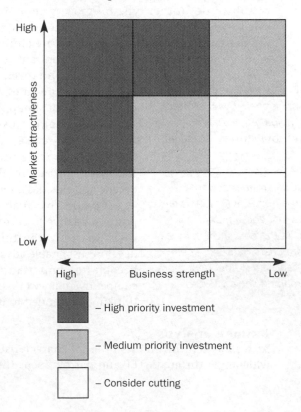

The resulting matrix divides into nine sectors. SBUs falling into those occupying the top left-hand three merit investment, those in the middle are less of a priority, those in the lower right-hand three need to be looked at with a view to halting their drain on company resources.

While planning frameworks in general, and portfolio models in particular, are useful tools, their use needs to be tempered with caution. A brief summary of the strengths and weaknesses of such tools is as follows.

Strengths

▶ Check-lists mean that nothing gets left out.
▶ Frameworks help the organisation look at itself dispassionately, and take the customer viewpoint.
▶ Models facilitate shared information and test assumptions.
▶ Models access accumulated experience from a wide range of industries.

Weaknesses

▶ Accurate information is difficult to establish and input satisfactorily.
▶ Models may be based on inappropriate experience (e.g. service industries are under-represented and growth markets are no longer the norm).
▶ Misdiagnosing the position of an SBU on a matrix may lead to costly mistakes.
▶ Implementing recommendations to divest or harvest an SBU can have dire social consequences in job losses and factory closures.

Where do we want to go?

The various forms of analysis covered should identify some key issues about the way an organisation is going. In turn this should facilitate the formation of some definite objectives, to steer the enterprise to where it wants to go. In order to be useful objectives need to be SMART:

▶ *Specific*: Raising sales by 10 per cent is better than raising sales. And raising sales in a particular section of the market (e.g. through cash and carries or through multiple grocers) helps focus effort effectively.
▶ *Measurable*: The outcomes being sought by the objective need to be quantifiable. If the effect of marketing effort is not measurable in some way it is impossible to learn from experience and to control the implementation of a strategy. Measures of success need to be considered at the same time as the objectives are set.
▶ *Achievable*: There is no point in setting an objective if it cannot be achieved. Careful analysis of all the factors that might contribute to the achievement of an objective, weighed against all the factors working against it, can help to flush out objectives whose time has not yet come.
▶ *Relevant*: The objective needs to be related to the issues identified in the situational analysis. The fewer objectives there are, the more chance there is of achieving them. Prioritising the most important ones is essential.
▶ *Time-related*: Marketing takes place in the real world, and time is an inescapable factor. Marketing objectives need to take this into account,

especially as speed becomes more important in establishing differential advantage. Being first into a market has traditionally carried benefits (hence the emphasis on innovation which is discussed in Chapter 8), but a time frame for the achievement of any kind of objective helps to focus the effort and resources necessary.

KEY SKILLS
ACTIVITY **14.2**
••••••••••••••••
**Improving own
learning and
performance**

Objectionable objectives?

All planners agree on the importance of objectives. After all, if you don't know where you are trying to go, you are hardly likely to get there! But getting the objectives themselves right is a vital first step in any kind of enterprise – whether it's marketing or learning or both.

Consider the following objectives. How do you rate them and how might they be improved? Measure them against the SMART criteria and suggest rewording or refor-mulation as necessary.

1   Increase brand awareness and expand market share.
2   Increase sales value by 10 per cent in two years.
3   Make every child a wanted child.
4   Delight the customer.
5   Improve quality by 10 per cent in a year.

Forecasting

In order to render objectives more credible, planners have to be able to envisage the future. This is not the scientific discipline it sometimes appears to be. Forecasts are not judged by how accurate they are, but by how useful they are. They can help create greater cohesion among the managers of an organisation as assumptions are exposed and a common vision of the future is established. The value of the exercise is not whether things turn out exactly as expected, but whether you can anticipate major problems before they get the better of you.

There are six commonly-used methods of forecasting. They can be divided into quantitative methods and qualitative methods.

Quantitative forecasting methods

Extrapolation
This is simply taking a statistical trend and extending it into the future as if it were a line on a graph. So, if your business in the late 1990s was in selling VHS video tapes, extrapolating the trend in the increase in sales of DVDs soon after their introduction would have led you to the conclusion that tapes were on the way out. This kind of technological substitution is often depicted by what is known as an 'S' curve. (See Figure 14.5.) The line is not straight, as the rate of substitution of one technology by another is gradual to begin with, accelerates, and then slows down again as the available market saturates.

figure 14.5
'S' curve

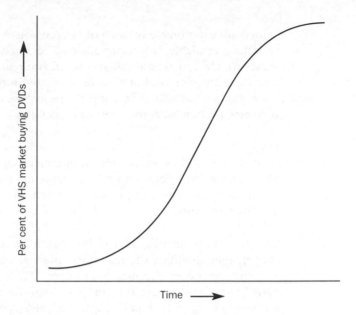

Leading indicator

It may be that you can anticipate increases in sales of your product or service by watching a related product or service. The price and availability of paper, for example, is a useful leading indicator for book sales. An overall drop in share prices or a rise in interest rates is a commonly accepted leading indicator of the level of economic activity of a country, hence the prominence given to such information in news and current affairs.

Model building

This forecasting technique aims to include all the main factors that will influence an organisation's costs and sales, and assemble them in a logical way that recognises their interdependence. Even though computer power and statistical information have enabled some very complex models to be built, their sophistication should not disguise the fact that they are judgemental in the relationships they include and assume.

Qualitative methods

Scenario building

Pioneered in the 1970s by Shell, and enjoying something of a renaissance among today's corporate planners and political strategists, this technique assumes that it is impossible to forecast the future. Instead it presents managers with a number of alternative visions of what may happen. Confronted by possible futures, managers can break free of their conventional expectations and prepare for the unexpected. One result of its use of the technique has been Shell's decentralisation in advance of its competitors to match an increasingly fragmented world market.

Delphi technique

Named after the oracle in ancient Greece where expert (if confusing!) advice was always available, this technique collects forecasts individually from a panel of experts. The forecasts are then collated and replayed back to the experts, who then have another shot at a more concerted forecast. The result is a kind of consensus of what is likely to happen. The experts concerned may be salespeople, managers, customers, consultants or academics.

Judgement

Probably the most important forecasting method, and one that the other methods can make better but not replace. Marketing is, after all, human activity and so a humanistic, intuitive judgement based on sound experience is central to effective forecasting.

Not all of these techniques will be feasible or relevant for all organisations. They neither eliminate the risk of business failure, nor do they guarantee success. Too heavy an emphasis on them can lead to what has been called analysis-paralysis, where the company is so busy contemplating the choices available to it that it becomes incapable of snatching the initiative. But appropriate analysis on a regular basis is a sure sign that an organisation is externally oriented, seeking ways of providing customer satisfactions more effectively and efficiently than its competition.

CASE STUDY **14.4**

Sailing to success

Pearl Motor Yachts is the brainchild of 33-year-old Iain Smallridge. Having skippered yachts in the South of France in the mid-1990s, Smallridge fell in love with the idea of luxury boats and returned to Britain with the idea of making his own vessel. This he did – in his then partner's garage – and eventually sold the craft for £240,000. What started out as a boat-building project had crystallised into a business idea.

1998 saw the launch of the Pearl 45, a 45-foot aft-cabin yacht, at the Southampton Boat Show. Backers for the new venture materialised over the next 18 months, during which time he collected two new business partners and £1.8 million in investment. The company produced eight boats in 2001, and a dozen in 2002. It now occupies purpose-built premises just outside Stratford.

Aft-cabin craft have more internal space than the more common fly-bridge designs on which British boat-builders have concentrated in their pursuit of the Mediterranean market. Fly-bridge designs emphasise lots of external sun space at the expense of internal accommodation, giving them a jet-setting, glamorous image. Aft-cabin designs had become a relatively neglected area, giving Smallridge the opportunity to explore a gap in the market. By employing a talented design team, and concentrating on the highest quality fittings and finish for the new boats, Pearl Motor Yachts has managed to make the aft-cabin sexy again with a range of highly-desirable models at 43, 47 and 55 feet long. World-renowned naval architect Bill Dixon has been drafted in to design the revolutionary hull for the 55-footer, and all of the boats' sumptuous interiors (finished in materials such as suede and cherrywood) have been designed by Evan K. Marshall, an internationally famous nautical stylist. An important plank in the boats' marketing is for the yachts to be seen, so Pearl moored its latest offerings at high-profile sites in Portsmouth and Majorca.

There has been something of a renaissance in the British yacht-building industry over the last 10 years. Big UK firms such as Riva, Sunseeker International and Princess, are among the world's most successful luxury manufacturers and build seriously big boats for the seriously rich customer. The target market for Pearl's boats is not the super-rich jet setter pursued by bigger companies, but the self-made professional man in his mid-forties, who still has enough disposable income to afford over half a million pounds for a boat he may only use for three weeks of the year.

An interesting aspect of the boat business is the strong personal relationship which each company builds with the customer – offering expert service and support – which encourages customers to stay with the brand and to trade up to more powerful or luxurious models when changing boats. Smallridge believes very strongly in the power of branding in order to help compete against larger companies with his niche product. The Pearl logo – three white spheres side by side – is an important design motif throughout the vessels, and there are plans to launch a range of merchandise and clothing as well as to establish a network of international dealerships and a sea sailing school.

Questions

1   Explain, with reference to the case study, what is meant by niche marketing.
2   How might an understanding of customer motivation help Pearl Motor Yachts market its boats successfully? What kind of marketing research might it carry out to increase this understanding?
3   What factors are likely to have an effect on demand for Pearl Motor Yachts in the next decade and what forecasting techniques would you recommend it uses to explore them?

Source: Winn (2003).

How do we get there?

Functional strategy

This part of the process is all about finalising functional marketing strategy. As we have seen, this needs to support the corporate strategy articulated in the mission statement and overall direction of the company. The role of each marketing mix element in achieving the objectives needs to be assessed. Pricing strategy, as we have seen in Chapter 9, can be focused on one of four main areas: income, volume, market share and societal value, and strategic options revolve around setting prices high (skimming) or low (penetration). Skill and experience will guide the marketing planner to the most likely strategic alternative in order to achieve the objectives in view.

Tactics

The functional strategy needs to be broken down into time-related, costed actions. Time and money are scarce resources, and a line has to be drawn between what you would ideally like to have (given the nature of the task) and what you can afford. Assumptions on costs and trends need to be worked into this thinking. The appropriateness of organisational structure to implementing plans successfully is a crucial issue which we will examine in greater detail later

figure 14.6
Gantt chart

ACTIVITY: XMAS Biscuit Gifts	Jan	Feb	Mar	Apr	May	Jun	Jul	Aug	Sep	Oct	Nov	Dec
Commission pack design	■											
Approve design		■										
Go to artwork			■									
Approve artwork					■							
Print materials						■	■					
Manufacture promo stock								■	■			
Sales meeting announcement								■				
Pack promo stock										■		
Deliver to warehouse											■	■

in this chapter. Executive responsibility needs to be assigned, and control and review mechanisms put into place. Project management software is increasingly used to keep track of tactical progress towards strategic goals. Many offer visual aids based on the simple Gantt chart – a horizontal bar chart which maps out over time periods what work is to be done and by whom. (See Figure 14.6.) The original was dreamt up in 1917 by Henry L. Gantt, an American social scientist and engineer. Potential bottlenecks are clearly predicted in this simple visual format, and a critical path established of what needs to be done by when. Gantt charts are helpful psychologically. Like many other planning tools they can help share information quickly and effectively, and keep everyone's attention on the task in hand.

Writing the marketing plan

One of the advantages of marketing planning is that it allows the organisation to agree and communicate its programme of action internally. The main instrument of this communication is a written marketing plan. The precise format of the plan will vary from one organisation to another, but it will usually cover a year's activity, and represent the fine-tuning of longer-range plans (usually three-year and five-year plans, which can take full account of the environmental trends brought to light by STEP analysis). Planning becomes easier and more meaningful as a process once it is established as a continuous cycle.

The main presentation components of a written marketing plan are as follows:

1 *Executive summary*: A short synopsis of the rationale, implementation and costs of the plan designed to provide an instant overview for executives who need to know what the plan contains but do not need detail.
2 *Mission statement and business strategy*: This should provide a context for what follows in terms of the organisation's overall direction and aims.

3   *Situational analysis*: This section presents the findings of the SWOT, STEP and competitive analyses which we have reviewed earlier in the chapter. Detail of the analyses themselves is best consigned to an appendix. The main body of the report should be reserved for what is important. From this the key issues that emerge should be stated. What are the main opportunities that face the organisation, and what threats does it need to overcome to take advantage of them?

4   *Statement of marketing objectives*: These objectives should fall naturally out of the key issues identified in the situational analysis. Their number should reflect what can be realistically achieved in the planning period, so they will reflect the highest priorities of the organisation.

5   *Marketing strategy*: This statement of functional strategy should relate the role of each element of the marketing mix to the achievement of the objectives.

6   *Marketing tactics*: Detailed plans with timings, costs and responsibilities. This is likely to be the bulkiest part of the plan itself, following on from the strategies to their implementation over the course of the planned period of activity.

7   *Controls and evaluation*: The plan should make it clear what measurements are implicit in its objectives. It should specify how and when these measurements are to be applied to evaluate the success of the plan in its various stages, and the mechanisms for corrective action as necessary. This aspect of marketing planning is dealt with in greater detail later in the chapter.

Marketing organisation

An organisation is a collection of individuals and resources who are united in the conscious pursuit of a common purpose. Concepts like planning and strategy are part of our conception of organisation, as they provide and articulate the unifying purpose that binds the organisation together. How effectively and appropriately the organisation is structured will therefore determine its success in achieving its purpose.

There are a number of ways of organising for marketing in a company. In Chapter 12 we looked at several options for organising a salesforce, a promotional decision that has much in common with human resources management. The conclusion reached there, that there is no one blueprint for a successful sales operation, can be transferred to marketing organisation as a whole. It is necessary to understand the strengths and weaknesses of a number of alternatives to cope with a changing customer environment.

Some Japanese companies have dispensed with marketing departments altogether. Their very literal interpretation of marketing is that it is everybody's business, so it should not be hived off into a separate management function. However, even though they may not have the M-word in their job title, senior executives in such organisations will have responsibilities for determining customer needs and wants and integrating the organisation's efforts towards satisfying them.

Marketing organisation will be a function of the overall organisational culture prevailing in an enterprise. Centralised cultures work by what is known as top-down management. Policy and aims are decided by top management and handed down to the organisation itself to be implemented. Decentralised cultures, on the other hand, work by a bottom-up management policy whereby major decisions are delegated to the relevant managers themselves. Both approaches have their advantages. With a centralised approach lines of communication are clear and marketing plans are readily implemented. It works well in a packaged goods environment, where quality can be built into the product at the manufacturing end of the chain. Decentralisation facilitates innovation and flexibility, but can create confusion in marketing policy and blur accountability. It works well in a service environment, where autonomy at the point of delivery to the customer can make all the difference to repeat business.

The issues are most clearly observable in international marketing. Choosing whether to standardise a company's offerings throughout its markets (symptomatic with centralised management) or adapt them to individual market conditions (a decentralised management ploy) is an ongoing dilemma for many organisations. Some highly effective international marketing companies manage to derive the best from both worlds, with structures that combine centralised corporate strategy with delegated marketing strategy.

CASE STUDY **14.5**

Consulting the Oracle

If sometimes it seems as if Bill Gates is the only name in software it probably means that you either don't work for a large company or you are not interested in international yacht racing. Gates' sworn rival is the founder and CEO of global business software supplier Oracle, Larry Ellison – famous for his immense personal wealth, outrageous charm, energetically expensive tastes and obsessive desire to win the Americas Cup (his team pulled it off in 2002 – after he had invested over $50 million of his personal fortune in the process). He's a marketing genius whose high-pressure management style has led to an extraordinary record of company expansion.

Ellison's argument is that if all companies bought the same software package (even if it was more sophisticated than they currently needed) their IT bills would tumble. In a recent presentation to customers he explained that over the years software companies have made and marketed too many products, and customers themselves have bought too many for the wrong reasons. As a result, there are three huge problems currently besetting business and hampering its entry into the riches of the information age. First of all there are too many incompatible products vying with each other even within companies. Second, the information which companies have on their various databases is hopelessly fragmented to the point where people cannot find the data they need to make decisions. Finally, Ellison underlines the fact that there are still yawning gaps in functionality within commercially-available business software. As a result, a company can spend up to 10 times more than it did on the original software on hiring consultants to write tailor-made software for them which works alongside it in order to achieve the results they need.

Ellison's solution is simple. Instead of buying bits and pieces of software from different suppliers and installing it as a customised patchwork which is never the same from one company to another, he wants to sell everyone exactly the same 'one-size-fits-all' package. This will, of course, mean that companies will buy software within the package that they rarely or never use. But it also means that whatever they buy will be guaranteed to work together. Furthermore, it will allow companies to store and locate all their information in one place, and it will offer comprehensive functionality to the point where additional 'tailor made' software will become redundant. Ellison's vision has been compared to that of Henry Ford, who made a fortune by only offering customers one car, the Model T, in one famous colour, black.

Ellison points to the fact that since Oracle itself adopted such an approach to its own software systems its IT costs have halved and its profitability has soared. On the other hand, critics of the 'e-business suite' approach have commented that what works for Oracle may not work for companies which are less centralised, and whose local markets may differ significantly from each other. After all, Oracle specialises in large business customers on a global basis, and their needs are pretty homogeneous. Other companies may be getting better results by picking and choosing software according to their specific market needs.

Ellison counters this argument by pointing to cost and complexity. It may well be that a more bespoke approach to software yields higher quality results, but it's a disproportionately expensive option. Oracle's first major advertising push for the e-business suite dangled a carrot of $1 billion a year savings in software costs, based on its own experience. So far a number of large-scale customers, including General Electric, Alcoa and the State Government of Texas, have signed up to the idea. Ellison argues that the only way to bring business software costs down and to improve quality and reliability is to follow the 'one-size-fits-all' route. 'Every child should be unique,' he avers, 'but not every software system.'

Questions

1   Assess the argument that a standard software suite offers better value for money than a 'pick and mix' solution (you may want to revisit some of the material in Chapter 13 about standardisation vs adaptation when answering this question).
2   Does concentrating on one software product mean that market segmentation is no longer relevant to Oracle?
3   Discuss the role of personal selling in business-to-business marketing from evidence in the case study.

Sources: *The Economist* (2003); Kawamoto et al. (2001); Oracle (2002).

Major alternatives for organising the marketing function

If marketing management is to fulfil its role of co-ordinating and integrating an organisation's customer orientation, it needs to work closely with other departments. It is essential that marketing makes itself felt throughout an organisation. Marketing-oriented companies can be identified by the presence of people with marketing experience at the highest levels of management, as well as by the lines of communication between marketing and other departments. Less genuinely marketing-oriented firms may well have marketing

figure 14.7
**Functional
organisation**

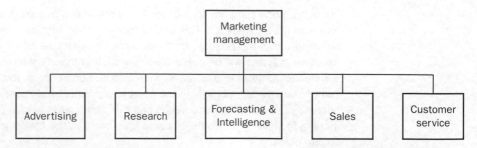

departments, but will limit their role to one of strictly functional responsibility for promotion and selling. Whatever a company's commitment to marketing, however, its marketers have the job of internal marketing as well as dealing with external customers. In other words, marketing departments need to establish the customer's place at the heart of the organisation through training and development, clear communication, reliable systems and explicit professionalism.

As for the marketing department itself, there are three major organisational principles: by function, by products and by customer.

Organising by function

Functional organisation divides the marketing task into its separate constituents – advertising, research, market intelligence, market forecasting, and so on. Executives responsible for each function report to marketing management. The structure is straightforward and clear, and suits the need of organisations with a unified product line and a centralised culture. Business-to-business marketers often find it an appropriate structure because they tend to specialise in one type of product or service, and the boundaries of their markets are clearly defined. (See Figure 14.7.)

Organising by product

Fast-moving consumer goods companies often have a number of different products or groups of products in their overall portfolio. This diversity encourages them to make product rather than function the unit of organisation, as the circumstances faced by one set of products may be quite different from those faced by another group in the same company. (See Figure 14.8.) Product-based organisation has the disadvantage of proliferating numbers in marketing departments, with costly consequences for the wage bill. But, for all its expense, this kind of organisation permits a great deal of flexibility in responding to the particular demands of different product markets.

The brand manager

Product-based organisation has been responsible for the creation of the classic marketing role of the brand manager. Brand managers are usually people relatively young in the organisation whose responsibility is to look after the brand as if it were their own business. As the personal advocates of the brand within the organisation they are responsible for making things happen in the process of maintaining and improving long-term profitability. It's a popular developmental position for ambitious executives keen to progress in a company, as the brand manager has to have a finger in every pie in the organisation.

figure 14.8
Product-based organisation

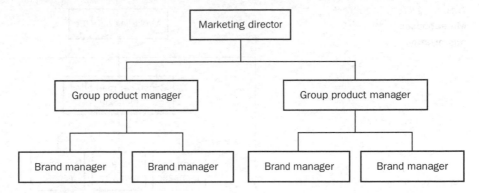

Brand management is not without its critics, however. There follows a brief account of its good and bad points.

Good points

- ▶ Provides the brand with a personal advocate inside the company.
- ▶ Developmental role for future senior management.
- ▶ Regular turnover of brand managers provides a stream of fresh ideas and energy.

Bad points

- ▶ Expensive and labour intensive.
- ▶ Brand managers have a great deal of responsibility but less authority than more senior staff.
- ▶ Short-term involvement by brand managers (who may only spend two years on the brand before moving on) can be detrimental to the long-term health of the brand.

The value of products and services is vested in their brand personalities. For all the debate about brand management, it has the enduring appeal of being an appropriately personal way of managing these valuable assets.

Organisation by market

Firms whose businesses are concentrated in a number of different markets, geographical regions or customer types will organise themselves accordingly. (See Figure 14.9.) Dividing a marketing department between consumer and industrial markets, for example, is an intelligent response to the different kinds of channel, product size and pricing decision involved in each. This is especially the case in different national markets, where a considerable portion of marketing time is occupied by the management and recruitment of intermediaries unique to each market. It is also becoming more important to

figure 14.9
Market-based organisation

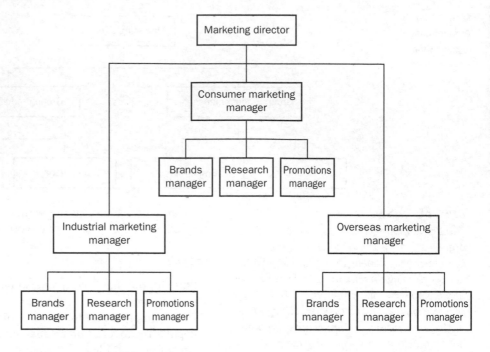

organise by customer type in response to the growth of retailer power discussed in Chapter 10. Companies operating in the packaged grocery sector need to pay special attention to servicing the demands of these powerful customers. This requires allocating marketing and sales executives dedicated to servicing their needs, as in the salesforce structure outlined in Chapter 12.

Matrix organisation

Function, product and market influences often feature together in the make-up of a pragmatic, adaptive marketing structure. A company that organises mainly according to function could have a further grouping within it dedicated to product innovation, drawing its membership from various functions. This would be a combination of product and function organisation. Similarly, most FMCG companies, while organising their marketing departments on product group lines, will organise their sales departments on customer types. This kind of multi-stranded organisation is known as matrix organisation. Its advantages are that it allows flexibility and innovation. Its disadvantages are that lines of responsibility are not always clear, creating conflict and inefficiency. However, compared to the tall hierarchies of the traditional centralised organisation (where layers of management report up functional lines to senior decision-makers), it can be less expensive and more responsive to customer demands.

Marketing control

There is many a slip between cup and lip, according to the proverb. Part of the marketing function is to monitor the successful implementation of marketing plans, and to take corrective action if necessary.

Monthly checks: sales by period

The most obvious way of doing this is to assess performance against objectives on a regular basis. Most manufacturing companies divide their year into sales periods of four weeks each (making a 13-period year). Meetings between sales planning and marketing at the end of each period provide a means of updating planned sales with actual sales. Price moves by competitors, promotional activity, unforeseen price increases, even factors like the weather, can all affect demand and therefore the level of stocks in distribution channels. Production planning needs to be tailored to how things are going – making more if sales are exceeding expectation, and cutting back if the reverse is true in order to save on inventory costs. The need for remedial action may be clear – whether a burst of promotion activity brought forward to support a drooping brand or the delaying of a price increase to make the product better value.

The 'Z' chart

A very useful format for graphing the periodic sales progress of a brand in a way that focuses on long-term trends rather than short-term blips or seasonal distortion is the 'Z' chart. (See Figure 14.10.) This involves the plotting of three lines (or 'curves' as they are known). When the chart is complete, after a year of observation, the three lines are joined in a way that resembles a 'Z', hence the name. The lines are as follows:

▶ *Moving annual total*: Calculated by adding the current sales period's total sales to those of the periods for the last 12 months. This reveals long-term trends in the brand's performance very well.

figure 14.10
'Z' chart

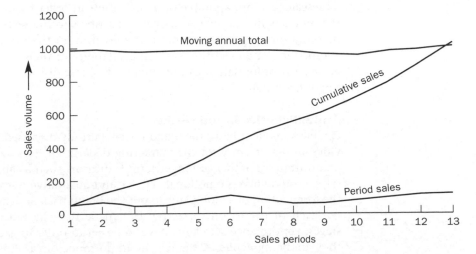

▶ *Periodic sales*: Sales for each period are graphed on a monthly basis. This helps diagnose seasonality and other short-term peaks and troughs.

▶ *Cumulative periodic sales*: This curve moves diagonally up the chart from left to right, connecting the parallel lines of the 'Z'. Compared to the target curve this can be a very revealing indicator.

KEY SKILLS
ACTIVITY **14.3**
••••••••••••••••

Application of number

A picture of success?

Making sense of numerical information is often easier when you create pictures from data. This exercise gives you practice in working out moving annual totals and cumulative totals by period before combining them with period-by-period figures in a chart.

Using the following periodic sales data, draw a 'Z' chart for year 3 and comment on the overall trends it reveals.

Sales period	Sales (tonnes) by four-week period:		
	Year 1	Year 2	Year 3
1	1,200	1,210	1,200
2	1,210	1,210	1,200
3	1,300	1,250	1,200
4	1,200	1,200	1,000
5	1,100	1,100	900
6	1,000	1,010	1,000
7	1,000	900	900
8	850	900	850
9	900	850	850
10	1,000	850	950
11	1,300	1,200	1,100
12	1,250	1,200	1,150
13	1,100	1,000	1,000

Retail audit

Another regular source of control feedback for FMCG companies is the retail audit. This is a service provided by a specialist research company which sends its researchers into a sample of retail outlets in order to gauge the sales rate of the products in a particular market. Subscribers to the service are given regular presentations, updating them on the position of their brands relative to the competition and even the levels of availability of their brands to shoppers by outlet. This information can be used to diagnose distribution problems in time to put them right.

Annual checks: brand review

On a less frequent basis, the brand review (already discussed in Chapter 11) provides an opportunity for the marketing department to assess the health of its brand from a number of longer-term indicators such as annual market share, sales, profitability, promotional activity and qualitative research. This can assist the formulation of action plans to put the brand back on its strategic track.

Each of these control activities can be flowcharted to reveal common stages. Performance standards have to be set in order to gauge whether or not they are being achieved (hence the importance of careful objective setting).

figure 14.11
Control process loop

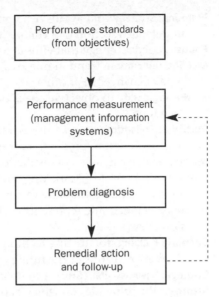

Information systems have to be sensitive and timely in order to show up variances from plan. Diagnosis has to be accurate – it can be counter-productive to cure the wrong ill. And responsibility for the improvement needs to be clearly delineated and followed up. (See Figure 14.11.)

Marketing audits

Marketing is as subject to external or internal audit as any other business process. An audit is a systematic and rigorous examination of systems and their effectiveness. Because the marketing environment is ever changing, external marketing audits carried out by independent consultants are good practice every three to five years to reassess the relevance of the organisation and its procedures.

In an effective marketing organisation a less formal kind of audit should be an ongoing part of the general orientation towards planning and organising with the customer in mind. It will contribute to the kind of situational analysis we have discussed as fundamental to the marketing planning process, particularly in terms of a relevant SWOT analysis.

Key concepts
••••••••••••••••

Centralised/decentralised organisation: alternative management styles where decisions are taken by top management (centralised) or delegated to those responsible for implementation (decentralised).

Cost leadership: strategic use of economies of scale to undercut competition on price.

Delphi technique: forecasting method involving a panel of expert opinion.

Differentiation: generic strategy that concentrates on non-price factors.

Extrapolation: predicting the future by assuming that past trends will continue.

Flanking: strategy that avoids head-on confrontation to concentrate on an undefended section of a competitor's business.

Focus: generic strategy that aims at a particular niche market.

Leading indicator: a trend in one area of the economy that can be used to predict changes in another.

Marketing audit: an objective check on the systems and activities of a marketing operation.

Matrix organisation: an organisation that is structured on two or more principles (e.g. by function, product, market).

Mission statement: a verbal distillation of an organisation's corporate strategy.

PIMS: Profit Impact of Marketing Strategy, a long-running research project that aims to relate profitability to a number of alternative marketing strategies.

'S' curve: graphed line representing change that starts slowly, accelerates and slows down again.

Scenario building: forecasting technique that presents a number of radically alternative visions of the future.

Strategic business unit (SBU): a component of an organisation's business structure.

Strategy: the principles on which activity is founded.

Tactics: the day-to-day activities resulting from strategy.

'Z' chart: a graph representing sales as moving annual total, periodic actual and cumulative.

SELF-CHECK QUESTIONS

1 Corporate strategy is:
   a Decided by functional marketing strategy.
   b Reactive to short-term competitive activity.
   c The framework for functional marketing strategy.
   d The implementation of plans to achieve long-term aims.
   e More specific and practical than marketing strategy.

2 Which of the following statements are not true of market challengers?
   a They often direct their competitive activity at smaller firms.
   b They tend to use penetration as a way of expanding their existing business without excessive risk to market share.
   c They carry out flanking activity.
   d They have a vested interest in the status quo.
   e Their success suggests that high profitability is a consequence of either very high or very low market share.

3 PIMS stands for:
   a Profit Isolation from Market Saturation.
   b Product Impact of Marketing Solutions.
   c Profit Impact of Marketing Strategy.
   d Projected Implications for Marketing Science.
   e Positional Intelligence in Motivational Situations.

4 Which of the following forecasting techniques are quantitative rather than qualitative?
   a Scenario building.
   b Model building.

  c Extrapolation.

  d Leading indicator.

  e Delphi technique.

5 Put the following elements of a marketing plan into the order in which you would expect to find them in the written document:

  a Tactics.

  b Situational analysis.

  c Controls and evaluation.

  d Strategy.

  e Statement of objectives.

Which of the following statements are true and which are false?

6 The overall organisational culture prevailing in an enterprise will be a function of its marketing organisation.

7 Top-down management has the advantage of allowing important decisions to be delegated to those who will implement them.

8 Departments structured on a functional basis can often work well in business-to-business marketing.

9 Brand management gives a lot of power but relatively little responsibility to comparatively junior managers.

10 Retail audit services can expose weaknesses in distribution.

Discuss the following

11 To fail to plan is to plan to fail.

12 The key to differential advantage lies in product quality.

13 How can small companies defend themselves against aggression from larger rivals? Illustrate your answer with examples.

14 Forecasting is all about persuading other people of your vision of the future.

15 The brand manager is an endangered species, not worth preserving.

Further study
. . . .

Ansoff, H.I. (1961) *Corporate Strategy*, Penguin Books.
The man who put business strategy on the academic agenda in the 1950s and still highly relevant.

McDonald, M. (2002) *Marketing Plans: How To Prepare Them How To Use Them*, 5th edn, Heinemann.
Professor McDonald, a marketing director of Canada Dry before he entered academia, has established himself as the doyen of British marketing planning.

Keller, K. (ed.) (2002) *Harvard Business Review on Marketing*, Harvard Business Review Press.
A useful and accessible collection of practitoner-focused articles.

Piercy, N. (2001) *Market-led Strategic Change,* 3rd edn, Butterworth-Heinemann.
A very intelligent guide to strategy from a marketing point of view.

Ringland, G. (1998) *Scenario Planning: Managing the Future*, John Wiley.
A recent guide to this interesting planning methodology.

References

Ansoff, I. (1987) *Corporate Strategy*, revised edn, Penguin.

Buzzell, R.D. and Gale, B.T. (1987) *The PIMS Principles: Linking Strategy to Performance*, Free Press.

CIM (2002) 'Marketers in the money as salaries edge higher', Press Release, 3 October, Chartered Institute of Marketing, available at: http://www.cim.co.uk/cim/new/html/newArt.cfm?objectID=5B5DA98D-CECF-430B-9683B9BC0E58816A

Davey, J. (2003) 'Benetton's bid to run Italy's roads', *The Times,* 1 January, p.21.

Day, P. (2002) 'Fly move', *In Business*, BBC Radio 4, broadcast 26 September.

Economist (2003) 'Face value: jolly boating weather', *The Economist,* 4 January, p.55.

Kawamoto, D., Wong, W. and Farmer, M.A. (2001) 'Buying into trouble', *Tech News,* 29 June, available at: http://news.com.com/2009-1017-269001.html

Kotler, P. and Armstrong, G. (1998) *Principles of Marketing*, 8th edn, Prentice Hall.

McIntyre, P. (2002) 'Forget branding, now integration makes mark', *The Australian*, 22 August, p.11.

Oracle (2002) *OracleWorld Keynote: Larry Ellison Discusses 3 Greatest Challenges Facing IT,* available at: http://www.oracle.com

Porter, M.E. (1980) *Competitive Strategy: Techniques for Analyzing Industries and Competitors*, Free Press.

Smith, P. (2002) 'Electricals set to be the fastest growing retail area', *Financial Times,* 4 March, p.3.

Winn, S. (2003) 'How to launch a brand into the luxury market', *Management Today,* January, pp.56–8.

Answers to self-check questions

Chapter 1
•••••••••••

Multiple-choice

1 e Marketing-led firms recognise that without customers they have no reason to be in business!

2 b The functional role of marketing extends beyond the task of promotion: it encompasses analysis, strategy, tactics (of which promotion is one, but 'product', 'price' and 'place' are also important) and management.

3 d Only firms that embrace all three of these can be described as adopting the marketing concept: they are prerequisites to 'creating and keeping profitable customers'.

4 d Organisations that emphasise 'getting the sale' are in danger of losing out when it comes to building long-term relationships with customers.

5 a When organisations keep an eye on what is going on in the world outside, they are in a better position to anticipate changes in demand and to react to them.

True/False

6 True. Income will probably determine the quality and style they can afford and age is likely to influence their functional needs: young single people in their first homes may value style while those with young children may be looking for durability.

7 True. Retailers are the most common type of intermediary used to get grocery products from the factory to the consumer.

8 False. The purpose of marketing control is to identify any departure from the plan to enable corrective action to be taken if necessary.

9 False. Marketing principles are relevant to all organisations that have customers.

10 True. The concept of internal marketing, although quite new, is helpful in encouraging organisations to integrate their efforts in improving service levels.

Discussion

11 A firm might adopt a sales orientation if it is concerned with 'making the sale' but isn't too worried as to whether its customers are satisfied with their purchases. This may occur if the product being sold is unlikely to be a repeat purchase (e.g. double glazing, fitted kitchens and encyclopaedias). It could be argued that financial services salesmen have also been guilty of adopting this approach to selling pensions, which are a good example of a one-off purchase. The discovery of large-scale mis-selling of private pension plans throughout the whole industry (to members of corporate pension schemes who would have been better off staying in their company schemes) has led to regulation to force the companies concerned to compensate the victims of their hard-sell. The question of whether the approach is excusable depends, perhaps, on one's ethical stand point. One might be persuaded that it is excusable particularly as governments use it to attract voters in elections! As to whether or not it is desirable, the fact that bad word-of-mouth travels faster than good is a sufficient deterrent for most businesses, whose interests are usually better served by a more customer-focused ethos.

12 The most commonly cited fifth 'P' is that of *people*, though this can be thought of as an integral part of the product rather than a separate element of the marketing mix. Particularly in service industries, employee performance has a direct influence over the way the customer experiences the product. 'Processes' and 'planning' are other additions that are sometimes made to the marketing mix, but it could be argued that this is inappropriate, as manufacturing processes are primarily the responsibility of the production function and planning is a central activity and not just a marketing tool. Nonetheless, people, processes and planning can all affect demand for an organisation's products, and marketing-oriented firms will consider them all with customer needs in mind.

13 Public utilities such as British Gas, the water companies and the electricity companies are in very similar situations as other industries in that they depend on satisfied customers for continued revenues and profits. It is in their own interests to attempt to 'create and keep profitable customers'. If they do not, they are vulnerable to either takeover bids or liquidation (though the government would almost certainly intervene if there were any threat of the latter). They may also be subject to price controls if governments perceive them to be failing to deliver a fair deal to customers. Only in situations of pure monopoly, where consumers have no choice (and are unlikely ever to have any choice) as to whom to buy from might it be possible for public utilities to ignore the marketing concept. Even then there is a risk that the environment will change and leave the business in jeopardy.

14 There is an argument that universities should be 'product' oriented, providing courses that are believed to be *worthwhile* rather than responding to demand for places. Universities themselves may be tempted to be 'production' oriented, and strive to be more efficient. They may accept large numbers of students to increase their revenues in order to cover their fixed costs, even if this has a negative impact on the quality of the student experience. A 'sales' orientation may be evident during Clearing, when places need to be sold to students to make courses viable, even if they do not match the students' ambitions or qualifications very well. But the best institutions recognise that there has to be a balance between their own objectives and the needs of the student if they are to thrive and maintain their good reputations in the market.

15 While the marketing mix for toothpaste and political parties is likely to be very different, the application of the other principles of marketing will bear remarkable similarities. Both toothpaste manufacturers and politicians have to understand their environments and the ways in which they are changing, and they are likely to use market research (or opinion polls) to help them do this. Both are likely to identify key target markets and attempt to present themselves in a better light than the competition (or opposition), though there is some debate as to whether their target markets comprise 'citizens' or 'customers' (the latter being arguably more passive than the former). They will prepare plans (or manifestos) that will give direction to their activities and attempt to use limited resources in the most effective way possible to increase their market shares (or share of the vote).

Chapter 2
. . . .

Multiple-choice

1 e Effective use of resources towards organisational objectives. As to the other answers: **a** Non-profits are not interested in profitability in the traditional sense. **b** Marketing is likely to increase costs (at least in the short term) because of salaries and expenditure. **c** This is arguable but fundraising is only part of marketing. **d** Efficiency is all very well if it is helping the organisation achieve its objectives – but sometimes it can be a misplaced emphasis.

2 a and **d.**

3 d.

4 a, c, d and **e.** Some would add **b** but most non-profits do charge for their services, even at non-commercial rates.

5 d While this might seem like common sense, there are problems about deciding on the membership of 'the greatest number of people' group. Even utilitarians have families, friends and reciprocal ties with individuals such as long-standing customers. Should they not receive preferential treatment?

True/False

6 False. They are in the market for benefits rather than how they are conveyed. However, marketers can convey benefits more effectively through an understanding of the emphases due to services and products respectively.

7 True. Such as souvenirs and merchandise.

8 False. This is the job of buyers.

9 True. As in the Potteries, or Silicon Valley. However this is not a hard-and-fast rule.

10 False. It is equally if not more concerned with keeping customers.

Discussion

11 Marketing religion raises interesting issues. It could be argued that marketing can only go so far because of the nature of the 'benefits' involved in this exchange relationship. To answer this question properly will require you to think hard about product analysis and targeting strategy.

12 While many of their attributes will be similar, industrial salespeople are usually called on to play more of a technical role than their consumer counterparts. Beware in discussing this question of falling into a stereotypical view of salespeople.

13 It is certainly true that good customer service depends on good staff, so quality control from the first is essential. Not only recruitment but also training (very often part of the same department) can play a decisive role in equipping an organisation for differential advantage through service.

14 This view is based on an adversarial conception of the relationship between staff and managers. It might be argued that such a view is out of date. Certainly, the rise of internal communications in businesses in the late twentieth century coincided with a decline in union membership. Some of the role of the unions in informing the workforce was assumed by management through internal communications and marketing. On the other hand, because marketing requires there to be a mutuality of interest between parties to the exchange, it would be a misnomer to call it mind control.

15 Some customers do. They don't want ongoing contact with companies, they just want to be left alone. Some feel that techniques such as direct marketing are unacceptably intrusive. Legislation in some European countries follows this principle. If it were adopted in the UK, it might seriously hamper direct marketing. Technology may be the answer here, with sophisticated software able to target and contact reluctant customers less frequently.

Chapter 3

Multiple-choice

1 e These types of competitor are in the same industry but are not trying to gain business from exactly the same customers, so they are only competing indirectly.

2 c Both of these can enable suppliers to charge high prices which businesses may have no choice but to pay.

3 e Patents are one of the ways in which innovators are rewarded to compensate them for their research and development costs.

4 c Action should be taken at this stage, but the type of action will depend on the nature of the environmental change.

5 e When inflation threatens an economy, governments may raise interest rates to dampen excess demand and break the price/wage increase spiral.

True/False

6 False. Although their price brackets may be similar, consumers will use different decision criteria as the two purchases meet different consumer needs.

7 False. These decisions will affect levels of customer service, and are therefore of interest to marketers.

8 True. This is a heavily branded market with highly differentiated products that their producers hope will be perceived as unique by their customers.

9 False. Demographics are concerned with the size and composition of populations, over which businesses have virtually no control.

10 True. Innovation can be triggered by new needs and wants in society, but can also lead to changing values and lifestyles.

Discussion

11 As a promotional tool, the Internet offers opportunities to a wide range of industries which wish to provide information to customers. Some industries have enjoyed more success than others in using it as a marketing tool for sales. Tickets (for entertainment and travel), recorded music and books, software and electronics have led the field in terms of consumer interest. It could be argued that the Internet threatens existing forms of distribution channel and communication media, but consumers tend to prefer multiple ways of accessing products and services and of communicating, which suggests that the high street, telephone and letter are here for a while yet.

12 In an oligopoly a business feels some protection from new entrants, as the few large firms in the industry tend to deter them by heavy expenditure on promotion to reinforce the popularity of their brands, or investment in capital goods which make them highly efficient. They are, however, vulnerable to the activities of existing competitors, particularly on pricing strategy. Firms fear losing market share if their prices are higher than their competitors, so a price cut by one firm tends to be followed by all the others. This can ultimately lead to reduced profit margins in the industry as a whole unless cost savings can be made by improved efficiency.

13 Tobacco companies have diversified out of purely tobacco product manufacture; they are mainly conglomerates now, selling financial services, cosmetics and food products as well as tobacco. By creating a portfolio of products they have protected themselves from the decline in tobacco sales being experienced in many Western markets following extensive publicity about the health risks of smoking (first publicised seriously in the 1960s). They have also made efforts to penetrate foreign markets, particularly some less developed countries where the consumption of tobacco is still buoyant, consumer and government health concerns are less aggressive and taxation less punitive. More recently, they have attempted to stop the decline in consumption in Western markets by cutting prices (a move that seems to have worked: for the first time since the early 1960s the American cigarette market has stopped shrinking).

14 The big supermarkets have a very high share of the grocery retailing market. Consequently, if food manufacturers wish to reach the mass market in the UK, they must persuade the big retailers to stock their products. But the big retailers buy in bulk, so they insist on very low prices. Also, they will only stock products if they are sure that consumers will buy them, and will resist all but the most successful brands. Supermarkets also buy unbranded products which are then given their own label and placed to compete with branded alternatives on the shelves. If they are not satisfied with their supplier, they can change without the end-user customer even knowing that there is any difference in the product. Marks & Spencer uses the second of these strategies only. All of its products are bought unbranded, and given its own name. This enables it to choose its suppliers carefully and dispense with those that do not meet its exacting quality standards.

15 Traditional university and college students are recent school-leavers in their late teens and early twenties. A dip in the birth rate will therefore reduce the size of the school-leaver market some 20 years later and can create recruitment difficulties for educational institutions unless governments intervene by introducing policies that encourage greater participation in further and higher education. Strategies that target mature students are one response to this problem. By recruiting across a wider age-band, educational institutions are less exposed to the more intense competition for students that can otherwise occur. Another response is to engage more aggressively in head-on competition. Some universities have increased their marketing budgets substantially, and now include TV advertising among the promotional techniques they use to recruit more 18–21 year olds.

Chapter 4
••••••••••••

Multiple-choice

1 c Income, education, wealth and occupation are the most commonly used, with occupation being the easiest to identify.

2 b Derived demand is the term used to describe the fact that businesses only buy products and services because consumers or other businesses demand their products and services.

3 b A straight rebuy is a purchase class in organisational buying.

4 e Children are unlikely to be initiators, deciders or buyers in this product category, though they may influence the decision and will almost certainly use the product!

5 c Recession occurs when there is a down-turn in demand in the economy, leading to lower levels of business.

True/False

6 False. Modified rebuy situations usually require new information sources so that established purchasing habits can be reviewed.

7 False. Personal characteristics such as personality, buying style and risk tolerance will all influence decisions.

8 True. Consumers refer to the behaviour of peers to ensure that they themselves will remain accepted members of the group.

9 False. It is likely that consumers will use commercial as well as personal and public sources of information for this type of decision.

10 True. MOSAIC and ACORN are both systems that attempt to relate lifestyles to postcode districts.

Discussion

11 Evidence suggests that advertising has little impact on consumer perceptions of a product at the time it is actually seen; however, if it is creatively presented, it may be subject to selective retention that can increase the likelihood of a consumer trying the product. After trial, advertising can be more influential still. When consumers who have seen products advertised actually sample them, they are more likely to be favourably impressed, having been positively influenced by the expectations that the advert has planted (A. Mitchell (1994) 'Rephrasing the question', *Marketing*, 10 March: 25–6).

12 Central purchasing is likely to be the most efficient means of procurement for products that are required throughout a large organisation and for which discounts can be negotiated from suppliers for large quantities. Company car fleets, for example, are usually purchased centrally in big companies and stationery supplies are often ordered on an annual contract. Products required by only one division of an organisation, or those that are technically complex or specifically related to a particular production process, may be more effectively purchased at a local level where the product knowledge is greatest. In these situations, the role of a central buyer may still exist, but simply to process the transaction rather than make an informed input into the decision-making process.

13 The decision-making process for a critical purchase, such as a house, is likely to involve a sizeable decision-making unit. The initiator could be a parent, whose job has been relocated, but the decision to move and which house to buy may be influenced by children, parents, building societies and professional experts such as surveyors and solicitors. In a family unit, the final decision is likely to be a joint one by the adults of the household, but the transaction itself is likely to be conducted in conjunction with a mortgage lender who will provide some of the money for the purchase.

14 Social class is a construct that cuts across many other determinants of consumer behaviour, including income, education, wealth and occupation. In days gone by (and in some countries today) social classes were relatively easy to identify or measure as these four features often ran in parallel, with the wealthiest members of society having been educated for the longest and getting well-paid jobs in the professions. But changes in social structures have altered this pattern and have made it very difficult to classify social groups in this way. In the future, an examination of lifestyle is likely to give a better indicator of the beliefs, values and purchasing behaviour of different sub-groups of society.

15 Just like consumers, organisational buyers are likely to investigate four sources of information:

► Their own experience of previously buying computers (Were they reliable?, Did they deliver on time?, Was the back-up service adequate?).
► Opinions of others, particularly other members of the decision-making unit who may be experts in this field.
► Public information, including reports in computer magazines and the trade press. These provide a relatively unbiased perspective on the alternatives available.
► Promotional literature, and also face-to-face interaction with salespeople, who can provide product feature information.

Chapter 5
. . . .

Multiple-choice

1 b The others are not available within the organisation itself, but can be obtained from other sources (note, however, that even a customer database is an external source of data if it is purchased from a list-broker rather than generated internally).

2 c Respondents are being asked to place their views on a scale, hence the term 'scaled question'.

3 b The frequencies of response to each question are the summation of the responses of all individuals in the sample; further statistical analysis can be undertaken when the frequencies have been calculated.

4 d This is the only objective that implies a general investigation rather than more specific description or the need for experimentation.

5 d Focus group discussion should be led by a trained moderator who can orchestrate the debate around key issues of relevance to the objectives of the research.

True/False

6 False. There may be no need to conduct any primary research if the answers can be found in the secondary data.

7 False. Randomness means that the sample is more likely to represent the views of the whole population, so fewer respondents are needed.

8 False. Qualitative research does not even try to be statistically reliable. It seeks to identify attitudes, feelings and motivations, rather than to measure their occurrence.

9 True. Data are simply facts and figures, whereas information is produced when these facts and figures are interpreted with reference to the objectives of the research.

10 False. It isn't possible to compare the two for reliability. They are likely to be used in different circumstances and for different purposes; their reliability will depend on their appropriate use in the right circumstances to achieve specific objectives.

Discussion

11 Buying syndicated research is a very useful way of obtaining market information that would otherwise be unavailable. It can be particularly useful when it would be too expensive for a single firm to undertake the research individually, as in the case of regular large sample consumer surveys such as the TGI. The findings of the research are, however, publicly available to all the competitors in an industry, so the strategic use of the findings to gain a competitive advantage is difficult. It is also possible that the research methodology, the nature of the sample or the timing of the research may not fit the information needs of the company very precisely, and that personalised *ad hoc* research is the only way of obtaining relevant information.

12 Before this question can be answered, more specific objectives have to be set so that data requirements can be identified. It is likely that the sample should contain both users and non-users of catering outlets to give a balanced view. You may choose a cluster sample, such as all the students from a particular year group or course, chosen at random from all the courses in your institution. For the most statistically accurate findings you could use a random sample from the list of all registered students. Alternatively, you could try a stratified sample, which selects groups of respondents in direct proportion to the number of male, female, full-time and part-time students. There is no hard-and-fast rule; the sample must simply be adequate to provide the information required with an acceptable level of accuracy.

13 Telephone surveys are useful in research where it is likely that the population is easily contactable by phone (so that the sample will not be biased). It is also a good way of reaching a geographically spread sample, when it would be logistically difficult to contact a balanced sample face to face. What is more, in comparison with face-to-face interviewing, this technique is both cheap and fast. These two factors contribute to the relatively heavy use of this technique in business-to-business research as opposed to consumer research.

14 The mean is useful for gaining an impression of the overall tendencies of the sample in a scaled question. When used in conjunction with the standard deviation it indicates the extent to which the respondents have similar views – the wider the deviation, the fewer the similarities between respondents. The mode indicates the most popular responses to a question. If there are two different, but equally popular, responses, this implies that there are two distinct segments within the population under investigation. The median is simply the 'middle person's' response. The category into which this response falls can be thought of as the half-way point in public opinion.

15 'Paralysis by analysis' is an expression that refers to the way in which some organisations generate so much information that they are overwhelmed with facts and figures and feel unable to act on any of them. 'Data distress' is one example of this. Marketing information is only useful if it is a cost-effective way of improving decision-making and helping the organisation to achieve its objectives. It is not a substitute for action.

Chapter 6
....

Multiple-choice

1 b While income is a demographic basis for segmentation, price is a *response* to the target market, i.e. part of the marketing mix.

2 c Although these systems use demographic and geographic characteristics to *analyse* the population, their findings enable marketers to *segment* the population on the basis of the lifestyle implied by these characteristics.

3 b When the different positions of their competitors are identified, organisations are better able to design appropriate competitive strategies.

4 b The number of competitors in different market segments is unlikely to have a major impact on the viability of a new market segment unless they subsequently adopt a head-on competition strategy.

5 d In this situation, avoiding the competition may not be a viable option.

True/False

6 True. Product differentiated marketing tries to find product versions that appeal to a wide range of people whereas multi-segment marketing strategies involve producing different products to reflect the different characteristics and needs of different groups within the total market.

7 True. This may take lots of different forms, and a number of examples are given in this chapter.

8 True. These concepts both imply a focus on a single market segment.

9 False. Figure 6.1 demonstrates how marketing mix decisions arise as a result of segmentation, targeting *and* positioning.

10 True. Segmentation based on purchase patterns such as this can be very useful.

Discussion
....

11 Demographic segmentation has been used extensively by toiletries manufacturers. For example, there are brands aimed at women (Lux and Camay), at men (Lynx), at young people (Clearasil) and at babies (Johnsons). However, demographic segmentation is by no means the whole story. A further level of segmentation by benefit sought is apparent in each of these brands – namely good complexion, personal hygiene, prevention of spots, and gentleness. Other brands are not segmented on demographics at all, but focus on segments based, for example, on purpose of use (Fairy household soap), ease of use (liquid soap), natural ingredients (Body Shop), moisturising properties (Dove) or freedom from irritation (Simple).

12 Rotators need to be exposed to consistent promotional activity to maintain the standing of a brand in the eyes of consumers, encouraging them to select it above the others on their short-lists. Distribution should match, or better that of, the competition, but prices need not necessarily be lower, simply in an acceptable band. Deal-sensitive consumers are attracted by low prices, so price rather than brand should be emphasised in promotional messages. Distribution needs to be good, but these consumers may be willing to shop around to some extent in search of a bargain.

13 Store loyalty cards enable supermarkets to identify students and make them promotional offers that can be denied to other more affluent segments of their market. This makes the student segment more accessible and therefore more viable. The student market holds good potential for future business too, as this segment is likely to be more affluent than average in later life. To attract the student market to its loyalty card scheme, Tesco launched a Student Clubcard which it promoted at 75 universities, and which required a lower minimum spend than its normal Clubcard.

14 Owner-managed businesses with limited resources competing against much larger companies tend to be the most successful niche marketers, particularly if they target small segments that are not viable for a larger competitor with higher overheads. Success produces a dilemma for these businesses. They are vulnerable to aggressive competitors if their market starts to grow, as they do not have a portfolio of markets to fall back on if they lose ground.

15 The answer to this can only be identified through research, and care should be taken to ensure that the market is a homogeneous one. Three common characteristics cited are 'error protection', 'number of functions' and 'ease of learning', but the most important of these might depend on the purpose of use. Home-workers may be willing to sacrifice ease of learning for a wide variety of special commands, but parents buying software for their children may rate ease of learning number one, followed by error protection. The two more important characteristics for each target market are the ones that should be placed on each axis.

Chapter 7
. . . .

Multiple-choice

1 c It is intangible in that it does not offer physical benefits when the purchase is made, only reassurance, so it is part of the extended product, not the core or actual product.

2 d Stars need cash investment for promotional activities which will help them to extend their markets and sustain their market shares into maturity.

3 a.

4 b Customers go through a very short decision-making process for convenience products. All the product categories except impulse products are likely to engage customers in longer deliberations.

5 c All the brand names given except Campari are associated with product lines as opposed to single products.

True/False

6 False. Saturation occurs at the maturity stage when no new customers enter the market.

7 False. The original equipment manufacturer is a major purchaser of components.

8 True. Under these circumstances 'dogs' have little long-term potential for profitability.

9 True. The intangible features are described as being part of the extended product.

10 True. Many supermarkets, for example, sell their own-brands as well as manufacturer brands.

Discussion

11 Groceries are usually categorised as staples, or FMCGs, as they are generally purchased on a regular basis, with a tendency for consumers to repeat purchase brands that they are happy with. But consumers may be tempted to 'shop around' when they buy a product class for the first time, or if they become dissatisfied with their usual brand, perhaps due to a new recipe which they don't like, or an increase in price. Speciality products might be sought as specific ingredients for recipes or, for example, if preferred foreign brands are not generally available except through delicatessens.

12 The aftermarket purchases for resale and repair, so potential buyers tend to be more numerous and smaller in size than OEMs. This means that buyers in the aftermarket usually have minimal buying power over their supplier, who can charge them prices that generate a reasonable profit margin. Suppliers to OEMs tend to rely heavily on the business from just a few customers and, in the face of hostile competition, are more likely to cut prices rather than risk losing business upon which their firms depend.

13 The product life-cycle for recorded music began with trumpet-shaped gramophone players and vinyl records. The market moved into growth, as the only alternative was live music which was not always convenient or practical. Records were soon joined and replaced by tapes and ultimately CDs, and the market has moved into a relatively stable period of what appears to be a long-term maturity. There are no signs yet that the market for recorded music is moving into decline. Tape cassettes, on the other hand, were not introduced at the very start yet have already passed through a growth phase (particularly during the expansion of in-car hi-fi and personal stereos), into maturity and more recently into steep decline since the launch of the CD format.

14 Although a question mark is a product that is failing to gain market share in a growing market, it may be worth sustaining. The environment may be changing, perhaps improving its future potential. Competitors may be passive, leaving the door open for a good promotional campaign to turn the tide. There may be potential for the product to thrive in a specialist niche, aimed only at a small segment of the total market. It could be that the question mark is an essential complement to another product line and serves to keep customers loyal by enabling the company to offer a full product mix. Finally, it may fill production capacity that would otherwise be spare, and therefore make a useful contribution towards overheads.

15 The two main reasons are risk and money. Family branding and brand extensions are supported by the corporate image and can reduce the psychological fears customers have of trying something new. Costs of promotion can also be lower. New brands can sometimes share the space purchased for their sister products or at least benefit from the media exposure of the family brand name.

Chapter 8
•••••••••••

Multiple-choice

1 b Employees are *internal* sources of new product ideas, as they work for the organisation that will produce the new product.

2 e The product is 'dropped' too soon in the innovation process.

3 c Financial assessment takes places along with a marketing assessment at the business analysis stage.

4 b Opinion leaders are respected in society for their views and are unlikely to take the kinds of risk that innovators do in buying new products, so they tend to be early adopters.

5 e Trial is a typical part of the process people go through in adopting a new product.

True/False

6 False. It is known as a 'me-too' product.

7 False. It may start with a brainstorming session, but there are many other sources of new ideas too.

8 False. They are sometimes made at the concept testing stage, and usually at the product development and testing stage.

9 True. This is because test-markets are often impractical for the types of product and sales pattern experienced in industrial markets.

10 False. Laggards are the last group within a target market to adopt the product, but they get there eventually!

Discussion

11 Product line extensions are a relatively low-cost, low-risk way of providing consumers with more choice. It is a common route to NPD in recession when businesses are short of cash and more risk-averse. They are useful for filling a gap where a competitor could potentially enter, or where a competitor is strong and no one else is supplying that product. However, there are several drawbacks. Product line extensions do not always meet new customer needs, so may add unnecessary complexity to the market and incur higher costs for the business but fail to create any greater competitive advantage. Sometimes companies are diverted by product line extensions while competitors are getting on with the job of real innovation.

12 There is no right answer here. It depends on circumstances. Drop-errors imply a missed opportunity. This is likely to be the more serious of the two for large organisations who can afford to take risks and fail from time to time. It is a particular problem if the error allows new competitors to enter or existing competitors to increase their presence significantly in a market. Go-errors are a big problem for organisations with limited resources who cannot afford to fail. Fear of them increases the hesitancy of smaller organisations to become involved in NPD.

13 The size and resources of the company are an important factor, as a global launch is very expensive. The nature of the distribution network is also important. It is rare to be able to launch a new product on a wide scale into a completely new network. The nature of the market is also a factor to consider. If 80 per cent of demand is likely to come from 20 per cent of the market, it is more sensible to concentrate on this proportion first. Finally, it will also depend on customer needs across geographical areas. A global launch is only sensible if customer needs vary little between areas.

14 Laggards are the last group to adopt a product; 84 per cent of the total market for a product is already using it by the time laggards come along, so the cost-effectiveness of specifically targeting promotions at this group can be doubtful. It may be more appropriate to use reminder advertising, for example, which is aimed at retaining the loyalty of existing users but will overspill to the laggards who are likely to be influenced by the actions of others. Alternatively, if new and better products are already coming along by the time this group is ready to adopt, the promotional budget may be better spent on securing a foothold for the new products.

15 With me-too products, the business analysis stage is usually the starting point in the decision-making process, the idea and the concept having already proved successful in the market. Product development and testing, and a limited amount of market testing are also necessary, though it is unlikely that a test-market will be cost-effective.

Chapter 9
....

Multiple-choice

1 a, c and **e** These are all strategies that concentrate on earnings in the short term.

2 a, c and **e** Penetration pricing concentrates on buying volume, so the investment needs to hold out promise of a good return.

3 d and **e.**

4 b.

5 c.

True/False

6 True. And it can mean that the cheapest product in a particular category is not the best selling choice.

7 True. However, there are exceptions, such as cigarettes and alcohol, where higher prices are used to limit consumption.

8 True. An example is the practice of selling consumer durables at near cost price in order to make money on warranties.

9 True. According to A.C. Ehrenberg's research at least.

10 False. What the market will bear is more important in the long run.

Discussion

11 Customers expect transparent dealings from manufacturers and service providers. Strong attention to public relations and a proactively ethical trading stance are two ways of assuring customers of good faith.

12 Distribution, product quality and promotion are all capable of softening the impact of price. But money is not the only thing that consumers exchange for benefits. Inconvenience, time and energy are just some of the other non-financial price factors. By manipulating the other elements of the marketing mix to heighten consumer utility, sustainable competitive advantage can be created without sacrificing revenue.

13 Pricing decisions should never be taken in isolation. These three marketing areas offer plenty of scope for illustrating how price interacts with the other elements. Pricing services is, as we have seen in the chapter, a particularly delicate process.

14 While the tactic of the RPO might run the risk of cheapening a product's reputation, it is nevertheless a highly effective way of generating volume. The strength of any promotional idea, however, lies in its originality. Once price promotion becomes the done thing, manufacturers are in a very dangerous position. This can be a spur to greater creativity in promotional thinking, and an attempt to bolster brand values rather than simply cut price.

15 Price elasticity is important to know because it can help predict the effect of planned price changes. It can be learned only through careful observation over a number of years. Computer modelling can help to amplify the effects of such empirical observation.

Chapter 10
....

Multiple-choice

1 Sorting, accumulation, breaking down bulk, assortment, convenience, promotion.

2 a While some common patterns emerge, distribution decisions need to be taken on a case-by-case basis, and regularly reviewed.

  b Many buyers and sellers will use several different distribution systems at the same time (e.g. a retailer may use a traditional wholesaler and a cash and carry, depending on stock fluctuations and timing).

  c Push promotion is aimed at the trade rather than at the consumer.

3 d They do, however, offer convenient opening hours.

4 e.

5 d.

True/False

6 True. Along with customers and product characteristics.
7 False. While it is common with luxury goods and expensive cars, exclusive distribution also applies to items like Body Shop cosmetics.
8 True.
9 False. The minimum is 100,000 square feet.
10 True. By reducing the amount of stock in the system, snags are exposed.

Discussion

11 Merchant intermediaries (such as retailers and wholesalers) actually buy and own what they resell, whereas functional intermediaries (such as agents and transport providers) are rewarded by commission or a fee. Merchants take more risk but can look forward to greater returns.
12 Intensive (e.g. batteries), selective (e.g. electric kettles) and exclusive (e.g. Porsche cars).
13 a A specialist discount retailer aiming for a monopoly in its category.
   b Confectioner tobacconist newsagent, like a traditional corner sweet and paper shop.
   c An independent grocer who allies with others in order to increase their buying power.
   d A go-between connecting buyers and sellers.
   e The range and amount of stock carried.
14 The Wheel of Retailing sees retailers as having a life-cycle whereby they start as discounters and then try to move up-market to a more profitable positioning. Meanwhile new discounters enter at the bottom of the market and the process renews itself.
15 Order processing, materials handling, warehousing, inventory management, transport.

Chapter 11
• • • • • • • • • • • • • •

Multiple-choice

1 d Although technological advances (as in e) have facilitated its development.
2 e.
3 b David Ogilvy described it as a product's 'first-class ticket through life'.
4 c.
5 d.

True/False

6 False. Some of it is aimed at activity other than buying things, and some of it takes place on a corporate rather than product level where there is no obvious purchase to be made.
7 True.

8 False. This is the job of the production department.
9 True. As opposed to 'burst' which is shorter but more intense.
10 False. The reverse is true.

Discussion

11 This is becoming an increasingly vexed question as new opportunities for selective targeting presented by developing media become available. New ways of reaching consumers may not offer vast numbers of viewers, readers or listeners, but they can be a very efficient way of accessing otherwise extremely elusive audiences.
12 Sales may not be the immediate object of the advertising, but it remains true that an idea is being 'sold' to you every time you look at an advertisement. Perhaps finding some examples of advertising for non-commercial causes might help clarify an answer to this question.
13 Many large advertisers (Heinz and Nestlé among them) have made significant moves in this direction. To some extent it is sabre-rattling against the large retailers (whose stranglehold on distribution is a danger to manufacturers) and to media owners (who need to be reminded from time to time that there are alternative ways of reaching the public rather than through their expensive vehicles).
14 Radio and posters are surprisingly similar in a number of ways. Press is the odd one out here. As ever with advertising essays or discussion, examples are a useful way of highlighting the real issues.
15 Self-regulation depends on there being a need for regulation itself in communicating with consumers. Some would argue that the market can take care of itself and does not need norms of good taste or fairness imposed on it. A medium addressing smaller and more self-assured publics does not have the same power to offend viewers, readers or listeners who have made a conscious choice to be their audience. On the other hand, advertisers are extremely sensitive about the possibility of negative publicity, so might be reluctant to abandon any kinds of control.

Chapter 12

Multiple-choice

1 b.
2 c.
3 b.
4 b.
5 c.

True/False

6 True. In spite of the traditional idea of an adversarial sales encounter, successful salespeople are like business partners with their customers.

7 True. They are particularly important early on in the sales interview.

8 False. Good salespeople listen a lot.

9 True. Part of their effectiveness derives from their being temporary.

10 False. Leave opinions to journalists, but facts to the press release.

Discussion

11 Training is essential for salespeople to develop their potential and to keep in touch with ideas and techniques. However, most people would agree that while there is no definite selling 'type', a successful salesperson needs to have the potential in the first place.

12 This quote, from a very commercially successful novelist, reminds us that selling is a basic human activity. Trying to convince other people of one's ideas in an argument is a selling job of sorts, as is going for an interview or having a date.

13 This might have been a widely held opinion 20 years ago, but the medium has matured into a highly regarded technique that can consolidate branding on a strategic level, especially if integrated with other techniques.

14 PR is capable of abuse, like any other tool, but this view of it is too extreme. It is also naive to expect an objective view of the world from journalists, each of whom will have opinions and convictions that will inform his or her outlook.

15 The VNR is certainly a powerful device, but there is a discernible backlash against it from TV news editors for a number of reasons. One of the most important ones is that there are now a lot of VNRs being sent to newsrooms and so they can afford to be more choosy. On the other hand, technology seems to be driving us towards an increasingly visual culture, so perhaps the VNR or something like it in a digital set-up will be setting the agenda for the future.

Chapter 13
. . . .

Multiple-choice

1 a Many companies whose own marketing is entirely domestic will use plant and equipment made in other countries.

2 c Product quality is a *sine qua non* of any kind of marketing, but the other aspects of marketing management are particularly problematic in the international environment.

3 e In spite of the fact that personal grooming is an intensely cultural phenomenon, hair type is something that we are born with and is therefore demographic rather than cultural. **d** is an arguable answer here, but studies show a high correlation between educational achievements and earning power.

4 c, a, d, e and **b.**

5 d.

True/False

6 False. Experience with joint ventures suggests that they are unlikely to remain stable in the long term.

7 True. All of these industries provide good examples of 'global' brands.

8 True. Manufacturers need to have a presence in such markets to keep abreast of developments.

9 True. Such branding eliminates the difficulties caused by language.

10 False. The final stage is when exporters face competition in their domestic markets from imports.

Discussion

11 Small- to medium-sized businesses need, like any other business aiming at international markets, to be sure that there is a genuine opportunity out there. So research is necessary – especially on a personal basis. There is often much valuable information available from organisations such as chambers of commerce or trade bodies. In Europe, the SME has a privileged position in EU commercial legislation, so advantage may be taken of this. Partnerships with other companies are a good way of compensating for the disadvantages of size relative to larger competitors.

12 Promotional management is a difficult area at the best of times, but in the international context it presents peculiar difficulties. This is because of the cultural, technological and legal environments, all of which may be significantly different from country to country. There is no simple answer to this problem. Promotional managers should not assume that they can merely extend a successful domestic strategy to a new market without careful research. The growth of multinational agencies in the worlds of advertising and public relations recognises this new need. Many multinational companies get good results through using local agencies which follow agreed overall strategies, but have a large amount of flexibility as to their detailed implementation.

13 Marketing research is more difficult to co-ordinate and carry out in the international arena. People in some cultures are not used to being asked questions about consumption. In this case confusion and unreliable data may result from an attempt to carry out the kind of research that would be straightforward in the domestic market. Secondary research, too, can be dogged by problems of continuity of data or its comparability with other data. This kind of confusion can extend to demographic statistics. For example, the population of Nigeria is thought by some analysts to be something like three times the official estimate. Like other marketing services, research is beginning to organise itself on the lines of international networks, but the area is still fraught with difficulties.

14 The marketing manager of the twenty-first century will need to be more comfortable in a multicultural environment. Forward-thinking educators in the EU, for example, recognise the value of student mobility between countries in order to prepare them for this new challenge. This is the point of the various programmes run under the SOCRATES-ERASMUS scheme.

Working, living and studying in a number of cultures – and being proficient in a number of languages – are all likely to be characteristics of employable graduates in the twenty-first century. As we have seen at the beginning of Chapter 13, international marketing makes more searching demands than even domestic marketing. So the new breed of marketing manager needs to be in position to respond on each count.

15 This question is best answered by reference to an actual example. Nestlé's marketing of infant formula in the developing world is a particularly well-documented example, as it has led to two widespread boycotts of Nestlé products. Examination of the issues demonstrates that, emotive as the subject may be, it is by no means clear-cut. On the one hand, the kind of assumptions it is easy to make in the West about the infrastructure of clean water, literacy and standard of living are impossible to extend to many developing countries. On the other hand, consumers in those countries should not be denied choices that the developed world considers appropriate for itself. Other good examples include global brands like McDonalds, Coca-Cola (in markets such as the Phillipines), or the international marketing activities of cigarette companies.

Chapter 14

Multiple-choice

1 c Marketing strategy supports corporate strategy.
2 b This strategy is more in keeping with the behaviour of market leaders.
  d Market followers are happy with the status quo, but challengers challenge by their nature.
  e Niche marketers manage to get high profits from very low market share.
3 c.
4 b, c and **d** But all methods of forecasting need to be combined with qualitative judgement.
5 b, e, d, a and **c.**

True/False

6 False. It's the other way round.
7 False. Top-down (centralised) management has the advantage of giving clear instructions on decisions already taken.
8 True. Because of the concentration usually associated with industrial markets and product/service ranges.
9 False. Brand managers get a lot of responsibility without a lot of power.
10 True.

Discussion

11 Whether or not you agree with the pithy sentiment expressed here, it is certainly true that it would be very difficult to understand the concept of success without first having an idea of what it meant to be successful (i.e. objectives). Failure to plan means that success becomes impossible. However, it is a time-consuming and challenging process, which diverts energy from the immediate task in hand.

12 Although this sounds as if it should be true, the chapter has provided examples of differential advantage sourced from two other areas as well – company capability and relationships with customers. There may well be more kinds of source – again, examples of successful companies can help elucidate the principles involved.

13 There are a number of strategies available. The two most obvious ones, perhaps, are niching and flanking. Market segmentation is extremely important here.

14 In spite of its trappings of statistics and science, forecasting is a very approximate art. Therefore it needs to be done with confidence that your opinion (based on judgement and analysis) is valid. Scenario building, for example, works not because it is accurate, but because it allows a number of different visions of the future to be tried out.

15 Certainly the nature of the brand is changing, with the growth in retailer power and the developing technological environment. Brand managers are expensive, moreover, and many companies are seeking to downsize. However, it would be surprising if the function did not survive in some way because of its peculiar appropriateness to marketing.

Index